HASIDIC STUDIES

THE LITTMAN LIBRARY OF
JEWISH CIVILIZATION

Dedicated to the memory of
LOUIS THOMAS SIDNEY LITTMAN
who founded the Littman Library for the love of God
and as an act of charity in memory of his father
JOSEPH AARON LITTMAN
and to the memory of
ROBERT JOSEPH LITTMAN
who continued what his father Louis had begun
יהא זכרם ברוך

'Get wisdom, get understanding:
Forsake her not and she shall preserve thee'
PROV. 4: 5

HASIDIC STUDIES

Essays in History and Gender

◆

ADA RAPOPORT-ALBERT

The Littman Library of Jewish Civilization
in association with Liverpool University Press
2018

The Littman Library of Jewish Civilization
in association with Liverpool University Press
4 Cambridge Street, Liverpool L69 7ZU, UK
www.liverpooluniversitypress.co.uk/littman

Managing Editor: Connie Webber

Distributed in North America by
Oxford University Press Inc., 198 Madison Avenue,
New York, NY 10016, USA

Catalogue records for this book are available from the
British Library and the Library of Congress

ISBN 978-1-906764-82-1

Publishing co-ordinator: Janet Moth
Copy-editing: Agnes Erdos
Proof-reading: Laura Macy
Index: Sarah Ereira
Production, design, and typesetting by
Pete Russell, Faringdon, Oxon.

Printed in Great Britain on acid-free paper by
TJ International Ltd., Padstow, Cornwall

Preface

◆

THE initiative for assembling the essays comprising the present volume came from the Littman Library on the advice of Shaul Stampfer—a fellow Littman author, longstanding colleague, and friend. I am immensely grateful to him for proposing the idea, and to Connie Webber, Littman's managing editor, for putting it to me in the most generous of terms, which relieved me of much of the labour entailed while allowing me a free hand to revise the essays—originally published as independent studies over some four decades—wherever I felt this to be most necessary and appropriate. The result is that each of the chapters has largely retained its original substance and form while undergoing a certain measure of bibliographical updating and stylistic or, occasionally, substantive modification. As before, unless otherwise stated, all translations of source materials into English are my own.

I am no less grateful to Moshe Rosman—yet another Littman author, colleague, and friend—who graciously agreed to write what turned out to be a truly humbling introduction to the volume.

Special thanks are due to my copy-editor, Agi Erdos, whose light touch, good sense, and sound judgement turned what I feared might be a battleground into a wholly pleasurable mutual learning experience.

Other members of the Littman team—Janet Moth, the publishing co-ordinator, Pete Russell, the designer, and Ludo Craddock, the chief executive officer, have all given generously of their experience and skill, together creating the most congenial professional environment that any author could wish for.

March 2017 A.R.-A.

Acknowledgements

The essays in this volume were originally published as detailed below.

CHAPTER 1: 'Hasidism after 1772: Structural Continuity and Change', in Ada Rapoport-Albert (ed.), *Hasidism Reappraised* (London: Littman Library of Jewish Civilization, 1996), 76–140. © The Littman Library of Jewish Civilization 1996.

CHAPTER 2: 'God and the Zaddik as the Two Focal Points of Hasidic Worship', *History of Religions*, 18/4 (1979), 296–325; repr. in G. D. Hundert (ed.), *Essential Papers on Hasidism: Origins to Present* (New York, 1991), 299–329.

CHAPTER 3: 'Confession in the Circle of R. Nahman of Braslav', *Bulletin of the Institute of Jewish Studies*, 1 (1973–5), 65–96.

CHAPTER 4: 'Hagiography with Footnotes: Edifying Tales and the Writing of History in Hasidism', *History and Theory*, 27 (1988), 119–59. © 1988 by Wesleyan University.

CHAPTER 5: 'Conclusion: From Sabbatianism to Hasidism', in Ada Rapoport-Albert, *Women and the Messianic Heresy of Sabbatai Zevi, 1666–1816* (Oxford: Littman Library of Jewish Civilization, 2011), 258–96.

CHAPTER 6: 'On Women in Hasidism: S. A. Horodecky and the Maid of Ludmir Tradition', in Ada Rapoport-Albert and Steven J. Zipperstein (eds.), *Jewish History: Essays in Honour of Chimen Abramsky* (London: Peter Halban, 1988), 508–9, 524–5.

CHAPTER 7: 'The Emergence of a Female Constituency in Twentieth-Century Habad Hasidism', in David Assaf and Ada Rapoport-Albert (eds.), *Let the Old Make Way for the New: Studies in the Social and Cultural History of Eastern European Jewry Presented to Immanuel Etkes*, i: *Hasidism and the Musar Movement* [Yashan mipenei ḥadash: meḥkarim betoledot yehudei mizraḥ eiropah uvetarbutam, shai le'imanuel etkes, i: ḥasidim ve'anshei ma'aseh] (Hebrew and English) (Jerusalem: Zalman Shazar Center, 2009), English section, 7*–68*.

CHAPTER 8: 'From Woman as Hasid to Woman as "Tsadik" in the Teachings of the Last Two Lubavitcher Rebbes', *Jewish History*, 27/3–4 (2013), 435–73. Reproduced by permission of Springer.

Contents

Note on Transliteration and Conventions Used in the Text xi

INTRODUCTION

Changing the Narrative of the History of Hasidism 1

MOSHE ROSMAN

PART I

HISTORY

BECOMING A MOVEMENT

1. Hasidism after 1772: Structural Continuity and Change 23

CONCEPTUALIZING LEADERSHIP

2. God and the Tsadik as the Two Focal Points of Hasidic Worship 124

3. Confession in the Circle of R. Nahman of Bratslav 161

FASHIONING THE PAST

4. Hagiography with Footnotes: Edifying Tales and the Writing of History in Hasidism 199

PART II

GENDER

WOMEN OUT?

5. From Prophetess to Madwoman: The Displacement of Female Spirituality in the Post-Sabbatian Era 269

6. On Women in Hasidism: S. A. Horodetsky and the Maid of Ludmir Tradition 318

WOMEN IN?

7. The Emergence of a Female Constituency in Twentieth-Century Habad Hasidism 368

8. From Woman as Hasid to Woman as 'Tsadik' in the Teachings of the Last Two Lubavitcher Rebbes 427

Bibliography 471

Index 503

Note on Transliteration and Conventions Used in the Text

◆

Hebrew

The transliteration of Hebrew in this book reflects consideration of the type of book it is, its content, purpose, and readership. The system adopted therefore reflects a broad approach to transcription, rather than the narrower approaches found in the *Encyclopaedia Judaica* or other systems developed for text-based or linguistic studies. The aim has been to reflect the pronunciation prescribed for modern Hebrew, rather than the spelling or Hebrew word structure, and to do so using conventions that are generally familiar to the English-speaking reader.

In accordance with this approach, no attempt is made to indicate the distinctions between *alef* and *ayin*, *tet* and *taf*, *kaf* and *kuf*, *sin* and *samekh*, since these are not relevant to pronunciation; likewise, the *dagesh* is not indicated except where it affects pronunciation. Following the principle of using conventions familiar to the majority of readers, however, transcriptions that are well established have been retained even when they are not fully consistent with the transliteration system adopted. On similar grounds, the *tsadi* is rendered by 'tz' in such familiar words as barmitzvah. Likewise, the distinction between *ḥet* and *khaf* has been retained, using *ḥ* for the former and *kh* for the latter; the associated forms are generally familiar to readers, even if the distinction is not actually borne out in pronunciation, and for the same reason the final *heh* is indicated too. As in Hebrew, no capital letters are used, except that an initial capital has been retained in transliterating titles of published works (for example, *Shulḥan arukh*).

Since no distinction is made between *alef* and *ayin*, they are indicated by an apostrophe only in intervocalic positions where a failure to do so could lead an English-speaking reader to pronounce the vowel-cluster as a diphthong—as, for example, in *ha'ir*—or otherwise mispronounce the word.

The *sheva na* is indicated by an *e*—*perikat ol*, *reshut*—except, again, when established convention dictates otherwise.

The *yod* is represented by *i* when it occurs as a vowel (*bereshit*), by *y* when it occurs as a consonant (*yesodot*), and by *yi* when it occurs as both (*yisra'el*).

Names have generally been left in their familiar forms, even when this is inconsistent with the overall system.

Yiddish

The transcription of Yiddish in this volume follows the conventions of the YIVO Institute.

INTRODUCTION

Changing the Narrative of the History of Hasidism

MOSHE ROSMAN

THE PURPOSE OF THIS INTRODUCTION is fourfold. The first section is intended to explain the historiographical context in which Ada Rapoport-Albert's research has been conducted. By understanding the scholarship which preceded her, readers may come to a better appreciation of how her work has altered the narrative of the history of hasidism. The second purpose is to provide links between the essays presented in this volume. While they were originally written and published independently I think they fit together in shaping a new perspective on hasidism. By articulating how they do so I hope that this anthology will take on the aspect of an integral book with a consistent argument and point of view.

In addition, the essays have been summarized and the larger import of each highlighted. There are no footnotes, which should provide readers with a straightforward roadmap through the sophisticated scholarly oeuvre this volume presents. Virtually every point referred to in this introduction can be found in the text or footnotes of the essays themselves.

The introduction concludes by alluding to Professor Rapoport-Albert's academic work beyond the studies published herein.

THE HISTORIOGRAPHICAL CONTEXT

When Ada Rapoport-Albert began studying hasidism in the mid-1960s, several figures towered over academic hasidic scholarship. The first was Simon Dubnow (1860–1941) whose classic history of hasidism, based on his late nineteenth-century work in Russian, appeared in both Hebrew and German editions in 1931. In his book Dubnow proposed a construction of hasidic history that still influences both academic and popular notions of how hasidism arose and developed.

The Dubnovian Paradigm

For Dubnow the key element in the background of hasidism was crisis. This crisis began with the 1648 uprising of Cossacks and Ukrainian (Ruthenian) peasants against Polish rule of Ukraine, led by Bohdan Khmelnytsky, subsequently a Ukrainian national hero. The rebels made Jews a main target of their attacks, and approximately half of Ukraine's 40,000 Jews were killed while thousands more were wounded or uprooted. For Jews, Khmelnytsky was a villain and these events were referred to as Gezerot Tah-Tat (the persecutions of 1648–9). They segued into a series of invasions and wars, and, Dubnow claimed, resulted in an overwhelming multidimensional crisis for Polish Jewry lasting well into the eighteenth century and constituting the context for the rise of hasidism. Dubnow emphasized that the first half of the eighteenth century had witnessed 'a frenzy of blood libels'. This corresponded to the lifetime of Israel ben Eliezer, the Ba'al Shem Tov, usually credited with founding the hasidic movement. He was often identified, using the acronym of his title, as Israel Besht, or simply the Besht.

The term *ba'al shem tov* means 'master of the good [i.e. divine] name'. Israel Ba'al Shem Tov was indeed someone who knew how to communicate with God and use the divine name in incantations, amulets, and mystical rituals in order to help people with their physical ailments, material poverty, and social problems. As such he ranked low in the hierarchy of religious functionaries and scholars who enjoyed prominence in the Jewish community. Dubnow, however, insisted that the Besht was actually a sophisticated religious innovator who applied 'mystical pantheism' to everyday Judaism. With common conversation, stories, and folk sayings as his tools, he forged a religious ethos based on love, spirituality, joy, religious emotion, and ethics. Dubnow contrasted the Besht's warm, practical approach to Judaism and Jews with the legalism and insensitivity of the establishment rabbis. He proffered psychological and spiritual healing (*tikun*) and relief from the collective melancholy that gripped the persecution-weary Jews. The rabbis thought only of pedantic religious texts and rituals, ignoring people's real problems. The Besht's personality and modus operandi attracted a huge following and, as Dubnow told it, by the time of his death in 1760 on the festival of Shavuot, he had launched a new, original, authentically Jewish mass movement, complete with doctrines and organization. It drew on the semi-learned and unlearned for its membership. It was they, together with the Besht's disciples at the time, who composed the first generation of hasidism.

For Dubnow the second generation of hasidism began when Dov Ber, the Magid (preacher) of Mezhirech (Międzyrzecz), became the leader of the new hasidic movement, having inherited the Besht's mantle. He moved his court away from the Besht's town, Międzybóż, to the more centrally located Mezhirech. The Magid sent out young men to recruit new souls to the movement. In addition he propounded its doctrines, which seemed to compete with different ideas set forth in a series of three books authored by the Magid's supposed rival for the movement's leadership, Jacob Joseph of Połonne (d.1784), another disciple of the Besht. Jacob Joseph's books quoted hundreds of sayings in the name of the Besht as well as presenting interpretations of the Torah inspired by hasidic teaching. These books were the first steps in the formation of a hasidic literary canon.

The Magid's disciples, such as Elimelekh of Lizhensk (Leżajsk), Levi Isaac of Berdichev (Berdyczów), Abraham of Kalisk (Kołyszki), Menahem Mendel of Vitebsk (Witebsk), and Shneur Zalman of Liady, were, for Dubnow, the third hasidic generation. After the Magid's death they spread, but also split, the heretofore unified movement by founding their own autonomous courts in far-flung areas of the Russian Jewish Pale of Settlement and Poland. They managed to maintain organizational and doctrinal loyalty to the birthright they had received from the Magid (and the Besht); still, each developed a distinctive leadership style and doctrinal inflections. According to Dubnow, this decentralization of both structure and doctrine made hasidism more accessible to an ever-growing swathe of the Jewish community, until it soon came to rule the Jewish street, at least in the southerly reaches of what had been the Polish–Lithuanian Commonwealth. The price, however, for this absence of a central authority was a lack of standards and oversight, sowing the seeds of later degeneration.

Dubnow considered these first three generations of the movement's leadership—the Besht, the Magid (and Jacob Joseph, Pinhas of Korets, etc.), the Magid's disciples—to be the classic period of hasidism. During this time the movement was at its creative peak and virtually free of corruption. Scholars adopted the term 'early hasidism' to denote the activity beginning with the Besht's 'revelation' as a bona fide *ba'al shem* circa 1736 (preceding his move to Międzybóż) until 1815, by which year all of the Magid's students had died.

After 1815, something scholars have called 'late' (i.e. non-classic) hasidism set in. The movement divided and subdivided into numerous dynasties and their tributaries, whose leaders could do—and order their followers to do—as they pleased. Dubnow called this tsadikism (from the word 'tsadik', denoting the leader of a hasidic court), a perversion of the original movement now being led by shallow, and even corrupt, men of no ideological inspiration or theological depth. What energy they had was largely misdirected to a vain struggle against modernity in the form of the Haskalah (Jewish Enlightenment). After 1870 the degeneration became even worse and Dubnow called it 'the period of absolute decline'.

Opposition from traditionalist circles (*mitnagedim*) to the new hasidism was the subject of almost a third of Dubnow's history. He asserted that opposition accompanied the new movement virtually from its inception in the 1740s. The opposition became organized and intensive in 1772 under the leadership of Elijah ben Solomon Zalman, the Vilna Gaon (1720–97). However, after initial successes it subsided somewhat, to be succeeded by two more periods of acute opposition: 1781–4, mainly in reaction to the publication of Jacob Joseph's books; and 1797–1801, initially in response to the outrageously disrespectful behaviour of some hasidim at the news of the Vilna Gaon's death on Sukkot of 1797.

Dinur's Twists

Dubnow's saga of hasidism and the halo of its influence was somewhat modified by the one-time dean of Israeli modern Jewish historians, Ben-Zion Dinur (1884–1973). Dinur agreed with Dubnow's paradigm of a three-generation classic movement. Also like Dubnow, he was convinced that hasidism arose within a context of crisis; however, unlike Dubnow, he considered the crisis to have been rooted in the corruption of the Jewish communal institutions, including the rabbinate. Corruption caused those institutions to malfunction and the leadership to lose its legitimacy. Into the breach rushed the hasidic leadership, deriving its legitimacy from charisma and introducing voluntary rather than coercive institutions.

These were leaders who believed in social justice and fought for the simple Jew. Hasidism turned out to be a vehicle for coalescing and activating opposition to a corrupt establishment.

Buber–Scholem Hasidism

Martin Buber (1878–1965) and Gershom Scholem (1897–1982) were intent upon locating the essence of hasidic doctrine. Their fundamental question: wherein lies the innovation of hasidism? Buber's answer: hasidism is 'kabbalah become ethos'. This meant that hasidism converted mystical truths into righteous action without, however, crossing halakhic red lines. The charisma of hasidic leaders served to animate their followers' routine behaviour, shaping it into the contours of a just society.

Scholem gave multiple responses to the question of the innovative essence of hasidism. He considered the movement to be 'the latest phase' of Jewish mysticism. It differed by neutralizing the acute messianism that had infused the Lurianic kabbalah which preceded it, yet preserving those aspects of kabbalah with the potential for inspiring the masses. At one time Scholem apparently agreed with Buber that the charismatic hasidic tsadik translated the kabbalah into ethical values suitable for application through halakhic means in common people's everyday life. Later he decided that Buber was mistaken. The actual mission of hasidism was to introduce novel kabbalistic ideas.

Chief among these was the concept of *devekut*, communion with God. The idea of *unio mystica*, mystical union with the Divine, was a foundational concept of all religious mysticism, not least kabbalah. According to Scholem, the Ba'al Shem Tov had profoundly changed the place of *devekut* in the Jewish religious quest. For traditional Jewish mystics, *devekut* was a remote ideal that only a select few adepts might realize after completing the arduous, at times Sisyphean, task of distilling the sparks of holiness dissolved in the materiality of this world. It was the ultimate state of being, to be attained—if at all—only after a lifetime of spiritual striving.

In Scholem's conception the Besht and his successors, basing themselves on the zoharic notion that *leit atar panui mineh*, no place is devoid of God, emphasized God's radical immanence. Holiness suffused and infused everything everywhere and might be engaged at any time. What was required was merely the individual's decision to seek out and commune with the godliness that surrounded him. *Devekut* was not an objective; it was a mode of existence. It was available to anyone willing to commit to it.

Scholem's framing of hasidism as advocating such a 'democratic' approach to the religious life, making the highest form of spirituality available to everyone, echoed Dubnow's image of a folksy yet profound Ba'al Shem Tov who ministered to the downtrodden, persecuted masses. It also matched up with Dinur's early hasidism, which took up the cause of the common people against the oppressive, corrupt establishment; or with Buber's hasidism, which turned the elitist kabbalah into an ethical way of life for the masses.

Scholem, in addition to highlighting what many came to accept as the doctrinal essence of hasidism, *devekut*, also anchored Dubnow's claim that the opposition to hasidism began in response to the Ba'al Shem Tov's activities. Scholem published texts which he thought expressed criticism of the new Beshtian hasidim as early as the 1740s.

In the mid-1960s Ada Rapoport-Albert came to the study of hasidism. At first she served as the student amanuensis of Professor Joseph Weiss, an assignment that soon transformed into a unique tutorial with the erudite, intense, creative scholar. Lacking background in the subject, she was faced with a fully articulated portrayal of the rise and development of the hasidic movement in the eighteenth century. Its main points, which were to be most relevant to her subsequent research, were:

- Hasidism arose in response to some crisis.
- The Besht started a centralized, institutionalized, mass religious-social movement.
- The three-generation chronology of the Besht, the Magid, and the Magid's disciples constituted early or classic hasidism.
- The Magid inherited the leadership of the unified, centralized movement from the Besht; it then split into various courts in the third generation.
- Opposition to hasidism began in the generation of the Besht and became institutionalized in the generation of the Magid.
- The key theological doctrine of hasidism was the conversion of *devekut* from an ultimate objective to be achieved through a lifetime's striving to

a mode of living which any person might commit to. It meant that, with the inspiration of the tsadik, even simple people could become spiritual experts and be connected directly to God. It 'democratized' spirituality.

- Hasidism was primarily a popular movement, aimed at raising the status of the common people, enhancing their lives, giving them a voice. It even exhibited certain democratic tendencies.

There was one other dimension of hasidism that, consonant with the reigning assumptions and prejudices of the time, had been virtually ignored by the main academic scholars but which had gained at least one famous treatment. This was the issue of the place of women in the history of the movement.

Only Samuel Abba Horodetsky, scion of prominent hasidic families, Zionist intellectual, and writer of popular histories, had turned scholarly attention to the relationship of hasidism to women. In 1923 he asserted that 'the Jewish woman was given complete equality in the emotional, mystical religious life of Beshtian hasidism'. Expanding on a short 1909 article he had written in Russian concerning Hannah Rachel Verbermacher, the so-called Maid of Ludmir, who had briefly functioned as a hasidic quasi-tsadik, Horodetsky extolled hasidism as having promoted women's position in both the family and the community. First of all, it enabled women to establish a direct relationship with the hasidic master, the tsadik who led their particular hasidic group, paralleling that of men. Secondly, it fostered the development of a Yiddish religious literature which offered women the possibility of becoming religiously literate hasidic Jews, like men. Finally, and most dramatically, it allowed talented, learned women to become leaders within the movement, even assuming the role of tsadik, like Verbermacher, the Maid.

Horodetsky's pronouncement of the elevation of women in hasidism to parity with men was influential. It became a common, if unexamined, assumption of both scholarship and popular lore. The reigning assessment of hasidism incorporated it as one of its secondary themes.

Beginning with the fresh perspective of a newcomer to the study of hasidism, Ada Rapoport-Albert immersed herself in the subject. Since the 1970s she has been subjecting the conventional assessment to critical examination. As a result she has been a main partner in the profound transformation of the history of hasidism that has taken shape over the past generation or so. No one has done more to effect such a transformation than she. The essays in the present collection represent her oeuvre in this field.

ADA RAPOPORT-ALBERT'S ESSAYS

◆

CONCEPTUALIZING LEADERSHIP

'God and the Tsadik as the Two Focal Points of Hasidic Worship'

'Confession in the Circle of R. Nahman of Bratslav'

In these two early essays, written in the 1970s, Rapoport-Albert lent a new perspective on the role of the tsadik in hasidism. She insisted on reading the primary sources, especially Jacob Joseph's material and Nathan Sternharz's written records of Nahman of Bratslav's teachings, *tabula rasa*, independently of the interpretations of previous scholars. What she discovered both contradicted some of the key points of the Dubnovian paradigm delineated above and qualified Gershom Scholem's famous conclusion with respect to *devekut* as the essence of hasidism.

Rapoport-Albert emphasized how the Besht and his associates all believed in the dichotomy between the 'men of matter' (*anshei ḥomer*) and the 'men of form' (*anshei tsurah*). Most people were 'men of matter' and could never hope to secure the status of 'men of spirituality', a condition reserved for the spiritual elite, the tsadikim, alone. It was not democracy, but hierarchy: 'Received from the Besht: Each man should conduct himself according to his own rank. For, if he adopts the conduct befitting another man's rank, he fails to comply either with his own or with the other man's standard.'

Hasidism, then, began as an elitist movement, not popular and certainly not populist. Techniques for attaining the state of *devekut*, such as 'worship through corporeality' (*avodah begashmiyut*) and bonding with the inner holiness of the letters of sacred texts, could only be mastered by members of the spiritual elite. *Devekut* itself was out of reach of common people.

Hasidism did, however, offer the 'men of matter' something new. They could transcend their corporeality and maintain contact with the Divine not by emulating the spiritual elite, but by cleaving to it. Their objective should not be communicating with God, but rather attaching themselves to the holiness of the men of spirit, the tsadikim. As Rapoport-Albert put it, 'Just as God is the focus of the tsadik's religious life, so the tsadik is the focus of the ordinary person's religiosity.'

This notion of the tsadik as a surrogate for God in the hasid's life reached its apotheosis with Nahman of Bratslav. He went so far as to project some of God's attributes, such as 'withdrawal' (*tsimtsum*) and inaccessibility, onto himself. Perhaps the ultimate expression of the tsadik's substitution for God was the role of confession in Nahman of Bratslav's court. Confession, to Nahman, was not a sign of atonement, prompting the tsadik's prescription of a course of penance. Rather, the very act of confession to the tsadik brought absolution from the sin and enabled the person confessing to approach the 'state of the World to Come'. This innovation assigned the tsadik quasi-divine power.

Rapoport-Albert's conception of the tsadik and his relationship to his hasidim did confirm that hasidism raised the status of the common person. It did so, however, by making him the object of spiritual attention on the part of the spiritual elite, the tsadikim. There was no democratization of true spirituality, which remained the province of the elite. *Devekut* may have changed from life goal to mode of living, but it was not a mode available to everyone. Early hasidism did not abolish spiritual—or, in its wake, social—hierarchy.

BECOMING A MOVEMENT

'Hasidism after 1772: Structural Continuity and Change'

By implication, the 1970s essays undermined the conventional, Dubnow-originated portrayal of hasidism. In her pivotal study 'Hasidism after 1772' Rapoport-Albert attacked the old schema head-on: she proved that the three-generation construct was untenable, because there was nothing that could be termed a new hasidic 'movement' until the end of the Magid's life (December 1772) and the onset of the so-called third generation. Thus the 'early' pristine versus 'late' decadent hasidism dichotomy was outmoded and most of the rest of Dubnow's paradigm collapsed alongside it.

Rapoport-Albert demonstrated that in the time of the Besht and for most of the Magid's period there was no self-conscious, collective group identity, no articulated institutions, no unique hasidic ideology, no proprietary hasidic customs, and no literary canon. Thus it was anachronistic to speak of an eighteenth-century centralized, institutionalized, popular mass movement founded by Israel Ba'al Shem Tov, which he headed as formal leader and which was further developed by the Magid. All such descriptions were a later reading into the eighteenth-century *Sitz im Leben* of characteristics of the mature nineteenth-century hasidic movement. In the mid-eighteenth century hasidism was amorphous and embryonic. It was only as it emerged as an identifiable entity in the late eighteenth century that the Besht and the Magid were assigned the role of its founding leaders.

Moreover, the context of the formation of hasidism in the eighteenth century was not crisis. Like the Besht, Jacob Joseph, Pinhas of Korets, and the Magid, who were later seen as members of a distinctive hasidic movement, had originally stemmed from circles of mystical pietists, also called hasidim (their hasidism will be referred to below as 'ascetic-mystical hasidism'). These associates of the Besht continued to practise a normatively bounded style of pietistic Judaism but inflected their traditional pietism with a few unconventional features, such as rejection of asceticism and acceptance of non-elitist members. They did not attract unusual attention until the Vilna Gaon defined them as sectarian. Until then there was no organized opposition to a hasidism still barely distinguishable from conventional ascetic-mystical hasidism. The Gaon decided that what had been seen as another style of pietism should be labelled the Other.

In response to the Gaon's turning them into a targeted enemy, a chief manifestation of evil whose elimination was vital to the perfection of all society, the hasidim started to distinguish themselves in various ways from established entities. They began developing doctrines and institutions, and became conscious of themselves as a distinct group. They always continued, however, to maintain a relatively conservative halakhic stance and gradually penetrated established local Jewish institutions. Given the decentralized nature of Jewish communal life in general and the difficulty of finding technical halakhic fault with the behaviour of hasidim, on the whole their resistance to the *mitnagedim* was rather successful.

The Ba'al Shem Tov, then, did not found anything. He was prominent and influential among a network of charismatic spiritual leaders, each of whom was not his 'disciple' but was himself surrounded by a group of disciples. Each of them was articulating some version of traditional ascetic-mystical 'hasidic' pietism. The decentralization that had been heralded by academic scholars as a hallmark of the so-called 'late' hasidism was actually present from the origins of the movement and mirrored the decentralization of the Polish Jewish community and the Polish polity as well.

Since the early movement was not centralized, institutionalized, or even self-conscious, there was never any 'leadership of the movement' to inherit—or to fight over. Early disputes and feuds among members of the network of leaders in the 1760s and 1770s concerned personal animosities and turf struggles, not doctrines or power within the 'movement'. It was only as the individual hasidic courts multiplied in the late eighteenth century that the question of leadership and its transmission arose and was contested. The issue, however, was always the leadership of a given court or dynasty. From its inception there never was a battle over some—non-existent—supreme leadership of the movement as a whole. The pluralist, non-institutionalized nature of the larger incipient movement encouraged the proliferation of many branch groups, which themselves became progressively more tightly knit, centralist, and institutionalized, while maintaining a loose non-hierarchical relationship between groups.

The greater significance of Rapoport-Albert's interpretation was that the decentralized but institutionalized hasidism of the nineteenth century was not hasidism in its degenerate period, but rather in its mature form. The Magid's disciples, who had conventionally been viewed as the 'third generation' of a movement founded thirty or so years earlier, were actually the first self-conscious generation of the new hasidic movement. There was no rooted movement united under the leadership of the Besht and the Magid. The leaders of the new hasidism in the last third of the eighteenth century were experimenting with different forms of organization and developing various doctrines that would shape their emerging movement.

In addition, as already noted, hasidism was not fashioned in response to some crisis and did not meet with opposition in the time of the Ba'al Shem Tov. It gradually differentiated itself from the existing ascetic-mystical hasidism. The opposition galvanized by the Vilna Gaon in the early 1770s, more than a decade after the Besht had died and less than a year before the

Magid did, catalysed hasidim's own leap from identification with conventional pietism to self-consciousness as a separate movement.

Paradoxically, opposition to hasidism was the crucial step in defining the new movement, and this process of self-conscious definition did not begin until after both the Besht and the Magid had made their mark. Moreover, this new hasidism maintained fundamental fealty to both the halakhah and the Jewish community.

FASHIONING THE PAST

'Hagiography with Footnotes: Edifying Tales and the Writing of History in Hasidism'

Every construction of hasidic history is based on sources, but the vexing question of which ones—written and oral—are legitimate for the uses of historiography and how they should be utilized has dogged the writing of this history ever since it began. As its full title implies, in this essay Ada Rapoport-Albert explored the relationship between hasidic history and hasidic hagiography.

At the outset she distinguished between 'archaeological truth' and 'historical truth'. The former is what the evidence indicates; the latter is what collective memory has construed. It is this 'historical truth', or historical collective memory, that serves as the basis for people's beliefs and actions. Hasidic historical sources, Rapoport-Albert posited, were interested in propagating historical memory, not what she referred to as archaeological truth.

It is scarcely surprising, then, that the best-known and most utilized source for the history of the Ba'al Shem Tov and early hasidism has been the book *Shivḥei habesht* (In Praise of the Ba'al Shem Tov). This is a collection of some 200 stories transcribed, compiled, and edited from oral sources about the Besht and his associates. The book has gone through complicated compiling, editing, and publication processes. Its title announces the genre to which it belongs: hagiography (*hagios* = holy, *graphos* = writing, i.e. writing praising holy figures). As the original compiler of the stories, Dov Ber of Linits (Ilintsy), and Rapoport-Albert both emphasized, the intention of *Shivḥei habesht*, as of all hagiography, was to use the life of the holy man to instil in readers a sense of awe and motivate them towards a life of morality and piety. It was *not* to convey history in the conventional sense, but rather to transmit to posterity a historical image that people could cherish and be inspired by.

Rapoport-Albert insisted, however, that the tales 'do not set out to falsify the facts or to make them up'. Once again drawing a paradox, she asserted, 'But it is precisely the historically casual nature of the tales, the fact that their conscious "agenda" is pietistic, not historiographical, that lends credibility to such concrete items of historical information as they still contain.' By this she meant that names, dates, specific events, and other 'hard facts' mentioned in passing in these hagiographical stories should be taken at face value unless proven otherwise.

Ironically, then, hasidic hagiography may prove to be a useful source for the facts of hasidic history despite itself. At the same time, other hasidic historical sources and history-writing, while consciously attempting to mimic modern, academically sanctioned archival sources and historiographical scholarship, are nothing more than 'hagiography with footnotes'. The bulk of the essay illustrates this thesis with two related examples: the letters of the infamous Kherson *genizah* and the extensive historiographical writings of the sixth leader, or *admor*, of Habad hasidism, Joseph Isaac Schneersohn (1880–1950).

The Kherson *genizah* is a collection of hundreds of letters purporting to be the correspondence of the Ba'al Shem Tov and his associates in the eighteenth century. Virtually all academic and even most hasidic authorities—apart from Habad—agree that these documents are forgeries concocted around the time of the First World War. Rapoport-Albert analysed the contents and demonstrated that the documents were carefully contrived to serve as glosses on existing hasidic hagiography and oral traditions. Keenly aware of problems with the traditional written and oral sources, the 'letters' attempt to resolve these, corroborating, filling in gaps, explaining inconsistencies, and harmonizing discrepancies between current hasidic practice and what seemed to obtain 150 or so years earlier as reflected in the traditional material.

The Admor Joseph Isaac, the most enthusiastic defender of the authenticity of the Kherson *genizah*, made extensive use of these documents to write what he hoped would be the authoritative history of hasidism, perpetuating the traditional image based on collective hasidic historical memory. The Admor also drew on another source: his own secret activities reinforcing Jewish religion in general and Habad in particular in the face of early Soviet repression of both.

The Admor construed his own clandestine initiatives for spreading Jewish belief and practice in the Soviet Union in the 1920s as typological activity characteristic of hasidic leaders beginning with the Besht and continuing with Shneur Zalman of Liady and his successors. Joseph Isaac thus projected what he himself had done onto the Besht, and constructed a historical Besht who appeared to foreshadow his own persona and career.

For Rapoport-Albert the key historical significance of the Kherson archive and Joseph Isaac's historiography was that both felt the necessity to dress up what was essentially hagiography to appear to be academically legitimate historiography. This was indicative of how sensitive at least some hasidic circles had become to secular critiques of the movement and how they sought to neutralize academic attacks by answering them in their own style. But more than being a response to outside criticism, the adoption of a simulated academic pose was a measure of how much modern secular values had infiltrated the traditional world, leading people to abandon it in droves. In order to retain the loyalty of their followers, religious leaders had to lend their claims authority by expressing them in terms that at least appeared to satisfy modern criteria for truth assertion. By this time many traditionally inclined people shared certain epistemological assumptions current in society at large. In order to preserve the traditional portrait of the past, the method of portrayal had to change.

WOMEN OUT?

'From Prophetess to Madwoman: The Displacement of Female Spirituality in the Post-Sabbatian Era'

'On Women in Hasidism: S. A. Horodetsky and the Maid of Ludmir Tradition'

The subject of women and hasidism had been sorely neglected by conventional scholarship. Horodetsky's lone study, cited above, held sway without ever having been subject to critical review. Here Rapoport-Albert engaged in a revision that was more aggressive and even more sweeping than she had accomplished with respect to the Dubnovian paradigm concerning the origins and development of the movement.

The reader will recall Horodetsky's claim that by bringing women into the tsadik's court, providing them with religious literature, and enabling talented women to reach leadership positions, hasidism had brought women to equality in religious life. This became the common scholarly orthodoxy for some sixty years. In 1988 Rapoport-Albert challenged every one of Horodetsky's contentions in an essay which has become a classic of Jewish feminist scholarship. In this essay she demonstrated that hasidism related only to the spiritual life of men, not only ignoring women religiously but adding to their domestic burdens. Contrary to Horodetsky's statement, she proved that, notwithstanding the possibility that some individual women might have been able to gain a personal interview with a tsadik, women in general were excluded from the arenas of court activity that counted in hasidism. Again contradicting Horodetsky, she demonstrated that there was no hasidic literature for or about women before the twentieth century.

Most dramatically, she demolished Horodetsky's central thesis, based on the example of the Maid of Ludmir, that women could even be tsadikim. She showed that this one example was unique, *sui generis*, never replicated. More important, she argued, the case of the Maid actually proved the limitations on women's participation in hasidic life. Verbermacher had come to stand at the head of a following of hasidim only by virtue of her abandonment of the gender markers of femininity. Only a woman who violated the gender boundary and did not behave as a 'real' woman might lead. However, even this was not to be tolerated by the male establishment. Tremendous pressure was brought to bear upon the Maid to 'act like a woman'—first and foremost to marry (she subsequently divorced)—and thereby relinquish any pretensions to the male role of tsadik. She could not be both a 'real' woman and a tsadik. Hasidism, then, did not make women equal to men, but perpetuated and even strengthened the traditional gender hierarchy.

For Rapoport-Albert the question was, 'Why?' In her research on Sabbatianism she discovered that there actually was a tradition of messianic prophecy by Jewish women beginning in the wake of the Spanish Expulsion, flourishing in sixteenth-century Safed, reaching a climax with female Sabbatian prophets in the seventeenth and eighteenth centuries, and continuing in some form until the last gasps of Sabbatianism in the 1800s.

In hasidism women had no spiritual agency. With the partial exception of prominent women relatives of important hasidic figures (such as Feyge, granddaughter of the Besht and mother of Nahman of Bratslav, held to be like 'one of the prophetesses'), spiritual, prophetic women disappeared. They were replaced, in hasidic lore, by women who were possessed by evil spirits or who were sinners themselves. Hasidic homiletical literature was never addressed to women. When they did appear in the literature they were never presented as actual women. Instead they were allegorized as representing something else, like the 'men of matter' or the Jewish people.

Why was it that hasidism, which shared many of the characteristics of Sabbatianism (e.g. geographical location in eastern Europe, kabbalistic legacy, charismatic leadership) and pioneered new, unconventional paths to holiness, did not include the cultivation of female spirituality and leadership among its innovations? Why did it perpetuate gender hierarchy rather than an inclusive, egalitarian attitude towards women?

Rapoport-Albert's answer, in a word, is: sex. Traditionally women were defined by an inherent sexuality. Sabbatianism in its various incarnations had shown that if women were admitted to the circle of spiritual activism, they brought their sexuality with them. This led to libertinism and sexual depravity. As it was, the enemies of hasidism libelled it as an offshoot of Sabbatianism. The hasidim dared not flirt with the sexual threat that women represented. Rather than summon them to transcend their sexual nature (a main theme of hasidic doctrine with respect to men), better to allegorize real women out of doctrinal consciousness. Meanwhile the place for flesh-and-blood women was in out-of-focus facilitative roles at home or at the margins of the tsadik's court.

WOMEN IN?

'The Emergence of a Female Constituency in Twentieth-Century Habad'

'From Woman as Hasid to Woman as "Tsadik" in the Teachings of the Last Two Lubavitcher Rebbes'

We have seen how Rapoport-Albert skilfully used the example of 'hagiography with footnotes' to illustrate the sensitivity of at least some hasidim, and especially of Habad, to the inroads that modern sensibilities were making into traditional society. In these two studies about women and twentieth-century Habad, she highlighted how the traditional stance towards women, elucidated in the previous section, was inadequate to the social and cultural circumstances of the twentieth century. In response, the role of women in Habad hasidism underwent a radical transformation.

In these essays Rapoport-Albert continued developing the theme that in hasidism, from its origins in the eighteenth century, there was no provision for a collective spiritual experience for women. Technically a woman could not even be a 'hasid'; wife of, sister of, daughter of a hasid, but not a hasid herself—no matter how distinguished her lineage. Even the one venue of female contact with the tsadik, the private interview (*yehides*), was restricted. Some tsadikim, notably all of the first five leaders of Habad, refused even this expedient.

The refusal to include women was only indirectly relaxed in Habad beginning with Shalom Dovber (1860–1920), who consented to his wife, Shterna Sarah (1860–1942), presenting him with the petitions of women supplicants. Eventually he decided that Shterna Sarah should found a women's philanthropic group to support the students of the Habad Tomkhei Temimim yeshiva. Still, Shalom Dovber never directly addressed women. After all, he believed that 'Satan dances among the women' and blamed them as primarily responsible for the large-scale secularization and assimilation of his day.

It was Shalom Dovber's son, the sixth *admor* of Habad, Joseph Isaac, who realized that women were an untapped resource that could supply much-needed human capital to reinforce the traditional Judaism that was under attack. He was the first *admor* to speak to women directly and collectively. He sought to organize women's groups promoting halakhic observance, and created frameworks for exposing them to Habad teachings in a limited way.

Menachem Mendel Schneerson (1902–94), Joseph Isaac's son-in-law and successor, went much further. He saw women as full partners in the messianic project, which more and more became the ultimate focus of Habad under his leadership. Towards that end he institutionalized women's education and roles in the movement. He often taught women's groups personally and granted many women private audiences. Initial resistance to this stance on the part of men did not deter him.

This empowerment of women as full-fledged hasidim and messianic catalysts was also calculated to combat contemporary feminism. To Menachem Mendel feminism subverted women's divinely endowed nature and divinely assigned roles and was destructive to traditional society as a whole. Rapoport-Albert posited that by transvaluing women's traditional virtues and roles Menachem Mendel had created a powerful counter-feminism that was a key factor in the success of his movement.

Once more hasidism, or at least its Habad iteration, proved its sensitivity to the shifting modern context. It demonstrated its ability to innovate in the name of tradition, appropriating, yet transmuting, feminism—that most modern of cultural trends—as a means of protecting tradition.

CONCLUSION

Ada Rapoport-Albert has rewritten the master-narrative of early hasidic history. Thanks to her we now know that eighteenth-century hasidism did not represent the movement's 'classic period' and was not a project of democratization, ameliorating the hierarchical structuring of religion and spirituality. Evolving in a context of intense spirituality rather than of political, social, economic, or religious crisis, eighteenth-century hasidism is more accurately described as the gestational prelude to the mature movement of the nineteenth century. The new hasidism, initially neither institutionalized nor centralized, was characterized by a process of differentiating itself from conventional ascetic-mystical hasidism. Its elite leaders only became conscious of a distinctive group identity long after the Ba'al Shem Tov's death and at the very end of the Magid's career.

Ironically, this newfound consciousness emerged in response to the Vilna Gaon's demonization of the hasidim. They subsequently spent the last decades of the eighteenth and the first decades of the nineteenth century experimenting with various forms of doctrine, literature, organization, leadership, and transfer of authority. The experimentation was, however, always within the bounds of halakhah and with an eye towards remaining integrated in the established Jewish community.

Somewhat surprisingly, this experimentation did not include the revision of women's status and role. Rapoport-Albert has emphasized that, contrary to the thrust of hasidism towards spiritualization of the physical, the movement persisted in identifying women with an irredeemable materiality. They could never escape their inherent sexuality and attain spiritual heights. Therefore gender hierarchy persisted and, formally speaking, for the first 150 years or so of the existence of hasidism women were not counted as members of the group. Real women, as opposed to generic allegorized or symbolic women, were invisible in hasidic doctrine and marginal to hasidic life.

Looking at twentieth-century hasidism through the prism of Habad, Rapoport-Albert has revealed its negotiation with modernity. Understanding the changes in all post-Enlightenment people's epistemological universe, Habad's modern leaders adapted their modes of communication and rhetoric to appeal to modern sensibilities. They also responded to modernist feminism by re-evaluating and recalibrating the role of women in their movement. As they (mis-)appropriated modern rhetorical strategies to defend tradition, so did they adopt certain feminist postulates in order to create a counter-feminism that would empower women without flouting traditional fundamental gender roles.

The essays that appear here represent Rapoport-Albert's scholarship, with its felicitous combination of erudition and creativity. She has never lacked the courage to question conventions, but neither has she overturned them lightly. The rabbinic admonition of 'respect but suspect' is an apt epigraph for her approach to the scholarly legacy to which she has been heir. The conclusions of her innovative scholarship have been incorporated in the collectively authored *Hasidism: A New History*, published by Princeton University Press.

Research and writing, however, do not exhaust Rapoport-Albert's contribution to scholarship and education. As the perennial long line of students outside her University College London office testifies, she has become a figure to whom students—and colleagues—look for guidance, criticism, advice, and inspiration. Projecting a quiet authority and subtle charisma, she has made her mark in every area of academic endeavour: research, writing, teaching, editing, speaking, reviewing, evaluating, recommending, conferencing, administrating, organizing, grantsmanship, and fundraising.

The decision of the Littman Library to bring together the essays in this volume is a fitting statement of Ada Rapoport-Albert's importance to the fields of research she has undertaken, to the institutions with which she has been associated, to Jewish studies as a whole, and to the academic scrutiny of religion.

Jerusalem, July 2017 (Av 5777)

PART I

HISTORY

ONE

Hasidism after 1772: Structural Continuity and Change

1. The Problem

The year 1772 is generally regarded as a critical one, or at least an important turning point, in the history of hasidism. Three decisive events took place in that year which altered both the ideological and the organizational course on which the movement had originally embarked. The spring brought with it the first outbreak of bitter hostilities between the *mitnagedim* and the hasidim in Vilna, whence the dispute quickly spread to other Jewish communities in Lithuania and Galicia. During the summer months Belarus was annexed to Russia, and Galicia to Austria, in the first partition of the disintegrating Polish–Lithuanian Commonwealth; as a result, parts of the Jewish (and hasidic) community in Poland, which until then had formed a single cultural and political entity, found themselves arbitrarily separated. At the end of the year, in December, the supreme leader of hasidism, R. Dov Ber, the Magid of Mezhirech (Międzyrzecz), died without leaving an heir to take charge of the movement in his place.

In the light of this historic combination of circumstances, the scholarly literature on hasidism has tended to divide the history of the movement, especially from the point of view of its organizational structure, into two periods separated by a clear line of demarcation: (*a*) from the foundation of the movement to the death of the Magid of Mezhirech, the period of centralized leadership under a single universally acknowledged head (first the founder, Israel Ba'al Shem Tov (the Besht), and then his disciple and successor, the Magid of Mezhirech); (*b*) the period beginning immediately after the death of the Magid in 1772, which was marked by the onset of decentralization: the leadership split up, and the movement began to function as a loose affiliation of distinct communities connected, it is true, by the common legacy of the Besht and the Magid of Mezhirech, but independent of each other, and each led by its own tsadik.

This periodization scheme underlies every major historical study of hasidism. Explicit discussions of it, however, have been scarce and lacking in rigour, since the organizational development of hasidism, as distinct from the evolution of its doctrines, has not received much critical scholarly attention. Processes of organizational change, inasmuch as they are observed at all, are treated casually, and up to now no systematic attempt has been made to identify their causes.[1]

It is surprising that the many historians who posited such an abrupt and extensive change in the organizational structure of hasidism as this transition, following the death of the Magid, from central leadership to a multiplicity of independent centres showed so little curiosity as to its causes. In most cases they contented themselves with the assumption that the son of the Magid, R. Abraham the Angel, either did not want or was not competent to succeed to his father's place, and that therefore the leadership passed to a group of the Magid's disciples and became fragmented.[2] The late Shmuel Ettinger, who did recognize the decentralization of the hasidic leadership after the death of the Magid of Mezhirech as an intriguing historical question, labelled it 'a paradoxical element in the formative stages of the movement':

> Rabbi Dov Ber of Meseritz, the Great Magid, the well known figure called by his disciples the 'Rabbi of all the sons of the Diaspora', who was a leader of authoritarian views . . . directed the movement into . . . decentralization. He set up group after group with a pupil at the head of almost every one, with the result that after his death there was no single agreed leader of the movement.[3]

In his search for an answer to this question Ettinger suggested that 'the tradition of autonomous activity in the local Jewish communities must have assisted the decentralizing tendency in the movement',[4] and he was undoubtedly right in this. But his answer itself raises new, and equally intriguing, questions: if hasidism emerged on a landscape of which autonomous units of communal organization had traditionally formed a natural feature, why, then, did it adopt in its initial stages such an 'unnatural' framework of central control, and why did it abandon this novel structure immediately after the death of the Magid?

In order to give these questions proper consideration, the assumptions from which they have sprung must be examined first: did hasidism really undergo a swift and clear-cut transition from centralized organization to a loose association of autonomous units? In other words, was the leadership centralized in the first place? Did the death of the Magid really create a void, and was it only because no suitable successor could be found that this void came to be filled by a group of the Magid's disciples? Was it only at this stage that the process of decentralization was set in train?

There is no doubt that hasidism did eventually develop as a thoroughly non-centralist movement, and that it has remained so up to the present day. The sphere of influence of each tsadik, though not formally fixed, was well defined and zealously guarded, just like the formal boundaries of the areas that fell within the jurisdiction of each of the *kehalim*, the traditional governing bodies of the communities,[5] or—and this factor should not be underestimated—the oft-disputed boundaries of the independent estates of the Polish aristocracy in eighteenth-century Poland.[6] Ettinger rightly pointed out that the boundaries of each of the autonomous units which together constituted the expanding hasidic movement did not match those of the areas that were traditionally subject to the jurisdiction of each of the *kehalim*. The hasidic fraternities drew their membership from extensive regions which might include any number of established communities (*kehilot*), some of them large and important, while their charismatic leaders might be resident in remote little towns, away from the major traditional seats of rabbinic and communal authority.[7] But in spite of the fact that the boundaries of the two types of autonomous unit—those within the regime of the *kehalim* and those that constituted the hasidic movement—did not correspond, it is clear that we are dealing with two equally non-centralist systems. The independence of the various hasidic courts from each other found expression not only in the exclusive relationship of each hasidic fraternity to its own tsadik and his particular teachings but also in the realm of everyday life: for example, as Chone Shmeruk has shown, each court had its own *shoḥet*, and meat slaughtered by a 'foreign' hasidic *shoḥet* was regarded as if slaughtered by a non-hasidic one.[8]

Since, as all agree, hasidism ultimately adopted a highly fragmented organizational structure, it is particularly important to re-examine its structure in the earliest stages, during which it is generally assumed to have been highly centralized. How far was leadership of the hasidic movement in fact concentrated at that time in the person of the Besht and, after him, the Magid of Mezhirech?

2. The Leadership in the Time of the Ba'al Shem Tov

The method by which hasidism recorded its spiritual debt to its two first and most profoundly revered leaders has, to some extent, obscured the facts. Hasidic literature consistently presents the Besht as the founder and sole leader of the movement in his day, exercising supreme control from the centre. The following quotation, chosen almost at random from among dozens of similar passages, clearly reflects the traditional hasidic evaluation of the Ba'al Shem Tov's leadership:

The rabbi, our teacher, R. Israel Ba'al Shem Tov, of blessed memory, father of the hasidim and chief of those holy tsadikim, the light of whose *torah* and righteousness has continued to shine up to the present day, and all the tsadikim there have been since the time of the Besht, of blessed memory, have but drawn from the well of his instruction. And even though his disciples have gone their various ways, nevertheless they all drink their fill from his unfailing source alone; all are his disciples, and the disciples of his disciples, who cast their light on the world to teach the people the ways of the Lord, to love Him and fear Him with heart and soul.[9]

Similarly *Shivḥei habesht* declares: 'The crown of Israel's glory, the rabbi, our teacher R. Israel Ba'al Shem Tov, may his merit protect us and all Israel, and his holy and pure disciples who dwelt in his shadow and sheltered under his wing and sat in the dust of his feet, to drink in his words with thirst'.[10] The whole of *Shivḥei habesht* reflects this attitude when it portrays all the Ba'al Shem Tov's associates as his subservient disciples, repeatedly emphasizing not only their spiritual inferiority to him but also their willing recognition of this fact (even if they were sometimes slow to appreciate his full spiritual stature). But this picture is incomplete and somewhat distorted. In a series of biographical studies, A. J. Heschel sketched the character of several members of the Besht's circle on the basis of *Shivḥei habesht* and other sources which are independent of it. These studies call for a re-evaluation of R. Pinhas of Korets (Korzec), R. Nahman of Kosów, R. Isaac of Drohobycz, as well as quite a few others, and of the complex pattern of their relations with the Besht. It is clear that they were not merely 'disciples' humbling themselves before their master and 'sitting in the dust of his feet to drink in his words with thirst' but charismatic figures in their own right, charged with enormous spiritual power and claiming the same freedom of access to the upper worlds as the Besht himself.[11] Ben-Zion Dinur and Joseph Weiss furnished further support for this assessment of the Besht's circle in the first generation of hasidism.[12] *Shivḥei habesht* itself drops occasional hints on the position of the Besht in the circle of his intimates which depart from the express tendency of that book to glorify him and exalt him above all his contemporaries. It describes R. Nahman of Kosów, for example, as a man who headed his own circle of hasidim and who opposed, and even persecuted, the Besht. The scene in which he finally acknowledges the spiritual stature of the Besht and appears to be submitting to his authority in fact refers to a test of the pneumatic powers of the Besht forced upon him by R. Nahman, whose own powers were already tried and tested.[13] Only after the Besht had passed this test was R. Nahman ready to treat him as a colleague and an equal:

The rabbi, our teacher and rabbi Naḥman of Kosów, was an opponent of the Besht. (I heard that the Besht stems from the soul of King David, may he rest in peace, and the rabbi, our teacher and rabbi, Naḥman stems from the soul of King Saul, may he rest in peace. Therefore Rabbi Naḥman always hated this David.)

Once the Besht said: 'The rabbi, our teacher and rabbi, Naḥman, pursues me to kill me.' (It is known that in bowing down [*nefilat apayim*] there is the *kavvanah* of killing one's enemies.) 'But with the help of God he will not get me.'

Once the disciples of our teacher and rabbi, Naḥman, went to their rabbi and said to him: 'Why is it that all the world goes to the rabbi, the Besht, and everyone praises him highly? Why don't you come to an agreement and learn his true nature so that we will know where the truth lies, why let him be a snare for us?'

He listened to their words and he went to the holy community of Medzhibozh to the rabbi, the Besht, who received him with great honor. Afterwards both of them entered a special room, and everyone was excluded from the room save one who hid himself in a certain place. The rabbi, our teacher and rabbi, Naḥman, said: 'Israel, is it true you say that you know people's thoughts?'

He said to him: 'Yes.'

He said to him: 'Do you know what I am thinking now?'

The rabbi answered: 'It is known that thought is not fixed. It wanders from one point to another and is continually transformed. If you concentrate your thought on one thing, then I will be able to know.'

The rabbi, our teacher and rabbi, Naḥman, did so.

The Besht said: 'The name of YAHWEH is in your thoughts.'

The rabbi, our teacher and rabbi, Naḥman, said: 'You would know this anyhow, for I must always keep this thought. As it is written: *I have set the Lord* [YAHWEH] *always before me* [Ps. 16: 8]. Whenever I remove all thought and concentrate on one thing, the name of the Presence is before my eyes.'

The Besht said: 'But there are several holy names, and you could have concentrated on any that you like.'

Then the rabbi, our rabbi and teacher, admitted that it was as the Besht had said. After that they discussed the secrets of the Torah.[14]

Even after R. Nahman recognized the spiritual powers of the Besht, he did not humble himself before him. It appears that he continued to maintain a circle of his own followers and these were inclined to be scornful of the Besht in spite of the improvement in the personal relations between him and their master.[15] According to *Shivḥei habesht*, R. Nahman rebuked his people 'for speaking ill of the Besht', and described his relations with him in these terms: 'The quarrel between the Besht and myself is a very old one. It is the quarrel that was between King Saul and David, may they rest in peace, and the quarrel that was between Hillel and Shammai. How can you dare to butt into it?'[16] Although *Shivḥei habesht* seeks to glorify the status of the Besht as sole leader, R. Nahman of Kosów emerges from between the lines as a pneumatic personality in his own right, independent of the Besht and not subject to his authority.[17]

Unlike such men as R. Nahman of Kosów and R. Pinhas of Korets, who had their own circles of disciples and regarded themselves as colleagues of the Besht, R. Aryeh Judah Leyb, the Mokhiah (preacher) of Połonne, accepted the Besht as his teacher, as is shown by all the stories about him in *Shivḥei habesht*. All the same, according to those accounts, R. Aryeh Judah Leyb was gifted with a power 'to annul judgements' which was not inferior to that of the Besht, and which, in one case at least, exceeded it and was exercised in order to render ineffective an action taken by the Besht in the upper worlds.[18] In another incident it was said of the Mokhiah that he had heard a proclamation by a heavenly herald which led him to foretell the destruction of Shargorod (Szarogród). The Besht, who was present, 'shouted at the Preacher and said: "Fool. *You*, too, hear heralds?"',[19] but later admitted to R. Jacob Joseph of Połonne: 'Did you think that the Preacher was lying, God forbid, when he said he heard the herald's voice? He truly did hear the herald.'[20] It is clear therefore that the Mokhiah of

Połonne could hear heavenly proclamations and exert influence in the upper worlds just like his master, the Besht. Clearly, he was not 'one of the common people' or 'a man of matter', to use the terminology employed by hasidism from its beginnings to describe the ordinary hasid and to distinguish him from the tsadik, the 'man of form' or the leader, who was 'a man of the spirit'.[21]

Later hasidic tradition could hardly fail to recognize this. In spite of its anachronistic tendency to turn the Besht—primarily a pietist, a pneumatic, and a *ba'al shem*, one who can manipulate divine names to utilize their supernatural powers—into a latter-day, full-fledged hasidic leader, or tsadik, and to present all his associates as his subservient disciples and 'courtiers', it does not deny those 'disciples' their status as charismatic figures in their own right, quite like the Besht himself:

And in this generation, too, it has been revealed that the Besht had the Holy Spirit and the revelation of Elijah and other exalted spiritual qualities, and he disclosed the secrets of the Torah to his disciples (may their souls rest in Paradise), who also had the Holy Spirit, as, for example, his brother-in-law R. Gershon of Kuty and R. Nahman of Kosów and his other famous disciples, the wondrous greatness of whose deeds was recognized by all who saw them and whose prayer was heard from afar, and at the end of his days he handed on the principles of the Torah to the holy rabbi, R. Dov of Mezhirech, who had the Holy Spirit, which he attained by means of great affliction, as we have explained; and now, in this generation, all the tsadikim are his [presumably the Besht's] disciples and we drink his waters.[22]

We see, then, that the picture of the Besht's circle, even as portrayed in *Shivḥei habesht* and later hasidic tradition, is far removed from the typical image of the hasidic court in which one spiritually outstanding personality dominates a congregation of ordinary hasidim who, by their very nature, are 'common people' from the spiritual point of view (though not necessarily from the point of view of education, intellectual capacity, material wealth, or anything else), and who are totally dependent on the personality of the leader and his mediation to realize their own spirituality. Rather, the whole of the Besht's circle is charged with high spiritual tension. As was shown above, several of his associates were clearly endowed with pneumatic qualities like his and even attracted disciples of their own, although the definition of 'disciple' in this context is, of course, fluid: a person could regard himself as someone's disciple and at the same time be regarded as the teacher and leader of others.[23] Later hasidic tradition could hardly ignore this fact; nor has it escaped the attention of modern scholars. Distinguishing 'primitive' hasidism (after the model of 'primitive Christianity') from, on the one hand, the exclusive circles of 'aristocratic' kabbalists which preceded it—whose members segregated themselves from the community at large—and, on the other hand, from the popular 'cult of tsadikism' into which it was soon to degenerate—a cult which elevated the tsadikim over the community at large—scholars concluded that 'primitive hasidism' brought about, if only briefly, something of a democratization of religious life, inviting the whole community to strive towards the highest spiritual and mystical goals which it had set forth.[24] This, then, was taken as the truly vital, original, creative stage in the history of hasidism, an initial period of purity, before the novel egalitarian ideals of the founders were corrupted under the compulsion of reality. For once the common people adopted the 'spiritual' mannerisms of the holy men, they inevitably reduced them to no more than empty gestures. This in turn was seen as the factor which prompted the leadership to reassess its methods and goals, a process which culminated in the rise of the institution of tsadikism. Hasidism now drew a fundamental distinction between the spiritual ideals which the tsadik alone could realize and the completely different spiritual possibilities which were open to the ordinary hasid.

This picture of a spiritually ambitious, egalitarian, 'democratic' hasidism, however attractive to the modern eye, does not square with one solid historical fact to which I have already alluded: it was precisely in this initial period that hasidism formulated the sharp distinction between the 'men of matter' and the 'men of form', between 'the ordinary organs of the body of the people' and the 'spiritual men' who were 'its head'. How is it possible to reconcile an image of egalitarian spiritual comradeship, such as is so commonly associated with early hasidism, with an anthropological doctrine which divides mankind (or rather, the Jewish component of mankind) into two clear-cut sections: a small minority, purely spiritual in nature, on one side, and, on the other, the great majority, characterized by crude materiality or corporeality (the ideal of the bond between the two sections which hasidism set up for itself, far from obscuring this fundamental distinction, is actually based on it and takes it as its starting point).[25] If hasidism, in its initial stages, did indeed throw open the gates of spiritual-mystical religiosity equally to everyone, whom did R. Jacob Joseph have in mind when he introduced the concepts and coined the various phrases and terms which have ever since served the hasidic movement to distinguish between the two sections of humanity which he had defined? The only possible answer to this question seems to be that the Besht and the 'spiritual' members of his circle all regarded themselves as representatives of the section described as 'the head', the leaders. It was only within that circle, not outside it, that they called for the fulfilment of such mystical ideals as the requirement of constant *devekut*, the state of 'cleaving', that is, focusing at all times on nothing other than God; worship 'through corporeality', even by means of material or mundane preoccupations; the elevation of 'straying thoughts'—distractions from focus on the Divine—and so on. The 'corporeal' common people were situated on the margins of the circle or outside it, and the call directed to them, from the outset, was completely different: the masses were instructed, above all, to cleave [*lidbok*] to the leaders of their generation but not to mimic them. Thus, on the subject of the ideal of worship through corporeality, R. Jacob Joseph writes as follows, pointing out that this is a tradition which 'I believe I heard from my teacher', the Besht:

And it is in that sense that we should understand 'And warm yourself by the fire [Heb. *or*—'light'] of the wise',[26] that is to say, it is while the wise are in the superior spiritual state of *gadlut* [expanded consciousness] and occupied with the light [*or*] of Torah and prayer, when they are literally aflame with the light of fire, that you should warm yourself by their fire. But 'beware of their embers',[27] that is to say, when they are in the lesser state of *katnut* [diminished consciousness], when they have no light to kindle them with an inner fire, a condition to which we apply the word 'embers', [when they are] devoid of inner fire. The disciple wishes to learn from his master how he occupies himself with material things, but he does not know that the master is, at the same time, fulfilling [the ideal expressed by the verse] 'I have hidden Your words in my heart',[28] occupying himself with material things but with an inner spiritual purpose. Thus *all that the disciple manages to learn from* [*his master*] *is to occupy himself on the material level, and he will be punished* [*for this*], 'for their bite is the bite of a fox and their sting is the sting of a scorpion'.[29] That is to say, he [the master] . . . is bringing seven [heavenly] levels . . . closer to their [spiritual, divine] root.[30] But the disciple knows nothing of this and thinks his master is simply occupied with material things. And these are the words of a wise man.[31] (emphasis mine—A.R-A.)

The traditions that have come down to us from that circle of the founders of hasidism often stress that the call to fulfil the mystical ideals is limited to 'the men of the spirit'. Sometimes they make this explicit, as in the passage quoted above; sometimes they do not spell out the limitation but it is clear that they regard it as self-evident, or else it is slipped in here and there, in some of the parallel traditions which have been preserved.[32] It is true that, at this stage of the development of the movement, there was not yet a standard terminology by which to refer to the leaders, and they were variously called 'men of form', 'scholars', 'men of understanding', 'men of knowledge', 'heads of the generation', 'the tsadikim', 'those of Israel who are perfect in their faith', and so on, but the collective consciousness of leadership which was shared within the circle is clear beyond all doubt, and, as we have seen, it is not focused at this stage on the figure of a single leader, not even on that of the Besht.[33]

Shivḥei habesht (literally, 'The Praises of the Besht'), a hagiography dedicated to the personality of the Besht, is also, in some measure, a hagiography of R. Gershon of Kuty, R. Jacob Joseph of Połonne, R. Aryeh Leyb the preacher of Połonne, R. Dov Ber of Mezhirech, R. Pinhas of Korets, and all the other extraordinary figures who populate its pages. Although overshadowed by the Besht, they clearly belong to his superior category of humanity. The qualitative difference between him and them is insignificant when compared to the qualitative difference between the Besht and his circle, taken as one category, and the category comprising 'the common people', 'the men of matter', whose presence in *Shivḥei habesht*, however dimly perceived, is not to be overlooked. True, *Shivḥei habesht* is not concerned to portray the personalities of these 'common people' in any detail. Rarely even named, they serve only as a background, a narrative means of enhancing the spiritual quality and supernatural powers of the heroes. But they perform an important function, in that the Besht and his associates can only operate through them or on their behalf.[34] This tendency to highlight the individual personality of the heroes while letting the ordinary mortals who witness, and benefit from, their actions speak only from the shadows is natural to the hagiographic genre, but it should not conceal from us the fact that all those others who are obscure as individuals have a collective 'otherness' perceived with great clarity. The picture of society in the early days of hasidism as it emerges from *Shivḥei habesht* is, then, that of a group of spiritual teachers who maintain a certain level of communication among themselves while at the same time maintaining an altogether different level of communication with a wider public among whom they operate but from whom they are conscious of being utterly different in every aspect of their spiritual constitution[35]—a picture which is wholly compatible with the anthropological doctrine of R. Jacob Joseph of Połonne.

If we seek to uncover the historical reality which underlies R. Jacob Joseph's observations concerning the 'body', or the corporeal nature, of 'the common people', and to relate his speculative teachings to some concrete state of society in his day, *Shivḥei habesht* supplies the answer in stories about the tax farmers, tradespeople, *ḥeder* teachers, and ritual slaughterers, men and women from all walks of life, who, lacking all 'spirituality' of their own, were passive witnesses of the wonderful deeds performed by the Besht and his colleagues and came under the influence of their powers. And if a parallel is to be drawn between the fully developed hasidic community of recent generations, with the tsadik at its head, and any organizational structure in the first generation of hasidism, the lines will not run from the latter-day tsadik to the Besht and from the Besht's circle of associates and disciples to the latter-day hasidic community, as has generally been assumed in the historiography both within the hasidic movement and in the scholarly literature outside it. Rather, the parallel lines will run from the latter-day tsadik to the entire circle of the Besht and his associates, and from the latter-day hasidic community to the wider public within which the Besht's circle operated.

The clarification of these issues has a direct bearing on the question which formed the starting point of the present discussion, namely, whether leadership of the hasidic movement in the time of the Besht was, in fact, centralized. There is no doubt that the Besht's circle of associates and colleagues was influenced by his teachings,[36] and it is reasonable to assume that in his time he was regarded as the most prominent personality in that circle. From this point of view it is understandable and legitimate that he should have been perpetuated in the collective memory of the movement as the chief or only leader of his day. But from an organizational point of view it is quite clear that he did not act as the supreme leader in any hierarchical framework. Rather, he belonged to a whole network of charismatic personalities who were accepted by the wider community as teachers and spiritual leaders, and who, indeed, saw themselves in that light. Hasidism in its early stages did not create any centralized organizational framework, and its leadership structure in the generation of its founders was no less fragmented than it is generally taken to have been in later generations. The chain of events immediately after the death of the Besht highlights the absence of any centralized framework of leadership. If the Besht had, indeed, served in his lifetime as the supreme leader of the whole movement in the same way as every tsadik in succeeding generations was to act as sole leader of his own congregation of hasidim, we would expect an immediate successor to have been found, acceptable to the majority, if not to all, of the hasidim (although the appointment of such a successor might have followed a short contest for the position by a number of candidates from among his sons or his disciples). For were it not so, the movement as such would have broken up and disappeared from the arena of history, as did many hasidic congregations, whose distinctive identity was weakened to the point of extinction after the death of their founder in the absence of an 'heir' to succeed him. True, it is generally assumed that the Magid of Mezhirech inherited the leadership in precisely this way, either on the strength of an explicit nomination by the Besht before he died or through being 'elected' to office by the other disciples, because, so the argument goes, the natural candidate, R. Zevi, the son of the Besht, was either unfit for leadership or unwilling to accept it.[37] However, the evidence for all this is meagre and problematic: the Magid of Mezhirech was certainly not the natural candidate for the succession, since he came to hasidism only a short time before the Besht died.[38] As was demonstrated by Heschel, he was not acceptable to everyone; the majority of the disciples and associates of the Besht did not regard the Magid as their leader and were not numbered among his disciples. But Heschel's suggestion, which was intended to resolve this question, is far from satisfactory: 'The followers of the Besht, *who apparently were unaware that he had chosen R. Ber*, refused to accept his authority. Only two or three of the youngest disciples attached themselves to him' (emphasis mine—A.R-A.).[39] It is hard to believe that the Besht's associates and disciples, who were his most intimate companions, would not have known of a decision so important for all of them as his nomination of the Magid to be his successor. It is also hard to conceive of any reason why such a decision should have been kept intentionally secret, for by its very nature its sole purpose would have been to legitimize the succession by making it public. This question mark over the circumstances of the transfer of leadership from the Besht to the Magid also gave rise to the conjecture that the Magid was not recognized as leader of the movement until the year

1766, about six years after the death of the Besht, and that during those six years a strenuous contest for the leadership was waged between the Magid of Mezhirech and R. Jacob Joseph of Połonne, and perhaps also R. Menahem Mendel of Przemyślany.[40]

The notion of a long-drawn-out struggle for the succession to the leadership is unconvincing: if hasidism in the generation of the Besht had indeed crystallized around its 'tsadik' like a hasidic congregation of more recent times, it is hard to imagine that it could have survived as a movement for fully six years in the absence of the leader who was, after all, the source of its vitality and the focus for its distinctive identity; it would certainly have disintegrated or split up, earlier rather than later, into separate and even mutually hostile congregations in the course of the protracted struggle between the rival claimants to the succession. Moreover, this hypothesis has no support in the sources. The facts and factors to which Heschel and Rubinstein drew attention are, indeed, correct and reasonable in themselves, but they do not necessarily combine to present us with a picture of a struggle for 'the crown of leadership' between the Magid, R. Jacob Joseph, and R. Menahem Mendel of Przemyślany. All that we know is: (*a*) that the Magid of Mezhirech was accepted at some stage as the leader of a large circle of hasidim; (*b*) that R. Jacob Joseph of Połonne and R. Pinhas of Korets explicitly, and some of the other intimates of the Besht by implication (as we are prompted to conclude from the absence of their names from any list of the Magid's disciples), were critical of the Magid as leader and did not join his circle after the death of the Besht;[41] (*c*) that the Magid of Mezhirech, and still more so some of his disciples, rejected the hasidic path taught by R. Pinhas of Korets;[42] (*d*) that R. Pinhas of Korets and R. Jacob Joseph of Połonne were on terms of affection and mutual respect;[43] (*e*) that R. Menahem Mendel of Przemyślany, whether or not in accordance with his own wishes, was also accepted as spiritual leader by a section of the public until he left for Erets Yisra'el in 1764.

If we do not start with the hypothesis of a struggle for the leadership which allegedly delayed the final decision for a full six years, the information at our disposal does not in the least point to the creation of full-blown pressure groups fighting to advance R. Jacob Joseph, R. Pinhas of Korets, R. Menahem Mendel of Przemyślany, or anyone else to the position of supreme leader of hasidism, and the facts are open to a different interpretation. Heschel himself formulates his opinion cautiously and presents it only as a conjecture,[44] although it seems that both he and Dresner, who quotes him in full,[45] are convinced that it is correct. But this conjecture raises more problems than it solves: why did the majority of the Besht's disciples reject or ignore his nomination of the Magid as his successor? Indeed, why did the Besht not choose a disciple who was of longer standing and closer to him, like R. Jacob Joseph of Połonne? And if, in fact, R. Jacob Joseph was considered unfit for leadership because of his difficult character,[46] just as R. Zevi, the son of the Besht, may have been considered unsuitable for high office (though it may be questioned whether such considerations would have been enough to oust a natural heir from his rightful position), why did the obvious talents of the Magid of Mezhirech fail to earn him universal and immediate recognition?

The unlikely conjectures which have been offered in explanation of the allegedly irregular procedures following the death of the Besht stem from the anachronistic expectation that the leadership should have passed immediately and directly from him to the Magid of Mezhirech, just as it did eventually pass from father to son, son-in-law, or some other natural heir in the hasidic dynasties which developed later on. This expectation, which is common to both internal hasidic and critical scholarly historiography, has grown out of the no less anachronistic assumption that the Besht acted as the sole central leader of an established community of 'his' hasidim. In fact, the Besht was only one prominent personality among others in a circle of charismatics and pneumatics, whose members all shared his supernatural qualities and his claims to spiritual leadership of the age, although it is quite likely that many of them drew their inspiration from him. We must therefore reject the conjectures outlined above; the facts in our possession will then fit without difficulty into an alternative reconstruction of the circumstances which followed the death of the Besht: the Magid of Mezhirech did not 'inherit' the leadership of hasidism as a result of a secret or controversial 'nomination' by the Besht; nor was he 'elected' to office by a majority of the Ba'al Shem Tov's disciples as has generally been assumed either explicitly or implicitly despite the absence of any evidence for this in the sources.[47] His accession to power was spontaneous, and it was based on his own charismatic personality, not on any formal, rational procedures, such that had not yet crystallized in hasidism. It is very probable that not many people saw him as a leader in the period immediately following the death of the Besht, perhaps until 1766.[48] In other words, the status of the Magid as the heir of the Besht was not that of a direct, immediate, and formally instituted successor but of an heir in the broadest sense of the word: he came to be regarded as the greatest hasidic leader of his time, just as the Besht had been regarded before him. The existence of an heir in this latter sense would not, in principle—and, as we know, did not in practice—necessitate the removal from the scene of other hasidic leaders who did not accept the authority of the Magid, in just the same way as the activity of the Besht had not curbed the independent operations of his colleagues and their disciples in the preceding two decades.

This interpretation of the facts also relieves us of the need to cast R. Jacob Joseph in the unlikely role of an unsuccessful rival candidate for the leadership, when there is no evidence of any efforts by him in that direction, unless his well-known reservations with regard to the leadership of the Magid were to be so construed.[49] That this is most unlikely becomes evident if we bear in mind that there were many internal controversies in the hasidic camp, and that the opposing parties entertained mutual reservations of various kinds in regard to worship, personal conduct, or distinct styles of communal leadership. These did not necessarily indicate the existence of a struggle for the 'crown' of supreme authority over the hasidic movement as a whole: indeed, in most cases they certainly did not. This is as true of the beginnings of hasidism as of its subsequent stages of development even up to the present day, when tensions and ideological or territorial disputes between the various hasidic courts have become commonplace, without ever turning upon the subject of rival claims to the supreme leadership of the entire movement, and without challenging the pluralistic principle which underlay the organizational structure of the movement from the start.[50]

One final point is worth noting in this connection: the Lithuanian *magid* R. Israel Löbel, a zealous opponent of hasidism,[51] in his German tract on the hasidic 'sect' said: 'After the death of R. Israel Ba'al Shem, both the external and the internal government of the sect took on a new form. Instead of one supreme leader, many were chosen.'[52] Admittedly R. Israel Löbel's account, written at the end of the 1790s, is imprecise on the historical details of the beginnings of hasidism, and it is clear that his knowledge of the Besht is defective.[53] But he was a contemporary of many of the disciples of the Magid of Mezhirech, and it is significant that he located the apparent decentralization of the hasidic leadership in the more distant past, after the death of the Besht, rather than associating the process with the situation he knew at first hand, following the death of the Magid of Mezhirech. So far as he was aware, the hasidic movement had been governed by many leaders as far back as anyone could remember. It is not impossible that his picture of a fragmented leadership faithfully reflects the historical situation which existed in the 1760s and early 1770s—particularly as it was perceived in the strongholds of the *mitnagedim* in Lithuania; for the few hasidic centres in mitnagdic Lithuania, notably the one at Karlin, were as notorious as the hasidic centre at Mezhirech, and they were certainly regarded not as secondary branches but as important centres in their own right (see more on this directly below).

3. The Leadership in the Time of the Magid

The enormous influence of the Magid of Mezhirech on his many disciples in the leadership of hasidism is so well documented as to be beyond dispute. It is precisely this that will throw into sharper relief the claim that the hasidic movement of his day was not centralized and did not produce any organizational framework for supreme leadership by the Magid or anyone else.

The decisive influence of the Magid is attested in hasidic literature both directly, in explicit acknowledgements, and indirectly, through the reflections of his views in the teachings of his disciples and their disciples. His influence, like that of the Besht, has become fixed in the historical memory of the movement. Hasidic historians present the Magid as the second link in a chain of transmission of charismatic authority in hasidism which began with the Besht and continued through the Magid to all the latter's disciples. Thus, instead of descending link by link from one generation to another, charismatic authority was seen as branching out in the third generation from the first two links, the Besht and the Magid, into several ancillary chains of transmission. Aaron Walden, for example, author of *Shem hagedolim heḥadash*, described the ramification of charismatic authority after the Magid of Mezhirech as follows: 'He drew living water from the well of that holy old man, the saintly, holy, and awe-inspiring rabbi, the holy of holies, Israel Ba'al Shem Tov of Międzybóż, and gave all the holy and pure disciples to drink of it, and through them all the earth was illuminated.'[54]

The picture of a chain that was broken up, its first two links—the Besht and the Magid—jointly connecting their numerous 'heirs' to the source of charismatic authority, naturally contributed to the assumption that in the generation of the Magid's disciples there was a pronounced organizational shift from central leadership by a single figure to a decentralized structure of leadership by many. However, this picture does not differentiate the strong personal and ideological connection which undoubtedly existed between the links from the loose organizational connection between them.

It is clear that the disciples of the Magid of Mezhirech were fully conscious of their ties to their common master. Not only did many of them continue to regard him as their teacher, and to acknowledge this proudly on numerous occasions even long after they had begun to lead their own hasidic communities; in addition, the teachings of the Magid certainly played a decisive part in the subsequent development of all the speculative doctrines of hasidism. Notably, at least one sharp ideological dispute between two hasidic leaders of the generation of the Magid's disciples was perceived by the protagonists as primarily a clash between two conflicting interpretations of the original teaching of the Magid. This was the dispute between R. Abraham of Kalisk (Kołyszki) and R. Shneur Zalman of Liady (Lyady), in which R. Levi Isaac of Berdyczów was also involved, and which spilt over into the struggle for control of the funds raised for the hasidic community in Erets Yisra'el.[55]

But the influence of the Magid as a teacher was not such as to inhibit the existence of independent hasidic centres away from Mezhirech. New courts were set up, not only after 1772 but also during his lifetime and apparently on his initiative, in the years when, supposedly, he functioned as the sole leader of the whole hasidic movement and exercised central control.

Although the Magid, as we have seen, was not accepted by all the intimates of the Besht as the heir to the leadership,[56] a whole generation of hasidic leaders had spent some time at his court and regarded him as their foremost teacher and master. At the same time, apart from those of the Besht's associates who never affiliated themselves to the Magid and continued independently to maintain circles of their own followers, there were some disciples of the Magid who established communities of hasidim during the lifetime of their teacher, and each of them was regarded in his own court as its sole leader. Thus R. Abraham of Kalisk, for example, in spite of his personal deference to his teacher the Magid, was already heading his own congregation of hasidim in Belarus in 1770, more than two years before the death of the Magid, and from one document it appears that his leadership of the hasidim in Kalisk may have begun as early as 1768.[57]

So, too, in 1772, while the Magid was still living, R. Menahem Mendel of Vitebsk became known as the leader of a community of hasidim in Minsk, and he acquired a reputation among the *mitnagedim* for the attraction he held for hasidic pilgrims.[58] R. Aaron of Karlin, too, established a centre of hasidism, the first in Lithuania, during the lifetime of the Magid.[59] In fact, although he is usually counted among the Magid's disciples and 'heirs' as a member of the third generation, he could only have served as a hasidic leader while the Magid was still alive: he himself died in Nisan 5532 (1772), a few months before the death of the Magid in Kislev of the following year.[60] According to all the available evidence, the Lithuanian hasidic centre in Karlin was not regarded as a subsidiary of the 'headquarters' of the movement in Volhynia, even though R. Aaron was known as a disciple of the great Magid.[61] To outside observers of hasidism during this period of expansion, the court at Karlin appeared as a centre in its own right. In the same period (that is, before 1772) the movement established a number of other centres in various regions, and all were known as places to which hasidim were drawn on pilgrimages to their leaders' courts. Solomon Maimon, for example, reports on that period: 'Therefore it naturally occurred that those who were attracted to this sect increased greatly in numbers in a short time. They used to go to K[arlin], M[ezhirech], and other holy places where the leaders, teachers, and luminaries of this sect lived . . . to visit the exalted rebbes and to hear them expound the new doctrine.'[62] He mentions Mezhirech and Karlin in the same breath, along with other, unnamed hasidic centres, without suggesting any hierarchical connection between them.[63]

A similar conclusion can be drawn from the anti-hasidic anthology *Zemir aritsim veḥarvot tsurim*: even before 1772 the hasidim were known collectively, at least in Lithuania, not only as 'Mezheritsher' but also as 'Karliner', and the two names were used indiscriminately.[64]

The following hasidic tale about R. Zusya of Annopol will illustrate the ambivalent status—disciple and teacher—of all the Magid's disciples who led their own hasidic communities while their own master was still living. The tale points to a level of personal relationship on which the Magid remained, and was known to be, the spiritual teacher and mentor of his distinguished disciple even after the latter had left his court and set up a hasidic community of his own; but at the same time the tale makes it quite clear that for the hasidim of the Magid's disciple it was that disciple, and he alone, who was their spiritual teacher and mentor, and all access to the supreme authority of the great Magid of Mezhirech was barred to them from the outset:

A man who lived in the same town as Rabbi Zusya saw that he was very poor. So each day he put twenty pennies into the little bag in which Zusya kept his phylacteries, so that he and his family might buy the necessaries of life. From that time on, the man grew richer and richer. The more he had, the more he gave Zusya, and the more he gave Zusya, the more he had.

But once he recalled that Zusya was the disciple of a great Magid, and it occurred to him that if what he gave the disciple was so lavishly rewarded, he might become even more prosperous if he made presents to the master himself. So he travelled to Mezritch and induced Rabbi Baer to accept a substantial gift from him. From this time on, his means shrank until he had lost all the profits he had made during the more fortunate period. He took his trouble to Rabbi Zusya, told him the whole story, and asked him what his present predicament was due to. For had not the rabbi himself told him that his master was immeasurably greater than he?

Zusya replied: 'Look! As long as you gave and did not bother to whom, whether to Zusya or another, God gave to you and did not bother to whom. But when you began to seek out especially noble and distinguished recipients, God did exactly the same.'[65]

This attempt by the hasid, once he had made his way in the world, to bypass the lesser authority of R. Zusya in order to affiliate himself directly to the supreme authority of the Magid appears to reflect a hierarchical outlook which can be understood in terms of the social dynamics of personal success. However, whether the details of the story are historically accurate or not,[66] there is no doubt that it warned against any deviation from the norm which required of every hasid that he should be 'connected' to his own rebbe and no other. The story castigates in the strongest terms the ambition to establish direct links with a supreme authority at the centre. It undoubtedly reflects the non-centralist organizational structure of the movement, even during the lifetime of the Magid, a structure which permitted every leader to be in sole charge of his own hasidim without in the least calling into question the spiritual supremacy of the Magid.

We see, then, that the conventional and convenient chronological division of the early hasidic leadership into three discrete generations, namely, those of the Besht, the Magid, and the Magid's disciples, is arbitrary and rather misleading. The generations overlapped to a considerable extent, and it is certainly difficult to separate the generation of the Magid's disciples, which began while he was still living, from that of the Magid himself, which only lasted between six and twelve years.

Moreover, it appears that no machinery for overall supervision of the movement was ever set up in the Mezhirech centre. To the best of our knowledge the Magid's disciples, who, at the end of their apprenticeship at his court, went back to their home towns or left for other places in order to establish and head hasidic communities of their own, rarely visited him and did not maintain any links by regular correspondence with him.[67] Nor did any tradition develop of regular meetings of hasidic leaders in Mezhirech or general assemblies there of hasidim from the other hasidic communities.[68] The only event of this kind was the meeting of the disciples of the Magid at his court in Równe in the summer of 1772, a few months before his death. This meeting, which is mentioned in R. Shneur Zalman of Liady's letter to R. Abraham of Kalisk,[69] was called in response to the first proclamation of the *ḥerem* (excommunication) against the hasidim, which had been issued in Lithuania and Galicia earlier that year. It appears that the meeting was convened in order to enable the hasidic leaders to consult on the campaign of the *mitnagedim* and co-ordinate their attitude to it. All those who attended were disciples and intimates of the Magid, and all of them of course regarded him as their spiritual master, even though some had already begun to lead hasidic congregations of their own. According to R. Shneur Zalman, the Magid rebuked R. Abraham of Kalisk for his wildly ecstatic style of worship and for the contempt for scholars which he had instilled into his hasidim, and it seems that he charged him with causing the outbreak of the dispute with the *mitnagedim*.[70] The relations between the Magid and R. Abraham are described as extremely strained, to the point where R. Abraham was afraid to enter the city of Równe. He presented himself before the Magid only after R. Yehiel Mikhl of Złoczów and R. Menahem Mendel of Vitebsk had interceded on his behalf and to some extent allayed the Magid's wrath.

R. Shneur Zalman's testimony presents R. Abraham of Kalisk as a disciple who submitted to the authority of the Magid even after leaving his court. But at the same time it reinforces the claim that by this time R. Abraham was already serving as the established leader of a group of like-minded people, on whom his personality and teaching had left their mark. Clearly he had founded a type of hasidism which was quite distinct from the hasidism of others and which, in some measure, was even opposed to it.

However angry the Magid was with R. Abraham of Kalisk, the only recourse open to him was to persuade R. Abraham to mend his ways, and his only weapon was the force of his own personality. He had no formal powers under which to dismiss the controversial leader from his office or ensure that he moderated his activity among his hasidim, as one might have expected to happen if the Magid had really stood at the head of a centralist hierarchical organization. If the whole hasidic movement had functioned at that time as the personal court of the Magid of Mezhirech, as the hypothesis of a centralized leadership in his time would require us to believe, the situation of R. Abraham of Kalisk would have corresponded to that of a disciple who is a functionary of the court or the broader organization of the particular hasidic community: the court *gabai*, the head of the hasidic yeshiva in recent generations, or the town's rabbi who defers to the spiritual authority of his rebbe, and other such emissaries of the tsadik, all of whom he can appoint or dismiss at will, and whose authority stems mainly from him. It is obvious that this was not the situation of R. Abraham: he was already in sole charge of a community of hasidim, which he led in his own way.

The meeting of the Magid's disciples in Równe, apparently the only one of its kind during the lifetime of R. Dov Ber, was no doubt called in response to the emergency created by the first clash with the *mitnagedim*. On the face of it, it could be construed as a centralist initiative stemming from the organizational headquarters of the movement. But we must not forget that even many years after the death of the Magid of Mezhirech, by which time all agree that the organization of the movement was fragmented, the leaders of hasidism would meet from time to time to discuss matters of joint concern or internal disputes. No one would think of ascribing to such meetings an intention to centralize the leadership or undermine the pluralistic principle whereby each hasidic master was fully acknowledged as a leader of his own hasidic following.[71]

From another point of view, too, it is quite evident that we cannot base any reconstruction of the organization of hasidism in its early stages, and especially in the lifetime of the Magid of Mezhirech, on the pattern of the particular hasidic court of the nineteenth century and its central dynastic leader. The Magid's disciples founded their own courts while he was still living, and they did not need to compete with him, oppose him, or sour their relations with him in order to declare their independence as leaders of their own hasidim. To the best of our knowledge, their parting from the Magid was not marked by any tension or controversy and may well have had his blessing.[72] By contrast, in the fully developed, centralized organization of the hasidic court in the nineteenth century this could not be tolerated. Since it was only possible to join the hasidic camp by personal affiliation—*hitkarvut*—with one of its leaders, the nineteenth-century courts necessarily continued to receive into their midst some disciples whose magnetic personalities and spiritual powers sooner or later bore witness to the fact that they, too, were natural leaders of men. By its nature, the institutionalized hasidic court could only contain one dominant charismatic personality of this sort. The presence of other such personalities in the capacity of disciples charged the atmosphere of the court with tension,[73] and was liable to result in open conflict with the reigning tsadik, or, after his death, with the dynastic heir to the leadership. These clashes could take an ideological form, and would eventually lead to the emergence of new courts whose distinct identity, at least to begin with, was based precisely on the difference, or even the hostility, between them and the courts from which they had seceded.[74]

We can therefore draw a distinction at two stages between the non-centralist organization of the entire hasidic movement in the generation of the Magid, on the one hand, and on the other hand the centralist pattern of organization which became characteristic of each particular court in the course of the nineteenth century. First there is the stage when the disciples begin to lead their own hasidic communities in the lifetime of their master: in the institutionalized centralist court this would generally be accompanied by a fierce dispute and rivalry over hasidim, whereas in the circle of the Magid the rise of the disciples to leadership does not appear to have generated any tension of this sort. The second stage is when the disciples claim the leadership after the death of their master: in the institutionalized centralist court, a quarrel would break out between the charismatic disciple who was gathering hasidim to himself and the 'natural' dynastic heir to the leadership. In the circle of the Magid's disciples, on the other hand, no claim was ever laid by a 'natural' heir and there was no dispute among the disciples over the inheritance. Such a dispute could not have developed at this time, partly because R. Abraham the Angel, the Magid's son, took no part in public life and did not aspire to leadership,[75] but mainly because at that stage in the organizational development of hasidism, when the role of the tsadik had not yet crystallized into institutional office within a clearly demarcated territory and a fixed pattern of obligations and privileges, there was no expectation that a direct successor would step into such a role.

4. The Structure of the Leadership after 1772

The Besht and the Magid, then, both operated within a non-centralist framework which found its natural continuation in the fragmented structure of the hasidic leadership after 1772. It was precisely the existence of such a loose framework of organization that prevented the occurrence of any acute crises of leadership after the death of the Besht in 1760, and again after the death of the Magid in 1772. Although their deaths were undoubtedly felt as a great personal loss by their respective circles of associates, neither left a void in the leadership of hasidism, for a network of leaders, each with his own followers, was operating while they were still alive. Pinhas of Korets, Nahman of Horodenka, Menahem Mendel of Przemyślany, the Magid of Mezhirech, and the other members of the Besht's circle, who fell into the category of charismatic 'men of spirit', ensured the continuity of the leadership without there being any need to fill the place of the Besht by the appointment of a direct successor. Similarly, the disciples of the Magid of Mezhirech, who were actively engaged in hasidic agitation during his lifetime, did not cease their operations when he died, and those of them who began to lead hasidic communities in various places after his death did not 'inherit' his position in the dynastic sense of the word but became integrated into the existing network of leaders just as others had done while he was alive.

Although I have contended here that hasidism did not undergo a drastic organizational change with the alleged decentralization of 1772, and that its fragmented structure thereafter simply continued a situation which had existed even before the death of the Magid of Mezhirech, it is not my purpose to suggest that the movement did not experience any organizational change during this period. On the contrary, extensive changes did occur in the organization of hasidism at the end of the eighteenth century and during the first half of the nineteenth. The anachronistic view of the structure of the movement in its early stages, which pictures a centralist leadership that broke up, does not exaggerate the extent of the change but offers a mistaken diagnosis of its nature. According to that view, the hasidic leadership, at its beginnings, was set up as a dynastic, centralist institution which somehow malfunctioned from the outset: as a result of chance circumstances, when the founder of the movement died, and again at the death of his 'unnatural' heir in the 'second generation', there were no natural heirs to the leadership. In both cases, we are asked to believe, matters went awry and the 'natural' hereditary processes for the transfer of authority from generation to generation were abandoned in favour of improvised, and not altogether satisfactory, ad hoc solutions to the problem of succession. The failure of the initial pattern of a centralist dynastic succession is thus assumed to have led to the fundamental structural change which found expression in decentralization.[76] But this supposed sequence of frustrated natural expectations, procedural irregularities, and unorthodox solutions is highly improbable in a novel situation in which set expectations, regular procedures, and orthodox practice have not yet had time to emerge. The very fact that the supposedly dynastic pattern of succession failed to secure the 'natural' continuity of the leadership in the generation of the founders should give us pause: why should this pattern and no other have been adopted, in circumstances to which it was so blatantly unsuited—the absence of natural heirs on the first two occasions when the leadership of the hasidic movement had to be passed on? From what has been said in the preceding sections it will be clear that this, too, is an anachronism—the application of later circumstances to an earlier situation, in which these circumstances evidently did not obtain. There is no doubt that the hereditary principle of succession had not yet gained currency in the leadership of hasidism during the generation of the founders. In fact, the decisive change in the organization of the movement did not take the form of an abrupt transition from a hereditary and centralist to a hereditary but decentralized leadership structure: rather, it was a shift from a loose, informal leadership structure which was neither hereditary nor centralist to an established institution which remained non-centralist in its overall structure but whose very consolidation was owed, in large measure, precisely to the adoption of the hereditary principle of succession in each one of its proliferating centres. The new structure could thus generate a multiplicity of dynastic leaders, each exerting supreme authority from the centre at his court over his own community of followers, and each associated with his fellows within an overall framework which remained loosely knit, non-centralist, and capable of giving rise to further proliferation.

The hereditary principle of succession became accepted gradually, and not everywhere, at the end of the eighteenth and the beginning of the nineteenth centuries. Since the hasidic leadership had first entered the arena as a group of individuals distinguished by the gift of personal charisma, the hereditary principle, and indeed any alternative rational measure of suitability for high office, were inherently foreign to it at the start. Only in the course of the nineteenth century did the leadership crystallize into a network of dynasties which availed themselves of the hereditary principle as a matter of course for the purpose of transmitting authority from one generation to the next and preserving the distinct character and identity of each dynasty within hasidism. The result was a movement which can be characterized as combining two different, if not diametrically opposed, modes of operation: the overall structure had always been, and remained, loose, pluralistic, and non-centralist—an association of independent groups, each headed by its own charismatic leader. But in each of the constituent groups within that structure there developed the tightly knit and highly centralized organization of the court, whose sole head now drew his authority not only from any personal charismatic gifts he might possess but also from the routinized charisma he inherited from his predecessors in office.[77]

There is no doubt that the lines along which the movement expanded during the first half of the nineteenth century were non-centralist. Considering the historical circumstances—the non-centralist traditional regime of the autonomous *kehalim*, the abolition of the central Council of Four Lands, and the disintegration of the Polish–Lithuanian Commonwealth—out of which hasidism grew and by which it was affected during its period of growth,[78] this is not surprising, and indeed it is hard to imagine that any other modes of expansion were open to it. But it should not be concluded from this that the growth in numbers and the geographical expansion during the last decades of the eighteenth century had forced the movement into a drastic revision of its organizational structure and led inevitably to the fragmentation of a leadership which had been centralist so long as its sphere of influence was small. On the contrary, the movement had its beginnings in a distinctly non-centralist organizational framework, and the course of its expansion merely enhanced and brought to the fore the pluralistic tendency which had been inherent in it from the start.

Nor is there any substance in the claim that the partitions of Poland in 1772, 1783, and 1795 cut off the 'headquarters' of the hasidic movement from its branches and made it impossible to continue the leadership in its original centralist form[79]—a claim which has contributed to the generally accepted view that three decisive factors had combined to bring about the decentralization of the leadership in 1772.[80] The fact that by pure chance the first partition of Poland, the outbreak of the controversy with the *mitnagedim*, and the death of the Magid of Mezhirech occurred in a single year has created the illusion of a significant combination of circumstances sufficient to explain what appeared to be an abrupt organizational change. But once this explanation is shown to be misplaced—it purports to account for a decentralization which neither took place nor could have done, since no central institution of hasidic leadership had existed before 1772—the triad of 'factors' can be resolved into its separate and unrelated components, none of which could have changed the course of the organizational development of the hasidic movement in the aftermath of 1772.

The possibility that the death of the Magid of Mezhirech without leaving a natural successor might have led to the fragmentation of the leadership was examined above (section 3) and rejected: the examination revealed that the movement had been fragmented even during his lifetime, and that his death did not alter the leadership structure but rather exposed and highlighted its non-centralist character. The remaining two 'factors'—the partition of Poland and the controversy with the *mitnagedim*—can similarly be shown to have had little effect on the structure of the hasidic leadership during this period. Indeed, it is remarkable how slight was the imprint of these dramatic events on the organization of the hasidic movement in the last decades of the eighteenth century. Both must be seen against the same background of overall disintegration and fragmentation from which hasidism itself had sprung, and both similarly reflect its inherent pluralistic tendency rather than determine it.

The impact of the partitions of Poland on the structure of the movement was limited. The new political boundaries did not break the bonds between hasidic leaders and their followers, just as they did not halt the expansion of hasidism far beyond its areas of provenance.[81] In 1784, some seven years after settling in Erets Yisra'el, R. Menahem Mendel of Vitebsk advised his hasidim in Belarus not to appoint 'some righteous man over them from among the famous men, the great tsadikim, and bring him to the lands of Russia'.[82] From what he went on to say it is clear that he meant a tsadik from Poland, that is, 'the lands of Volhynia and Lithuania',[83] which, in 1784, in the period between the first and second partitions of Poland, were still within the borders of the Polish state, while Belarus, where R. Menahem Mendel's hasidim lived, had been annexed to Russia in 1772. As we know, R. Menahem Mendel of Vitebsk and R. Abraham of Kalisk failed in their attempt to maintain their leadership in Belarus through the sole medium of correspondence from overseas. Their 'orphaned' hasidim began to visit courts in Poland across the border,[84] or tried to import a tsadik from there to lead them in their own locality. True, most of them eventually took the advice of their leaders in Erets Yisra'el and accepted local tsadikim, of whom the most important was R. Shneur Zalman of Liady.[85] But it was not the new political boundary which restrained them but the instructions of their spiritual mentors and the tradition of their particular form of hasidism, which the leaders in Erets Yisra'el wanted to preserve, as is clear from all their pastoral letters. The 'Polish' tsadik who was approached by the hasidim of Belarus in spite of the political break created by the first partition of Poland was the Lithuanian R. Shelomoh of Karlin. He frequently visited his new hasidim across the border, and, as is evident from his letter to his followers in Shklov, he tried to retain their allegiance even after they had ceased to visit his court and begun to attach themselves to R. Shneur Zalman of Liady.[86]

If the hasidic movement as a whole had functioned as a centralist organization during that period, the partitions of Poland would undoubtedly not have broken the link between the centre and its offshoots. After all, they did not disturb the contact between the tsadik and his hasidim in those institutional frameworks in which centralist patterns of organization are known to have been established, namely, in the growing numbers of particular courts, whose leaders had succeeded in maintaining their connection with their followers across political boundaries in spite of the vicissitudes of the time. Thus, for example, Abraham Ber Gottlober describes the area of influence of Habad in the middle of the nineteenth century as follows: 'The Habad sect in general is prominent in Lithuania (and there are some of them in Moldavia and Wallachia, and a few in Volhynia under the rule of R. Menahem Mendel)'.[87] The leader referred to was the Tsemah Tsedek, who led

Habad from 1828 until his death in 1866.[88] In the middle of the nineteenth century Lithuania and Volhynia formed part of a single political unit within the Russian Empire, but the distant territories of Moldavia and Wallachia had passed through a long period of political instability before they were united to form the independent state of Romania in 1858. The frequent changes of boundaries did not put an end to the existence of the Habad enclave in Romania, nor did they weaken the bond between the Habad hasidim there and their rebbe in Belarus. Similarly Gottlober reports on the movements of R. Israel of Ruzhin and his hasidim:

R. Israel of Ruzhin increased the glory of his household so greatly that the eyes of the government were opened towards him [i.e. he lived a life of such luxury that he attracted the attention of the government], and certain other occurrences also contributed to his downfall, and he was taken from there and imprisoned in a fortress for many days. And after he had been released he feared for his life lest he be taken prisoner again, and he fled to the land of Galicia and dwelt for some years in Sadagora, which is in Bukovina. Thereupon his hasidim in our country began to visit him there.[89]

R. Israel of Ruzhin, after his imprisonment in Kamenets-Podolsky and Kiev, fled from Russia in 1838,[90] and settled in a district within the jurisdiction of the Austro-Hungarian empire. This did not prevent his followers from continuing to make the journey to see him, and hasidim from Russia maintained this tradition of crossing the Austrian border even after his death, when the leadership had passed to his sons. According to the hostile account of the *maskil* Gottlober, the motives for these frequent crossings of the frontier were not purely hasidic:

They arise and cross the border of the country to bring merchandise from a foreign land contrary to the king's laws, hoping thereby to amass wealth without much exertion and without work, to which they are unaccustomed. (We have seen such and we know for a certainty that some of these people who call themselves hasidim travel to Galicia to their rebbe, one of the sons of R. Israel of Ruzhin, [the R. Israel] who had fled thither, and on their return they bring with them some of the merchandise of that country, and that is virtually all that they want, and their journey to the rebbe is only a pretext.)[91]

It is clear, at any rate, that it was easy enough to cross the frontier, which the hasidim did frequently. And just as the nineteenth-century political borders did not prevent the passage of hasidim from Russian territory to their tsadikim in Galicia, so, too, they did not prevent the hasidim from bringing their 'obscurantist' books into the enlightened province of Galicia in spite of the vain attempts of the Austrian censorship—prompted by *maskilim* headed by Joseph Perl—to prohibit this.[92]

In parallel with the spread of hasidism across the changing political borders, mitnagdism spread too: the frontiers presented no barrier to either. The first *ḥerem* of Vilna was declared about four months before the first partition of Poland,[93] and it is therefore not surprising that the proclamation issued by the Vilna Gaon[94] became known throughout Lithuania, Belarus, and Galicia, which still formed a single political unit within Poland.[95] But the severance of Galicia and Belarus from the other regions of Poland (especially Lithuania) in the summer of 1772 did not hamper the distribution of the documents of excommunication across the new frontiers, nor did it halt the first controversy or hold back the waves of controversy which followed; they, too, encompassed Austrian Galicia no less than Polish Lithuania and Russian Belarus.[96]

The fact is that all the excommunications and accusations, the denunciations to the authorities, the dismissals from office, and even the full weight of personal authority exerted by the Gaon of Vilna did not avail the *mitnagedim* in their attempt to stamp out the hasidic 'sect'. But their failure did not stem from the political dismemberment of the Polish–Lithuanian Commonwealth, which took place during those years. The partitions could not sever the links between the Jewish units of population which had previously been Polish, and therefore they did not interfere with the activities of the *mitnagedim*, any more than they did with the activities of the hasidim throughout the former territories of Poland. The failure of the *mitnagedim* to eradicate hasidism was largely due precisely to the tradition of non-centralist communal organization from which both hasidism and mitnagdism grew—the tradition of the autonomous *kehilot*, each of which had been self-governing for centuries, and whose centralized institutions had gradually degenerated until they were finally abolished in 1764.[97] The traditionally non-centralist character of Jewish self-government in Poland was reinforced rather than undermined by the political disintegration of the Commonwealth. This served the interests of hasidism well but worked against the interests of the *mitnagedim*. The pluralistic pattern of communal organization provided the hasidic movement with a mode of growth and expansion which was natural and extremely convenient for it.[98] On the other hand, the efforts of the *mitnagedim* to ban the hasidim and excommunicate them were frustrated time and again precisely because of the absence of any centralist organizational framework through which the anti-hasidic measures could be implemented effectively in all the diverse and widely spread communities in which the 'heresy' had taken root. The Gaon of Vilna could not secure the implementation of the *ḥerem* in all the *kehilot* of Poland, or even in all those of Lithuania. In fact, he himself, having no official position in the *kahal* of Vilna, could only operate behind the scenes, spurring on his intimates and urging the official leadership to take action against the hasidim in their city. As for the other *kehilot*, he could only exert influence on them unofficially; no machinery was available to him by which to force his will on the Jewish community as a whole.[99] The *mitnagedim* themselves were well aware of this limitation. The proclamation of the *ḥerem* by the *kahal* of Brody against the hasidic sect on 20 Sivan 5532 (1772) states:

Although our *kehilah* has no power to bind other honourable *kehilot* to undertake an investigation likewise and issue their own *ḥerem* in that regard, and we can only address a request to them for the sake of the glory of the Lord, blessed be He, the Holy One of Israel, all *kehilot* should be zealous for the Lord of Hosts; they and we are all children of one Father, children of the living God. And seeing that our *kehilah* is the largest community, the best Jewish city in the land . . . we have found ourselves obliged to take our place among those who arouse and penetrate the innermost feelings of all our brethren, the house of Israel. And we shall send this proclamation to all the borders of Israel.[100]

The recognition of the difficulty is accompanied by a nostalgic reference to the centralist institution of the Council of Four Lands, which had dealt more efficiently with the heretics of its day:

Some years ago there were such wicked men in the world; there were also, at that time, the wisest men of their generations, leaders of the Four Lands, who pursued them and made their infamous conduct widely known, until they had been got rid of, but today the mitre has been removed and the crown taken away, the men of faith have perished and there is no one to contend for us with evildoers.[101]

Of course, organizational structure was not the only factor responsible for the failure of the mitnagdic campaign against hasidism. Other factors helped the hasidic movement to withstand the attempt of the *mitnagedim* to eradicate it: on the one hand, its evident halakhic conservatism, which lessened the opposition to it, and on the other hand its gradual penetration of existing communal institutions without challenging them by a frontal assault—a method which facilitated the hasidic 'conquests' in eastern Europe.[102] Above all, the personal magnetism of the hasidic leaders and the new frameworks of religious life which they created were genuinely attractive and offered a viable alternative to the traditional values upheld by the *mitnagedim*. However, the importance of the structural and organizational factor should not be underestimated.

It appears, then, that the non-centralist, pluralistic structure which has become one of the hallmarks of the hasidic movement was not forced upon it at a certain moment, as a result of the events of 1772, by external factors such as the partitions of Poland or the controversy with the Lithuanian *mitnagedim*, nor was it determined by a pure coincidence such as the absence of a natural successor to the Magid of Mezhirech. This structure was dictated by the internal dynamic of the long-established tradition of non-centralist Jewish communal organization in eastern Europe, and it underlay the patterns of organization and expansion which were characteristic of hasidism from the outset. The events of 1772 simply exposed and reinforced this underlying structure, but they certainly did not divert the movement from a centralist organizational path into the multiple byways which came to typify it. The assumption that there was a centralist stage in the first two 'generations' of the leadership, until 1772, derives, as was shown above, from the anachronistic application of the nineteenth- and twentieth-century model of the individual hasidic court—a centrally led, dynastic institution—to a whole group of loosely associated circles which constituted the hasidic movement at its very beginnings, in the middle decades of the eighteenth century.

5. Centralist Tendencies in the Leadership after 1772?

If indeed the hasidic movement was never headed by a supreme central leader, even in the first two 'generations' of the founders, then it is important to carefully examine those apparently anomalous cases in subsequent generations, after the alleged decentralization of 1772, which have been taken by historians to represent a lingering presence of the original centralist tendency in the organization of the movement. These cases have been interpreted as expressions of longing, or even explicit demands, for the restoration of central authority to the descendants of the founders, and, in particular, to the line of the Besht. But since, as was argued above, neither the Magid nor the Besht ever exercised exclusive central control, how are we to explain the apparent claims by the grandson of the Besht, R. Barukh of Międzybóż,[103] and even more so by his great-grandson, the one and only 'tsadik of the generation', R. Nahman of Bratslav, to the sole leadership of the movement on a hereditary and centralist basis?[104]

R. Barukh of Międzybóż, a son of the Besht's daughter, has often been portrayed by historians as 'an arrogant man, ambitious for authority, honour and riches', 'of limited intelligence and bad character', who wished 'to exploit the status of a grandson of the Besht . . . to lord it over the people and even over the tsadikim of his generation'.[105] And in more restrained and objective terms: 'Rabbi Barukh saw himself as the man to continue the path of his grandfather the Besht. The Magid of Mezhirech's disciples, who had established new hasidic dynasties, refused to recognize R. Barukh of Międzybóż as supreme leader, and because of this grave disputes broke out between him and the tsadikim of the generation.'[106]

The view that R. Barukh tried (and failed) to preserve in hasidism a tradition of centralist leadership as the hereditary prerogative of the line of the Besht is founded on a tendentious interpretation of evidence which itself is of very doubtful reliability. R. Barukh did not leave an extensive body of teachings or writings of his own, and all we have is a collection of statements by or about him, which was published long after his death.[107] From the few items of evidence about him that remain, he appears as a tsadik relying on the merit of his grandfather the Besht, and it is very probable that he saw himself as his successor.[108] But his ambition to take the place of his grandfather in Międzybóż was not necessarily inspired by any aspiration to centralist leadership over the whole hasidic movement of his day. That interpretation of his ambition is conditioned by the view of the Besht himself as supreme leader, exercising control from the centre, but there is no compelling evidence for it whatsoever in the traditions relating to R. Barukh.[109] As soon as we drop the assumption that the Besht was a supreme overseer of the hasidism of his time, there cease to be grounds on which to ascribe to R. Barukh any centralist-monopolistic claim to the leadership of hasidism by right of hereditary entitlement. The provocative declarations he is alleged to have made, which have been represented in the scholarly literature as reflecting his desire to assume his grandfather's 'crown' as leader of all the tsadikim, do not survive critical examination. Some of them have been taken out of context and interpreted without sufficient regard for their plain meaning, and others were set down by writers and compilers who lived scores of years after his time. They shared the anachronistic view of the leadership of the Besht, attributing to it, and therefore also to the leadership of his grandson, the exclusive centralist quality discussed above. Horodetsky, for example, describes R. Barukh as follows: 'And in his great self-confidence . . . he waged his war with all the tsadikim, and was not ashamed even to pray: *velehevei ana pekida bego tsadikaya*'—which Horodetsky translates as 'I desire to be in charge of the tsadikim.'[110] The book *Butsina dinehora* brought together the sayings of R. Barukh and his few teachings. This work, contrary to what was said by the publisher in the foreword, appears never to have existed as an original and complete manuscript but was compiled from a variety of sources, including, apparently, the works of others, shortly before its publication in 1880.[111] In the book R. Barukh's declaration appears in a different context: 'Once he said "*ulemehevei ana pekuda bego tsadikei*—Master of the universe, may I be numbered among the tsadikim.[112] I do not mean them; I mean with the holy rabbi R. Pinhas of Ostrog and with the holy rabbi of Połonne."'[113] Only in what follows there do we find the play upon words which allows *pekuda* to be understood as 'appointed over the tsadikim' and not simply as 'numbered with them'—a double meaning firmly embedded in the perception which all hasidim have of their tsadik: they laud his superiority over all other tsadikim without going so far as to deny the right of the others to independent authority over their own followers.[114]

It is clear, at any rate, that the friction between R. Barukh and a number of his contemporaries in the leadership arose from clashes over territory and from his fears of encroachment by others, not from any fundamental opposition by R. Barukh to the right of others to lead hasidim within their own borders.[115] A well-known tradition purports to record a pertinent exchange of words between R. Barukh and R. Shneur Zalman of Liady on the occasion of R. Shneur Zalman's visit to R. Barukh. This tradition has been taken as reflecting a fundamental disagreement between them on the principle which should determine how the authority of the leader was to be transmitted, whether from father to son or from teacher to disciple.[116] However, not only is the tradition itself of doubtful reliability but even as it stands, if it is read carefully, it can hardly be construed as evidence for such a clash over two alternative principles of succession in the central leadership of hasidism. According to the tradition, 'Finally our rabbi [R. Barukh] became angry and said, "I am the grandson of the Besht and I should be shown respect." The rabbi [R. Shneur Zalman] answered: "I, too, am the grandson of the Besht, his spiritual grandson, for the great Magid was an outstanding disciple of the Besht and I am a disciple of the Magid."'[117] This conversation appears in the book *Butsina dinehora hashalem*, which was published, edited, collated from various sources, and even, in part, composed by Rabbi Reuben Margaliot during the 1920s.[118] The book includes the whole of the 1880 edition of *Butsina dinehora*, the reliability of whose contents and even their connection with R. Barukh is in doubt, as indicated above.[119] To that material Rabbi Margaliot made numerous additions from later sources, some of which are even more questionable. Thus, for example, he drew heavily on the documents of the forged Kherson *genizah*.[120] He appears to have extracted the conversation between R. Barukh and R. Shneur Zalman of Liady from Michael Levi Rodkinson's hagiographical work on the latter entitled *Shivḥei harav*,[121] and he inserted it as a direct continuation of an authentic letter he quoted in which R. Shneur Zalman reported his dispute with R. Barukh.[122] Thus was created the false impression that the account of the exchange of words between the biological grandson, R. Barukh, and the 'spiritual grandson', R. Shneur Zalman, was written by the founder of Habad himself in his letter. In fact, I have not found any reference to this matter in any source earlier than Rodkinson's book. It seems to be a piece of fictional writing by Rodkinson, inspired by the dynastic outlook which had become characteristic of Habad by the second half of the nineteenth century, when the group had developed a strong sense of its unique position in the history of the hasidic movement, claiming to be the one school which maintained an unbroken and exceptionally intimate connection with the Besht and the Magid of Mezhirech, and thus preserved more authentically than any other school the original teaching of hasidism.[123] In any event, this sort of controversy over the 'legacy' of central leadership in hasidism is the fruit of the anachronistic imagination of recent generations, and has no basis in the earlier historical reality in which R. Barukh and R. Shneur Zalman actually operated.[124]

As for R. Nahman of Bratslav's claim to the supreme leadership, he indeed regarded himself, and was regarded by his followers, as 'the tsadik of the generation'. But his claim needs to be examined in its peculiar ideological context. R. Nahman's status as 'tsadik of the generation' or 'the true tsadik' was undoubtedly connected with his messianic view of himself. On this level the quality of his leadership was indeed seen as unique, in that it alone could trigger off the messianic advent by effecting the *tikun* (restoration to a state of perfection) of the entire generation—his own handful of hasidim, all the other tsadikim, 'and even the nations of the world'.[125] But these exaltations of R. Nahman's unique messianic mission were never meant to undermine the position of other tsadikim in the contemporary hasidic leadership. On the level of sober consciousness he recognized his overt position in the reality of pre-messianic existence as the obverse of his messianic status, which was to remain concealed for the time being. And so not only did he accept as legitimate the existence of other tsadikim in the leadership but he also recognized the superior qualities of some of them (though he sharply criticized the way of life of others), and acknowledged their success compared to his own failure as a controversial leader whose hasidim were few and persecuted. R. Nathan Sternharz, R. Nahman's literary secretary, offers this explanation of *torah* 56 in *Likutei moharan*, part I,[126] which R. Nahman 'said' on Shavuot 5565 (1805):

And he then delivered [the] wondrous teaching on the verse 'And on the day of the first fruits' [Num. 28: 26], [which is to be found in] *torah* 56 [of *Likutei moharan*, pt. I], beginning 'For in each member of Israel there is a quality of kingship'. After he had delivered this teaching, in which he discussed the quality of kingship which is in every Jew etc., and [distinguished between] 'revealed kingship' and 'concealed kingship' etc., and [spoke about] 'one man who has no revealed dominion, and yet in concealment' etc., he then said explicitly about himself: 'To you [my hasidim] it seems that I have no dominion except over you. In truth I rule even over all the tsadikim of the generation, but this is in concealment.'[127]

A clear distinction must be drawn between R. Nahman's consciousness of concealed or secret kingship and his consciousness of revealed kingship. 'In great concealment and secrecy he rules over the whole generation and even over every tsadik of the generation. For their souls are all under his dominion and kingship and all of them submit to him and are subjected to him.'[128] But this conception is far removed in its inner logic and origins from any concrete claim to the position of supreme central leader by right of direct descent from the Besht.[129] R. Nahman's messianic leadership 'in great secrecy' is a metaphysical and cosmic leadership, not a concrete organizational one, and what inspires it is his consciousness of his absolute and extraordinary uniqueness, not his dynastic connection with the line of the Besht. This 'concealed' leadership operates not only horizontally, over all the tsadikim of his own generation, but also vertically, over all his predecessors in hasidism (including the Besht, the alleged source of his supreme authority), and even over the leaders who ruled in the distant past—all the distinguished personalities in the history of the nation who had failed to bring the messianic project to fruition; he alone would fulfil it, either during his life or in the more distant future, after his death.[130] On this plane of consciousness he could claim that not only his colleagues, the tsadikim of his own generation, but also 'all the sages of Israel are as nothing compared to me'.[131] In this way he actually shook off the legacy of leadership of the Besht:

I have heard it reported in his name that he said, 'The world thinks that it is because I am the [great-]grandson of the Besht that I have attained this eminence. Not so. Only through one thing have I succeeded, and through it I have been able to ascend and achieve what I have.' And he repeated in Yiddish: 'With one thing I have succeeded.'[132]

Without denying the fact of his family connection with the Besht, R. Nahman stood the relationship between them on its head: rather than that he needed the Besht, the Besht needed him. He expressed himself to that effect while on his visit to Międzybóż before leaving for Erets Yisra'el in 1798:

And when he came to Międzybóż to the house of his righteous father and mother, may their memory be for a blessing, and they rejoiced greatly at his coming, his mother said to him: 'My son, when will you go to your grandfather the Besht?' meaning, to his holy grave.[133] Our rabbi, may his memory be for a blessing, replied: 'If my grandfather wants to see me let him come here.'[134]

On the *madregah* (spiritual rank) of the Besht, on the metaphysical source from which he drew his teaching, and on the efficacy of his advice to his hasidim, his esoteric writings and his power to effect the *tikun* of the world, R. Nahman repeatedly commented with condescension, express or implied.[135] In doing so he even incurred the wrath of his uncle, R. Barukh of Międzybóż, who took his remarks as a personal insult (rightly so, since R. Barukh's claim to the leadership rested on his descent from the Besht), and the incident was to mark the start of a lifelong quarrel between them. Thus, for example, R. Nahman declared to his uncle that he himself had overtaken the spiritual rank of the Besht when he was only 13 years old:

And our rabbi (may the memory of that righteous and holy man be for a blessing) came to the rabbi R. Barukh, and when our rabbi sat down next to him our rabbi sighed. And R. Barukh said to him, 'Why are you sighing?' And our rabbi answered: 'Because I long to reach your *madregah* [spiritual rank].' He then listed the *madregot* attained by various tsadikim, and finally mentioned the *madregah* of the Besht, may his memory be for a blessing, and our rabbi said that he had attained his *madregah* too, and had done so at the age of 13 (and then R. Barukh pushed him so that he almost fell from the upper room, until his mother, mistress Feyge, may her memory be for a blessing, came from the upper world and saved him from falling), and from that time the quarrel between them began.[136]

On the other hand, on the plane of consciousness of his 'revealed' existence, R. Nahman took for granted the presence on the scene of other tsadikim and did not in the least object to it. On this plane he held a sober view of himself as a man 'who has no dominion', who was 'poorer than all the great men: one has property, another has money, another owns towns, and I—I have nothing'.[137] His attitude to the tsadikim of his generation was very matter-of-fact. With some he clashed, others he despised, but for some he had great respect. He maintained working 'diplomatic' relations with other hasidic courts and took part in the internal politics of contemporary hasidism as a member of a pluralistic system of leadership which he regarded as valid in itself, despite his strong disagreement with some of its other members.

The list of tsadikim who met with R. Nahman's approval was headed by R. Levi Isaac of Berdiczów, of whom he said, 'The rabbi of Berdiczów is very great in my eyes',[138] and he even called him 'unique in this generation'[139] and 'the glory of Israel'.[140] He praised his virtues so highly that his eulogy after R. Levi Isaac's death was taken as alluding to his own virtues.[141] He made the acquaintance of R. Abraham of Kalisk in Tiberias on the occasion of his visit to Erets Yisra'el in 1798, and the two developed a friendship based on mutual respect.[142] He also made friends with R. Samson of Shepetovka in the course of the same visit, and even succeeded in establishing peace between him and R. Abraham of Kalisk.[143] On his return from Erets Yisra'el he travelled to the court of R. Shneur Zalman of Liady,[144] 'and spoke much with him about the people of Erets Yisra'el'.[145] It appears that he approached R. Shneur Zalman on behalf of R. Abraham of Kalisk and asked him not to hold up the funds raised for the hasidim of Erets Yisra'el but to hand them over to R. Abraham's emissary.[146] To R. Shneur Zalman himself R. Nahman's attitude was somewhat ambivalent: he was undoubtedly impressed by his large following. When R. Shneur Zalman visited him in Bratslav, on the way to his famous meeting with R. Barukh of Międzybóż,[147]

Our master, may the memory of that righteous and holy man be for a blessing, said to his people concerning the rabbi [Shneur Zalman]: Show honour to 'a ruler of a thousand' [cf. Exod. 18: 21]. And our master asked the rabbi: Is it true, as they say about you, that you have eighty thousand hasidim? And the rabbi said to him that he had hasidim who were teachers and each one had a charity box for him, and since the youngsters gave charity for him they would presumably not be opposed to him.[148]

R. Nahman felt a sense of comradeship with R. Shneur Zalman on account of the situation in which they both found themselves, for both were involved in a bitter quarrel with R. Nahman's uncle, R. Barukh of Międzybóż. Two late traditions, apparently independent of each other, record R. Nahman's mocking humour at the expense of his uncle in conversation with R. Shneur Zalman of Liady.[149] On the other hand, he did not accept the hasidic doctrine of R. Shneur Zalman and did not hesitate to make this plain in front of the latter's disciples.[150] Shortly after his return from Erets Yisra'el R. Nahman also visited the courts of R. Mordecai of Neshchiz, R. Zevi Aryeh of Ołyka, and R. Aryeh Leyb, the Zeyde ('grandfather') of Shpola (Szpoła); at that time, before the outbreak of the controversy between them, R. Aryeh Leyb regarded R. Nahman with great respect.[151] R. Nahman despised the popular tsadikism of these hasidic leaders, and emphasized the difference between their kind of leadership and his:

Could I not have been 'a famous one' and a leader of the kind called a *guter yid* [lit. 'a good Jew'], to whom the hasidim journey and do not know for what purpose they journey? They come again and again without knowing why they have come. But I wanted nothing to do with any of that. I simply committed myself to this task in order to bring you back to a better way of life.[152]

It is clear, however, that he did not regard all the tsadikim of his generation in this light, and that his objection was not to the multiplicity of tsadikim in itself but to the type of leadership offered by a particular kind of tsadik: the miracle-workers, the men without learning, 'who have made gatherings to eat and drink the main feature of the worship of the Lord, blessed be He'.[153]

It is probable that, together with other factors, R. Nahman's hasidic lineage—his descent from the Besht—helped, from the start, to develop in him a sense of his unique and extraordinary qualities. As a child he often prayed at the grave of the Besht, 'asking his grandfather to help him to draw near to the Lord, blessed be He',[154] and in his first contacts with other tsadikim they all showed him great respect as 'the seed of the Besht'.[155] The value of lineage and ancestral merit was one of east European Jewry's most ancient Ashkenazi legacies,[156] and it is hard to imagine that R. Nahman's sense of his special mission was not fostered by his pedigree when he started out on the path of tsadikism. But once this sense of mission had crystallized, not only did it extend far beyond the hereditary link with the Besht but it actually led R. Nahman to reject that link, which did not accord with his conception of himself as a *ḥidush*—an extraordinary phenomenon the like of which the world had never seen.[157] He saw himself as a unique messianic *ḥidush* whose dominion extended over all creation, and not as a supreme leader within the prosaic framework of a hierarchical organization, for which, as we have seen, there was no precedent in the actual historical circumstances of his environment. By contrast, in his day-to-day activities as a tsadik, his position was simply that of a constituent part of the large network of hasidic leaders of his time. The particular messianic dimension of his leadership 'in concealment' found concrete historical expression not in opposition to the pluralistic principle which allowed all other tsadikim to lead their own followers, but in the rejection, within the Bratslav school itself, of the dynastic solution to the problem of preserving the distinctive identity of the school after the death of its founder. Most hasidic communities were beginning at that time to adopt the dynastic solution to this problem. In most cases it ensured their organizational continuity and maintained their original identity (and those communities that did not adopt this method disappeared from the scene with the death of their founders). Alone of all the hasidic circles and schools (at least until the demise of the last Lubavitcher Rebbe in 1994, which the Habad school has survived, maintaining its identity, if not quite its cohesion, without appointing a successor), the Bratslav community, which had been nurtured on the sense of R. Nahman's unique messianic role, was able to preserve its own cohesiveness and distinct identity, without anyone succeeding R. Nahman to the leadership, by regarding his death as a temporary stage of further 'concealment' in which he continued to have dominion over them, and by waiting patiently for the extension throughout the world of his 'revealed' dominion in the messianic time to come.

6. Conferences of Tsadikim

Apart from the alleged claims of individuals to supreme leadership, which were discussed above and shown to have been misconstrued as such, it is important to examine yet another possible indication of the apparent survival of centralist traditions in the leadership of post-1772 hasidism from the days of its founders. I refer to the meetings of the hasidic leaders of one region or another which were convened from time to time for a variety of reasons, and which could be construed as the remnants of an institution facilitating control from the centre, first established by the Magid of Mezhirech.

The disciples of the Magid appear to have come together only once, in Równe, towards the end of their master's life, in the summer of 1772. This we gather from R. Shneur Zalman of Liady's letter to R. Abraham of Kalisk, written at the end of 1805 or in 1806.[158] The letter was intended, among other things, to remind R. Abraham, who was in dispute with R. Shneur Zalman, of the sins of his youth, when he incurred the wrath of the Magid and had to ask the Rabbi of Liady to intercede on his behalf.[159] Admittedly, some doubt has been cast on the reliability of the hasidic historiographical tradition and the sources on which it was based, starting with the correspondence between the hasidic leaders who emigrated to Erets Yisra'el and their contemporaries, through the literature of the polemic between the hasidim and the *mitnagedim*, to the early hagiographical tales of hasidism. It is claimed that all these bodies of literature emanated from the Habad school and reflect the particularly biased perspective of Habad, in much the same way as does the internal historiography of Habad in the twentieth century.[160] It is, however, difficult to treat these diverse sources as a homogeneous literary tradition simply on the grounds of the Habad thread which runs through them all, and they certainly do not all display the tendentiousness which has marked Habad historiography in recent decades.[161]

Although all our information on the Równe meeting of the Magid's disciples is derived from Habad sources, there is no good reason to suspect its reliability. The purpose of the meeting as recorded by R. Shneur Zalman in his letter, namely, 'to take counsel' in response to the outbreak of the controversy with the *mitnagedim*, seems entirely reasonable.

We have no knowledge of any other conferences or assemblies of the Magid's disciples during his lifetime, or of any regular meetings of hasidic leaders after his death which might have been convened by one or other of them in order to determine the policy of the hasidic movement as a whole.[162] On the other hand, we know that hasidic leaders did occasionally come together under various circumstances to deal with topical issues and also to argue out disputes between opposing hasidic camps. However, none of these conferences placed any obligation on the participants, and no individual leader ever emerged as a sufficiently dominant figure to impose his authority on the others. It is quite clear that the organizational framework within which these meetings took place did not offer any machinery for the imposition of central control.

Conferences of this kind took place in Berdiczów at the beginning of the first decade of the nineteenth century. Gottlober reports on a meeting of communal leaders, most of them hasidic, invited by R. Levi Isaac of Berdiczów to his town 'to consult together and defend their lives' on account of 'a great calamity' and 'a day of darkness' the nature of which he does not specify.[163] Dubnow identified this calamity as the establishment, by order of Tsar Alexander I, of the Committee for the Amelioration of the Jews in St Petersburg in 1802,[164] a committee which, in December 1804, issued the notorious 'Statute Concerning the Organization of the Jews', excluding the Jews from their traditional rural occupations and expelling them from the villages and hamlets in a vast area in which they had long been resident.[165] Dubnow put forward the hypothesis that R. Levi Isaac of Berdiczów called his fellow hasidic leaders together in his town in order to forestall this misfortune and plan joint action, and he therefore conjectured that the meeting was held in 1802 or 1803.[166] Israel Halpern, however, observed that the internal chronology of Gottlober's account was problematic and did not necessarily point to the date proposed by Dubnow.[167] It appears that Gottlober himself supposed the meeting to have taken place in 1809, though the accuracy of his memory at the time of writing may be questionable. Just as in the case of the Równe meeting of 1772—as reported in R. Shneur Zalman's letter[168]—so, too, on this occasion it appears that the leaders were called together in the first place in response to a grave external danger facing them all, but the meeting became the arena for an internal dispute: in Równe the Magid of Mezhirech and some of his intimates fell out with R. Abraham of Kalisk, and in Berdiczów some thirty years later R. Barukh of Międzybóż, the grandson of the Besht, was in dispute with R. Aryeh Leyb, the Zeyde of Shpola.

Another description of a conference of hasidic leaders in Berdiczów during the same period appears in the biography of R. Nahman of Bratslav by his disciple, R. Nathan Sternharz.[169] According to that account the conference of the tsadikim in Berdiczów took place 'in the summer of 1802' on the occasion of the wedding of the son of one of the 'great men'. In spite of the obvious difference between Gottlober's account of the circumstances of the undated Berdiczów conference and the report in *Ḥayei moharan* on the meeting in the same town which was held in the summer of 1802, they share one detail in common: on both occasions the hostility of the participants was focused on the figure of the Zeyde of Shpola. He was insulted and publicly humiliated by R. Barukh of Międzybóż, according to Gottlober,[170] while according to R. Nathan Sternharz, the majority of those present in Berdiczów came close to excommunicating him for his intrigues against R. Nahman, and he was only saved from this censure by the intervention of R. Levi Isaac himself.[171] In Gottlober's account the precise date and circumstances are unclear; the Bratslav source is patently tendentious and polemical—it places the dispute between the Shpola Zeyde and R. Nahman at the centre of events and may well have neglected to report additional items of information which lie outside the immediate concern of the author. Dubnow's hypothesis that the Berdiczów conference mentioned by Gottlober was held in 1802 or 1803 is not an easy one to maintain in the face of all the difficulties advanced against it by Halpern, but Halpern does not altogether reject it, and prefers to leave the matter open until such time as fresh evidence on the question may come to light.[172] Given all these uncertainties it is just possible that the 1802 conference in Berdiczów described in *Ḥayei moharan* and the one reported by Gottlober, which may be tentatively dated to 1802/3, are one and the same.[173]

Another large meeting of hasidic leaders is known to us almost exclusively from the hagiographical sources,[174] although the fact that it took place is not in doubt. This meeting, too, was occasioned by a marriage in the household of a famous tsadik—the wedding of a grandson of the rebbe of Apta (Opatów) in Ustila (Uścilug), and it, too, apparently became the arena for a sharp dispute between the assembled guests. In the nature of things, the marriages of tsadikim and of their children provided opportunities for a number of hasidic leaders to meet in one court, especially as there was a great deal of intermarriage between the dynasties in the course of the nineteenth century. All our information on such meetings and conferences, far from reflecting the presence of a certain centralist, hierarchical mode of operation, actually emphasizes the degree of independence of each court, and, at times, the high level of tension and mutual hostility which characterized the relations between the courts even when their leaders came together under the roof of their host to discuss matters of common concern.

In contrast to all the sources mentioned above, there exists a single body of source material which attributes a distinctly centralist tendency to the hasidic leadership not only during the lifetime of the Besht and the Magid of Mezhirech—as has been the general assumption—but even in the period following the death of the Magid, in the 1770s and 1780s. These sources mention regular conventions of all the Magid's disciples, who place in charge over themselves a 'managing committee' and other centralist institutions which 'oversee' the internal administration of the movement as well as the wider dissemination of its teachings. The sources in question are the internal historiography of Habad, of which the most systematic and prolific exponent was the *admor* Joseph Isaac Schneersohn.[175] In his historical writings the figure which stands out among the disciples of the Magid as the leader who was chosen by his colleagues to 'oversee' the affairs of the movement is, of course, R. Shneur Zalman of Liady.

Contrary to the picture which emerges from the evidence considered above of a leadership structure which was fragmented from the start, and contrary, too, to the view—which has prevailed both in the scholarly literature and in later hasidic writings—that the leadership was decentralized after 1772, R. Joseph Isaac reconstructs the events which followed the death of the Magid, and the outbreak of the controversy with the *mitnagedim*, as follows:

The situation at the time required that in charge of affairs there should be a man with the spirit to speak plainly to the opponents and not take fright at the noise of the excommunications and proclamations fired off by the opponents at the followers of hasidism. Accordingly it was decided then to elect a management committee, with a general organizer—authorized by the holy rabbi, R. Abraham,[176] and the entire holy fraternity—having power and authority to act on his own responsibility and to give such instructions to all the centres as seemed to him necessary for the good of the cause. And the holy fraternity—in general session—elected our venerable and holy Old Rebbe [*der alter rebe*][177] to be the general organizer [investing him] with full authority, and they empowered him to organize the work of all the centres and the work of propaganda throughout the country, and also to visit from time to time the places of residence of the disciples of our teacher, may his soul rest in Eden.[178] For about three years—from 1773 to 1776—the Old Rebbe was engaged in various journeys to various places to examine the situation of the disciples of the Magid and to see whether the work carried out in the centres was in accordance with the arrangements prescribed by the management committee.[179]

This reconstruction is clearly anachronistic: the model of the centralized Habad court, and its characteristic concern with 'organization' and 'propaganda', which marked especially the difficult and heroic leadership of the author from the end of the 1920s until his death in 1950,[180] is applied retrospectively to the structure of the entire hasidic movement of the 1770s. The account is out of step with everything we know from other sources: there is no reference in the contemporary writings of members of 'the holy fraternity' themselves to any such centralized organizational activity on their part, nor to R. Shneur Zalman of Liady's exalted position at the centre of affairs, particularly during this early period, at the beginning and in the middle of the 1770s. He had not yet become leader of the hasidim of Belarus at that time, and certainly did not attain this position before the departure for Erets Yisra'el, in 1777, of R. Menahem Mendel of Vitebsk and R. Abraham of Kalisk—the two disciples of the Magid of Mezhirech who led the hasidic communities of the region during the Magid's lifetime. R. Shneur Zalman's rise to leadership was a long-drawn-out process, and it was not completed until the end of the 1780s, with the death of R. Menahem Mendel of Vitebsk in Erets Yisra'el.[181] What is more, his leadership, even when established, did not extend over all the areas of influence of the Magid's disciples throughout the crumbling Polish–Lithuanian Commonwealth, as would appear from the *admor*'s remarks quoted above. The rabbi of Liady served as leader of his hasidim in his own area, like the Magid's other disciples and the other tsadikim in their own areas and for their own hasidim. The only centralized function which can be attributed to him—

the collection of money on behalf of the hasidim in Erets Yisra'el—was itself not exclusive to him, for he was never the sole 'authorized person' in charge of this task in all the regional territories of hasidism;[182] and in any event, there were those who objected to his having even this authority, and the matter became a bone of contention.[183]

In addition to ascribing to R. Shneur Zalman of Liady the status of supreme leader at this time—an heir, as it were, to the Magid of Mezhirech's leadership,[184] the centralist nature of which is taken for granted—Habad tradition attributes to the hasidic leadership during those years a formal centralist structure which was expressed, above all, in regular and fairly frequent—almost annual—conventions of all the Magid's disciples. In his 'historical' writings the *admor* Joseph Isaac claims that such conventions were held at least in 1773, 1776, 1777, 1779, and 1782.[185] According to him, they constituted the forum at which the policy of the hasidic movement as a whole was formulated, and the decisions of the leaders who attended were binding upon everyone. Thus, for example, it was decided at the meeting in 1776 that R. Menahem Mendel of Vitebsk should go to Erets Yisra'el, and also that R. Shneur Zalman should be appointed to the positions of *nasi* (head) of the hasidim in Lithuania and 'general organizer' of the entire movement.[186] At the meeting in 1777 the 'fraternity' said farewell to R. Menahem Mendel, who was about to leave for Erets Yisra'el; undertook to see to the maintenance of 'our masters who are journeying to the Holy Land, and their families'; acknowledged the principle that 'every member of the fraternity is head [*nasi*] in his place and in his district' (which is as much as to say that the phenomenon of decentralization was itself the result of a policy formulated in the upper echelon of the central leadership); fixed the limits of R. Shneur Zalman's authority in Lithuania and Belarus; and also appointed him supreme head (*nesi hanesi'im*) in the matter of the collection of funds for Erets Yisra'el, and general 'organizer' of the whole fraternity for a period of five years.[187] The meetings were always held in the area where the Magid of Mezhirech had lived, and the rabbi of Liady was repeatedly obliged to travel to 'Volhynia, the region which the holy fraternity fixed for their assembly'.[188] This reflects the assumption of the writer that the institution of the regular conventions of the Magid's disciples began during the lifetime of their master, when they would doubtless have met in his court (even after they began to lead their own congregations of hasidim), in the same way as they had met once in Równe in 1772, according to the famous letter of R. Shneur Zalman of Liady. It is clear that the historic meeting in Równe, which was apparently an ad hoc gathering to consider the unprecedented problem of the controversy with the *mitnagedim*, served the *admor* Joseph Isaac as a peg on which to hang his reconstruction of events in the 1770s and 1780s from the Habad perspective. There is no mention of most of the details of his reconstruction in contemporary sources; and however much he may employ the professional mannerisms of the historian, his work both serves and reflects the internal needs of Habad more than it suggests any interest in the writing of history as such. R. Joseph Isaac, who was not a professional historian but the leader of a large community in extremely difficult circumstances, subordinated the writing and documentation of history to the needs of the making of history, in which he took an active part indeed. Fuller consideration is given below to his seemingly historiographical activity as part of the courageous enterprise of rehabilitating and consolidating the Habad movement in conditions of crisis,[189] an enterprise which was inspired by his view that the 'travails' of the time heralded the coming of the messiah.

7. The Ideological Framework in Relation to the Realities of Organizational Change

The hasidic movement, then, operated as a network of separate congregations of hasidim, each under the exclusive leadership and central control of its own charismatic leader, which, however, did not infringe on the no less exclusive and central authority of other tsadikim over their hasidim. This organizational structure found ideological expression in various formulations of the doctrine of the affinity of souls—souls which had their origin in the same 'root' or 'family' in Heaven. The doctrine, which sprang from medieval kabbalah,[190] reached its full development in the sixteenth-century kabbalah of Safed.[191] It provided hasidism with a means of explaining and legitimizing, in terms of well-known kabbalistic ideas, the novel leadership structure of the movement and the intricate relationships within it: each tsadik is capable of drawing to himself, reforming (effecting the *tikun* of), and elevating only the individual souls which belong to the root of his soul, and this leaves the field open for the activity of other tsadikim, whose souls are derived from other roots. R. Elimelekh of Lizhensk (Leżajsk) formulates the principle of the affinity between the roots of the souls of the tsadik and his particular hasidim as follows:

'If your brother becomes poor and sells [part] of his property [Heb. *umakhar me'aḥuzato*] etc.' [Lev. 25: 25]. The meaning of *umakhar* is 'he sells himself'; *me'aḥuzato*, 'out of his property', is the upper world from which he was hewn, and which is his true possession. For example, we observe that a person who is not yet grown up is greatly attached to his father by bonds of love, but as he grows and his understanding in matters of corporeal, worldly affairs is strengthened, he gradually becomes detached from his father until he is entirely separated and he leaves his father and becomes like a different person. Similarly with the soul, when it first comes to this world it still has bonds with the upper world, for it was hewn from that world . . . but later, when a person has become part of the corporeality of this world . . . his mind separates itself from the service of the Creator . . . and he sells himself and is deprived of the Lord, blessed be He, [as is alluded to in the verse] 'and they were brought low for their iniquity' [Ps. 106: 43]. That is what is meant by *umakhar me'aḥuzato*. And what is its remedy? 'His kinsman who is nearest to him shall come and redeem what his brother has sold' [ibid.], and he, his kinsman, is the tsadik nearest to him in the Garden of Eden, their souls being attached to each other because they stem from the same root. 'And shall redeem what his brother has sold', i.e. he shall aid and assist him to separate himself from this lowly world and to attach himself to the upper worlds. And that is the meaning of the verse 'Better is a neighbour who is near than a brother who is far off' [Prov. 27: 10]. 'A neighbour who is near' refers to the affinity of souls; although in this world they appear to be distant from each other, nevertheless they are near to each other in the upper world, and that is better than 'a brother who is far off', someone who is a brother in this world but is distant from him in the upper world,[192] for such a brother can avail him nothing, whereas the tsadik, who is with him in one and the same root, he is his true redeemer [*go'el*, which also means 'kinsman']. And that is the meaning of 'shall redeem what his brother has sold'; see above.[193]

Such statements provide a theoretical basis for the demarcation of the 'territory' of each tsadik and for the exclusive links between him and his own hasidim. Thus it is related of a man who was a hasid of R. David of Lelów, one of the disciples of R. Elimelekh of Lizhensk, but who decided to try out another rebbe by joining the ranks of Habad:

One day it occurred to him to journey to the holy Eminence, the author of the *Tanya* (may the memory of that righteous and holy man be for a blessing) in

Liozno, and he did so, but when he arrived he could not go in to see him for eight days. On the eighth day the 'Tanya' himself came to him and greeted him and said to him, 'Go to the rabbi, R. David of Lelów, for the root of your soul does not belong to me but to him.'[194]

On this R. Mordecai Brokman, compiler of the hagiographical anthology *Migdal david*, observes: 'It is well known that every soul is drawn to its root, for it goes to the tsadik together with whom it previously existed in the upper world, and as is mentioned in *No*[*am*] *e*[*limelekh*] on the verse "If your brother becomes poor", your brother from the upper world: see what is said there.'[195]

In its original kabbalistic context the doctrine of the affinity between the roots of souls is linked with that of transmigration, the means by which souls return to their families, their tribes, or their roots in the upper world.[196] On the other hand, in the hasidic versions of the doctrine transmigration is displaced from its central position and, instead, emphasis is placed on the ability of the tsadik to elevate the souls of his hasidim to their root through his *devekut*. While he is in the state of *devekut* his soul becomes bound up with theirs, in exactly the same way that it becomes bound up with all the captive divine 'sparks' in his immediate material environment—his food, his utensils, his animals—which also belong to the root of his soul and achieve their *tikun* through him.[197] On the evidence of the tales cited above about tsadikim who were able to tell that certain hasidim who sought to approach them actually 'belonged' to other tsadikim,[198] every tsadik can identify the original heavenly root of every soul, be it destined to be perfected by him or by one of his colleagues. This view springs from the belief that the tsadikim possess such exalted souls that they have already accomplished their own *tikun* and returned to their root; they descend to the world only in order to perfect and redeem the lowly souls which are dependent on them. Underlying this view is the elitist consciousness shared by kabbalists of previous generations who saw themselves collectively as a vanguard, 'the exalted souls which were the first to ascend and have already been perfected, then they descend to guide and set straight those lowly souls in order that they [too] may be perfected'.[199]

The doctrine of the root-affinity between the souls of the hasidic leader and his followers not only enabled every tsadik to draw towards him only those hasidim whom he recognized as being from the root of his own soul and reject others with 'foreign' souls: it also explained and legitimized the search of every hasid for a leader who suited his own disposition; for 'the young people' (*benei hane'urim*)—the early recruits to hasidism during its first period of expansion—were apparently given to wandering from court to court before attaching themselves permanently to the 'right' master. We shall return to this below.

It follows, then, that the kabbalistic doctrine of the root-affinity between particular souls, which, in origin, was unquestionably deterministic, was transformed by early hasidism, in effect if not in fully articulated theory, into the doctrine of voluntary association between individuals: the approach to hasidism was a process of mutual choice between particular hasidim and particular tsadikim who knew each other personally. It is true that, on the face of it, the choice was not a free one but was simply a matter of identifying the primordial link between the roots of their souls, a link which had been established in the upper worlds during the initial stages of Creation. Actually, however, as soon as this link was put to the test of immediate personal contact between the spiritual leader and the 'lowly souls' which were dependent on him, the deterministic element was displaced by the element of free will. In contrast to the kabbalistic elite who restored souls to their root by spiritual action which did not require personal contact with their individual embodiment, every hasidic tsadik restored the souls related to him to their roots through direct contact with their owners, within the concrete social framework of his congregation.

The doctrine of the affinity between the root of every tsadik's soul and that of his particular hasidim was formulated in parallel in the teachings of several hasidic leaders at the end of the eighteenth and the beginning of the nineteenth centuries.[200] That was precisely the period in which the hasidic circles were emerging as fully institutionalized and distinct courts, each under an undoubtedly centralist leadership which was beginning, at least in some cases, to show a tendency towards dynasticism.[201] But in the selfsame period there also developed a sense of cohesion and interconnection which bound the various courts together within the framework of the whole of hasidism, now newly perceived as a coherent movement. For the 'primitive' hasidism of the 1750s and 1760s had neither felt itself to be a movement nor been looked upon as one until it came up against mitnagdism and learnt from its opponents to regard itself as a 'sect'.[202] At the outset it merely consisted of a cluster of charismatic individuals and 'holy fraternities' whose relationship to each other and to the wider public was unstructured, personal, and spontaneous.[203] Admittedly the Besht, R. Pinhas of Korets, R. Nahman of Kosów, R. Isaac of Drohobycz, R. Aryeh Leyb the Mokhiah of Połonne, R. Jacob Joseph of Połonne, the Magid of Mezhirech, and other members of what historians have termed 'the circle of the Besht' knew each other, spoke to each other, and influenced each other significantly, as is evident from the traditions quoted in their name and about them. But at the same time it is very doubtful whether they saw themselves as the standard-bearers of a newly established movement with a coherent ideology and social framework such as might define, on the one hand, the exclusive sphere of influence of each one over his own followers and, on the other, some common ideological platform and mode of operation that would distinguish them collectively from the non-hasidic community.

It is not without significance that the theme of the exclusive nature of the bond between the soul of each tsadik and the souls of his particular hasidim is totally absent from R. Jacob Joseph's discussions of the root-affinity between the souls of the spiritual leaders and those of the common people; and his discussions may be taken as representative of the views prevalent within the early 'circle' of the Besht. As was noted by Weiss: 'In the generation of the "circle" the connecting line is generally drawn between Tsadikim and common people in the nation at large. The social collectivity to which the doctrine of leadership applies is not, as yet, the hasidic congregation specifically but the whole nation, the whole generation.'[204] R. Jacob Joseph puts the point as follows:

And afterwards, in speaking words of correction and rebuke to the inhabitants of his town, let him see to it that he first binds himself to Him, blessed be He, and then let him see to it that he attaches and binds himself to them by way of complete unity and incorporation with them, for the leaders of the generation and the members of his [*sic*] generation have one and the same root,[205] and if he does this, the Lord his God will be with him and he will ascend [lit. 'he has ascended'] with them in order to attach them to Him, blessed be He.[206]

It is true that the leader's words of correction and rebuke are here directed at a more specific audience defined as 'the inhabitants of his town'; but the choice of this wording undoubtedly stems from the personal experience of the writer, who served for the greater part of his life as communal rabbi in various towns,[207] and 'the inhabitants of the town' were his natural professional environment. None the less, those who are linked with the leaders of the generation by the principle of the root-affinity of their souls are clearly all 'the members of his generation'—the whole of Jewry, without any distinction between the hasidim of one tsadik and another or between hasidim and non-hasidim. From this point of view the link between the hasidic leader and the community at this stage in the history of hasidism was the direct continuation of the traditional link—close in the upper worlds but free from direct personal involvement—between the kabbalists and the souls of the generation. This is a far cry from the relationship of later hasidic leaders with their own clearly differentiated and personally affiliated hasidim. There is not a trace here of any sense of belonging to a sect or movement, either in the internal relations between individuals within the loosely knit network of 'leaders of the generation'—the circle of the Besht and his associates—or in their external relations with the wider public within which and for the benefit of which they worked. In fact, the demarcation between 'exterior' and 'interior', that is, between non-hasidic and hasidic, at this stage was rather blurred: the operative distinction was between the anthropological category of the 'spiritual men'—those exalted people who were 'leaders of the generation'—and that of the 'common people', to which the rest of Jewry belonged; and the two categories were called upon to bind themselves to each other in a bond of mutual dependence.

It was not until the 1770s and 1780s that hasidism first began to display some signs of a budding collective identity as a movement, and this at precisely the same time as each of the proliferating hasidic centres which constituted the movement was crystallizing its separate identity within it. These two processes, each accelerated by interaction with the other, can be understood as nothing other than manifestations of a new self-awareness which was aroused and sharpened by the external stimulus of the controversy with the *mitnagedim*; for it was in the writings of the *mitnagedim* that the hasidim and their leaders, their diverse prayer groups and fraternities, as well as various types of individuals who were sympathetic to them, were first treated as a coherent 'sect',[208] and it was in the proclamations of *ḥerem* that all these varied expressions of the new spiritual awakening were first lumped together. Thus, for example, the Vilna proclamation of 1781 excommunicates a whole range of 'deviant' groups and individuals who are identified with hasidism but who do not necessarily have any connection with each other:

In regard to this the chiefs and princes of the holy congregation [of Vilna] have been aroused . . . and have renewed the great *ḥerem* . . . against the aforesaid sect in every place where there are groups of the aforesaid people and [those] who follow their practices, and also to individuals who follow their practices and customs in their homes and in secret; also the[ir] branches, and those who assist and advise them and protect them, and of course those who believe in them, [to those people] all the aforesaid *ḥaramot* apply.[209]

Until the outbreak of the controversy with the *mitnagedim* it was possible to sample the hasidic experience—to take the measure of its leaders, join its prayer groups, or adopt some of its customs—out of curiosity or a spirit of adventure, without being obliged to undergo a complete change of identity or a clear-cut transfer from one camp to another. In *Shivḥei habesht* there are many descriptions of individuals joining the Besht and his circle, as well as of visits with a less clear motive by people who came on their own initiative, or were sent, to find out what sort of men the new leaders were and test their powers. These descriptions contain no hint of any upset in the family life of the visitors or any break with their previous social environment.[210] On the contrary, it emerges from the story of how the Magid of Mezhirech became a disciple of the Besht that 'his relatives pressed him to go to the Besht' in the hope that he would find a cure for his illness there.[211] R. Abraham, the father of R. Pinhas of Korets, did not disown his son—in fact, it seems that his relations with him remained extremely good—in spite of the fact that he knew of his son's links with the Besht, whom R. Abraham considered 'insignificant'.[212] Similarly it appears from the autobiography of Solomon Maimon that his association with hasidism in the court of the Magid of Mezhirech was not attended by any family crisis or by a break, recognized either by him or by those around him, with the pattern of his earlier life. When he made the acquaintance of a young man with leanings towards hasidism, and who aroused his curiosity and fanned the flames of his spiritual and intellectual unrest, he got up and went to Mezhirech. Even his prolonged absence from home was nothing out of the ordinary for him, for in any event he had to live in other people's houses and away from his home town in the course of earning his living as a children's tutor.[213] And when he grew tired of Mezhirech hasidism he went back peacefully to his home. If any alarm or anger had been occasioned among the members of his household (especially his motherin-law, whom he describes as a Xanthippe[214]) by the fact that he had been attracted to the new 'sect' of hasidism, we could have expected to find some reference to this in his book, for he has a great deal to say about dramatic domestic incidents, and says it very well. Actually he appears to have regarded his connection with hasidism at this stage as unremarkable and not involving him in any obligation. That, indeed, is how the matter was presented to him by the young man who had first introduced him to hasidism: 'As far as the mode of admission was concerned . . . he assured me that that was the simplest thing in the world. Any man who felt a desire for perfection but did not know how to satisfy it . . . had nothing to do but apply to the superiors of the society, and automatically he became a member.'[215]

Unlike these contacts, which were free of any hint of crisis, the act of conversion to hasidism in the period following the outbreak of the controversy with the *mitnagedim* involved a transformation of consciousness which demanded the total isolation of the convert from his old environment and the adoption of a new identity. In the unique hasidic autobiography *Yemei moharnat*, R. Nathan Sternharz, the literary secretary of R. Nahman of Bratslav, documents his conversion from *mitnaged* to hasid at the end of the 1790s, some twenty-five years after Solomon Maimon's visit to Mezhirech:

And at that time I was a great opponent [*mitnaged*] of the hasidim because my father-in-law strongly disagreed with them and spoke a great deal about them to me and his other sons-in-law and the members of his household and said that his whole intention in speaking to us was to distance us from them. Afterwards I left Sh"g [Szarogród] at Sukkot, at the beginning of 5556 [1796], and came to the holy congregation of Nemirov together with my wife and boarded at my late father's table, and I joined with my late friend to study during the winter. He had been brought up from childhood among the hasidim and had spent some time with a number of tsadikim, and he spoke with me a great deal, arguing that the hasidim were God-fearing and that their famous tsadikim were men of very great eminence and served the Lord, blessed be He, in truth (as indeed they do). And other people, too, argued with me about this but I nevertheless remained firm and determined in my opposition . . . and because of this, during the whole of the winter I spent in Nemirov, I was still opposed to them. Subsequently, as a result of my friend's and other people's continuing to press their arguments, I realized the truth and was privileged to be initiated into the belief in the sages. I agreed with the hasidim that it was good to associate with the famous tsadikim, the great men of the hasidim, because they are men of truth and the Lord is with them, and then, to some extent, the fear of Heaven was drawn down upon me and I changed for the better in regard to several matters known to me. But in spite of this I was still wandering aimlessly and did not know my right hand from my left, for I had no one to lead me properly, and it would take too long to tell everything that happened to me during that time.

In the year 5562 [1802] in the month of Elul I was privileged to become a follower of the holy and awe-inspiring *admor*, the true teacher, Moharan [R. Nahman], may the memory of that righteous and holy man be for a blessing . . . and it is impossible to imagine how many obstacles and afflictions I endured in that year, namely 5562, for everyone was opposed to me, both my wife and my father, may his light shine, and all the members of his household and all the household of my late grandfather . . . and immediately, that winter, my father, may his light shine, drove me away from his table and I was obliged to eat in my grandfather's home and my wife ate with my father, may his light shine.[216]

Although both Maimon's and R. Nathan's autobiographical accounts were written many years after the events that they describe,[217] the difference between them illustrates very well the enormous change of consciousness which had occurred in the twenty-five years that had elapsed between their respective initiations into hasidism. Maimon, at the very beginning of his book, defines himself as belonging to the well-to-do learned class, whose values he is still able to regard as an absolute and universal norm for the Jewish world. R. Nathan indicates that his identity at the outset was conditioned by his membership of the selfsame class. But he expresses this by defining himself as 'a great *mitnaged*'—a relative definition of an identity which has meaning only in reference, and by opposition, to a clearly defined alternative hasidic identity. It is true that in his general, preliminary remarks at the start of the chapter which he entitles 'On a Secret Society and Therefore a Long Chapter' Maimon refers to hasidism as 'a sect of my nation called the "new hasidim"',[218] and introduces it as a distinctive movement, but this does not square with the main substance of the chapter, where he describes the details of his affiliation to the hasidic fraternity at Mezhirech. The sectarian terminology of the introductory section apparently reflects his later sensitivity, at the time of writing in Berlin, to 'secret societies' (such as the Freemasons) which were then in vogue, and in the context of which he saw the rise of hasidism among the Jews.[219] In contrast to Maimon's free movement into hasidism and out again, which had no repercussions on his status in the society in which he had grown up, R. Nathan was ejected from his family circle and deprived of his status the moment they became aware of his conversion to hasidism. The breakdown of relations between them, which ultimately led to his financial ruin, is alluded to in brief comments scattered throughout the autobiography, and is documented in detail in the later literature of the Bratslav circle.[220]

The attempt of the *mitnagedim* to exclude the various kinds of 'new hasidim' from the body of the Jewish community (the fact that in the end they failed is irrelevant for our present purpose) introduced into the hitherto holistic, integrative hasidic outlook a keen sense of the boundary between the world of hasidism 'within' and the hostile community 'without', thus generating the new consciousness of hasidism as a movement.[221] One of the first manifestations of this enhanced awareness was the meeting of the disciples of the Magid of Mezhirech at Równe in the summer of 1772, shortly before his death. They came together 'to take counsel' and to consider the threat from the *mitnagedim* which faced them all.[222] No doubt the personal links between the assembled tsadikim, founded on their association with their common master, created a natural and convenient framework in which to consider their common predicament, and fostered their newly awakened sense of belonging collectively to a tangible organization. But this feeling was determined in the first instance by their new relationship to the outside world, a world which had now revealed itself as distinct from the world of hasidism 'within', and even hostile to it. This orientation was in marked contrast to the all-embracing view of the world held in the previous generation by the circle of the Besht, which had drawn no distinction whatsoever between 'without' and 'within', and whose field of vision still encompassed the nation or the 'generation' as a whole.

The awakening of this collective consciousness of belonging to one movement among the disciples of the Magid of Mezhirech was in apparent conflict with the sense of the unique identity of each of the individual courts which developed simultaneously after the outbreak of the controversy with the *mitnagedim*. The meeting at Równe was not only the first collective initiative of hasidism as a movement. It was also the arena for the first internal struggle between different factions within it. The special identity of each faction was all the more keenly felt precisely as a result of their growing awareness that they shared a common destiny as a movement: for example R. Abraham of Kalisk's style of hasidism was revealed at the meeting as distinctive and controversial enough to be regarded by the others as deviant, and it was denounced under pressure of the collective interest in appeasing the *mitnagedim*.[223] R. Abraham later levelled the same charge against his attackers, chief among them R. Shneur Zalman of Liady.[224] Once the dynamic of delimitation of boundaries and the growing recognition of distinctive identity began to work, it operated not just on the conception of the world 'outside' as against the world 'within' hasidism but also on the sense of distinctive identity within hasidism itself. The crystallization of the disjointed world of hasidism as a clearly defined and coherent entity, under the pressure of the controversy from 'without', necessarily heightened the awareness of those 'within' that their world was a complex one, and it led to the conscious differentiation of its constituent parts from each other; for until the whole was recognized as such, its parts would be perceived as single items only randomly interconnected, so that there would be no need or reason to define them in relation to one another. This is precisely how the tensions between individual leaders in the generation of the Besht may be understood. They occurred during the period which preceded the consolidation of discrete hasidic fraternities into a cohesive movement in response to the campaign of the *mitnagedim*. The antagonism between R. Nahman of Kosów and the Besht,[225] for example, or between R. Jacob Joseph of Połonne and R. Pinhas of Korets on the one hand and the Magid of Mezhirech on the other,[226] was not centred on a struggle for the legacy of the supposedly centralist leadership of the Besht, as has been suggested by historians,[227] and it certainly did not go beyond personal rivalry or disagreement between individuals with different religious temperaments. The tense relationships between them, where they occurred, were incidental and did not define their individual religious identities. By contrast, the internal divisions within hasidism which occurred later, such as the clashes between R. Abraham of Kalisk and R. Shneur Zalman of Liady,[228] between R. Nahman of Bratslav and his uncle R. Barukh, and between R. Nahman and his great enemy the Zeyde of Shpola,[229] as well as many other disputes which took place in the period following 1772, were the products of a novel sense of mutual accountability within the movement as a whole. The component parts of the movement were now essentially related to one another, however tense this relation might be. These disputes were concerned with conflicting claims of authenticity and loyalty to a common spiritual legacy, and they were fought out on both the ideological and the organizational planes. On the ideological plane, the speculative doctrine of the Magid of Mezhirech was the common legacy of all his disciples in the leadership of hasidism after 1772, and the disputes between them were perceived as turning upon the proper interpretation of his teachings.[230] The leaders of other hasidic factions, who had not served their apprenticeship at the court of the Magid, developed not only a sense of their own interrelationship but also an affinity with the disciples of the Magid through the connecting link of the Besht, who was seen as the mentor of the Magid of Mezhirech and the teacher of them all.[231] On the organizational plane, the hasidic leaders of that generation disagreed over encroachments on each other's preserves concerning both their influence over hasidim and the joint collection of funds for the hasidic community in Erets Yisra'el.[232]

The emergence of a distinctive identity in each one of the hasidic courts alongside their collective identity as a movement was clearly discernible by the end of the 1790s and the beginning of the nineteenth century. The process is reflected quite well in the account cited above of R. Nathan's conversion to hasidism. R. Nathan himself distinguishes two stages in his transition from *mitnaged* to hasid: in the first stage 'I was privileged to be initiated into the belief in the sages. I agreed with the hasidim that it was good to associate with the famous tsadikim, the great men of the hasidim . . . But in spite of this I was still wandering aimlessly and did not know my right hand from my left, for I had no one to lead me properly.'[233] In other words, in the first stage R. Nathan shook off his identity as a *mitnaged* and adopted a new but internally undifferentiated identity as a hasid. At that time, then—1796—it was possible to be identified as a hasid in one's relations with the world which lay outside hasidism (and to suffer all the consequences which that involved) without necessarily being identified in one's intra-hasidic relations as a committed follower of a particular tsadik. From 1796 until he associated himself with R. Nahman of Bratslav in Elul 5562 (1802), R. Nathan wandered from one hasidic court to another without finding a leader after his own heart. He himself does not detail the names of the tsadikim to whom he attached himself temporarily. There is no doubt that he regarded the whole of his life up to the time that he became a follower of R. Nahman—both his time as a *mitnaged* and his time as a hasid—as quite meaningless, and he devotes no more than one and a half pages to it, apart from some brief remarks scattered here and there in his autobiography. However, later Bratslav hasidism—which, as we know, preserved old traditions and (unlike R. Nathan) did not hesitate to disseminate them in print—elaborated R. Nathan's summary account, out of admiration for him as a remarkable and saintly man, second only to R. Nahman himself. Bratslav tradition invests with meaning all the episodes of R. Nathan's life and records them as fully as possible. It thus enumerates 'R. Zusya, of blessed memory, and the righteous rabbi R. Levi Isaac of Berdiczów, and the holy rabbi R. Barukh, of blessed memory, and the tsadik R. Gedaliah of Linits [Ilintsy], of blessed memory, and the righteous rabbi R. Shalom of Pogrebishche [Pogrebishchenski], of blessed memory, and other great men, may their memory be for a blessing',[234] as leaders whose courts were all visited by R. Nathan during those years. A parallel tradition adds to this list R. Pinhas of Korets, R. Yehiel Mikhl of Złoczów, and R. Mordecai of Krzemieniec.[235] Not until 1802, after six years of searching for someone 'to lead me properly', did R. Nathan have the good fortune 'to become a follower of the holy and awe-inspiring *admor*, the true teacher, Moharan, may the memory of that righteous and holy man be for a blessing'.[236] Only then, in the second stage of the process of his conversion to hasidism, did he adopt the specific identity of a Bratslav hasid.

It appears that this two-stage process was typical of the young recruits to hasidism during this period.[237] And it is no wonder that the hasidic adaptation of the kabbalistic doctrine which identified the root-affinity between the souls of particular tsadikim and particular hasidim was emerging precisely at that time, for this version of the doctrine reflected the process of mutual choice between tsadikim and hasidim and served it very well. However, once it had established itself in hasidism it never lost its hold, even when the circumstances which it had served and mirrored altered during the early decades of the nineteenth century with the evolution of the hasidic leadership into a hereditary institution.

The hereditary principle under which the leadership of hasidism began to be transmitted within dynasties from one generation to the next[238] was also applied at the level of the ordinary hasidim to their affiliation with a particular court and leader. This affiliation was now beginning to be transmitted from generation to generation as an established family tradition. It is not impossible that the dynastic pattern on which the hasidic courts came to be modelled at this stage, as well as the hereditary pattern of affiliation to particular courts, and even the very practice of referring to the residence of the hasidic leader as his 'court'—*dwór* in Polish and other Slavonic languages, where the term refers to the manorial seat of the nobleman on his estate—reflected the feudal pattern of relationships on the Polish-Russian estates, with their proprietors, the noblemen who inherited the estates from their forefathers, and their tenants, the peasants who had 'belonged' to the estates for generations.[239] The period in which R. Nathan Sternharz's conversion to hasidism took place was characterized by the two-stage process in which a complete transformation of outlook, from *mitnaged* to hasid, was followed by the free choice of one tsadik out of many. But in the course of the nineteenth century, with the institutionalization of dynastic tsadikism and the stabilization, by heredity, of the community of followers within the framework of the court over a period of several generations, the hasidic identity of those who frequented each one of the courts became the product of a sense of continuity rather than severance and transformation of consciousness. The voluntary act of conversion by individuals was replaced by an inherited affiliation to hasidism of whole families, and even whole populations, in localities which had come to belong by tradition to the sphere of influence of a particular dynasty of leaders. Just as the leadership passed by inheritance, so, too, did the particular hasidic identity of the followers. At the same time, the collective hasidic identity, clearly differentiated from the non-hasidic or anti-hasidic world 'without', but undifferentiated by particular affiliations 'within' (as in the first stage of R. Nathan Sternharz's conversion to hasidism, before he became a follower specifically of R. Nahman of Bratslav), grew steadily less distinct. The usually inherited affiliation of the follower with a particular hasidic leader became the essential component of his identity as a hasid. From then on one could be born or become the hasid of a specific court but one could not be simply a hasid of no one in particular. That was the process which led to the virtual displacement of the old, absolute meaning of the title 'hasid' by its new, relative meaning.[240]

It appears that at this stage, when the place of the individual within hasidism had become a matter of inheritance rather than choice, the doctrine of the common roots of the soul which linked every tsadik exclusively with his own hasidim—a doctrine deterministic in its original kabbalistic form, but harnessed to the service of the novel principle of mutual choice in pre-dynastic hasidism—continued to confer legitimacy on the multiplicity of rival courts and their leaders in spite of the fact that the scope for free choice between hasidim and tsadikim had been restricted. Thus, for example, R. Hayim Meir Heilman, author of the well-known history of Habad, *Beit rabi*, makes use of this doctrine in his protest about the internal rivalries and disputes among the diverse branches of the hasidic movement of his time. In the preface to his book he writes:

> And this is the underlying cause of the division between hasidim, that one of them journeys to one tsadik and another journeys to a different tsadik (each according to the root of his soul), and each one thinks that the tsadik to whom he journeys is the only tsadik of the generation. But should we therefore speak ill, heaven forbid, of the other tsadikim of the generation . . . Let each one journey to the place to which his heart draws him, and let him drink living, flowing water from his well etc. And let him be bound to that place with cords of love, so that he may never be moved. And let him look with kindness and compassion on others and not set them at naught or interfere with their worship.[241]

Heilman here treats the link of each hasid with 'his' tsadik as a voluntary link 'to the place to which his heart draws him'. But in fact, when those words were written, at the beginning of the twentieth century, the link with the tsadik was no longer open to the free choice of the hasid. In most cases his heart was drawn to none other than the court to which his parents and grandparents had been attached, and he inherited his connection from them.

At this stage, when the hereditary link between every tsadik and his hasidim had become stable enough to restrict their freedom of mutual choice, there was no longer any need to reinforce and legitimize the internally differentiated hasidic identity of each court by means of the doctrine of the exclusive affinity between the roots of the souls of each community of hasidim and their particular tsadik. This affinity was now taken for granted. The sentiment which was, in fact, undermined as a result of the processes of hereditary stabilization within each one of the courts was the sense of the collective identity and solidarity of the hasidim within the movement at large, and it was this sentiment that the author of *Beit rabi* felt called upon to strengthen. By the beginning of the twentieth century the sense of belonging to hasidism as a movement had given way to the more vital sense of belonging to a particular hasidic court. New political and ideological divides were now cutting across the hasidic camp, aligning some of its factions with non-hasidic forces in Orthodoxy, with which hasidism had become identified through the struggle against secularization and modernity. The boundary between the Orthodox world 'within' and the Orthodox world outside hasidism was becoming blurred once again, while the internal divisions between the hasidic courts were felt as acutely as ever. Yet the collective identity of hasidism as a movement could continue to draw strength from the very doctrine which in its time had supplied the kabbalistic basis for legitimizing the opposite process of differentiating the individual courts from one another. *Beit rabi* makes use of this doctrine to ease the growing tension between the hasidic factions of its day, each one of which tended to see itself and its leader as the only authentic embodiment of the hasidic teaching while questioning the authenticity and piety of the others. This is clearly the context in which to explain not only the tendency of each hasidic community to regard its leader as 'the only tsadik of the generation' and to 'speak ill, Heaven forbid, of the other tsadikim of the generation'. It is also quite clearly the context in which to place the tendency of several hasidic communities, chief among them Habad, to adopt the Besht and the Magid of Mezhirech (who, from the outset, had constituted the basis of the collective identity of hasidism as a movement) as an integral part of their own particular history, and to appropriate them as an asset to which they claim exclusive title.[242]

In order to invoke the kabbalistic doctrine of the root-affinity between souls in support of the call to strengthen the now much weakened sense of collective hasidic identity, it was necessary to forgo one of the original components of the doctrine—the principle that 'most of the children are not from one root',[243] that is to say, that kinship between blood relatives is unlikely to be matched by common association with one 'root' or one 'family' of souls. Once the association between a given tsadik and his followers had become hereditary and therefore not subject to choice, the doctrine of the root-affinity between the souls of the tsadik and his own hasidim reverted to its deterministic origin—with the difference that the predetermined root-affinity now tended to overlap with the hereditary family link, apparently as a self-evident truth which did not need to be pitted against the previous incarnations of the idea.

Notes

1 See e.g. S. Dubnow, *The History of Hasidism* [Toledot haḥasidut] [Tel Aviv, 1930–1] (Tel Aviv, 1960), 87, 126; S. A. Horodetsky, *Hasidism and Its Adherents* [Haḥasidut vehaḥasidim] (Tel Aviv, 1928–43), i. 83, 102; ii. 8; M. Teitelbaum, *The Rabbi of Liady and the Habad Faction* [Harav miliadi umifleget ḥabad] (Warsaw, 1910), i. 32; A. Rubinstein, 'Studies in the History of Hasidism' (Heb.), in id. (ed.), *Studies in Hasidism* [Perakim betorat haḥasidut uvetoledoteiha] (Jerusalem, 1977), 242, 245.

2 As e.g. in Dubnow, *The History of Hasidism* (Heb.), 213. It is hardly necessary to point out that this assumption alone is not enough to explain the fragmentation of the leadership after the death of the Magid. As hasidic history itself demonstrates, in later generations, once the leadership had become a hereditary institution, the absence of a suitable candidate for the succession did not necessarily entail a break in the dynasty; witness the cases in which infants served as heads of hasidic communities, or a son-in-law, brother, or pupil was found to continue the leadership of the community and preserve its particular identity. So, too, with regard to the transmission of the leadership from the Besht to the Magid and from the Magid to his disciples, it is customary to assume that R. Zevi, the son of the Besht, was unsuited for office, and that therefore the Magid was elected or appointed to succeed his master; and that after the death of the Magid his office was divided among several of his disciples as a result of the 'refusal' of his son R. Abraham to take his father's place. In both cases (and in some others too) this is no more than an anachronistic expectation that the son would inherit the tsadik's position. It is clear that in the first generations of hasidism this expectation had not yet gained currency. It does, indeed, appear that R. Zevi was unfitted for leadership, in spite of his depiction in the hagiographical literature as a most saintly man. And R. Abraham the Angel, too, appears to have shunned public affairs and led the life of an ascetic kabbalist in the manner of earlier generations, rather than that of a hasidic leader of the new type. But there is no doubt that the unsuitability of both for the role of leader was not regarded at the time as precipitating a crisis or upsetting any established procedures so far as concerned leadership. See more on this on pp. 34ff. and 38ff. above.

Quite the opposite view has been taken in the internal historiography of Habad produced in recent generations. Most of this is the work of the *admor* Joseph Isaac Schneersohn (the sixth *admor* of the Habad dynasty, father-in-law and predecessor of the last *admor*, Menachem Mendel Schneerson, who died in 1994). On his historiographical writings and their historical value see Ch. 4 below, as well as n. 76 and Section 6 of the present chapter; R. Elior, 'The Minsk Debate' (Heb.), in *Jerusalem Studies in Jewish Thought*, 1/4 (1981–2), 181–3; Z. Gries, 'From Myth to Ethos: Towards a Portrait of R. Abraham of

Kalisk' (Heb.), in S. Ettinger (ed.), *A Nation and Its History*, ii: *The Modern Era* [Umah vetoledoteiha, ii: Ha'et haḥadashah] (Jerusalem, 1984), 130–1 n. 41. The *admor* Joseph Isaac Schneersohn repeatedly treats the first stages in the development of the hasidic movement as if they were governed by the regular procedures, sound organizational structure, and relative institutional stability which are characteristic of Habad. In his writings both of the sons with doubtful qualifications for the succession—the son of the Besht and the son of the Magid—are credited with short periods in office as supreme leaders of hasidism, each immediately after the death of his father. On the year-long leadership of R. Zevi, the son of the Besht, see J. I. Schneersohn, 'Avot haḥasidut', *Hatamim* (Kefar Habad, 1975), i. 140, ch. 6; and cf. id., *Sefer hazikhronot* (Kefar Habad, 1985), i. 39–41. On the two-year leadership of R. Abraham the Angel, son of the Magid, see Joseph Isaac's letter of 1935 to his daughter Mushka, in R. N. Kahan, *Shemuot vesipurim meraboteinu hakedoshim* (Kefar Habad, 1974–7), iii. 10–11, repr. in *Igerot kodesh . . . yosef yitsḥak* (Brooklyn, 1982–5), iii. 162–3. And see below, n. 76.

3 See S. Ettinger, 'The Hasidic Movement: Reality and Ideals', in H. H. Ben-Sasson and S. Ettinger (eds.), *Jewish Society through the Ages* (New York, 1971), 251–66 (originally published in *Cahiers d'histoire mondiale: Journal of World History*, 11/1–2 (1968), 262; repr. in G. D. Hundert (ed.), *Essential Papers on Hasidism* (New York, 1991), 238).

4 Ibid.

5 The principle of the multiplicity of hasidic courts was accepted by most hasidic leaders and their followers (see Section 7 below), but the encroachment of one tsadik on the sphere of influence of another was not tolerated, and when it did occasionally occur, whether accidentally or by design, it led to serious clashes. A case in point was that of R. Asher of Karlin. After the death of his master R. Shelomoh in 1792, he spent some time at the courts of R. Barukh of Międzybóż and R. Israel of Kozienice. On his return he was at first reluctant to settle in Karlin again, for fear, it seems, of the anti-hasidic activity of R. Avigdor of Pińsk (who had been dismissed from his position as local rabbi, apparently in 1793). He therefore settled temporarily in Żelechów, where he occupied the position of town rabbi for a time. Żelechów, however, 'belonged' to R. Levi Isaac of Berdiczów, and on this account a dispute arose between him and R. Asher. As a result of this R. Asher was obliged to move from Żelechów to Stolin, whence he returned to Karlin. See W. Z. Rabinowitsch, *Lithuanian Hasidism* (London, 1970), 49, 69. Similarly, in the 1780s Karlin hasidism experienced a period of crisis. Under the pressure of the campaign by the *mitnagedim* against Lithuanian hasidism on the one hand, and, on the other hand, faced with the growing influence of R. Shneur Zalman of Liady in Lithuania, and in Karlin itself in particular, R. Shelomoh of Karlin was forced to remove

his court from Karlin and look for a new place of residence. According to hasidic tradition, he first tried to settle in the small town of Beshenkovichi in Belarus, where there was a small concentration of his hasidim. This town adjoined the area of influence of R. Shneur Zalman of Liady, and R. Shelomoh was obliged to seek his permission to settle there. R. Shneur Zalman attached several conditions to his consent and R. Shelomoh refused to accept one of them. He therefore abandoned his plan to settle in Belarus and moved to Ludmir (Włodzimierz). See ibid. 35; H. M. Heilman, *Beit rabi* [Berdiczów, 1902] (Tel Aviv, n.d.), 128 (= 64*b*) n. *b*. Another territorial clash involved R. Shneur Zalman of Liady and R. Barukh of Międzybóż; on this see pp. 55–6 above. The well-known dispute between R. Aryeh Leyb, the Shpola Zeyde, and R. Nahman of Bratslav also appears to have been the result of encroachment on a neighbour's preserves, R. Nahman having entered the Zeyde's area of influence by settling in Zlatopol just before Rosh Hashanah 5560 (1800). See N. Sternharz, *Ḥayei moharan*, i (Jerusalem, 1947), 'Mekom yeshivato unesiotav', 54–5 §11.

6 On the disintegration of the Polish–Lithuanian Commonwealth, a process which began in the 17th century and reached its climax in the partitions of the 18th century, see S. Kieniewicz et al. (eds.), *History of Poland* (Warsaw, 1968), 223–4; N. Davies, *God's Playground: A History of Poland* (Oxford, 1981), i. 492–546; O. Halecki, *A History of Poland* (London, 1978), 177–213; W. Reddaway et al. (eds.), *The Cambridge History of Poland* (New York, 1978), ii. 1–176. During that period, while central government in other European countries such as France and Austria was being strengthened, Poland underwent a process of decentralization. The elected kings, their army, and the central parliament of the state—the Sejm—gradually lost their power, and in practice the landowning aristocracy, with their private armies and their local parliaments, ran the affairs of the state as they saw fit.

On the tradition of non-centralist Jewish communal organization which prevailed in Europe from the beginning of the second millennium, see e.g. S. W. Baron, *The Jewish Community* (Philadelphia, 1945), i. 206, 231, 326, 372; ii. 20. There were several attempts to set up centralist institutions above the level of the individual community councils, the best known of these being the Council of Four Lands and the Council of the Land of Lithuania, which branched off from it. During the period of their existence these councils succeeded in imposing their central authority, but not without a certain measure of strain and opposition on the part of the *kehilot*, who were not happy to sacrifice their traditional sovereignty. See on this H. H. Ben-Sasson, *Ideology and Leadership: Views of Society among Polish Jews at the End of the Middle Ages* [Hagut vehanhagah: hashkafoteihem haḥevratiyot shel yehudei polin beshalhei yemei habeinayim] (Jerusalem, 1959), 38–9; I. Levitats, *The Jewish Com-*

munity in Russia, 1772–1884 (New York, 1943), 71–91; see also J. Katz, *Tradition and Crisis*, trans. B. D. Cooperman (New York, 1993), 65–112. It must be remembered that, in parallel with the dwindling power of the central Polish government, the central councils of the Jewish communities grew weaker from the second half of the 17th century and during the 18th, until they were abolished by government order in 1764. See Dubnow, *The History of Hasidism* (Heb.), 20–1. The hasidic movement was therefore born into an environment which was marked by the disintegration of centralized organizational frameworks, whether we consider the decline of the Polish monarchy or the collapse of the Jewish Council of Four Lands.

7 See Ettinger, 'The Hasidic Movement', 262.

8 See C. Shmeruk, 'The Social Implications of Hasidic Ritual Slaughtering' (Heb.), *Zion*, 20 (1955), 70–1, repr. in id., *A Call for a Prophet*, ed. I. Bartal (Jerusalem, 1999).

9 M. M. Bodek, *Seder hadorot mitalmidei habesht z"l* (Lublin, 1927), 5.

10 From the title page of Dov Ber ben Shemuel of Linits, *Shivḥei habesht* (Berdiczów edn., 1815), and also (with slight variations) in the Kopys edition (1814). Facsimiles of the two title pages were included in B. Mintz's edition of *Shivḥei habesht* (Tel Aviv, 1961). The well-known statement of R. Menahem Mendel of Vitebsk: 'Thus it was that the word of God was given to the Ba'al Shem. He was the one. None of the ancients were like him, nor will there be any like him upon earth', which was quoted in the printer's preface to the 1814 Kopys edition of *Shivḥei habesht* (p. 2 in the English edn., *In Praise of the Baal Shem Tov*, ed. D. Ben-Amos and J. R. Mintz (Bloomington, Ind., 1970)), was clearly taken by the printer as a declaration of the unique 'greatness and glory' of the Besht, in the spirit of the hagiographical evaluation of his leadership, which became prevalent in later hasidism. At first sight this statement appears, then, to provide conclusive evidence, dating from relatively close to the time of the events in question—some twenty-five years after the death of the Besht—as to his unique status within the organizational framework of the hasidic leadership of his day. But it is doubtful if this was the intention of R. Menahem Mendel of Vitebsk. His statement needs to be examined in its original context rather than being severed from it, as it is in R. Israel ben Isaac Yofeh's introduction to the Kopys edition of *Shivḥei habesht*. R. Menahem Mendel's statement occurs in his letter of 1786, addressed from Tiberias to R. Jacob of Smiła, who was in charge of fundraising for the benefit of the hasidic community in Erets Yisra'el. In response to R. Jacob's personal request that he should intercede (with heaven) on his behalf in the matter of 'children' and ensure that he would be granted viable offspring, R. Menahem Mendel launched into an attack on 'some great men among the tsadikim of our generation' who acceded to such requests from their hasidim. He stressed his strong

objection to the claims of some of his colleagues in the hasidic leadership to perform miracles for their followers. It is in this polemical context that his remarks on the Besht appear: only the Besht could act in this way and alter the laws of nature; no one after him had been granted these powers, and it would be better if the tsadikim of the generation gave up this contemptible practice:

> But to return to the matter of his request for children: having seen the fervency of his prayer and his prostration before us and his strong pleas . . . I was covered in shame. For am I in the place of God? [cf. Gen. 30: 2]. Thus it was that the word of God was given to the Ba'al Shem. He could decree and it would come to pass. He was the one. None of the ancients were like him, nor will there be any like him on earth, even though some of the great ones among the tsadikim in our generation are big talkers and make such claims. That is not how I see myself. (*Peri ha'arets* [Zhitomir, 1867] (Jerusalem, 1970), 60; also published in J. Barnai, *Letters of Hasidim from the Land of Israel* [Igerot ḥasidim me'erets yisra'el] (Jerusalem, 1980), 154 no. 35)

This polemical statement, which evokes the unique spiritual stature and supernatural powers of the Besht in order to condemn the practice of miracle-working, which was becoming the hallmark of popular tsadikism at that time, is certainly not to be taken as hard evidence of the status of the Besht within the overall structure of the hasidic leadership of his day.

11 See A. J. Heschel, *The Circle of the Baal Shem Tov: Studies in Hasidism*, ed. S. H. Dresner (Chicago, 1985).

12 See B.-Z. Dinur, *With the Turn of the Generations* [Bemifneh hadorot] (Jerusalem, 1955), 159–70. An English translation of parts of Dinur's study appeared in Hundert (ed.), *Essential Papers on Hasidism*, 159–72, 203–8. See also J. Weiss, 'The Beginnings of Hasidism' (Heb.), *Zion*, 16 (1951), 46–9 (repr. in Rubinstein (ed.), *Studies in Hasidism* (Heb.), 122–5); J. Weiss, 'A Circle of Pneumatics in Pre-Hasidism', *Journal of Jewish Studies*, 8 (1957), 199–213 (repr. in id., *Studies in Eastern European Jewish Mysticism* (Oxford, 1985), 27–42). M. Piekarz, in *The Beginning of Hasidism: Intellectual Trends in Derush and Musar Literature* [Biyemei tsemiḥat haḥasidut: megamot ra'ayoniyot besifrei derush umusar] (Jerusalem, 1978), 22–33, criticizes the methodology and conclusions of Heschel and Weiss in these studies. His criticisms, particularly those dealing with their analysis of the traditions relating to R. Nahman of Kosów, are justified for the most part, but do not invalidate their observations on the network of personal relationships and the balance of power among the members of the circle, with which we are here concerned.

13 *In Praise of the Baal Shem Tov*, ed. Ben-Amos and Mintz, 208–10; *Shivḥei habesht*, ed. A. Rubinstein (Jerusalem, 1991), 264–6. This is, of course, a standard motif in *Shivḥei habesht* and in hagiographical literature in general. The accounts lay stress on the dramatic transition from a hostile, suspicious, or dismissive attitude to one of admiration for the saintly man, which was experienced sooner or later by most of his associates. See J. Dan, *The Hasidic Tale: Its History and Development* [Hasipur haḥasidi] (Jerusalem, 1975), 123–8.

14 *In Praise of the Baal Shem Tov*, ed. Ben-Amos and Mintz, 234–5; *Shivḥei habesht*, ed. Rubinstein, 291. This tale is missing from the Yiddish edition of *Shivḥei habesht* [Korzec, 1816] (Jerusalem, 1965) and from the manuscript version published by Y. Mondshine, *Sefer shivḥei habesht: faksimil miketav-hayad hayeḥidi hanoda lanu veshinuyei nusaḥav le'umat nusaḥ hadefus* (Jerusalem, 1982).

15 *Shivḥei habesht* relates how 'Harav Moharan [R. Nahman of Kosów] once heard some of his people [*anashav*] speaking ill of the Besht' (text according to B. Mintz's Hebrew edn. (Jerusalem, 1969), p. 150. Horodetsky's edition (Tel Aviv, 1947) (p. 93) and Rubinstein's (p. 292) read: 'Harav Moharan once heard some of his intimates [taking the abbreviation *an"sh* as *anshei shelomo*, but see below]', while the English version, *In Praise of the Baal Shem Tov*, offers: 'our own people' (p. 236) (evidently taking the same abbreviation as *anshei shelomenu*). This tale, too, does not appear either in the Yiddish version or in the Mondshine edition. Examination of the first editions yields *an"sh* in the Kopys and Berdiczów prints of 1814 and 1815 respectively, and *anash*[*av*] in the Łaszczów edition of 1815. The Mintz edition therefore corresponds to the Łaszczów text, while the Horodetsky and Rubinstein editions correspond to the Kopys and Berdiczów versions. It is clear from the context that the reference is to R. Nahman's intimate associates, *anshei shelomo*, the 'disciples' who regarded him as their master, which is what we are told in the other tale quoted above, and not to the collective *anshei shelomenu*, 'our people', as the English version has it, for what is in question is the opposition of a particular group to the Besht. The version *anashav*, 'his people', appears to be the better one, and of course the *an"sh* of the Kopys edition can be interpreted as *anshei shelomo* ('his people') and not necessarily as *anshei shelomenu* ('our people'). I am grateful to Rachel Elior, who kindly checked the text of the editions not available to me in London libraries from the copies in the National Library in Jerusalem.

16 *In Praise of the Baal Shem Tov*, ed. Ben-Amos and Mintz, 236–7; *Shivḥei habesht*, ed. Rubinstein, 292. In the Yiddish edition of *Shivḥei habesht* the tale appears in a somewhat extended version, but without the comparison of the dispute between R. Nahman and the Besht to the dispute between Saul and David and Hillel and Shammai. See pp. 31*b*–32*a* of that version. A. Ya'ari, 'Two Basic Editions of *Shivḥei habesht*' (Heb.), *Kiryat sefer*, 39 (1964), 554–5, compares the Yiddish and Hebrew versions of this tale, and the conclusion which he draws from this comparison supports the conclusion of his article as a whole, namely, that this Yiddish version is independent of the Hebrew one and may even be the earlier of the two. For this reason he assumes that the passage missing in the Yiddish edition is a later addition to the Hebrew version of the tale. But see

Y. Mondshine's critical remarks on Ya'ari's study in the introduction to the Mondshine edn. of *Shivḥei habesht*, 22–47. In any event, in all the versions of the tale R. Nahman of Kosów and the Besht are portrayed as equals.

17 J. G. Weiss, in his article 'A Circle of Pneumatics in Pre-Hasidism', drew a character sketch of R. Nahman of Kosów's 'holy fraternity' (*ḥavurta kadishta*). Unlike Dinur, who regarded R. Nahman as the leader of this fraternity (see Dinur, *With the Turn of the Generations* (Heb.), 160–1), Weiss emphasizes that R. Nahman of Kosów did not serve as leader of the group in any sense comparable to the institutionalized leadership of the tsadik which was developed in the hasidic movement later on. Rather, he belonged to a pre-hasidic circle of ascetic kabbalists gifted with supernatural spiritual powers. Weiss was inclined to identify this circle with the exclusive group known as the 'hasidim' of Kuty, which also numbered among its members R. Moses, head of the rabbinical court of Kuty, and R. Gershon, the brother-in-law of the Besht (see Weiss, 'A Circle of Pneumatics in Pre-Hasidism', 203 ff.). Weiss's analysis of the complex of relations between the various members of this group of pneumatics serves well to clarify the links between the circles of kabbalists and Sabbatians of that period and the early hasidic masters who emerged from within their ranks, but the resultant chronology is not compatible with the facts. The term 'pre-hasidism' which Weiss coined is helpful as a typological category but chronologically misleading. It implies that those circles of kabbalists and pneumatics preceded the foundation of the hasidic movement by the Besht. But in fact they operated contemporaneously, and to some extent overlapped, with the Besht and his associates in hasidism. All the information we have about those circles and the individuals who were active in them relates to the same period as that in which the Besht was active. Moreover, according to hasidic tradition, it was precisely the members of those circles who were the early disciples of the Besht, his intimates, and his colleagues. As we have seen, not all of them humbled themselves before him and accepted him as their leader. In fact, it appears that the relations between him and them were not unlike those outlined by Weiss in his descriptions of the pre-hasidic circles in his article. The difference between those 'pre-hasidic' circles of kabbalists and the circle in which the Besht operated consists only in the active involvement of the Besht's circle with the wider public and their mundane affairs, as contrasted with the reclusiveness of the fraternities of the Kuty type. The conclusion this invites is that the activity of the Besht among the members of his circle, as it is described in the works of R. Jacob Joseph of Połonne and in *Shivḥei habesht*, likewise belongs to the 'pre-hasidic' stage from the point of view of its leadership structure, in which there is not yet an institutionalized court and a single tsadik who is the focus of all its activities. See more on this below.

18 See *In Praise of the Baal Shem Tov*, ed. Ben-Amos and Mintz, 202–3; *Shivḥei habesht*, ed. Rubinstein, 259–60.

19 *In Praise of the Baal Shem Tov*, ed. Ben-Amos and Mintz, 62–3; *Shivḥei habesht*, ed. Rubinstein, 100–1.

20 *In Praise of the Baal Shem Tov*, ed. Ben-Amos and Mintz, 66–7; *Shivḥei habesht*, ed. Rubinstein, 106–8.

21 On this see below, n. 25, and at nn. 31–3.

22 *Matsref ha'avodah* [Zhitomir, 1865] (1st edn. Königsberg, 1858), 58. See also the corresponding passage in *Vikuḥa rabah* (Munkács, 1894), 32*a*. On the connection between the two works and on their author see Y. Mondshine, 'The books of *Matsref ha'avodah* and *Vikuḥa rabah*' (Heb.), *Alei sefer*, 5 (1978), 165–75.

23 This applies also to the circle of the disciples of the Magid of Mezhirech. See below, Section 3.

24 I deal with this *in extenso* in Ch. 2 below.

25 On the formulations of these distinctions in the works of R. Jacob Joseph of Połonne see G. Nigal, *Leader and Congregation: Opinions and Parables in the Beginning of Hasidism According to the Writings of R. Jacob Joseph of Połonne* [Manhig ve'edah: de'ot umeshalim bereshit haḥasidut al pi kitvei r. ya'akov yosef mipolna'ah] (Jerusalem, 1962), 50–65; S. H. Dresner, *The Zaddik* (New York, 1960), 113–90.

26 Mishnah *Avot* 2: 10.

27 Ibid.

28 Ps. 119: 11.

29 Mishnah *Avot* 2: 10.

30 That is to say, while the tsadik is working on the material level, he is in reality occupied with perfecting the upper worlds: in a play on the Hebrew word for scorpion (*akrav*), he is said to bring closer (*mekarev*, containing the last three letters of *akrav*) seven levels, each one of which consists of ten—the first letter of *akrav* being the letter *ayin*, which in *gematriyah* has the value of 70, i.e. 7 × 10—and thus he raises them to their spiritual root. See G. Nigal, *Rabbi Jacob Joseph of Połonne (Polna): Selected Writings* [Torot ba'al hatoledot: derashot rabi ya'akov yosef mipolna'ah lefi nose'ei yesod] (Jerusalem, 1974), 119.

31 Jacob Joseph of Połonne, *Tsafenat pa'ne'aḥ* [Korzec, 1782] (New York, 1954), 32*a*. Cf. also id., *Ben porat yosef* (New York, 1954), 127*a*.

32 I discuss this more fully in Ch. 2 below; in that chapter I try to look beyond the literal sense of what appears to be a conflicting directive, which occurs here and there in the early hasidic sources. This is the appeal, expressly directed at everyone, to aspire to the highest degree of spiritual perfection, offering an assurance that this goal is within everyone's reach. I point out there that this appeal, whose ethical-didactic motives are self-evident, appears at times even

in the teachings of R. Nahman of Bratslav alongside his more characteristic teachings, which are unquestionably 'tsadikist' inasmuch as they draw the sharpest possible distinction between the tsadik's religious norms and those that define the much more limited scope for spiritual action by ordinary men. There can be no doubt that it was the latter that reflected his true position. One must therefore be extremely cautious in assessing the implications of these apparently egalitarian demands for radical spirituality, and not attach to them any programmatic significance beyond the purpose of not discouraging the public in their aspiration to realize their (inherently limited) spiritual potential to the full. See pp. 130–2 below.

33 Weiss, in 'The Beginnings of Hasidism' (Heb.), 84–5, dealt with various expressions which alternate in parallel formulations of the earliest teachings relating to the status of the leaders. He pointed out that some of them, though certainly not most, spoke of 'the great man of the generation' (*gedol hador*) or 'the tsadik' in the singular. He considered the possibility that these formulations may reflect a tendency to attribute supreme leadership to one personality out of the group that collectively comprises 'the great men of the generation' (*gedolei hador*), and he tried to demonstrate a connection between this tendency—if indeed its existence could be proved—and the Besht. But Weiss himself recognized the limitations of this approach, for often the singular appears in one text and the plural in the parallel version of the same teaching in another. Occasionally it seems that it is the framework of midrashic associations interspersed with biblical verses that dictates the random choice between singular and plural. Weiss's general conclusion is correct: 'By the very nature of the traditions it is clear that we must not attempt to draw too many fine distinctions from the language used, and it is impossible to subject the wording of these oral traditions to the sort of textual analysis which is customary in the interpretation of written speculative works' (ibid. 87). It may be that we should adopt the same attitude towards one such statement by R. Jacob Joseph of Połonne, to which Ettinger ('The Hasidic Movement', 130) attributed programmatic significance:

> And so, too, we should interpret the other plagues, up to the plagues of *arbeh* [locusts], the Targum of which is *gova* [locust] and also *bor* [Hebrew for 'pit'; the Aramaic *guba*, a pit, has the same consonants as *gova*], for it is a plural, as it is written: 'I will multiply [*arbeh*, same spelling as for 'locust'] your seed etc.' [Gen. 16: 10; 22: 17], and the fact that there is a plurality of leaders [*manhigim*] is so that there should not be only one leader [*dabar*] for the generation but rather the contrary, that they should all be heads and leaders, for I have heard that that was the blessing bestowed by Elijah on a certain town, namely, that they should all be leaders, etc., and then a change came about from a single *dabar* to *dever* [pestilence, the fifth plague], Heaven forbid, or to hail [the seventh plague, *barad*, the same

> three consonants], and through this 'it covered the eye of the earth' [a literal reading of Exod. 10: 5]. He who was the eye of the earth was, as it were, the eyes of the congregation, for he was fitted to watch over the earth, [but] when these many people were created leaders the result was that they 'covered the eye of the earth' and he could not see the earth so as to watch over them, as I have written on the verse 'And the eyes of Israel were dim with age, and he could not see etc.' [Gen. 48: 10] And also, what is meant by 'and they [the locusts] shall eat what is left to you after the hail' [Exod. 10: 5] is that when there was one leader [*dabar*] for a generation there was blessing, but when a change came and many leaders [*manhigim*] were created, *dabar* became *barad*, hail, which ruins what is left. This is easy to understand. (Jacob Joseph of Połonne, *Toledot ya'akov yosef* [Korzec, 1780] (Jerusalem, 1966), 'Bo' (Exod. 10 ff.), 39*c–d*)

On the face of it R. Jacob Joseph is here arguing for leadership by a single person (presumably the Besht) and attacking the multiplicity of leaders in his generation. And indeed, Ettinger has suggested that in what R. Jacob Joseph says we can perhaps detect an echo of some criticism of the Besht by members of his own circle, a criticism which R. Jacob Joseph is seeking to rebut. In fact, however, this passage, which appears in the middle of a long sermon interspersed with scriptural quotations, need not be understood as a piece of polemic, especially as on the next page of the same sermon R. Jacob Joseph again speaks of 'the eyes of the congregation'—its leaders—in the plural as a desirable group, as he does elsewhere in his writings, e.g. *Toledot ya'akov yosef*, 'Vayetse' (Gen. 28: 10 ff.), 224. And further on in the same sermon, on 'Bo' (43*b*), he makes the following recommendation: 'And that is how "Be a tail to lions" [Mishnah *Avot* 4: 15] should be understood: like a tail hanging behind him, so you should follow a lion, that is, righteous men [*anashim tsadikim*]', and a few lines further: '"Why is the land ruined" etc., "Because they have forsaken My law which I set before them" [Jer. 9: 12], that is to say, they have forsaken the exalted spiritual qualities of the men of Torah who are before them.' Here he actually expounds a singular noun ('My law', 'lion') by a plural equivalent ('men of Torah', 'righteous men'). If he had wanted to emphasize the oneness of 'the tsadik of the generation', he could easily have kept to the singular with which the verse supplied him. Furthermore, there is not necessarily any contradiction between the view of a society divided into two groups, spiritual leaders and the worldly masses, and the view that in every generation one tsadik appears who is the head of them all and is spiritually superior to them all. His superiority need not find expression in supreme leadership within a hierarchical system. See Weiss, 'The Beginnings of Hasidism' (Heb.), 85, and compare with the explicit formulation of the problem in the foreword to Heilman, *Beit rabi*, 14–15:

> Now it is true that in every generation there is certainly a particular tsadik

> who is called the tsadik of the generation. And this is the secret of the division between the hasidim, that one journeys to one tsadik and another to another tsadik (each according to the root of his soul) and each one thinks that the tsadik to whom he journeys is the particular tsadik of the generation. But should we therefore speak ill, Heaven forbid, of the other tsadikim of the generation?

See also below, Section 7.

34 These people are the 'tax farmer' (*arendator*) (*In Praise of the Baal Shem Tov*, ed. Ben-Amos and Mintz, 35–8; *Shivḥei habesht*, ed. Rubinstein, 65–70); 'a certain great merchant and his son' (*In Praise of the Baal Shem Tov*, 48; *Shivḥei habesht*, ed. Rubinstein, 83); 'the wealthy man, Aizik' and his sick daughter (*In Praise of the Baal Shem Tov*, 77; *Shivḥei habesht*, ed. Rubinstein, 121); 'two litigants' (*In Praise of the Baal Shem Tov*, 88; *Shivḥei habesht*, ed. Rubinstein, 136); a 'treasurer' (*gabai*) (*In Praise of the Baal Shem Tov*, 90; *Shivḥei habesht*, ed. Rubinstein, 138); 'a *shoḥet* who was very frivolous and a drunkard' (*In Praise of the Baal Shem Tov*, 90; *Shivḥei habesht*, ed. Rubinstein, 138), and many others throughout the book. On the relationship between the spiritual leader and his congregation in this initial period as distinct from later developments, see I. Etkes, 'Hasidism as a Movement: The First Stage', in B. Safran (ed.), *Hasidism: Continuity or Innovation?* (Cambridge, Mass., 1988), 1–26.

35 Consciousness of this gap of course engendered the distinctly hasidic methods of bridging it: the doctrine of the descent of the tsadik in its hasidic versions, the doctrine of the leader as a 'channel' or intermediary between upper and lower worlds, etc. Were it not for this, it would be hard to explain the enormous success of hasidism, whose leaders came from elitist circles but which nevertheless attracted to itself great numbers of 'simple' people, as it defined them, who found in it the opportunity to lead a vital and rich religious life. It is important to remember, however, that what was in question was the throwing of a bridge over the gap and not the closing of the gap.

36 For example, it is told of R. Nahman of Horodenka that he said: 'When I was a great hasid I went every day to a cold *mikveh* . . . Despite this I could not rid myself of wayward thoughts, until I turned to the wisdom of the Besht' (*In Praise of the Baal Shem Tov*, ed. Ben-Amos and Mintz, 156; *Shivḥei habesht*, ed. Rubinstein, 205). And, according to the traditions relating to R. Pinhas of Korets (Korzec), R. Pinhas himself testified that 'from the day that I was with the Besht, God helped me toward the truth, and I walk in the path of King David, may he rest in peace.' And similarly: 'Since the time when people began to follow the way of the Baal Shem Tov, many customs instituted by R. Judah the Hasid have been abrogated' (see 'R. Pinḥas of Korzec' in Heschel, *The Circle of the Baal Shem Tov*, 10–14). And if this is true of R. Nahman of Horodenka, and even more so of R. Pinhas of Korets, both of whom preserved a certain distance in their relations with the Besht, maintained their own circles of hasidim, and dared to differ from the Besht's opinion at times, it is certainly true of people who were beyond doubt disciples of the Besht, for example R. Jacob Joseph of Połonne, who consistently calls him 'my teacher' and acts as a mouthpiece for his teachings.

37 See e.g. Dubnow, *The History of Hasidism* (Heb.), 69, 80; Horodetsky, *Hasidism and Its Adherents* (Heb.), i. 80; D. Kahana, *A History of the Kabbalists, the Sabbatians, and the Hasidim* [Toledot hamekubalim, hashabeta'im vehaḥasidim], ii (Tel Aviv, 1926–7), *Even ofel*, 82.

38 See n. 2 above and nn. 47, 76 below.

39 Heschel, 'R. Pinḥas of Korzec', 16.

40 See A. Rubinstein, 'A Praise from *Shivḥei habesht*' (Heb.), *Tarbiz*, 35 (1966), 178–80. He relies mainly on the testimony of the *mitnaged* R. David of Maków: first, the remark in R. David's letter to R. Solomon Zalman Lipschitz of Nasielsk that 'only in 5526 [1776] did R. Berush [= Ber] become famous, and a number of rabbis and eminent scholars journeyed to him' (ibid. 179 n. 23; and see also M. Wilensky, *Hasidim and Mitnagedim* [Ḥasidim umitnagedim] (Jerusalem, 1970), ii. 235); and secondly, the wording of R. David's will, from which it can be inferred that R. Levi Isaac of Berdiczów entered into association with the Magid of Mezhirech only in 1776 (Rubinstein, 'A Praise from *Shivḥei habesht*' (Heb.), 178–80; Wilensky, *Hasidim and Mitnagedim* (Heb.), ii. 244). In the opinion of Rubinstein, Menahem Mendel of Przemyślany was one of the contenders for the succession in the years between the death of the Besht (1760) and the establishment of the leadership of the Magid (1766). He infers this from the document which he published and in which R. Menahem Mendel is said to have 'journeyed to the Holy Land [in 1764; A.R.-A.] because people had begun to journey to see him for the purpose of engaging in business' (Rubinstein, 'A Praise from *Shivḥei habesht*' (Heb.), 177, 191). Rubinstein offers the reasonable explanation that this sentence indicates that 'the author was referring to people who used to visit Mendel as a wonder-working tsadik for the sake of their business interests [but] R. Mendel turned his back on his visitors and journeyed to Erets Yisra'el' ('A Praise from *Shivḥei habesht*' (Heb.), 177). Y. Mondshine's dismissal of Rubinstein's conclusions ('Is It Really a Praise from *Shivḥei habesht*?' (Heb.), *Tarbiz*, 51 (1982), 673–7, to which Rubinstein replied (ibid. 677–80), does not affect the matter we are considering one way or the other unless we accept his hypothesis that the 'document' relating to R. Mendel's journey was a piece of fiction authored by the *maskil* Joseph Perl—a hypothesis which would deprive it of all historical value as evidence of the status of R. Menahem Mendel of Przemyślany.

41 Heschel, 'R. Pinḥas of Korzec', 16 ff.

42 Ibid. 21 ff.

43 Ibid. 17.

44 Ibid. 16.

45 See Dresner, *The Zaddik*, 60–2.

46 Ibid. 61.

47 The assumption that the Magid was 'appointed' to the leadership by the Besht and even 'ordained' by him by the laying on of hands is based principally on the story of the commencement of the Magid's association with the Besht in the version given in *Shivḥei habesht* (*In Praise of the Baal Shem Tov*, ed. Ben-Amos and Mintz, 81–4; *Shivḥei habesht*, ed. Rubinstein, 126–9; ed. Mondshine 169–11; Yid. version, ch. 23, 11*a–b;* Ya'ari, 'Two Basic Editions of *Shivḥei habesht*' (Heb.), 405; and see e.g. Dresner, *The Zaddik*, 59–60), but it has no foundation in fact. The story in *Shivḥei habesht* expressly concerns the Magid's initiation into the circle of the Besht on the occasion of his first visit to him, and it is certainly not to be interpreted as describing a ceremony in which the succession to the leadership was bestowed on the chosen disciple. Nor does the exchange of blessings between them, or the laying of the hand upon his head, which is described at the end of the story, suggest ordination (*semikhah*) to the leadership. At most it can be understood as emphasizing the relations of equality between the Magid and the Besht, with the object of providing *ex post facto* support for the position of the Magid as leader after the death of the Besht (see also Dan, *The Hasidic Tale* (Heb.), 128). It should be pointed out that, in a second version of the story (Aaron of Opatów, *Keter shem tov* [Zholkva (Żółkiew), 1794–5] (Brooklyn, NY, 1972), pt. II, 124–5 §24), the exchange of blessings does not appear at all. As for the suggestion that the other disciples of the Besht 'elected' the Magid to the leadership (see e.g. Kahana, *A History of the Kabbalists, the Sabbatians, and the Hasidim* (Heb.), ii, *Even ofel*, 82), that, too, has no support in the sources, for there is no trace at all in hasidism of any official electoral procedures such as were customary, for example, in the institutions of the *kahal*. Moreover, it is clear that the majority of the Besht's senior disciples had reservations as regards the Magid's authority and did not accept his leadership. In the absence of clear evidence of the 'appointment', 'ordination', or 'election' of the Magid to office by the Besht or any of the Besht's disciples, *Shivḥei habesht* relies on the following tradition:

> I heard this from the rabbi, the hasid, R. Jehiel Mikhel of the holy community of Zolochev. When he visited here in the town of Ilintsy for the wedding of his son, our teacher Ze'ev, he said that he was ordered from Heaven to accept the Besht as his rabbi and to go and learn from him. They showed him the 'streams of wisdom' which led to the Besht. When the Besht passed away he was ordered to accept the Great Maggid, Rabbi Dov, as his rabbi. They showed him that the same 'streams of wisdom' that formerly ran to the Besht now led to the rabbi, the Maggid, God bless his memory. (*In Praise of the Baal Shem Tov*, ed. Ben-Amos and Mintz, 185; *Shivḥei habesht*, ed. Rubinstein, 238)

The authority of the Magid, according to this tradition, came direct from Heaven, and did not derive from the authority of his predecessor or the collective authority of the hasidim. This places it clearly within the definition of pure charismatic authority, and there is no doubt that the authority of the Magid fell within that category just as had that of the Besht. It is interesting to note that, apart from the stories of the Magid's entry into association with the Besht, which were interpreted with excessive licence as referring to his 'ordination' to the leadership, the only documents in our possession indicating that the Besht expressly appointed the Magid to succeed him as leader are the letters found in the Kherson *genizah*, which are universally regarded as forgeries. It seems that it was precisely the absence of early evidence for such an appointment that created the need to 'document' it in unambiguous terms. In fact, the very existence of these letters in the Kherson *genizah* could serve as further proof of the weakness of the hasidic tradition regarding the appointment of the Magid to office, for this *genizah* is particularly sensitive to the missing historical links in the hagiographical sources and shows considerable concern to 'supply' them. For such letters see C. E. Bichovsky, *Ginzei nistarot* (Jerusalem, 1924), 'Or yisra'el', 7 no. 21, 8 no. 23, 13 no. 46, 15 no. 52, 19 no. 61. See also *Hatamim*, i. 121 no. 260, and cf. my discussion in Ch. 4 below, pp. 217–19.

48 This is asserted by R. David of Maków, and the remarks of A. Rubinstein on the interval between the death of the Besht and the emergence of the Magid as a leader are reasonable enough in themselves, although the notion of struggles for the succession is essentially anachronistic (see above, at n. 40).

49 It certainly undermines the even weaker claim that R. Menahem Mendel of Przemyślany was a candidate for the *supreme* leadership (Rubinstein, 'A Praise from *Shivḥei habesht*' (Heb.), 180). All that is known on this question from the document published by Rubinstein is that R. Menahem Mendel, like several other members of the Besht's circle, was accepted by the public as a spiritual leader in his own right, *alongside* the others and not necessarily as their head.

50 On this see also below, Section 7.

51 See Dubnow, *The History of Hasidism* (Heb.), 278–86; G. Scholem, 'On Israel Löbel and His Anti-Hasidic Polemics' (Heb.), *The Latest Phase: Essays on Hasidism by Gershom Scholem* [Hashalav ha'aḥaron: meḥkerei haḥasidut shel gershom shalom], ed. D. Assaf and E. Liebes (Jerusalem, 2008), 164–76; Wilensky, *Hasidim and Mitnagedim* (Heb.), ii. 253–342.

52 From Wilensky's Hebrew translation in *Hasidim and Mitnagedim* (Heb.), ii. 328.

53 For example he states that the Besht became famous in the years 1760–5, i.e. in the five years following the known date of his death. See ibid. 259, 326. Wilensky, the translator and editor of Israel Löbel's tract, comments here (ibid. 328 n. 12) that, in fact, 'after the death of the Besht, R. Dov Ber, the Magid of

Mezhirech, became the leader of the sect, and it was only after his death that "instead of one supreme leader, many were chosen"'. Wilensky is 'correcting' Israel Löbel's 'mistake', offering us the conventional view of the matter, but see below.

54 A. Walden, *Shem hagedolim heḥadash* (Warsaw, 1870), 11*a* §24; and cf. Bodek, *Seder hadorot mitalmidei habesht z"l*, 16–17.

55 Heilman, *Beit rabi*, 43*a*–*b* (= 85–6); D. Z. Hillman, *Letters by the Author of the Tanya and His Contemporaries* [Igerot ba'al hatanya uvenei doro] (Jerusalem, 1953), 105 and 167–79. For a discussion of the dispute among the disciples of the Magid over his spiritual legacy, see Elior, 'The Minsk Debate' (Heb.), 189–99; Gries, 'From Myth to Ethos' (Heb.), 126–32.

56 See above, pp. 34–5.

57 See Rabinowitsch, *Lithuanian Hasidism*, 15. The year 5530 (1770) was apparently the year which saw the emergence of a fully fledged congregation of R. Abraham's hasidim in Kalisk (Kołyszki), as is shown by the designation *ḥasidei talk* (the Hebrew letters *tav-lamed-kuf*, whose numerical value is 530, represents the year [5]530), which is embodied in the Yiddish saying *Der talk iz on a talk* (the hasidism of Talk is without any order, i.e. is disordered). The name 'Talk' is mentioned in the letter of 1801 from R. Abraham of Kalisk to R. Shneur Zalman of Liady, in which he complains that the associates of R. Shneur Zalman are persecuting him (Hillman, *Letters by the Author of the Tanya* (Heb.), 156 no. 94; and see Hillman's remarks in p. 160 n. 4, where he quotes the Habad tradition on this matter in the name of the *admor* Joseph Isaac of Lubavitch. See also M. Wilensky's comment in *Kiryat sefer*, 1 (1924–5), 240). This chronology accords well with the testimony of R. Shneur Zalman in his letter to R. Abraham of Kalisk. He tells there of the meeting of the Magid's disciples in Równe in the summer of 1772, when the Magid delivered his well-known rebuke to R. Abraham 'on his bad behaviour towards our colleagues in Russia', and he reminds R. Abraham that R. Menahem Mendel of Vitebsk, too, 'was angry with the rabbi [addressing R. Abraham in the third person] and with his conduct and with his associates' (see Hillman, *Letters by the Author of the Tanya* (Heb.), 175–6 no. 103). Hence R. Abraham was already known in 1772 as head of his own congregation of hasidim, which he led in his own way.

58 See Rabinowitsch, *Lithuanian Hasidism*, 25, and see also R. Shneur Zalman's letter to R. Abraham of Kalisk, in which he said of R. Menahem Mendel of Vitebsk that 'in the summer of 5532'—i.e. as early as 1772, at the time of the Równe conference of the Magid's disciples—'the late rabbi was well established by then in the holy congregation of Minsk' (Hillman, *Letters by the Author of the Tanya* (Heb.), 175).

59 Rabinowitsch, *Lithuanian Hasidism*, 8–22.

60 Ibid. 17, 23.

61 Solomon Maimon took the trouble, as we know, to travel from his native Lithuania to distant Mezhirech in Volhynia in order to see 'the superior B.' in person (see *The Autobiography of Solomon Maimon*, trans. J. Clark Murray (London, 1954), 175, repr. in Hundert (ed.), *Essential Papers on Hasidism*, 9). He refers to the Magid as *der hohe Obere* B.—'the exalted leader B.' (a description which is somewhat blurred in the English translation: see *Salomon Maimons Lebensgeschichte* (Munich, 1911), 202). His use of this term confirms the widely accepted assumption that the Magid of Mezhirech had indeed established a reputation for himself as the greatest of the hasidic leaders of his time. But we are not entitled to conclude from this that the Magid served as the supreme leader of the whole hasidic movement, exercising control from the centre, any more than we are entitled to conclude, for example, that the Gaon of Vilna served as 'chief rabbi' of Lithuania from the fact that he had earned the reputation of being the greatest rabbinic authority of his generation.

62 Maimon, *Salomon Maimons Lebensgeschichte*, 135. The English translation (*Autobiography*, 167–8) omits the references to 'K' and 'M'.

63 Maimon wrote this about twenty years after the event. The historical details in his testimony therefore call for meticulous scrutiny. But in this case critical examination only serves to confirm the reliability of his statement: he left Poland almost immediately after his visit to Mezhirech, severing all his connections with the Jewish community in that part of the world and with hasidism (his latest information on the movement relates to the rising tide of mitnagdism in Lithuania, headed by the Gaon of Vilna. Maimon innocently believed that this meant the end for hasidism; ibid. 179). For that very reason he preserved the memory of the situation as it had been at the time of his last stay in the area, and there is no reason to suspect him of having drawn an anachronistic picture coloured by the situation as it existed at the time he was writing, when the hasidic movement had 'split' into many congregations, according to the prevailing view.

64 See e.g. Wilensky, *Hasidim and Mitnagedim* (Heb.), i. 64, 274–7. On the extension of the name 'Karliner' or, in Hebrew, 'Karliniyim' to hasidim in general, see also A. B. Gottlober, *Memoirs and Travels* [Zikhronot umasa'ot], ed. R. Goldberg (Jerusalem, 1976), i. 142.

65 M. Buber, *Tales of the Hasidim* (New York, 1972), i. 238–9, on the basis of E. Z. Stern, *Siḥot yekarim* (Satu-Mare, n.d.).

66 Buber points out that in *Ohel elimelekh* the role of R. Zusya in the story is mistakenly given to R. Elimelekh of Lizhensk, R. Zusya's younger brother (M. Buber, *Or haganuz* (Tel Aviv, 1977), 480); and cf. Abraham H. S. B. Michelsohn, *Ohel elimelekh* (Przemyśl, 1910), 13 §44.

67 It is, of course, possible that such letters were written but have not survived. At any rate, the Kherson *genizah*, which applies the actual organization of the

hasidic community at the end of the 19th and the beginning of the 20th centuries retrospectively to the relations between the Magid and his disciples in the 1770s, is sensitive, in this instance also, to the dearth of historical material that would document the presumed state of affairs, and it 'supplies' a lively correspondence between the Magid's disciples and their master. See Bichovsky, *Ginzei nistarot*, 'Or ne'erav', 1–7. A fuller collection of letters from the Kherson *genizah* was published in the Habad periodical *Hatamim*; see esp. ii. 563–71, 651–64.

68 See below, Section 6 of this chapter. The difficulties of communication and travel over long distances at the end of the 18th century are likely to have contributed to the weakening of personal contacts between the Magid and his scattered disciples, but these factors were not decisive. Within the framework of a centralist organization such as was constituted by each separate hasidic court, the hasidim overcame these difficulties and preserved their personal links with their leader. Thus, for example, R. Menahem Mendel of Vitebsk and R. Abraham of Kalisk kept up a correspondence with their disciples in Belarus until the end of their days. The disciples of R. Menahem Mendel of Vitebsk, who were not content with this link and looked round for a tsadik to whom they could have personal access—a vital ingredient of the system of relations between the tsadik and his hasidim—began travelling to Karlin, and later to Ludmir, both situated a long way away, in order to visit the court of R. Shelomoh of Karlin (see Heilman, *Beit rabi*, 12*b* (= 24), 64*b* (= 128); Rabinowitsch, *Lithuanian Hasidism*, 26–7). When R. Israel of Ruzhin was imprisoned and subsequently banished from the Ukraine, his hasidim continued to make the long journey to his new court in Sadagora, in the Bukovina region, which at that time was on the other side of the border, under Austrian sovereignty (see D. Assaf, *The Regal Way: The Life and Times of Rabbi Israel of Ruzhin* (Stanford, 2002), 69–172; R. Mahler, *Hasidism and the Jewish Enlightenment* (Philadelphia, 1985), 129–34; Gottlober, *Memoirs and Travels* (Heb.), i. 153, 190). See also pp. 48–53 above.

69 See Hillman, *Letters by the Author of the Tanya* (Heb.), 175, and cf. n. 57 above.

70 But see Gries, 'From Myth to Ethos' (Heb.), 126 ff.

71 See Section 6 below.

72 R. Shneur Zalman of Liady's letter shows that it was not the fact of R. Abraham of Kalisk's leadership that aroused the anger of the Magid at the Równe conference in 1772 but the particular manner of his leadership, which fanned the flames of the controversy with the *mitnagedim*. The Magid's displeasure does not indicate any intention to cast doubt on the legitimacy of R. Abraham's position as a tsadik in his own right.

73 For example, according to one tradition, even before the outbreak of the dispute between the Seer of Lublin and his great disciple, 'the Jew of Pshischa

[Przysucha]', some of the Seer's disciples, and even his wife, used to peddle reports to him that 'the Jew' was planning to turn him out of his position and take his place. See Buber, *Tales of the Hasidim*, 226–7 (extracted from *Tiferet hayehudi*). Similarly, R. Shneur Zalman is said to have foreseen the dispute that would erupt between his son and heir R. Dober [Dov Ber] and his favourite disciple, R. Aaron Halevi of Starosielce, at a time when the pair were still very close friends. See Heilman, *Beit rabi*, 94*a* (= 187) n. *a*. And indeed, a few years before R. Shneur Zalman died, a 'calumny' and a 'grave accusation' concerning R. Aaron were brought to his notice, apparently by members of R. Shneur Zalman's own family circle, with the result that R. Aaron was forced to leave Liady (Lyady) and return to his native city of Orsha, although he continued to visit his master's court in Liady 'from time to time'. Heilman, *Beit rabi*, 67*b* (= 134), 94*a* (= 187).

74 The final rift between R. Jacob Isaac, 'the Jew of Pshiskhah', and the court of his master R. Jacob Isaac Horowitz, the Seer of Lublin, will serve as an example of this. See U. Gellman, 'Hasidism in Poland in the First Half of the Nineteenth Century: Typologies of Leadership and Devotees' (Heb.) [Haḥasidut bepolin bamaḥatsit harishonah shel hame'ah hatesha-esreh: tipologyah shel manhigut ve'edah], unpublished Ph.D. diss. (Hebrew University, 2011), 217–31; A. Z. Aescoly, *Hasidism in Poland* [Haḥasidut bepolin], intr. D. Assaf, Mivḥar: Studies and Sources in the History and Culture of Eastern European Jewry (Jerusalem, 1999), 50–5. And the beginning of the Seer of Lublin's career as a leader during the lifetime of his master, R. Elimelekh of Lizhensk, may have been similarly charged with tension between the master and his departing disciple. See R. Elior, 'Between *Yesh* and *Ayin:* The Doctrine of the Zaddik in the Works of Jacob Isaac, the Seer of Lublin', in A. Rapoport-Albert and S. J. Zipperstein (eds.), *Jewish History: Essays in Honour of Chimen Abramsky* (London, 1988), 396–7. Cf., however, Gellman, 'Hasidism in Poland' (Heb.), 25–7, who acknowledges the 19th-century hagiographical sources which claim that such tension existed between the two, but who has found no contemporary evidence for it and who suspects that it may be anachronistically projected onto a late 18th-century hasidic landscape, where the distinction between master and disciple was still rather fluid. On the other hand, the dispute between R. Aaron Halevi of Starosielce and the son of R. Shneur Zalman, Dov Ber, the 'Mitteler Rebbe', in the second generation of the Habad leadership certainly does belong in this same category. See R. Elior, 'The Dispute over the Habad Legacy' (Heb.), *Tarbiz*, 49 (1980), 166–8; ead., *The Theory of Divinity of Hasidut Habad: Second Generation* [Torat ha'elohut bador hasheni shel ḥasidut ḥabad] (Jerusalem, 1982), 5–14; N. Loewenthal, *Communicating the Infinite: The Emergence of the Habad School* (Chicago, 1990), 100–38; L. Jacobs, *Seeker of Unity: The Life and Works of Aaron of Starosselje* (London, 1966), 11–13.

75 See n. 2 above.

76 It is interesting to note that Habad historiography, which consistently applies the fully developed organizational frameworks of the Habad movement retrospectively to the initial stages of hasidism, ascribes a short period as *nasi* at the head of the movement, immediately following the death of their fathers, to each of the two sons with doubtful qualifications for the succession—R. Zevi, the son of the Besht, and R. Abraham, the son of the Magid. Thus they are represented as having assured the institutional continuity of the hasidic leadership, even though there is no evidence to back this in any other sources. With regard to the period of about a year allegedly spent by R. Zevi as *nasi*, the *admor* Joseph Isaac writes as follows in his essay 'Avot haḥasidut':

> After the decease of our teacher the Besht, his son the rabbi and tsadik R. Zevi was chosen as *nasi* and leader. However, when the first year had gone by, the holy company could see that the son of their teacher and master was a weak man while the situation at that time required strength and power and a man who had the spirit to stand at the head of the leadership, and they were very worried. At the festive meal on the second day of Shavuot, which was a day after the first *yahrzeit* of our teacher the Besht, the holy rabbi and tsadik R. Zevi was sitting at the head of the table dressed in the holy garments of his saintly father, our teacher the Besht, surrounded by all the holy company. When he had finished speaking words of Torah he rose to his full height and said: 'Today my saintly father came to me and told me that the retinue of Heaven and their servants, who were wont to accompany him, have today gone over to our holy and awe-inspiring teacher and master R. Berinyu [affectionate form of the name Ber, here in reference to the Magid, Dov Ber] son of R. Abraham; therefore, my son, hand over to him the office of *nasi* in the presence of all the holy company, and he will sit in my place at the head of the table and you, my son, will sit in his place. And know that you [the holy company] will be twice as successful through his spirit.' And as he spoke he turned to the holy rabbi, R. Dov Ber, to congratulate him and took off his coat and gave it to our holy master, R. Dov Ber, and put on the holy R. Dov Ber's coat and sat in his place. And forthwith the holy rabbi, R. Dov Ber, sat down at the head of the table, and all the holy company rose to their feet to hear the words of Torah which the new *nasi* would utter. (*Hatamim* (Kefar Habad, 1975), i. 140–1, ch. 6)

On R. Abraham the Angel's position as head of the movement during the two years immediately following the death of the Magid, Joseph Isaac writes as follows in the letter he wrote to his daughter Mushka in 1935:

> After the decease of the Magid of Mezhirech on 19 Kislev 5533, the holy company of disciples of the Magid accepted the holy rabbi, the learned rabbi, the righteous rabbi, the holy Angel, R. Abraham, as their rebbe . . . [His] *nesiut*, to our sorrow, did not last long, it lasted about two years, and

in 5535 [1775] the holy and righteous rabbi, the holy Angel, passed away. (R. N. Kahan, *Shemuot vesipurim*, iii. 10–11 (the letter is published in Hebrew translation alongside the original Yiddish); and see also *Igerot kodesh . . . yosef yitsḥak* (Brooklyn, 1983), iii. 162–3)

These accounts are based on the letters from the Kherson *genizah* (see Joseph Isaac's explicit endorsement of the Kherson letters, *Hatamim*, i. 12. I have been unable to identify the Kherson letter in which the *admor* says this particular matter is 'fully' explained, but there are several letters in the collection printed in *Hatamim* which deal with the leadership of R. Abraham the Angel. See e.g. *Hatamim*, ii. 664–6, nos. 247, 249, 255.)

77 It is clear that not all 19th-century hasidic congregations developed a centralist dynastic leadership. Where a centralist dynasty had not come into existence the congregation dispersed after the death of its founder or was split up among a number of successors until it lost its original identity. The only exception was the Bratslav congregation, which preserved its distinctiveness even without a dynasty of tsadikim, and crystallized its independent identity round the messianic figure of the dead R. Nahman. The question of the dynasties in general, and the anomalous case of Bratslav in particular, are beyond the scope of the present study. For a detailed account of the Chernobyl dynasty see G. Sagiv, *Dynasty: The Chernobyl Hasidic Dynasty and Its Place in the History of Hasidism* (Heb.) [Hashoshelet: beit chernobil umekomo betoledot haḥasidut] (Jerusalem, 2014). For the routinization of charisma in the institutionalised, dynastic hasidic leadership see S. Sharot, *Messianism, Mysticism, and Magic: A Sociological Analysis of Jewish and Religious Movements* (Chapel Hill, NC, 1982), 155–88.

78 See the opening pages of the present chapter, and n. 6 above.

79 See Rubinstein, 'Studies in the History of Hasidism' (Heb.), 242, 245.

80 See the beginning of the present chapter.

81 On the spread of hasidism in spite of the new political borders and the changes of regime in the parts of Poland which were annexed to the various powers, see Dubnow, *The History of Hasidism* (Heb.), 175, 177. On the travels back and forth of scholars and rabbis and their activities in the areas which were cut off from each other politically but retained a sense of their cultural unity until the middle of the 19th century, see A. Shulvass, 'Torah Study in Poland and Lithuania' (Heb.), in I. Halpern (ed.), *The Jewish People in Poland* [Beit yisra'el bepolin] (Jerusalem, 1953), ii. 26. See also Rabinowitsch, *Lithuanian Hasidism*, 23, 26. The relative ease of movement across the new political borders may be illustrated by the following anecdote, which appeared in a hasidic collection of Bratslav traditions transmitted by Levi Isaac Bender (1897–1989):

In the days of Moharnat [Nathan Sternharz, R. Nahman of Bratslav's disciple and scribe, who led the Bratslav circle after the death of its founder without ever claiming for himself the title of rebbe], if a man wished to travel [from the formerly Polish Ukrainian territories annexed by Russia] to the territory of [Congress] Poland, he would need a permit and a passport, but Moharnat had no alternative but to travel there, with [his disciple] R. Nahman of Tulchin, without a passport or a permit. At that time the border police did not normally search hasidic leaders and rabbis to establish whether they carried a passport; they would simply ask them whether they had one, and if they replied that they were in possession of valid papers, they would enquire no further. When the border guards asked R. Nahman [of Tulchin] whether he had a passport, he replied: 'Would one travel without a passport these days?', and thus he crossed the border safely. (*Siaḥ sarfei kodesh* (Jerusalem, 1994), ii. 121)

82 Barnai, *Letters of Hasidim* (Heb.), 108.

83 Ibid.

84 Ibid. 92–3, 96, 166.

85 Ibid. 93; and see also I. Etkes, *Rabbi Shneur Zalman of Liady: The Origins of Chabad Hasidism* (Waltham, Mass., 2015), 9–21.

86 Heilman, *Beit rabi*, 64*b* (= 128); Rabinowitsch, *Lithuanian Hasidism*, 26–7.

87 Gottlober, *Memoirs and Travels* (Heb.), i. 152.

88 It is evident from this that Gottlober wrote this part of his memoirs before 1866, the year in which the Tsemah Tsedek died. This accords with the information on his p. 158, where he specifies the date of writing as 'in the year 5625 [1865], 22 Marheshvan'.

89 Gottlober, *Memoirs and Travels* (Heb.), i. 190.

90 On this episode see Mahler, *Hasidism and the Jewish Enlightenment*, 99, 129–34; D. Assaf, *The Regal Way*, 105–62. Here, too, the picture agrees with the time at which Gottlober was writing, the year 1865: R. Israel of Ruzhin died in 1851, and during the 1860s the leadership was in the hands of his sons.

91 Gottlober, *Memoirs and Travels* (Heb.), i. 153.

92 See Dubnow, *The History of Hasidism* (Heb.), 200; Mahler, *Hasidism and the Jewish Enlightenment*, 105 ff.

93 Dubnow, *The History of Hasidism* (Heb.), 126.

94 See I. Etkes, *The Gaon of Vilna: The Man and His Image* (Berkeley, Calif., 2002), 73–95.

95 On the diffusion of the decrees of *ḥerem* from Vilna during the first dispute see Dubnow, *The History of Hasidism* (Heb.), 107–37; Wilensky, *Hasidim and Mitnagedim* (Heb.), vol. i, *passim*.

96 See Wilensky, *Hasidim and Mitnagedim* (Heb.), and also Dubnow, *The History of Hasidism* (Heb.), 138–69, 242–89. The third dispute, which broke out in

1796, was the only one to occur after the reunification of Lithuania and Belarus as part of the Russian empire, in the Third Partition of Poland in 1795. But Galicia, which was no less active (see Dubnow, *The History of Hasidism* (Heb.), 283–6, on the activity of the Lithuanian *magid* Israel Loebel in Galicia), remained under the rule of the Austrian Empire.

97 See n. 6 above.

98 See pp. 45–8 above.

99 On the position of the Gaon of Vilna and his influence on various communities in the campaign against hasidism, see H. H. Ben-Sasson, 'The Personality and Historical Impact of the Gra' (Heb.), *Zion*, 31 (1966), 39–86, 197–216; Etkes, *The Gaon of Vilna*, 73–95; E. Stern, *The Genius: Elijah of Vilna and the Making of Modern Judaism* (New Haven, 2013), 83–114.

100 Wilensky, *Hasidim and Mitnagedim* (Heb.), i. 49. Cf. Dubnow, *The History of Hasidism* (Heb.), 122.

101 Dubnow, *The History of Hasidism* (Heb.), 120; Wilensky, *Hasidim and Mitnagedim* (Heb.), i. 46. The 'wicked men' that the Council of Four Lands succeeded in getting rid of were no doubt the Sabbatians and the Frankists, but the statement exaggerates the power of that centralist institution to suppress and root out the heresy. In reality, the communities did not 'get rid of' the Sabbatians and Frankists until these 'heretics' apostatized and so, by their own act, removed themselves from the Jewish fold. The pluralistic and non-centralist structure of the medieval Jewish communities in Europe, unlike the centralist and hierarchical structure of the medieval Church, was not conducive to the formation of heretical sects as such within the bounds of their own religion, precisely because there was no central apparatus for identifying and defining them as sects, or orchestrating a campaign against them in the way that the Church was able to campaign, successfully, against its own heretical groups. The structure of the autonomous *kehilot*, even within the framework of the central councils, was flexible enough to prevent schismatic sectarianism: on the one hand, their pluralistic framework was able to assimilate local differences of custom and tradition and allow considerable scope for groups which would have broken out of a more homogeneous centralist structure; on the other hand, this fragmented framework deprived the communal organizations of the centralist power they would have required in order to eradicate 'sectarian' deviations. Moderate Sabbatianism, which did not follow the path of apostasy and did not break away from the Jewish community, was not suppressed or eradicated, even by 'the wisest men of their generations, the leaders of the Four Lands', as we might have deduced from the nostalgic tone of the proclamation.

102 See I. Halpern, 'Torah and Mitsvah Societies and the Expanding Hasidic Movement' (Heb.), in id., *Eastern European Jewry: Historical Studies* [Yehudim veyahadut bemizraḥ eiropah] (Jerusalem, 1968), 313–32.

103 That is how his claims were interpreted by Dubnow (*The History of Hasidism* (Heb.), 212–13), Horodetsky (*Hasidism and Its Adherents* (Heb.), iii. 13), A. Kahana (*Sefer haḥasidut* (Warsaw, 1922), 317), and Ettinger ('The Hasidic Movement', 263, or 239 of the *Essential Papers on Hasidism* reprint).

104 For this view of R. Nahman as laying claim to sole leadership see Dubnow, *The History of Hasidism* (Heb.), 295, 304; Ettinger, 'The Hasidic Movement', 264, or 240 of the *Essential Papers on Hasidism* reprint.

105 Dubnow, *The History of Hasidism* (Heb.), 208, 212–13; and cf. Kahana, *Sefer haḥasidut*, and Horodetsky, *Hasidism and Its Adherents* (Heb.).

106 Y. Alfasi, *Encyclopedia of Hasidism: Personalities* [Entsiklopedyah laḥasidut: ishim], ed. Y. Rafael (Jerusalem, 1986), col. 375; and cf. Ettinger, 'The Hasidic Movement', 263, or 239 of the *Essential Papers on Hasidism* reprint.

107 See directly below, and n. 111.

108 See *Butsina dinehora* (Lemberg, 1884), 58–9.

109 See the letter from R. Barukh to R. Menahem Mendel of Vitebsk in which he describes the circumstances of his rise to leadership. It appears from this that, against his own inclinations, R. Barukh acceded to pressure from local people to become their 'head' and settled in Tulchin. It is clear that there was no question of centralist leadership extending beyond his own locality. The letter was published at the end of *Butsina dinehora*, 65. Cf. *Butsina dinehora hashalem* (Biłgoraj, n.d.), 10–11 §4, and the remarks of the editor, Reuben Margaliot, on p. 10, setting the letter in its context.

110 Horodetsky, *Hasidism and Its Adherents* (Heb.), iii. 13, relying on the collection of the sayings and teachings of R. Barukh in *Butsina dinehora*, and see below.

111 See A. Schischa Halevi, 'On the Book *Butsina dinehora*' (Heb.), *Alei sefer*, 8 (1980), 155–7.

112 See Zohar ii. 206*a*: *velehevei ana avdakh pekida bego tsadikaya* ('may I, Your servant, be numbered among the tsadikim'), and cf. I. Tishby, *Mishnat hazohar* (1971), published in English as *The Wisdom of the Zohar: An Anthology of Texts*, trans. D. Goldstein (Oxford, 1989), iii. 1037. This quotation from the Zohar is very well known because it is incorporated in the order of service; it is to be recited when the Torah scroll is taken out of the ark for the reading of the Law.

113 *Butsina dinehora*, 49.

114 Ibid.

115 See the famous letter of R. Shneur Zalman of Liady, written in 1810, on his quarrel with R. Barukh: 'And I asked him: "Then why are you angry with me?" And he replied: "Why did you come to our province?" [i.e. why have you invaded my territory?]'; Hillman, *Letters by the Author of the Tanya* (Heb.), 192 no. 113, and cf. *Igerot kodesh admor hazaken, admor ha'emtsa'i, admor hatsemaḥ tsedek*, i. 142 no. 60.

116 See Ettinger, 'The Hasidic Movement', 263, or 239 of the *Essential Papers on Hasidism* reprint.

117 *Butsina dinehora hashalem*, the part entitled 'Mekor barukh', §§9, 24.

118 The part entitled 'Mekor barukh' was published by Reuben Margaliot in Zamość in 1931 as a separate pamphlet from the matrices of the Biłgoraj edition of *Butsina dinehora hashalem*, which had been published, without a date, a few years previously. I should like to thank Mr Avraham Schischa Halevi for his help in clarifying this point. See also Alfasi, *Encyclopedia of Hasidism: Personalities* (Heb.), cols. 377–8; S. H. Porush, *Encyclopedia of Hasidism: Works* [Entsiklopedyah laḥasidut: Sefarim], ed. Y. Rafael (Jerusalem, 1980), col. 416, no. 2; col. 418, no. 7.

119 See n. 111 above.

120 Published by C. E. Bichovsky in *Ginzei nistarot* (Jerusalem, 1924). See e.g. *Butsina dinehora hashalem*, 'Mekor barukh', 7 §1, which reproduces the text of 'a note from the members of the Besht's household' taken from *Ginzei nistarot*, 'Or yisra'el', 19 no. 60; 'Mekor barukh', 8 §2, reproducing the letter of R. Barukh's brother R. Ephraim of Sudyłków from *Ginzei nistarot*, 'Or ne'erav', 14 no. 31; 'Mekor barukh', 20–1 §8, reproducing the letter from R. Barukh to R. Abraham of Kalisk from *Ginzei nistarot*, 'Or ne'erav', 10 no. 24; etc. And see the letter of R. Hayim Issachar Gross of Mukachevo (Munkács), 'Ḥayim uverakhah', printed at the end of *Butsina dinehora hashalem*, 88 §§4, 9, in which he criticizes Reuben Margaliot's use of the suspect Kherson letters.

121 On Michael Levi Frumkin-Rodkinson, his works, and his 'conversion' to Haskalah see G. Nigal, *The Hasidic Tale*, trans. E. Levin (Oxford, 2008), 22–5; id., 'A Chapter in the History of the Hasidic Tale' (Heb.), in *Sefer sipurei kedoshim*, ed. G. Nigal (Jerusalem, 1977), 87–109; and cf. Dan, *The Hasidic Tale* (Heb.), 195 ff. For a comprehensive study of Rodkinson's career see J. Meir, *Michael Levi Rodkinson* [Shivḥei rodkinson] (Jerusalem, 2012). Rodkinson's first work was published for the first time in 1864 (see Nigal, *The Hasidic Tale*, 23). I had before me the Jerusalem edition (n.d.), in which the conversation in question appears on p. 33. The whole episode was reprinted by Rodkinson in his later book *Toledot amudei ḥabad* (Königsberg, 1876), 81–2. Reuben Margaliot could have drawn the conversation directly from the works of Rodkinson, and also from Kahana's *Sefer haḥasidut*, which was published a few years before *Butsina dinehora hashalem* and which reproduced the whole conversation in the chapter headed 'Divrei agadah' ('Hagiographical Traditions') on R. Shneur Zalman of Liady, 217.

122 On this letter see n. 115 above.

123 It seems that Rodkinson both reflects and nourishes this self-perception on the part of Habad. His stories, being among the first, and very few, on the history of Habad hasidism, contributed to Habad's sense of its privileged position as the central stream and most authentic representative of hasidism. That is how modern Habad historiography, which stems from the sixth *admor*, Joseph Isaac Schneersohn (see nn. 2 and 76 above), came to accept the tradition that R. Shneur Zalman used to call the Besht *zeyde*, as if the Besht were his grandfather. This tradition appears dozens of times in R. Joseph Isaac's writings, from which it has found its way into all the rich and varied Habad literature of the present day. For example, it is transmitted as follows by the *admor* Joseph Isaac in his memoirs: 'The Old *Admor*, R. Shneur Zalman, used to refer to the Besht as "the grandfather". This was because he was the disciple of his disciple . . . R. Shneur Zalman regarded himself as the "grandson" of the Besht, and used to say: "R. Barukh [of Międzybóż] is the physical grandson of the Besht, whereas I am the spiritual grandson of the Besht"' (*Sefer hazikhronot*, i. 37). Since this version does not appear anywhere in the published writings of the Shneur Zalman of Liady, not even in relation to his dispute with R. Barukh (n. 124 below), it is not impossible that the *admor* Joseph Isaac, like Margaliot in *Butsina dinehora hashalem*, drew upon Rodkinson's *Shivḥei harav* for the notion of R. Shneur Zalman's spiritual descent from the Besht, as against R. Barukh's physical descent.

Further testimony (dating, like *Shivḥei harav*, from the second half of the 19th century) to the consciousness in Habad of a special and intimate relationship with the founders of hasidism is furnished by another Habad hasid, R. Jacob Kadaner, in his hagiographical anthology *Sipurim nora'im* (on this book see Nigal, *The Hasidic Tale*, 31–2; on the author and his other works see Mondshine, 'The books of *Matsref ha'avodah* and *Vikuḥa rabah*' (Heb.), 165–75). In one of his stories about R. Shneur Zalman's time as a pupil in Mezhirech (*Sipurim nora'im* (Lemberg, 1875), pages unnumbered; pp. 59–61 according to my count), Kadaner eulogizes 'the holiness of the young R. Shneur Zalman', which the Magid found it difficult to reveal to the other disciples when they wondered what sort of person he was. When the Magid died 'the disciples immersed his holy body in a *mikveh* of running water and drew lots to determine who should hold each body part, and it fell out that he [R. Shneur Zalman] should hold his head. And all the disciples were greatly moved by this and realized that he [the Magid] had bequeathed the whole of his *torah* to him [R. Shneur Zalman].' This story, too, is incorporated in the historical writings of the *admor* Joseph Isaac (see his 'Avot haḥasidut', *Hatamim*, i. 143, ch. 9), in which it is quoted as an oral tradition which had passed from R. Shneur Zalman to his grandson the Tsemah Tsedek, and from him—presumably—through the generations of the Habad leadership to the *admor* Joseph Isaac himself. The *admor* makes no reference at all to the version published in Kadaner's book, which may have served him as a source, just as did Rodkinson's stories.

124 Indeed, R. Shneur Zalman's genuine letter (n. 115 above) on his quarrel with

R. Barukh of Międzybóż itself demonstrates how foreign to his view of himself was the claim to be the 'spiritual grandson' of the Besht. On his connection with the founder of hasidism he writes in that letter:

> On the two occasions that I was in P–b [St Petersburg] it was for *his* [R. Barukh's] *grandfather* the Besht, may he be remembered for life in the World to Come, and I could have said '*His grandson* is very much alive, let him come and explain all the difficulties raised against him', and I did not say 'Who am I that the teaching of the Besht should be sanctified by me'. (emphasis mine—A.R.-A.)

It is evident that these turns of phrase by R. Shneur Zalman could have engendered the claim on his behalf to the status of 'grandson' in the imagination of anyone brought up in a tradition that regarded R. Shneur Zalman as the principal bearer of the hasidic legacy of the Besht (the tradition whereby there is an almost dynastic continuity in the hasidic leadership, which passed from the Besht to the Magid of Mezhirech and from him to R. Shneur Zalman and, after him, to all the subsequent leaders of Habad, on which see n. 184 below). However, it is also clear that it did not occur to Shneur Zalman of Liady himself to use the term 'grandson' in anything other than its simple biological meaning. His reference to R. Barukh as a grandson is unambiguous, and however much he identifies with the teaching of the Besht, even to the extent of defending and 'sanctifying' it in the face of the attack by the *mitnagedim*, he is entirely free of the proprietary attitude displayed by R. Barukh, to which he alludes with a certain measure of irony.

125 See e.g. Sternharz, *Ḥayei moharan*, ii: *Shivḥei moharan* (Jerusalem, 1947), 'Gedulat hasagato', 9 §§8, 10–11; and cf. ibid., vol. i, 'Nesiato le'erets yisra'el', 65 §20. For a discussion of R. Nahman's messianic leadership see e.g. A. Green, *Tormented Master: A Life of Rabbi Nahman of Bratslav* (Tuscaloosa, Ala., 1979), 116–23, 182–220; Z. Mark, *The Scroll of Secrets: The Hidden Messianic Vision of R. Nachman of Breslav* (Brighton, Mass., 2010).

126 Nahman of Bratslav, *Likutei moharan* (New York, 1966), pt. I, *torah* 56, pp. 150–6.

127 Sternharz, *Ḥayei moharan*, i, 'Siḥot hashayakhim lehatorot', 15 §22.

128 Nahman of Bratslav, *Likutei moharan*, pt. I, *torah* 56, p. 150.

129 On this interpretation of R. Nahman's view of his leadership see n. 104 above.

130 See Sternharz, *Ḥayei moharan*, ii, 'Ma'alat torato usefarav hakedoshim', 26 §14; ibid. 29 §34; ibid., 'Gedulat hasagato', 16 §50; ibid. i, 'Nesiato viyeshivato be'uman', 90 §45.

131 Ibid. ii, 'Gedulat hasagato', 16 §50. R. Nahman here uses, word for word, Ben Azai's well-known statement (BT *Bekh.* 58*a*) and hints that, unlike Ben Azai, who excepted 'this baldhead' (Rashi explains: R. Akiva) from the generality of the sages of Israel, who were worthless compared to him, he, R. Nahman, could make no exception.

132 N. Sternharz, *Siḥot haran* [with *Shivḥei haran*] (Lemberg, 1901), 60*b* §166; and cf. *Shivḥei haran*, 6*b* §25.

133 As a child he had, in fact, frequently prayed at the grave of the Besht and felt the need to ask for his guidance. See below, at n. 154.

134 Sternharz, *Ḥayei moharan*, i, 'Nesiato le'erets yisra'el', 61 §1.

135 On R. Nahman's sense of superiority to the Besht, asserting his independence and uniqueness as a hasidic leader—as it were, 'a new thing the like of which the world had never seen'—see Sternharz, *Siḥot haran*, 73*b* §239; ibid., 'Seder hanesiah shelo le'erets yisra'el', 7*b* §4; Sternharz, *Ḥayei moharan*, i, 'Nesiato le'erets yisra'el', 63 §11; ibid. ii, 'Ma'alot torato usefarav hakedoshim', 29 §34; Abraham Hazan of Tulchin, *Avaneiha barzel* (in the volume entitled *Sefer kokhevei or*) (Jerusalem, 1961), 17 §15. And cf. n. 132 above. Similarly, R. Nahman contemptuously shrugged off the heritage of his maternal grandfather, R. Nahman of Horodenka (see Sternharz, *Siḥot haran*, 68*b* §210). Whether or not his rejection of his links with the latter grandfather was in the nature of a defence against allegations that he was tainted with Sabbatianism (see Weiss, 'The Beginnings of Hasidism' (Heb.), 89–90 n. 14; and cf. Y. Liebes, 'R. Nahman's General *Tikun* and His Attitude to Sabbatianism' (Heb.), *Zion*, 45/3 (1980), 226–7 n. 93), it is clear that his dissociation of himself from the legacy of his grandfather was bound up with Nahman's view of his own uniquely wondrous quality and his 'concealed' superiority (*be'itkasya*) to the leaders of every generation, in the past, the present, and even the future. This feeling of superiority undoubtedly stands in complete contrast to the sense of the 'continual decline of the generations' (*holekh ufoḥet*), which is a universal perception, characteristic of Jewish tradition and Western culture in general. On the consciousness of 'continual decline' as the ideology which legitimized the promotion in hasidism of the tale and of mundane conversation to the highest level of the tsadik's spirituality, see M. Piekarz, *Braslav Hasidism* [Ḥasidut bratslav] (Jerusalem, 1972), 102–4. On the tension between the sense of 'continual decline' and the sense of spiritual and prophetic innovation in hasidism, see L. Jacobs, 'Hasidism and the Dogma of the Decline of the Generations', in A. Rapoport-Albert (ed.), *Hasidism Reappraised* (London, 1996), 208–13.

136 *Avaneiha barzel*, 17 §15.

137 Sternharz, *Ḥayei moharan*, i, 'Nesiato le'erets yisra'el', 65 §19; and cf. id., *Yemei moharnat* (Benei Berak, 1956), pt. I, 46*b*.

138 Sternharz, *Ḥayei moharan*, ii, 'Gedulat hasagato', 12 §30.

139 Ibid., 'Avodat hashem', 65–6 §105.

140 Sternharz, *Yemei moharnat*, pt. I, 29*a*.

141 See ibid. 30*b*, and cf. J. Weiss, *Studies in Braslav Hasidism* [Meḥkarim beḥasidut bratslav] (Jerusalem, 1974), 36–41.

142 See N. Sternharz, *Shivḥei haran*, 'Seder hanesiah shelo le'erets yisra'el', 12*a*–13*b* §§19–20, and also R. Abraham's letter to R. Nahman in Sternharz, *Ḥayei moharan*, i, 'Nesiato le'erets yisra'el', 66.

143 Sternharz, *Shivḥei haran*, 'Seder hanesiah shelo le'erets yisra'el', 13*b* §20.

144 According to R. Nathan's account (n. 145 below), R. Nahman went to 'the holy congregation of Liady' to see R. Shneur Zalman 'immediately on his arrival from Erets Yisra'el', i.e. in the summer of 5559 (1799), apparently after the release of R. Shneur Zalman in Kislev of that year from his first spell of imprisonment. At the time R. Shneur Zalman was still living in Liozno, for in his petition addressed to the emperor in August 1801 he still signs as 'the rabbi of Liozno' (see Dubnow, *The History of Hasidism* (Heb.), 278), and it seems that he did not move to Liady until after his return from St Petersburg for the second time, in 5562 (1802) (ibid. 332–3). R. Nathan Sternharz recorded these events in *Ḥayei moharan* many years after their occurrence, when R. Shneur Zalman had become known as 'the rabbi of Liady', and he was clearly mistaken in locating the rabbi's court in 5559 (1799) at Liady instead of Liozno.

145 Sternharz, *Ḥayei moharan*, i, 'Mekom yeshivato unesiotav', 52–3 §10; and cf. *Avaneiha barzel*, 33–4 §46.

146 See R. Abraham of Kalisk's letter to R. Nahman (n. 142 above).

147 See above, at nn. 115–24.

148 *Avaneiha barzel*, 34 §46.

149 See Gottlober, *Memoirs and Travels* (Heb.), i. 168; and cf. *Avaneiha barzel*, 34 §46.

150 See *Avaneiha barzel*, 34 §46, and cf. Sternharz, *Ḥayei moharan*, i, 'Nesiato le'erets yisra'el', 61–2 §4. It is unlikely that R. Nahman was unaware of the fundamental difference between his own outlook on hasidism and that of R. Shneur Zalman as expressed in his published work, *Tanya*, a difference so pronounced that it provided hasidic scholarship with the typological distinction between the hasidism of 'faith' and 'contemplative' or 'mystical' hasidism. See Weiss, *Studies in Braslav Hasidism* (Heb.), 87–95; Eng. version in Weiss, *Studies in Eastern European Jewish Mysticism*, 43–55.

151 See Sternharz, *Ḥayei moharan*, i, 'Mekom yeshivato unesiotav', 52–4 §10; and see the discussion of this point in Green, *Tormented Master*, 99–100.

152 Sternharz, *Ḥayei moharan*, ii, 'Ma'alat hamitkarvim elav', 22 §95; and cf. *Avaneiha barzel*, 8 §6; Nahman of Bratslav, *Likutei moharan*, pt. II, *torah* 15, pp. 46–7. In the latter *torah* R. Nahman distinguishes between 'those who falsely boast of great deeds and wonders, as if nothing is beyond their ability and everything is within their powers, and some of them are [the] leaders of

the generation', and, on the other hand, 'true tsadikim, of great spiritual eminence, whose mouth is holy and its way is to utter great and wondrous things, and they can truly serve the Lord through anything in the world, through eating, drinking and other things'. As he often does in expressing himself on the subject of 'the true tsadikim', he slips from 'tsadikim' in the plural to 'tsadik' in the singular, and there is no doubt that in doing so he is alluding to his own pre-eminence as 'the tsadik of the generation'. But one should not underestimate the reality in R. Nahman's mind of 'the true tsadikim' as a whole group whose existence is clearly 'revealed' to the world, and which is distinct from the group of 'lying hypocrites who mimic [the true tsadikim] like an ape'. The legitimate and 'revealed' status of the true tsadikim is as real to him as his own 'concealed' status as tsadik of the generation. It is interesting to note that R. Nathan Sternharz enumerates a long list of tsadikim which includes almost indiscriminately all of R. Nahman's predecessors in the hasidic movement as well as many of his contemporaries, for all of whom R. Nahman allegedly felt great respect and on whose holiness he lavished praise. This contrasts with his caustic and derisive comments (likewise recorded by R. Nathan), in various other contexts, on 'all the sages of Israel' in general and many of his fellow hasidic leaders in particular. From the fact that the list even includes R. Nahman's uncle and adversary, 'the holy rabbi, R. Barukh, of blessed memory', it is evident that it is an exercise in apologetics, serving, as it were, as a reply to claims that R. Nahman exalted himself above other people. Genuine praise, such as the expression of R. Nahman's high regard for R. Levi Isaac of Berdiczów, appears in it alongside vague statements in praise of all the great hasidic personages of the generation. See Sternharz, *Ḥayei moharan*, ii, 65–6 §105.

153 *Avaneiha barzel*, 8 §6.

154 Sternharz, *Shivḥei haran*, 5*a* §19; and see also ibid., §20.

155 See e.g. ibid., 'Seder hanesiah shelo le'erets yisra'el', 12*b* §19.

156 See A. Grossman, 'Family Pedigree and Its Role in Early Ashkenazi Jewish Society' (Heb.), in I. Etkes and Y. Salmon (eds.), *Studies in the History of Jewish Society in the Middle Ages and in the Modern Period* [Perakim betoledot haḥevrah hayehudit biyemei habeinayim uva'et haḥadashah, mukdashim leya'akov kats] (Jerusalem, 1980), 9–23.

157 See Sternharz, *Ḥayei moharan*, ii, 'Gedulat hasagato', 9 §7.

158 See Hillman, *Letters by the Author of the Tanya* (Heb.), 175 no. 103; and, on p. 177, Hillman's comment on the date when this was written. *Igerot kodesh admor hazaken, admor ha'emtsa'i, admor hatsemaḥ tsedek*, 125–6 no. 51; and see the presumed date (Elul 5565 = 1805) given on p. 120.

159 See p. 40 above, and n. 57.

160 See Z. Gries, 'Hasidism: The Present State of Research and Some Desirable Priorities', *Numen*, 34/1 (1987), 101–3.

161 On Habad historiography in the 20th century, and especially on the writings of the *admor* Joseph Isaac Schneersohn, see nn. 2 and 76 above, and Ch. 4 below. But it is hard to accept the claim that *Shivḥei habesht*, for example, reflects a distinctly Habad perspective on the personalities and events it describes, or that it betrays a characteristic Habad predilection for 'organization and propaganda' (see Gries, 'Hasidism', 102–3), simply because the book was published by R. Israel Yofeh, who was a follower of R. Shneur Zalman of Liady. Notably, R. Shneur Zalman and his family are not mentioned at all in the tales of *Shivḥei habesht*, whereas the Habad historiography stemming from Joseph Isaac places them at the very centre of the entire hasidic movement from its earliest beginnings in the time of the Besht, and even alleges that the Belarusian town of Lubavitch was an underground centre of hasidism during the Besht's lifetime (see *Sefer hazikhronot*, pt. I, 28–36, and below, Ch. 4, p. 236). Nor is there any trace in *Shivḥei habesht* of the fondness for 'organization and propaganda'—among the hallmarks of Joseph Isaac's style of leadership, which in his quasi-historical reconstructions he projected onto the early beginnings of hasidism (see nn. 2 and 75 above, and Ch. 4 below). In fact, the tales of *Shivḥei habesht* reflect a very weak organizational framework and mention what might be construed as 'propaganda' activities only incidentally. As to the letters that passed between the leaders of Belarusian hasidism in Erets Yisra'el and their hasidim back home, which were likewise preserved and distributed primarily by Habad, these, too, lack the tendentiousness typical of later Habad historiography: rather than purporting to reflect the contemporary state of hasidism as a whole while presenting its Belarusian branch, and ultimately Habad, as the headquarters of the entire movement and its most important centre, the letters actually document only internal developments in Belarusian hasidism as such.

162 The writings of the *admor* Joseph Isaac Schneersohn are an exception. They tell of regular and fairly frequent meetings of the disciples of the Magid, presided over by R. Shneur Zalman. On this see more below.

163 Gottlober, *Memoirs and Travels* (Heb.), i. 173–8.

164 Dubnow, *The History of Hasidism* (Heb.), 310.

165 See also S. Dubnow, *History of the Jews in Russia and Poland* (Philadelphia, 1916–20), i. 335 ff.; J. D. Klier, *Russia Gathers her Jews* (Dekalb, Ill., 1986), 116–43.

166 And cf. the editor's note 103 in Gottlober, *Memoirs and Travels* (Heb.), i. 173.

167 'R. Levi Isaac of Berdiczów and the Decrees of the State in His Time' (Heb.), in Halpern, *Eastern European Jewry* (Heb.), 345–6.

168 See n. 57 above.

169 Sternharz, *Ḥayei moharan*, i, 'Mekom yeshivato unesiotav', 58 §19; and cf. *Pe'ulat hatsadik* (Jerusalem, 1981), 142 §379.

170 Gottlober, *Memoirs and Travels* (Heb.), i. 177–8.

171 See Sternharz, *Ḥayei moharan*, i, 'Mekom yeshivato unesiotav', 58 §19.

172 Halpern, *Eastern European Jewry* (Heb.), 347.

173 But cf. Green, *Tormented Master*, 110, 140. He takes the two accounts of a conference in Berdiczów as relating to two separate events, and surmises that R. Nahman was not present at the conference described by Gottlober.

174 See e.g. Buber, *Tales of the Hasidim*, ii. 258–9. For an analysis of the process by which the concrete event of the Ustila wedding in 1821 acquired mythological dimensions in the rich hagiographical and neo-hasidic literature of the 19th and early 20th centuries, see now U. Gellman, 'The Great Wedding at Ustila: The History of a Hasidic Myth' (Heb.), *Tarbiz*, 80/4 (2013), 567–94. For the hagiographical traditions on inter-dynastic weddings as a means of constructing the distinctive identities of each of the hasidic parties involved, see the index in G. Sagiv, *Dynasty: The Chernobyl Hasidic Dynasty and Its Place in the History of Hasidism* [Hashoshelet: beit chernobyl umekomo betoledot haḥasidut] (Jerusalem, 2014), s.v. *ḥatunah*, *ḥatunot bein shoshalot*.

175 See n. 2 above and, in particular, Ch. 4, pp. 219–43 below.

176 The reference is to the son of the Magid, R. Abraham the Angel, who is presented as having inherited his father's position as supreme leader of the hasidic movement (see nn. 2, 76 above) but being incapable of actually exercising that function because of his temperamental preference for the reclusive life of the ascetic. This is why he had to delegate the practice of leadership to the various institutions and office-holders described in the remainder of the passage quoted.

177 The reference is to R. Shneur Zalman.

178 The Magid of Mezhirech.

179 J. I. Schneersohn, 'Avot haḥasidut', *Hatamim*, i. 144, ch. 10.

180 The *admor* Joseph Isaac led his hasidim in Russia during the period of oppression by the Soviet regime under Stalin. He was imprisoned, persecuted, and expelled on account of his covert activity aimed at preserving traditional Jewish religious life in Communist Russia. He persisted in these efforts even after he escaped to Latvia, then to Poland, and later, during the Second World War, to the USA. There he rehabilitated the Habad movement, establishing it on a new basis in a new world. All this is documented in his prolific writings, and especially in the many volumes of his letters, which have been published in New York in recent decades. Basing himself on the *admor*'s own writings, R. Abraham H. Glitzenstein wrote his biography—*Sefer hatoladot: rabi yosef yitsḥak schneersohn, admor morenu harav yosef yitsḥak*, 4 vols. in 3 (1971–4). Vol-

ume III (for the years 1921–8, spanning his activity up to the time he left Russia) and Volume IV (1928–50, up to his death in New York) relate to the period with which we are concerned. In addition, the central part played by Joseph Isaac, at considerable danger to himself, in the struggle to preserve Judaism in Russia during those years is documented in works quite independent of the official hagiographic literature of Habad. See e.g. A. A. Gershuni, *Judaism in Soviet Russia: Towards a History of Religious Persecution* [Yahadut berusyah hasovietit: lekorot redifot hadat] (Jerusalem, 1961), 156–207; J. Rothenberg, *The Jewish Religion in the Soviet Union* (New York, 1971), 161, 178.

181 For a detailed reconstruction of this process see Etkes, *Rabbi Shneur Zalman of Liady*, 9–21.

182 Ibid. 12.

183 See Heilman, *Beit rabi*, 81–90 (= 41*a*–45*b*); A. J. Brawer, 'On the Dispute Between R. Shneur Zalman of Liady and R. Abraham Hakohen of Kalisk' (Heb.), *Kiryat sefer*, 1 (1924–5), 142–50, 226–38; Elior, 'The Minsk Debate' (Heb.), 198–9.

184 On the view of R. Shneur Zalman as the Magid's successor to the central leadership of hasidism as a whole and as the most authentic representative of the hasidic path laid down by the founders of the movement, see e.g. the claim implicit in the dynastic chart 'Shalshelet nesi'ei haḥasidut hakelalit unesi'ei ḥasidei ḥabad' ('The chain of hasidic leaders in general and of the leaders of Habad hasidism'), which has been printed on the title pages of many Habad books in both Hebrew and English (e.g. all the biographies of the Habad leaders written by Abraham H. Glitzenstein). In the chart the Besht and the Magid of Mezhirech are counted as the 'first generation' and 'second generation', R. Shneur Zalman is named immediately after them as the 'third generation', and after him come all his successors as leaders of Habad down to the last *admor*, who was the 'ninth generation' in the leadership of hasidism. See also above, p. 56 and n. 123. It is not only in Habad hasidism that there appears this tendency to credit the Besht and the Magid of Mezhirech with the parentage of a particular hasidic dynasty, whose founder is regarded as their sole or principal heir. Thus, for example, hagiographical tradition presents R. Elimelekh of Lizhensk as a disciple who was chosen to succeed his master, the Magid of Mezhirech, as the leader of the whole of the hasidic movement of his day. See *Ohel elimelekh*, 49–50 §24:

> For after the decease of the rabbi, R. Ber of Mezhirech, may the memory of that righteous and holy man be for a blessing, all his associates came there to pay their last respects to him. Among them were the rabbi R. Elimelekh and his brother, the rabbi R. Zusya of Annopol, may their merit protect us, who, too, had previously journeyed to the rabbi, R. Ber, may his merit protect us; and after the 'holy ark' [coffin] of the rabbi,

> R. Ber, was buried, it was proposed in the course of discussion among his disciples that they should place themselves under the authority of a new master, who would take the place of the rabbi, R. Ber, may his merit protect us. And they began to conduct enquiries as to whether there was such a man among them who would be worthy to take the place of the rabbi, R. Ber. And they all agreed to accept as their master the rabbi, R. Elimelekh of Lizhensk. And forthwith they placed the crown of sovereignty on his head and all cried, 'Long live our *admor* the rabbi, R. Elimelekh' . . . and they said, 'Then blessed be the Lord, who has not left us like sheep without a shepherd. For he is truly worthy to take the place of the rabbi, R. Ber, may his merit protect us.'

A tradition of the Gur dynasty ascribed a similar status to the Seer of Lublin. See Aescoly, 'Hasidism in Poland' (Heb.), 128. This proprietary sense with regard to the legacy of the Besht and the Magid of Mezhirech as the central leaders of the whole of the hasidic movement descends also, via R. Elimelekh of Lizhensk and the Seer of Lublin, to R. Isaac Judah Yehiel Safrin of Komarno, and finds expression in his *Megilat setarim*, ed. N. Ben-Menahem (Jerusalem, 1944), 51.

185 See 'Avot haḥasidut', *Hatamim*, i. 144, chs. 10–11; Elior, 'The Minsk Debate' (Heb.), 211, 214, 218, 219.

186 'Avot haḥasidut', *Hatamim*, i. 144, chs. 10–11.

187 Elior, 'The Minsk Debate' (Heb.), 214–15. It is interesting to note that the *admor* Joseph Isaac does not mention R. Abraham of Kalisk in this connection, even though he was one of the leaders of Belarusian hasidism and a colleague of R. Menahem Mendel of Vitebsk, with whom he emigrated to Erets Yisra'el. Surely, it might have been expected that, in the *admor*'s version of events, the disciples would decide on R. Abraham's departure also and would take leave of him, too, as they did with his travelling companion R. Menahem Mendel of Vitebsk. Joseph Isaac's peculiar silence on all this may well be intended to serve as an implicit reminder of, in the first instance, the Magid and his disciples' disapproval of R. Abraham on account of his wild and disgraceful behaviour in 1772, which had angered the Magid and also, according to R. Shneur Zalman, aroused the wrath of the *mitnagedim* (see n. 57 above, and also n. 70, which draws attention to Z. Gries's reservations in this regard). But, in addition, it constitutes an implicit condemnation by Habad of R. Abraham of Kalisk for his subsequent dispute with R. Shneur Zalman of Liady (see n. 183 above). It is this, above all, that lies behind the silence of Joseph Isaac on R. Abraham of Kalisk's role in the alleged events of 1777.

188 In this acknowledgement of the awkward distance between the historic geographical centre of the hasidic movement in Volhynia, where the Magid of Mezhirech and many of his disciples lived, and the relatively isolated centre of Habad hasidism in Belarus, we may detect a certain consciousness on the part of the *admor* Joseph Isaac—a consciousness to which he gives more explicit expression elsewhere—that 'Polish' hasidism, which he often contrasts with the hasidism of Habad, enjoys a certain emotional affinity with, and has some sort of historical 'proprietary' right over, the original founders of hasidism, who all began their activities in Polish Podolia and Volhynia. See e.g. the *admor*'s long letter to his son-in-law Menachem Mendel, the last *admor* of Habad, sent to Berlin from Riga in 1932. The letter was first published in *Hatamim* and is now included in *Igerot kodesh . . . yosef yitsḥak* (Brooklyn, 1983), ii. 371–7. The special affinity of 'Polish' hasidism to the Besht and the Magid of Mezhirech requires an explanation from the Habad point of view, since it clashes with Habad's view of itself as the hasidic school with the strongest claim to be the legitimate and most authentic heir to the tradition of the founders of the movement. Notably, this sensitivity to the closer geographical, and, in some respects, temperamental ties between 'Polish' hasidism and the founders of the movement appears to have found its strongest expression in the period when Habad was uprooted from its historical centre in Belarus and, under the leadership of Joseph Isaac, was exposed for the first time to intensive contact with a large and vigorous Polish hasidic world in interwar Warsaw. See on this A. Rapoport-Albert and G. Sagiv, 'Chabad versus "Polish Hasidism": Towards the History of a Dichotomy' (Heb.), in J. Meir and G. Sagiv (eds.), *Chabad: History, Thought, Image* [Ḥabad: historyah, hagut, dimuy] (Jerusalem, 2016).

189 See Ch. 4 below, and Rapoport-Albert and Sagiv, 'Chabad versus "Polish Hasidism"' (Heb.).

190 See G. Scholem, *On the Mystical Shape of the Godhead: Basic Concepts in the Kabbalah* (New York, 1991), 215 ff., 223–6, 231–5.

191 Ibid. 223–5, 231 ff.; B. Sack, 'Three Times of Redemption in R. Moses Cordovero's *Or yakar*' (Heb.), in Z. Baras (ed.), *Messianism and Eschatology* [Meshiḥiyut ve'eskhatologyah] (Jerusalem, 1984), 282; ead., 'Man as Mirror and the Theory of Mutual Responsibility' (Heb.), *Da'at*, 12 (1984), 37.

192 On the idea, expressed by R. Hayim Vital, that bonds of family kinship do not necessarily coincide with the bonds of affinity of the roots of souls, see e.g. *Sha'ar hamitsvot* (Tel Aviv, 1962), 'Yitro', 33–5:

> But it has long been known that most children are not from one root, but one [stems] from Loving-kindness [the *sefirah* Hesed] and another from Might [the *sefirah* Din] and so on, and this is particularly so with regard to those who have undergone *gilgul* [transmigration of the soul], for in most cases they have no connection with their ancestors, neither do they have any connection or affinity whatsoever with the souls of their fathers and mothers . . . and there is no connection between father and son or between

> the son and his father and mother and his elder brother. Each one goes to his own root, but when their souls are all from one root then kinsfolk are joined together as they were at first.

Cf. H. Vital, *Sha'ar hagilgulim* (Tel Aviv, 1963), 34, *hakdamah* 10; and see Scholem, *On the Mystical Shape of the Godhead*, 235.

193 Elimelekh of Lizhensk, *No'am elimelekh* [Lemberg, 1788], ed. G. Nigal (Jerusalem, 1978), ii. 65*c* (p. 350), 'Behar'; and cf. i. 37*c* (p. 198), 'Bo', and see the editor's remarks in the introduction, p. 22. See also R. Schatz-Uffenheimer, 'On the Nature of the Tsadik in Hasidism' (Heb.), *Molad*, 18/144–5 (1960), 375.

194 M. Brokman, *Migdal david* (Piotrków, 1930), repr. in *Sefarim kedoshim migedolei talmidei ba'al shem tov hakadosh* (Brooklyn, NY, 1981), iii. 50. This motif also appears in the tale quoted by Buber in *Tales of the Hasidim*, ii. 108–10. According to this tale, which originated in the circle of R. Moses Leyb of Sasów, R. Abraham Joshua Heschel of Apta (Opatów) became a disciple of R. Elimelekh of Lizhensk on the instructions of R. Levi Isaac of Berdiczów and R. Moses Leyb of Sasów, who had both recognized that he belonged to the root of R. Elimelekh's soul.

195 *Migdal david*, 50. On *Migdal david* and its author see Nigal, *The Hasidic Tale*, 47. For the references in *No'am elimelekh* see n. 193 above.

196 See Scholem, *On the Mystical Shape of the Godhead*, 218 ff.

197 Ibid. 241 ff.

198 See n. 194 above.

199 Vital, *Sha'ar hagilgulim*, 24, *hakdamah* 5; and see Sack, 'Man as Mirror' (Heb.), 43.

200 In addition to the remarks of R. Elimelekh of Lizhensk (p. 69 above and n. 193), see e.g. Nahman of Bratslav, *Likutei moharan*, pt. II, *torah* 1, 'Tike'u memshalah', §3:

> In order to bind oneself to the roots of all the souls of Israel one has to know the origin of all souls and the source of their vitality, whence every single soul receives its vitality, and the most important thing is to know all the famous men of the generation, for if you cannot know and bind yourself individually to each and every soul you must bind yourself to all the famous men and leaders of the generation, for the souls are distributed among them; for every famous man and leader of the generation has a number of souls who belong to his allotted portion, and when you bind yourself to the famous men, you are bound together with all the individual souls of Israel.

Admittedly this statement is made from the peculiar viewpoint of R. Nahman —the messianic tsadik of the generation who aspires to form a bond, directly or indirectly, with the souls of all Israel—but it is clear that the doctrine of the special affinity between the sparks of every leader's soul and of his 'private' hasidim underlies his view on the existence of a bond between the tsadik of the generation and every soul. Another formulation of the same doctrine appears in R. Kalonymos Kalman Epstein of Kraków's *Ma'or vashemesh* [Breslau, 1842] (Jerusalem, 1986), pt. II, 'Ḥukat', 59–60:

> And so, too, every tsadik has people who journey to him to join themselves to him, and they are branches of the root of his soul. And inasmuch as they affiliate with him he raises up their soul and binds it to their root above, for they are his sparks, which must be raised up . . . The tsadik must take the greatest care to distance himself from those individuals who are not of the root of his soul. That is to say, he must certainly love every Jew, but he must be careful not to weary himself to raise them [all] up and bind them to their root, for by doing so the tsadik could fall, Heaven forbid, below his [spiritual] level, and he must therefore greatly beware of them. The enlightened man will understand this.

201 The dynastic solution to the problem of preserving the special identity of a hasidic community which had formed round a particular founder even after his death makes its first appearance in the hasidism of Chernobyl, where R. Mordecai succeeded to the leadership on the death of his father, R. Menahem Nahum, in 1798. In Karlin hasidism it was a disciple, R. Shelomoh, who first succeeded to the leadership of the community on the death of its founder, R. Aaron of Karlin, in 1772. After the death of R. Shelomoh in 1792, the leadership passed to the founder's grandson, R. Asher of Karlin-Stolin, and from him to his sons. In Habad hasidism R. Dov Ber succeeded to the leadership after the death of his father, R. Shneur Zalman of Liady, in 1813. In Lizhensk hasidism, when R. Elimelekh died in 1786, the leadership of his community was shared by his two sons, though they were not particularly successful in that role. In the hasidic community founded by R. Israel, the Magid of Kozienice, who died in 1814, the Magid was succeeded by his sons. In Lelów hasidism R. Moses inherited the leadership from his father, R. David, who died in 1813. See also Aescoly, 'Hasidism in Poland' (Heb.), 96. Cf. the genealogical chart of the leading hasidic dynasties in *Encyclopaedia Judaica* (Jerusalem, 1972), i. 160–7. For a discussion of the dynastic principle in the hasidic leadership in its sociological context, see Sharot, *Messianism, Mysticism, and Magic*, the chapter on 'Hasidism and the Routinization of Charisma', 155–88. For a pioneering critical history of the Chernobyl dynasty see Sagiv, *Dynasty: The Chernobyl Hasidic Dynasty* (Heb.).

202 See pp. 73–9 above.

203 Unlike the literature of the organized mitnagdic campaigns against hasidism during the 1770s and 1780s, the earliest references—for the most part hostile —to groups of pietists described as hasidim (regarded by most scholars as 'proto-hasidic') in the time of the Besht still relate to the activity of individuals. See the remarks of R. Jacob of Satanów in *Mishmeret hakodesh* and of R. Solomon of Chełm in *Mirkevet hamishneh*, both quoted in G. Scholem, 'The First Two Testimonies on Hasidic Groups and the Besht' (Heb.), in id., *The Latest Phase: Essays on Hasidism* (Heb.), ed. D. Assaf and E. Liebes, 64–90, although it is not clear whether they actually refer to the Besht and his circle. On this subject see also H. Lieberman, 'How Hasidism Is "Studied" in Israel' (Heb.), in id., *Ohel raḥel* (New York, 1980–4), i. 12–49; G. Scholem, 'The Polemic against Hasidism and Its Leaders in the Book *Nezed ha-Dema*' (Heb.), in id., *The Latest Phase* (Heb.), 91–105; Piekarz, *The Beginning of Hasidism* (Heb.), 131 ff.

204 Weiss, 'The Beginnings of Hasidism' (Heb.), 149.

205 On the interchange of singular and plural in R. Jacob Joseph's references to the leaders of the generation, see n. 33 above.

206 *Toledot ya'akov yosef*, 'Mishpatim', 29*a*; and cf. ibid., 'Ḥayei sarah', 18*b*:

> for the tsadik, after ascending to the upper world, descends again in order to raise up [other] levels in accordance with the mystical principle [which underlies the verse] 'The righteous man falls seven times and rises again' [a literal rendering of Prov. 24: 16] . . . and this applies [to his activities] both in this world and in the World to Come, for he returns [by means of *gilgul*] reincarnated in order to raise up the levels of the people who are his sparks and his branches, so that they may all achieve *tikun*.

Cf. also *Degel maḥaneh efrayim* (Zhitomir, 1875), 'Noaḥ', 6*a*.

207 See Dubnow, *The History of Hasidism* (Heb.), 93–6.

208 See e.g. Wilensky, *Hasidim and Mitnagedim* (Heb.), i. 59, 62, 63, 67, and *passim*.

209 Ibid. 104. And in this connection see Z. Gries, 'The Hasidic Conduct (*Hanhagot*) Literature from the Mid-Eighteenth Century to the 1830s' (Heb.), *Zion*, 46 (1981), 233, where he points out that the wide circulation of the booklets of *hanhagot* (rules of conduct) up to the year 1800 confirms the existence of a variegated pattern of affiliation with hasidism, comprising many different forms and either more or less intense shades of commitment.

210 On the *hitkarvut* of the Magid of Mezhirech see *In Praise of the Baal Shem Tov*, ed. Ben-Amos and Mintz, 81–4 (*Shivḥei habesht*, ed. Rubinstein, 126–9); On the *hitkarvut* of R. Jacob Joseph of Połonne see *In Praise of the Baal Shem Tov*, 61–3 (*Shivḥei habesht*, ed. Rubinstein, 99–101). On the *hitkarvut* of 'R. David, the preacher of the holy congregation of Kolomyya' see *In Praise of the Baal Shem Tov*, 45–6 (*Shivḥei habesht*, ed. Rubinstein, 79–81); On two visits designed to take the measure of the Besht see *In Praise of the Baal Shem Tov*, 105–6 (*Shivḥei habesht*, ed. Rubinstein, 152–4). See also *In Praise of the Baal Shem Tov*, 146–9 (*Shivḥei habesht*, ed. Rubinstein, 194–6) on the meeting between R. Abraham—the father of R. Pinhas of Korets—and the Besht, which took place in spite of R. Abraham's contempt for the Besht and his objection to the relations between the Besht and R. Pinhas. *Shivḥei habesht* does indeed report that R. Jacob Joseph was expelled from his position as rabbi of Shargorod (Szarogród), apparently as early as 1748, because he had begun 'to consort with hasidim', and that he 'persisted in his righteous course' for a long time. However, at this time and in this environment the expulsion of rabbis from their posts was not a rare phenomenon (see e.g. S. Assaf, 'On the History of the Rabbinate (Heb.), in id., *Be'oholei ya'akov* (Jerusalem, 1943), 56–9), and the precise background to R. Jacob Joseph's expulsion from Shargorod is not known from any other source. *Shivḥei habesht*, which was compiled many decades after the events described here and in full familiarity with the mitnagdic controversy of the 1770s and 1780s, was quite capable of explaining the expulsion of R. Jacob Joseph as a self-evident consequence of his affiliation with hasidism. In any event it is clear, even from what we are told, that the relations between R. Jacob Joseph and his congregation deteriorated gradually, and only culminated in his expulsion after some time. This was not an immediate reaction to his identification as a hasid.

211 *In Praise of the Baal Shem Tov*, ed. Ben-Amos and Mintz, 82 (*Shivḥei habesht*, ed. Rubinstein, 126).

212 *In Praise of the Baal Shem Tov*, ed. Ben-Amos and Mintz, 147 (*Shivḥei habesht*, ed. Rubinstein, 195).

213 See *The Autobiography of Solomon Maimon*, 175 (19 of the *Essential Papers on Hasidism* reprint), 89 (not reprinted).

214 Ibid. 53 (not reprinted).

215 Ibid. 173 (18 of the *Essential Papers on Hasidism* reprint).

216 Sternharz, *Yemei moharnat*, pt. I, *6a–7b*.

217 Solomon Maimon finished writing his autobiography in 1792, when he was almost 40 years old, whereas the episode of his affiliation with hasidism occurred during his youth, apparently at the end of the 1760s or the beginning of the 1770s, and in any event before the death of the Magid of Mezhirech in 1772 (see P. Lachower's introduction to Maimon, *Autobiography* [Ḥayei shelomoh maimon] (Tel Aviv, 1942), 35, 48). *Yemei moharnat* concludes with a description of the episode of R. Nathan's journey to Erets Yisra'el in 1822. It appears to have been written over a period of many years (R. Nathan died in 1845). In it, dated diary entries are randomly interspersed with sections which are more in the nature of memoirs.

218 See e.g. *The Autobiography of Solomon Maimon*, 166 (11 of the *Essential Papers on Hasidism* reprint).

219 See e.g. ibid. 168 n. 1 (23 of the *Essential Papers on Hasidism* reprint); 184–5 (not reprinted), and p. 34 of Lachower's introduction to the Hebrew edition.

220 See e.g. Abraham Hazan of Tulchin, *Sefer kokhevei or*, 'Anshei moharan', 9–11; id., *Avaneiha barzel*, 3 ff. See also Weiss, *Studies in Braslav Hasidism* (Heb.), 66–77.

221 The emergence of this consciousness completes the process the beginning of which was described by Jacob Katz (*Tradition and Crisis*, 239–40) as the 'dissociation' of the hasidim from the public at large, which was perceived as sectarian separatism and gave rise to mitnagdism. But the separatism of the hasidim in the period leading up to the campaign against them found expression only in the initiatives of individuals in various communities who adopted certain pietistic norms which had been current in kabbalistic circles for generations. These norms did not originate in a coherent policy of any new 'movement' as such, and the relationship between the various individuals and circles that adopted them was rather loose at that stage. See also above, pp. 26 ff.

222 See above, n. 57, and cf. Section 6 above.

223 See n. 57 and Section 6.

224 See n. 55 above and cf. Gries, 'From Myth to Ethos' (Heb.), 126–32.

225 See above, pp. 27–8 and n. 14.

226 See above, pp. 34–5 and nn. 42–3.

227 See p. 35 above.

228 See above, p. 39 and nn. 55, 57.

229 See end of n. 5 above, and cf. Green, *Tormented Master*, 94–134.

230 See above, p. 39 and n. 55.

231 See above, pp. 26–30, 38–9.

232 See pp. 55–6, 59–61, 63–5 above.

233 See pp. 75–6 above.

234 Abraham Hazan of Tulchin, *Sefer kokhevei or*, 9 §2.

235 Id., *Avaneiha barzel*, 46 §2.

236 See p. 76 above.

237 Weiss, *Studies in Braslav Hasidism* (Heb.), 70–2.

238 See above, n. 201.

239 See above, p. 25 and n. 6. On the shift from a spontaneous, voluntary association to a fixed hereditary link between the hasid and his tsadik, see Rubinstein, 'Studies in the History of Hasidism' (Heb.), 246–7. The matter has not been addressed by scholars, but the institutionalization of the hereditary principle in both tsadikism and hasidism should not be taken as self-explanatory.

240 See A. Green, 'Typologies of Leadership and the Hasidic Zaddik', in id. (ed.), *Jewish Spirituality*, ii: *From the Sixteenth Century Revival to the Present* (New York, 1987), 153 n. 2. Green's observation that the term 'hasid' at first denoted

affiliation only to the hasidic movement and not to a particular hasidic leader is perfectly compatible with, and may even be explained by, the suggestion that, at the end of the 18th century and the beginning of the 19th, it was still usual for youngsters joining the hasidic movement to wander from court to court and be known as 'hasidim' without associating themselves permanently with a particular hasidic master. Only when permanent affiliation with a particular master ceased to be a voluntary act by individuals who had reached the end of one stage of their spiritual journey, and became an established family tradition into which one was initiated at birth, could the term 'hasid' assume its later relative meaning of disciple or adherent of a particular hasidic leader.

241 Heilman, *Beit rabi*, the author's 'Address to the Readers' (Heb.), 14–15.

242 See above, nn. 123, 127, 184.

243 See above, n. 192; this is how R. Elimelekh of Lizhensk still understood this principle as it operated in the period of voluntary attachment and effective freedom of choice between the tsadik and his hasidim. Cf. pp. 68–71 above.

TWO

God and the Tsadik as the Two Focal Points of Hasidic Worship

IT IS GENERALLY ACCEPTED NOW, following a seminal essay by Gershom Scholem, that *devekut*—mystical adherence or cleaving, which he defined as 'communion with God'—was adopted by hasidism from earlier kabbalistic traditions and became the highest religious ideal of the movement. It was towards the fulfilment of this ideal that every hasid was expected to concentrate all his mental faculties at all times.[1] The notion that *devekut* could and should be maintained at all times is present already in the earlier kabbalistic formulations of this ideal, notably in Nahmanides' comment on Deuteronomy 11: 22: 'To love the Lord your God, to walk in all His ways and to cleave unto Him'. Nahmanides interprets the last section of this verse, 'and to cleave unto Him', as a command, in contrast to Ibn Ezra, who sees it as the end achieved by those who have already fulfilled the previous two commands listed in the verse. Nahmanides' comment reads as follows: 'This cleaving to God may well consist of remembering God and His love always. One must not allow one's consciousness to part from Him at any time, not even when one is walking, sleeping, or rising. Thus when a man engages his mouth and tongue in conversation with his fellow men, his heart should not be occupied with them but rather it should rest before God.'

While Nahmanides is suggesting that *devekut* should be sustained even through mundane, non-devotional activities, he still considers such activities as a hindrance, which the true mystic may and should overcome not by renouncing worldly life but by transcending it. For him the ideal state is of seclusion with God through the expulsion from one's higher conscious-

This essay was first read at the conference on the Jewish Religious Tradition held at the Divinity School of the University of Chicago, 17–20 April 1977.

ness, if not always from one's concrete circumstances, of all concerns with the profane material or corporeal dimension of earthly existence. The true mystic may achieve this by applying the technique of dividing his consciousness, to enable one part of it (his mouth and tongue) to carry out mundane tasks, while the other, more elevated part (his heart) continues to be absorbed in contemplation of God.[2]

In hasidism there are some early traditions that reflect practically no departure from this notion of *devekut*, insisting that it should be maintained at all times, despite the need to engage also in profane activities, which are essential for the preservation of life. But other traditions, especially those that are associated with the Besht, introduce a more positive evaluation of the profane by presenting it as a ground which is just as fertile for the cultivation of *devekut* as are devotional engagements with the sacred.

If man's contact with the Divine is conceived of as *devekut* then worship is that practice or activity that leads to its attainment. Under the call to strive for *devekut* at all times, including the times of 'walking, sleeping, or rising' or of profane conversation with one's fellowman—that is, activities which are religiously neutral or, if this notion is to be pursued to its logical conclusion, even activities which are religiously negative—then every human activity, whatever it is, becomes a potential vehicle for *devekut*. Thus the concept of worship in hasidism, particularly in the first generation of the movement, assumes a totality of scope which it had rarely entertained before. As presented by the Besht and his associates, the ideal of constant *devekut* extended the arena on which devotional activities could take place beyond the traditional rabbinic norm of study and prayer, or the traditional kabbalistic norm of ascetic practice and solitary contemplation. And even though mundane occupations had been recognized previously as an obstacle which did not necessarily preclude *devekut* because it could be divorced from the contemplative consciousness, now such occupations were proclaimed, at least by some hasidic masters, as a legitimate mode of worship in *devekut*. This was achieved by the introduction of the practice of worship by means (or in a state) of corporeality (*avodah begashmiyut*).

In the circle of the Besht R. Nahman of Kosów was one of the main advocates of constant *devekut*, which the mystic could maintain even while being engaged in mundane tasks such as business transactions:

I have heard it said of our master, R. Nahman Kosover, that he used to reproach people for not fulfilling [the request indicated by the verse in Ps. 16: 8] 'I have set the Lord always before me', even while they are dealing in merchandise and are concerned with business affairs. And if one asks how this might be possible, [the answer is that] just as a man praying in the synagogue may be thinking of various kinds of merchandise and business affairs, so it is possible to do the opposite.[3]

Notably, R. Nahman of Kosów, a tax farmer and merchant, was the only one of the Besht's associates who earned his living by pursuing a mundane occupation rather than serving, like most of them, in the 'spiritual' capacity of preacher, rabbi, or teacher.[4] The gulf between his profane occupation and his spiritual life may have heightened his sensitivity to the scope for worship that lay in 'dealing in merchandise and business affairs'—his personal response to the call for *devekut* at all times, which was shared by the entire circle. But while R. Nahman of Kosów, in allowing for the possibility of maintaining *devekut* even during commercial dealings, still resorts to the split of consciousness recommended by Nahmanides ('the opposite' of the practice he reproaches being the conduct of business affairs while at the same time thinking only of God),[5] the Besht disposes of the need for such a split by suggesting that profane conversation may itself be just as conducive to *devekut* as any sacred utterance:

I have heard it from my master [the Besht] . . . that 'unifications' [*yiḥudim*] are inherent in [all] words, whether these are words of Torah and prayer or [of] conversation with one's fellow man in the market place. Each man according to his level may be 'joined' and uplifted, either by means of sacred words or by means of profane words, which are [all] comprised of the 22 letters [of the Hebrew alphabet] etc.[6]

With the aid, in this case, of the Lurianic technique of *yiḥudim*—contemplation of the various permutations of Hebrew letters yielding divine names, into which every word in the Hebrew language may be reduced, and by which one may unite, and oneself be united with, all the apparently disparate realities of the divine realms—the Besht sees no need for divorcing man's higher consciousness from his profane speech in order to enable him to maintain his *devekut* during mundane conversation. This is because every profane utterance, in just the same way as a recitation of sacred words, is nothing but an articulated permutation of the twenty-two letters of the Hebrew alphabet. These letters are traditionally viewed by the kabbalists as a tangible manifestation of the divine presence in the material world, and thus they provide a vehicle for the ascent to God. Man's higher consciousness should therefore embrace, not discard or transcend, the profane utterance, which lends itself just as well to the realization of *devekut*.

One qualification should be stressed in this connection. Profane utterances are presented as a positive means to worship in *devekut*, not on account of their profanity as such, which is taken to be just an 'outer garment', a 'partition', or a disguise, but rather because their inner core and ultimate reality are divine. This connects them to the unity of God, which is present, albeit in disguise, throughout the universe at all times. The following passage highlights the unreality of the profane as it manifests itself in mundane activities or in 'straying thoughts' (*maḥshavot zarot*)—the mundane or illicit thoughts that distract the individual from his study and prayer, obstructing his spiritual endeavours to reach God:

A teaching received from the Besht: He who cleaves to one part of the unity cleaves to the whole. And the same applies to the opposite condition: 'I sought him whom my soul loveth, I sought him, but I found him not' [S. of S. 3: 1]. The meaning is that the great King, King of all Kings, the Holy One, blessed be He, conceals himself behind several garments and partitions, such as straying thoughts and the cessation of study and prayer. . . . But for the men of knowledge, who know that no place is empty of Him, these are not true disguises.[7]

However, there are traditions ascribed to the Besht, as well as to other members of his circle, which offer an alternative legitimation of profane activities, presenting them as a means to attaining *devekut* without denying either their profanity or their essential reality. One source for this view is the following parable:

Received from the Besht: A king had a son whom he wanted to teach various wisdoms necessary [for a prince]. He hired a number of scholars to study with him, but the prince did not learn anything. Finally, the scholars despaired of ever teaching him, and only one of them remained with the prince. One day the prince saw a young girl and desired her beauty. The scholar reported this to the king and complained. But the king said: Since he has experienced desire, even in this way, through his physical desire, he will attain all wisdoms. The king summoned the girl to court and instructed her not to submit herself to the prince until he has acquired one wisdom. The girl followed the king's instructions. On each subsequent occasion she demanded that the prince should acquire an additional wisdom, and so eventually he acquired them all. Once he became a scholar, he dismissed the girl, for he was to marry a princess of his own rank. The meaning of the parable is clear. . . . In the name of R. Sa'adyah Gaon: It is befitting for a man to learn from his desire for physical things how to desire the service of God and His love.[8]

The reference to Sa'adyah at the conclusion of the passage is inappropriate as, while Sa'adyah does describe intense physical desire in bold language, he actually condemns it as excessive, and rejects altogether the view—regrettably held by some 'ignorant fools'—that physical desire is commendable in that it teaches man how to desire God and to crave for submission to him—precisely the view that the Besht advocates in his name![9] However, even the view he falsely attributes to Sa'adyah is not quite in harmony with the Besht's parable. For while Sa'adyah allegedly presents physical desire as an allegory of the spiritual desire for God, the intensity with which it is felt serving as a measure of the intensity with which God should be desired, the Besht's parable establishes a concrete link between the two types of desire: physical desire is itself instrumental in awakening the spiritual desire for God. The girl is not an apparition, nor does she turn out in the end to be essentially spiritual and 'wise'. She is physical, profane to the core; and it is precisely in that capacity that she is enlisted in the service of a purely spiritual cause. The satisfaction of physical desire is thus rendered a precondition of the spiritual desire to know God.

Similarly, a famous parable recorded by R. Jacob Joseph of Połonne in the names of both the Besht and R. Menahem Mendel, the Magid of Bar, presents the satisfaction of a need which is irredeemably physical and profane as serving the cause of spiritual joy in God:

I have heard the following parable from my master [the Besht]: A prince was once expelled to distant lands and settled in a village inhabited by inferior men. After he had been there for a long time, a letter from his father the king reached him. The prince longed to rejoice in this letter, but he was inhibited by the villagers, who might have ridiculed him, saying, what is so special about this day and what has brought about this joy? Therefore he summoned the villagers, bought them wine and other intoxicating drinks, so that they rejoiced in the wine and he was free to rejoice in his father.[10]

Although the parable, in almost all its versions, serves to illustrate the request, addressed to every Jew, to celebrate the sabbath and festivals with both the physical pleasure of his body and the spiritual joy of his soul, once the meaning is extended to apply (as in R. Jacob Joseph of Połonne's language a little further on in the same passage) to the universal 'body' and 'soul', namely, to the ontological categories of 'matter' and 'form', or the anthropological categories of 'men of matter' and 'men of form', physical pleasure is ascribed to the former while spiritual joy appears to be the prerogative of the latter. Notably, not once does the prince of the parable himself become intoxicated with drink in order to induce his spiritual joy in the king's letter. However, other traditions suggest that this distinction is not essential to the message whereby satisfaction of the body's desires facilitates the satisfaction of the soul's yearnings.[11] Most likely, the formulation of the idea in the parable is one of several, but inconsistent, attempts to idealize the spirituality of the 'men of spirit' and to distinguish it as sharply as possible from the vulgar corporeality of 'men of matter', to the point of denying the former even the slightest awareness of their physical needs, while denying the latter the capacity for spiritual yearnings.[12] What emerges clearly as the view behind this idealized picture is that, already in the circle of the Besht, men of spirit, such as the prince who acquired wisdom through satisfying his physical desire for a beautiful girl, were thought to be capable of utilizing profane activities and thoughts (in which they engaged quite openly) to achieve the spiritual joy of *devekut*. Men of matter, on the other hand, enjoyed a more limited scope for divine service, from which were excluded all profane activities and thoughts. Paradoxically, then, although the men of matter were defined as being incapable of spiritual joy, the religious path that was set out for them consisted entirely of normative spiritual activities, in which study, and especially prayer, featured most prominently. As for their engagement in profane activities, they were expected to call a spade a spade, to accept profanity at its face value and not to attempt the impossible by investing it, as do the men of spirit, with spirituality and holiness. The original version of the parable of the prince takes up this issue more explicitly than the abridged version of *Keter shem tov*.[13] It insists that this route to *devekut* lies entirely outside the capabilities of 'commoners', in whom the satisfaction of physical desire is plainly that; it leads them no further and is simply the product of their evil inclination:

> However, all this happened only through the 'wise man', namely, the king, who could tell the outcome of the matter in advance. For this is the quality of the wise man, who can see into the future[14] and alter human nature from evil to good . . . which is not the case with the 'non-wise' man, who would have remained true to his nature, susceptible to all manner of evil desires and transgressions.[15]

Likewise, the Besht is reported to have warned:

Received from the Besht: Each man should conduct himself according to his own rank. For, if he adopts the conduct befitting another man's rank, he fails to comply either with his own or with the other man's standard. In this connection it was said: 'Many a man had done as R. Simeon bar Yohai, but failed.'[16] The meaning is that they were not of his rank but modelled themselves on him . . . and this is why they failed.'[17]

And R. Jacob Joseph of Połonne, who in this case is not, apparently, recording the view of the Besht, but whose own view seems to be in harmony with it, states specifically in connection with the practice of worship through corporeality:

In this way may be understood the saying 'Warm thyself by the fire of the wise',[18] meaning when they are in the state of *gadlut* [the 'major' or 'expansive' state of *devekut*], occupied with the fire of Torah and prayer . . . 'but beware of their glowing coals' on the days when they are in *katnut* [the 'minor' or 'diminished' state of *devekut*, which is when they engage in profane activities], for at such times they do not glow with inner fire and are therefore called a coal without inner fire. A pupil might want to emulate such a wise man when he carries out corporeal tasks. But the pupil does not know that at such times his teacher is fulfilling [the request implied in the verse] 'Thy word have I hid in mine heart' [Ps. 119: 11], namely, that he is occupied with corporeal things while at the same time contemplating their inner, spiritual core. Thus, the pupil may emulate the outer appearance of his teacher's corporeal activities and be punished.[19]

There are, it is true, quite a number of traditions which do not distinguish, at least not explicitly, between the category of 'corporeal' or 'material' men and the qualitatively different, superior category of 'men of spirit'. They thus create the impression of calling on every Jew to practise *devekut* even as he engages in profane activities. Other traditions ascribed to the Besht and some of his associates go even further by expressly inviting every individual to take responsibility for himself, securing his own path to God by subduing the forces of evil rather than trusting 'great men' to do this on his behalf. For example:

'Blessed is the people that know the joyful sound' [Ps. 89: 16]. The Besht interpreted this verse with the following parable: There was a country in which there lived a hero. All the inhabitants of that country relied on him [to fight for them] and did not learn the art of warfare. Eventually war broke. The hero wanted to prepare his weapons, but the enemy tricked him and stole all his weapons one by one, so that the hero had nothing with which to fight, and all the inhabitants of that country who had relied on him were captured with him. This is the meaning alluded to in the verse 'Blessed is the people that know the joyful sound,' namely, when the people do not rely on the hero but they know the joyful sound of war for themselves. Then 'they shall walk, O Lord, in the light of thy countenance' [ibid.] 'to meet the king' [probably 2 Sam. 19: 16].[20]

Likewise, even R. Jacob Joseph of Połonne, the chief exponent of the dichotomy between the 'spiritual' elite and the 'corporeal' masses, appears to suggest that every Jew is capable of achieving the spiritual purity and prophetic empowerment attained uniquely by Moses:

Furthermore, no pentateuchal portions other than 'Vayakhel' [Exod. 35: 1–38: 20] and 'Kedoshim tihyu' [Lev. 19–20] begin with the request for Moses to gather the entire nation together.[21] The matter has already been explained, for Moses, may he rest in peace, had said: 'Enviest thou for my sake? Would God that all the Lord's people were prophets' [Num. 11: 29], etc. Moses . . . wished the whole of Israel to attain the rank which he had attained. And this is not impossible. For man can freely choose to purify his corporeal nature to the point of reaching the rank of Moses, may he rest in peace. And Moses was distinguished from all other prophets by one other quality, namely . . . that the Shekhinah [divine presence] itself spoke through his throat. This rank also may be reached by every Israelite once he has sanctified himself with God's holiness.[22]

However, all these qualifications of the deterministic division of society into the few who naturally have and the many who cannot possibly attain the spiritual quality that would grant them direct access to God do not cancel it out. They are prompted by a genuine concern not to discourage the majority who are striving for a connection with the Divine even though they belong to the class of the spiritual 'have-nots'. But there is little doubt as to which is the truly operative notion. To exemplify this, reference might be made to a tsadik, such as R. Nahman of Bratslav two generations later. In his view of himself as a supreme tsadik, utterly different in essence and therefore in all his conduct from ordinary folk and fellow tsadikim alike, this categorization of society found one of its most extreme expressions in the entire literature of the hasidic movement. Nevertheless, R. Nahman was still able to reproach his followers on one occasion for entertaining the thought that 'the rank of the tsadik and his achievement derive only from his being endowed with a sublime soul. But he said that this was not so, for they derive mostly from good deeds, endeavour, and works. And he said explicitly that every individual can attain to the highest rank, for this depends entirely on his free will.'[23] If taken seriously, this statement would stand in stark contrast to R. Nahman's numerous declarations of the exceptional qualities and status of the tsadik, which betray his profound sense of himself as a 'unique phenomenon [*ḥidush*] the like of which the world has never seen', superior not only to other tsadikim but even to all the spiritual heroes of Israel's past.[24] For obvious didactic reasons he is challenging his followers to confront the age-old dilemma of predestination versus the doctrine of free will, but there is no doubt that he is all too aware of their inherent limitations.

Admittedly, while it stressed the corporeal vulgarity of the masses time and again, early hasidism did promise them the possibility of transcending it. Without this promise it would be hard to explain the immense success of the movement. But, with the exception of a few relatively marginal trends in the early generations, as well as the singular exception of Habad,[25] the masses were being urged to realize this promise not by emulating the spiritual elite but by 'cleaving' or 'adhering' to it, that is, by setting at the focus of their inherently limited religiosity not God but rather the figure of the 'man of spirit', who was eventually defined institutionally as the tsadik. The true scope for exercising their free will lay, for the masses, in either choosing or failing to choose to adhere with unquestioning faith to their particular tsadik, and it is not by accident that precisely the same terms as were used in respect of the tsadik's connection to God were used also in respect of the connection of ordinary hasidim to their tsadik.

It is important to consider all this alongside the suggestion, made more than once, that early or 'primitive' hasidism not only widened the scope for worship in *devekut* to cover the full range of human experience, but that it also opened up the possibility of fulfilling this ideal to every single Jew.[26] As Gershom Scholem famously claimed: 'Hasidic *Devekut* is no longer an extreme ideal to be realized by some rare and sublime spirits at the end of the path. It is no longer the last rung in the ladder of ascent, as in Kabbalism, but the first. Everything begins with man's decision to cleave to God. *Devekut* is the starting point and not the end. Everyone is able to realize it instantaneously.'[27] However, Scholem himself sensed that this was an oversimplification of the hasidic departure from the kabbalistic ideal and, a little further on in the same work, he injected a note of ambivalence to his earlier observation:

> It sounds very simple and anyone might start practicing it, but it is extremely difficult to attain as a sustained state of communion. Why should not anyone be able to concentrate all the inwardness of the spiritual element in everything? As a matter of fact, it is a counsel given not to the accomplished Kabbalist at the end of his path, but repeatedly addressed to everybody. Yet, it has the unmistakable ring of a mystical practice which has its esoteric side and is by no means as easy to carry out as it appears to be.[28]

It would seem, in fact, that, already in the first generation of hasidism, the ideal of *devekut* was conceived of as anything but capable of universal fulfilment or, rather, it was viewed as something that could not be fulfilled by everyone in the same way. Although the gap between ordinary people and 'spiritual men' could be bridged over (on which more below), it was so fundamental that it would be misleading to deny its existence altogether with the claim that 'early hasidism' had democratized the old elitist ideal of *devekut*. Right from the start, the Besht and his associates, almost without exception, were so conscious of the spiritual qualities that distinguished them from everyone else that at times they seem to have taken the distinction for granted. Admittedly, not all of them were as preoccupied as was R. Jacob Joseph of Połonne with the dichotomy between the 'spiritual' elite and the 'corporeal' or 'material' majority. But even if we cannot entirely trust the language in which their pronouncements have been preserved, especially since so many of them were recorded by R. Jacob Joseph himself (who might be suspected of allowing his own sensibilities to colour the views he attributed to others), they still betray a shared notion of the dichotomy between the two classes and its implication for their respective modes of worship. For example, R. Jacob Joseph seems to favour the terms 'men of matter' (*anshei ḥomer*) and 'men of form' (*anshei tsurah*); he contrasts them time and again and often analogizes them to the correspondingly dichotomous categories of 'body' and 'soul'. But the juxtaposition of 'vulgar masses' (*hamonei am*) with 'men of spirituality' (*anshei haruḥani*) is ascribed with some measure of consistence to R. Nahman of Horodenka.[29] And in the traditions recorded specifically in the name of the Besht, the terms 'men of knowledge' (*anshei da'at*), 'men of understanding' (*anshei binah*), 'the perfect man' (*ha'adam hashalem*),[30] as well as the more standard terms 'scholar' (*talmid ḥakham*), 'teacher' (*rav*), and 'righteous man' (*tsadik*), which was widely used but as yet devoid of institutional connotations, all alternate in reference to the ideal mode of worship in *devekut*, distinguishing it either explicitly or implicitly from the devotional practices and aspirations that are appropriate for ordinary people. To show that the ideal state of *devekut* applied only to the superior category of 'spiritual men' even when this was not stated explicitly, we may return to a tradition, cited earlier on, which was recorded more than once by R. Jacob Joseph of Połonne in the name of the Besht. This was the warning, clearly addressed to ordinary people, urging them not to emulate the 'scholars' when the latter are engaged in profane activities while still maintaining their *devekut*, albeit in the diminished state of *katnut*.[31] The warning appears at the end of a longer passage whose central theme is the difference between *katnut* and *gadlut*, the minor and major states of *devekut*.[32] The entire passage is an explanation of the saying in Mishnah *Avot* 2: 10: 'Warm thyself by the fire of the wise but beware of their glowing coals, lest thou be burnt,' with which the discussion opens and concludes. The description, in this passage, of *devekut* as it is practised during each of the two states (*katnut* and *gadlut*) can be read as if it was intended for universal application: the subject is plain 'man', and one of the opportunities for worship in *katnut* is 'idle conversation with one's fellow man' (*sipurim shemesaper im ḥavero*), as if all were equally capable of transforming idle talk into an act of worship. Only at the end of the paragraph, which still forms part of the tradition reported in the name of the Besht, do we learn that it is only the idle talk of the 'wise man', the 'sage', or the 'scholar' that qualifies as a devotional act, while his 'pupil'—the ordinary person—who cannot see beyond the apparent corporeality of his master's actions, is warned not to emulate him when he seems to be engaging in profane activities.[33] Likewise, a teaching by R. Jacob Joseph of Połonne, in which he points out the lowest starting point of the ascent to *devekut*, would seem at first sight to be addressed to any 'man', although it soon becomes clear that this was by no means the author's intention. The passage reads as follows:

> 'Thus [with this] shall Aaron come into the Holy Place' [Lev. 16: 3]. The meaning is that 'this' is . . . the lowest rung of the ten sublime *sefirot* [i.e. Malkhut] with which the world was created. And when *man* is at this low rung, either worshipping or engaged in the affairs of this world, such as business affairs etc., the following advice may be given to the *perfect man*: He should realize that this is the rung of Shekhinah [God's immanence; Malkhut]. He should then pray from this

low level, which is called 'this', and from there he may ascend further, into the holy place.[34]

Universal 'man' becomes 'the perfect man' almost incidentally, indicating the real addressees of the author's advice. Occasionally R. Jacob Joseph, who is unquestionably the most insistent on the distinction between the two classes, does highlight it when he interprets the somewhat less explicit traditions which he records in the name of others. He does this, for example, on one of the many occasions when he reports R. Judah Leyb Pistiner's interpretation of the verse (Ps. 12: 2) 'for the faithful fail from among the children of men':

I have already mentioned in the name of the late pietist [*ḥasid*], R. Judah Leyb Pistiner, the meaning of the verse . . . 'Help, Lord, for the godly man ceaseth; for the faithful fail from among the children of men' etc. The verse may be interpreted in two ways, either from the beginning to the end or from the end to the beginning. Thus, because the 'godly man', the [category of] men of form, ceases, therefore ordinary 'children of men', that is, the men of matter, have no faith. And vice versa: The reason why the 'godly man' ceases is that ordinary men have no faith.[35]

It is quite likely that R. Jacob Joseph himself added to R. Judah Leyb's interpretation the identification of the 'godly man' with the 'man of form', and that of the 'children of men' with ordinary 'men of matter'. But this addition by no means distorts the original interpretation; it only translates it into R. Jacob Joseph's favourite terms. And even where there is no mention at all of the distinction between the two categories of men or of their respective modes of worship, it is still clear that, more often than not, when the ideal of *devekut* is set as a target, the expectation of fulfilment is restricted to those who are capable of exercising exceptional spiritual powers. For example the following tradition is ascribed to the Besht: 'Received from the Besht: One should adhere [*yadbik*] one's thought to the infinite Divine Light which is contained in the letters. . . . This is an important rule to be applied to the study of Torah and to prayer. Furthermore, it enables one to cancel evil judgments.'[36] Similarly, another tradition concerning the Besht's special method of attaining *devekut* during Torah study and prayer by means of 'cleaving' or 'adhering' to the Hebrew letters cannot possibly have meant to apply to ordinary people, even though he does not exclude them explicitly:

According to a tradition received from my master [the Besht], the essence of Torah and prayer is for a man to cleave to the inner aspect and spirituality of the infinite Divine Light contained in the letters of the text of Torah and prayer. This is called study [of Torah] for its own sake. Concerning this R. Meir said: 'Whosoever labours in the Torah for its own sake merits many things . . . to him the secrets of the Torah are revealed' etc. [Mishnah *Avot* 6: 1] This means that from the Torah he will know the future and all that will happen to him.[37]

In both these cases the Besht attributes pneumatic powers to his method of Torah study and prayer, which utilizes the Hebrew letters of which such texts are made up as a means of attaining the ideal state of *devekut*.[38] There is no doubt that these powers were thought to be supernatural. The Besht possessed them, as did a number of his immediate associates, but not the mass of ordinary people who marvelled at their miraculous feats. Nor could just anyone strive to acquire such extraordinary powers. The promise that one would gain the ability to cancel 'evil judgments' or to see into the future surely was not made to everyone. These powers were thought at the time of the Besht, just as they seem to us now, to be available only to those who are born to be receptive of them, even though, through the failure to state this explicitly, the Besht appears to be inviting everyone to exercise clairvoyance and to avert divinely ordained suffering.

Where the distinction between the scope for *devekut* that was open respectively to the elect few and, quite differently, to the majority of ordinary people remained implicit in the earliest literature of hasidism, this was so simply because it was unnecessary to state what was so deeply and naturally felt as to be taken for granted.[39] The reasons for this become evident when one examines critically (inasmuch as this is possible, given the anachronistic perspective of the later sources) the nature of the affiliation between the Besht and his associates, as well as the relationship between R. Dov Ber, the Magid of Mezhirech (Międzyrzecz), and his disciples and followers in what is commonly, if somewhat misleadingly, termed the first two 'generations' of hasidism.

Through the efforts of a number of distinguished scholars in the past, the origins and organization of these early hasidic circles have become better known. Ben-Zion Dinur drew attention to the existence of groups of pietists known as hasidim both before and during the time of the Besht. He argued that the Beshtian hasidic movement must be viewed within the context of these proto-hasidic circles, since some of their members, mentioned in the works of R. Jacob Joseph of Połonne and others of his generation, as well as in *Shivḥei habesht*, subsequently came to be seen as the Besht's disciples.[40] J. G. Weiss further advanced our understanding of the conditions from which the new hasidic leadership arose, by portraying the Besht as a member, and not necessarily the one and only leader, of a circle whose views and activities later became associated primarily with him.[41] Finally, and most convincingly, A. J. Heschel provided abundant evidence to show that several of the Besht's early associates, who had been described as his faithful devotees by later hasidic hagiographers and historians alike,[42] were, in fact, independent hasidim who, in some cases, commanded their own following and regarded the Besht as their equal, if not, indeed, as their rival or as inferior to themselves.[43] This can be read between the lines even of *Shivḥei habesht*, which is heavily biased in favour of the Besht's supreme leadership of the entire circle, projecting the distinctive organizational reality of its own time of composition onto a period that preceded it by several decades.[44] Clearly, the inconsistent use in the early sources of interchangeable terms such as 'men of form' or 'spiritual', 'perfect', 'righteous', or even 'learned' men, in reference to the superior category of the 'heads', namely, the spiritual leaders, reflects the fluidity of the situation at a time when it was far from clear who was considered a spiritual master by whom and in relation to whom, and who was seen as a mere 'material', 'corporeal', or ordinary man. Surely, R. Pinhas of Korets (Korzec), R. Aryeh Leyb of Połonne, R. Nahman of Kosów, and others of their ilk cannot be classified as 'ordinary'—devoid of spiritual insight and powers of their own—in relation to the Besht. And, with some qualifications, the same can be said of a significant number of the Magid of Mezhirech's disciples. While he was acknowledged by many in his day as their spiritual mentor, some of the Besht's associates, notably R. Jacob Joseph of Połonne and R. Pinhas of Korets, rejected his leadership,[45] while others who did accept it clearly belonged to his own 'spiritual' category and proceeded, already during his lifetime and with his blessing, to establish their own circles of followers and to operate, for all intents and purposes, as full-fledged tsadikim in their own right.[46] However, in the zeal to dispel the misguided notion that all these early charismatic figures were submissive disciples, first of the Besht and subsequently of the Magid of Mezhirech, the scholars who so aptly stressed that many among them were, in fact, no less spiritually endowed than either of the two allegedly supreme leaders overshot their mark when they drew from it the conclusion—seemingly warranted by the dearth of evidence on the concrete circumstances and manner in which spiritual authority was exercised at the time—that the Besht, and following him the Magid, 'democratized' mystical ideals which had previously been accessible only to a small kabbalistic elite. Moreover, this putative democratization has been presented as being particularly striking, given that it constituted a radical, albeit short-lived, departure,[47] not only from the elitist exclusivity of the past, but also from the rapid reinstatement of the elitist framework in the almost immediate future, as with the rise of institutionalized tsadikism a generation or two later, the direct mystical path to God, which had been briefly opened up to admit all and sundry, was once again barred to the rank-and-file followers of hasidism.[48]

This appreciation of 'primitive' hasidism must be modified, particularly in view of the lingering currency of popular, uncritical designations of the nascent movement as a religion 'of the people', proclaiming the dignity of common man and putting within his reach the spiritual quality of religious life which had been denied him by both the corrupt oligarchic regime that governed Jewish communal life in eighteenth-century Poland and the exclusive 'aristocratic' circles of kabbalistic adepts. Thus we read, for example, that 'the Ari [R. Isaac Luria] lifted God up to Heaven, where He resides remote from the lower world of life and action. Then came the Besht and brought God down to earth, restoring Him to the people, to all His living creatures. The Besht's God is the folk's God, even though He "disguises" Himself . . . while the Ari's God is aristocratic;' or 'The broad social basis of hasidism was made up of the petty bourgeoisie . . . and the poor, who played no part in the economy. It was this Jewish population, in the villages and small provincial towns, that invested hasidism with its democratic character and stamped it with its folkish hallmark;' or 'The implication of the divine presence being everywhere and accessible to all people was a blurring of distinctions between Jews: all were . . . capable of revealing God in every thought and action . . . Whereas the kabbalistic tradition saw access to the Divine as restricted to a knowledgeable elite, hasidism saw it as open to all.'[49]

There is a fusion here of two quite distinct pairs of conflicting ideas: divine immanence as against transcendence on the one hand, and a democratic as against an aristocratic religious doctrine on the other. It is generally true that Luria's God is transcendent while the Besht's God is immanent.[50] But in effect, Luria's notion of God's relation to the created world is much more egalitarian than the Besht's. Ultimately his God is equally inaccessible to all, in that he has removed himself from this world in order to create it. For the Besht, on the other hand, God is directly accessible, but only to those who can see through his earthly disguises. And to see through God's disguises, to experience his immediate presence, one has to be exceptionally endowed with spiritual insight. The Besht does not consider himself, nor is he considered by others, as 'an average scholar and a simple man, no more'.[51] He is indeed an average scholar, perhaps worse, and a simple man, but the crucial fact is that he is, and is recognized to be, much more than that: he has, for the lack of a better term, that elusive quality we call charisma; he can perform supernatural acts; he can read people's minds and see into the future; he can interfere with God's schemes and alter their outcome. What is more, as has been shown by Dinur, Weiss, and Heschel, he is not the only one. Quite a few of his associates, the progenitors of hasidism, are endowed with these extraordinary qualities. The circle exudes a collective sense of its own uniqueness.[52] This is neither the exclusivity that marked the traditional kabbalistic elite, nor the sense of privilege shared by the products of the age-old alliance between rabbinic scholarship and wealth, who traditionally made up the ruling classes of the Jewish communities, but it is all the same the clear sense of constituting an elite group. The novelty it represents is not in discarding the elitist framework as such but rather in altering the criteria by which membership of the elite was to be defined, substituting intellectuality with emotionality, and reclusive asceticism with direct engagement with the lives of ordinary people and the affairs of this world. Far from bringing God down to the people, hasidism, right from the start, effectively did precisely the opposite: it blocked entirely and a priori the ordinary person's direct route to God by placing in the middle of that route a superior class of charismatic men whom it depicted as being 'righteous', 'wise', or 'perfect', as 'men of form', of 'spirit', or of 'understanding', who would eventually come to be designated tsadikim. To put the point more poignantly at the risk, perhaps, of being a little unfair, it can be said that in 'primitive' just as much as in 'mature' hasidism, the majority of ordinary people could not follow the direct route to God precisely because a minority of extraordinary people were blocking it, insisting that every contact with God should be regulated or 'channelled' by them. As R. Nahman of Bratslav, a great-grandson of the

Besht, was to state only a few decades later, 'Before the True Tsadik [a designation by which he commonly alluded to himself] came into the world, it was possible to attach oneself to God Himself. But now that the True Tsadik is in the world, it is truly impossible to attach oneself to God by any means other than the merit of attaching oneself to the Tsadik.'[53] The only difference in this respect between the early and the mature stage in the development of hasidism lay in the loosely defined and as yet uninstitutional nature of the spiritual elite in the earlier stage.[54]

The collective elitist consciousness of the early circle explains the inconsistent articulation of such restrictions as were being imposed on the accessibility of the highest mystical goal of *devekut*. That direct contact with God, and all the powers which ensue from it, could be attained only by the spiritually endowed was self-evident and did not need to be stated explicitly to an intimate audience consisting predominantly of equally endowed men. Moreover, the elitist consciousness which characterizes the entire circle is in perfect harmony with the atmosphere prevalent in the pre-Beshtian hasidic circles, which, as is now acknowledged by all, were the immediate ancestors of the new hasidic movement.[55] For these pietistic circles were pronouncedly elitist. And it is important to remember that, at the very start of his career as a spiritual master, the Besht could conceive of no other validation of his spiritual prowess but admission into one of these highly exclusive circles of pietistic kabbalists.[56] In fact, far from the demotic figure he is so often said to have been, the Besht can be described as an aspiring elitist and a religious-social climber. He was rejected by the Brody circle at first because he did not conform to the traditional qualifications for admission, but eventually the entire circle, as *Shivḥei habesht* testifies, perhaps hyperbolically, swung round to his distinctive style of worship while retaining—and this is the crucial point—its traditional elitist framework. Surely, without some unequivocal evidence that the barriers separating the masses from the elite were being programmatically eradicated by the Besht and his charismatic associates, it is much more plausible to assume continuity, in this respect, from the immediate precursors to the immediate successors of 'primitive' hasidism than it is to stipulate a sudden break from the traditionally exclusive framework, which was soon after, with the alleged degeneration of hasidism into a cult of the tsadikim, reinstated so completely as to reinforce its elitist nature and even to inject it with extra vigour and rigidity.

Perhaps the best test of the extent to which the elitist framework was retained despite the fact that its boundaries were being redefined is the fate of the Lurianic *kavanot* of prayer in early hasidism. It has been shown that, without ever opposing it explicitly, the Besht effectively abandoned the practice of this highly technical system of contemplation aids, which had been used by generations of kabbalists since Luria, including the circles of kabbalistic hasidim from whose ranks the early hasidic leadership arose.[57] The Besht apparently substituted Luria's *kavanot* with his own, whose precise nature is not quite clear. From the time of the Magid of Mezhirech on, explicit objections to the system of the Lurianic *kavanot* were raised, mostly on the grounds that they did not enhance but rather obstructed the endeavour to realize the new hasidic ideal of *devekut*. Joseph Weiss, who first observed the phasing out of Luria's *kavanot* in hasidism, described them as 'an aristocratic art' and suggested that

> The practice of the elaborate technique of the Lurianic Kavvanoth was by necessity confined to the limited number of a spiritual elite who could cope with the immense intellectual task of countless contemplative flying visits to precisely charted points of the Sephirotic Universe. . . . It is very doubtful whether Israel Baalshem himself was fully qualified as a Kabbalist to become one of those initiated into the mysteries of meditative prayer life.[58]

Implied in this is the misleading suggestion that, since the Lurianic *kavanot* were beyond his grasp and might have offended his spontaneous religiosity, the Besht devised a simplified system which was more accessible to all those who did not belong to the traditional kabbalistic elite. In fact, from the descriptions of the Besht's prayer as they appear in *Shivḥei habesht* it emerges quite clearly that his method was even less accessible to the uninitiated and required greater and more exceptional spiritual powers than Luria's *kavanot*.[59] On one occasion, meditation during his extraordinarily prolonged prayer entailed conversations with myriads of souls of the dead and the endeavour to effect *tikunim* (restore them to purity and wholeness) for all of them.[60] On a second occasion he lingered in meditation, of a distinctly non-Lurianic type, over one verse from the psalms which is normally recited during the morning service, engaging in clairvoyance with the object of averting an event threatening the life of a certain Jew.[61] Surely, this cannot possibly be construed as a popular practice substituting an elitist one. In principle the Lurianic *kavanot* could be studied by anyone willing to devote the time and effort required for mastering them. The books prescribing these *kavanot* in detail were available and could be consulted, which is precisely what R. Elijah of Sokołówka—the young man who witnessed the second instance of the Besht at prayer mentioned above—proceeded to do when he was puzzled by the Besht's lengthy meditation on the Psalms verse, wrongly assuming it to be a Lurianic *kavanah* unknown to him. But the Besht's own method was beyond his grasp; it clearly could not be followed by the uninspired.

The most famous pronouncement on the Lurianic *kavanot* by the Magid of Mezhirech is the following: 'This resembles a door which may be opened with a key. But there are thieves who open it with something which can break iron. Thus the ancients used to employ in meditation the appropriate *kavanah* for each thing. Now, however, we have no *kavanah*. Only the breaking of the heart opens [the door] to everything.'[62] The Magid, too, rejects the *kavanot* of Luria, not because they are an elitist practice but because they offend his religious sensibility. As a true spiritualist for whom prayer in *devekut* entails total loss of individual self-awareness, he considers the *kavanot* to be too restrictive, too demanding of the intellect to allow the self to be extinguished as it strives to merge with the Divine.[63] But this is not to say that his ideal of prayer in *devekut* is any easier to realize or more widely accessible than prayer with Luria's *kavanot*. On the contrary, anyone can open a locked door by turning the key. But when the key is not available, the truly ordinary, uninspired man simply stays out (unless, as we shall see, he can rely on someone else to unlock the door for him). The ingenious thief, on the other hand, who is highly skilled in his own way, is able to overcome the problem by tackling the lock and breaking in. Alternatively, if the dominant image here is not that of the thief's ingenuity and skill but rather the impatient impulsivity and brute force of the burglar who smashes the door down with 'something which can break iron', then the ideal is still the prerogative only of those who are endowed with immense spiritual force.

It is quite clear that the line of demarcation that separated those who could fulfil this ideal from those who could not (at least not without the intermediacy of others) was not drawn around the hasidic community as a whole to the exclusion of anyone who remained outside it, but rather, it cut across the entire Jewish community, distinguishing the spiritual supermen from the masses with greater rigour than was ever invested in the division between the followers of hasidism and those who either ignored or opposed it.[64] For the emergent hasidic movement was markedly not what has sometimes been called an 'introversionist' sect,[65] feeding on a collective sense of its own election while holding all outsiders doomed to eternal damnation. Rather, its vision of society, or at least of Jewish society, was all-embracing. As the deterministic division between the spiritually gifted and the irredeemably ordinary person was more operative than the traditional doctrine of free will, the distinction between those who exercised their free will badly by failing to adhere to the hasidic masters and those who exercised it well by subjecting themselves to their authority never acquired the force of the distinction between the spiritual types, who formed the hasidic leadership, and the ordinary people, who made up the bulk of their followers.

The few, and relatively marginal, exceptions to this rule (apart from Habad, which, constituting a unique case, deserves special treatment and is therefore excluded from the present discussion) confirm the general picture by their very marginality and isolation.

Thus R. Meshulam Feibush Heller of Zbaraż sensed the elitist undertones of the Besht's, and especially the Magid's, pronouncements on worship in *devekut* and rejected not only the Lurianic *kavanot* of prayer[66] but also the hasidic ideal of *devekut*,[67] which had originally ousted them, particularly *devekut* as it was to be achieved through corporeal, profane activities.[68] R. Meshulam argued that the *kavanot* of Luria on the one hand, and *devekut* on the other, had been intended for a select group of supreme religious authorities of the past, but not for himself or his contemporaries. As Rivka Schatz-Uffenheimer has rightly observed, R. Meshulam appears to have substituted an ethical ideal of his own, capable of universal application, for the more radical mystical ideal of *devekut*.[69] Notably, he contrasts non-hasidic Torah study as practised by members of the rabbinic elite, who have been accused in hasidism of abusing their learning for the sake of self-aggrandizement, not—as one would have expected—with the Besht's (and the Magid's) method of attaining *devekut* during Torah study by means of contemplating the letters of the alphabet comprising the text, but rather with his own ideal of study in constant 'fear of sin' leading to humility, of which he conceives not in the Magid's sense of mystical self-nullification but in the traditional ethical sense of self-abasement.[70]

In summing up, it is appropriate to pose the question again: If, right from the start, hasidism confined the possibility of direct access to God to a small elite of spiritual men while denying it to the ordinary person, then what did it offer the ordinary person that seemed attractive enough to account for the movement's rapidly increasing popularity? As was suggested earlier on, while it denied him direct access, it guaranteed the ordinary person access to God by means of his adherence to those who experienced it directly. It may be argued that the present discussion so far has been inclined to overlook the crucial importance of this point. Indeed, from the viewpoint of the potential recruit to hasidism, does it matter very much whether he is guaranteed the means of 'cleaving' to God directly or through the intermediacy of a direct recipient of divine grace? Whatever admissions of his inherent limitations it required of the ordinary person a priori, it is clear that the doctrine was effective in injecting him with the sense of his own communion with God.

Of the way in which this worked, we read in the writings of R. Jacob Joseph of Połonne: 'There are two kinds of *devekut*: one is that of the learned, who cleave to God directly, and the other is that of the common people, who do not know how to cleave to the Lord directly. Therefore the Torah commands them, "thou shalt cleave unto him" [Deut. 10: 20], meaning, to cleave to the learned, which is like cleaving to God.'[71] There is no need here to expound this important doctrine further. With regard to the writings of R. Jacob Joseph of Połonne, the topic has been given exhaustive coverage by Samuel Dresner in his work *The Zaddik*.[72] As for the Magid of Mezhirech, although several studies have focused on particular aspects of his mystical teaching,[73] there is as yet no analysis of the social setting in which he operated, and we are still unclear about the nature of the audiences he addressed, or of his relationship with the hasidic leaders who considered themselves his disciples. However, owing to the virtual absence from the compilations of his sermons of the doctrine of the descent of the tsadik or his mission on behalf of all ordinary people, a doctrine which is so prominent in the writings of R. Jacob Joseph of Połonne (and, inasmuch as this is possible to ascertain, also in the original teachings of the Besht), it has been suggested that

> no activity which he [the Magid] attributes to the tsadik is unique to him. Such activities . . . are, in fact, the duty of every Jew. The only difference is that the tsadik is certain to be more successful than anyone else in carrying them out. In other words: the tsadik appears here as an ideal figure, the model for everyone

else's behaviour. Whatever the tsadik does, anyone can and should do. The Magid renounces in principle the unique religious status of the tsadik.[74]

This representation of the Magid's position seems far too extreme. The conspicuous absence from his teachings of the social dimension of the tsadik's role can be attributed to his lack of interest in this dimension of the role—which is so marked, by contrast, in the writings of R. Jacob Joseph of Połonne—more plausibly than to any conscious renunciation on his part of the tsadik's unique quality. The difference between his religious temperament and that of R. Jacob Joseph of Połonne can entirely account for the Magid's silence on such issues as the structure of society or the responsibility towards the wider community of the spiritually gifted man. For him, the responsibility of the true mystic was towards himself in God; it was his task to renounce all sense of himself in order to be incorporated in the divine 'nothingness', to the point of merging with it completely. It is difficult to imagine that he was so out of touch with reality as to believe everyone to be capable of achieving this goal. More likely, addressing a group of intimate disciples-associates, who clearly belonged to his own class of spiritual men, and of whom many were soon to acquire, or had already acquired, a following of their own, he did not feel the need to dwell on the exclusion of others from the practices he advocated within his circle. Moreover, as Weiss himself noted, the doctrine of the descent of the tsadik from the height of *devekut* to the level of ordinary people's mundane or even sinful existence, a doctrine which was obviously not taught in the school of the Magid, was instantly and enthusiastically adopted by the self-same school shortly after his death. It was incorporated into its main body of teachings as soon as it became known through the publication, in 1780–1, of the works of R. Jacob Joseph of Połonne, where it featured so prominently, often in the name of the Besht.[75] Surely, if this doctrine, which was based entirely on the supposition that ordinary people were incapable of fulfilling the mystical ideal for themselves, had been out of tune with the Magid's own teaching, it would not have been integrated so smoothly and unapologetically into the teachings of the majority of his disciples.

It seems, then, that right from the start, and more unequivocally so with the institutionalization of the leadership of hasidism, it was the duty of a minority of spiritually endowed men to 'cleave' to God, while the duty of all ordinary people was to 'cleave' to their leaders. As was mentioned above, it is not by accident that the same weighty term, 'to cleave', is used to describe the nature of the connection in both cases: the ordinary person stands in relation to the tsadik as the tsadik stands in relation to God. Just as God is the focus of the tsadik's religious life, so the tsadik is the focus of the ordinary person's religiosity. To convey the concrete sense of the ordinary person's cleaving to the tsadik as his only point of access to the deity, the following passage may be quoted, advising on how to facilitate the 'cleaving' to God (in this case the term *hitkasherut*—'bonding'—is used, which is synonymous to *devekut*) at the time of prayer:

> Even though he cannot pray with awe and love, his prayer may be uplifted by means of his bonding himself [*hitkasherut*], when he says: I hereby undertake to fulfil the positive commandment of 'Love your fellow man as you love yourself' [JT *Ned.* 9*d*]. With perfect love he should incorporate himself in the holy souls [of] those righteous men [*tsadikim*] of the generation with whose physiognomy he is familiar. At such times he should visualize their physiognomy in his mind. This is of great and special benefit.[76]

At times of prayer the man who cannot pray with true 'awe and love' of God is advised to contemplate the familiar face of his tsadik.

There is little wonder therefore that the hasidim were so fond of such turns of phrase as allowed them, on the one hand, to analogize the figure of the tsadik to God and, on the other hand, to depict him as partaking of God's tasks, all within the perfectly legitimate tradition of rabbinic and kabbalistic literature.[77] One such example is the reference to the tsadik as creator of the world. Rabbinic tradition bestows the title of 'God's partner in Creation' on individuals who distinguish themselves in righteousness and piety.[78] The Zohar attributes to the righteous the ability to create new worlds by their wise utterances, an ability which is portrayed as analogous to God's creation of the world by means of his Ten Utterances of Creation.[79] In hasidic literature the motif recurs often. Echoing all these earlier traditions, the Magid of Mezhirech, for example, taught:

> 'Unto thee, O Lord, belongeth mercy; for thou renderest to every man according to his work' [Ps. 63: 13]. This may be understood by way of analogy to a craftsman who works for an employer. What reward does he receive if not the wage of his labour? For, surely, the employer does not award him the full value of his labour. This is comparable to a country where a king has been appointed to rule.

The king rewards the princes [who appointed him] and pays each one according to the value of his effort. But he cannot reward them as they had done for him, by bestowing the crown of kingship on any one of them. By contrast the Holy One, blessed be He, does reward measure for measure: he who proclaims God king, God makes him king over all the universes; God decrees and he cancels the decree, and the righteous create worlds[80] [and resurrect the dead and call upon infertile women].[81]

R. Elimelekh of Lizhensk (Leżajsk), a disciple of the Magid of Mezhirech and the man who is often described as the chief theoretician of institutionalized tsadikism, employs the notion of the tsadik as creator to explain the means by which he can, according to rabbinic tradition, overrule God and cancel his decrees:

For God created and made His world, and He does with it as He pleases. On the other hand, God created the tsadik, who is able to cancel his decrees. How is it possible that he [the tsadik] is able to cancel the decrees which had been decreed in Heaven, in the upper worlds? This may be explained . . . by the verse 'By the word of the Lord were the heavens made' [Ps. 33: 6], that is, by means of the tsadik's pursuit of Torah [i.e. the Lord's word] for its own sake, and by his new interpretations of it, new heavens are created, and he performs the act of Creation. The decrees are thus cancelled of themselves [*mimeila*], for they are not included in those newly created worlds.[82]

The same author returns to this subject in an attempt, once again, to explain the tsadik's ability to cancel God's decrees. He portrays him as a partner, with God and the Shekhinah, in the creation of man:

The Talmud says: 'There are three partners in [the creation of] each human being: The Holy One, blessed be He, his father, and his mother' [BT *Kid.* 30*b*]. This means that the tsadik is his father, for he is called 'father', as [in the case of] Elisha, who said to Elijah: 'My father, my father, the chariot of Israel' [2 Kgs 2: 12]. And his mother, that is to say, *keneset yisra'el* [the congregation of Israel] is the Shekhinah. 'His father ejaculates the white semen', that is, the tsadik whitewashes transgressions and converts judgments into mercy.[83]

Louis Jacobs, who refers to this passage in his book on hasidic prayer,[84] describes 'R. Elimelech's zeal for Zaddikism' as 'bordering on the blasphemous'. Indeed, R. Elimelekh, as all others within the movement who sensed the tsadik to be the real focus of religious life, bordered on blasphemy without ever quite falling into it. The tsadik was never deified; he never became the object of worship in his own right, despite such stark statements as, for example, 'It is possible that in the [messianic] future everyone will refer to the tsadikim by the [divine] name El',[85] or 'The tsadik is the image of God for his generation.'[86] It is not impossible that such attempts as we do occasionally hear of, to worship a hasidic master even after his death instead of seeking another living tsadik to adhere to, were curtailed with at least an unconscious awareness of the possible degeneration of such devotion to an otherworldly tsadik into a cult of leaders who are venerated as quasi-deities, which the tsadikim fell decidedly, but not by far, short of becoming. The following tradition may be mentioned in this connection: After the death (in 1813) of Jacob Isaac, 'the Jew' of Pshischa (Przysucha), R. Mendel of Kotsk (Kock) was anxious to find a new teacher. 'The Jew' appeared to him in a dream and offered to remain his teacher even after death. R. Mendel replied: 'I do not wish for a teacher from the World to Come.'[87] Whether or not this late story is authentic, it reflects a clear preference for personal contact with a living tsadik down here, on earth, over communion with a dead tsadik who is, uncomfortably, a little too proximate to God in Heaven.

It is not a coincidence that the one hasidic circle in whose writings the formal analogy between the tsadik and God is most frequently and unequivocally stated is also the circle which, alone in the entire hasidic camp (until the demise, in 1994, of the last Lubavitcher Rebbe, who was never succeeded and who has, indeed, become—at least for the 'messianist' faction within Habad hasidism—the focus of a cult in which the tsadik's messianic and divine dimensions have been fused together), and controversially so, still continues to worship its eighteenth-century founder, R. Nahman of Bratslav, as their one and only True Tsadik, who would never be succeeded, despite the fact that he died in 1810. In the teachings of R. Nahman, as well as in the works of subsequent Bratslav authors, the Lurianic myth of God's withdrawal from this world (*tsimtsum*), and his paradoxical mode of self-revelation, were applied wholesale to the tsadik—R. Nahman.[88] The parallel between God and R. Nahman was perceived so vividly that, at times, it would appear that God ceased to be the original of whom R. Nahman was the replica, to become himself a divine replica of the original, R. Nahman. Thus, for example, a certain feature of R. Nahman's biography, namely, his controversy with a neighbouring fellow tsadik, R. Aryeh Leyb of Shpola (Szpoła), was interpreted as a manifestation of *tsimtsum* and projected onto God's biography according to Luria.[89] R. Nahman sensed God's transcendence in relation to this world with the full severity of the literal meaning of Luria's notion of *tsimtsum*, while at the same time acknowledging the clash between this sensibility and the overriding hasidic perception of God's immanence, albeit in a state of concealment. He believed that this contradiction would be resolved, that is, that God's all-pervasive presence would shine through his apparent absence, but only at the end of days, in the messianic era.[90] And it was this notion of God's concealment as his only mode of self-revelation in the present that R. Nahman projected onto himself: he likewise underwent *tsimtsum* and was capable of fully revealing himself to his followers only by means of withdrawal or concealment, apparently beyond their reach.[91] It is not surprising that his death was seen by his hasidim as one such act of 'withdrawal', by which alone he was able to reveal himself to the world, at least until such time as he would return to earth, to complete the messianic project that he never managed to accomplish in his lifetime.[92] *Likutei tefilot*, the collection of prayers composed by R. Nahman's disciple and scribe, Nathan Sternharz, after the death of his master and by direct inspiration from his recorded teachings as they appeared in the collection of his sermons, *Likutei moharan*, contains adaptations of most of the sermons into prayer form—a unique type of composition for which R. Nathan was attacked by Bratslav's hasidic opponents.[93] It is interesting to compare R. Nahman's teaching on *tsimtsum* in *Likutei moharan* with the prayer in *Likutei tefilot* which was modelled on it. The teaching begins with a stark statement of the literal meaning (*peshat*) of the Lurianic concept of God's transcendence through *tsimtsum*:

> For God created the world out of His compassion, which He wished to reveal. For had He not created the world, to whom would He have revealed His compassion? . . . And when God wished to create the world there was no space in which to create it, for everywhere was [His] infinity. For this reason God withdrew [*tsimtsem*] His [infinite] light sideways, and by means of this withdrawal the empty space was formed. In this empty space . . . was Creation.[94]

The clear implication of this is that the world exists in a space which is empty of God.

Notably, *Likutei tefilot* more often than not adheres to the text of R. Nahman's *Likutei moharan* quite closely, simply converting his statements into supplications. In this case, however, it digresses from its source by introducing the prayer corresponding to the sermon that inspired it with precisely the opposite of R. Nahman's own introductory remarks, launching the prayer with a series of standard biblical, hasidic, and kabbalistic proclamations of God's immanence: '"Which does great things past finding out; yea, and wonders without number" [Job 9: 10]. Master of all, "above all things, and nothing is above you", "He who fills all the universes and surrounds them"; "He who is above all universes and below them and in between them". "There is no place that is empty of you".'[95] One has the impression that in this case—as, indeed, throughout the book *Likutei tefilot*—the dominant perception (of necessity, since the book, after all, is a collection of prayers addressed to God) is of God's immanence rather than, as in *Likutei moharan*, of his transcendence. The prayers are replete with appeals to God as an intimate presence, pleading with him to restore the lost access to the absent, transcendent, 'true tsadikim' of the generation—a plural form which alternates with the singular and is without a doubt an invocation of the departed R. Nahman, the only True Tsadik of all times. For example:

> 'Stir the heart of the true tsadikim of our generation, and give them the strength to receive our prayers and raise them up to you . . . But what shall we do now, oh God, our Lord, for we have been orphaned of our father, and there is no one to stand for us . . . We have been left bereft, devoid of all that is good . . . And even though there surely are true tsadikim even in the present generation, they are concealed, invisible to us, and we are not able to know of them and to connect ourselves to them.[96]

The focus of all sense of transcendence seems to have shifted from God to R. Nahman, who, already in his lifetime, but certainly now after his death, has 'withdrawn his light', a light which will be revealed only in the messianic World to Come.

Notes

1 See G. Scholem, 'Devekut, or Communion with God', in id., *The Messianic Idea in Judaism* (London, 1971), 203–27.

2 See ibid. 205; J. G. Weiss, 'The Beginnings of Hasidism' (Heb.), *Zion*, 16 (1951), 63.

3 Jacob Joseph of Połonne, *Toledot ya'akov yosef* (Korzec, 1780), 17*b*, quoted in Weiss, 'The Beginnings of Hasidism' (Heb.), 61.

4 See B. Dinur, *With the Turn of the Generations* [Bemifneh hadorot] (Jerusalem, 1955), 141–2; A. J. Heschel, *The Circle of the Baal Shem Tov: Studies in Hasidism*, ed. S. H. Dresner (Chicago, 1985), 118.

5 Cf. Jacob Joseph of Połonne, *Tsafenat pa'ne'aḥ* (New York, 1954), 31*b* (Korzec edn. [1782], 24*b*): '"Thy word have I hid in mine heart" [Ps. 119: 11], while outwardly he carries out material affairs.'

6 Ibid. 76*a* (Korzec edn., 60*a*), quoted in Weiss, 'The Beginnings of Hasidism' (Heb.), 64.

7 *Keter shem tov* (Jerusalem, 1968), 15. For the numerous parallels in the writings of R. Jacob Joseph and in Ephraim of Sudyłków's *Degel maḥaneh efrayim*, see Weiss, 'The Beginnings of Hasidism' (Heb.), 97–9.

8 *Keter shem tov*, 14–15. For the original version of the parable in the writing of R. Jacob Joseph, see his *Ben porat yosef* (New York, 1954), 85*a* (Korzec edn. [1781], 66*b*). This parable is reminiscent of, and was probably inspired by, the parable of the king, his son, and the beautiful harlot who was sent to seduce him, by which the Zohar (ii. 163*a*) shows the evil inclination to be acting as a divine agent. However, while the zoharic version has the prince gain his father's favour by resisting temptation, in the hasidic version he gains it by satisfying his desire. For an annotated English rendition of the zoharic parable see I. Tishby, *The Wisdom of the Zohar: An Anthology of Texts*, trans. D. Goldstein (Oxford, 1989), ii. 806; *The Zohar: Pritzker Edition*, trans. D. C. Matt (Stanford, Calif., 2009), v. 441.

9 See *Emunot vede'ot*, ed. Slucki (Leipzig, 1864), ch. 10, p. 150 §4. G. Scholem, in his *Major Trends in Jewish Mysticism* (New York, 1961), 96, and in nn. 56–7 on p. 373, quotes the passage in which the Besht ascribes this view to Sa'adyah Gaon, implying, particularly in the note, that he was indeed the Besht's source for 'such erotic imagery for Israel's love for God'. Following him, Weiss ('The Beginnings of Hasidism' (Heb.), 101), who likewise quoted the passage, referred the reader to Scholem on the origin of the idea. As he testifies, Scholem quotes the statement attributed to the Besht not directly from its original source—the books of R. Jacob Joseph of Połonne—nor from the anthology *Keter shem tov*, which reproduced it shortly after the publication of R. Jacob Joseph's works, but rather from a relatively late source, M. L. Rodkinson's *Toledot ba'alei shem tov* (Königsberg, 1876). Although in a subsequent Hebrew work ('The Historical Figure of R. Israel Ba'al Shem Tov' (Heb.), in G. Scholem, *Explications and Implications: Writings on Jewish Heritage and Renaissance* [Devarim bego: pirkei morashah uteḥiyah] (Tel Aviv, 1975), 321, previously published in *Molad*, 144–5 (1960), 355) he does clarify this point, Scholem does not note here, first, that Sa'adyah's vivid description of physical desire is not an allegory of Israel's love for God but a strong denunciation of physical desire as such, which he considers to be devoid of any merit, physical

or spiritual, and an impediment to, rather than a model for, man's spiritual love for God. Second, Scholem does not mention the fact that Rodkinson himself, having paraphrased (not quoted) the passage from *Keter shem tov*, pointed out the discrepancy between Sa'adyah's actual view and the one ascribed to him by the Besht. Rodkinson noted that the question had first been raised by 'R. E. Katz' (Eliezer Zvi Hakohen Zweifel), who had searched in vain for such a view in Sa'adyah's writings and finally resolved the difficulty by admitting that the Besht must have been so inspired by Sa'adyah's lively description of physical desire that he himself analogized it approvingly to spiritual passion for God (see M. L. Rodkinson, *Toledot ba'alei shem tov* (Königsberg, 1876), 96–9; E. Z. Hakohen Zweifel, *Shalom al yisra'el* (Jerusalem, 1972; 1st edn. Zhitomir, 1868–73), i. 110–13). M. Piekarz, in *The Beginning of Hasidism: Intellectual Trends in Derush and Musar Literature* [Biyemei tsemiḥat haḥasidut: megamot ra'ayoniyot besifrei derush umusar] (Jerusalem, 1978), 21, 207–8, similarly observes the discrepancy between Sa'adyah's view and that ascribed to him by the Besht, and he notes that such false attributions to medieval authorities are not at all uncommon in the homiletical writings of the early modern period, including the literature of hasidism, although he has not encountered this particular false attribution elsewhere.

10 *Toledot ya'akov yosef*, 195*b*, quoted by Weiss in 'The Beginnings of Hasidism' (Heb.), 66–8, with several parallels.

11 Cf. e.g. Weiss, 'The Beginnings of Hasidism' (Heb.), 51.

12 Cf. e.g. *Tsafenat pa'ne'aḥ*, 29*a* (Korzec edn., 22*a*).

13 Quoted above, at n. 8.

14 BT *Tam.* 32*a*.

15 *Ben porat yosef*, 85*a* (Korzec edn., p. 66*b*).

16 BT *Ber.* 35*b*.

17 *Keter shem tov*, 5.

18 Mishnah *Avot* 2: 10.

19 *Tsafenat pa'ne'aḥ*, 32*a* (Korzec edn., 24*b*–*c*); cf. *Ben porat yosef*, at the end, 127*a*. Another clear statement to this effect appears in the collection of traditions attributed to R. Barukh of Międzybóż, a grandson of the Besht:

> He said that . . . the tsadikim, the Almighty's holy men, conduct themselves like everyone else when they eat, drink, pray a little, and talk mostly about worldly affairs. Yet this is how they serve God, and no one should model themselves on them, for the tsadik is holy and pure from infancy, and all his thoughts are focused exclusively on the Holy One, blessed be He; he does not need to engage as much [as ordinary people] in the battle against the Evil Inclination. For this reason, even by means of his [apparently] undemanding mode of worship he cleaves and connects his pure thoughts

to the Holy One, blessed be He. But the [ordinary] person, who has to mend his ways, if he observes the tsadik and desires to serve God in the same manner, will be prevented from doing so by the Evil Inclination, for he has to be much stronger [than he is] in order to refrain from committing an evil deed. (*Butsina dinehora* (Lemberg, 1884), 9)

20 *Keter shem tov*, 29; cf. pp. 10, 59.

21 Cf. *Midrash vayikra rabah*, 24: 5.

22 *Toledot ya'akov yosef*, 67*a*.

23 N. Sternharz, *Shivḥei haran* [with *Siḥot haran*] (Lemberg, 1901), 6*b* §26; cf. 60*b* §165; 61*a* §170.

24 See N. Sternharz, *Ḥayei moharan*, ii: *Shivḥei moharan* (Jerusalem, 1947), 'Gedulat hasagato', 16 §50; 9 §7.

25 On some of the features that make Habad an exception, and on its view of itself as such, see below, Chs. 6–8.

26 See R. Elior, '"The World is Filled with His Glory" and "All Men": Spiritual Renewal and Social Change in Early Hasidism' (Heb.), in M. Hallamish (ed.), *Alei shefer: Studies in Jewish Thought in Honour of Alexander Shafran* [Alei shefer: meḥkarim besifrut hehagut hayehudit, mugashim likhvod harav dr aleksander shafran] (Ramat Gan, 1990), 29–40; ead., *The Mystical Origins of Hasidism* (Oxford, 2006), 37–40, 115–16.

27 Scholem, 'Devekut, or Communion with God', 208.

28 Ibid. 212.

29 See Weiss, 'The Beginnings of Hasidism' (Heb.), 51.

30 See *Keter shem tov*, 15, 21, 22.

31 Cf. above, p. 130.

32 For these two qualifications of the state of *devekut* see Scholem, 'Devekut, or Communion with God', 218–22.

33 See *Tsafenat pa'ne'aḥ*, 32*a* (Korzec edn., 24*b*–*c*); cf. the parallel at the end of *Ben porat yosef*.

34 *Toledot ya'akov yosef*, 78*c* (emphases mine; A.R.-A).

35 Ibid. 56*c*.

36 *Keter shem tov*, 22.

37 *Toledot ya'akov yosef*, 25*a*.

38 For the Besht's method of study 'for its own sake' see J. G. Weiss, 'The Besht's Method of Torah Study' (Heb.), in H. J. Zimmels, J. Rabbinowitz, and I. Feinstein (eds.), *Essays Presented to Chief Rabbi Israel Brody on the Occasion of His Seventieth Birthday* (London, 1968), 155–6, 163–4, 167; M. Idel, 'Modes of Cleaving to the Letters in the Teachings of Israel Baal Shem Tov: A Sample Analysis', *Jewish History*, 27/2–4 (2013), 299–317.

39 Sharing the view that the ideal of *devekut* in early hasidism was open for all to fulfil, while at the same time drawing attention to the frequently asserted distinction between the 'spiritual' and 'corporeal' human categories in early hasidic writings, Weiss ('The Beginnings of Hasidism' (Heb.), 84–5) rightly raised the question of the historical origins of this notion of society.

40 See B. Dinur, *With the Turn of the Generations* (Heb.), 159–70. For more on this see now M. Rosman, *Founder of Hasidism: A Quest for the Historical Ba'al Shem Tov* (Oxford, 2013 (1st edn. Berkeley, Calif., 1996)), 27–41; I. Etkes, *The Besht: Magician, Mystic and Leader* (Waltham, Mass., 2005), 152–202.

41 See Weiss, 'The Beginnings of Hasidism' (Heb.), 46–9 and *passim*, and 'A Circle of Pneumatics in Pre-Hasidism', *Journal of Jewish Studies*, 8/3–4 (1957), 199–213 (repr. in id., *Studies in Eastern European Jewish Mysticism* (Oxford, 1985), 27–42).

42 See e.g. A. Walden, *Shem hagedolim heḥadash* (Warsaw, 1870), 35*a* §234, 65*a* §25); M. M. Bodek, *Seder hadorot mitalmidei habesht z"l* (Lublin, 1927), 12–13; Rodkinson, *Toledot ba'alei shem tov*, 30, 35, 38, 43; S. A. Horodetsky, *Hasidism and Its Adherents* [Haḥasidut vehaḥasidim] (Tel Aviv, 1927), vol. i *passim*; S. Dubnow, *The History of Hasidism* [Toledot haḥasidut] (Tel Aviv, 1960), 59, 63.

43 See A. J. Heschel, *The Circle of the Baal Shem Tov*, 1–112, 152–81.

44 See e.g. *In Praise of the Baal Shem Tov*, trans. and ed. D. Ben-Amos and J. R. Mintz (Bloomington, 1970), 156–60, 175–6, 195–6, 222–3.

45 See Heschel, *The Circle of the Baal Shem Tov*, 14–29.

46 For the activities of R. Aaron of Karlin in Lithuania during the lifetime of the Magid, see W. Z. Rabinowitsch, *Lithuanian Hasidism* (London, 1970), 10. For the equal status of Karlin to Mezhirech (Międzyrzecz) as a hasidic centre during this period, see S. Maimon, *Lebensgeschichte*, ed. J. Fromer (Munich, 1911), 188. The allusive reference to these two hasidic centres as 'K. M.' (alongside other 'holy places where the enlightened leaders of the sect lived') is missing from the English edition, *The Autobiography of Solomon Maimon*, trans. J. Clark Murray (London, 1954), 168. As an echo of the fluidity of the situation, and the relativity of the titles 'leader' and 'follower', the following tradition may be quoted, received in the name of R. Yehiel Mikhl of Złoczów, a disciple of the Magid of Mezhirech:

> Indeed, I have heard from R. Yehiel Mikhl, of blessed memory, that he said: Before the start of each prayer I connect myself [*mitkasher*—synonymous with 'cleave', *davek*] to the entire nation of Israel, both to those who are superior to me and to those who are my inferiors. For the benefit of connecting myself to my superiors lies in that, through this, my thought may be uplifted. And the benefit of connecting myself to my inferiors lies in that, through this, they may be uplifted. (Meshulam Feibush of Zbaraż, *Derekh ha'emet (Yosher divrei emet)* (Jerusalem, n.d.), 42)

R. Yehiel Mikhl was one of the disciples of the Magid of Mezhirech who became a hasidic master in his own right, commanding a following of his own.

47 Scholem, who points out that it was virtually impossible to expect everyone to fulfil the highest ideal of *devekut* even though this was demanded, or, 'in a way, forced upon the masses', concludes therefore that

> it was bound to assume rather crude and vulgar forms. Once the radical slogan 'Judaism without *Devekut* is idolatry' was accepted, its very radicalism already contained the germ of decay, a dialectic typical of radical and spiritualist movements. Since not everyone was able to attain that state of mind by introspection and contemplation, external stimulants, even liquor, had to be employed. ('Devekut, or Communion with God', 209)

48 For this view see e.g. Weiss, 'The Beginnings of Hasidism' (Heb.), 64–5 n. 61; Dubnow, *The History of Hasidism* (Heb.), 59.

49 Respectively, Horodetsky, *Hasidism and Its Adherents* (Heb.), iv. 22; R. Mahler, *Hasidism and Haskalah* [Haḥasidut vehahaskalah begalitsyah uvepolin hakongresa'it bamaḥatsit harishonah shel hame'ah hatesha-esreh] (Merhavyah, 1961), 21 (missing from the abridged English edition of this work, *Hasidism and Jewish Enlightenment: Their Confrontation in Galicia and Poland in the First Half of the Nineteenth Century*, trans. E. Orenstein, A. Klein, and J. Machlowitz Klein (Philadelphia, 1985), 10); Elior, *The Mystical Origins of Hasidism*, 84.

50 For an exhaustive analysis of the tension between the immanentist and the transcendentist perceptions of God's relationship to the created world, as they found expression in a wide range of early hasidic sources, see T. Kaufman, *In All Your Ways Know Him: The Concept of God and Avodah Be-Gashmiyut in the Early Stages of Hasidism* [Bekhol derakheikha da'ehu: tefisat ha'elohut veha'avodah begashmiyut bereshit haḥasidut] (Ramat Gan, 2009).

51 Horodetsky, *Hasidism and Its Adherents* (Heb.), iv. 48.

52 A possible exception is R. Menahem Mendel of Przemyślany, whose pamphlet *Darkhei yesharim* (Zhitomir, 1805) does appear to request direct *devekut* from everyone. There is not a single reference in the pamphlet to the division, so often stated by R. Jacob Joseph of Połonne and others, between ordinary 'corporeal' people and the supreme group of 'spiritual men'. On the contrary, R. Menahem Mendel seems to advocate the complete equality in *devekut* of all creatures before God:

> And let not a man say to himself that he is greater than his fellow man since he can worship in greater *devekut*. For he, as all other creatures, was created in order to worship God. Has God not given his fellow a mind such as he gave to him? By what is he more important than a mere worm? For the worm also worships God with all its might and mind, and man likewise is a worm. (*Darkhei yesharim*, 9*a*)

R. Menahem Mendel acknowledges that it is very difficult to maintain his own extreme version of the ideal of *devekut*, and therefore he advises everyone to refrain as much as possible from all activities which are not directly conducive to it. Notably, unlike the Besht, he considers study, and sometimes even prayer, a hindrance, not a potential vehicle, for *devekut*, which can be achieved in total silence and seclusion. For his attitude to study see J. G. Weiss, 'The Besht's Method of Torah Study' (Heb.), in H. J. Zimmels, J. Rabbinowitz, and I. Feinstein (eds.), *Essays Presented to Chief Rabbi Israel Brodie on the Occasion of His Seventieth Birthday* (London, 1968), 158–62. See, however, Ze'ev Gries's conclusion (*Conduct Literature* [Sifrut hahanhagot: toledoteiha umekomah beḥayei ḥasidei r. yisra'el ba'al shem tov] (Jerusalem, 1989), 156–81) that *Darkhei yesharim* was not actually authored by Menahem Mendel of Przemyślany but rather constitutes a recension of the Magid of Mezhirech's 'conduct' instructions.

53 Sternharz, *Ḥayei moharan*, ii, 'Gedulat hasagato', 17 §59.

54 With this in mind, it would be instructive to consider the question, raised by Weiss, of the traditions attributed to the Besht in the writings of his grandson, R. Ephraim of Sudyłków. Weiss compared two parallel traditions transmitted in the name of the Besht, one recorded by R. Jacob Joseph in *Tsafenat pa'ne'aḥ* and the other by R. Ephraim of Sudyłków in his *Degel maḥaneh efrayim*. He recognized in the latter a paraphrase of the former:

> into which R. Ephraim had inserted a few words to sharpen the general idea of the Besht by confining it to the activities of the tsadik only. . . . This passage does not properly belong to the Beshtian stage of transmission but rather to a later development in the history of hasidic ideas, when the tendency came to prevail of limiting to the tsadik what was everyone's entitlement according to the teachings of the Besht. ('The Beginnings of Hasidism' (Heb.), 64–6)

However, a careful examination of the two texts will show that R. Ephraim did not depart from the Besht's ideas as recorded by R. Jacob Joseph in any way other than the introduction of the term 'tsadik', which for him had a clear institutional meaning, and possibly also by emphasizing something which his grandfather may not have felt the need to stress, namely, that only the tsadik could ever realize the ideal. But the clear division between the man who can 'raise' and the man who may 'be raised' is present in the original version of *Tsafenat pa'ne'aḥ*. The Besht himself clearly identifies with the man who can 'raise', and there is no question of the two distinct roles being interchangeable.

55 See e.g. Weiss, 'A Circle of Pneumatics in Pre-Hasidism'; Rosman, *Founder of Hasidism*, 27–41; Etkes, *The Besht*, 152–202.

56 For the Besht's attempt to gain recognition from the circle of the 'great hasidim' in Brody, see *In Praise of the Baal Shem* Tov, ed. Ben-Amos and Mintz, 30–1.

57 See J. G. Weiss, 'The Kavvanoth of Prayer in Early Hasidism', *Journal of Jewish Studies*, 9 (1958), 163–92 (repr. in id., *East European Jewish Mysticism*, 95–125); R. Schatz-Uffenheimer, *Hasidism as Mysticism: Quietistic Elements in Eighteenth-Century Hasidic Thought* (Princeton, NJ, 1993), 215–41; L. Jacobs, *Hasidic Prayer* (London, 1972), 74–81; M. Idel, *Hasidism: Between Ecstasy and Magic* (Albany, New York, 1995), 149–70; and cf. M. Kallus, 'The Relation of the Baal Shem Tov to the Practice of Lurianic Kavvanot in Light of his Comments on the Siddur Rashkov', *Kabbalah: Journal for the Study of Jewish Mystical Texts*, 2 (1997), 151–67.

58 Weiss, 'The Kavvanoth of Prayer in Early Hasidism', 168 (100 in the repr. edn.).

59 See *In Praise of the Baal Shem Tov*, ed. Ben-Amos and Mintz, 60–1, 195–6.

60 See ibid. 61.

61 See ibid. 195.

62 *Or ha'emet*, 14*b*, quoted by Weiss (with a slight omission) in 'The Kavvanoth of Prayer in Early Hasidism', 177.

63 See *Or ha'emet*, 64*a*; Weiss, 'The Kavvanoth of Prayer in Early Hasidism', 178.

64 This, of course, was particularly true of what is often called the 'first' and 'second' generations of hasidism and, at any rate, before the outbreak of the campaign against the movement by its opponents. But even subsequently, while the opponents regarded hasidism as a deviating sect and attempted to sever it from the main body of Judaism, the hasidic response was remarkably harmonistic, stressing its sense of belonging to the wider community and conforming with its values, rather than breaking away from it (see e.g. M. Wilensky, *Hasidim and Mitnagedim* [Ḥasidim umitnagedim] (Jerusalem, 1970), i. 84–100, 161–76, 296–313).

65 See e.g. B. R. Wilson, 'A Typology of Sects', in R. Robertson (ed.), *Sociology of Religion* (London, 1969), 366–7.

66 See Weiss, 'The Kavvanoth of Prayer in Early Hasidism', 185–92 (105–8 in the repr. edn.).

67 See Schatz-Uffenheimer, *Hasidism as Mysticism*, 228, 238–41.

68 For his rejection specifically of this ideal of *devekut* through 'corporeality' as being inapplicable to 'our generation', see *Derekh emet*, 61, 66.

69 See Schatz-Uffenheimer, *Hasidism as Mysticism*, 226, 239. See also M. Krassen, *Uniter of Heaven and Earth: Rabbi Meshullam Feibush Heller of Zbarazh and the Rise of Hasidism in Eastern Galicia* (Albany, NY, 1998), 107–61; I. Etkes, 'R. Meshullam Feibush Heller and His Conversion to Hasidism', *Studia Judaica*, 3 (1994), 78–90, esp. 85–6.

70 See *Derekh emet*, 76–7, but cf. 49–50.

71 *Tsafenat pa'ne'aḥ* (Korzec edn.), 30*b*, quoted in S. H. Dresner, *The Zaddik* (New York, 1960), 129.

72 For the cleaving of the common people to their spiritual leader rather than directly to God, see Dresner, *The Zaddik*, 113–41. Dresner, however, argues that the Ba'al Shem Tov and R. Jacob Joseph of Połonne did not advocate the complete dependence of the ordinary person on the tsadik, and that in this respect one can detect 'a difference in attitude towards the Zaddik between the earlier and later generations of Hasidism' (pp. 133–6). But the sources he quotes for this are not entirely convincing and could easily be explained as a token acknowledgment of the doctrine of free will and an awareness of the obligation not to discourage anyone from attempting his best (cf. above, at nn. 20–4). Significantly, the most powerful evidence he adduces for the desire to minimize ordinary people's dependence on the tsadik is not taken from any hasidic text but from Martin Buber's interpretation of a hasidic text (see ibid. 134–6). The argument here is not that the ordinary person was encouraged to surrender his free will and become a passive dependent on the tsadik's mediation with God on his behalf, but rather that right from the very beginning (and not only in the 'later generations of Hasidism') the tsadik's mediation was seen as the only means to the ordinary person's experience of genuine communion with the Divine. For another exposition, and an anthology of sermons dealing with this doctrine in the works of R. Jacob Joseph of Połonne, see G. Nigal, *Leader and Congregation: Opinions and Parables in the Beginning of Hasidism According to the Writings of R. Jacob Joseph of Połonne* [Manhig ve'edah: de'ot umeshalim bereshit haḥasidut al pi kitvei r. ya'akov yosef mipolna'ah] (Jerusalem, 1962); id., *Rabbi Jacob Joseph of Połonne (Polna): Selected Writings* [Torot ba'al hatoledot: derashot rabi ya'akov yosef mipolna'ah lefi nose'ei yesod] (Jerusalem, 1974).

73 See e.g. A. Y. (Arthur) Green, 'Around the Maggid's Table: *Tsadik*, Leadership, and Popularization in the Circle of Dov Baer of Miedzyrzecz' (Heb.), *Zion*, 78/1 (2013), 73–106, and A. Green with E. Leader, A. E. Mayse, and O. N. Rose (eds.), *Speaking Torah: Spiritual Teachings from around the Maggid's Table*, 2 vols. (Woodstock, Vt., 2013), both of which use the concrete image of 'the Magid's table' as an imaginary construct, and can only speculate on the actual social setting in which the teachings of the Magid and his 'school' came into being. For studies of particular aspects of these mystical teachings see E. Drescher Mayse, 'Beyond the Letters: The Question of Language in the Teachings of Rabbi Dov Baer of Mezritch', Ph.D. diss. (Harvard University, 2015); M. Lorberbaum, '"Attain the Attribute of *Ayin*": The Mystical Religiosity of *Magid devarav leya'akov*' (Heb.), *Kabbalah: Journal for the Study of Jewish Mystical Texts*, 31 (2014), 169–235; O. Michaelis, 'The Path of Love and Awe in the Doctrine of the Magid R. Ber of Mezhirech' [Ahavah veyir'ah betorat hamagid mimezrich], MA thesis (Tel Aviv University, 2013).

74 J. G. Weiss, *Studies in Braslav Hasidism* [Meḥkarim beḥasidut bratslav] (Jerusalem, 1974), 104.

75 See ibid. 105–7.

76 *Derekh emet*, 42. For a similar recommendation see Moses Elyakim Briah Hofstein of Kozienice, *Vayeḥal mosheh* (Lemberg, 1863), 4*a*, the comment on Ps. 16 (quoted by G. Nigal in 'Hasidic Doctrine in the Writings of R. Elimelekh of Lizhensk and His Contemporaries' [Mishnat haḥasidut bekhitvei rabi elimelekh milizhensk uvenei doro], Ph.D. diss. (Hebrew University, Jerusalem, 1972), 200–1). In *Derekh emet* R. Meshulam Feibush refers the reader, at the end of the passage quoted above, to the book *Ḥesed le'avraham* by Abraham Azulai (1570–1643) as a source in which the matter is explained further. Indeed, in *Ḥesed le'avraham* (Amsterdam, 1685), *ma'yan* 2, *ein hakore*, *nahar* 33, p. 18*a–b*, Azulai writes: 'It is forbidden to look at idols, for that shape damages the mind. And this is the secret meaning of the prohibition on looking at the face of a wicked man. Conversely, if the form of an honourable man is drawn up in a man's mind, he may rise to great and wondrous eminence.' However, when he speaks of the man who achieves the status of someone much closer to God than himself, Azulai uses the example of Elisha and Elijah and prescribes a somewhat different technique whereby the lesser man, Elisha, causes his own form to be drawn up in the mind of the greater man, Elijah, thus himself 'coming to stand before God', like Elijah. Altogether, Azulai's ideas in this connection are somewhat less striking in that they are free of the hasidic context, where the tsadik functions as the focus of the ordinary person's devotion.

77 See e.g. BT *BB* 75*b*, *Pes*. 68*a*, *MK* 16*b*, *Shab*. 63*a*; *Midrash shir hashirim rabah*, 1: 31; Zohar i. 45*b*, 114*b* (*Midrash hane'elam*), 135*a* (*Midrash hane'elam*).

78 *Midrash tanḥuma*, ed. Buber, 'Toledot', 11.

79 Zohar, introduction, 5*a–b*.

80 This is clearly an allusion to the Zohar text referred to above in n. 79, just as the attribution to the tsadikim of the power to resurrect the dead and to cure the infertility of women is based on the rabbinic sources referred to in n. 77.

81 *Magid devarav leya'akov*, ed. R. Schatz-Uffenheimer (Jerusalem, 1976), 285 no. 185.

82 *No'am elimelekh*, ed. G. Nigal (Jerusalem, 1975), ii. 510, 'Ki tetse'.

83 Ibid. 469, 'Devarim'.

84 Jacobs, *Hasidic Prayer*, 131.

85 *Likutim yekarim* (Jerusalem, 1975; 1st edn. Lemberg, 1792), 85*b*.

86 Nahman of Bratslav, *Sefer hamidot* (New York, 1965; 1st edn. Mohilev, 1811), 262.

87 Adapted by M. Buber from *Nifle'ot hayehudi* in his *Or haganuz* (Tel Aviv, 1976),

429 (Eng. edn. *Tales of the Hasidim*, ii: *The Later Masters*, 271–2). For an account of a Jew who remained loyal to the Besht even after his death and refused to accept another master, see A. Kahana, *Sefer haḥasidut* (Warsaw, 1922), 24.

88 For preliminary comments on this see Weiss, *Studies in Braslav Hasidism* (Heb.), 152–4; see also M. Piekarz, *Braslav Hasidism* [Ḥasidut braslav: perakim beḥayei meḥolelah uvikhtaveiha] (Jerusalem, 1972), 112–17. Cf. the same theme in writings of the Seer of Lublin as discussed in R. Elior, 'Between *Yesh* and *Ayin*: The Doctrine of the Zaddik in the Works of Jacob Isaac, the Seer of Lublin', in A. Rapoport-Albert and S. J. Zipperstein (eds.), *Jewish History: Essays in Honour of Chimen Abramsky* (London, 1988), 420–5.

89 See Nahman of Bratslav, *Likutei moharan* (New York, 1966), pt. I, *torah* 64, §4. Here, too, the passage from the introduction to the Zohar which was referred to above, depicting the righteous as creators, is the source for the attribution of this power to the tsadikim.

90 See ibid., §1.

91 See e.g. ibid., *torah* 63, where the tsadik's mode of self-revelation is, paradoxically, concealment and disguise 'in small things', since the full force of his undisguised 'mind' cannot be revealed at all. This is a clear echo of the classic hasidic interpretation of the Lurianic *tsimtsum* in reference to God, who, equally paradoxically, conceals or disguises himself in base materiality, because this is his only way of exposing himself to the world without instantly annihilating it (see also ibid., *torah* 140, and Piekarz, *Braslav Hasidism* (Heb.), 139).

92 For the belief that R. Nahman's death was merely his 'withdrawal' or 'concealment', which was due to last for forty-five years, after which time he was expected to return to earth, see Abraham Hazan of Tulchin, *Sefer kokhevei or* (Jerusalem, 1961), 'Ḥokhmah uvinah', 119–20, and Piekarz, *Braslav Hasidism* (Heb.), 139.

93 See N. Sternharz, *Yemei moharnat* (Benei Berak, 1956), pt. II, 85 §5. On the book *Likutei tefilot* see J. Meir, 'The Politics of Printing *Sefer likutei tefilot*' (Heb.), *Zion*, 80/1 (2015), 43–68.

94 Nahman of Bratslav, *Likutei moharan*, pt. I, *torah* 64, the beginning of §1.

95 N. Sternharz, *Likutei tefilot* (Jerusalem, 1957), pt. I, prayer no. 64, the beginning of §1, p. 231. The entire first section of the prayer is made up of a string of hasidism's immanentist slogans.

96 Ibid., prayer no. 2, p. 3, and prayer no. 4, pp. 6–7.

THREE

Confession in the Circle of R. Nahman of Bratslav

IN JUDAISM the confession of sins is traditionally made directly to God by the sinner himself or, in the case of communal sins, by an individual representing the whole community. In the Pentateuch, confession constitutes part of a ritual of atonement which necessitates the offering of sacrifices.[1] When the sacrifices were abolished confession passed over to the liturgy and was seen by the rabbis as a stage in the process of complete repentance which ultimately, in most cases, secured atonement. In the Talmud various formulae of confession were suggested,[2] and there were debates as to whether or not sins should be confessed in detail.[3] Maimonides, in his 'Hilkhot teshuvah', rules that sins concerning God alone might not be made known in public, and should be confessed in detail before God only, whereas sins committed against one's fellow man should be confessed in public and in detail.[4] The notion underlying the requirement to confess such sins in public was not that the public, or certain individuals included therein, had the power to grant atonement. Rather, it was for the sake of peaceful relations in the community that the sinner was directed to admit his sins to those whom he had wronged, thus also making it harder for him to repeat them.

When the practice of private confession before an ordained priest gradually spread throughout Europe and became obligatory on all Christians (a trend which was finally given the official Church stamp by the Fourth Lateran Council of 1215),[5] the Jews living in Christian lands were confronted by yet another conspicuous difference between their own religious practice and that of their neighbours. Discussion concerning the

The notes to this essay, originally numbered by page, are numbered in a single sequence in the present version.

absence in Judaism of institutionalized confessions before a priest occurs in a number of public as well as private Judaeo-Christian disputations of that period. The Jews mostly ridiculed the notion that a mere human being, no matter how high his position in the Church hierarchy, should be credited with the power to absolve sins. When confronted by the Christian representatives with such biblical verses as 'He that covereth his sins shall not prosper; but whoso confesseth and forsaketh them shall have mercy' (Prov. 28: 13), they countered by quoting 'Blessed is he whose transgression is forgiven, whose sin is covered' (Ps. 32: 1), and harmonized the blatant contradiction between the two verses by interpreting the first as being a command not to conceal one's sins from God, and the second as an order not to reveal them to man. When they did not base their arguments on exegesis, the Jewish representatives reasoned on ethical grounds that the priests, being accustomed to hearing confessions of sins, would themselves become corrupt, and that absolution of sins immediately following confession at fixed, regular intervals offered a great temptation to sin freely in the intervening period. They stressed that the absence in Judaism of institutionalized confession before a priest represented an implicit command that each Jew must be constantly scrutinizing his own behaviour and confessing each one of his transgressions, if necessary many times a day, before God himself.[6]

As a result of such confrontations, European Jewry in the Middle Ages developed a consciously negative, though somewhat apologetic, attitude towards confession as it was practised by Christians.[7] Indeed, it is interesting to note that even the Jewish pietists known as *ḥasidim* in twelfth- and thirteenth-century Ashkenaz (Germany), who absorbed so many customs and beliefs from their Christian environment and adopted almost in its entirety the Christian practice of penance, did not, in the final analysis, accept the Christian institution of confession.[8] In the *Sefer ḥasidim* there are, it is true, numerous descriptions of typical confession situations. We read: 'Three men went to a wise man to confess, so that he might show them the righteous way',[9] or: 'A man who had committed a major transgression came before a wise man and asked him what he should do in order to atone for a minor sin',[10] and so on. Nevertheless, it should be noted that the wise man (*ḥakham*) in these situations was not endowed with the power to grant atonement for the sin. He was simply an expert in *teshuvat hamishkal* (appropriately graded penances), and was consulted rather as a doctor might be consulted on matters concerning physical health. He could prescribe a remedy within the rules of a system with which he was familiar, but he could not guarantee the result. There was no intrinsic value in a confession uttered specifically before the *ḥakham*. The fact that it was necessary merely indicated a concession to reality, the majority of people not being expert in the intricacies of *teshuvat hamishkal*. In other words, among the medieval Ashkenazi *ḥasidim* (and in subsequent generations) confession before the *ḥakham* was not in itself a religious duty. It was only a means to the end of fulfilling the religious duty of penance. Confession before the *ḥakham* was permitted, or at the most encouraged, in those cases where the sinner himself was ignorant of the appropriate penance for his sin and had to learn it from the *ḥakham*. Thus, for example, the eighteenth-century rabbi Meir Eisenstadt ruled in one of his responsa that 'it is forbidden to recount sins in detail except when one is alone. And even before death one should not recount one's sins in public; rather, one should confess in private to God. But if a man does not know the appropriate penance for his sin he is permitted to consult a *ḥakham* as to which penance is appropriate for his sin.'[11]

Against the background of this type of reluctant and rather limited rabbinic sanction, the mystical tradition has credited the illustrious sixteenth-century Safed kabbalist Isaac Luria (known by the acronym of his title and name as the Ari) with the gift of physiognomy, which gave him instant insight into people's minds. This would elicit from all of them detailed confessions of their covert sins, and he would prescribe for each one a bespoke penance that would result in full expiation of his sinful past:

> He would tell a person [on merely looking at his face] all the sins he had committed even twenty years since, [uncovering] his most secret actions and innermost thoughts . . . People would take flight when they saw him . . . to prevent him from looking at their faces . . . but many would come and prostrate themselves before him, asking him to look at their faces and tell them where they had gone wrong, in order to guide them in repentance by prescribing a penance. He would list all their transgressions one by one and would even remind them of the place where each was committed, in whose company, and other such details, until they would confess everything to him, and he would give each one of them a penance that was specific to his sins and to his soul, so that in the end no trace would remain of all their earlier transgressions.[12]

This ability was clearly considered to be quite exceptional. It was attributed to a uniquely holy man, and most likely the practice of eliciting such confessions was confined to the circle of Luria's immediate associates. But the tradition that circulated about his exceptional powers as a confessor may well have provided the model for the subsequent attribution of these powers to other distinguished kabbalists and prophetically inspired charismatic figures, including at least some of the eighteenth-century leaders of the emergent hasidic movement.

It is important to note from the outset that even among the hasidim institutionalized confession before the tsadik was not a widespread practice. As the late Joseph Weiss observed: 'The custom of confession before the *Ṣaddik* is to be found here and there in the Hasidic movement. But more surprising than the fact that it is found at all is the fact that it is not found in far greater measure and force in an atmosphere so heavily charged with emotion and in an area in which the Christian practice of confession prevailed throughout.'[13]

There are, however, some reports of confession before the tsadik in the anti-hasidic writings of both *mitnagedim* (i.e. rabbinically orthodox opponents of hasidism) and *maskilim* (advocates of Jewish Enlightenment), as well as in some of the hasidic sources themselves. One such report by an avowed *mitnaged* appears in the petition against the tsadik Shneur Zalman of Liady (Lyady), submitted in 1800 to Tsar Paul I by Avigdor, the deposed rabbi of Pinsk, who wrote as follows:

> I have also heard that when a man wants to join the Karliner sect he must first of all come to their rebbe and hand him a list of all the transgressions, sins, and crimes he has committed from the day when he was born to the present day. The list must be signed in his own handwriting. Then he must resign his soul to the rebbe, for the rebbe has said that his own soul includes all the souls of those who have come to adhere [*devukim*] to him. And then he must give the rebbe as much money as he demands, for he is afraid of the rebbe, because he has possession of that signed list.[14]

This is no doubt a somewhat distorted but still recognizable description of confessions before the 'rebbe of the Karliners'—a very general term which could be applied to a number of the disciples of the Magid of Mezhirech (Międzyrzecz). Another *mitnaged*, R. David of Maków, in his polemical tract against the hasidic movement, is more specific in his allegations. With regard to confession, he writes of R. Hayim Haykl of Amdur's hasidic emissaries that they entice innocent people to sin, so as to send them afterwards to confess before their rebbe. He describes them as saying:

Come to our rebbe Ra Hayke [a rather clumsy pun on *ra*, meaning evil, and *rav*, meaning rebbe], to his innermost chamber, and confess to him all the sins you have committed from the day when you were born to the present day. He will give you a *tikun* [penitential instructions] and will make you a *pidyon* [will charge you a certain sum of money as 'redemption' of your soul] so that your sin will be wiped off and atoned for.[15]

The *maskilim*, who appropriated many of the *mitnagedim*'s arguments against hasidism, were no less critical of the practice of confession before the tsadik. In his anti-hasidic satire *Emek refa'im* (Valley of Ghosts), the *maskil* Isaac Ber Levinson described confession as a manipulative exercise designed to secure the hasid's total submission to his rebbe: 'When someone comes to you to seek advice, or for any other reason, you should first of all order him to confess his sins to you, and once he has disclosed them, he would always be afraid of you and submit himself to you.'[16]

In the hasidic sources the practice of confession before the tsadik is rarely mentioned. One relatively late work, which appears to preserve an early tradition, associates confession with R. Yehiel Mikhl of Złoczów, a disciple of the Magid of Mezhirech. As reported by one of his followers,

penitents would come to confess before him, and he would ask them how and what they had done, when, and with whom. If he could tell from what he heard that a person was genuinely seeking to repent and to comply with his remedial instructions, he would admit him to his circle of followers and prescribe for him a penance that would heal both his body and his soul. But if he could tell that that person had come for an ulterior motive, prompted by some misfortune and believing that once he had confessed, his circumstances would change for the better, he would not admit him to his circle, not even for all the money in the world.[17]

By far the most detailed descriptions of the institution of confession in any hasidic group are to be found in the Bratslav literature. In the circle of R. Nahman of Bratslav, as in the courts of R. Hayim Haykl, R. Yehiel Mikhl, and the 'Karliners' rebbe', confession constituted part of the initiation ceremony for new disciples. Up to the time when he settled in Medvedevka in 1792, R. Nahman used to recruit his followers by travelling through the villages neighbouring the town of Husiatyn, where he had been living in his father-in-law's house since his marriage in 1786. Those few who were attracted to him at that time started visiting him there occasionally. His circle was not organized, and affiliation with it did not necessitate any formal initiation. It was only in Medvedevka, where R. Nahman first set himself up as a tsadik, that he started holding semi-formal initiation ceremonies, which all shared one feature in common: at a certain point during his first meeting alone with R. Nahman, the new recruit would confess all his sins to him, and R. Nahman would instruct him on the appropriate steps he should take to amend them, granting him pardon and atonement. Thus we read about the initiation of R. Yudl, one of R. Nahman's earliest disciples, in Medvedevka:

Now R. Yudl was a man of some importance in his town, and he was versed in the writings of R. Isaac Luria (for he was the son-in-law of the saintly tsadik R. Leyb of Strestinitz, and had studied the Lurianic kabbalah with his father-in-law). When he first came to *adumor*[18] he addressed him in a haughty manner and said: 'Let Our Rebbe show us a way to worship the Creator, blessed be He.' And *adumor* replied quizzically: '"That thy way may be known upon earth" [Ps. 67: 2].'[19] . . . Then *adumor* inspired him with the most terrible fear, until he stepped back terrified and stood by the door, too scared to come near *adumor*. Then *adumor* began to smile at him, and somewhat relieved him of his fear . . . This was repeated several times, until *adumor* ordered him to confess all that had happened to him (as he used to order all his close disciples, and he would give each one of them remedial instructions according to the root of his soul, as mentioned in his holy books). And from that time on R. Yudl and R. Samuel Isaac became very closely bound to *adumor*.[20]

According to this account, R. Yudl's 'initiation' (*hitkarvut*[21]) and his confession took place on the same occasion, his first meeting with R. Nahman in Medvedevka, but a different tradition was preserved by R. Abraham Sternharz (R. Nathan's great-grandson) in his book *Tovot zikhronot*. Though it confirms that the actual initiation had already taken place in Medvedevka, this tradition dates R. Yudl's confession to R. Nahman's Zlatopol period.[22] And while the version of *Sefer kokhevei or* describes in detail a confession by R. Yudl, and only at the very end introduces the name of R. Samuel Isaac, the account in *Tovot zikhronot* refers to confessions by three disciples, R. Yudl, R. Samuel Isaac, and R. Aaron,[23] suggesting that all three occurred on the same day, immediately after Pentecost, in Zlatopol. According to *Tovot zikhronot*, although all three disciples had been associated with R. Nahman since his days in Medvedevka, none of them was asked to confess before him until after his move to Zlatopol. Even when he first hinted to them that confessions might be necessary, they understood him to mean that the requirement only applied to new recruits but not to themselves, who had been with R. Nahman for quite some time.[24] It was only after Pentecost, when R. Nahman delivered his teaching which specifically dealt with the absolute necessity for confession in the relationship between the tsadik and his followers, that they finally realized his true intention, and one by one went to him to confess.[25] The account reads as follows:

It is known that *torah* 4, 'Anokhi', was delivered on Pentecost in Zlatopol. And it is known that when he delivered this teaching he told a story about the Besht and his associate who refused to confess. The Besht said to him: 'Tell me that which God knows, and you and I know.' And the man, although he was pious and devout, refused, for he was too ashamed to confess before the Besht. And it so happened that he later suffered so much from bone-aches that he died from this illness.[26] Now R. Samuel Isaac and R. Yudl and R. Aaron were also present on that Pentecost. They had already become R. Nahman's disciples in Medvedevka, and had already given him *pidyonot*.[27] Nevertheless they did not as yet know about confession before the tsadik . . . Since the time of their *hitkarvut* they had visited R. Nahman several times, and he had treated them with wondrous wisdom, but he did not tell them anything about confession. However, on that occasion, when a number of people had gathered for the festival, and two of the guests had been suffering from bone-aches . . . R. Yudl, R. Samuel Isaac, and R. Aaron understood from the story which R. Nahman had told them about the Besht and his associate who refused to confess that it was R. Nahman's intention that they, too, should do so. But since they had already visited R. Nahman many times they imagined that because of their importance and piety he did not ask them to confess . . . However, when on Pentecost they heard that teaching . . . immediately after the festival they came before *adumor*, and each one of them confessed to him in private, weeping and broken-hearted.[28]

According to this tradition, institutionalized confession was not introduced into R. Nahman's circle until after his move to Zlatopol in 1800. Although the text does not explicitly state this, it clearly implies that it was on that occasion, immediately after Pentecost in Zlatopol, that R. Nahman first heard confessions from his disciples. Why else should R. Yudl and R. Samuel Isaac, on the one hand, and R. Aaron, on the other, have been grouped together to confess for the first time on the same occasion? We know that there was a gap of several years between their respective 'initiations', and if confession had already been practised in Medvedevka all three of them (but most certainly R. Yudl and R. Samuel Isaac) would have long since undergone the ceremony. Their initial reaction to R. Nahman's hints at the need to confess before him likewise indicates that the matter was entirely new to them; and if it was new to them, who were among his oldest and most intimate disciples, it could not have been known to or practised by others. Furthermore, the earliest reports of R. Nahman's followers being called *viduynikes*,[29] as well as his first and most important teaching about confession, all date from the Zlatopol period.[30] The discrepancy between this account and the description in *Sefer kokhevei or* of R. Yudl's *hitkarvut* and confession in Medvedevka can, perhaps, be ironed out if we regard the version in *Sefer kokhevei or* as a description, first, of R. Yudl's initiation in Medvedevka, and then of his confession before R. Nahman several years later in Zlatopol. Unlike *Tovot zikhronot*, *Sefer kokhevei or* is not, in this section, particularly interested in the chronological order of events; rather, it is concerned with the personality of R. Yudl.

Nevertheless, *Tovot zikhronot* itself suggests that while formal, institutionalized confessions were introduced only after the move to Zlatopol, R. Nahman had already begun to hear informal confessions from at least some of his disciples at the end of his stay in Medvedevka. In the account of R. Aaron's *hitkarvut* (which is explicitly said to have taken place during the period when 'Our Rebbe' was 'still resident and living in Medvedevka', and which is separated from the account of his confession alongside R. Samuel Isaac and R. Yudl a few years later) we read:

> And since on that night R. Aaron revealed before R. Nahman all that was hidden in his heart, *as in a confession*,[31] all that had happened to him from the day when he first became conscious of his acts until his arrival at R. Nahman's, R. Nahman knew, and later told his disciples that he knew, that R. Aaron had entered his bridal chamber on his wedding night in a clean shirt [*mit a reyn hemd*]; and let this suffice for the wise.[32]

Although this passage describes a very early, confession-like situation, it contains the only clue we have as to the content of the confessions, which evidently included details of the disciples' sexual lives. Nowhere else is there any account of the nature of the things confessed before R. Nahman.[33]

R. Aaron's informal, apparently spontaneous confession on the occasion of his *hitkarvut* was not considered sufficient. When R. Nahman decided to introduce confessions a few years later as an obligatory part of the initiation ceremony, R. Aaron, along with R. Yudl and R. Samuel Isaac, was asked to confess again, this time in order to comply with the new, formal regulation.

That confession became an obligatory, and perhaps the most important, part of the initiation ceremony is apparent from a number of accounts. For example: whilst visiting Kamenets-Podolsky on the Fast of Esther (the year is not mentioned), R. Nahman wished to spend the night in the house of the local *shoḥet* (ritual slaughterer). The *shoḥet*, who was not one of R. Nahman's followers, refused to let him stay since he was too busy with preparations for the festival of Purim. Later on, however, when he realized that R. Nahman was a man of some importance, he changed his mind, and invited him to his house. R. Nahman then refused to come, claiming that the *shoḥet* had been using a ritually defective slaughtering knife. This was investigated and found to be true, whereupon the terrified *shoḥet* fainted. When he regained consciousness, R. Nahman, realizing that he had impressed the *shoḥet* sufficiently to make him a potential follower, told him to come to his court on the following New Year's day—the most important of the three annual gatherings of his followers. After several years' delay the *shoḥet* finally came to R. Nahman for the New Year festival, and on that occasion was ordered to confess. As in most other accounts of confession before R. Nahman, the story ends here, with the cryptic 'etc.' (*vekhulei*) standing for the proceedings of the confession itself. However, it is clear that it was only after he had confessed that the *shoḥet* was officially regarded as a follower of R. Nahman.[34]

Another account, in which confession never actually takes place, clearly demonstrates the importance of the institution in R. Nahman's circle. R. Nahman once (again, no date is given) happened to pass through a village in which the brother of one of his followers was living. The brother did not know him but was impressed with his appearance, and hesitantly approached him. R. Nahman encouraged the young man to visit him on the following New Year—again, as in the case of the *shoḥet* of Kamenets, a clear invitation to join his circle formally. The man was asked to come to

R. Nahman on the day of the biggest annual gathering of his followers, the time of year in which most initiation ceremonies must have taken place. The young man promptly came to R. Nahman's court on the following New Year. When he arrived, he saw a large number of people entering R. Nahman's *shtibl* (approximately 'conventicle') carrying gifts (*pidyonot*). He asked what they were doing and was told *she'osin viduy devarim*—they were going in to confess before R. Nahman. When he noticed that each one of them came out of the room red-faced and crying he became afraid, and regretted having come. Finally, he gathered enough courage to push his way in together with one other man. But R. Nahman ordered the other man to leave the room, locked the door behind him, and said: 'Well, tell me that which God knows, and you and I know.'[35] The man, however, refused to confess. The text reads as follows:

But he refused, and said that he had nothing to confess. R. Nahman repeated to him several times: 'Say' [i.e. confess], but he replied each time, 'there is nothing to confess'. Finally R. Nahman said to him: 'Are you trying to make a fool of *me*? [*Mikh vesdu narren*?]' And I have heard that when R. Nahman said these words, he struck his nose with his finger, and said, with great deliberation, '*Mikh vesdu narren*? Do I not know all that happens to you, even when you are lying in your bed?' Then [when the man still would not confess] R. Nahman pushed him out of the room, and after the New Year festival he returned to his home.[36]

A few years later the man, who still wished to become a follower of R. Nahman, returned to his court, but because he had once refused to confess R. Nahman deliberately ridiculed him in front of his other followers, so that he was offended and never returned.

We can see from this story that without confession before R. Nahman, no matter how great the desire may have been to become his follower it was quite impossible to join his circle. A new candidate was not allowed a period of novitiate during which to convince himself that R. Nahman was indeed a great tsadik and the most suitable one for him. In order to be admitted to the circle he had to be so certain of this from the start that he would be prepared to entrust R. Nahman with his most intimate secrets.[37] Confession was, effectively, a test of the candidate's *emunah*—faith in R. Nahman. If he failed the test, he was rejected.

The fact that at New Year and, to a lesser extent, during the other two annual gatherings of R. Nahman's followers, quite a number of people are said to have come to confess before him might suggest that he held confessions regularly on those occasions—not only for new recruits, but also for all his old disciples. However, without exception, all the accounts we have of people confessing before R. Nahman are in fact descriptions of their initiation into the circle. There is not a single reference to any confession other than the initial one on the occasion of *hitkarvut*. No definite conclusion can, of course, be drawn from this, as the period during which R. Nahman practised confession was relatively short, and its documentation is extremely fragmentary. But it is at least reasonable to assume on the basis of the evidence we have that he was not always available for all to confess. Confessions were held infrequently, not more than three times a year, and were, quite possibly, expected from new disciples only. The fairly large concentration of people awaiting confession in the story related above can be explained if we bear in mind that it was R. Nahman's technique in recruiting new followers to invite those who had approached him in the course of his travels to come to his court at the next fixed gathering of his disciples.[38] On that occasion their association with him would be formalized by individual ceremonies of initiation, including confession. Thus, on each of the three annual occasions, and particularly on New Year—the most important—quite a number of prospective disciples would gather who had first approached R. Nahman at different times during the intervening months.

Another description of an initiation ceremony in which confession features prominently is that of R. Isaac, the son-in-law of the Magid of Tirhavitsa (Trushivtsi), one of R. Nahman's earliest disciples. Once again, the account of R. Isaac's *hitkarvut* exists in two versions, one in *Sefer kokhevei or* and the other in *Tovot zikhronot*.[39] Both versions agree in featuring R. Isaac's confession as the climax of the initiation ceremony, but they contradict each other on almost every other detail. The shorter version, in *Sefer kokhevei or*, reads as follows:

R. Isaac, the son-in-law of the Magid [of Tirhavitsa], was an excellent man of perfect qualities, a great scholar and a hasid all his life.[40] He was brought up in the house of the tsadik R. Zusya. Before the death of that great tsadik, R. Isaac asked him: 'With which tsadik should I associate myself now?' And R. Zusya replied: 'With the tsadik who deals with confessions, that is, the tsadik who orders his followers to confess before him and gives them *tikunim* [corrective instructions by way of penance] for each sin.' Now he had heard that R. Nahman's followers[41] were called *di viduynikes* [the confessors].[42] When he first came to R. Nahman he saw that his followers were coming out of confession with tears running down their cheeks. He went to the *beit midrash*, where he found many other people. R. Nahman signalled to all of them to leave, and they all took off their *talit* and *tefilin* and went out. R. Isaac then wanted to leave too, but R. Nahman took the key and locked the door, so that no one else was left inside apart from *adumor* and R. Isaac. R. Nahman started smoking his pipe and pacing up and down the room, until R. Isaac was struck by the most terrible fear, and he began to remember all that had happened to him from his childhood to that day. Then R. Nahman approached him and said in the following words: '*Heynt zog* [now tell]', and R. Isaac started confessing before him all that was in his heart. R. Nahman then said to him whatever he said, and from that time on R. Isaac became a very close disciple of his.[43]

This version presents R. Isaac as a great scholar and as a hasid of R. Zusya, in whose house he is supposed to have grown up. This R. Zusya is no doubt R. Zusya of Annopol, brother of R. Elimelekh of Lizhensk (Leżajsk). R. Zusya instructs his protégé R. Isaac to approach, after his own death, the tsadik-confessor, a term which is understood by the narrator—as, indeed, by R. Isaac himself—as a reference to R. Nahman.[44]

The second version, which is longer and more detailed, presents R. Isaac's *hitkarvut* as the setting of R. Nahman's teaching 'Or haganuz'.[45] According to this version R. Nahman delivered that teaching in Zlatopol a few weeks after the *hitkarvut* of R. Isaac, which had inspired it.[46] While the version in *Sefer kokhevei or* describes R. Isaac as a devoted disciple of R. Zusya in the years prior to his *hitkarvut*, in this version not only is there no mention at all of R. Zusya, but R. Isaac is represented as a traditional scholar, altogether divorced from the world of hasidism, if not actually opposed to it. We read:

The son-in-law of the Magid, R. Isaac, was a great scholar, but he was not a member of the hasidic sect; rather, he was one of the pious, righteous scholars [in other words, although he was not a hasid, he was not an active opponent of the movement]. However, since he was the son-in-law of the Magid [who was an old disciple of R. Nahman], he often heard his father-in-law praise R. Nahman's understanding of both open and hidden matters in Torah [i.e. both talmudic and kabbalistic studies]. He had already heard this when R. Nahman was living in Medvedevka, and later in Zlatopol. Nevertheless he showed no enthusiasm, since he was of such high birth and a great scholar, etc.[47]

Other differences between the two versions are numerous, and it would be pointless to compare them in detail as it is impossible to determine which of the two has preserved the more authentic traditions. Some confusion may have arisen with regard to the identity of R. Isaac, since another man by the same name was also initiated into the circle round about the same period,[48] and either R. Abraham Hazan or R. Abraham Sternharz (both of whom belong to the fourth generation of Bratslav) may have confused the two homonyms of the second generation. Be that as it may, the section which concerns us most in both accounts, that is, the one dealing with the confession itself, is similar in both. The *Tovot zikhronot* version reads:

> When he [R. Isaac] came to Zlatopol he did not know in which house *adumor* was living. He asked someone there and was shown the house . . . R. Nahman had deliberately locked the door from inside and gone upstairs. R. Isaac knocked once and then again, until R. Nahman opened up . . . [there follows a long account of R. Nahman's conversation with R. Isaac, which consists mostly of sections of what was to become—a few weeks later—the *torah* 'Or haganuz']. And when R. Nahman finished talking . . . R. Isaac fainted . . . for he was so terrified and astounded that he collapsed in a faint . . . And even when he came round he was still afraid . . . And he started to weep and cry before *adumor*, and confessed all that had ever happened to him. For R. Nahman had dealt with him with such wondrous wisdom that although he did not tell him to confess, R. Isaac became so excited that his heart broke down of its own accord and he made a *viduy devarim* [confession] before R. Nahman.[49]

Although in this version R. Isaac's confession is almost spontaneous whereas in *Sefer kokhevei or* he is explicitly asked to confess, his emotional experience is identical in both versions: R. Nahman inspires him with the most terrible fear, he breaks down, and in an outburst of weeping confesses before him 'all that had ever happened to him'. This agrees with all other accounts of confession before R. Nahman. Invariably it is induced by fear; the disciples coming out of confession are always described as 'red-faced' or 'with tears rolling down their cheeks', and some of them also faint. Similarly, all these sessions are held in private, R. Nahman taking special care to be left alone with the person making confession.

It is worthy of note that, while all the accounts which we have of confession before R. Nahman contain detailed descriptions of his interview with each initiated disciple up to the point of the confession, they speak of the confession itself—which is always the emotional climax of the interview—

in very general terms, and say practically nothing about its content. The account of R. Yudl's *hitkarvut*, which up to that point is circumstantially elaborate, ends vaguely with the statement: 'until R. Nahman ordered him to confess before him all that had happened to him, and from that time on he and R. Samuel Isaac became very closely associated with the *adumor*'.[50] The account of the confession of R. Yudl, R. Samuel Isaac, and R. Aaron in Zlatopol is equally vague in this respect.[51] The description of the *hitkarvut* of the *shoḥet* of Kamenets is interrupted by *vekhulei* ('etc.') when it comes to the details of his confession.[52] Similarly, the first version of R. Isaac's *hitkarvut* seems evasive about the contents of the confession: 'R. Nahman then said to him whatever he said [*diber imo mah shediber*], and from that time on R. Isaac became a very close associate of his.' The second version simply resorts to the use of the technical term 'And he made a *viduy devarim* before R. Nahman', anticipating familiarity on the part of the reader with the details of the procedure. This in itself might be the reason why these accounts, primarily written for internal circulation, contain no detailed descriptions of the confessions. It can also be argued that since they were strictly private, these confessions could not have been known to the authors in such detail as they knew and reported the preceding parts of the initiation ceremonies. Indeed, from R. Nathan's interpretation, in his *Likutei halakhot*, of R. Nahman's teaching on confession, it is clear that he considered the entire experience to be a matter which could not be discussed at all.[53]

It is for one of these reasons, and perhaps all of them, that the accounts of confession in the Bratslav sources all fail to mention (along with the omission of details of the sins confessed and the remedies prescribed by R. Nahman) one other important element, and a most powerful incentive to confession, namely, the final granting of absolution by R. Nahman. That he did not merely hear confessions in order to prescribe appropriate *tikunim* but actually granted his followers pardon and atonement for their sins is apparent from *torah* 4, 'Anokhi', in *Likutei moharan* I.

According to this teaching, the absolution of his followers' sins by the tsadik—R. Nahman—means, in fact, the abolition of the impact of those sins on the metaphysical world of the divine *sefirot*. All sins are atoned for in *olam haba*—the World to Come. In order to attain, already in this world, 'a state like that of the *olam haba*', in which one knows that all events that befall one are for one's own good, one must help bring about the redemption of the *sefirah* Malkhut, Sovereignty, from its present exile among the heathen (i.e. the kabbalistic 'evil husks', the *kelipot*) by confessing one's sins before the tsadik:

When a man knows that all events that befall him are for his own good, this is a state like the *olam haba* . . . And it is impossible to attain this state except by raising the *sefirah* Malkhut of holiness from its exile among the heathen; for at the present time the kingdom and government are in the hands of the heathen [kingdom being understood as Kingdom, i.e. Malkhut, Sovereignty, and heathen as Heathen, i.e. the *kelipot*, although the sentence also, of course, retains its plain political import] . . . And it is impossible to restore the kingdom to the Holy One, blessed be He [i.e. to deliver Malkhut from its captivity in the hands of the Heathen, the *kelipot*] except by *viduy devarim* [confession] before a scholar [i.e. the tsadik]. Through this he amends and raises the *sefirah* Malkhut to its root.[54]

The connection between confession, the raising of Malkhut, and atonement for sins is expounded in one of the Bratslav commentaries on *Likutei moharan*:

And it is impossible to attain this state except by raising the *sefirah* Malkhut from its exile: this means that by one's sins one sends the *sefirah* Malkhut of holiness into exile, and then all one's sufferings [punishment for sins] derive from the *kelipot*, on the principle of 'thine own wickedness shall prove the instrument of thine own correction' [Jer. 2: 19]. Therefore [the sinner] cannot grasp that all events which befall him are for his own good . . . But when he raises the *sefirah* Malkhut of holiness from its exile by confessing before the tsadik, then all his transgressions are atoned for of themselves [*mimeila*]. For the primary evil caused by his transgressions is that he sends Malkhut of holiness into exile. But when he raises Malkhut of holiness up from exile, his transgressions are atoned for of themselves. Then, even if he experiences sufferings, his sufferings derive from holiness, and they are a token of love, on the principle of 'whomsoever the Lord loveth he correcteth' [Prov. 3: 12]. Therefore he can grasp and understand all the good which is disguised in them.[55]

The fundamental consequence of sin is the sinking of Malkhut into the realm of the *kelipot*. Thus, the primary purpose of confession is not to secure the personal salvation of the sinner, but rather to effect the redemption of Malkhut. The expiation of sin, and the subsequent transformation of all sufferings into a token of God's love, both follow 'of themselves'—almost incidentally—from the restoration of Malkhut to its state of holiness.

R. Nahman explains exactly how the effect upon Malkhut of every sin is effaced, and the sin atoned for, through confession before the tsadik. The word signifying each sin, and each precept, is articulated as a correspondingly evil or good particular permutation of letters of the Hebrew alphabet.[56] Every sin committed by man destroys the good permutation of letters signifying the precept whose transgression it constitutes, and creates in its stead an evil permutation of letters, signifying a sin. There follow two consequences. The precept (*dibur*) is sunk into the realm of *tum'ah* (impurity, defilement, the *kelipot*), that is, Malkhut (identified with *dibur*[57]) is sent into exile; and at the same time the evil permutation of letters constituting the sin becomes engraved on the sinner's bones and wreaks vengeance on him.[58] Only confession can reverse both these consequences. By confessing, the sinner removes from his bones the evil permutation of the letters of his sin, for it is these letters that make up the words and sentences of his verbal confession. This instantly destroys the evil permutation of letters and reconstructs the good permutation signifying the precept, that is, it restores Malkhut to its holiness:

A man's transgressions are on his bones, as it is written, 'But their iniquities shall be engraved upon their bones' [Ezek. 32: 27]. And each transgression has a combination of letters. When a man commits a certain transgression, an evil combination is engraved on his bones, and through this he puts the *dibur* [divine *pronunciamento*] of the negative commandment which he has transgressed into defilement. That is, he puts Malkhut [Sovereignty], which is a *dabar* [spokesman, leader] for each generation, into the realm of the heathen, and gives the heathen power to rule. For example, if he transgresses the negative commandment 'Thou shalt have none [other gods before me]' he destroys the good combination of the commandment and builds an evil combination. This combination becomes engraved on his bones and takes vengeance on him, as it is written: 'Your iniquities have turned away these things' [Jer. 5: 25], and it is written: 'Evil shall prove the death of the wicked' [Ps. 34: 22].[59] But through confession the letters which are engraved on his bones depart from them, and from these letters the *dibur* [utterance] of the confession is made up. For the *dibur* comes from his very bones; as it is written: 'All my bones shall say' [Ps. 35: 10]. It destroys the evil combination, and builds out of it the Malkhut of holiness.[60]

It is not, however, the mere traditional utterance of confession before God that disposes of the consequences of sin in the realm of the *sefirot*. The confession must be uttered specifically before the tsadik, R. Nahman, who alone possesses the special quality—perfect humility (*anavah*)—that facilitates this result:

And this is the meaning of the verse 'The wrath of a king is as messengers of death' [Prov. 16: 14]: for the wrath of the Holy One, blessed be He, on behalf of Malkhut, which he [the sinner] has sunk by his iniquities—'a wise man [*ish ḥakham*] will pacify [lit. atone] it'; that is, the *talmid ḥakham*, who is Moses,[61] will atone for him [the sinner], as it is written, 'and passeth by the transgression of [lit. 'to'] the remnant [*she'erit*]' [Mic. 7: 18], to him who abases himself as [low as] broken remains of food [*shirayim*].[62] Consequently, when he comes before the *talmid ḥakham* and brings out all his permutations before the *talmid ḥakham*, the *talmid ḥakham* is like Moses, who abased himself as [low as] broken meats; as it is written: 'Now the man Moses was very meek' [Num. 12: 3]. This is why he is called a wise man; as it is written: 'But wisdom shall be found from *ayin* [nothingness]' [Job 28: 12].[63] And through this [i.e. through his meekness, his setting himself as low as the remains of broken foodstuffs] the *talmid ḥakham* has the power to atone. As it is said, 'a wise man will pacify [atone] it'.[64]

Anavah (meekness) and *ayin* (nothingness) are here understood in the sense of mystical self-annihilation.[65] It is through this 'meekness', through the fact that his special brand of 'wisdom' enables him to undergo mystical self-annihilation, that the tsadik can atone for his followers' sins. Having entirely emptied himself of any sense of his own being, he can fill the vacuum thus created with the divine *ayin*—nothingness—a realm which is devoid of all oppositions and contradictions. When he achieves this state he becomes part of the divine Ein Sof (infinity), where there ceases to be any incompatibility between *ḥesed* (mercy) and *din* (judgment),[66] that is, between those aspects of the Deity that represent respectively its expansive, benevolent mode of operation and its stern measure of judgment, with which it inflicts all sufferings on man. In other words, by becoming enfolded within the divine Ein Sof the tsadik attains a state in which there is no difference between suffering and joy, where one can grasp that all events are for man's good and derive from God's love for him. This is the 'state of the world to come' (*beḥinat olam haba*), or 'like the world to come' (*me'ein olam haba*), which his followers, too, can attain by adhering to him when they confess before him: 'Whenever he [a follower] comes to the *talmid ḥakham* and tells him all that is in his heart [i.e. confesses], the *talmid ḥakham* is as Moses, who is as *ayin*, as Scripture says: "But wisdom shall be found from *ayin*", and through this you [the follower] are incorporated in the divine Ein Sof.'[67] For R. Nahman's followers are *devukim*, mystically adhered to their tsadik. When he hears their confessions he undergoes self-annihilation, so that they, who are not capable of his 'meekness' but who have adhered to him at that same time, become themselves incorporated in the divine Ein Sof. Thus they, too, can grasp, as in the World to Come, that there is no distinction between God's *ḥesed* and his *din*, or, as the idea is expressed here, between the two divine names that correspond to these two divine aspects, namely, Adonai and Elohim: 'And this is [evident in] what Moses said to his generation, "Unto thee it was shewed, that thou mightest know that the Lord [Heb. Adonai], *he* is God" [Heb. Elohim] [Deut. 4: 35]. For Moses is as *ayin*, and as for his generation, who adhere [*devukim*] to him, it befits them to know . . . [that] Adonai, *he* is Elohim.'[68]

It is not quite clear from this teaching precisely what 'adherence' to the tsadik requires of the confessing party at the time of confession. Does he stand in relation to the tsadik as the tsadik stands in relation to Ein Sof? Does he, too, have to experience mystical self-annihilation so as to fill himself with the being of the tsadik, who at that moment is part of the Ein Sof? R. Nahman's chief disciple and scribe, Nathan Sternharz, certainly understands it in this way, as is evident from his interpretation in his own work, *Likutei halakhot*, of the following passage from his master's teaching on confession: 'And at the time when he annihilates himself in relation to Ein Sof, the verse "but no man knoweth" [Deut. 34: 6] applies to him; for even he does not know himself.'[69] R. Nathan reads this passage as referring to the confessing disciple, not to the tsadik. He writes: 'For it is impossible to talk of it [of confession] to one's friends; for the glittering of the light of Ein Sof which shines in the knowledge of the Israelite who has had the merit of associating himself [i.e. who has been initiated through *hitkarvut*] with the True Tsadik . . . is impossible to discuss; for at the time of annihilation he himself "does not know".'[70] R. Nahman, however, almost certainly has the tsadik in mind in this, as in any other passage in this *torah* where he speaks of self-annihilation—*anavah*, *ayin*, *bitul* (annulment), or *hitpashetut hagashmiyut* (stripping away of corporeality). One would have accepted R. Nathan's interpretation without question if it were certain that his presentation of confession from the point of view of the confessing disciple was based on personal experience. But his description in *Likutei halakhot* is textually dependent on *Likutei moharan*, and it does not add a single detail which might have been based on his own recollections of the experience.

This corroborates other evidence to the effect that his own familiarity with the institution was purely literary.[71]

If we compare *viduy devarim* before R. Nahman with confession before the *ḥakham* as it was practised among the medieval Ashkenazi *ḥasidim* and in subsequent generations, two important differences emerge. First, confession before the *ḥakham* served a simple, practical purpose: The *ḥakham* had to hear it in order to know what penance to prescribe for each sin. Had the sinner himself been sufficiently learned in compensating penitence (*teshuvat hamishkal*) he would not have been under the necessity of confessing to anyone. But R. Nahman had no need to hear the confession in order to learn the nature of the sin. In most cases he made it quite clear that he knew all about his disciple's sins even before the confession was made. We may recall his words to the man who refused to confess before him: 'Do I not know all that happens to you, even when you are lying in your bed?'[72] and on several occasions he intimated to his followers that it was time to make confession by saying: 'Well, tell me that which God knows, and you and I know.' However, R. Nahman's foreknowledge of the confessing party's sins did not render confession superfluous, as it would have done in the case of the traditional *ḥakham*. For it was the very utterance of the confession in his presence that removed the evil letter permutation of the sin from the confessor's bones, destroyed it, and constructed out of the same letters a holy combination yielding a *dibur* (precept), thus redeeming Malkhut by effectively undoing the theurgic impact of the sin.

This leads us to the second difference between traditional confession before the *ḥakham* and *viduy devarim* before R. Nahman. In the case of the former, confession on its own did not guarantee expiation of the sin. Only when the sinner had carried out his penance in its entirety could he expect his sin to be atoned for. But in the circle of R. Nahman it was the confession itself that accounted for complete expiation. The subsequent *tikun*—the remedial penitential instructions which R. Nahman gave each confessing party in accordance with 'the root of his soul'—had nothing to do with atonement for the sins confessed. *Tikunim* were meant to guide the disciples in the future, but the sins they had committed up to the day of their *hitkarvut* were all wiped out and atoned for from the moment when they articulated their confession before R. Nahman.

The *tikunim* which R. Nahman gave to each new disciple at the end of his confession were presumably chosen according to the man's past sins.

There is no record of them, just as there is no detailed record of the confessions themselves. One can only speculate as to their nature. Most likely they were instructions to recite especially relevant prayers or combinations of psalms, such as the only published *tikun lemikreh lailah—tikun* for 'an accident of the night' (the traditional euphemism for nocturnal emission of semen). In addition, it is not impossible that R. Nahman occasionally prescribed some such measures of self-mortification as had been widely practised both by the medieval Ashkenazi hasidim and by those ascetic pietists (also known as hasidim) who were the immediate predecessors of the 'new', Beshtian hasidism—fasting, rolling in the snow (*gilgul sheleg*), and the like. He himself had strong ascetic tendencies, and had practised all these in his youth.[73] Although he was officially said to have abandoned this line in later life, there is some scattered evidence in Bratslav sources indicating (although not in connection with confession) that he did continue to prescribe such measures for his followers.[74]

In his later years R. Nahman discontinued the practice of hearing confessions altogether. We never learn from the Bratslav literature why or exactly when the institution was interrupted. In the years when the controversy between R. Nahman and R. Aryeh Leyb of Shpola (Szpoła; the Shpola Zeyde) was at its height, confessions were still going on in Bratslav. We know that when R. Nahman moved (or possibly fled) from Zlatopol to Bratslav in 1802, he was still accustomed to hearing confessions from his followers:

Our Rebbe . . . came to Bratslav on a Tuesday [at the beginning of the month of Elul 5562 (1802)], which was a market day. People gathered together and said of him that he had rejected the customs of the Famous Ones [*mefursamim*, i.e. tsadikim], who serve the Lord mostly by feasting, with food and drink . . . But Our Rebbe speaks of nothing else but Torah and prayer, and he commands [his followers] to make confession before him. And one man there . . . said of one of Our Rebbe's followers: 'I have seen a *viduynik*'; and he meant it in a derogatory sense, by way of mockery.[75]

The next time we hear anything of confessions in Bratslav it is only to learn that they had already been stopped. We read:

R. Judah Eliezer, who travelled to Palestine with R. Nathan, became associated [i.e. was initiated by *hitkarvut*] with R. Nahman towards the end of his [R. Nahman's] life. He began to make confession before him, but by that time

R. Nahman, for secret reasons of his own, would no longer hear confessions. R. Judah Eliezer did not know this, and began to confess. R. Nahman interrupted him, and informed him that he had abandoned that practice. But since R. Judah had already begun to confess, he gave him a few *tikunim*, and bade him discuss the rest with R. Nathan (and only in general, without recounting the sins in detail).[76]

It is not impossible that confessions were abolished very soon after R. Nahman's move from Zlatopol to Bratslav and before R. Nathan's *hitkarvut* a few weeks later. R. Abraham Sternharz, when describing his great-grandfather's *hitkarvut*, writes of the attempts made by R. Nathan's family and friends in Nemirov to prevent him from joining the hasidic movement in general, and particularly R. Nahman's circle. He explains their opposition thus: 'For his father and father-in-law were of the sect of the "Pharisees", and particularly since those who used to travel to Our Rebbe *beforehand* [*mikodem*] were nicknamed *viduynikes*, and were considered a shame and a disgrace by the *mitnagedim*.'[77] The use of the word 'beforehand' might imply that confessions had been practised in R. Nahman's circle before R. Nathan's *hitkarvut*, but not during or after it. Indeed, it is remarkable that nowhere in the numerous accounts of the *hitkarvut* of R. Nathan, given by himself and by others, is there any mention of a confession he might have made before R. Nahman.[78]

Later Bratslav authors seem to be as ignorant as we are of the reasons for R. Nahman's decision to discontinue the practice of confession. Nor does the account (in *Siḥot vesipurim*), which informs us of this decision, specify whether the task of hearing confessions in some modified form ('without recounting the sins in detail') was permanently entrusted to R. Nathan, or whether his hearing of R. Judah Eliezer's modified confession was an exceptional event. But since we hear of no confessions made before R. Nathan in the years when he was himself the effective leader of Bratslav, it may be assumed that the practice was entirely abandoned.

Indeed, *Sefer likutei tefilot* provides some support for this assumption. In the prayer which is based on, and corresponds to, the *torah* on confession (entitled 'Anokhi') in *Likutei moharan* I, R. Nathan clearly indicates that in the absence of R. Nahman—whose death he bitterly mourns—since no other tsadik has yet emerged who could replace him in his capacity of father-confessor, members of the group are to confess directly to God. He seems, however, to regard such confessions (addressed to God directly) as being inferior in their power of atonement to confessions before 'the

True Tsadik'—R. Nahman—as is evident from his express wish: 'And may the *viduy devarim* which I have confessed before Thee be considered before Thee as acceptable and as pleasing as if I had confessed it before the Wise Man and True Tsadik of the generation.'[79] R. Nathan claims that this state of affairs, in which confessions are to be addressed directly to God, is temporary only, and that he is awaiting the emergence of new True Tsadikim, who would be capable of hearing confessions and atoning for sins just as R. Nahman could do. He even says that he believes such tsadikim to be alive in his own time, but that they are hidden and unrecognizable: 'It is certain that there are True Tsadikim even in this generation, but they are hidden and disguised from our eyes.'[80] However, these statements are not necessarily to be taken at their face value. First, though he refers to the existence of several, and perhaps even many such True Tsadikim—in the plural—it is almost certain that he really has in mind only one True Tsadik of this quality, as his occasional slips into the singular betray: 'All as one man are wishing and yearning, awaiting and expecting to associate themselves with the True Tsadik, in order that he may make them repent of their iniquities and amend their crimes, and show us the way to follow and the right way to act.'[81] And again, with both singular and plural occurring in one sentence:

> And all the good qualities and attributes . . . which we could have gained through the True Tsadikim . . . help us, O Lord our God, to attain them all . . . for it is revealed and known before Thee that my will and desire to associate myself with the True Tsadikim are very strong, but through my numerous iniquities I have not had the merit to know who he is and where he is. O would that I had known this and had found him! I would have come leaping upon the mountains, skipping upon the hills [after S. of S. 2: 8], to associate myself with him; I would have declared unto him the number of my steps [after Job 31: 37].[82]

These 'slips' occur in all editions of *Likutei tefilot*, and seem to be but a reminder to the reader that the numerous references to the plurality of present and future True Tsadikim are, in fact, a disguise for the genuine belief in the one and only such True Tsadik. Speculations as to the identity of this one True Tsadik cannot be substantiated by any direct evidence. It can only be observed here that expectations of the appearance in the future of any tsadik other than R. Nahman, a tsadik who would fully replace him in his capacity of confessor or, for that matter, in any other capacity, are totally alien to Bratslav. This is quite clear from the following, as well as from many other passages in the Bratslav literature:

Concerning this matter we have found with *adumor* . . . that he also said explicitly in the following words: 'Why should you be afraid that I should go before you?'; namely, that Our Rebbe . . . *who is himself the True Tsadik, to the end of all generations*, had warned and promised us that he would go before us, even before such lowly ones as ourselves in the present generations. He goes before us always, to show us the way we should follow. He straightens the way for us and removes from it all kinds of snares and thorns, snakes and scorpions; for his strength now is as his strength then, in his holy lifetime. And it is certain that his strength and his merit now are much greater, for 'tsadikim are greater when they die than when they are alive' [BT *Hul.* 7*b*].[83]

The use interchangeably of the plural and singular True Tsadik or the Tsadik of the Generation is already found in *Likutei moharan*. For example:

There are True Tsadikim of great standing, and they have holy mouths, and it is their manner to speak great and wonderful things . . . And there are True Tsadikim who can effect a *pidyon* through their eating, etc. But because of the boasting of these great tsadikim which comes out of their holy mouths, there are other hypocrites and liars who ape them, and they, too, boast with the same boasting words which come out of the holy mouth of the True Tsadik . . . But in truth it is to the advantage of the True Tsadik that there exist such liars who imitate them.[84]

It is impossible to tell with certainty whether this apparent confusion between singular and plural was in R. Nahman's own language, or whether it was introduced by R. Nathan, the scribe. It is, however, quite clear from the continuation of the teaching from which the above quotation is taken that R. Nahman regarded all the tsadikim in the world as arranged in a certain hierarchical order. According to him, there are some who are altogether false tsadikim; others who are indeed true tsadikim, but who speak highly of their own greatness and thereby diminish it: there are some true tsadikim whose degree of piety is even greater, since they do not boast of it; and at the top of the order there stands *the* True Tsadik—one who is much greater than all the other true tsadikim. R. Nahman's belief that there is one such supreme tsadik is implicit in numerous passages in his teachings. For example: 'The world says that there is no need to search for great things. But I say that, on the contrary, one must search for great things; one must look and search for the greatest tsadik of all. And it is further explained in his book that one must search especially for the tsadik and rebbe who is the greatest one of all.'[85] There is little doubt as to whom R. Nahman had in mind when he spoke of the greatest tsadik of all: 'And then he said explicitly about himself: "You imagine that I have no power except over you. In fact I have power even over all the tsadikim of the generation; but my power is in disguise."'[86] Such statements would naturally have been provocative and have given offence to other hasidic leaders. It is not impossible that the occasional confusion in *Likutei moharan* between True Tsadik and True Tsadikim was a careful modification introduced by R. Nathan (no doubt with R. Nahman's approval), or perhaps even by R. Nahman himself, with deliberate inconsistency so as not to obliterate entirely the real import of the text.

There is a much stronger case for this suggestion when it comes to *Likutei tefilot*. R. Nathan started turning R. Nahman's teachings into prayers in 1815. By 1817 he had begun to circulate them in manuscript form among members of the group, so that they could copy and use them.[87] A collection of twenty-two prayers was first published by R. Nathan's son Shekhna in 1822; but some time before this publication, during the five years while the prayers were still circulating in manuscript, it appears that *mitnagedim*—hasidic opponents of Bratslav—managed to get hold of them. They must have found the prayers particularly offensive, since R. Nathan records that as a result of this the controversy against Bratslav erupted with greater force: 'At that time I gave the prayers out to be copied, and they spread among Our People until the *mitnagedim* found out, and through this, too, the controversy became more acute.'[88] It is not exactly clear who these *mitnagedim* were, as the old controversy with the Shpola Zeyde must have died out after the death of the Zeyde himself in 1812, shortly after R. Nahman's own death, and the controversy with R. Moses Zevi of Savran did not start until 1835. The book *Likutei tefilot*, even before it was published, must have aroused sufficient opposition to reopen the controversy. The accusation laid against its author, R. Nathan, seems to have been that it was blasphemous to compose prayers without possession of divine inspiration. This can be reconstructed from the following account:

I have heard from the veteran [Bratslav member] R. Nahman Tulchiner . . . that once . . . R. Nathan was by his [R. Nahman's] shrine and recited the prayer which begins with the words 'Thou hast created' in *Likutei tefilot* II, §36. And after he had left, he said quizzically: the *mitnagedim* ask if there is divine inspiration in the prayers; in fact they are above divine inspiration, for they derive from the fiftieth gate.[89]

R. Nathan's own introduction to *Likutei tefilot* also echoes this line of accusation:

The composition of prayers is no exceptional thing. Many authorities, greater and less, have preceded me in doing this. Even the *piyutim*, *seliḥot*, and *zemirot* [liturgical compositions] were not composed by the ancient prophets or by the *tana'im*, who were in possession of divine inspiration; rather they were composed by more recent authorities, who lived long after the cessation of divine inspiration in Israel. For surely, any educated man would understand that just as writers of all other kinds of books do not necessarily have to be in possession of divine inspiration, so those who compose prayers are not forbidden to do so if they are not in possession of divine inspiration . . . On the contrary, the composition of prayers demands no responsibility, and it is not as potentially dangerous as the writing of other kinds of books . . . Surely, even those who are not of very high standing ought not to be prevented from composing prayers, especially these prayers, which stand on a firm basis . . . on the words of the holy teachings of Our Rebbe . . . all of whose words were uttered with the highest degree of divine inspiration.[90]

It is therefore reasonable to assume that R. Nathan would have toned down radical doctrines particularly in this book, which, even before it was published, came under special attack from the opponents of the group. It seems that this is what lies behind the confusion between singular and plural in the prayer based on the *torah* 'Anokhi'.

This prayer clearly demonstrates that the duty of hearing confessions was not permanently delegated to R. Nathan or continued by him after R. Nahman's death. Rather, confession had been abandoned altogether in Bratslav already in R. Nahman's lifetime, and most certainly after his death. However, it is odd that R. Nahman's decision to stop hearing confessions is totally ignored in *Likutei tefilot*. The prayer implies that confessions ceased with R. Nahman's death only, and as a result of it, but not that they had been discontinued by him a few years earlier. It does not wish the reason (whatever it may have been) for abolishing confession to be removed, but rather it expresses the desire for a suitable tsadik to appear who would be capable of resuming the role of confessor:

With Thy great mercy Thou hast shown us . . . to confess before the *talmid ḥakham* and True Tsadik of the generation, so that through this Thou mayest effect atonement for all our iniquities and crimes . . . But what are we to do now, O Lord our God, for we have been left fatherless orphans, and there is no one to stand for us? . . . The True Tsadikim and wise men of the generation, who had this power that I have mentioned before Thee, and even more, have departed from us because of our many iniquities . . . Woe to us, for we have been robbed . . . The desire of our eyes, the restorer of our life, has been taken away from us . . . Therefore I have come before Thee, O Lord my God and the God of my ancestors . . . that Thou mayest pity me and have mercy on me and send us True Tsadikim, who may have the power to amend us and make us repent and amend our souls and atone for our iniquities . . . Make us . . . worthy of having *viduy devarim* before the True Tsadik and Wise Man of the generation, so that we may confess all our sins, iniquities and crimes before him . . . in order that he should atone for us by his wisdom and meekness.[91]

Finally there remains the question of the origin of the institution of confession in Bratslav. It is undeniable that in its external form, that of private confession before a man who grants absolution from sin, this type of confession is absent from Jewish tradition and is very similar to the Christian sacrament of confession. But this, it seems, is where the similarity ends. There is no trace of the Christian doctrine of confession in R. Nahman's teaching, and his practice of *viduy* was more likely to have been inspired by the hagiographical traditions about the Ari as confessor. Needless to say, it is highly unlikely that he had access to any Christian theological treatises on confession. His concepts, terminology, and imagery are deeply rooted in the kabbalistic tradition. As in kabbalah (and in contradistinction to the Christian doctrine), R. Nahman hardly discusses sins and their expiation on the moral or theological level. He is interested in them primarily from the theurgic point of view of their effect on the condition of the *sefirot*. Thus atonement does not cancel out the sin by extra prayer, a good deed, self-mortification, or similar. Indeed, atonement does not even seem to require forgiveness. It is a quasi-magical linguistic operation by which Malkhut is restored to the state it had enjoyed before the sin was committed. In other words, through confession, the sin—or rather its impact on Malkhut—is undone, wiped off, as if it had never been committed.

Whilst in the Lurianic kabbalah confession still forms part of the liturgy and is addressed directly to God, R. Nahman introduces the tsadik as an intermediary between the confessing hasid and the Deity. Without him confession would not have the effect of annulling the impact of the sin, and the sinner would not be included in the 'state of the world to come', where the difference between mercy and judgement is effaced. The introduction of the tsadik as an intermediary in confession is R. Nahman's innovation; and it is, after all, a very natural innovation within a movement in which the concept of the tsadik as an intermediary between ordinary folk and God is so fundamental. It is, indeed, surprising, as Weiss observed, that this step was not taken by many more hasidic leaders. One can only assume that the persistence of the medieval tradition, as manifest in the literature of interfaith disputation, of Jewish opposition to, and contempt for, the superficially similar Christian institution, prevented the widespread practice of confession in the hasidic movement.

Why was R. Nahman among those few tsadikim who did, nevertheless, institute the practice of confession? He belonged to that school of thought in the hasidic leadership which saw the tsadik as a being qualitatively, even ontologically, different from his followers—a man distinguished in essence from ordinary people. In his teachings this concept of the tsadik found one of its strongest expressions in the hasidic movement.[92] Where the tsadik was seen in such a light, his position as an intermediary between God and man in confession was, perhaps, the more easily acceptable. Significantly, R. Nahman introduced confession into his circle shortly after his return from Palestine. His journey there is often marked in the Bratslav literature as a turning point in his life, which radically changed his concept of himself as a tsadik.[93] It is not impossible that his subsequent abolition of the institution was similarly connected with some crisis in his concept of his own tsadikism, a crisis of which there are some traces in his later *siḥot* and *torot*. But the exact reasons for his decision to stop hearing confessions remain for us, as they were to his immediate disciples, his own secret.

Notes

1 See Lev. 5: 1–5; Num. 5: 6–7.

2 See e.g. JT *Yoma* 3: 7, 8: 7.

3 Ibid.; also BT *Ber.* 34*b*; *Sot.* 7*b*. For the role of confession in the rabbinic concept of atonement see E. E. Urbach, *The Sages: Their Concepts and Beliefs* (Cambridge, Mass., 1987), ch. 15, particularly pp. 433 ff.; A. Büchler, *Studies in Sin and Atonement* (Oxford, 1928).

4 Maimonides, *Mishneh torah*, 'Hilkhot teshuvah', 1–2.

5 For the history of the institution of confession in the Christian Church see O. D. Watkins, *A History of Penance*, 2 vols. (London, 1920); R. C. Mortimer, *The Origins of Private Penance in the Western Church* (Oxford, 1939); P. F. Palmer (ed.), *Sacraments and Forgiveness: History and Doctrinal Development of Penance, Extreme Unction and Indulgences*, Sources of Christian Theology 2 (Westminster, Md., 1960).

6 See E. E. Urbach, 'Études sur la littérature polémique au moyen-age', *Revue des études juives*, 197–8 (1935), 70–1; J. Rosenthal, *Sefer yosef hamekane* (Jerusalem, 1970), 85–6 §§92, 92*a*; 104–5 §114; Meir ben Simeon of Narbonne, *Milḥemet mitsvah*, MS Parma, 85*a–b*, 219*b*–220*a*; D. Berger, *The Jewish–Christian Debate in the High Middle Ages: A Critical Edition of the Nizzahon Vetus* (Philadelphia, 1979), 22–3, 223–4, 339.

7 See R. Chazan, *Fashioning Jewish Identity in Medieval Western Christendom* (Cambridge, 2004), 308–10.

8 J. Dan, *The Esoteric Theology of Ashkenazi Hasidism* [Torat hasod shel ḥasidut ashkenaz] (Jerusalem, 1968), 37; Y. F. Baer, 'The Religious Social Tendency of *Sefer ḥasidim*' (Heb.), *Zion*, 3 (1938), 18.

9 *Sefer ḥasidim*, ed. J. Wistinetzki (Frankfurt am Main, 1924), 44–5 §52.

10 Ibid. 25 §19.

11 M. Eisenstadt, *Panim me'irot* (Sulzbach, 1733), pt. II, 104*b* §178. R. Meir Eisenstadt is here replying to a question concerning the legitimacy of public confession, a practice which he rejects as a recent outside or heretical influence, deviating from the tradition of private confession before God. See in this connection A. J. Heschel, 'R. Gershon Kutover: His Life and Emigration to the Land of Israel' (Heb.), *Hebrew Union College Annual* 23, pt. II (1951), 247. (The relevant passage was omitted from the English version of this article, in id., *The Circle of the Baal Shem tov: Studies in Hasidism*, ed. S. H. Dresner (Chicago, 1985.)

12 S. Dreznits, *Shivḥei ha'ari* (Warsaw, 1863), 11*a–b*. See also *Toledot ha'ari*, ed. M. Benayahu (Jerusalem, 1967), 238–9. For a comprehensive discussion of the Ari's powers as diagnostician of sinful souls, see L. Fine, *Physician of the Soul, Healer of the Cosmos* (Stanford, Calif., 2001), 150–86.

13 J. G. Weiss, 'R. Abraham Kalisker's Concept of Communion with God and Man', *Journal of Jewish Studies*, 6 (1955), 99 (repr. in id., *Studies in East European Jewish Mysticism and Hasidism* (London, 1997), 166).

14 M. Wilensky, *Hasidim and Mitnagedim* [Ḥasidim umitnagedim] (Jerusalem, 1970), i. 276.

15 Ibid. ii. 161–2.

16 I. B. Levinson, *Emek refa'im*, in id., *Yalkut rival* (Warsaw, 1878), 127. For another maskilic reference to confession before the tsadik, see J. Perl, *Uiber das*

Wesen der Sekte Chassidim aus ihren eigenen Schriften gezogen im Jahre 1816, ed. A. Rubinstein (Jerusalem, 1977), 129.

17 Yeruham Hayim Halevi Segal, *Beit halevi* (Lemberg, 1910), 22, cited in M. M. Foigel, 'The Holy Rabbi Zevi Hirsh of Nadvorna and His Disciples' (Heb.), *Kovets siftei tsadikim*, 7 (Kislev 5755 [1994]), 53. This reference was brought to my attention by the late Yehoshua Mondshine.

18 The Hebrew acronym of *adonenu umorenu*—our master and teacher—a title often used in the Bratslav sources in reference to R. Nahman. The form *adumor* differs slightly from that conventional in most other hasidic circles, *admor*.

19 R. Nahman's intention in quoting this verse to R. Yudl and his interpretation of it are clarified by the following passage, written by his chief disciple and scribe, R. Nathan Sternharz:

> They have told me his [R. Nahman's] holy disquisition on the occasion when a certain hasid of some importance came before him. He [that hasid] was by then quite old, and was familiar with the writings of Isaac Luria. He wished to associate himself with Our Rebbe of Blessed Memory [another title often used in the Bratslav sources in reference to R. Nahman]. He began to speak to Our Rebbe in the manner of the important hasidim and said to him: 'Let Our Rebbe show us a way to worship the Creator.' Our Rebbe . . . answered quizzically: 'That thy way may be known upon earth [Ps. 67: 2]'. That is to say, would one who is still steeped in total 'earthliness' like to know a way to approach the Holy One, blessed be He? And it is understood from this story that he [R. Nahman] reproached him [R. Yudl] because he had spoken to him in a haughty manner, saying that he wished to know a way to the Holy One, blessed be He; as though all he lacked was knowledge of such ways. For Our Rebbe wanted him to speak truthfully. (N. Sternharz, *Siḥot haran* [with *Shivḥei haran*] (Lemberg, 1901), 80 §290)

Although R. Yudl's name is not mentioned here at all, there is no doubt that the passage deals with his initiation. As was his custom in all his writings, R. Nathan, who no doubt knew the identity of the hasid in question, preferred to refer to him vaguely as 'a certain hasid of some importance'. It is only the later report by R. Abraham Hazan of Tulchin in *Sefer kokhevei or* that provides us with the name of that hasid. The version of the account in *Sefer kokhevei or* is very close to that of the account, as far as it goes, in *Siḥot haran*, and was almost certainly based on it. But it contains many additional details which were not reported by R. Nathan, and which were possibly known to him.

20 *Sefer kokhevei or* (Jerusalem, 1961), 'Anshei moharan', 26–7 §23.

21 The technical Hebrew term for initiation in Bratslav hasidism is *hitkarvut*—'drawing near'. The verb 'to draw near' will hereafter be translated as 'to associate oneself with' the tsadik. The noun will mostly be left in its Hebrew form.

22 R. Nahman moved to Zlatopol in 1800 (Elul 5560) and stayed there for two years, until his move to Bratslav; see Sternharz, *Ḥayei moharan*, i (Jerusalem, 1947), 'Mekom yeshivato unesiotav', 45 §11.

23 As a result of R. Nahman's intervention on his behalf, R. Aaron later became the rabbi of Bratslav (see Avraham Kokhav Lev [Sternharz], *Tovot zikhronot* [appended to Nahman of Cherin's *Yeraḥ ha'eitanim*] (Jerusalem, 1951), 124). His success in promoting the appointment of one of his followers as rabbi of the town can serve as an indication of R. Nahman's popularity and influence there.

24 R. Yudl and R. Samuel Isaac became R. Nahman's associates some time before his journey from Medvedevka to Palestine in 1798. By that time R. Yudl was sufficiently close to R. Nahman to be consulted about his plans for the journey (see Sternharz, *Ḥayei moharan*, i, 'Nesiato le'erets yisra'el', 62 §7). R. Aaron first came to R. Nahman shortly after the latter's return from Palestine, and before his move from Medvedevka to Zlatopol in 1800 (see *Tovot zikhronot*, 121–4).

25 The *torah* in question is 'Anokhi', no. 4 in *Likutei moharan*, i. For its contents, see below.

26 For the full version of this story see Sternharz, *Ḥayei moharan*, i, 'Siḥot hashayakhim lehatorot', 28 §58. I have not been able to find any comparable story outside the Bratslav literature representing the Besht as confessor, and, as far as I am aware, the Besht did not practise confession. It would seem that by connecting the Besht with confession R. Nahman was providing this novel and rather unusual practice with a legitimate, traditional basis in hasidism. For the notion of bone-aches which could only be alleviated by confession, see below, at nn. 57–9.

27 The Hebrew plural of *pidyon*. See p. 165 above.

28 *Tovot zikhronot*, 106.

29 Meaning, in Yiddish, 'confession-mongers'; see n. 42 below.

30 The dating in *Tovot zikhronot* of the *torah* 'Anokhi' (*Likutei moharan*, pt. I, *torah* 4) to Pentecost in Zlatopol agrees with the date suggested in Nathan Sternharz's list in *Ḥayei moharan* of the dates on which most of the *torot* in *Likutei moharan* were delivered. See Sternharz, *Ḥayei moharan*, i, 'Siḥot hashayakhim lehatorot', 28 §59. A later Bratslav tradition, which opens with the declaration 'It is well known that *torah* 4 in *Likutei moharan*, part I was delivered in Zlatopol during Pentecost', proceeds to describe yet another *hitkarvut*, of an unnamed new recruit, which took place on the same occasion. Arriving in Zlatopol for his first audience with R. Nahman on the eve of the festival and unaware that he was expected to confess his sins, he recounted all his mundane troubles at some considerable length. R. Nahman interrupted the audience

and instructed him to return on the next day. Only then, immediately after hearing R. Nahman deliver his *torah* 'Anokhi' and understanding its implications, did he make his full confession during a fresh private audience with R. Nahman, from which point on he became one of his most dedicated and ardent followers. See *Siaḥ sarfei kodesh* (Jerusalem, 1994), i. 217–19 §506; this work, published anonymously, is based primarily on Bratslav traditions transmitted by R. Levi Isaac Bender (1897–1989).

31 The Hebrew text reads *kemo viduy devarim*.

32 *Tovot zikhronot*, 123. The 'clean shirt' is a euphemistic reference to sexual purity.

33 For more on this see n. 37 below.

34 See *Sefer kokhevei or*, 'Anshei moharan', 40 §4.

35 This phrase, which, according to R. Nahman, the Besht had also used in order to instruct his associate to confess (see at n. 26 above), seems to have been the formula with which R. Nahman often opened the confessional proceedings.

36 *Avaneiha barzel* (printed with *Sefer kokhevei or*), 40 §61.

37 If we are to go by the few clues we have as to the content of the confessions, such as R. Aaron's confession of having entered his bridal chamber wearing a clean shirt, and R. Nahman's remark to the young man who refused to confess that he knew all that happened to him even when he was lying on his bed (see p. 170 above), it is evident that the confessions included, and perhaps even focused on, the most intimate details of the disciples' sexual lives. This is corroborated by a 19th-century account of the hasidic practice of confession, written by Eliezer Zvi Hakohen Zweifel, a *maskil* who was well acquainted with hasidic life in his native Russia, and whose book *Shalom al yisra'el*, published in four volumes during the 1860s and 1870s, was a pioneering maskilic defence of hasidism. In it he addresses the question

> why hasidism is stricter about the 'sin of youth' [*ḥatat ne'urim*—a euphemism for involuntary nocturnal emission and masturbation] than about all the other grave transgressions mentioned in the Torah, so much so that, more often than not, all those who come before the tsadik to confess do not even mention most of the transgressions that carry the punishment of *karet* [extirpation—punishment at the hands of Heaven, e.g. premature death, for transgressions committed deliberately] . . . and only the 'sin of the phallus' [*pegam haberit*—literally, and euphemistically, 'the blemished covenant'] is considered by them the gravest of all transgressions. (*Shalom al yisra'el* (Vilna, 1873), iii, pt. II, 30–1)

See on this source A. Rapoport-Albert, *Studies in Hasidism, Sabbatianism, and Gender* [Ḥasidim veshabeta'im, anashim venashim] (Jerusalem, 2015), 197–8 and nn. 6–9.

38 Apart from his sudden journeys, which were irregular, but for a time rather frequent, and never explained to anyone (see on this J. G. Weiss, 'Megilat setarim' (Heb.), *Kiryat sefer*, 44 (1969), 186), R. Nahman used to travel at fixed times of the year to visit the three towns where most of his followers were concentrated: Cherin (Chigirin, Czehryń), Tirhavitsa (Trushivtsi), and Medvedevka (see Sternharz, *Ḥayei moharan*, i, 'Siḥot hashayakhim lehatorot', 16 §26; ibid., 'Mekom yeshivato unesiotav', 59 §24, 60 §25). These regular journeys were, however, discontinued in 1808, soon after his return from a sudden trip to Lemberg, where his illness became more acute, so that he could no longer travel long distances (see ibid. 60 §26). A late Bratslav tradition, transmitted by R. Levi Isaac Bender in the name of Abraham [ben Nahman] Hazan of Tulchin, seems to imply that perhaps not only new recruits but older disciples as well were expected to confess during the New Year festival—the largest annual gathering at R. Nahman's court. The tradition attempts to explain

> the wondrous phenomenon we witnessed during the years when Our Rebbe still conducted confessions: how could the hundreds of people who visited him for the New Year all come before him to make their confessions and present their supplications, and how could Our Rebbe set out for each one the appropriate path to repentence during the short time available on the eve of the New Year? He [R. Abraham Hazan] explained that according to what we know, confessions were conducted in the following manner: Our Rebbe would be standing in his room facing the wall. The person coming to confess would enter and begin his confession, but after mentioning two or three details, Our Rebbe would raise his hand to signal that he has heard enough, at which point the person would instantly recall everything that had ever befallen him and would be greatly stirred, weeping copiously, and leave the room. All this did not take any more than a very short time. (*Siaḥ sarfei kodesh* (Jerusaem, 1990), iii. 40 §95)

It is difficult to imagine that even at the large New Year gathering hundreds of new recruits would be arriving at R. Nahman's court, and it is impossible to tell how reliable this late tradition might be.

39 The *Tovot zikhronot* account is also printed at the very end of several editions of *Ḥayei moharan*. The traditions preserved in the four booklets which constitute the volume entitled *Sefer kokhevei or*, all of which were written by R. Abraham Hazan or by his pupils, often differ from (and sometimes contradict) the traditions of R. Abraham Sternharz in *Tovot zikhronot*. R. Abraham Hazan usually quotes his father, R. Nahman of Tulchin, as his source. (R. Nahman of Tulchin was R. Nathan's closest disciple and eventual successor in the leadership of Bratslav.) R. Abraham Sternharz's sources are his great-grandfather, R. Nathan, and his maternal grandfather, R. Nahman of Cherin. In most cases it is impossible to determine which traditions are the more authentic.

40 The Hebrew text reads: *ve'asak ba'avodat hashem kol yamav*. The terms *avodat hashem* and *oved hashem* seem to have been synonymous at that time with the terms *ḥasidut* and *ḥasid*. See on this point I. Halpern, *Eastern European Jewry: Historical Studies* [Yehudim veyahadut bemizraḥḥ eiropah] (Jerusalem, 1968), 316–17.

41 The Hebrew expression used is *anshei shelomenu*.

42 The term *viduynikes* (confessors, or those who confess) appears to have been derogatory, and used mostly by the hasidic opponents of R. Nahman and his circle. This emerges from such passages as the following: 'And one man . . . said of one of Our Rebbe's followers, "I have seen a *viduynik*", and he meant it in a derogatory sense, by way of mockery' (*Avaneiha barzel*, 8 §6); 'particularly since those who used to travel to Our Rebbe before were nicknamed *viduynikes*, and they were considered an abomination by the *mitnagedim*' (*Tovot zikhronot*, 109). See also Weiss, 'R. Abraham Kalisker's Concept of Communion', 166; A. Green, *Tormented Master: The Life of Rabbi Nahman of Bratslav* (Alabama, 1979), 45, 60 nn. 78–9. *Mitnagedim* in the Bratslav sources usually indicates the hasidic opponents of the group, rather than orthodox opponents of the hasidic movement as a whole, for example:

> R. Ozer . . . of Uman was first a member of the sect of the *mitnagedim*; later the Holy One, blessed be He, helped him to recognize the truth of Our Teacher Moharnat, until his heart was burning [with desire] to associate himself with him . . . But when this became known to his family, *who were among the important and respectable hasidim of the town*, they literally wanted to kill him. (*Sefer kokhevei or*, 33 §31)

The 'sect of the *mitnagedim*' here undoubtedly means the hasidic opponents of Bratslav, for R. Ozer and his family were hasidim long before his *hitkarvut* to R. Nathan. It is most unlikely that R. Ozer was a *mitnaged* in the usual anti-hasidic sense, while the rest of his family in Uman were hasidim. And even if we assume this to have been the case, had he been an opponent of the hasidic movement the clash between him and his hasidic family would have occurred much earlier, and would have concerned hasidism as a whole, and not his affiliation to the hasidic Bratslav circle. The rabbinic opponents of hasidism are sometimes called in Bratslav *perushim* (Pharisees, separatists, and/or ascetics, that is, those who separate themselves from the world—the term by which the disciples of hasidism's chief rabbinic opponent, the Gaon of Vilna, became known), as, for example, in the account in *Tovot zikhronot*, which explains why R. Nathan's family so strongly opposed his association with R. Nahman: 'For his father and father-in-law were of the sect of the "Pharisees"' (*Tovot zikhronot*, 108). From other sources we know that R. Nathan's family were opponents of hasidism in general.

43 *Sefer kokhevei or*, 29–30 §24.

44 This, however, does not necessarily mean that R. Nahman was the only 'tsadik-confessor' at that time. Nor does the nickname *viduynikes*, by which his followers had become known, indicate that they were the only group in the hasidic camp to practise confession. See at nn. 14–17 above.

45 Nahman of Bratslav, *Likutei moharan*, pt. I, *torah* 15.

46 This dating can be partially verified by comparison with the list of dated *torot* provided in *Ḥayei moharan*, i, 'Siḥot hashayakhim lehatorot', 28–30. Although the list in its present form cannot have been edited by R. Nathan, the author of *Ḥayei moharan*, since he is referred to in it several times in the third person, it was certainly based on R. Nathan's notes. Most of the *torot* for which exact dates are provided were delivered by R. Nahman during the eight years of R. Nathan's association with him. For the earlier *torot* there are either no dates at all, or else vague approximations, preceded by cautious statements such as 'It is thought that' or 'I have heard that'. The date for *torah* 15, 'Or haganuz', is conspicuously missing in this list. All the teachings in *Likutei moharan* immediately preceding and following it (i.e. from *torah* 3 to 14, and from *torah* 16 on) are meticulously dated, and were all delivered during the last eight years of R. Nahman's lifetime. But *torah* 15 is missed out, since it obviously belonged to the period prior to R. Nathan's *hitkarvut*. This agrees with R. Abraham Sternharz's tradition, which connects this teaching with R. Isaac's *hitkarvut* and dates it to R. Nahman's Zlatopol period, about two years before the *hitkarvut* of R. Nathan.

47 *Tovot zikhronot*, 119.

48 See *Sefer kokhevei or*, 30 §25; Sternharz, *Ḥayei moharan*, i, 'Mekom yeshivato unesiotav', 55 §11.

49 *Tovot zikhronot*, 120.

50 See at n. 21 above.

51 See above, at nn. 23–8.

52 See at n. 34 above.

53 See at n. 70 below.

54 Nahman of Bratslav, *Likutei moharan*, pt. I, *torah* 4, 'Anokhi', §§1–3.

55 *Be'ibei hanaḥal* [supplement to *Likutei moharan*] (New York, 1966), 124.

56 This echoes a principle, first articulated in the ancient *Sefer yetsirah* (Book of Creation), whereby clusters of letters—constituting manifestations of the Divine in creation—may be reordered so as to yield each other's opposite: 'The twenty-two letters . . . are fixed on a wheel . . . The wheel rotates backwards and forwards. And this is a sign for the matter: if for the good, above pleasure, and if for evil, below pain' (A. P. Hayman, *Sefer Yeṣira*, Texts and Studies in Ancient Judaism 104 (Tübingen, 2004), 98 §18).

57 R. Nahman explains this traditional kabbalistic designation of the *sefirah* Malkhut in an earlier section of the *torah*, where he writes: 'This [*dibur*] is the

sefirah Malkhut, as in "one *dabar* only for each generation" [BT *San*. 8*a*]. *Dabar* means spokesman, that is, leader and ruler' (*torah* 4, §3). *Malkhut*, meaning kingdom or sovereignty, is identified with *dibur*, meaning (divinely uttered) commandment, through the occurrence in BT *Sanhedrin* of the term *dabar* (both words deriving from the root *d-v/b-r* = speak, command).

58 Hence the reference (above, at nn. 26–8) to bone-aches, from which ailment the Besht's disciple who refused to confess allegedly died, and from which some of R. Nahman's guests on Pentecost in Zlatopol are said to have suffered until they confessed before him. The connection between sins and bones, which is traceable to Ezek. 32: 27—'but their iniquities shall be upon their bones'—reverberates in the subsequent rabbinic and kabbalistic sources, e.g. BT *Ta'an*. 30*b*: 'He who eats meat and drinks wine on the eve of Tishah Be'av, his iniquities are engraved on his bones'; Zohar iii. 275*a*: 'The wicked, his iniquities are engraved on his bones; the righteous, his merits are engraved on his bones', and M. Cordovero, *Pardes rimonim* (Jerusalem, 1962), gate 8, end of ch. 1, quoting the talmudic statement and its scriptural anchor as above, while adding the explanation that 'This is because the soul imprints its actions on [the bones], and its blemishes manifest themselves in the body.'

59 It is to be noted that the foregoing verse (21) in the same psalm, referring to the righteous person (tsadik), reads: 'He [God] keepeth all his bones, not one of them is broken'.

60 Nahman of Bratslav, *Likutei moharan*, pt. I, *torah* 4, §5.

61 R. Nahman often identifies himself with Moses (see e.g. *Likutei moharan*, pt. I, *torah* 64, §§3, 5, 6; ibid., pt. II, *torah* 7, §13), and there is no doubt that he does so here too. The *talmid ḥakham* (scholar) = Moses = the tsadik = R. Nahman. At the basis of this equation lies the assumption that, more often than not, when R. Nahman speaks of the tsadik, the tsadik of the generation, or the leader of the generation, he has in mind none other than himself. This was first suggested as a key to the understanding of some of R. Nahman's teachings by the late J. G. Weiss, and it is here accepted throughout.

62 See BT *Meg*. 15*b*:

> The Holy One, blessed be He, will be [for] a crown on the head of each and every righteous person [*tsadik*], as Scripture says: 'In that day shall the Lord of Hosts be for a crown of glory and for a diadem of beauty unto the residue of his people' [Isa. 28: 5]. One might take this to apply to everyone, but the verse says 'unto the residue of his people'—[only] to him who abases himself as [low as] broken remains of food.

See also Zohar ii. 54*a*: 'The world would not exist if not for those who abase themselves as [low as] broken remains of food.'

63 The Hebrew verse reads *vehaḥokhmah me'ayin timatse* ('But whence shall wisdom be found?'), but R. Nahman, in line with the traditional hasidic inter-

pretation of this verse, treats the Hebrew *me'ayin*, meaning 'whence?', as 'from *ayin*', meaning nothingness.

64 Nahman of Bratslav, *Likutei moharan*, pt. I, *torah* 4, §7.

65 The word *anavah*—meekness—had been used in the sense of mystical self-annihilation (although it also retained its ethical meaning of humility) by various hasidic writers since the Magid of Mezhirech, who had first formulated the quietistic doctrine of *ayin* in hasidism. See J. G. Weiss, 'R. Abraham Kalisker's Concept of Communion', 88. For an extensive discussion of this doctrine in the teachings of the Magid of Mezhirech, see R. Schatz-Uffenheimer, *Hasidism as Mysticism: Quietistic Elements in Eighteenth-Century Hasidic Thought* (Jerusalem, 1993), 65–92; M. Lorberbaum, '"Attain the Attribute of *Ayin*": The Mystical Religiosity of *Magid devarav leya'akov* (Heb.), *Kabbalah: Journal for the Study of Jewish Mystical Texts*, 31 (2014), 169–235.

66 In the text *ḥesed* and *din* are often taken to be indicated by their corresponding divine names, Adonai and Elohim. These designations of the *sefirot* Hesed and Din are based on the rabbinic observation that the Tetragrammaton, vocalized Adonai, is usually employed in the Bible whenever God acts with his quality of *ḥesed*, whereas the name Elohim seems to occur when he acts with the quality of *din*. The visualization of the World to Come as a world in which the distinction between these two qualities ceases to be meaningful is, once again, a rabbinic tradition, which appears here in its kabbalistic guise.

67 Nahman of Bratslav, *Likutei moharan*, pt. I, *torah* 4, §9.

68 Ibid.

69 Ibid.

70 *Likutei halakhot*, 'Ḥoshen mishpat', 'Geviyot ḥov miyetomim', 4 §3. See also R. Nathan's *Likutei tefilot* (Jerusalem, 1957), 9 §4:

> For all this, grant us . . . the merit of confessing before the True Tsadik and Wise Man of the generation . . . so that he would atone for us by means of his wisdom and his meekness . . . and by means of him, grant us the merit of being incorporated in the Ein Sof, the merit of genuinely annihilating ourselves, to the point of divesting ourselves of corporeality.

71 See below, at nn. 77, 78.

72 See above, at n. 36.

73 See e.g. Sternharz, *Shivḥei haran*, 1*b* §1, 2*b* §9, 3*b* §16, 5*a* §19, 5*a–b* §21, 6*a* §24.

74 See *Sefer kokhevei or*, 'Anshei moharan', 6*a* §43; Sternharz, *Ḥayei moharan*, ii, 'Avodat hashem', 55–6 §45; id., *Siḥot haran*, 63*b* §184.

75 *Avaneiha barzel*, 8 §6. It seems that the practice of confession in Bratslav was singled out for ridicule by the opponents of the group. See also *Tovot zikhronot*, 108–9.

76 *Siḥot vesipurim* (in *Sefer kokhevei or*), 143–4 §56. A late tradition recorded in *Siaḥ sarfei kodesh* (Jerusalem, 1994), ii. 109 §326 refers to the passage above from *Siḥot vesipurim* and adds: 'When Our Rebbe abandoned the path of confession . . . it stopped entirely; and even on the New Year's eve, when Our People would enter [his room], they would come with nothing but *kvitlekh* [the slips of paper on which personal petitions would normally be inscribed], on which nothing would be written other than the name of the person entering'.

77 See above, n. 42.

78 According to *Sefer kokhevei or*, 'Anshei moharan', 12 §4, a few days after his very first visit to R. Nahman during the New Year festival, on one of the ten penitential days between New Year and the Day of Atonement, 'he entered R. Nahman's chamber alone and told him everying that was in his heart'. This was clearly not a formal initiation by way of confession—a practice which R. Nahman had already abandoned by this time, but it seems to be the closest that R. Nathan ever got to the experience. In his own rather moving eyewitness account of the death of R. Nahman, he notes that as soon as his master's soul departed, before the ritual preparations for his burial began, 'I entered his chamber and sat on the floor next to him, and spoke in his ear, saying on this occasion everything I yearned but did not manage to tell him when he was alive' (*Yemei moharnat*, pt. I, 44*b*). This may allude to his regret that he had missed by some two years the opportunity, enjoyed by several of R. Nahman's older disciples, as he was surely aware, to undergo the full cleansing experience of confession before their master.

79 *Likutei tefilot*, 9.

80 Ibid. 7.

81 Ibid.

82 Ibid. 9–10.

83 *Tovot zikhronot*, 148; R. Nahman's question, 'Why should you be afraid that I should go before you?', is in Yiddish (*Vos hat ir mora tsu hoben az ikh geh var oykh*?). The remainder is in Hebrew. The obvious parallel with sundry well-known New Testament passages (John 13: 36, 14: 2 f., 18 f., 27–8; cf. Matt. 28: 7, Mark 16: 7) is striking. Deliberate allusion on the part of R. Nahman to the New Testament is inconceivable, but the whole question lies beyond the scope of the present study. For the Christological resonance of R. Nahman's self-construction see S. Magid's pioneering study, *Hasidism Incarnate: Hasidism, Christianity, and the Construction of Modern Judaism* (Stanford, Calif., 2014), 31–50 and *passim*.

84 Nahman of Bratslav, *Likutei moharan*, pt. II, *torah* 15.

85 Sternharz, *Siḥot haran* (in *Shivḥei haran*), 33*a* §51.

86 Sternharz, *Ḥayei moharan*, i, 'Siḥot hashayakhim lehatorot', 15 §24. See also ibid. ii, 'Gedulat hasagato', 10.

87 See N. Sternharz, *Yemei moharnat* (Benei Berak, 1956), pt. I, 55*a*.

88 Ibid. ii. 85 §5. For the history of this book see now J. Meir, 'The Politics of Printing *Sefer likutei tefilot*' (Heb.), *Zion*, 80/1 (2015), 43–68.

89 *Sefer kokhevei or*, 'Anshei moharan', 77 §25.

90 *Likutei tefilot*, introduction.

91 Ibid. 6–9. The prayer may well be alluding to the expectation that R. Nahman would return from the dead or re-emerge from his 'concealment' or 'withdrawal' to complete his messianic mission. For the currency of this belief in Bratslav circles, see above, p. 160 n. 92.

92 Because he is so different in essence from his followers, R. Nahman is often permitted (and is sometimes under a special obligation) to undertake tasks which are specifically forbidden to them. See e.g. Sternharz, *Ḥayei moharan*, ii, 'Lehitraḥek meḥakirot', 38–9 §6; Nahman of Bratslav, *Likutei moharan*, pt. I, *torah* 64, §3; ibid., pt. II, *torah* 19; ibid., *torah* 116.

93 See e.g. Sternharz, *Ḥayei moharan*, i, 'Nesiato le'erets yisra'el', 62 §§6–7; R. Nathan's introduction to *Likutei moharan*, towards the end; Sternharz, *Shivḥei haran*, 'Seder hanesiah shelo le'erets yisra'el', 18*b* §29; id., *Siḥot haran*, 61*b*–62*a* §173.

FOUR

Hagiography with Footnotes: Edifying Tales and the Writing of History in Hasidism

THE ROLE of the heroic personality in history entered the historical discourse of the nineteenth century and became the subject of popular debate in connection with the publication in 1840 of Thomas Carlyle's famous book on this topic.[1] Dismissing the debate as a futile expenditure of scholarly energy, Ahad Ha'am,[2] in the introduction to his quasi-biographical essay on Moses first published in *Hashilo'aḥ* in 1904, wrote:

> Surely it is obvious that the real great men of history, the men, that is, who have become forces in the life of humanity, are not actual, concrete persons who existed in a certain age. There is not a single great man in history of whom popular fancy has not drawn a picture entirely different from the actual man; and it is this imaginary conception, created by the masses to suit their needs and inclinations, that is the real great man . . . this, and not the concrete original. . . . And so it is when learned scholars burrow in the dust of ancient books and manuscripts, in order to raise the great men of history from the grave in their true shapes; believing the while that they are sacrificing their eyesight for the sake of 'historical truth' . . . These scholars will not appreciate the simple fact that not every archaeological truth is also a historical truth.[3]

The distinction between 'archaeological' truth, namely, documentary or material evidence, and the 'historical' truth of the heroic personality which is formed in the popular imagination and becomes an active force in history, served Ahad Ha'am well in his attempt to capture the impact of the mythical personality of Moses, for whose concrete existence, 'archaeologically' speaking, there was virtually no retrievable evidence at all.

It is remarkable, however, that Ahad Ha'am's framework of interpretation, designed to cope with the state of the evidence on Moses—a figure who, according to tradition, lived more than three millennia ago—should have been found suitable, albeit as a self-conscious literary bow in the direction of Ahad Ha'am, for the reconstruction of the life of the founder of modern hasidism, Israel Ba'al Shem Tov, who, after all, lived only two and a half centuries ago, in an age with which we are all, relatively speaking, at home, and about which we are, on the whole, extremely well informed.

Echoing Ahad Ha'am's methodological remarks, with which, like all Zionist intellectuals of his generation, he was bound to have been familiar, Ignacy Schiper, a social and economic historian of Polish Jewry, who died in a concentration camp in 1943, wrote an essay in Yiddish entitled 'R. Israel Ba'al Shem Tov and His Image in Early Hasidic Literature'.[4] The essay appeared in Warsaw in 1939 and was eventually translated into Hebrew and published posthumously in 1960.[5] In it Schiper sharply distinguished between the 'archaeological' truth about the alleged founder of hasidism and the network of fanciful fabrications and confusions which have created the legend of his 'historical' truth. Unlike Ahad Ha'am, however, as a professional historian he was more concerned to identify the true core of 'archaeological' data than to trace the 'historical' impact of the myth. He argued that all the literary sources which had traditionally served the historians of hasidism as the basis for their reconstructions of the Ba'al Shem Tov's life and works were virtually worthless in that they were written long after his death, by men who were either unacquainted with him personally or else motivated by a desire to obscure the true origins of hasidism. The real 'archaeological' founder of the hasidic movement was not Israel Ba'al Shem Tov at all but a fellow *ba'al shem*, a certain Joel of Nemirov—a contemporary rabbi and kabbalist who, like his colleague Israel Ba'al Shem Tov of Międzybóż, possessed the secret knowledge of divine names and could manipulate them to perform supernatural feats, as the title *ba'al shem tov* implies.[6] According to Schiper, this 'archaeological' fact, which was still known in the second generation of hasidism at the court of Dov Ber, the Magid of Mezhirech (Międzyrzecz), was effectively obliterated by the machinations of R. Jacob Joseph of Połonne, a personal disciple of Israel Ba'al Shem Tov and a rival of Dov Ber. It was he who began the process which eventually ousted R. Joel Ba'al Shem and promoted Israel Ba'al Shem Tov in the collective memory of the movement to the 'historical' position of founder and first leader of hasidism.

This extraordinary piece of detection contains not a grain of truth, 'archaeological' or 'historical'. It is as confused and as fanciful as many of the hasidic tales whose authenticity the author was out to deny so catagorically, and it was never taken seriously, as far as I know, by any subsequent student of the history of hasidism.[7] But the sensibility which had inspired it—a sense of the historically problematic nature of the hasidic sources for the lives of Israel Ba'al Shem Tov and all his associates—was shared by all but the most naive or apologetic historians of the movement. It led such scholars as Aaron Zeev Aescoly—a historian, among other things, of Jewish sectarianism, messianic movements, and hasidism—to conclude in his doctoral dissertation, published in Paris in 1928, that 'the Besht[8] had played no part whatsoever' in the formation of the hasidic movement,[9] that he was 'a legendary figure in the history of hasidism whose historical value rested on the sole fact that his legend had been set up at the head of the hasidic tradition',[10] that only 'after his death, when the hasidic movement proper was begun by his disciples and followers, did the mysterious Besht become the central figure and later on the alleged creator of the movement',[11] and that 'the followers of hasidism had created their own master'.[12] Even Simon Dubnow, who laid the foundation of the scholarly investigation of hasidic history,[13] introduced his chapter on Israel Besht with the following pessimistic remarks:

> The historical figure of the creator of hasidism appears to us out of a mist, the mist of fanciful tales with which folk tradition had adorned the head of its beloved hero. A thick screen, woven in the imagination of both contemporaries and subsequent generations, conceals from our eyes the true image of the Besht, so that at times it appears as if this man had never existed but was a mere fable, a name made up for the factor initiating a religious movement which was to shake the Jewish world.[14]

Dubnow nevertheless proceeded to dismiss the notion that the Ba'al Shem Tov never existed as absurd, rightly pointing out that (*a*) he was mentioned not only by venerating hasidic disciples and colleagues long after his death, but also by a number of contemporary outsiders or even opponents of hasidism who could not be associated with the construction of the hasidic legend of the Besht, and that (*b*) even his legendary biography,

Shivḥei habesht (In Praise of the Ba'al Shem Tov),[15] admittedly published as late as 1814, well over fifty years after his death, could nevertheless yield a considerable amount of verifiable historical evidence if read critically.[16]

The problem of the sources is, however, serious, both for the life of Israel Ba'al Shem Tov and for the precise nature of his teaching. For his life—the problem of identifying his authentic teaching lies outside the scope of the present discussion—we do not possess any of the raw materials which biographers (at least biographers of mid-eighteenth-century CE Europeans, if not of thirteenth-century BCE Egyptians) might expect to find easily and abundantly; there is no autobiography or 'confessions' by the Besht, no diary, no memoirs, no 'journal', nor a substantial body of letters to be scrutinized for psychological insight or even for sheer, elementary facts such as his dates of birth and marriages, his educational career, his places of residence and employment, and other landmarks in his physical or spiritual life.[17] This dearth of autobiographical material is intriguing and should, perhaps, be seen in the context of the overall poverty of Jewish biographical and, more generally, historiographical output until as late as the nineteenth century,[18] as well as, and more particularly, of that 'personal reticence' which has been identified as characteristic of most Jewish mystics, in contrast to the often autobiographically prolific mystical exponents of other religious traditions.[19] The Ba'al Shem Tov and his colleagues would have had no literary models for such an enterprise, no access to any eastern European Jewish literary tradition of spiritual autobiography or 'confessions'.

The sources to which one has to turn for information about his life, and the lives of most other hasidic masters, are not autobiographical or, strictly speaking, biographical, but can be classified as belonging to the hagiographical genre—edifying tales about the extraordinary lives of holy men or saints. Many of these are truly fanciful, echoing literary motifs which are the common stock of folktales the world over: magical transformations of inanimate objects and animals, encounters with witches, demons, werewolves, and other mythical creatures; miraculous healings and resuscitations by the saint; the ability to travel through time or to ordain the future; and so on.[20] While all this fills the pages of *Shivḥei habesht*, and all the subsequent hasidic hagiographical collections which were modelled on it, with reading material which is as entertaining as it is morally and spiritually edifying, it reduces the historical credibility of the tales to a matter of religious belief and piety.

Moreover, the hagiographical tales are not only fantastical in parts and so historically or 'archaeologically' implausible, they also conform to a typology of saintly lives which had been established in the literature long before the publication of the first hasidic hagiographical work in 1814, or even before the very emergence on the historical arena of Israel Ba'al Shem Tov himself in the 1740s.[21] *Shivḥei habesht* takes its generic inspiration, right down to its title, from the 'praises' or tales of the lives of eminent scholars and saintly personalities of the medieval and early modern period. Such tales were being compiled as coherent literary works from the end of the sixteenth century. The most immediate typological model for the life of Israel Ba'al Shem Tov was the kabbalist Isaac Luria, the 'Holy Ari', whose 'praises' constitute the first such comprehensive cycle of hagiographical tales. These began to circulate as a literary unit in the first decade of the seventeenth century and became known as *In Praise of the Ari*.[22] Some of the biographical details related by *Shivḥei habesht* to Israel Ba'al Shem are too close to the details of Isaac Luria's life as related in *Shivḥei ha'ari* to be considered mere coincidences. For example, both figures are said to have spent several years in seclusion prior to the public disclosure of their true spiritual stature; both are said to have been conceived 'in purity'—without sexual desire on the part of their parents; both are credited with the superhuman knowledge of the languages of 'animals, birds, and palm trees'. Although the esoteric concept of mastering the speech of animals and palm or other trees (as well as plants, mountains and valleys, angels, and demons) is of talmudic origin,[23] the mention specifically of palm trees, which seems natural enough against the setting of the Ari's life in Palestine and Egypt, is almost as unnatural in the case of the Ba'al Shem Tov as the very power of speaking the language of trees, since it has to be set against the background of his experiences in the Carpathian mountains and the forests of Podolia. It was clearly grafted onto his life story from the earlier Lurianic context as a ready-made measure of extraordinary spiritual powers.[24]

It is not impossible, however, that the parallels between the praises of the Ari and the praises of the Besht are not a purely literary phenomenon. The Besht himself may have wished to conform to the existing typology of mystical saintly lives and might have modelled himself on his illustrious predecessor, re-enacting certain scenes from the life of the Ari as recorded in the *In Praise of the Ari*.[25] We know with greater certainty, for example, that a later hasidic master, R. Nahman of Bratslav, had interpreted certain incidents in his own life as a repetition of events in the life of the Ari, with whom he identified in some respects as an earlier manifestation of the same mystical-messianic soul with which he himself, and other distinguished figures of the historic past, had been endowed.[26]

To complicate matters further, *In Praise of the Ba'al Shem Tov* appeared in several editions, both Hebrew and Yiddish, close to the time of the first publication of the Hebrew version in 1814.[27] The editions vary from one another to some extent, and the question whether the Yiddish version represents an independent recension of the material or is a free translation of the Hebrew text remains controversial.[28] We do not as yet possess a critical edition of the text—a prerequisite for any systematic attempt to extract historical information from the tales—and, for the time being, the standard, if flawed, edition is Avraham Rubinstein's, which was published posthumously in Jerusalem in 1991.[29]

As fanciful and typologically prescribed as they are, and however problematic from the textual point of view, the tales nevertheless have been sensed by most scholars to contain many echoes of the historical reality of their heroes. Since for the most part they form the richest, if not the only, repository of biographical source material about the Besht and his circle of associates, historians of hasidism, however sceptical, could not but grapple with the problem of sorting out fact from fiction without any clear methodological guidelines beyond the obvious search for corroboration from extraneous sources.[30]

Such corroboration has been found for the references in the tales to the ritual blood accusation in Pavlitch (Pawołocz) in 1753,[31] or to the value of various units of currency during the first half of the eighteenth century, which is mentioned incidentally in *Shivḥei habesht* and agrees with what is known from other sources about the rates of exchange current in Poland at the time.[32] The same is true of the tale which describes the involvement of the Ba'al Shem Tov with the brothers Samuel and Gedaliah Itskovitch, who were Prince Radziwiłł's chief tax farmers on his estates in Lithuania. Some of the information about them as it features in *Shivḥei habesht* is corroborated by several non-hasidic sources and reflects quite accurately the historical background of the peasant rebellion against the prince and his powerful Jews during the 1740s, a rebellion which became known by the name of its leader as the Woszczyło revolt.[33] The historical details supplied by one of the tales in connection with the immigration to the Holy Land of R. Eleazar of Amsterdam in 1740 have likewise been verified by comparison with other sources, and the tale can, on the whole, be taken as a record of authentic events.[34] The same applies to a number of other tales concerning personalities and events in the Holy Land, which could have been based on communications from the hasidic emigrants to the Holy Land during the eighteenth century, and have been shown to be valuable and reliable complements to other sources.[35] Most dramatically, on the basis of an independent Polish archival source, the very fact of the Ba'al Shem Tov's existence at the time and place at which hasidic tradition had always located him has been established by Moshe Rosman firmly and unequivocally enough as to demolish once and for all the case, however contestable, for his purely 'historical' but not 'archaeological' reality.[36] Rosman examined the archive of the noble Polish Czartoryski family, who owned the town of Międzybóż, where, according to *Shivḥei habesht*, the Ba'al Shem Tov was resident during a substantial part of his career as a public figure, from 1740 until his death in 1760. The archive, now kept in Kraków, covers the middle decades of the eighteenth century and contains material concerning the large Jewish population of the town. This includes lists of ratepayers which were updated almost annually and arranged by order of the houses in each street. One house, close to the town's synagogue, is listed as owned by the Jewish community council and therefore exempt from rates. Nevertheless, the Czartoryski officials occasionally noted the identity of its occupants in much the same way as they regularly did for all the other rate-paying residences in the town. From 1740 until 1760, precisely the period of the Ba'al Shem Tov's residence in Międzybóż according to hasidic 'legend', the occupant of this house is identified in the Polish documents variously as *kabalista* (a kabbalist), *Balsem* or *Balsam*, and finally *Balszam Doktor*, all of which can refer to no one other than Israel Ba'al Shem Tov, who was indeed a kabbalist and a healer, that is, a 'doctor'. In 1763, three years after his death, the house was listed as being occupied by a certain Herszko, who must be identified with Zevi Hirsch, the Ba'al Shem Tov's son according to hasidic tradition. Other names can likewise be identified with members of the Besht's family and his close associates, precisely as depicted in *Shivḥei habesht*.[37]

While Rosman's discoveries have removed such doubts as might have been entertained by ardent sceptics such as Aescoly and Schiper about the factual basis of the hasidic legend of the Besht, they suggest the need for a drastic revision of all received notions of his role and status, and highlight at least one of the biases which characterize the modern, secular, scholarly historiography of hasidism, biases which make this historiography as problematic in its way as the hagiographical hasidic sources are in theirs.[38]

Clearly, the hasidic narrators of the tales do not share the historians' concern with 'archaeological' data. To the extent that they refer to specific historical facts—events, dates, names, locations and the distances between them, currency units, and so on—they do so incidentally and casually. Their conscious purpose is to record the spiritual achievements of the saints, and to inspire the readers with a sense of awe and piety. Notably, the author or editor of *Shivḥei habesht*, clearly an heir to a tradition which ascribes little value to the writing of history as such,[39] prefaced the volume with an apology in which he disavowed any historiographical intent:

> Let me explain . . . so that the reader will not question my decision or wonder what brought me to write meaningless narratives . . . The reader should realize that I wrote all this not as histories nor as stories. In each tale he should perceive His awesome deeds. He should infer the moral of each tale, so that he will be able to attach his heart to the fear of God, the beliefs of the sages and the power of the holy Torah.[40]

But it is precisely the historically casual nature of the tales, the fact that their conscious 'agenda' is pietistic, not historiographical, that lends credibility to such concrete items of historical information as they still contain. The weight of their self-proclaimed commitment to the value of edification rests elsewhere, and this renders the historical pegs to which the tales are casually tied an indifferent component of the work, one in which little effort of value-charged, tendentious interpretation or embellishment has been invested.

The tales of *Shivḥei habesht* may seem fanciful to the modern, scientifically critical reader; their credibility may depend on the belief in supernatural forces; the printed texts in which they have come down to us may have been corrupted in the course of transmission; and some of the tales may have been disconnected in time from the factual ground in which they were once rooted; but they do not set out to falsify the facts or to make them up. Often enough, as we have seen, the historical framework to which they point incidentally seems authentic and is compatible with extra-hasidic evidence.

In addition to the hagiographical tradition, which can yield much authentic historical and biographical information, however inadvertently, the historiography of hasidism has had to contend with a body of fabrications and falsifications of evidence which is quite distinct from the tales in both provenance and intent, although it bears a certain relationship to them.

The earliest instance of manufactured evidence which can be demonstrated to be false is a report by a certain Podolian Jew, Abraham of Szarogród, recorded in good faith by the famous talmudic scholar, kabbalist, and anti-Sabbatian polemicist Jacob Emden, who published it in Altona in 1769. According to this report, Israel Ba'al Shem Tov was one of the main delegates, alongside some of the most eminent rabbinic authorities in Poland at the time, who was chosen to represent the rabbinic side in the disputation with the Frankist heretics (followers of the messianic sectarian Jacob Frank) taking place in the town of Lwów (Lviv) in 1759.[41] The report was taken at face value and accepted as historical fact by the early historians of hasidism,[42] as well as by subsequent manufacturers of false documentary evidence on the career of the Besht (on which more below).[43] But all other reports of the disputation, both Jewish and Polish, including eyewitness accounts whose authenticity is beyond doubt, fail to mention the Ba'al Shem Tov while providing a full list of the leading Jewish participants.[44] It is clear that the Ba'al Shem Tov did not take part in the official disputation with the Frankists, which is hardly surprising, given that he was not one of the first-rank rabbinic scholars of the day, and it is difficult to imagine that any communal body would have elected him to defend rabbinic Judaism on behalf of Polish Jewry. Admittedly, the hagiographical tradition of hasidism celebrates the Ba'al Shem Tov as a national hero, able time and again to astonish everyone who came in contact with him not only by his supernatural powers but also his unrivalled mastery of every branch of traditional Jewish knowledge. In reality, however, he was hardly mentioned, either favourably or disparagingly, in the learned writings of his well-known contemporaries outside the hasidic camp. It is true that a handful of critical reports by rabbinic observers from near his time and place, denouncing some unnamed 'new hasidim' whose activities resembled those associated with him, have been interpreted as referring to none other than the Ba'al Shem Tov and his associates. But this interpretation remains controversial, and it is far from certain that the critics were indeed referring specifically to the Besht or to anyone in his circle.[45] Moreover, the concerted efforts to eradicate hasidism as a subversive sect began not in Podolia, the Ba'al Shem Tov's region of residence, but rather in distant Lithuania, where the rabbinic opponents of the movement, who came to be known as the *mitnagedim*, launched their campaign against it only in the spring of 1772, some twelve years after the death of the Besht, and without ever placing his personality or teaching at the heart of their campaign. This, indeed, was one of the puzzling facts which had led such scholars as Aescoly and Schiper to the speculation that the 'archaeological' Ba'al Shem Tov, if he ever existed, could not have been the true founder of hasidism.

The interpolation of the Ba'al Shem Tov's name in the list of delegates to the disputation in Lwów could have been made only by someone who, like Abraham of Szarogród, had come from the Ba'al Shem Tov's immediate regional environment, where alone he might have gained some public recognition during his lifetime or shortly after his death. Notably, while counting 'Israel Międzybóż Ba'al Shem' among the rabbinic disputants, Abraham of Szarogród did not present him as their chief spokesman or otherwise turn him into a central figure in his account of the event. At most, his testimony suggests a certain awareness of the Besht as a local hero, coupled with a naive belief that his reputation must have spread throughout Poland, or else with the desire to promote this reputation beyond its region of provenance, against the possible background of the Besht's admittedly humble, if inspired, origins, which may have attracted some local criticism or scorn. Whatever his motives, by adding the Besht's name to the list of eminent disputants, Abraham of Szarogród would seem to have anticipated the apologetic tendency that was eventually to mark the whole of the hagiographical literature of hasidism; it 'provided' the Ba'al Shem Tov with the presumption of widely acknowledged rabbinic credentials, such that would magnify his stature and legitimate it by conventional criteria,[46] most likely in response to the notion that his brand of hasidism was the piety of ignoramuses and fools. In this respect we may regard Abraham of Szarogród's testimony as an embryonic 'praise', one that could easily have found its way into any of the hagiographical tales of hasidism, which tend to present the Ba'al Shem Tov as a superhero and to endow him with every traditional accomplishment. Such 'praises', originating in oral transmission, were assembled and edited in manuscript form, apparently during the 1790s, and eventually began to circulate in print from 1814–15 on, with the publication in several editions, both Hebrew and Yiddish, of *Shivḥei habesht*.

Abraham of Szarogród's fictional 'praise' must have been conceived shortly before its publication by Emden in 1769—that is, less than ten years after the death of the Ba'al Shem Tov in 1760 and long before the literary consolidation of the hasidic legend of his life. It appears to be quite independent of the hagiographical tradition of *Shivḥei habesht*, which never associates the Ba'al Shem Tov directly with the disputation in Lwów. Moreover, Abraham of Szarogród's false testimony indirectly supplies some confirmation of the essential historical credibility of *Shivḥei habesht*. For while the book portrays the Ba'al Shem Tov as being deeply concerned with the Sabbatian-Frankist heresy, and although it contains several tales which could provide a natural narrative framework for the interpolation of precisely such a 'praise' of the Ba'al Shem Tov, portraying him as the leading delegate to the disputation in Lwów,[47] *Shivḥei habesht* refrains from doing so while at the same time preserving the evidently authentic information that the Besht was not acquainted personally with at least one of his alleged (and truly celebrated) fellow disputants—R. Hayim Hakohen Rapoport, the rabbi of Lwów, whose own membership of the rabbinic delegation is beyond doubt.[48]

Nevertheless, Abraham of Szarogród's testimony as recorded by Emden has one significant feature in common with *Shivḥei habesht*: both are innocent of the modern historiographical sensibility that is suspicious of all hagiographical traditions, based as they are on rumour or hearsay, that is, on oral transmission, and treating such evidence as inadmissible if it cannot be supported by more rigorous 'archaeological' documentation. The editor of *Shivḥei habesht* and R. Jacob Emden are both equally confident that the information they have received and are transmitting is reliable, since they believe, and can clearly demonstrate, that it derives ultimately, if not always directly, from first-hand, eyewitness accounts. In the case of *Shivḥei habesht* this takes the form of carefully noted, uninterrupted chains of informants with which the editor introduces most of the tales in the anthology.[49] This device, after all, had served as a stamp of the authenticity and validity of tradition, however ancient, and, above all, as proof of the continuity of divine revelation in the literature of Judaism ever since the earliest classical rabbinic sources.[50] By the same token Emden assures the reader of the reliability of his account when he stresses that his informant had witnessed the events described with his own eyes, and that he himself has recorded his testimony with meticulous care for accuracy. In his preface to Abraham of Szarogród's report he presents these credentials as follows: 'I consider it desirable to publish here . . . the account of the event as it occurred, just as it was told to me recently by a person who was there, at the time and place at which that wondrous event occurred';[51] and he expands on the same point at the conclusion of the report: 'Thus far the account of the above-mentioned visitor, who spoke without ulterior motives [*hamesiaḥ lefi tumo*]. He related it to me in Yiddish and I wrote it down in Hebrew word for word (to the extent that a foreign tongue may be translated into Hebrew literally), without addition or omission.'[52] In both cases the credibility of the evidence is established beyond doubt (however unjustifiably, as it happens, at least in the case of R. Jacob Emden) by intrinsic criteria which had long governed the process of authentication in the Jewish literary tradition.

In stark contrast to this traditional method of validating the evidence, which was still the norm in the hasidic world of the late eighteenth and early nineteenth centuries, a more recent production of 'early' hasidic documentation, together with the bulk of the modern internal hasidic historiography that derives from it its stamp of authenticity and rigour, reflects a keen hasidic awareness of extrinsic historiographical sensibilities, and a novel, extraneously inspired sense of the inadequacy of hagiographical traditions as historical source material.

This enterprise, manufacturing what was now clearly sensed by all to be the awkwardly missing 'hard-core' evidence about the early founders of hasidism, is a vast collection of letters and other materials allegedly written by the Ba'al Shem Tov himself, members of his family, and other associates and disciples, all purporting to date from the period between the 1730s and the beginning of the nineteenth century. These 'documents' were discovered in mysterious circumstances shortly after the First World War in the Ukrainian town of Kherson, and have since become notorious as the Kherson *genizah* (a repository of disused books and manuscripts). It was celebrated at first not only by members of the hasidic community but also by prominent literary figures, including some historians, who pronounced the Kherson materials the most important discovery of the new century, and quickly began to publish them in various editions. But the documents soon aroused the suspicion of several scholars, who eventually, on the basis of internal contradictions, discrepancies with extraneously verifiable facts, anachronisms, and other technical pitfalls into which forgers are always liable to stumble, proved enough of them to be recent fabrications to cast serious doubts on the entire collection.[53] A number of hasidic leaders were quick to dissociate themselves from the discredited *genizah*,[54] while others continued to endorse it; in scholarly circles the condemnation of the letters as forgeries has become virtually universal.[55]

Neither the identity of the forgers nor their motivation is entirely clear.[56] They were certainly at home with the eastern European hasidic world and its literature of the turn of the nineteenth and twentieth centuries,[57] and are likely to have produced the documents not long before their discovery.[58] Their motivation might well have been sheer greed: by the beginning of the twentieth century, in what was now perceived within the hasidic camp no less than outside it as the dearth of reliable documentary evidence about the historical origins of the movement, such a treasure trove of ancient 'archival' materials was bound to fetch a high price on the market.[59] At the same time the forgers might have been motivated by the desire to reinforce with unchallengeable documentation 'sanctified' hasidic traditions which had by then been questioned or even dismissed by modern sceptics as superstitious nonsense.[60] The two motivations need not preclude each other. In one way or another the Kherson *genizah*, and particularly its endorsement and exploitation by those hasidic leaders who persisted in treating it as authentic,[61] are a response to the breakdown of wholesome faith and the encroachment of secularization, which manifested itself increasingly in the course of the nineteenth century not only in the emergence and growing attraction of secular political ideologies but also in the development of modern, critical Jewish historiography, first in western and eventually in eastern Europe.

This historiography developed as both a reaction to, and a direct by-product of, the Jewish Enlightenment of the eighteenth and early nineteenth centuries—a movement which, in its eastern European manifestation, was militantly opposed to hasidism as an obscurantist, regressive element in the Jewish society that the Enlighteners were striving to reform.[62] The modern Jewish historians of the nineteenth century had inherited the rationalistic world-view of their enlightened intellectual forebears and were embarrassed by all manifestations of irrational, emotional religiosity in Judaism, a religion which they were at pains to portray as essentially rational and perfectly compatible with, if not even central to, the civilized, liberal culture of nineteenth-century European society into which they were seeking full admission.[63]

By the end of the nineteenth century, near the likely time of the production of the Kherson forgeries, the hasidic movement and its hagiographical tradition had been exposed to a number of historiographical treatments which ranged from the cautiously sceptical to the devastatingly hostile, but which were all united in paying critical attention to the hagiographical tales—inevitably the main source for any historical characterization of the movement.[64] To convey the flavour of some of the most vehement historiographical critiques of hasidism, it is sufficient to quote from the chapter entitled 'The New Chassidism', first published in German in 1870, in the monumental *History of the Jews* by Heinrich Graetz, the most influential German Jewish historian of the nineteenth century:

It seems remarkable that, at the same time as Mendelssohn declared rational thought to be the essence of Judaism,[65] and in fact founded a widely-extended order of enlightened men, another banner was unfurled, the adherents of which announced the grossest superstition to be the fundamental principle of Judaism, and formed a special order of wonder-seeking confederates . . . The new sect, a daughter of darkness, was born in gloom, and even today proceeds stealthily on its mysterious ways . . . As ugly as the very name, Besht, was the form of the founder and the order that he called into existence. The Graces did not sit by his cradle, but the Spirit of Belief and Wonder-working, and his brain was so filled with fantastic images that he could not distinguish them from real, tangible beings. . . . Israel Miedziboz also boasted that he could see into the future, as secrets were unveiled to him. Was this a deliberate boast, or self-deception, or merely an over-estimation of morbid phenomena of the soul? There are persons, times and places, in which no line of demarcation can be drawn between trickery and self-delusion.[66]

Other historians, notably Simon Dubnow, were less passionately condemnatory but more explicitly critical of the hagiographical sources, which had to be stripped of their mythical elements and checked, as much as possible, against alternative sources before any historical use could be made of them.[67]

If hasidic hagiography was being subjected to critical scrutiny and found to fall short of historical credibility on the grounds that it lacked documentary proof and was altogether fanciful and too far-fetched, then the

Kherson *genizah* was to supply the missing documents so valued by the historians and their readers and thus to silence the sceptics in their own terms. The eagerness with which it was received at first, not only by professional historians (whose appetite for archival material could be taken for granted since it was built into the historiographical tradition in which they were rooted) but also by the followers of hasidism and their leaders, to whose hagiographical, essentially oral, tradition it was alien, would suggest that the *genizah* was recognized as a valuable weapon, not only in the struggle against the secular world which lay outside and around hasidism, but also, if not primarily, against the infiltration of its values into the heart of the hasidic world. This world began to encounter modernization, secularization, and acculturation through its clashes with the Enlighteners in the early decades of the nineteenth century. But by the second decade of the twentieth century, following the Russian pogroms of the 1880s and early 1900s, the First World War, and the Russian Revolution, all of which had resulted in the dislocation of vast numbers of Jews from the traditionalist environment in which they had been reared, the fear of secularization, and the sense of demoralization within their own depleting ranks was becoming a constant preoccupation for the leaders of Orthodox Jewry, hasidic or not.[68] The value of archival documentation belonged to the secular world, which was now encroaching forcefully on a disoriented, modern hasidic consciousness, hardly impervious to the challenge of the historiographical critique of its traditions. The forgeries of the Kherson *genizah* thus appear, in the first instance, to offer concrete documentary verification of the hagiographical tales, whose traditional method of authentication had lost its validity through the assimilation, however unconscious, of modern historiographical criteria, and whose miraculous elements were becoming less credible to the growing number of Jews, including hasidim, who were exposed to a modern scientific education.

Kherson letters which spring from the tales of *Shivḥei habesht* while purporting to corroborate them include, for example, the letter from the Ba'al Shem Tov to his eminent brother-in-law, R. Gershon of Kuty, which both reflects and 'confirms' a tale depicting him as adopting the false identity of an uneducated Jew (prior to his self-disclosure as a spiritual giant) and arousing R. Gershon's anger and frustration with his apparent uncouthness. As befits the guise of an ignorant Jew, the Ba'al Shem Tov's letter is not in Hebrew but in Yiddish, and it consists of his clumsy apology for irritating R. Gershon with his inappropriate conduct.[69] Other forged letters, in which the Ba'al Shem Tov urges the sickly Dov Ber of Mezhirech, depicted in one of the tales as being doubtful of the healing powers of the Besht, to come to Międzybóż and find out for himself, are clearly dependent on this very tale while appearing to provide it with independent corroboration.[70] Similar examples abound.

The Kherson letters likewise supply rigorous documentary evidence purporting to corroborate traditions which the forgers must have gleaned from other sources. The most blatant example of this is the 'document' which appears to verify Abraham of Szarogród's presentation of the Ba'al Shem Tov as one of the delegates to the disputation with the Frankists in Lwów.[71] The Kherson document makes him, alongside one of the genuine rabbinic delegates as well as several prominent hasidic figures who had nothing to do with it as far as we know, proud signatory to a joint proclamation celebrating their victory over the heretics.[72] This 'corroboration' of what had been established as a false 'eye witness' account—which is embellished, moreover, by the celebratory claim of victory when in reality all the evidence points to a defeat[73]—was in fact one of the first Kherson letters to arouse the suspicion of scholars and led to the exposure of the bulk of the 'documents' as plain forgeries.[74] Majer Bałaban, the historian who was chiefly responsible for the clarification of this particular issue, was able to demonstrate further that the forger of the proclamation from Lwów did not derive his information directly from Abraham of Szarogród's report as published by Emden in 1769 but rather at second or third hand, from an inaccurate version of the account which appeared in a scholarly history of hasidism published in 1914.[75] This suggested to Bałaban that the document, and possibly the rest of the Kherson material, was manufactured in or shortly after 1914[76]—a suggestion which is compatible with the circumstances of the Kherson discovery.

The Kherson documents are at their most creative when they fill in some of the intriguing gaps left by the hagiographical tales, which, while expanding—extravagantly at times—on the miraculous feats performed by their heroes, are not concerned to record their life stories systematically. As a result they are often laconic or simply silent on precisely those issues that interest modern historians most. One of these issues is the relationship between Israel Ba'al Shem Tov and the mysterious R. Adam, described in the Yiddish (though not in the printed Hebrew) version of *Shivḥei habesht* as a fellow-*ba'al shem*,[77] who had discovered in a cave a collection of ancient esoteric writings and was commanded by revelation from Heaven to pass them on to the Besht. These writings are presented as being extremely important inasmuch as they initiated the Besht, in the years prior to his 'disclosure', to 'the secrets and mysteries of the Torah' which were to qualify him for his future public role.[78] The tale clearly attempts to place the Ba'al Shem Tov within a long mystical tradition, conferring on his teaching the legitimacy and authority of antiquity. However, no one had ever heard of a historical Adam Ba'al Shem, and the information about him in *Shivḥei habesht*, which introduces him without naming his place of origin or providing any other tangible biographical landmarks, was too fantastical to suggest any possible identification. This led the late Gershom Scholem to the speculation that the writings in question were a kabbalistic work by the heretical Sabbatian prophet Heschel Zoref, and that the hagiographical tale had substituted his name with the pseudonymous Adam Ba'al Shem in order to disguise the embarrassing Sabbatian connections of the author.[79] But Scholem's speculation became wholly unconvincing with the discovery that an Adam Ba'al Shem did apparently exist in Prague in the late sixteenth century, if not as a concrete historical figure, at least as the hero of a seventeenth-century Yiddish hagiographical work, which would have been accessible to the author of the hasidic tale and must have inspired it.[80]

The forgers of the Kherson letters could not, of course, have been aware of these scholarly considerations, but they were just as eager to shed factual light on the relationship between Israel and Adam Ba'al Shem. To this end they produced a number of letters allegedly written by Adam Ba'al Shem—one to his unnamed son and the others to 'Israel son of . . . R. Eliezer . . . of Okopy',[81] all purporting to date from 1731–2. Since they knew nothing of the Prague connection of the actual or literary Adam Ba'al Shem, they located the 'Rabbi Adam' of *Shivḥei habesht* in the Galician town of Ropczyce (which they must have imagined as a hasidic or proto-hasidic stronghold already in the early 1700s, even though the town does not appear to have been associated with the movement until the beginning of the nineteenth century, with the appointment to the local rabbinate of Naftali of Ropczyce (1760–1827), one of the founding fathers of Galician hasidism). To account for the failure of Adam Ba'al Shem and Israel Besht to meet each other, and for the rather tortuous way by which, according to *Shivḥei habesht*, R. Adam's son eventually accomplished his mission,[82] they had R. Adam repeatedly complain in his letters to his younger colleague-to-be, Israel Besht, that he cannot find him anywhere, urging him to reveal his identity so as to enable him to deliver the writings to his hands.[83] The stipulation implied in these letters, that Israel Besht and his whereabouts should remain unknown to R. Adam all his life, is no doubt designed to accord with the claim of *Shivḥei habesht* that the secret writings were revealed to the Besht during his years of 'concealment', before he became a public figure whose identity and location could, presumably, be established easily enough. Adam Ba'al Shem eventually leaves the secret writings and his letters to the Besht in the hands of his son, whom he instructs on his deathbed to find Israel Besht and convey these materials to him. Curiously, and uncharacteristically, the forged documents depart at this point from the plot as it unfolds in *Shivḥei habesht*, offering instead quite a different version of events. According to all the editions, both Hebrew and Yiddish, of *Shivḥei habesht*, R. Adam's son managed to locate Israel Besht in Okopy, where he was employed at the time as a humble attendant in the local *beit midrash* (study house). He gave him the secret writings on condition that the Ba'al Shem Tov would study them together with him, but soon died as a result of thus being exposed to mystical experiences for which he was not spiritually fit.[84] The Kherson documents, on the other hand, have the Ba'al Shem Tov report in a letter to his brother-in-law, R. Gershon of Kuty, that he has found the secret writings with the help of a non-Jewish Wallachian shepherd where R. Adam's son had left them for him, 'under a stone in the mountains'[85]—a version which, to the best of my knowledge, is not attested anywhere in the hagiographical sources.

Although the authors of the Kherson letters often expand on the hagiographical tales and occasionally clash with them unwittingly on minor points, they are not in the habit of contradicting their narrative substance as blatantly as in this case. One can only assume that they were working from memory, without reference to the text of *Shivḥei habesht*, and had confused the reference to Adam Ba'al Shem's initial discovery of the writings in a cave[86] with a later reference to Israel Ba'al Shem Tov's ultimate concealment of the writings 'under a stone in the mountains',[87] entirely overlooking the account of his encounter with Adam Ba'al Shem's son, thus producing a new, hybrid version of the story.[88]

Another example of the creative originality of the forgeries is the correspondence of the Ba'al Shem Tov with a number of 'secret tsadikim' (righteous men) during his period of concealment. The concept of supremely righteous individuals (often numbered thirty-six) who inhabit the world at all times in the guise of simple men, without anyone recognizing their true stature or their ability to exercise supernatural powers, is rooted in ancient rabbinic sources and makes its first full-fledged appearance in hasidic literature with a single reference in the Yiddish version of *Shivḥei habesht*. But both the term and the theme became a commonplace in the hagiographical literature of hasidism only from the latter part of the nineteenth century.[89] The Kherson letters have Israel Ba'al Shem Tov, during the 1720s and 1730s—his years of concealment—belong to a confederacy of 'secret tsadikim' who are known to each other but not to anyone else and who engage in good works on behalf of the nation, out of the public eye.[90] The entire picture is anachronistic both terminologically and historically. The term 'secret tsadik' could not have gained currency in hasidism until after the term 'tsadik' itself had become the regular designation of the hasidic leader in the speculative literature of the movement. This literature became widely accessible in print only some fifty years after the period when the Besht was supposedly corresponding with his fellow 'secret tsadikim', and at least two decades after his death in 1760, with the publication of the first hasidic books in the last two decades of the eighteenth century.[91] Historically, too, the notion that during his years of concealment the Ba'al Shem Tov was associated with a group of pneumatics whose leader he was destined to become once his true nature was revealed to all is clearly modelled on, and anachronistically anticipates, what *Shivḥei habesht* depicts as his association with a cluster of fellow charismatics—colleagues, even rivals, some eventually becoming disciples—in the years that followed his public 'revelation' as a great spiritual master.[92] The hagiographical tradition of *Shivḥei habesht* on his years of self-imposed anonymity and seclusion has been displaced in the Kherson letters by a readily available late nineteenth-century literary trope, whereby a 'righteous man' in obscurity must surely be one of the 'secret tsadikim', whose solitary spiritual training for his eventual assumption of a public role must be reconfigured as a disguise for membership of that clandestine mythical fraternity.

Another 'gap' in the tales of *Shivḥei habesht* which the Kherson letters endeavour to fill is the bewildering silence of the book on the apparent failure of both the Ba'al Shem Tov's son, R. Zevi, and the son of the Magid of Mezhirech, R. Abraham the Angel, to succeed their fathers dynastically in their respective capacities of first and second central leaders of the hasidic movement as a whole. While altogether failing to address this issue directly, *Shivḥei habesht* confirms indirectly that its authors were not aware of any established procedure for the regulation of succession in the leadership of hasidism, or even of any informally designated successor, hereditary or not, by either the Besht or the Magid towards the end of their lives. Even more surprisingly, the book makes not the slightest reference to any crisis in the leadership of the movement, which might have occurred as a result of the two sons' failure to succeed.[93] To account for this apparent deviation from a putative hereditary 'norm', both sons are conventionally portrayed in the historiography of hasidism as unfit for leadership on the grounds of lack of personal talent or inclination.[94] However, as I have demonstrated elsewhere,[95] the very expectation, at this early stage, of dynastic succession in the leadership of a supposedly coherent, centrally governed, fully institutionalized movement is entirely anachronistic: it projects the nineteenth-century organizational structure of most of the hasidic courts, each of which was being governed centrally by its own hereditary leader, onto the totally different landscape of a hasidism that was as yet to develop into a movement, one which had never been, nor was ever to become, either coherent or centrally governed. From the organizational point of view neither the Ba'al Shem Tov nor the Magid of Mezhirech could have functioned as central leaders to the loosely affiliated, discrete circles of hasidim that operated in their day, although on the personal and spiritual levels the impact of their personalities and teachings was undoubtedly felt by both contemporary and subsequent hasidic leaders, some of whom may have served a period of discipleship at either of their courts and could have viewed themselves as their faithful disciples even as they were themselves heading their own independent circles of followers alongside, and during the lifetime of, the two great masters. The Kherson letters share with the bulk of the historiography of hasidism—critical-scholarly and internal-apologetic alike—the anachronistic perception of the organizational history of the movement. But whereas the historians have speculated casually, the Kherson letters again supply the missing 'hard-core' documentation which explains away the apparent irregularities of the first two successions in the leadership, while at the same time projecting a reassuring sense of dynastic continuity through the stipulation of an implicit designation, first by the Ba'al Shem Tov and later by the Magid of Mezhirech, of a chosen disciple who in each case would substitute for the son as a legitimate heir. In a number of Kherson letters the Ba'al Shem Tov addresses the Magid, or else refers to him in letters addressed to others, in the most intimate and yet respectful terms, appointing him to deputize for him during his own long periods of absence (on clandestine 'secret tsadikim' missions), and putting him in charge of all the affairs of the movement.[96] Similarly, Dov Ber of Mezhirech singles out R. Shneur Zalman of Liady (Lyady; 1745–1812, founder of the Habad school of hasidism[97]) as his most distinguished disciple, and reports in a letter to his son Abraham the Angel that the Ba'al Shem Tov had appeared to him in a dream and identified R. Shneur Zalman as a young man possessed of extraordinary spiritual powers. He goes on to say: 'For this reason, my beloved son, I am thankful for my good fortune and yours, for I have chosen him to be as a brother to you, and let this [hint] suffice for the wise; you should treat him with great respect, and from now on you should do whatever he tells you to do.'[98] Although in this case the Kherson letters cannot quite point to R. Shneur Zalman as the direct successor of the Magid,[99] they nevertheless supply 'documentation' that lends support to, and clearly reflects, the dynastic consciousness of the Habad school, which sees itself as the most authentic heir to the original hasidism of the founders.[100]

A certain affinity between the Kherson letters and the historical self-perception of the Habad school was noted by some of the scholars who had examined the *genizah* documents (if only to dismiss them as recent fabrications devoid of historical significance).[101] Indeed, like the Magid's letter just cited, the Kherson material often appears to reflect a peculiarly Habad perspective on the early history of hasidism, and to serve Habad interests by reinforcing this perspective with corroborative archival documentation.[102] While the identity of the forgers remains uncertain, and they cannot be shown to have come from within the Habad ranks, the affinity between the *genizah* and the school of Habad is highlighted by the fact that shortly after its discovery, in 1918, a large collection of the 'documents' was bought by a wealthy Habad follower who gave it as a present to the then leader of Habad, the fifth *admor*, Shalom Dovber (1860–1920). According to his son and heir, the *admor* Joseph Isaac Schneersohn (1880–1950), R. Shalom Dovber scrutinized the Kherson material at length, and, shortly before his death in 1920, declared that 'all the writings and letters are only copies of the original autographs but their contents are authentic. Even if they should be found to contradict some points of fact, this is insignificant in relation to their remarkable contents, and must be the result of errors by the copyists.'[103]

This defensive endorsement of the Kherson material anticipates the main arguments against the authenticity of the documents, including the laboratory tests carried out on the paper in the mid-1920s which conclusively proved that it could not have been produced before 1846.[104] The results of the tests were sent to the new *admor*, R. Joseph Isaac Schneersohn, and he responded in December 1929 by advancing the explanation that the extant letters were indeed only copies of the originals, while still endorsing their ultimate authenticity.[105] Since then the Habad leadership, right down to the last rebbe, Menachem Mendel Schneerson,[106] has remained committed to this stance against the growing conviction of most scholars that the documents were mere forgeries. Between 1935 and 1938 the *admor* Joseph Isaac Schneersohn initiated the publication in Warsaw of the most extensive collection of Kherson letters in the Habad periodical *Hatamim*. He prefaced it with a statement relating the circumstances of the discovery of the *genizah*, describing its contents and endorsing it again in both his father's name and his own.[107] His name has become firmly associated with the Kherson documents.

To those who are convinced that all these documents are worthless forgeries, even to sceptics who prefer to suspend judgment and pass over the entire episode in silence, the persistent endorsement of the *genizah* by the *admor* Joseph Isaac Schneersohn—indisputably a leader of remarkable abilities and insight, and a man of the world[108]—may seem foolhardy or naive. After all, he could easily have chosen a more cautious course of action by keeping the controversial documents in his private archives while refraining from publication,[109] so as not to draw attention to material which could—as in some quarters it did—damage the reputation of Habad by casting aspersions on its integrity. His decision to endorse and publish this material was clearly made quite freely rather than being dictated by an inherited commitment to the letters; although his father did receive and pronounce them to be authentic in substance, it was not he but the *admor* Joseph Isaac himself who gave publicity to this verdict. It could, had he so wished, have been suppressed and quickly forgotten. Joseph Isaac elected to risk discredit by association with the Kherson *genizah* because he clearly recognized its immense value to his novel historiographical enterprise.

He was extremely prolific in a variety of genres and had initiated an extensive publication programme of both his own writings and the writings of his Habad predecessors.[110] This programme was much enhanced by the official Habad publishing house which he founded in 1942, shortly after his escape from wartime Poland to the United States. His literary prolificacy and his publishing interests reflected not only his personal inclination and talents,[111] but also his understanding of the traditional Habad commitment to the wide dissemination of its teaching (including its most esoteric kabbalistic aspects) by means of communicating it at various levels of conceptualization, designed to be meaningful to a diversity of followers with widely ranging educational backgrounds and intellectual abilities.[112] But the *admor* Joseph Isaac was entirely original in embracing the writing of history, especially the history of hasidism, as an effective tool for the realization of this Habad mission, and he adopted the historiographical genre for many of his publications,[113] a genre in which none of his Habad or, indeed, any other hasidic predecessors had ever expressed himself.

His keen historical curiosity first displayed itself in early childhood, in the desire to hear historical tales from his grandmother,[114] and soon developed into a compulsive interest in the personal reminiscences and oral traditions of his father and other senior figures at the Lubavitch court, whom he would interrogate about the early history of hasidism.[115] He began to record these traditions in diary and other notes, and eventually published selections from them in a number of explicitly historiographical works, as well as introducing this material in the form of historical excurses of varying length into his speculative teachings and vast correspondence.[116] In addition to his own historiographical activities, he ascribed great value to the personal histories and reminiscences of the ordinary hasidim, and he urged his followers to record what they knew about the hasidic past.[117]

This rich historiographical output, which has been published in many editions and which underlies all the subsequent historiographical publications of Habad, has, on the whole, been ignored by the scholarly historians of hasidism, who have associated the *admor* Joseph Isaac with the Kherson forgeries and have mistrusted either his judgment or his integrity or both. By contrast, the two major histories of the Habad school, written at the beginning of the twentieth century, prior to the discovery of the

Kherson documents, by men who were closely associated with the Habad community through family connections as well as by consciousness, are generally taken to be reliable and have served as the basis for all the modern, scholarly reconstructions of the early history of Habad.[118]

In recent years a few attempts have been made to draw the attention of scholars to the historiographical literature of Habad and to examine it with an open mind: after all, given the paucity of historical records about the hasidic movement in its formative years, such historiography as has emerged from within the movement should be welcomed by historians and trusted, at least in the first instance, to be reliable and well informed through its greater access to sources, both written and oral, which may not be available to outsiders, or its greater insight, through intellectual and spiritual affinity if not actual proximity of time and place, to the events and personalities of the hasidic past.[119] Moreover, it could be argued methodologically that the burden of proving the historical value of information drawn from sources which yield it reluctantly, indirectly, or incidentally (such as the hagiographical tales of hasidism) must lie on the historian who proposes to use them for his or her own reconstructions and analysis. On the other hand, sources which are explicitly and self-consciously historiographical (such as the memoirs, diaries, and historical accounts written or generated by the *admor* Joseph Isaac) can be presumed to be reliable, and the burden of proving them otherwise must lie on anyone attempting a conflicting historical reconstruction.

This recent challenge to the historians of hasidism to address themselves seriously to the internal historiography of Habad has been accompanied by the attempt to dissociate it entirely from the admittedly forged documents of Kherson.[120] But this is a problematic proposition. The *admor* Joseph Isaac himself fully acknowledges his debt to the Kherson *genizah*, not only implicitly, by proclaiming its authenticity time and again, but by drawing from it explicitly, with full acknowledgments, in many of his own historical works. He writes, for example:

> And even before our master the Besht, may he rest in Eden, had revealed himself, while he was still in concealment, he and his colleagues, the secret tsadikim (some of whose names we find in the letters of the recently discovered *genizah*, such as R. Mordecai, R. Kehat, and others) were well organized.[121]

As we have already seen,[122] the very notion that the Ba'al Shem Tov was a member of an organized network of 'secret tsadikim' does not occur in the early hagiographical or any other hasidic sources, but makes its first appearance in the Kherson material. The *admor* is clearly drawing from it not only the additional detail of their names, fortuitously 'preserved' in the letters of the *genizah*, but also the very notion of their existence. The only alternative explanation for this affinity between his own account and the Kherson letters on this point is that both were drawing on authentic oral traditions; but this explanation is hardly compatible with the view that the Kherson letters are recent fabrications while the *admor* is making use of his unique access to old, authentic family traditions which would not have been available to anyone not intimately connected to the Habad court.

Even when he does not cite the Kherson documents explicitly, the *admor* can be shown to be drawing his information from no other source but them. He reports, for example, a conversation between the Magid of Mezhirech and R. Shneur Zalman of Liady, allegedly taking place on 18 Kislev 5533 (= 14 December 1772), in which the Magid, shortly before his death, commands his young disciple 'to do his utmost to ensure that his son, R. Abraham [the Angel] should accept the leadership [after his own death], and if he refuses they should appoint R. Menahem Mendel the Litvak instead'.[123] There is no mention of such a conversation or its contents in the writings of R. Shneur Zalman himself or anywhere in the later Habad literature except, once again, for the Kherson letters, which include what must be the *admor*'s direct source. This is a letter from R. Shneur Zalman to Abraham the Angel, the Magid's son, purporting to date from 1773—shortly after the death of the Magid—in which R. Shneur Zalman reports:

He [the Magid] said to me in the following holy words, on 18 Kislev, just before he died [and here the Magid's words are reported as spoken in Yiddish, not Hebrew—in which written communications would normally be put unless they were addressed to women or uneducated men—no doubt in order to enhance the authentic flavour of the message]: Do whatever you can, so that my Avreminyu, long may he live, would take my place. But in the event that he refuses, God forbid, let it be Mendele the Litvak.[124]

The alleged conversation is implausible, to say the least, when examined against the background of the organizational reality of hasidism at this stage. As was suggested above, the Magid of Mezhirech was not succeeded by a direct heir since his 'office' had not yet generated the expectation of dynastic succession, an institution which did not emerge in hasidism until the very end of the eighteenth or the beginning of the nineteenth century, and became established in the majority of the hasidic 'courts', each with its own hereditary leader or occasionally his substitute, only a few decades later.[125] The principle of succession suggested by this letter and by the *admor* Joseph Isaac's account is therefore entirely anachronistic. Nor, strictly speaking, did the Magid ever function as a central leader of a highly organized movement (although he was clearly regarded as the teacher and mentor of many other leaders of hasidism). The implication of the Kherson letter, and the *admor*'s reconstruction which must be based on it, is that Abraham the Angel, and if not him, R. Menahem Mendel of Vitebsk, was to succeed the Magid of Mezhirech to the leadership of the whole of the hasidic movement. This is not only implausible on the grounds of the pluralistic structure which underlay the organization of hasidism from its start, but it reflects clearly the implicit Habad 'appropriation' of the founders of hasidism. The portrayal of R. Menahem Mendel of Vitebsk as the Magid's own choice as the alternative candidate for succession is, from the Habad perspective, the next best thing to naming R. Shneur Zalman himself—a step which no Habad historian could take, since R. Menahem Mendel's seniority and his involvement in the eventual authorization of R. Shneur Zalman to lead the hasidic community of Belarus are well attested in the earliest hasidic and Habad sources and could not be ignored.[126]

R. Menahem Mendel of Vitebsk was one of a small group of the Magid's disciples who imported hasidism to their region of provenance in Belarus. He became the head of a hasidic circle, first in Minsk and eventually in Gorodok, in the province of Vitebsk,[127] and was the most senior figure in Belarusian hasidism, the branch from which the Habad school descends. To promote R. Menahem Mendel of Vitebsk to the position of the Magid's dynastic heir is to promote Belarusian hasidism, and ultimately Habad hasidism, to the position of the most authentic expression of Beshtian-Magidic hasidism, a posture which we have already encountered in the letters of Kherson.[128] In reality, however, each one of the Magid's disciples who led their own hasidic communities could have made a comparable claim of 'direct' inheritance from the great master, a claim which would be as morale-boosting internally but just as unfounded as the implicit Habad claim when judged by external criteria. Indeed, some such claims can be found in the hagiographical literatures of other hasidic circles,[129] although none have been as authoritative or as persistent as that of Habad, which was advanced through the exceptional historiographical endeavours of the *admor* Joseph Isaac.

In order to translate into more concrete, institutional, dynastic terms Habad's sense of itself as the direct heir and most authentic expression of original hasidism, the *admor* can be shown to have exploited not only the Kherson letters but also late Habad hagiographical sources whose reliability has been questioned even within the Habad school itself.[130] This applies, for example, to the frequent statements scattered throughout his writings that the founder of Habad, R. Shneur Zalman of Liady, was in the habit of referring to the Ba'al Shem Tov—the founder of hasidism—as 'granddad' (*zeyde* in Yiddish): 'The Old *Admor*, R. Shneur Zalman, used to call the Besht granddad. This was because he was his disciple's disciple . . . R. Shneur Zalman saw himself as the "grandson" of the Besht, and he used to say: "R. Barukh [of Międzybóż] is a physical grandson of the Besht, while I am a spiritual grandson".'[131] This formula, and the title 'granddad', do not occur anywhere in the published writings of R. Shneur Zalman of Liady or any other early hasidic sources. They appear to have been based on a hagiographical tale of the second half of the nineteenth century written by Michael Levi Frumkin-Rodkinson, a man who had been born into the Habad community but stepped out of the traditionalist fold and eventually emigrated to the United States.[132] The tale is a fictional embellishment of an authentic source—a letter by R. Shneur Zalman in which he reports on his quarrel with R. Barukh of Międzybóż, the Ba'al Shem Tov's grandson.[133] The original letter had clearly provided Rodkinson with a peg on which to hang his embellishment: R. Shneur Zalman pointedly addresses R. Barukh, reminding him that the Ba'al Shem Tov was *his* grandfather,[134] but nowhere does he employ the distinction between the 'physical' and the 'spiritual' grandson or claim for himself the status of a disciple's disciple who is 'spiritually' as good as a grandson. The tale, on the other hand, elaborates on the original exchange between the two as follows:

Then R. Barukh said: How dare you quarrel with me? Am I not the grandson of the Besht? The rabbi [Shneur Zalman] replied: You are his grandson in the physical sense while I am his grandson spiritually . . . For the Great Magid was a distinguished disciple of the Besht, blessed be he, and I was a distinguished disciple of the Magid.[135]

This hagiographical elaboration, which seems to be the fruit of the creative imagination of its author, distorts the original tenor of the dispute. It reflects and at the same time nourishes the late Habad tendency to present R. Shneur Zalman as the Ba'al Shem Tov's and the Magid of Mezhirech's direct successor and 'heir', a tendency which the *admor* Joseph Isaac shares and wishes to promote in making use of the tale. It is hardly likely that R. Shneur Zalman in his day would have thought of himself in these categories.[136]

The historical reconstructions of early hasidism by the *admor* Joseph Isaac are distinguished by a number of other traits, which reveal his overriding interest in promoting contemporary Habad values in response to contemporary events and trends, specifically through historiography. He exploited the medium for the promotion of these values at the cost—which, if he ever perceived it as such, he was certainly willing to pay—of ordering the past in certain categories and patterns which could be totally alien to it in reality. These categories and patterns were formed out of the harrowing experiences of his own period of office, from 1920 until his death in 1950.

The *admor* Joseph Isaac succeeded to office during the early post-revolutionary years of Soviet rule in Russia, when the Jewish 'sections' of the propaganda department of the Russian Communist Party were engaged in the systematic eradication of all national and religious institutions of Jewish life: community councils, synagogues, religious academies and schools, ritual baths, ritual slaughterhouses and butchers, Hebrew libraries and books were all being liquidated with the help of the internal security forces. Following the elimination of the traditionally bourgeois basis of Jewish economic activities, many were forced to seek new sources of livelihood in agriculture and the crafts, colonizing new territories in which there was no tradition of Jewish life nor any access to its resources.[137] The *admor* launched a courageous campaign for the preservation and dissemination of Jewish religious practice in perilous conditions. He conducted it as an underground operation, sending out secret emissaries—rabbis, teachers, ritual slaughterers, and other specialists in Jewish lore—as well as material resources to Jewish settlements which had been cut off and were becoming estranged from their tradition, not only by government oppression but also through the already established presence of secularist elements within the Jewish community itself. After a period of incarceration in 1927 he moved to Latvia, where he established a new centre of Habad. Seven years later he settled in Poland, creating a network of Habad religious academies, recruiting new followers, and setting up various organizations dedicated to the material support and religious welfare of Soviet Jews. During the Second World War he fled to the United States, forced, once again, to leave behind the bulk of his traditional following. From his new headquarters in Brooklyn he effected a remarkable rehabilitation of the Habad movement, setting up a large network of schools, academies, publications, and various other organizations and institutions actively engaged in hasidic-traditionalist propaganda.[138] He left to his son-in-law, the last Lubavitcher Rebbe, a movement which, unlike many of the hasidic schools of eastern and central Europe, had not only survived the war but became freshly invigorated, making an effective adaptation to the conditions of the new continent in the post-war period.

These experiences and achievements had clearly shaped the historical outlook of the *admor*. It was by the criteria of activism, propaganda, powerful centralistic organization, and heroic self-sacrifice that he assessed the hasidic leaders of the past. He identified these qualities in the personalities and styles of leadership of the three hasidic masters from whom he and Habad Lubavitch trace their direct descent—the Ba'al Shem Tov, the Magid of Mezhirech, and R. Shneur Zalman of Liady. He writes of the Ba'al Shem Tov's period of concealment, which he portrays along the lines suggested by the Kherson letters,[139] while at the same time echoing his own experience of underground organization in Soviet Russia:

> Since its earliest beginnings, organization and propaganda had always occupied a place of prime importance in the hasidic camp. Even before our master the Besht, may he rest in Eden, had revealed himself, while he was still in concealment, he and his colleagues, the secret tsadikim . . . were well organized and had set up centres at various locations. Each one would work at his own centre, and from time to time they would report in detail to the centre where our master the Besht, may he rest in Eden, was located.[140]

The same features characterize the Ba'al Shem Tov's leadership in its 'revealed' stage, which, again, corresponds well to the *admor*'s own style of operation once he left the Soviet Union, when he was able to set up a network of open centres in Poland and elsewhere while maintaining clandestine links with his underground operators inside Russia:

When our master the Besht was revealed, he set up open centres, and in each centre he established one of his close disciples, or he would set up a centre where a close disciple was resident. In the year 1740 we find our master the Besht surrounded by powerful disciples, all experts in the battle for *torah* [Jewish lore]. And in addition to his disciples and colleagues, the secret tsadikim, he now had openly revealed disciples, eminent men, highly organized and energetic, each at his own post, at the place designated for him by the Besht. This organization, and our master the Besht's inspired strategy of [realizing] the ideal of the love of Israel, together with the propaganda activities of his holy disciples, which were carried out with the utmost dedication to the point of willingness to die as martyrs, bore the result that within fifteen years the teaching of the Besht had spread and appealed to the Jews not only throughout Poland but also in Lithuania. . . . This high standard of order and discipline had yielded good results; the inspired success in spreading our master the Besht's teaching . . . was evident throughout.[141]

Such progress as was made at the time of the Besht was temporarily halted during the brief period when the leadership of the entire movement passed on to his son, R. Zevi. About R. Zevi's putative term of office there is no shred of evidence in any other sources, and it must be a figment of the *admor*'s creative imagination. He clearly felt the need to incorporate R. Zevi in the line of succession to the leadership of hasidism, which he envisaged, and wished to present, as being dynastic from the start. From his perspective, the Besht's son was destined to succeed his father, if only for a year, but since he turned out to be a 'weak man' he failed to leave his mark on the development of the movement, which is, implicitly, how the *admor* explains why there is no reference to his succession in the hagiographical tradition of *Shivḥei habesht*:

After the death of our master the Besht, his son, the righteous Rabbi Zevi, was elected supreme head and leader. However, at the end of his first year of office, the holy company realized that their master and rabbi's son was a weak man, while the situation required valiant strength and a man spirited enough to take charge of the leadership.[142]

But the brief crisis soon passed when R. Zevi, in response to a heavenly communication from his deceased father, stepped down and passed on the mantle of leadership to the Magid of Mezhirech,[143] whose own leadership was marked by the enhancement and intensification of precisely the same activities as those that had distinguished the leadership of the Besht:

'During the leadership of the holy rabbi, the Magid, propaganda activities were doubled and the organization was much improved.'[144]

In the 'third generation' of the leadership of hasidism we find R. Shneur Zalman of Liady similarly engaged in the same sort of activities, which the *admor* describes in identical terms:

The situation at that time required a supreme leader, who would be spirited enough to speak unequivocally to the *mitnagedim*. . . . In its general assembly, the holy company elected our Old Rebbe [R. Shneur Zalman of Liady] and authorized him to act as chief organizer . . . They gave him power and authority over the organization of all the centres and all the propaganda activities carried out throughout the land, [and they also authorized him] to visit from time to time all the places where the disciples of our master the Magid, may he rest in Eden, were resident. For approximately three years, from 1773 to 1776, our Old Rebbe was engaged in various journeys to various places, to supervise the condition of the disciples of the Magid and to inspect their activities at the centres, in order to ensure that they accorded with the decision of the central committee. Some of these journeys were made in the open while others were secret, when he made secret visits to Shklov, Minsk, and Vilna.[145]

These reconstructions are anachronistic and historically implausible in a number of ways.[146] But quite apart from this, what is most striking about them is the similarity of the terms in which the *admor* describes these three distinct generations of leadership, stretching over a period of some fifty years, during which the hasidic movement was entirely transformed organizationally and in other respects as well. His account blurs all distinctions and focuses on the similarities—precisely the opposite of the analytical procedure of the historian. In fact, his perception of the institution of hasidic leadership as it emerges from this account can be classified as typological rather than historical, and it is not unlike the perception of the career of the saintly hero in the hagiographical tales.[147]

The *admor*'s typological perception of personalities, institutions, processes, and events is evident throughout his historiographical work. He writes, for example, of the activities of the Ba'al Shem Tov and the 'secret tsadikim' in the 1720s:

At that time, around the year 1720, our master the Besht, together with his colleagues the secret tsadikim, embarked on a propaganda campaign among the Jews in the provinces of Podolia and neighbouring regions, [encouraging them] to move out of the cities and other densely populated areas into the villages and countryside settlements, and to work there in agriculture or the crafts, while the women should accustom themselves to weaving, keeping domestic animals or fowls, growing vegetables, etc.[148]

Elsewhere he adds: 'The secret tsadikim were not satisfied with merely directing the unemployed to take up productive trades; they made a living example of it themselves. This is why many of them became farmers.'[149] Now the issue of the 'productivization' of Jewish economic life through the move into farming or the crafts and away from the traditional occupation of leasing or managing the estates of the nobility made its first appearance on the horizon of Russian Jewry in the first two decades of the nineteenth century, as one of the many reforms which were attempted (without much success) by Alexander I.[150] The leader of the Habad community at that time, R. Dov Ber Shneuri of Lubavitch (R. Shneur Zalman's son and heir) responded positively to the tsarist government's initiative and actively encouraged his followers to become farmers and artisans, promoting the dignity of these productive occupations against the indignity of poverty and unemployment.[151] By the middle of the century, under Nicholas I, R. Menahem Mendel, the Tsemah Tsedek, the third dynastic leader of Habad, was fully committed to the policy of agricultural colonization, acquiring land and setting up Jewish farming communities in the region of Minsk.[152] The issue became topical again in the early years of the *admor* Joseph Isaac's own leadership, when the Soviet government was attempting to achieve the 'productivization' that the tsarist regime had failed to implement effectively by setting up new Jewish agricultural colonies and collectives in a number of regions throughout the Soviet Union.[153] The *admor* Joseph Isaac was deeply involved in the endeavour to extend pastoral care to these settlements.[154]

This evidently authentic concern in the Habad leadership over several generations for the amelioration of the material conditions of its flock through the shift towards 'productive' occupations on the land becomes an essential ingredient in the *admor* Joseph Isaac's typology of the ideal hasidic leader. It is perfectly natural for him, therefore, to identify this ingredient already in the leadership of the Besht and his fellow 'secret tsadikim' during the 1720s. The fact that this anticipates the earliest, and wholly unsuccessful, attempt at the agricultural settlement of the Jews in Austrian Galicia by some sixty years,[155] and in the Ba'al Shem Tov's more immediate Russian environment by another twenty at least, is hardly material. It was not the particular historical circumstances giving rise to such an ideology of 'productivization' in hasidism that interested the *admor*; what concerned him was the ideal of a caring leadership, one that is wholly committed to ensure the spiritual as well as the material well-being of its followers. This ideal is absolute, free from any ties to the changing circumstances of time and place, and as such it can be used to promote a morale-boosting, reassuring, and unifying message that transcends the particularities of historical reality. It was this ahistorical but edifying message that the *admor*'s reconstructions of hasidic history were striving to disseminate.

The same typological perception prompts the *admor* to place each one of the early leaders of hasidism, including Habad's founder and his successors, in a situation which is marked by deep crisis and confrontation, requiring time and again a leader who is 'spirited' enough to cope and to inspire his disciples by example, with his own utmost dedication, 'to the point of being ready to die a martyr's death'—a fixed pattern which fits well and most probably arises from the trials and tribulations of his own critical period in office. Thus he places the emergence of the Ba'al Shem Tov and his 'secret tsadikim' in the context of the aftermath of the Cossack uprising in Poland in 1648–9, an event which resulted in the massacre of thousands of Jews and the devastation of a large number of Jewish communities in the Ukraine and beyond:[156]

> The main objective of our master the Besht and his colleagues the secret tsadikim was to encourage the people of Israel and to strengthen their spirit. For after 1648–9, the years of the terrible persecution of the Jews, when thousands of lives were lost and all material assets plundered, the Jews began to concentrate in the towns and larger communities, as they were afraid to live in the villages. Most of them were unemployed and became impoverished, and with poverty came despair at their bitter exile.[157]

The element of confrontation which belongs in the same fixed patterning of events is identified in this case as follows: 'The opposition came from two directions: from those who were called the *mitnagedim*, who had begun to agitate against the new path already during the lifetime of the Besht, and from the Frankists, with whom the Besht and his disciples had conducted public disputations from which they emerged victorious.'[158]

With regard to the Frankists' alleged opposition to hasidism (of which nothing is known historically, as is the case with the hostilities of the as yet non-existent rabbinic *mitnagedim*), the *admor* explains elsewhere, revealing yet again his reliance on the Kherson *genizah* forgeries: 'Our master the Besht conducted a number of disputations with the Frankists until he won victory, as is explained at length in the letters of the above-mentioned [Kherson] *genizah*. This victory gave rise to a repressed hatred of our master the Besht and his holy disciples on the part of the Frankists.'[159]

The succession to the leadership of the Magid of Mezhirech in the early 1760s is marked by an intensification of the same anti-hasidic agitation on the part of the Lithuanian *mitnagedim* (which in reality was to begin only a decade later, shortly before the Magid's death, in 1772) and by further, and more damaging, hostilities on the part of the Frankists.[160] Subsequent leaders in the Habad line are similarly shown to be operating in the context of crisis and opposition. The Frankists eventually disappear from the arena but are replaced by the Enlighteners, against whom the third leader of Habad, R. Menahem Mendel, conducts a heroic campaign and triumphs.[161]

This typology of the ideal leader, who emerges at a time of crisis and spearheads a victorious campaign against militant opposition of one type or another, is truly rooted in the historical experience of Habad hasidism: its founder, R. Shneur Zalman, *was* at the centre of the confrontation with the *mitnagedim* in the final decade of the eighteenth century; they *did* bring false charges against him as a result of which he was arrested by the Russian authorities, only to emerge vindicated and 'victorious' (although his victory over the *mitnagedim* at a public disputation in Minsk, which is not attested anywhere beyond the historiographical works of the *admor* Joseph Isaac,[162] is more likely to be the fictional product of the *admor*'s typological patterning of R. Shneur Zalman's career, modelled, perhaps, on the Ba'al Shem Tov's alleged victory over the Frankists at the disputation in Lwów, or on R. Shneur Zalman's reference, in one of his authentic letters, to his own and his hasidic mentor Menahem Mendel of Vitebsk's failed attempts to engage in a disputation with the leaders of the *mitnagedim* in Vilna and Shklov,[163] than to have taken place in reality). His son, the second leader of Habad, was similarly the victim of false accusations by the *mitnagedim* and, like his father, was imprisoned and released; the third *admor*, R. Menahem Mendel, was indeed a militant campaigner against the *maskilim*, who denounced and persecuted him; and the reality of the career of the *admor*

Joseph Isaac himself, as we have seen, fits this heroic pattern extremely well. The point is that the typology which has emerged from this collective Habad experience of crisis and confrontation has become the principle by which the peculiarities of each experience and its context are organized in the historical narratives of the *admor*. This is particularly evident in his accounts of the more distant, pre-Habad hasidic past, the time of the Ba'al Shem Tov and the Magid of Mezhirech, who in reality could not, of course, have shared in the collective experience that is peculiar to Habad. It is here that the *admor*'s reconstructions are most at odds with all the facts which can be gleaned from other sources.

Notably, in his book of memoirs—which contains, despite its title, long cycles of plainly hagiographical tales about personalities and events predating his own lifetime by centuries—the *admor* alludes to the constructive propagandist value of his typological accounts of history. In a long and rather complex series of tales he presents R. Barukh, R. Shneur Zalman's father, as a young man brought up to identify with the rabbinic opponents of the Besht. But he is swayed from this stance to a sympathetic curiosity about hasidism when he first learns of the comparable rabbinic opposition to the pious sixteenth-century kabbalist R. Elijah, the Ba'al Shem of Worms. He finally arrives at the conclusion that 'just as there is no difference between R. Israel Ba'al Shem Tov, the founder of the hasidic movement, and the Ba'al Shem of Worms, so there is no difference . . . between the earlier opponents and the opponents of this generation'.[164] R. Barukh becomes a convert to hasidism once he realizes that the Ba'al Shem Tov and his 'holy company' of 'secret tsadikim' are not a recent aberration but the bearers of an ancient tradition in kabbalistic Judaism, which is characterized as having always attracted suspicion and contempt in rabbinic quarters, where it was viewed as forbidden magic or mere superstition.[165]

The typology of ongoing opposition which was directed, from one generation to the next, at all the chief exponents of the mystical-magical tradition of Judaism, from the sixteenth-century Ba'al Shem of Worms through to the Besht, the Magid of Mezhirech, R. Shneur Zalman of Liady, and all the subsequent leaders of Habad right down to the *admor* himself, validates the struggles of the present by reference to struggles in the past, which are all enlisted in the service of contemporary causes.[166] The *admor*'s cause, to which he harnessed all his historical writings, was the critical struggle against what he perceived as the latest and most destructive manifestations of that age-old oppositional tradition: the suppression of religion in the Soviet Union, the liquidation of European Jewry in the Holocaust, and the accelerated secularization of Jewish life that he encountered on arrival in the United States. His goal at every stage of his struggle to counter these 'oppositional' forces was 'to bring the Jews closer to the Creator and to instil in them a love of Torah and a desire to observe its precepts.'[167]

This use of the past to validate the aims of the present is no different from the one made by the original redactor of the hagiographical *Shivḥei habesht*, who explained his rationale for producing the book as follows:

'Because of our many sins the faith has decreased and heresy has been spread in the world . . . Therefore I was careful to write down all the awesome things that I heard from truthful people . . . I wrote it down as a remembrance for my children and their children, so that it would be a reminder for them and for all to cling to God, blessed be He, and His Torah, to strengthen their faith in God and his tsaddikim, and so they would see how His Torah purifies the souls of its students so that a man can reach higher stages . . . In each tale he should perceive His awesome deeds. He should infer the moral of each tale, so that he will be able to attach his heart to the fear of God, the beliefs of the sages and the power of the holy Torah.'[168]

What is different, however, between this and the *admor*'s approach to his task is that, in the final decade of the eighteenth century, the first editor-author of *Shivḥei habesht* still needed to apologize for writing apparently 'meaningless narratives', 'history', or mere 'stories', and to derive the legitimacy of this medium from the value of religious edification which he believed it would promote. But by the first half of the twentieth century, the *admor* Joseph Isaac could take for granted the full legitimacy, indeed, the authority, of the historiographical medium; it was the eroded religious values of God-fearing, the beliefs of the sages, and the power of the holy Torah that needed to be expressed in this medium if they were to be validated and promoted effectively.

The status and function of history had been transformed in the course of the nineteenth century, as a new consciousness of the Jewish past was emerging in response to the breakdown of traditional belief and practice:

The modern effort to reconstruct the Jewish past begins at a time that witnesses a sharp break in the continuity of Jewish living and hence also an ever-growing decay of Jewish group memory. In this sense, if for no other, history becomes what it had never been before—the faith of fallen Jews. For the first time history, not a sacred text, becomes the arbiter of Judaism. Virtually all nineteenth-century Jewish ideologies, from Reform to Zionism, would feel a need to appeal to history for validation. Predictably, 'history' yielded the most varied conclusions to the appellants.[169]

Orthodoxy—a nineteenth-century ideology of which hasidism has been a militant exponent—was one of the appellants, and the *admor* Joseph Isaac was addressing 'fallen Jews', or Jews who were at risk of 'falling', or whose children seemed likely to 'fall', first in interwar Europe and eventually, and even more so, in the United States. In a letter written in 1932, he urged his followers to talk to their children about their hasidic past as a means of reinforcing their religious identity:

It is the duty and obligation of each one of 'our people' [*anshei shelomenu*, those who are affiliated with Habad] . . . to tell his children and members of his household what he had seen and heard at the homes of his hasidic father and grandfather. By means of such stories he would establish the value of God-fearing on a sound basis.[170]

Dozens of similar letters to both individuals and groups of followers encourage them not only to remember and talk of the past, but to write it down in the form of memoirs, histories, and stories, and to collect more information about it from the elderly, who can remember further back.[171] A number of letters point out the good effect of hasidic gatherings dedicated to the recollection of 'days of old', as a result of which individuals or groups of lapsed hasidic followers—people who had long abandoned the traditional Jewish way of life—were stirred and brought back to the fold.[172]

This exploitation of the past acquires a new dimension of nostalgia for the vanished 'old world' after the move to the United States during the war. In his first year in New York, urging a follower to record his 'recollections of the old-style hasidim you knew, and of the ordinary hasidim of that generation, and what you remember about your own ancestors, and the family of your late father-in-law', the *admor* writes movingly about the effect on his mood of his own historiographical activities:

I know for myself that when I read or write my memoirs, at that time it is as if I am back in my old situation, and a special, pleasant sensation overwhelms me . . . This must be the same for each one of our people when he remembers the days of old, while he was still living in an environment glowing with spiritual illumination.[173]

Nostalgia for the 'old world' is not only aroused by historiographical activity; it soon begins to nourish the work itself. In his book of memoirs, written after his arrival in the United States, the *admor* devotes several chapters to the Belarusian town of Lubavitch, which had served for over a century as the headquarters of the Habad movement, and with which its name has remained associated even after the evacuation of the town by the ruling Habad family during the First World War. The *admor* speaks of Lubavitch longingly, in the most affectionate terms, and he transforms the emotionally charged name, alluding to its literal meaning in Russian, into a 'symbol of the love of Israel, the love of humanity, and, above all, of course, the love of God, the Creator of all'.[174] Taking every liberty with chronology, geography, and the bounds of historical plausibility, he presents the town as the most important centre of clandestine hasidic agitation during the 'concealed' stage of the Ba'al Shem Tov's life, when he operated as a 'secret tsadik', thus turning the nineteenth-century 'capital' of Habad into the very birthplace of hasidism in the beginning of the eighteenth century —a theme which was not as yet present in his earlier, pre-war accounts of the same period dealing with the 'secret tsadikism' of the Besht.[175]

Altogether, the *admor* Joseph Isaac's *Memoirs*, first published in instalments in the Yiddish press during the war years in New York, and subsequently appearing as a substantial book and translated into several languages, are more boldly and imaginatively hagiographical than autobiographical in the conventional sense. His memory, as we have seen, is not confined to the experiences of his own past. It embodies a new collective memory of Habad hasidism, forging its post-war historical consciousness for the consolidation of a broader, more diverse, and newly based following, alien to the concrete reality of hasidism as it was in the 'old world'.

The book contains long cycles of quasi-historical, essentially hagiographical, tales,[176] many of them apparently new, about the prehistory of Habad hasidism. From the point of view of the *admor* and his followers, the value of the work as a historical record is beyond doubt; even its autobiographical title is distinctly modern, historiographical, rather than being drawn from the traditional stock of hagiographical book titles (the Praises, the Deeds, the Wonders, the Glory, the Tales of the tsadikim, and so on), and may suggest that a subtle, and not unconscious, blurring of generic categories has taken place. Indeed, the *admor* does not distinguish between 'memoirs', 'histories', and 'stories', terms which are often used interchangeably in his other writings.[177] He appears to be drawing on the now firmly established authority of the historiographical genre in order to bolster the hitherto questionable legitimacy of the hagiographical tales in the Habad tradition.

The hasidic tales did not only attract the sceptical scrutiny of modern historians; even within the hasidic camp, their status had been uncertain from the start.[178] Significantly, it was not with this genre, which was to become its popular hallmark, but rather with its speculative homiletic teachings that hasidism first launched itself in print during the 1780s and 1790s. It was this literature, not the hagiographical tales, that disseminated the novel message of hasidism just as it was expanding and cohering into a movement.[179] Although the oral transmission of the tales must have begun much earlier and was never interrupted, the publication of this hagiographical material was viewed with some ambivalence, as is evidenced by both the author's and the printer's apologetic introductions to *Shivḥei habesht*.[180]

Moreover, the embarrassment which was clearly felt in some hasidic quarters with regard to the more extravagantly wondrous elements of the hagiographical tales was compounded by an embarrassment with the wondrous deeds which had inspired them. While no one doubted the ability of a saint to perform miracles, a number of hasidic leaders had expressed their disdain for miracle-working tsadikim, defining their own leadership role in terms that precluded all miraculous interventions in mundane affairs, while focusing on the provision of moral and spiritual guidance to their fol-lowes.[181] This distaste for vulgar displays of miracle-work may have pre-conditioned a certain distaste for the tales that celebrated the extraordinary feats of miracle-working tsadikim.

In addition, the hasidim must have been aware—although the extent of this awareness is difficult to gauge—that their tales were attracting the hostile attention of the *maskilim*, who were quick to mock them. *Shivḥei habesht*, as well as R. Nahman of Bratslav's cycle of symbolic tales, *Sipurei ma'asiyot*, which were published within a year of each other (in 1814 and 1815 respectively), supplied them with powerful ammunition by exposing a particularly irrational face of hasidism, as is evident from the reaction of the Galician *maskil* Joseph Perl, who satirized both works in his *Megaleh temirin* (Revealer of Secrets), published in 1819.[182]

It is, perhaps, for all these reasons that after the publication of *Shivḥei habesht* the production of hasidic hagiography was arrested for a period of some fifty years, this despite the fact that *Shivḥei habesht* itself appears to have been in considerable demand, as it was repeatedly printed, in both Hebrew and Yiddish, during this period.[183] It was only from the mid-1860s on that newly assembled or newly composed tales began to be published again, with the genre soon achieving great popularity if never quite the full legitimacy that it lacked from the outset.[184] It is not impossible that the hagiographical works which appeared during this period were a response to the encroachment of Haskalah publications on the hasidic world. Their authors could believe that they were providing an edifying, pious historical literature for the masses as an antidote to the secular literature and the output of the Hebrew and Yiddish press, which were becoming increasingly available to them at the time.[185]

Curiously, even though two pioneers of this second-phase hasidic hagiography came out of the Habad camp and dedicated their works to the glorification of its leaders,[186] and although Habad's founder, R. Shneur Zalman of Liady, was associated, however indirectly, with the publication of *Shivḥei habesht* by one of his followers,[187] the Habad school did not contribute directly to the hagiographical literature that proliferated in the late nineteenth and early twentieth centuries, while at the same time producing a large body of speculative and halakhic writings.[188] Moreover, according to the (not necessarily reliable) testimony of Pesah Ruderman (1854–86), a Habad hasid who abandoned the fold and became a *maskil*, in Habad circles *Shivḥei habesht* was viewed as a mitnagdic or maskilic provocation, full of lies and designed for no other purpose but to mock and desecrate the memory of the Besht.[189] It should also be noted that the first two modern historians of Habad, writing at the beginning of the twentieth century as sympathetic observers who were attuned to the distinctive Habad perspective on its own history (however self-consciously and rigorously they were committed to their craft as historians), were blatantly critical of the hagiographical tales, especially those that concerned early Habad, and saw their own work as the answer to the countless exaggerations and deviations from the truth they had propagated.[190] In addition, it should be borne in mind that R. Shneur Zalman of Liady was one of the hasidic leaders who did not approve of the miracle-working aspect of tsadikism, insisting that his followers should address to him only requests that concerned their spiritual welfare, while disclaiming the power to intervene on their behalf supernaturally in mundane affairs.[191] If this posture was enough to inhibit the evolution of miraculous tales around his personality, such as were emerging in abundance around many other hasidic leaders in the late nineteenth and early twentieth centuries,[192] then it could go some way towards explaining the hagiographical reticence of Habad.

The *admor* Joseph Isaac was, of course, fully conscious and rather proud of this distinctive feature of his own hasidic tradition. According to him, Habad never held the recitation of wondrous tales 'in praise' of one tsadik or another to be the essence of hasidism. Rather, the Habad leaders had always encouraged their followers to strive for spiritual invigoration by engaging with, and fully internalizing, the guidance they provided in their speculative teachings. This definition of the Habad path—implicitly the path that captures the true spirit of hasidism—is often articulated in the *admor*'s writings by way of contrast with the passive reliance on the tsadik's spiritual endeavours on behalf of his followers, which is, as he claims, the defining characteristic of other hasidic schools. In this context he refers to all these other hasidic schools en masse, indiscriminately, employing the collective term 'Polish' (and occasionally Volhynian or Galician) hasidism —a monolithic designation which entirely blurs the distinctions between diverse hasidic schools, and an ambiguous one at best, given the historic instability of Poland's borders since the late eighteenth-century partitions of the Polish-Lithuanian Commonwealth. While prior to the first partition of 1772 the whole of hasidism, such as it was, could be referred to—in strictly geopolitical terms—as a 'Polish' phenomenon, after the partitions many hasidic courts, along with all their followers, found themselves in territories which were now either Russian or Austrian, and by the time when the *admor* was writing, in the interwar years of the twentieth century, not only had some of these territories become sovereign states in their own right, but hasidism had established itself in regions which had never belonged to Poland even in the pre-partitions era. Thus the term 'Polish hasidism' in the *admor*'s parlance is clearly a construct that has little to do with the history of hasidism or the geography of Poland; it serves to highlight his sense of Habad's unique status within the hasidic movement, and implies its superiority to all other varieties of hasidism. This sense must have been rooted in Habad's historic experience of 'splendid isolation', when for most of the nineteenth century it enjoyed unchallengeable pre-eminence throughout the north-eastern provinces of the Pale of Settlement, where its influence was such that it hardly had to contend with rival hasidic groups.

Habad's schematic juxtaposition with a notional 'Polish hasidism' occurs here and there already in the letters and 'talks' of the *admor*'s father, R. Shalom Dovber, but it features time and again throughout R. Joseph Isaac's own large corpus of writings, and must have come into sharp focus during his period of exile in Poland, when—driven by Communist persecution for his outlawed religious activism—he left his native Russia in 1927, settling first 'temporarily' in Riga, and from 1933 until his flight to the United States in 1940, in Warsaw and subsequently in the neighbouring resort town of Otwock. He clearly expected to find a permanent shelter in Poland, then home to the world's largest and most vibrant Jewish community, believing that the freedom of religion the Polish Republic offered, and the significant proportion of its Jewish population that was still religiously observant, provided the most conducive conditions for what was bound to be the effective recreation—and, as he hoped, restoration to past glory—of Habad hasidism, now denuded of the bulk of its large traditional following, which remained trapped in the Soviet Union, where religious practice was vigorously repressed, and was consequently facing the prospect of extinction. It was in this critical period that, for the first time in its history, the Habad leadership was exposed to the close and crowded proximity of numerous rival hasidic courts, all Polish in the sense that they were native to the territories that fell within the borders of the nineteenth-century Russian province known as the Kingdom of Poland, or had been Polish in the pre-partitions period and were annexed to the new Republic of Poland in the aftermath of the First World War. The encounter with all these Polish hasidic courts, some of them extremely large and wealthy, in their native environment—to which Habad was alien and where it wielded little power or influence—forced the *admor* to define Habad's identity by constant reference to the difference between his own and all the indigenous schools of hasidism, while at the same time targeting their institutions as fertile recruiting grounds for potential converts to Habad, who would replenish the drastically depleted ranks of his own followers.[193]

In a letter dispatched from Otwock in the summer of 1938, the *admor* formulated the difference between Habad and 'Polish' (here 'Volhynian', used synonymously) hasidism as follows: 'One of the fundamental principles of the hasidic teaching of Habad is that each one of its adherents must be diligently engaged in the work of hasidism, not as in the system of Volhynia, where the main point is the affiliation to the leader, and the leader lifts up those who are affiliated to him.'[194] And in a letter from Riga, written in 1932 to his son-in-law (the seventh and last *admor*, Menachem Mendel Schneerson), he associated this fundamental difference with two divergent approaches to the hagiographical tales of hasidism. The 'Polish' schools revolve entirely around the personality of the leader, whose miraculous feats are enthusiastically reported and recorded by his followers. They have thus produced a rich tradition of hagiographical tales. Habad, on the other hand, which places the burden of spiritual work on every hasid, must provide him with clear guidance, and this, while generating a large body of speculative literature, has suppressed the natural impulse—evident especially in the young—to glorify and celebrate the illustrious leaders with tales about their extraordinary lives and wondrous deeds:

> It is evident that the methods and teachings of the leaders of Volhynian, Polish, and Galician hasidism are closer than the Habad teaching to the method and teaching of our Master the Besht, especially as far as miracles are concerned . . . For our Master the Besht performed numerous miracles, both overt and covert, and this is the method pursued also by the hasidic leaders of Volhynia, Poland, and Galicia . . . [but] the foundation of Habad is to study in depth and to fully comprehend the ideas and concepts embedded in the holy teachings of the Habad leaders, which enhance the capacity for contemplative prayer and speculative thought . . . Five generations of Habad hasidim . . . have followed this path . . . The [Habad] students and youngsters are eager to hear the occasional miraculous tale, but the older hasidim rebuke them, since in the eyes of the eminent adherents of Habad, miracles degrade hasidism . . . The hasidim of Volhynia, Poland, and Galicia [on the other hand] have focused their attention on the lives of their leaders, their tales, and their deeds . . . For this reason, while the hasidim of Volhynia, Poland, and Galicia write down stories and [accounts of] events, providing us with whole books full of wonders, the Habad hasidim provide us with whole books of hasidic teachings—transcripts of our Masters' addresses, long expositions, and profound rational explanations.[195]

While he fully acknowledges that the Habad tradition had tended to frown on both wonders and their tales, the *admor* is far from condemning them outright. Remarkably for the spokesman of a hasidic school which insists on its intimate and exclusive affinity with the hasidism of the Besht and the

Magid of Mezhirech,[196] he admits that in respect of the attitude to miracles, 'Polish' hasidism is closer to the original path of the founders. Moreover, he detects the desire to hear miraculous tales even within the ranks of Habad, albeit in young students, not in the old and eminent hasidim. One cannot help feeling that his sympathies on this are mostly with the young, and that he disapproves of the doctrinaire attitude of the older generation. Indeed, near the conclusion of the letter he confesses:

> I cannot deny that I often regret it that the hasidic followers of Habad in every generation did not write down the tales and accounts of events which comprise numerous miracles and supernatural feats, even though I still prefer their books and their writings, which expound the teachings they had heard, each in his own time, to the wondrous tales they might have told us.[197]

The letter makes it quite clear that, despite the disapproval of the older hasidim, tales about the leaders of Habad continued to be 'whispered' even if they were not written down.[198]

Even at the time of writing this letter, and increasingly in the course of his term of office, particularly during the post-war period in the United States, the *admor* Joseph Isaac was committed to the rehabilitation of the tales in the Habad school. By blurring the distinction between stories and histories he was able to inaugurate a new era of hagiographical production in Habad, wholly 'modern' in its historical orientation, reinforced by the rigour of the Kherson 'documentation', but at the same time drawing on the rich resource of the orally transmitted tales, which clearly nourished his own imagination and underlies all his historical writings.

One of his early informants was his grandmother, the dowager Rebbetsin Rivkah (1834–1914). It is clear that tales about the hasidic past were transmitted by women in the Habad court,[199] a fact which would hardly have enhanced the questionable status of the genre, but one which the *admor* highlights repeatedly without a hint of embarrassment. On the contrary, he proudly admits to having listened eagerly to 'old wives' tales' in his youth, an admission which reflects not only his concern to establish the legitimacy of the hagiographical tales but also his equally novel project of integrating 'the wives and daughters of the hasidim' in his Habad constituency. He recognized that women, traditionally excluded from the spiritual life of the hasidic community, could make a crucial contribution to the preservation of Orthodox Jewish practice, appealing to them directly as the primary guardians of religious observance in the home, and mobilizing their energies for traditionalist propaganda and other forms of activism, especially in those spheres of life that are considered appropriate or specific to women; he even encouraged (albeit selectively) the initiation of women in the speculative teachings of Habad hasidism.[200]

The *admor* invested the tales with a higher degree of visibility and prestige by reporting, for example, that his father had always concluded the delivery of a formal discourse with a tale or a brief casual 'talk' when addressing an audience of 'simple' people who have not been initiated in the speculative teachings of Habad. This technique proved effective, since 'the teaching in general, and the casual talks and tales in particular, had the desired effect on the audience so that some of them began to engage in the hasidic style of worship, taking long over prayer and adopting the manners of the followers of [Habad] hasidism.'[201] As a method of recruitment or restoration into the Habad fold, the tales acquired the same status as the historical works into which they were woven and from which they were hardly distinguishable. The *admor*'s followers, and the present generation of Habad, have been committing them to writing and to print, taking both their inspiration and licence from him.[202]

The historiographical enterprise of the *admor* Joseph Isaac, typological, anachronistic, and uncritical of its sources as it is, was not the naive work of a dilettante historian. As a religious leader of ingenuity and vision, he borrowed the potent historiographical idiom in order to validate and harness to action a hagiographical tradition on whose power of edification he was compelled to draw in conditions of unprecedented crisis and change. He may not have uncovered the 'archaeological' truth, but that he created a new 'historical' truth of Habad is certain.

Notes

1 *On Heroes, Hero-Worship and the Heroic in History* (London, 1840).

2 *Nom de plume* of the Hebrew Zionist essayist Asher Hirsch Ginsberg (1856–1927).

3 *Selected Essays by Ahad Ha'am*, trans. L. Simon (Philadelphia, 1912), 306–7. For the background to Ahad Ha'am's ideas on this see E. Simon and J. E. Heller, *Ahad Ha'am: The Man and His Works* [Aḥad ha'am, ha'ish ufo'olo] (Jerusalem, 1955), ch. 2, esp. 145–56.

4 Schiper must have known Ahad Ha'am's essay on Moses, but the application of the categories 'archaeological' and 'historical' truth to the study of the Ba'al Shem Tov may have been suggested to him by Simon Dubnow's remarks in his *History of Hasidism* [Toledot haḥasidut] [1931] (Tel Aviv, 1960), 42 n. 2.

5 *Hado'ar*, 40/27 (1960), 525–32; 40/28 (1960), 551–3.

6 See G. Scholem, *Kabbalah* (Jerusalem, 1974), 310–11.

7 See G. Scholem, 'The Historical Figure of R. Israel Ba'al Shem Tov' (Heb.), in id., *The Latest Phase: Essays on Hasidism by Gershom Scholem* [Hashalav ha'aḥaron: meḥkerei haḥasidut shel gershom shalom], ed. D. Assaf and E. Liebes (Jerusalem, 2008), 106.

8 This is the acronym of the Hebrew *ba'al shem tov* and one of the most common designations of Israel Ba'al Shem Tov in the hasidic sources.

9 A. Z. Aescoly-Weintraub, *Introduction à l'étude des hérésies religieuses parmi les juifs: La Kabbale—Le Hassidisme* (Paris, 1928), 33–4.

10 Ibid. 40.

11 Ibid. 52.

12 Ibid. 51.

13 His *History of Hasidism* was first published in Russian during the 1880s and 1890s. See below, n. 67.

14 Dubnow, *The History of Hasidism* (Heb.), 41.

15 Unless otherwise stated, all references are to the English version: *In Praise of the Baal Shem Tov*, ed. D. Ben-Amos and J. R. Mintz (Bloomington, 1972).

16 Dubnow, *The History of Hasidism* (Heb.), 41–52, 59–75; cf. G. Scholem, 'The First Two Testimonies on the Relations between Hasidic Groups and the Ba'al Shem Tov' (Heb.), in id., *The Latest Phase* (Heb.), 64–81; id., 'The Historical Figure of R. Israel Ba'al Shem Tov' (Heb.), ibid. 106–38.

17 Only a handful of letters by the Besht have survived which can be presumed to be authentic, and even they are not unproblematic. For a critical evaluation of these letters see M. Rosman, 'The Besht's Letters: Towards a New Assessment' (Heb.), in D. Assaf, J. Dan, and I. Etkes (eds.), *Studies in Hasidism* [Meḥkerei ḥasidut] (Jerusalem, 1999), 1–14. For an English rendition of the most famous (and controversial) of these letters see L. Jacobs, *Jewish Mystical Testimonies* (New York, 1976), 148–55. See also M. Rosman, *Founder of Hasidism: A Quest for the Historical Ba'al Shem Tov* (Oxford, 2013), pp. xlviii–lvii, 97–126; I. Etkes, *The Besht: Magician, Mystic, and Leader* (Waltham, Mass., 2005), 282–8.

18 See Y. H. Yerushalmi, *Zakhor: Jewish History and Jewish Memory* (Seattle, 1982).

19 See G. Scholem, *Major Trends in Jewish Mysticism* (New York, 1961), 14–17. There were, of course, some exceptions, but personal accounts of mystical experience remained unpublished and never reached public circulation. Even

the mystical diaries of a number of prominent 16th-century Safed kabbalists have survived only in unique manuscripts, were not intended for public dissemination, and did not begin to circulate in print until the 20th century. One of the most remarkable exceptions in the hasidic context (and the hasidic masters did not write autobiographically, at least not until the 20th century; it was the Jewish Enlightenment that brought the autobiographical genre to eastern Europe) is Nathan Sternharz (1780–1845), R. Nahman of Bratslav's disciple and quasi-successor. His autobiography, which was published in two parts, in 1876 and 1904, is yet to be placed in its proper literary context. For the time being see M. Moseley, *Being For Myself Alone: Origins of Jewish Autobiography* (Stanford, Calif., 2005), 312–32. The mystical diary of the hasidic master Isaac Judah Yehiel Safrin of Komarno (1806–74), *Megilat setarim* (Scroll of Secrets), was printed for the first time only in the 20th century; see Naftali Ben-Menahem's edition, published in Jerusalem in 1944. For an English translation of that edition, under the title *Book of Secrets*, see *Jewish Mystical Autobiographies: Book of Visions and Book of Secrets*, trans. and introd. M. M. Faierstein (New York, 1999), 267–306.

20 See *In Praise of the Baal Shem Tov*, ed. Ben-Amos and Mintz, Index of Motifs, 290–305.

21 See ibid., introduction, p. xxv.

22 See J. Dan, *The Hasidic Tale: Its History and Development* [Hasipur haḥasidi] (Jerusalem, 1975), 29–35; id., *The Hebrew Story in the Middle Ages* [Hasipur ha'ivri biyemei habeinayim: iyunim betoledotav] (Jerusalem, 1974), 238–51; 'On the History of the "Praises" Literature' (Heb.), *Jerusalem Studies in Jewish Folklore*, 1 (1982), 82–100; G. Nigal, *The Hasidic Tale*, trans. E. Levin (Oxford, 2008), 18–21.

23 See BT *Suk*. 28*a*; cf. Zohar iii. 228*a*.

24 For other examples of this see Dan, *The Hasidic Tale* (Heb.), 68–74; Nigal, *The Hasidic Tale*, 19–21.

25 See Dan, *The Hasidic Tale* (Heb.), 71.

26 See A. Rapoport-Albert, '*Katnut*, *Peshitut*, and *Eini Yode'a* in Nahman of Bratslav' (Heb.), in S. Stein and R. Loewe (eds.), *Studies in Jewish Intellectual and Religious History Presented to Alexander Altmann* (Tuscaloosa, Ala., 1979), Hebrew section, 11; repr. in ead., *Studies in Hasidism, Sabbatianism, and Gender* [Ḥasidim veshabeta'im, anashim venashim] (Jerusalem, 2015), 102.

27 See A. Ya'ari, 'Two Basic Editions of *Shivḥei habesht*' (Heb.), *Kiryat sefer*, 39 (1964), 249–72, 394–407, 552–62.

28 See *Shivḥei habesht*, ed. Y. Mondshine (Jerusalem, 1982), 22–47.

29 *In Praise of the Ba'al Shem Tov [Shivhei Ha-Besht], with introduction and annotations by Avraham Rubinstein* [Shivḥei habesht: mahadurah mu'eret umevo'eret.

Avraham Rubinstein] (Jerusalem, 1991). The preface (pp. 4–9) provides a review of the various editions. A fully critical edition of the work is currently in preparation by Jonatan Meir.

30 See e.g. B. Dinur, *With the Turn of the Generations* [Bemifneh hadorot] (Jerusalem, 1955), 89–92; cf. Scholem, 'The Historical Figure of R. Israel Ba'al Shem Tov' (Heb.), 106–12.

31 See *In Praise of the Baal Shem Tov*, ed. Ben-Amos and Mintz, 161–3; cf. Dubnow, *The History of Hasidism* (Heb.), 64.

32 See *In Praise of the Baal Shem Tov*, ed. Ben-Amos and Mintz, 144–6, and cf. M. Rosman, 'Miedzyboz and Rabbi Israel Baal Shem Tov', in G. D. Hundert (ed.), *Essential Papers on Hasidism: Origins to Present* (New York, 1991), 210.

33 See *In Praise of the Baal Shem Tov*, ed. Ben-Amos and Mintz, 211–17, and cf. I. Halpern, *Eastern European Jewry: Historical Studies* [Yehudim veyahadut bemizraḥ eiropah] (Jerusalem, 1968), 277–88; Dan, *The Hasidic Tale* (Heb.), 113–18; A. Teller, 'The Słuck Tradition Concerning the Early Days of the Besht' (Heb.), in Assaf et al. (eds.), *Studies in Hasidism* (Heb.) 15–38.

34 See *In Praise of the Baal Shem Tov*, ed. Ben-Amos and Mintz, 84–5, 185, 334, and cf. I. Bartal, 'The Immigration of R. Eleazar of Amsterdam to the Land of Israel in 1740' (Heb.), in J. Michman (ed.), *Studies on the History of Dutch Jewry* [Meḥkarim al toledot yahadut holand] (Jerusalem, 1984), iv. 7–25 (repr. in id., *Exile in the Homeland* [Galut ba'arets: yishuv erets yisra'el beterem tsiyonut] (Jerusalem, 1994), 23–40).

35 See J. Barnai, 'Some Clarifications on the Land of Israel's Stories of "In Praise of the Baal Shem Tov"', *Revue des études juives*, 146 (1987), 367–80.

36 Scholem ('The Historical Figure of R. Israel Ba'al Shem Tov' (Heb.) and 'The First Two Testimonies' (Heb.)) had attempted to assemble all the contemporary extra-hasidic references to the Besht, but some of these were interpreted by others as unrelated to the founder of hasidism. See H. Lieberman, 'How Hasidism Is "Studied" in Israel' (Heb.), in id., *Ohel raḥel* (New York, 1980), i. 24–49.

37 See Rosman, 'Miedzyboz and Rabbi Israel Baal Shem Tov', 209–25.

38 See ibid. 216–21. Rosman's findings confirm, for example, the impression that the Ba'al Shem Tov was not a demotic, anti-establishment figure, the popular leader of a movement for the masses, as he has so often been portrayed in both the scholarly and the popular historiography of hasidism. As Rosman has shown, he was, rather, a functionary of the community and a member of its elite group. A number of studies in recent years have pointed independently to the same conclusion. See e.g. I. Etkes, 'Hasidism as a Movement: The First Stage', in B. Safran (ed.), *Hasidism: Continuity or Innovation?* (Cambridge, Mass., 1988), 1–26; M. Piekarz, *The Beginning of Hasidism: Intellectual Trends*

in Derush and Musar Literature [Biyemei tsemiḥat haḥasidut: megamot ra'ayoniyot besifrei derush umusar] (Jerusalem, 1978), 136–7, and my own Ch. 2 above, at nn. 50–61. For an analysis of this bias in the modern historiography of hasidism, focusing on the work of Simon Dubnow, see R. M. Seltzer, 'The Secular Appropriation of Hasidism by an East European Jewish Intellectual: Dubnow, Renan, and Besht', in A. Polonsky (ed.), *Poles and Jews: Renewing the Dialogue*, Polin: Studies in Polish Jewry 1 (1986), 151–62. For extensive re-evaluations of the Besht see M. Rosman, *Founder of Hasidism: A Quest for the Historical Ba'al Shem Tov* (Oxford, 2013); I. Etkes, *The Besht: Magician, Mystic, and Leader* (Waltham, Mass., 2005); R. Elior, *Israel Ba'al Shem Tov and His Contemporaries: Kabbalists, Sabbatians, Hasidim, and Mitnagedim* [Yisra'el ba'al shem tov uvenei doro: mekubalim, shabeta'im, ḥasidim umitnagedim], 2 vols. (Jerusalem, 2014).

39 See Yerushalmi, *Zakhor*, 33.

40 *In Praise of the Baal Shem Tov*, ed. Ben-Amos and Mintz, 3–5.

41 See Dubnow, *The History of Hasidism* (Heb.), 67–8. Abraham of Shargorod's Yiddish report first appeared in Jacob Emden's Hebrew translation under the tile 'A Dreadful Event in Podolia' [Ma'aseh nora bepodolyah], as an appendix to the anthology of medieval works entitled (after the first of these works, written by Sa'adyah Gaon), *The Book of Rescue and Deliverance* [Sefer hapedut vehapurkan], which Emden edited and published in his own printing press in Altona in 1769. This version was reprinted, together with an analysis of the whole affair, in M. Bałaban, *History of the Frankist Movement* [Letoledot hatenuah hafrankit] (Tel Aviv, 1935), pt. II, 295–320.

42 See Dubnow, *The History of Hasidism* (Heb.), 68 n. 2.

43 See above, pp. 210 ff.

44 See Bałaban, *History of the Frankist Movement* (Heb.), 306–11; A. Y. Braver, *Studies in Galician Jewry* [Galitsyah viyehudeiha] (Jerusalem, 1956), 225–66.

45 Cf. n. 36 above.

46 *Shivḥei habesht* contains a tale in which the Ba'al Shem Tov was subjected to an examination in ritual law by the most eminent rabbis of Poland, members of its Council of Four Lands (see *In Praise of the Baal Shem Tov*, ed. Ben-Amos and Mintz, 222–3). According to this tale, the Besht managed to impress them with his knowledge of the law, although he appeared to derive it from prophetically inspired insight rather than erudition. Interestingly, this tale is echoed in an anti-hasidic source which was published sixteen years before the first edition of *Shivḥei habesht*. See Dubnow, *The History of Hasidism* (Heb.), 65 n. 1. For another tale highlighting the Besht's credentials as a rabbinic scholar see *In Praise of the Baal Shem Tov*, ed. Ben-Amos and Mintz, 39–40.

47 See *In Praise of the Baal Shem Tov*, ed. Ben-Amos and Mintz, 54–9, 86–7, 155, 192.

48 See Scholem, 'The Historical Figure of R. Israel Ba'al Shem Tov' (Heb.), 121–3.

49 See *In Praise of the Baal Shem Tov*, ed. Ben-Amos and Mintz, e.g. the opening lines of tales 5, 17, 18, 19, 27, 28, 29, 30, 31, etc. throughout the book.

50 See e.g. Mishnah *Avot* 1. For a discussion of the 'chain of tradition' as a genre see G. Cohen, *The Book of Tradition by Abraham Ibn Daud* (London, 1967), introduction, l–lvii. Cf. Yerushalmi, *Zakhor*, 31–2.

51 Bałaban, *History of the Frankist Movement* (Heb.), 297.

52 Ibid. 304.

53 For a summary of the affair see Y. Rafael, 'The Kherson *Genizah*' (Heb.), in id., *On Hasidism and Its Adherents* [Al ḥasidut veḥasidim] (Jerusalem, 1991), 204–26, although the author himself would prefer to leave open the question of the authenticity of the documents (see ibid. 225–6).

54 See ibid. 224 n. 61.

55 The list of scholars who concluded that the documents were forged includes Bałaban, Dubnow, D. Z. Hillman, and Scholem. See ibid. 214–23.

56 R. Haim Lieberman, the Habad bibliographer who served for many years as private secretary to the sixth Lubavitcher Rebbe, Joseph Isaac Schneersohn (who never wavered from his endorsement of the *genizah* and was responsible for the most extensive publication of Kherson letters), is said to have known that they were forgeries and even to have been personally acquainted with the forger. See D. Assaf, *Untold Tales of the Hasidim: Crisis & Discontent in the History of Hasidism* (Hanover, 2010), 242 n. 65. For the suggestion that the forger was the Husiatyn hasid and bookseller Naftali Zevi Shapira of Odessa, see id., *The Regal Way: The Life and Times of R. Israel of Ruzhin* [Derekh hamalkhut: r. yisra'el meruzhin umekomo betoledot haḥhasidut] (Jerusalem, 1997), 202 (the relevant passage was omitted from the English edition of this work, *The Regal Way: The Life and Times of Rabbi Israel of Ruzhin* (Stanford, Calif., 2002)); S. Z. Havlin, 'Letter to the Editor' (Heb.), *Yeshurun: me'asef torani*, 4 (1998), 755–6.

57 See e.g. Dubnow, *The History of Hasidism* (Heb.), 431.

58 See above, p. 214.

59 As indeed it did. There are references to 'high prices' in the letter of the sixth Lubavitcher Rebbe, Joseph Isaac Schneersohn, whose father and predecessor, Shalom Dovber, had received a large collection of Kherson documents purchased for him by one of his wealthy followers. The letter was first published in Warsaw, in the Habad periodical *Hatamim*, 1 (1935), 11 and appears in the two-volume reprint of *Hatamim* (Kefar Habad, 1975), i. 11.

60 The view that the hagiographical traditions of *Shivḥei habesht* and of later collections of tales were regarded as sacred literature by the followers of

hasidism—a view which has been taken for granted by most scholars, even though they were aware of a certain ambivalence with regard to the publication of these traditions—was challenged by Y. Mondshine, who argued that the attitude to the tales within hasidism was much more casual. See *Shivḥei habesht*, ed. Mondshine, 52–7. From the point of view of the modern forgers, however, the tales represented the history of hasidism (sacred or not), and it was this that they were proposing to reinforce with 'archival' documentation.

61 On this see above, p. 219.

62 The most comprehensive work on the relationship between hasidism and the eastern European Haskalah is R. Mahler, *Hasidism and the Jewish Enlightenment* (Philadelphia, 1985). See also M. Wodziński, *Haskalah and Hasidism in the Kingdom of Poland: A History of Conflict* (Oxford, 2005); J. Perl, *Uiber das Wesen der Sekte Chassidim*, ed. with introd. and annotations by A. Rubinstein (Jerusalem, 1977); J. Meir, *Imagined Hasidism: The Anti-Hasidic Writings of Joseph Perl* [Ḥasidut medumah: iyunim bikhtavav hasatiriyim shel yosef perl] (Jerusalem, 2013).

63 See G. Scholem, 'The Science of Judaism: Then and Now', in id., *The Messianic Idea in Judaism* (London, 1971), 304–13; id., 'Reflections on *Wissenschaft des Judentums*' (Heb.), in id., *Explications and Implications: Writings on Jewish Heritage and Renaissance* [Devarim bego: pirkei morashah uteḥiyah] (Tel Aviv, 1975), 385–403; M. Wiener, *Judaism in the Era of Emancipation* [Hadat hayehudit bitekufat ha'emantsipatsyah], trans. from German to Hebrew by L. Zagagi (Jerusalem, 1974), 204–83; Yerushalmi, *Zakhor*, 81–103.

64 For a list of the historical studies of hasidism which would have been available before the First World War see Dubnow, *The History of Hasidism* (Heb.), 397–406. For a hasidic repudiation of the scholarly historiography of the movement, highlighting its hostile secular bias and mocking its scepticism with regard to the hagiographical sources, see n. 117 below.

65 Moses Mendelssohn (1729–86), leader of the German Jewish Enlightenment.

66 H. Graetz, *History of the Jews* (London, 1901), v. 397–9. The original German version appeared in 1870.

67 Dubnow's history of hasidism was first published in instalments in Russian, in the Russian Jewish periodical *Voskhod*, between 1881 and 1893. The relevant section appeared in 1888. See Seltzer, 'The Secular Appropriation of Hasidism', 160 n. 22.

68 For a survey of the scholarly literature which concerns these events and processes, see G. C. Bacon's bibliographical essay, 'East European Jewry from the First Partition to the Present', in G. D. Hundert and G. C. Bacon, *The Jews in Poland and Russia: Bibliographical Essays* (Bloomington, 1984), 158–70.

69 Cf. *In Praise of the Baal Shem Tov*, ed. Ben-Amos and Mintz, 19–22, with the

letter as published in *Hatamim*, i. 248 no. 1, and see Dubnow, *The History of Hasidism* (Heb.), 430.

70 Cf. *In Praise of the Baal Shem Tov*, ed. Ben-Amos and Mintz, 81–2, with the letters in *Hatamim*, i. 120–1.

71 See above, pp. 207–10.

72 See *Hatamim*, ii. 558–9 no. 175; cf. ibid. ii. 445 no. 115, and see Bałaban, *History of the Frankist Movement* (Heb.), 318.

73 See Dubnow, *The History of Hasidism* (Heb.), 428.

74 See Bałaban, *History of the Frankist Movement* (Heb.), 314–20.

75 This was David Kahana's *Even ofel*, which was eventually incorporated in volume 2 of his *History of the Kabbalists, the Sabbatians, and the Hasidim* [Toledot hamekubalim, hashabeta'im vehaḥasidim] (Tel Aviv, 1926–7). See Bałaban, *History of the Frankist Movement* (Heb.), 319–20.

76 Bałaban, *History of the Frankist Movement* (Heb.), 320.

77 See C. Shmeruk, *Yiddish Literature in Poland: Historical Studies and Perspectives* [Sifrut yidish bepolin: meḥkarim ve'iyunim historiyim] (Jerusalem, 1981), 126; *Shivḥei habesht*, ed. Mondshine, 30.

78 See *In Praise of the Baal Shem Tov*, ed. Ben-Amos and Mintz, 13–18.

79 G. Scholem, 'The Sabbatian Prophet R. Heschel Zoref—R. Adam Ba'al Shem' (Heb.), in id., *The Latest Phase* (Heb.) 41–55.

80 See Shmeruk, *Yiddish Literature in Poland* (Heb.), 119–39; *Shivḥei habesht*, ed. Mondshine, 58–65. See also *In Praise of the Baal Shem Tov*, ed. Ben-Amos and Mintz, 309–10 n. 1.

81 For the tradition that during this period the Ba'al Shem Tov was resident in the small Podolian town of Okopy, see *Shivḥei habesht*, ed. Rubnistein, 44, and editorial n. 36.

82 *In Praise of the Baal Shem Tov*, ed. Ben-Amos and Mintz, 15–18.

83 See *Hatamim*, i. 13–20.

84 See *In Praise of the Baal Shem Tov*, ed. Ben-Amos and Mintz, 18.

85 *Hatamim*, i. 19–20.

86 *In Praise of the Baal Shem Tov*, ed. Ben-Amos and Mintz, 13.

87 Ibid. 31–2.

88 Curiously, the official 'biography' of the Ba'al Shem Tov emanating from the hasidic school of Habad quotes extensively from one of the Kherson letters, in which the Besht reports to his brother-in-law the contents of one of R. Adam Ba'al Shem's letters, but the quotation ends abruptly, omitting precisely that section of the letter in which the Besht describes the circumstances of his discovery of the manuscripts with the help of a Wallachian shepherd (see A. H. Glitzenstein, *Rabbi Israel Ba'al Shem Tov* [Yisra'el ba'al shem tov] (Kefar

Habad, 1975), 27). The quotation is resumed immediately after the conclusion of the Besht's account of the discovery, with him confiding to his brother-in-law his reluctance to 'reveal himself'. (The same letter is, however, reproduced in full at the end of the book, where the entire collection of Kherson letters supposedly written by the Besht is published as an appendix. See ibid. 174–85.) The discreet omission of the middle part of the letter may suggest that the Habad biographer was reluctant to draw attention to the discrepancy between the Kherson letter's version and the account of the event in *Shivḥei habesht*. It is also curious that both the reference to Adam Ba'al Shem's discovery of the secret writings in a cave and the reference to the Ba'al Shem Tov's 'sealing' of them 'in a stone in a mountain', as well as the whole encounter between Adam Ba'al Shem's son and the Besht—precisely the elements in the account of *Shivḥei habesht* which are discrepant with the Kherson letter—are missing from the manuscript version of *Shiv(h.}ei habesht* which was published by Mondshine and which similarly stems from the Habad school, who consider the Kherson letters authentic. See *Shivḥei habesht*, ed. Mondshine, 144–5, 147. Although the manuscript contains only some 54 per cent of the material published in the printed versions of the work (see ibid. 7), and the omitted passages noted above are by no means the only ones missing, the omission on p. 144, which consists of a single sentence (referring to R. Adam's discovery of the secret writings in a cave) in what is otherwise an identical text, somewhat strengthens the impression that it may have arisen from the odd discrepancy with the Kherson version of the story (although it is not impossible that this was simply a scribal omission resulting from the occurrence of the Hebrew acronym *pe-alef* (standing for *pa'am aḥat* meaning 'once') in two consecutive sentences within the same paragraph).

89 See Nigal, *The Hasidic Tale*, 264–5.

90 See *Hatamim*, i. 20–5; i. 339 no. 38, i. 342 no. 53, i. 343 no. 60, i. 345 no. 71.

91 See G. Scholem, *The Mystical Shape of the Godhead* (New York, 1991), 120–2.

92 For this reconstruction of the Besht's relationship with his associates according to *Shivḥei habesht*, see Ch. 1, Section 2 above.

93 See *In Praise of the Baal Shem Tov*, ed. Ben-Amos and Mintz, 185:

> I heard this from the Rabbi, the Hasid, Rabbi Jehiel Mikhel of the holy community of Zolochev. When he visited here . . . he said that he was ordered from heaven to accept the Besht as his rabbi and to go and learn from him. They showed him the 'streams of wisdom' which led to the Besht. When the Besht passed away he was ordered to accept the Great Maggid, Rabbi Dov, as his rabbi. They showed him that the same 'streams of wisdom' that formerly ran to the Besht now led to the rabbi, the Maggid, God bless his memory.

R. Yehiel Mikhl, in *Shivḥei habesht*, would not have needed to resort to the vision of 'streams of wisdom' which flew first to the Besht and then to the Magid of Mezhirech, had he, or indeed the transmitter of the tale, possessed any information to the effect that the one was ever appointed by the other or succeeded him by virtue of any other procedural means. Rather, the tale points to the view that the Magid derived his charismatic authority directly from Heaven, in much the same way as did the Besht before him.

94 See e.g. Dubnow, *The History of Hasidism* (Heb.), 69, 80, 213; S. A. Horodetsky, *Hasidism and Its Adherents* [Haḥasidut vehaḥasidim] (Tel Aviv, 1927), i. 80; D. Kahana, *A History of the Kabbalists, the Sabbatians, and the Hasidim* (Heb.), ii, *Even ofel*, 82.

95 See Ch. 1, Sections 2–3.

96 See *Hatamim*, i. 120–2, 124, 349 no. 90; ii. 557–8 no. 172.

97 For a brief overview of this school see 'Habad' in *Encyclopaedia Judaica* (Jerusalem, 1972), vii. 1013–14; 'Lubavitch Hasidism', in *The YIVO Encyclopedia of Jews in Eastern Europe* (New Haven, 2008), i. 1094–7.

98 See *Hatamim*, ii. 659 no. 229.

99 See more on this above, p. 224.

100 See above, pp. 225–6.

101 See Scholem, 'The Historical Figure of R. Israel Ba'al Shem Tov' (Heb.), in id., *The Latest Phase* (Heb.), 108–9; Dubnow, *The History of Hasidism* (Heb.), 432.

102 It has been suggested that the bulk of the extant historiographical material relating to the formative stages in the development of hasidism—the hagiographical *Shivḥei habesht*, the pastoral letters of the two leaders of Belarusian hasidism, R. Menahem Mendel of Vitebsk and R. Abraham of Kalisk (Kołyszki), who had emigrated to the Holy Land in 1777, and those of R. Shneur Zalman of Liady, who succeeded them in that region, as well as the polemical hasidic responses to the accusations of the *mitnagedim*—has been preserved and published by the Habad school, which displayed from the start a keen historiographical interest, harnessed to the project of promoting Habad's centrality to the history and teaching of hasidism as a whole (see Z. Gries, 'Hasidism: The Present State of Research and Some Desirable Priorities', *Numen*, 34 (1987), 101–3). Although this can rightly be said of the internal historiography of Habad in the 20th century (on which see below), it is difficult to discern a particular Habad bias in *Shivḥei habesht*, for example, even though the printer of the first edition was a follower of Habad's founder, R. Shneur Zalman of Liady. In contrast to the Kherson letters and the modern historiography of Habad, which place R. Shneur Zalman and his family at the very heart of hasidism from its inception, *Shivḥei habesht* does not mention them at all. Nor does the correspondence between the Belarusian hasidim and their two leaders who settled in the Holy Land present itself as any more than a regional, Belarusian affair rather than a crucial stage in the development of the entire hasidic movement. The same applies to the hasidic responses to the hostilities generated by the *mitnagedim*: the fact that some of these responses stem from Habad and focus on Shneur Zalman of Liady is hardly surprising, as the Habad circle, more than most others, operated in proximity to the Lithuanian centres of opposition to hasidism. While Zeev Gries regards the internal historiography of Habad in the 20th century as a direct continuation and natural conclusion of the early Habad interest in the preservation and publication of historical source materials, I regard it as a break from the old tradition and a wholly original development, inspired by the peculiar historical circumstances of Habad in the early decades of the 20th century, and associated primarily with the personality of its leader from 1920 to 1950, the sixth *admor*, Joseph Isaac Schneersohn, on whom see above, pp. 226 ff.

103 *Hatamim*, i. 11–12. The letter was republished, together with additional material including the renewed endorsement of the *genizah* by the last Habad leader, the seventh *admor*, Menachem Mendel Schneerson (1902–94), as an appendix devoted to the Kherson *genizah* in *Igerot kodesh admor hazaken, admor ha'emtsa'i, admor hatsemaḥ tsedek*, i. 469–87.

104 See Rafael, 'The Kherson *Genizah*' (Heb.), 219.

105 This letter, first published as part of the same appendix in the periodical *Moznayim*, was printed again in *Igerot kodesh admor hazaken, admor ha'emtsa'i, admor hatsemaḥ tsedek*, i. 472–3.

106 See ibid. 473–5; cf. Rafael, 'The Kherson *Genizah*' (Heb.), 222–5.

107 See above, n. 105.

108 See his biography, based on his own writings, by A. H. Glitzenstein, *Sefer hatoladot: rabi yosef yitsḥak schneersohn, admor morenu harav yosef yitsḥak*, 4 vols. in 3 (Kefar Habad, 1972–6).

109 From the description of the contents of the Kherson documents received by his father, as it appeared in the *admor* Joseph Isaac's letter published in *Hatamim*, as well as from an explicit statement to this effect by the last *admor*, Menachem Mendel Schneerson (see *Igerot kodesh admor hazaken, admor ha'emtsa'i, admor hatsemaḥ tsedek*, i. 474), it appears that a considerable proportion of the letters remains unpublished in the Habad archive, particularly those which contain esoteric teachings rather than the more prosaic subject matter of the published letters.

110 For a detailed list of his publications, now out of date, see Glitzenstein, *Sefer hatoladot: rabi yosef yitsḥak*, iv. 317–47; for a more recent list see *Hayom Yom: From Day to Day* (Brooklyn, 1988), 18*a*–19; see also T. Blau, 'Writings of the *Admor* Joseph Isaac' (Heb.), in *Al hasifrut haḥabadit* (n.p., Kehot Publication Society, 1969), 57–61.

111 It must be noted that, as has always been the case in hasidism, an *admor*'s discourses and talks would be delivered orally and would later be written down by his disciples, although it seems that the *admor* Joseph Isaac used to edit them himself before publication. See e.g. Glitzenstein, *Sefer hatoladot: rabi yosef yitsḥak*, iv. 317, on the collection of 'talks' entitled *Likutei diburim*.

112 This is the subject of N. Loewenthal, *Communicating the Infinite: The Emergence of the Habad School* (Chicago, 1990). See also id., 'The Apotheosis of Action in Early Habad', *Daat*, 18 (1987), vi–viii; I. Etkes, *Rabbi Shneur Zalman of Liady: The Origins of Chabad Hasidism*, trans. J. M. Green (Waltham, Mass., 2015), 50–4.

113 These include a diary, a long historical essay entitled 'Avot haḥasidut' (Fathers of Hasidism), first published in *Hatamim* in instalments, a historical account of the encounter between the third leader of Habad, Menahem Mendel the Tsemah Tsedek, and the Russian Jewish Enlightenment, a book of memoirs, and a large number of letters which contain historical or autobiographical accounts. All this is unprecedented in the literary history of hasidism. Cf. above, p. 202 and n. 19.

114 See Glitzenstein, *Sefer hatoladot: rabi yosef yitsḥak*, i. 49 ff.

115 See 'Avot haḥasidut', *Hatamim*, i. 139–40, chs. 4–5.

116 For his own account of how he began to keep a diary in early childhood, chiefly in order not to forget the 'stories' about early hasidic and Habad figures, see Glitzenstein, *Sefer hatoladot: rabi yosef yitsḥak*, i. 117–19. For a large collection of 'diary entries' see ibid. ii. 143–279.

117 See e.g. his letters in *Igerot kodesh . . . yosef yitsḥak*, 17 vols. (Brooklyn, 1982–2011): i. 201 no. 98; iv. 109, iv. 124–6 nos. 938–9; xi. 187 no. 3886. In one long letter (ii. 498–504 no. 618), sent from Riga in the spring of 1933 to the Zionist educationalist and Hebrew publisher Shoshana Persitz in Tel Aviv, the *admor* Joseph Isaac reviews what he considers the sad state of hasidic historiography, traditionally produced, as he claims, by irreligious scholars who were both ignorant of and hostile to hasidism. This, he urges, must be countered with the genuine insight and knowledge that can come only from within the hasidic camp. He notes with approval, qualified by a certain measure of condescension, that

> in recent years, the scholarly world has begun to take a [renewed] interest in hasidism in general and in Habad in particular. A great deal has been written about it by way of glowing praise [on p. 501 he refers explicitly to the writings of such early 20th-century neo-hasidic authors as S. A. Horodetsky, H. Zeitlin, and the Habad historian H. I. Bunin], and, at any rate, in a way that is entirely the opposite of the deplorable style adopted by the 'offshoots of the *maskilim*', who had set it as their goal to destroy all that is holy and to deprecate illustrious Torah scholars . . . The early

> *maskilim*, struck by graphomania, had gone out of their way to outdo each other with . . . periodical publications . . . devoid of scientific and intellectual merit but wholly committed to the eradication of wholesome faith. They invited all manner of fantasists to contribute their mad delusions about the hasidic camp, and it is therefore hardly surprising that hundreds and thousands of hands became engaged in the production of defamatory writings about hasidism, its champions, their followers, and their customs . . . In the course of time they spawned a putrid body of writings which should be called 'Haman's Plot Publications' . . . We can see how deep these writers have sunk into the sea of lies, and how far they have been carried by the winds of folly, from such questions as they have asked, for example: 'Who can testify to us that a man called the Besht ever existed?', and 'Is it not the case that the hasidim and their masters have simply dreamt up that 120 years ago there was a man called by the name of our teacher R. Israel Besht, may he rest in Eden, who perfomed wonders and created a new school of thought?' [This last reference clearly echoes the scholarly scepticism about the very existence of the 'archaeological' Besht discussed at the beginning of this chapter].

See also pp. 236–7 above.

118 These are H. M. Heilman, *Beit rabi* (Berdiczów, [1902]), and M. Teitelbaum, *The Rabbi of Liady and the Habad Faction* [Harav miliadi umifleget ḥabad], 2 vols. (Warsaw, 1914). Both authors had close associations with Habad, both regarded themselves as professional historians, however sympathetic to Habad, and both were critical of the hagiographical tales, particularly those which concerned Habad's history, clearly differentiating their own approach from the cavalier approach of the hagiographers. Heilman, who was a follower of a splinter Habad dynasty, stresses in his introduction (pp. 3–6) that he intends to refrain as much as possible from using material derived from 'rumour' rather than from written documentation, and that whenever he cites an oral tradition he will identify it as such and register its degree of credibility. This represents a clear break from the essentially oral hagiographical tradition, and the genuine assimilation of modern, secular historiographical criteria, for which Heilman would have had numerous models in the modern Jewish historiography of his time. Nevertheless he still displays the apologetic tendency to suppress the evidence on such sensitive issues, from the hasidic point of view, as internal controversies, the clash between hasidism and its rabbinic opponents (pp. 6–15), or the embarrassing apostasy of R. Shneur Zalman of Liady's youngest son, Moses (p. 113). Teitelbaum's book was prefaced by the 'managing editor' Shemaryahu Schneersohn—a great-great-grandson of Habad's founder—and acquired thereby something approaching an informal Habad approbation. Yet he was even more self-consciously professional as a modern historian, criticizing Heilman for not checking his sources thoroughly enough and allowing hagiographical traditions to slip in (i. 250), while presenting his own work very systematically, setting it out not only in chronological but also in thematic order, with Volume I devoted to the biography of R. Shneur Zalman and Volume II to an analysis of his teaching. He states in the introduction to Volume I (p. xii): 'As for my own relation to the Rabbi [Shneur Zalman] and his views, I have been very careful to stay as objective as possible. All the facts and events presented to the reader are recorded and described as they were, free from any tendentious bias. My greatest wish has been to remain true to the spirit of history, which tolerates no blandishment, hypocrisy, or partiality.' For more on Heilman and his historiographical methodology, see N. Karlinsky, 'The Dawn of Hasidic-Haredi Historiography', *Modern Judaism*, 27/1 (2007), 20–46; Assaf, *Untold Tales of the Hasidim*, 77–8.

119 See R. Elior, 'The Minsk Debate' (Heb.), *Jerusalem Studies in Jewish Thought*, 1/4 (1982), 181–3; R. Foxbrunner, *The Hasidism of R. Shneur Zalman of Liady* (Northvale, NJ, 1993), 41–2.

120 See Elior, 'The Minsk Debate' (Heb.), 182–3, where she explicitly states:

> It should be noted that there is no connection between, [on the one hand,] the anonymous 'Kherson *genizah*', which aims to provide 'historical' verification for the beginnings of hasidism, and to shed light on the generation of the Magid of Mezhirech, which is shrouded in mist, by means of forging the correspondence between him and his disciples, and [on the other hand,] the Habad historiography, which offers family traditions preserved, from the middle of the 18th century on, in the memory of a chain of transmitters whose identity is known and whose books are readily available . . . There is no resemblance between the Kherson letters and the essay 'Avot haḥasidut' [by Joseph Isaac Schneersohn], neither in terms of style nor in the range of sources, the ultimate aim, or the historical background.

Foxbrunner, who is much more dogmatic and utterly uncritical of Habad's historiographical tradition, implicitly dissociates it from the Kherson letters by altogether refraining from any mention of their existence.

121 'Avot haḥasidut', *Hatamim*, i. 138, ch. 1. For other examples of direct quotations from, or explicit references to, the Kherson *genizah*, see e.g. ibid. 139 (with regard to the 'victory' over the Frankists at Lwów), and i. 10 (with regard to the election to the leadership of R. Abraham the Angel, the Magid of Mezhirech's son).

122 Above, pp. 216–17.

123 'Avot haḥasidut', *Hatamim*, i. 142, ch. 8. Menahem Mendel of Vitebsk is referred to here, and in the Kherson letter which underlies this passage, as 'the Lithuanian' (Litvak). This takes account of the Magid of Mezhirech's Volhynian perspective when referring to a Jew from Raysn—Belarus—which belonged to the region traditionally considered by Jews as Lite—Lithuania. See on this V. Levin and D. Staliūnas, '*Lite* in the Jewish Mental Maps', in D. Staliūnas (ed.), *Spatial Concepts of Lithuania in the Long Nineteenth Century* (Boston, 2016).

124 *Hatamim*, ii. 665 no. 249. See also the *admor*'s reference to the Kherson document in which all the Magid's disciples, headed by Judah Leyb Hakohen of Annopol (author of *Or haganuz*), Shneur Zalman of Liady, and Meshulam Zusya of Annopol, swear allegiance to R. Abraham the Angel, whom they accept as their leader after his father's death, in 'Avot haḥasidut', *Hatamim*, i. 142, ch. 8. Such a document, of which nothing is known elsewhere, appears in the Kherson collection, *Hatamim*, ii. 664 no. 247.

125 For a case study of dynastic succession in hasidism see G. Sagiv, *The Dynasty: The House of Chernobyl and Its Place in the History of Hasidism* [Hashoshelet: beit chernobyl umekomo betoledot haḥasidut] (Jerusalem, 2014).

126 For a careful reconstruction of R. Shneur Zalman of Liady's gradual ascent to leadership see Etkes, *Rabbi Shneur Zalman of Liady*, 9–21. Nevertheless, late Habad historiography tends to obscure the intermediaries between the leadership of the Magid of Mezhirech and R. Shneur Zalman's 'succession'. R. Menahem Mendel of Vitebsk is reported, for example, to have known all along that he was unsuitable for leadership (implicitly making way for the proper 'succession' by R. Shneur Zalman). See R. N. Kahan, *Shemuot vesipurim meraboteinu hakedoshim*, 3 vols. (Kefar Habad, 1974–7), i. 245–6, ii. 81–2 no. 105.

127 See Dubnow, *The History of Hasidism* (Heb.), 132; Heilman, *Beit rabi*, 11–12 (= *6a–b*).

128 See above, p. 219.

129 See e.g. the hagiographical anthology *Ohel elimelekh* (Jerusalem, 1968), 49–50 no. 124 for a tradition whereby R. Elimelekh of Lizhensk was elected to succeed the Magid of Mezhirech; cf. A. Z. Aescoly, 'Hasidism in Poland' (Heb.), in I. Halpern (ed.), *The Jewish People in Poland* [Beit yisra'el bepolin] (Jerusalem, 1953), ii. 128, for a similar tradition in the Ger (Góra Kalwaria) hasidic dynasty, whereby R. Jacob Isaac, the Seer of Lublin, was the Magid of Mezhirech's successor.

130 See Heilman, *Beit rabi*, the author's 'Address to the Readers', 3–6. Notably, the late Yehoshua Mondshine, the most outstanding, prolific, and important scholar of hasidism within the Habad school, consistently refrained from using the Kherson *genizah* materials, and hardly ever relied on the historical writings of the sixth *admor*, Joseph Isaac Schneersohn.

131 J. I. Schneersohn, *Sefer hazikhronot* (Heb.) (Kefar Habad, 1985), i. 37. This is common throughout his works. Cf. *Likutei diburim* (Yid.) (Brooklyn, 1984), ii. 695*a* (= 1389), where, in a talk dating from 1938, he reports that R. Shneur

Zalman of Liady used to call the Magid of Mezhirech 'father' and the Ba'al Shem Tov 'grandfather', articulating Habad's notion of the 'dynastic' relation between them in concrete terms that stand for intimate family kinship.

132 On Rodkinson (1845–1904) and his books see Nigal, *The Hasidic Tale*, 22–5; id., 'A Study in the History of the Hasidic Tale' (Heb.), in id. (ed.), *Sefer sipurei kedoshim* (Jerusalem, 1977), 87–109; cf. Dan, *The Hasidic Tale* (Heb.), 195 ff, and see the more recent comprehensive study by J. Meir, *In Praise of Rodkinson: Michael Levi Frumkin-Rodkinson and Hasidism* [Shivḥei rodkinson: mikha'el levi frumkin-rodkinson vehaḥasidut] (Tel Aviv, 2012).

133 D. Z. Hillman, *Letters by the Author of the Tanya and His Contemporaries* [Igerot ba'al hatanya uvenei doro] (Jerusalem, 1953), 192 no. 113; cf. *Igerot kodesh admor hazaken, admor ha'emtsa'i, admor hatsemaḥ tsedek*, i. 141–2 no. 60.

134 The only mention of the word 'grandson' in R. Shneur Zalman's letter (where it refers to R. Barukh, not to himself) is the following: 'On the contrary, I reproached R. Barukh for his ingratitude, for surely, my two stays in St Petersburg [referring to Shneur Zalman's two periods of incarceration following his denunciation to the Russian authorities by the *mitnagedim*] were for the sake of your grandfather the Besht . . . and I could have said: Is not his grandson [R. Barukh] alive and well?! Let *him* come and respond to all the questions [about hasidism] raised against me by my interrogators' (ibid.).

135 M. L. Rodkinson, *Shivḥei harav* [Lemberg, 1864] (Jerusalem, n.d.), 33.

136 For more on this see above, Ch. 1, Section 5, and the discussion there around nn. 109–127. Another example of the *admor* Joseph Isaac's probable integration of a late hagiographical tradition into his own historical memoirs is the account of R. Shneur Zalman's apparently random but evidently significant selection to attend to the ritual purification of the dead Magid's head (while other disciples had to be content with lesser parts of his body). This is mentioned by the *admor* in his historical essay 'Avot haḥasidut', *Hatamim*, i. 143, ch. 9 and ii. 793, but the story appears in full in Rodkinson, *Shivḥei harav*, 13 and in J. Kaidaner, *Sipurim nora'im* (Lemberg, 1875), 61 (my pagination; the book has none).

137 For the situation in Russia at the time, and its implications for the Jews, see S. M. Schwarz, *The Jews in the Soviet Union* (Syracuse, NY, 1952), 90–194; J. Lestchinsky, *The Jews in Soviet Russia: From the October Revolution to the Second World War* [Hayehudim berusyah hasovyetit: mimahapekhat oktober ad milḥemet ha'olam hasheniyah] (Tel Aviv, 1953); M. Altshuler, *Between Nationalism and Communism: The Evsektsia in the Soviet Union, 1918–1930* [Hayevsektsyah biverit hamo'atsot, bein le'umiyut lekomunizm] (Tel Aviv, 1980); A. A. Gershuni, *Judaism in Soviet Russia: Towards a History of Religious Persecution* [Yahadut berusyah hasovyetit: lekorot redifot hadat] (Jerusalem, 1961); J. Rothenberg, *The Jewish Religion in the Soviet Union* (New York, 1971).

138 The *admor*'s career as Habad's leader during his thirty years of office is assessed in detail in his quasi-official biography: Glitzenstein, *Sefer hatoladot: rabi yosef yitsḥak*, vols. iii, iv, and covered extensively in S. D. Levin, *The History of Habad in the Soviet Union, 1917–1950* [Toledot ḥabad berusyah hasovyetit [5]678–[5]710] (Brooklyn, 1989). His heroic role in the campaign for the preservation of Orthodox Jewish life in Soviet Russia is acknowledged outside Habad's own historiography as well as within. See e.g. D. Fishman, 'Preserving Tradition in the Land of Revolution: The Religious Leadership of Soviet Jewry, 1917–1930', in J. Wertheimer (ed.), *The Uses of Tradition: Jewish Continuity in the Modern Era* (New York, 1992); Gershuni, *Judaism in Soviet Russia* (Heb.), 156–207; Rothenberg, *The Jewish Religion in the Soviet Union*, 161, 178.

139 See above, pp. 222–3.

140 'Avot haḥasidut', *Hatamim*, i. 138, ch. 1.

141 Ibid. 139, ch. 3.

142 Ibid. 140, ch. 6, and cf. above, at n. 93.

143 Ibid. 140–1, ch. 7. The same story appears earlier in the collection of 'talks' by the *admor*'s father and predecessor, R. Shalom Dovber; see *Torat shalom* (Brooklyn, 1957), 83–4 no. 19. The story echoes the tale in *Shivḥei habesht* which spoke of heavenly 'streams of wisdom' flowing first to the Besht and then to the Magid of Mezhirech (see above, n. 93), but it subverts the notion of fresh charismatic authority by introducing as its regulator the deceased Ba'al Shem Tov, who irons out the difficulty of an unsuitable heir in order to secure the proper functioning of the dynasty.

144 'Avot haḥasidut', *Hatamim*, i. 141, ch. 7.

145 Ibid. 144, ch. 10. The secret journeys were to the Lithuanian strongholds of mitnagdism, where, according to this account, it was dangerous to spread hasidism openly.

146 For example, there is no trace of evidence for the emergence of 'secret' hasidism in Podolia, let alone in Lithuania, as early as the 1720s; the earliest indications of Beshtian hasidism are from the second half of the century (although it is, of course, as impossible to disprove conclusively the presence of a secret organization as it is to prove it). Similarly, there is no sign of opposition to hasidism in this period, and even for the 1750s and 1760s the evidence is uncertain; the anti-hasidic agitation in Lithuania and Galicia did not begin until the 1770s. Nor is there any evidence for the brief period in 'office' of R. Zevi, the Ba'al Shem Tov's son, who is presumed to have succeeded his father on the basis of the anachronistic projection of hereditary leadership onto this early period. The leadership of R. Shneur Zalman of Liady did not begin in the early 1770s, immediately after the death of the Magid of Mezhirech, nor even in the late 1770s, after the emigration to the Holy Land of the two senior figures in Belarusian hasidism (R. Menahem Mendel of Vitebsk and R. Abraham of Kalisk), but only in the 1780s, after the death of R. Menahem Mendel of Vitebsk, when R. Shneur Zalman was gradually emerging as the most powerful of the three figures, partially (and with some reluctance) authorized by the leaders in the Holy Land to look after their flock in their absence. See Etkes, *R. Shneur Zalman of Liady*, 9–21.

147 Subsequent Habad leaders are similarly described as 'systematic', excellent organizers, distinguished by a sense of 'order', and so on. See e.g. J. I. Schneersohn, *The 'Tzemach Tzedek' and the Haskala Movement* (Brooklyn, 1969), 8.

148 'Avot haḥasidut', *Hatamim*, i. 138, ch. 2.

149 *Sefer hazikhronot* (Heb.) (Brooklyn, 1985), i. 38.

150 For a detailed discussion of this see J. D. Klier, *Russia Gathers Her Jews: The Origin of the 'Jewish Question' in Russia, 1772–1825* (Dekalb, Ill., 1986), 150 ff.

151 See Heilman, *Beit rabi*, 185–6 (= 93*a*–*b*), n. *a*.

152 See Schneersohn, *The 'Tzemach Tzedek' and the Haskala*, 9. For the general background see M. Stanislawski, *Tsar Nicholas I and the Jews: The Transformation of Jewish Society in Russia, 1825–1855* (Philadelphia, 1983), 155 ff. The adoption of the cause of productivization by the Habad leadership in the 19th century was the appropriation of an extraneous value which was being advocated not only by the Russian authorities but also by the Jewish Enlighteners, with whom Habad was engaged in a series of bitter clashes (see Schneersohn, *The 'Tzemach Tzedek' and the Haskala*, and Stanislawski, *Tsar Nicholas I and the Jews*, 150–2). It was presented by the *admor* Joseph Isaac as the duty of the hasidic leader to concern himself not only with the spiritual but first of all with the material well-being of his followers:

> His holy eminence, our Old Rebbe [R. Shneur Zalman], told his grandson, my great-grandfather, the author of the *Tsemaḥ tsedek* [R. Menahem Mendel was thus named after the title of his major work] that his grandfather, our Master the Besht [for the Besht as R. Shneur Zalman's 'grandfather', see above, pp. 225–6] had said that the beginning of his work with his colleagues the secret tsadikim was to restore to health [Yid. *gezunt makhn*] the body of Israel and only later to restore to health their spirit and soul. That is why, so long as our Master the Besht was in concealment, he dedicated his work to helping Israel in matters concerning their livelihood, and most of his work was with simple folk, who are the body of Israel. Only later, when he was revealed, did he concern himself with students and scholars, who are the soul and spirit of Israel. ('Avot haḥasidut', *Hatamim*, i. 138, ch. 2)

This represents a departure in Habad from R. Shneur Zalman's conception of his leadership as confined to spiritual affairs only, and his refusal to attend, by way of miracle-work or prophetically inspired insight, to the more prosaic questions of livelihood and material affairs, which were becoming the major concern of other hasidic leaders at the time. However, there is evidence to suggest that this common characterization of R. Shneur Zalman's position, which is based on his own explicit statement on the matter, requires some modification, as he nevertheless apparently did provide guidance and help in respect of material concerns as well. See Y. Mondshine, *Migdal oz* (Kefar Habad, 1980), 320–72; Etkes, *R. Shneur Zalman of Liady*, 28–31.

153 See on this Schwarz, *The Jews in the Soviet Union*, 160–85; C. Shmeruk, 'The Jewish Community and Jewish Agricultural Settlement in Soviet Belorussia (1918–1932)' [Hakibuts hayehudi vehahityashevut hayehudit bebelorusyah hasovyetit] unpublished Ph.D. diss., Heb. with Eng. summary (Hebrew University, 1961).

154 See *Sefer hatoladot: yosef yitsḥak*, vols. iii (which deals with the years 1921–8) and iv, appendix, 397–413; Levin, *The History of Habad in the Soviet Union* (Heb.), 56–61.

155 See Braver, *Studies in Galician Jewry* (Heb.), 45, 165, 169 ff.; Mahler, *Hasidism and the Jewish Enlightenment*, 59–60, 195–7.

156 For the Cossack uprising and its consequences for the Jews see S. Dubnow, *History of the Jews in Russia and Poland* (Philadelphia, 1946), i. 144–53; B. D. Weinryb, *The Jews of Poland* (Philadelphia, 1973), 181–205. Interestingly, the *admor* Joseph Isaac appears, once again, to have assimilated a modern, secular historiographical perception of the background to the rise of hasidism, stemming from the wholly negative evaluation of the movement by the *maskilim*, which left its imprint on the scholarly historiography of hasidism in the 19th and early 20th centuries. This is the view of hasidism as a movement that was born into a situation of economic deprivation, moral degeneration, intellectual and spiritual decline, and the collapse of traditional communal and religious institutions (see e.g. Graetz, *History of the Jews*, v. 406, 408, 410–11). The implication was that only in such conditions of poverty, ignorance, and degradation could an obscurantist movement such as hasidism take root and flourish. The most persuasive and enduring portrayal of hasidism as the product of such conditions, precipitated by the Cossack uprising and the ensuing massacres of 1648, was by Simon Dubnow, who, in the introduction to his *History of Hasidism*, linked the rise of the movement to the social, economic, and religious bankruptcy of Polish Jewry in the first half of the 18th century, following the crisis of 1648, from which it never fully recovered (see Dubnow, *The History of Hasidism* (Heb.), 8–36). In recent years this view of the background to the rise of hasidism, which has dominated the historiography for many decades, has been undergoing a major revision. Younger historians, born or educated after the last war, and who had not directly shared in the predicaments of eastern European Jewry in the 20th century, were able to look at the evidence afresh and to dissociate the experience of 17th- and 18th-century Polish Jewry from its ultimate fate. Their findings have suggested a quicker and fuller recovery, both economically and culturally, from the catastrophe of 1648. By the first half of the 18th century Polish Jewry was enjoying relative—if by no means absolute—prosperity, security, power, and considerable intellectual prestige. See on this Foxbrunner, *The Hasidism of R. Shneur Zalman of Lyady*, 2–9; G. Hundert, 'Some Basic Characteristics of the Jewish Experience in Poland', in Polonsky (ed.), *Poles and Jews: Renewing the Dialogue*, Polin: Studies in Polish Jewry 1 (1986), 28–34; id., 'The Conditions in Jewish Society in the Polish-Lithuanian Commonwealth in the Middle Decades of the Eighteenth Century', in A. Rapoport-Albert (ed.), *Hasidism Reappraised* (London, 1996), 45–50; M. Rosman, 'Jewish Perceptions of Insecurity and Powerlessness in Sixteenth- to Eighteenth-Century Poland', in Polonsky (ed.), *Poles and Jews: Renewing the Dialogue*, 19–27; id., 'The Image of Poland as a Centre of Torah Learning after the 1648 Persecutions' (Heb.), *Zion*, 51 (1986), 435–48, and the additional bibliographical references he cites there (448 n. 58). (It should be noted, however, that Rachel Elior, in her *Israel Ba'al Shem Tov and His Contemporaries: Kabbalists, Sabbatians, Hasidim, and Mitnagedim* [Israel ba'al shem tov uvenei doro: mekubalim, shabeta'im, ḥasidim umitnagedim], 2 vols. (Jerusalem, 2014), has rejected this critique of Dubnow's view, re-embracing, and even radicalizing, his gloomy assessment of the existential condition of Polish Jewry in the middle of the 18th century.) The *admor* Joseph Isaac could not, of course, have been aware of this revisionist evaluation of the background against which hasidism grew. He had internalized the Dubnowian evaluation, implicitly negative about the origins of hasidism as it was, and placed the notion of a prolonged crisis (from 1648 to the 1720s) within his typological framework of crisis and the challenge of militant opposition as the 'natural setting' for the activities of the Ba'al Shem Tov and all subsequent hasidic leaders.

157 *'Avot haḥasidut'*, Hatamim, i. 138, ch. 1.

158 *Sefer hazikhronot* (Heb.), 1, 40.

159 *'Avot haḥasidut'*, Hatamim, i. 139, ch. 3.

160 Ibid., and i. 141–2 [47–8].

161 See *The 'Tzemach Tzedek' and the Haskala*.

162 See Elior, 'The Minsk Debate' (Heb.), 179–235.

163 See Hillman, *Letters by the Author of the Tanya* (Heb.), 95–6 no. 56.

164 *Sefer hazikhronot* (Heb.), 295.

165 The explanation whereby the opposition to hasidism was rooted in an age-old conflict between the kabbalists and a scholarly rabbinic establishment is both inaccurate and anachronistic. While it is true that in the course of the 19th century the kabbalah disappeared from the Lithuanian mitnagdic yeshiva curriculum (see e.g. I. Etkes, *Rabbi Israel Salanter and the Mussar Movement:*

Seeking the Torah of Truth (Philadelphia, 1993), 92–7, 120–1, 339 n. 10; S. Stampfer, *Lithuanian Yeshivas of the Nineteenth Century: Creating a Tradition of Learning* (Oxford, 2012), 42, 45, 52, 85), in the time of the Ba'al Shem Tov mastery of kabbalah was still within the rabbinical elite's range of standard accomplishments. Elijah, the Gaon of Vilna, the most venerated rabbinic authority of 18th-century Poland and the man who initiated the rabbinic opposition to hasidism in the 1770s and 1780s, was himself a proficient kabbalist. The *admor* Joseph Isaac's interpretation of the conflict represents, once again, his assimilation of the modern, secular depreciation of the kabbalah in the historiographical literature of his time (which was itself a legacy of the maskilic disdain for this 'occult science' in its hasidic garb). It is there, not in the proclamations of the *mitnagedim*, that the Ba'al Shem Tov and his followers were condemned as kabbalists—primitive purveyors of magic and superstition (see e.g. Graetz, *History of the Jews*, v. 397–400). The *admor* internalizes this negative perception and uses it to invest hasidism with the legitimacy of a kabbalistic tradition which had to contend with a hostile rabbinic establishment at every one of its historical manifestations.

166 This typological perception of the allegedly age-old conflict between a sober rabbinic establishment and the spiritually driven kabbalists is a mirror image of the mitnagdic view of hasidism (adopted by the *maskilim* as well) as a latter-day manifestation of the same tradition of heretical sectarianism that has plagued rabbinic Judaism since time immemorial—from the biblical rebels against God and his Torah, through the Samaritans and the Sadducees in Second Temple time, to the medieval Karaites and, finally, the Sabbatians and the Frankists. See e.g. M. Wilensky, *Hasidim and Mitnagedim* [Ḥasidim umitnagedim] (Jerusalem, 1970), i. 341–7; ii. 104, 209, 321. The same perception eventually surfaced even among rival hasidic groups engaged in conflict with each other, e.g. the school of Sanz (Nowy Sącz), whose campaign against Sadigura (Sadagora) hasidism was interpreted along these typological lines in the polemical tract *Keneset hagedolah vedivrei ḥakhamim* (Lemberg, 1869). See D. Assaf, *Beguiled by Knowledge: An Anatomy of a Hasidic Controversy* [Hetsits venifga: anatomyah shel maḥloket ḥasidit] (Haifa, 2012), 171–3.

167 *Sefer hazikhronot* (Heb.) i. 283.

168 *In Praise of the Baal Shem Tov*, ed. Ben-Amos and Mintz, 4–5. See also above, at n. 40.

169 Yerushalmi, *Zakhor*, 86.

170 *Igerot kodesh . . . yosef yitsḥak*, xi. 187 no. 3886.

171 See e.g. ibid. iv. 124 no. 938, 217–19 no. 975, 344 no. 1023, 393–4 no. 1050; ibid. v. 31–2 no. 1157, 97–9 no. 1210, 114–15 no. 1220, 152–3 no. 1250, 276 no. 1378, 334 no. 1424, 372 no. 1450, 393 no. 1463, 480 no. 1539.

172 See e.g. ibid. v. 107–10 no. 1218, 126 no. 1226.

173 Ibid. v. 115 no. 1220.

174 *Sefer hazikhronot* (Heb.), i. 3.

175 Ibid. 1–36; cf. 'Avot haḥasidut', *Hatamim*, i. 137–8, chs. 1–2.

176 Population statistics and precise geographical information appear side by side with accounts of the miraculous feats of the secret tsadikim. See e.g. *Sefer hazikhronot* (Heb.), i. 4, 7.

177 See e.g. *Igerot kodesh . . . yosef yitsḥak*, v. 32 no. 1157, 115 no. 1220, 151–2 no. 1250.

178 For a discussion of this see C. Shmeruk, *Yiddish Literature: Aspects of Its History* [Sifrut yidish: perakim letoledoteiha] (Tel Aviv, 1978), 203–13; *Shivḥei habesht*, ed. Mondshine, 52–7; Nigal, *The Hasidic Tale*, 17, 65–6; Elior, 'The Minsk Debate' (Heb.), 181; M. Piekarz, *Braslav Hasidism* [Ḥasidut braslav: perakim beḥayei meḥolelah uvikhtaveiha] (Jerusalem, 1972), 128–31.

179 For the first hasidic books to appear in print see Dubnow, *The History of Hasidism* (Heb.), 138 ff.

180 See above, p. 206, and cf. *In Praise of the Baal Shem Tov*, ed. Ben-Amos and Mintz, 1–6.

181 See R. Menahem Mendel of Vitebsk in *Peri ha'arets* (Zhitomir, 1867) (facs. edn. Jerusalem, 1970), 60 (also published in J. Barnai, *Letters of Hasidim from the Land of Israel* [Igerot ḥasidim me'erets yisra'el] (Jerusalem, 1980), 154 no. 35). For R. Nahman of Bratslav see J. G. Weiss, *Studies in Braslav Hasidism* [Meḥkarim beḥasidut bratslav] (Jerusalem, 1974), 146–8; A. Green, *Tormented Master: The Life and Spiritual Quest of Rabbi Nahman of Bratslav* (Tuscaloosa, Ala., 1979), 43. For Shneur Zalman of Liady see Hillman, *Letters by the Author of the Tanya* (Heb.), 60–3 no. 39 (also published in *Igerot kodesh admor hazaken, admor ha'emtsa'i, admor hatsemaḥ tsedek*, i. 53–8 no. 24); cf. Nigal, *The Hasidic Tale*, 66.

182 For an English version of Perl's satirical work see D. Taylor, *Joseph Perl's Revealer of Secrets: The First Hebrew Novel* (Boulder, Colo., 1996). For the attacks on the hasidic tales by the *maskilim* see S. Werses, *Joseph Perl and His Literary Legacy* [Ginzei yosef perl], ed. J. Meir (Tel Aviv, 2013), 9–29, 237–65; Shmeruk, *Yiddish Literature: Aspects of Its History* (Heb.), 234–60; cf. Dan, *The Hasidic Tale* (Heb.), 195; Meir, *Imagined Hasidism*, 28–61.

183 For a review of the editions, both Hebrew and Yiddish, published in the course of the 19th century, see *Sefer shivḥei habesht*, ed. B. Mintz (Jerusalem, 1969), 10–16; Rafael, 'Shivḥei habesht', in id., *On Hasidism and Its Adherents* (Heb.), 22–49; M. Rosman, 'In Praise of the Ba'al Shem Tov: A User's Guide to the Editions of *Shivhei haBesht*', in G. D. Hundert (ed.), *Jews in Early Modern Poland*, Polin: Studies in Polish Jewry 10 (1997), 183–99.

184 See Dan, *The Hasidic Tale* (Heb.), 189–95; Shmeruk, *Yiddish Literature: Aspects* *of Its History* (Heb.), 210–11; cf. *Shivḥei habesht*, ed. Mondshine, 55–6. For an example of more recent ambivalence about the publication of hasidic stories, see J. R. Mintz, *Legends of the Hasidim* (Chicago, 1968), 5–6.

185 See Nigal, *The Hasidic Tale*, 64–5. For the suggestion that the publication of various anthologies of hasidic tales in Yiddish was a reaction to the appearance in print of non-religious, 'heretical' Yiddish writings during this period, see H. Lieberman, *Ohel raḥel* (New York, 1980), iii. 6–7.

186 It would seem that the very first cycle of hasidic hagiographical tales to appear in print after the publication of *Shivḥei habesht* was a slim Yiddish volume dedicated to R. Shneur Zalman of Liady but written by a man who was not personally associated with the Habad school. This was E. Margaliot, *Ma'aseh nora'ah venifla'ah . . . merabi zalmina . . .* (Czernowitz, 1863). On this work see Shmeruk, *Yiddish Literature: Aspects of Its History* (Heb.), 212; Y. Mondshine, 'The Story of R. Zalmina: Fictional Tales about the Old *Admor*' (Heb.), *Kerem ḥabad*, 4/2 (1992), 247–65, where the full text of the work is reproduced. It was followed almost immediately, and possibly as a reaction to it, by *Shivḥei harav* (Lemberg, 1864) by Michael Levi Frumkin-Rodkinson (on him see above, n. 132), who published during the same period several other hagiographical collections as well as works in other literary genres. He returned to the same subject with a quasi-historical work written after his exposure to Haskalah, devoting the first part to the Ba'al Shem Tov and the second, entitled *Toledot amudei ḥabad* (Königsberg, 1876), to the Habad leadership. The other Habad hagiographer was Jacob Kaidaner with his *Sipurim nora'im* (Lemberg, 1875) (see above, n. 136). On this author see Nigal, *The Hasidic Tale*, 31–2; id. (ed.), *Jacob Kaidaner,* Sipurim nora'im*: The Tales of a Habad Hasid* [Ya'akov kaidaner, sipurim nora'im: sipurav shel ish ḥabad] (Jerusalem, 1992); Heilman, *Beit rabi*, 213 (= 107*a*).

187 See *Shivḥei habesht*, ed. Mondshine, 18–21; cf. Etkes, *Ba'al hatanya: Rabbi Shneur Zalman of Liady and the Origins of Habad Hasidism* [Ba'al hatanya; rabi shneur zalman milady vereshitah shel ḥasidut ḥabad] (Jerusalem, 2011), 62–4 (this passage was omitted from the English version of Etkes's book).

188 Y. Mondshine has assembled some references to, or short tales about, the early leaders of hasidism which are embedded in the speculative teachings of Habad. See Y. Mondshine, *Migdal oz* (Kefar Habad, 1980), 366–76. For comparable tales about the Ba'al Shem Tov see the second appendix to Mondshine's edition of *Shivḥei habesht*, 243–60. It is clear that such tales were being told but not published in Habad.

189 P. Ruderman, 'An Overall Perspective on the Tsadikim and on the Hasidim' (Heb.), *Hashaḥar*, 6 (1875), 92 n. 9, cited in *Shivḥei habesht*, ed. Mondshine, 52.

190 See above, n. 118.

191 For this stance (and its limitations) see above, n. 181 and the end of n. 152.

192 This might have checked the development of a hagiographical literature in Habad after the publication of Rodkinson's and Kaidaner's pioneering works, which were never embraced by the Habad leadership as 'official' hagiography, especially since Rodkinson's desertion of the traditionalist camp must have discredited him and his work. Nevertheless, it is reasonable to assume that tales 'in praise' of the Habad leaders of every generation did circulate among the hasidim as an oral tradition.

193 The view that the typical 'Polish' hasidic leader 'carries the flock' rather than urging every one of its members to 'carry' himself is ascribed to R. Shneur Zalman of Liady, apparently in reference to R. Shelomoh of Karlin. See Heilman, *Beit rabi*, 128 (= 64*b*), n. *b*. The *admor* Joseph Isaac's father, R. Shalom Dovber, in a letter dating from 1914, similarly contrasted 'the path of the Polish hasidim, who live by the glorification of their leaders' with the 'hasidic [i.e. Habad] path', which encourages them to take charge of their own spiritual development. See *Igerot kodesh . . . shalom dovber* (Brooklyn, 1982), ii. 756 no. 383 (reproduced in Mondshine, *Migdal oz*, 141). See also R. Shalom Dovber's *Torat shalom*, 23–4. In the writings of Joseph Isaac this becomes a recurrent topic. See A. Rapoport-Albert and G. Sagiv, 'Habad versus "Polish Hasidism": Towards the History of a Dichotomy' (Heb.), in J. Meir and G. Sagiv (eds.), *Chabad Hasidism: History, Thought, Image* (Jerusalem, 2016), 223–65.

194 *Igerot kodesh . . . yosef yitsḥak*, iv. 398 no. 1054.

195 Ibid. ii. 362–70 no. 552.

196 Cf. above, p. 225.

197 *Igerot kodesh . . . yosef yitsḥak*, ii. 377 no. 552.

198 Ibid. ii. 376 no. 552.

199 See above, at n. 114; *Sefer hatoladot: yosef yitsḥak*, ii. 17–18, 136–9; J. I. Schneersohn, *The History of the Rebbetsin Rivkah Schneersohn* [Divrei yemei harabanit rivkah shneurson] (Brooklyn, 2003).

200 See below, Ch. 6 (pp. 333–4 and p. 366 n. 84); Ch. 7 (esp. pp. 387–91); Ch. 8 (esp. p. 448, on the significant switch from the reference to women as 'the wives and daughters of the hasidim' to 'the wives and daughters of Habad').

201 *Igerot kodesh . . . yosef yitsḥak*, iv. 71 no. 906.

202 See e.g. the introductions to all three volumes of Kahan, *Shemuot vesipurim*, which feature 'talks' or letters by the *admor* Joseph Isaac in which he explains the importance of stories and histories in kabbalistic terms and stresses their power of edification.

PART II

GENDER

FIVE

From Prophetess to Madwoman: The Displacement of Female Spirituality in the Post-Sabbatian Era

SABBATIANISM, a messianic movement of unprecedented duration and scope, was centred on, and derived its name from, the charismatic personality of Sabbati Zevi (1626–76), a kabbalist from the Ottoman port town of Izmir (Smyrna), who, at the height of his international celebrity as the long-awaited Jewish messiah, abruptly converted to Islam in the autumn of 1666. While this might have been regarded as a shameful act of betrayal, as indeed it was instantly denounced by some, Sabbatai's conversion did not put an end to his remarkable career. Rather, it was quickly and persuasively explained in kabbalistic terms as the messiah's most difficult and trying task—preconceived as an integral part of his redemptive mission. Many of the 'believers', as his mass following was called, held on to their faith in the apostate messiah, and in some quarters he was also believed to be an incarnate aspect of the kabbalistic godhead. But the messianic frenzy that at first surrounded him subsided gradually with the passage of time, as it became increasingly evident that he had failed to accomplish his mission. When he died, in relative isolation, in the autumn of 1676, his death was interpreted as a mere 'occultation' and gave rise to the expectation of his imminent return. Some groups of 'believers', who had followed him into Islam, continued to maintain a secret but distinctive Sabbatian identity as an Islamic sect within the Ottoman empire and subsequently in modern Turkey, where their tradition apparently survives to the present day. In east-central Europe, too, the movement persisted at least until the second decade of the nineteenth century. Some of its adherents converted to Catholicism in the second half of the eighteenth century, and formed around their leader, Jacob Frank, a syncretistic sectarian-messianic cult that eventually assimilated into Polish society. But the majority of 'believers' did not apostatize. For them Sabbatianism became an underground current of kabbalistic Judaism. They operated clandestinely, in diverse sectarian groupings, each headed by its own charismatic 'prophet', who was often considered at the same time to be a fresh embodiment of the messiah's soul, and in some cases, as in Sabbatai Zevi's, also a human incarnation of the Divine.[1]

One of the most distinctive and persistent features of Sabbatianism was the high visibility of women within its ranks. They were among the movement's earliest and most ardent supporters—championing the messianic cause, proclaiming its gospel, and from time to time emerging as its chief protagonists. Admittedly, the evidence for this is fragmentary, and much of it is drawn from polemical sources, which are naturally marked by an anti-Sabbatian bias. Hostile authors were liable to exaggerate the involvement of women in the movement precisely in order to denigrate it and to besmirch its character. For the very mention of women's active involvement was enough to imply that Sabbatian messianism was far removed from the rabbinical world and its values, while at the same time suggesting, as a matter of course, its proclivity for sexual impropriety. And yet the extant documentation, problematic though it is, points to the conclusion that if the seed of any revolutionary 'feminism' ever germinated in a pre-modern Jewish milieu, it was in the Sabbatian and not in the hasidic movement.[2]

Throughout the century and a half of the viable existence of Sabbatianism, both within Judaism and—in its apostate form—still in close association with it, the liberation of women from the 'curse of Eve' formed an integral part of its redemptive vision. That vision was marked from the outset by two opposing if intertwined trends. The first was egalitarian, holding women's status to be wholly analogous to men's, and thus beckoning women to partake equally—in their own right, albeit apart from the men—in every aspect of the ritual and spiritual life of the messianic community. While this trend may be viewed as conservative inasmuch as it preserved the traditional segregation of the sexes from one another, it was undoubtedly revolutionary in that it tacitly established a novel ontological parity between them: the formal separation of the women from the men was conducive to the enhancement of their spiritual stature; it released them from the bounds of materiality, physicality, and above all their inherent sexuality, to which tradition had always anchored them, and by which it defined female nature in terms of 'body' or 'matter' as against male nature—'soul' or 'form'.[3] The result was that women could engage on an equal footing in the same range of messianically charged religious activities as the men. Evidence for this can be found, for example, in Sabbatai Zevi's two 'coronation' ceremonies, held in Smyrna in December 1665, in identical fashion on two consecutive days, one for men and the other for women; in the independent activity of his wife Sarah among the female messianic believers; in the sermons that Judah Hasid—a Sabbatian preacher from Poland who, in 1700, led a substantial group of immigrants to the Holy Land in the expectation of imminent messianic redemption—preached expressly in the 'women's synagogue', where he very likely also called them up to the reading from the Torah (as did Sabbatai Zevi in his day), for which he apparently brought them the traditional manuscript scroll; in the separate instruction of women in the Zohar; and in the symbolic juxtaposition, at the Frankist court, of the 'brothers' and 'sisters' in perfect symmetry, but always in two distinct groups and apart. We may conjecture that this trend could have drawn on eschatological traditions such as the Zohar's depiction of righteous women in Paradise, where—relegated to their own quarters, which are strictly off limits to righteous men (and even to angels!)—they occupy themselves with nothing other than the intellectual and spiritual pursuits of study and prayer.

The second trend was libertine. Its thrust was to cast off the burden of tradition and law, not least the laws of prohibited sexual unions. It set the relations between the sexes on an entirely new basis, drawing on midrashic traditions that envisage the 'slaying' of the evil impulse, the abrogation of the commandments, and the coming into effect of a new Torah in the messianic age. In kabbalistic tradition this idea was expressed in terms of progression from a world ordered by the Torah of Creation (*torah diberiah*), associated with the paradisal Tree of Knowledge and signifying the distinction between good and evil that engendered the restrictive system of halakhic prohibitions, to a state of perfected existence by order of the transcendent Torah of Emanation (*torah de'atsilut*), associated with the Tree of

Life and free from all distinctions, oppositions, and restrictions.[4] This libertine trend, which subverted the highly gendered structure of Jewish ritual law, established parity between the sexes by way of blurring the distinction between them. Men and women would function interchangeably or together in situations in which tradition had normally kept them apart. This manifested itself, for example, in Sabbatai Zevi's calling up to the reading from the Torah of both men and women, in front of a mixed congregation, when in December 1665 he forced his way into the sabbath service at the Portuguese synagogue of Smyrna; in Jacob Frank's declaration that women should carry swords, and his proclivity for surrounding himself with an armed female guard; and in the mixed-sex Zohar study groups that apparently met in Prague at the turn of the eighteenth and nineteenth centuries. It was most evident in the series of 'bizarre' acts, alluding to sexual transgression, which characterized Sabbatai Zevi's conduct almost from the start of his messianic career: his relations with his divorced wives, who were forbidden to him by Jewish law; the rumours of the virgins who were entrusted to him for mysterious purposes smacking of proscribed intimacy; and the affair of the 'sealed pouch' containing texts that called for the dissolution of the rules regulating sexual relations. This tendency persisted, and was even adopted as a sacred code of conduct, long after Sabbatai Zevi's demise, among those of the messianic sectarians who demonstrated their fealty to the 'Torah of Emanation' by consciously, deliberately, and ritually breaching the sexual restrictions of Jewish law.

The two trends, the egalitarian and the libertine, can be seen to have combined already in Sabbatai Zevi's personal address to women, as recorded by Thomas Coenen at the height of the messianic enthusiasm that erupted in Smyrna. In his address he promised to revoke the disabilities foisted upon women by the curse of Eve: to redeem them from the pain of childbirth, to free them from subjugation to their husbands, and so to make their wretched lot as happy as the lot of men. Thus far his egalitarian programme; but this was followed directly by the declaration that the messiah had come 'to annul the sin of Adam'—a promise which implied the libertine tidings of the abrogation of the restrictive Torah of good and evil. This Torah had come into effect only as a consequence of the primordial sin, and it was now becoming obsolete with the rescission of that sin and all its dire consequences.[5]

It was precisely in this sense, and in reference expressly to the abolition of sexual prohibitions, that Moses Hagiz, sworn enemy of Sabbatianism, interpreted the claim that Sabbatai Zevi had 'rectified' the sin of Adam. This, he said, was one of the two most widespread notions among the Sabbatians of his time, by means of which they validated and even sanctified the act of sexual transgression. He denounced these attitudes as 'the gall of evildoers' and a 'wicked belief' upon which it was best not to dwell so as not to 'sully the air':

Since, with the advent of their filthy redeemer[6] Sabbatai Zevi, the sin of Adam and Eve has already been rectified, and [good] nourishment has been sifted from [evil] refuse,[7] a new Torah has gone forth from him, permitting the sexual prohibitions and all manner of admixture of [the permitted and] the forbidden, for [as they claim,] the very notion of admixture is no longer tenable, since that which was accursed has become blessed, 'and everything is prepared for the feast'.[8]

This, it seems, is why the Sabbatian call for the liberation of women was ultimately silenced. The sexual depravity which had become a hallmark of the heretical messianic movement was tacitly linked to the high visibility of women within its ranks. For the mere presence of women had always signalled the danger of unbridled sexuality;[9] their active participation in the licentious eschatological 'feast' was perceived as the eruption of dark forces which were inherent in women and had to be subdued in order for sober propriety to be restored. It was above all its association with rampant sexuality that discredited the messianic spirituality of women. It put an end to the activities of the Sabbatian prophetesses, and with it to the tradition from which they had emerged—that tradition of messianic prophecy by women which predated Sabbatianism by at least a century and a half but was quickly harnessed to the Sabbatian cause to be entirely subsumed in it.

For surely, the Sabbatian prophetesses did not spring up out of nowhere, and their emergence in virtually every corner of the Sabbatian world can hardly be attributed to the influence of this or that factor alone in any one of their many and diverse surroundings. The origins of the phenomenon in the early modern era would seem to go back to the expulsion of the Jews from Spain at the turn of the fifteenth and sixteenth centuries. The experience of the Conversos who remained on Iberian soil inevitably positioned their women at the heart of what became an illicit, covert, and above all domestic practice of residual Judaism. This seems to have spurred the emergence from their ranks of an array of messianic prophetesses, and it is reasonable to assume some degree of continuity between their prophetic activity and the comparable activity, equally driven by urgent messianic hopes, of the female visionaries with whom Hayim Vital (1543–1620) came in contact in his Levantine milieu almost a century later. The women he describes, who all seem to have wielded considerable moral authority, were freely practising their prophetic craft in the Jewish communities of Safed, Jerusalem, and Damascus, where, throughout this period, the local population was exposed to the overwhelming cultural influence of a large tide of immigrants originating, either directly or indirectly, in the Converso population of Iberia. This Iberian connection may well account for the natural ease with which prophetically inspired women could be accepted—as evidently they were, at least by Hayim Vital, who was himself of Calabrian descent, which put him within the Judaeo-Spanish orbit—as belonging to a long-established tradition of messianic prophecy by women. Vital's attitude to the female visionaries he encountered can be inferred from the fact that he never doubted them or considered them in any way anomalous. His silence on this point suggests that he took their prophetic skill for granted, finding no need to hedge its credibility or to question its legitimacy. Rather, he seems to view the prophetesses of his acquaintance as in no way inferior, and in some cases decidedly superior, to their male counterparts such as himself.[10]

Less than a century later, the appearance of hundreds or even thousands of Sabbatian prophetesses—once again in an Ottoman milieu which had absorbed large numbers of Iberian immigrants—was, admittedly, perceived as extraordinary by all, and by the movement's few ardent opponents as defying both reason and tradition. But the masses of Jews who believed in Sabbatai Zevi did not doubt his female prophets any more than they doubted the male. More than anything else, it was the scale, not the nature of the phenomenon, that appeared so remarkable to everyone who witnessed it. Fragments of evidence—such as reports that in Livorno, long before the outbreak of messianic frenzy in Smyrna, Sarah, who was eventually to marry Sabbatai Zevi, was well known and much sought after as a skilful prophetess—suggest that the professional practice of prophecy by individual women, as described by Hayim Vital, never died out but rather was temporarily overrun by the unprecedented surge of prophetic inspiration that engulfed men, women, and children, who all began to prophesy en masse in response to the messiah's call. But individual Sabbatian prophetesses resurfaced and continued to operate long after the tide of mass messianic prophecy had subsided.[11]

Thus the visionary women in Vital's accounts seem to stand on a certain continuum that links them, at one end, with the Iberian prophetesses of the immediate aftermath of the expulsion, and at the other end with the women taking part in the Sabbatian eruption of mass prophecy.[12] When we view as contiguous all three apparently discrete manifestations of female prophetic spirituality, a tradition emerges of messianic prophecy by women that persisted for over 300 years, reaching its climax in the heyday of Sabbatianism, but surviving in one form or another right through to the last transmutations of the decaying messianic movement in the early 1800s.

One might have expected such a tradition to strike deep enough roots to ensure its future, and yet the demise of Sabbatianism coincided with the effective disappearance from the landscape of female visionaries and messianic prophetesses, or rather, as we shall see, with the delegitimization of any public display of female spirituality, which was now relegated to the domain of sorcery, spirit possession, or just plain madness.

That messianic prophecy as such should have subsided at this time is hardly surprising, given that the Sabbatian debacle, which had exposed the capacity of the messianic idea to undermine religious norms and morality, inevitably discredited, at least for a while, all manner of messianic agitation, and this applied to messianic prophecy by men and women alike.[13] Moreover, by the early nineteenth century, in several western and central European centres of Sabbatianism, the Jewish community was undergoing a transformation brought about by acculturation, the Enlightenment, and emancipation, which eroded old frameworks of religious life and led to a crisis of traditional faith.[14] This was accompanied by a growing distaste for mystical religiosity and kabbalah, which were associated with the discredited Sabbatian heresy, and which could not be reconciled with the rationalist thinking that governed the processes of modernization.[15] Under these circumstances, kabbalistic messianism, whether championed by men or by women, was doomed to extinction.

But in eastern Europe, at the same time and in the same regions where Sabbatianism was waning, hasidism was in the process of becoming a mass movement. It shared the kabbalistic legacy of Sabbatianism and adopted, or at least independently reproduced, its most distinctive mode of prophetic-charismatic leadership.[16] This gave rise to the still common perception that the hasidic movement was Sabbatianism's natural heir. Already in the late eighteenth century, the rabbinic opponents of hasidism denounced it as a latter-day offshoot of the messianic heresy, or else as its immediate successor within a long sectarian tradition, which had always been antithetical to rabbinic Judaism.[17] This was also the context in which the rise of hasidism was set by the Galician *maskilim*, who campaigned against it in the early decades of the nineteenth century;[18] and the same view was still being echoed by some of the movement's early historians,[19] while others presented hasidism as a dialectical response to Sabbatianism, and thus, too, its product.[20]

Given this line of descent, hasidism might have been expected to preserve the inclusive, egalitarian attitude to women that was such a distinctive feature of Sabbatianism. It might have produced its own array of prophetically inspired women, enabling them to play a prominent role in the charismatic leadership of the movement. Indeed, within certain limits, the hagiographical tradition of nineteenth- and especially twentieth-century hasidism does acknowledge the prophetic insight of some distinguished women, whom it also credits with supernatural powers, considerable authority, and prestige. But this is almost exclusively confined to women who were related by family ties to the most famous male leaders of the movement: their mothers, widows, daughters, or sisters, who derived from them such power and reputation as they possessed. This, after all, was no more than an extension of that ancient tradition in the rabbinical world whereby the female relatives of illustrious men could acquire a reputation for piety, erudition, and even expert knowledge in certain fields of halakhah, particularly those pertaining to the lives of women. It is hardly surprising therefore that hasidism—a movement that places the charismatic personality of the leader at the heart of both its doctrine and social organization—should have exploited this tradition to the full, allowing the leader's supernatural aura to reflect on all those who were closest to him, including his female relatives. But the revolutionary novelty of Sabbatianism—its promotion of some women in their own right to positions of authority as inspired prophetesses, and its full incorporation of all women as a constituency of the messianic community—was conspicuously absent from the emergent hasidic movement. The early hasidic fraternities effectively excluded women from their ranks; even when some of the hasidic courts—and by no means all of them—admitted women for the purpose of seeking a personal blessing from the leader (tsadik or rebbe), they denied them access to his 'table', where he continued to address his teachings to the exclusively male gatherings of his disciples and followers. As for the reports of independent female leaders functioning as rebbes in their own right—while being grounded in the probable historical reality of one extraordinary 'holy virgin', the celibate Maid of Ludmir, who may have attracted for a while a grassroots following of her own—they testify above all that the phenomenon, perceived as an intolerable aberration, was suppressed so quickly and so thoroughly as to have left no more than a faint imprint on the collective memory of the movement. This was preserved in oral tradition but eradicated from the vast literary output of hasidism until the early twentieth century, when it was rescued from oblivion, not by any of the movement's authentic literary spokesmen, but rather by one of its renegades: the westernized historian S. A. Horodetsky, who, viewing hasidism as a traditionalist model for Jewish national revival, construed what he believed to be the equal rights it offered women in the religious sphere in terms that matched the utopian egalitarianism inherent in the secular ideology of Zionism. Subsequently, female leaders of hasidism continued to feature from time to time in various genres of popular literature, as a mere curiosity at first, but eventually as an apologetic response to the challenges of modern feminism, and increasingly in our own time, as a focus for genuine spiritual stirrings and aspirations within feminist Orthodoxy and beyond.[21]

It is, perhaps, hardly surprising that, with the single, problematic exception of the case of the Maid of Ludmir, the hasidic movement did not adopt the institution of holy virginity as a legitimate mode of female charismatic leadership. After all, even within Sabbatianism this was never more than one—highly syncretistic and by no means universal—outlet for female prophetic spirituality, and it ran counter to a centuries-old tradition that rejected it in no uncertain terms.[22] It is more surprising, however, that the hasidic call for the sanctification of the profane—the endeavour to spiritualize every aspect of corporeal life, which defined the movement and lay at its doctrinal core—did not extend to encompass women as full participants in the enterprise. Perceived as physical, and above all sexual, they became the objects of spiritual transformation without ever being allowed to engage in it actively as subjects.[23] For inasmuch as the hasidic doctrine, drawing on earlier strands of kabbalistic thought, may be reduced to a single overriding idea, it is that the godhead is a constant and all-pervasive presence suffusing the whole of creation, reaching right down to its coarsest manifestations in man and in the base, material world that he inhabits.[24] Man's task is to harness his actions and thoughts to the enterprise of hallowing his mundane reality—converting the corporeal to the spiritual, matter to form[25]—which he does by stripping off its earthly exterior in order to expose the divine core that resides within it, animates and sustains it in existence. This transformation effectively disposes of the distinction between the sacred and the profane, since all existence is capable of being restored—albeit temporarily, until the final redemption—to its source in the undifferentiated unity and holiness of the godhead. Regardless of whether the material, the corporeal, and the mundane were sensed by the hasidic masters to exist in reality as such, or whether they held them to be merely an illusion that concealed the spiritual reality of the Divine, which alone was truly existent,[26] the effect of this fundamental insight was to turn the domain of earthly life into hasidism's central arena for transformative action. Rather than preaching retreat from the world, as previous generations of kabbalists had done, hasidism generally advocated active engagement with it, since every aspect of mundane reality, even its basest material manifestations, presented itself as a ready vehicle for the holy.[27]

It stands to reason therefore that women, who were traditionally perceived as occupying precisely the domain of material existence, should have been incorporated in, or even led, the hasidic project of world sanctification, for who was better able than them to embody the transformation of the corporeal to the spiritual? Curiously enough, the sublimation of female sexuality, its conversion from physical to purely spiritual energy, does occur as a theme in hasidic writings, as, for example, in the following teaching by Dov Ber, the great Magid of Mezhirech (Międzyrzecz):

If one suddenly sees a beautiful woman, one must consider the origin of her beauty. For surely, were she dead, she would not possess this [beautiful] face but rather would be utterly ugly. Where, then, does her beauty come from? It must come from the power of the Divine, which suffuses her and endows her face with its flush and beauty. It follows that the root of [physical] beauty is the power of the Divine. Why, then, should I be drawn to a single instance of this power? It is better for me to cling to the origin and root of all worlds, where all beauty is to be found.[28]

And again, in another of the Magid's teachings:

'Rachel came with her father's sheep' [Gen. 29: 9]. According to the Midrash, [Rachel came] in order [for Jacob] to cling to her [physical] beauty.[29] On the face of it, this [interpretation] is untenable [since one can hardly attribute to Jacob such a base motive], but the real meaning is that it refers to the upper Rachel [namely, to the female aspect of the kabbalistic godhead, the *sefirah* Malkhut], since the beauty of the lower Rachel derives entirely from the upper one. And similarly, this is the meaning [in the case] of . . . the righteous Joseph, who did not desire [the physical] beauty [of Potiphar's wife].[30] Rather, through her [lower] beauty he became excited and desired the upper beauty, which is the beauty of his father [Jacob], the Beauty of Israel [who signifies the divine *sefirah* of Tiferet]. This is the meaning of 'and [he] fled and got him out' [Gen. 39: 15], that is to say, he [Joseph] fled her corporeal beauty and was eager to get out, [namely] out of this world, so as to cling to the upper beauty. And this is the meaning of the verse: 'Go forth and behold, O ye daughters of Zion' etc. [S. of S. 3: 11]. The meaning is: go forth out of corporeality, and behold nothing but the inner core of the matter, not its [external] corporeality. This is why Scripture says, 'and behold, O ye daughters of Zion'. It refers to the example of a woman's beauty, and it calls the corporeality of this beauty 'daughters of Zion'; that is to say, [this beauty] is no more than a sign and a *tsiyun*[31] [pointing to] the beauty above . . . A man is [generally] not permitted to cling to this lower beauty, but if [a beautiful woman] suddenly comes towards him, by means of her beauty he should cling to the beauty above.[32]

Although in both examples the encounter with women triggers the encounter with the Divine, the women are quickly discarded once the lust they have aroused by their 'lower' beauty has been converted to a desire for the 'upper' beauty of the godhead. Notably, it is the impact of their physical beauty on men and not their own physicality that is at stake here. The Magid is not addressing himself to sexually arousing women, and certainly not to women who are themselves sexually aroused;[33] his teaching is targeted exclusively at his male audience. The sexuality of the women he refers to is being spiritualized only in the contemplative minds of the men who have been exposed to its potentially harmful effects.[34] The women themselves are oblivious of the transformation and totally excluded from the experience. Far from being summoned in their own right to transcend their sexual nature, they continue to embody it even as they serve to enable the men to transcend their own—unwittingly constituting the means to the end of sublimating male desire. This is particularly striking in the second example cited above, where one of the scriptural passages from which the

Magid is drawing this lesson does, in fact, expressly address the 'daughters of Zion' themselves, calling upon *them* to 'go forth and behold King Solomon', who is taken here to represent a certain aspect of the godhead. But the Magid instantly abandons the literal meaning by rendering the 'daughters of Zion' allegorically as 'corporeality' serving merely as 'a sign', a pointer to men in the direction that should lead to the spiritualization of their own desire. He clearly does not consider the possibility that the 'daughters of Zion' themselves might engage in the same spiritual exercise that he urges on his male adherents.

In fact, women are never addressed in the homiletical literature of hasidism. To the extent that they feature in it at all—either collectively, as the gender category 'female', or individually, in reference most commonly to female protagonists of the Hebrew Bible[35]—they are routinely allegorized. As such they may allude to one or the other of the female divine *sefirot*, to the restrictive, judgemental, or evil forces that emanate from the 'left-hand side', which is a feminine domain in the view of the kabbalists, or else they may signify one of the attributes traditionally marked by the philosophers as feminine—passivity, receptivity, and above all material corporeality—whereby as 'matter' or 'body' they are schematically juxtaposed with their standard male counterparts, 'form' and 'soul'.[36] To cite but a few formulaic examples: 'The female is matter and the male is form';[37] 'Daughter is called body . . . and son is called soul';[38] 'The soul is called Abraham, and the body is called Sarah';[39] 'It is known that form, which is the soul, is called Abraham, while the body, which is matter, is called Sarah';[40] 'This is why [Scripture says] "Then Jethro", having been highly regarded as Moses' father-in-law, "took [Zipporah], Moses' wife, after he had sent her back" [Exod. 18: 2]. This was the lesson of abasement, which was learnt from the materiality of the body that Moses had sent back';[41] '"If he has a wife" [Exod. 21: 3]—this alludes to the body, for he has rendered his body fit for divine service—"then his wife shall go out with him" [ibid.], that is to say, the body, too, will share in the pleasure of the soul';[42] '"If thou know not, O thou fairest among women" [S. of S. 1: 8] . . . "women" alludes to corporeality, which is feminine';[43] and so on. Even at the turn of the nineteenth and twentieth centuries, the fifth Lubavitcher Rebbe, Shalom Dovber, was still allegorizing women in the same way when he called on the students of the Tomekhei Temimim yeshiva, which he founded in 1897 as a means of combating Haskalah (the Jewish Enlightenment), Zionism, and other secular ideologies, to behave like soldiers on the eve of battle, of whom the rabbis had said that, in order not to render their wives *agunot* (deserted) in the event that they did not return home, '"everyone who went out in the wars of the house of David wrote a bill of divorcement for his wife" [BT *Shab.* 56*a*] . . . because to be a soldier in the war of the house of David one must first divorce [oneself from] all corporeal things in which worldly men engage'.[44]

Moreover, the hasidic masters often translate the ontological categories of male and female into a corresponding pair of anthropological categories, which are central to their view of society and their understanding of their relationship with their flock. These are, on the one hand, the minority category of 'men of form', of 'intellect' or 'spirit', also referred to as 'scholars', 'sages', 'priests', 'leaders', or 'heads', who eventually come to be consistently designated tsadikim, the spiritual elite which constitutes the leadership of hasidism; and on the other hand, the majority category of 'corporeal' or 'material men' (literally: 'men of body' or 'men of matter')—the ordinary masses who make up the bulk of the hasidic following.[45] 'Masculinity' is attributed to the former and 'femininity' to the latter in numerous statements scattered, for example, throughout the writings of Jacob Joseph of Połonne: 'It is known that the men of matter are called woman, and the men of form are called man';[46] 'It is known that men of form are called man, and men of matter, who are as feeble as the female, are called woman. This explains the verse, "The woman shall not wear that which pertains unto a man" [Deut. 22: 5], that is to say, one who is like a woman, and who does not possess the quality and piety of man, should not assume them. And likewise the reverse, "neither shall a man put on a woman's garment" [ibid.], which is the quality of men of matter. Rather, each should act in accordance with his appropriate quality';[47] 'Adam was created with two faces . . . male and female, one in front and the other behind,[48] and just as there are matter and form in every individual . . . so there are in the world at large men of matter and [men] of form';[49] 'This is the meaning of "If any man's wife go aside" [Num. 5: 12]: ["wife"] stands for men of matter, who are called woman, having turned aside and refused to listen to the scholar, who is called man';[50] 'The head of the city or of the generation is called man . . . while the inhabitants of his city are called woman, [and they are] comparable to matter as against form.'[51]

While it highlights the conventional gender hierarchy, which makes the female inferior to the male, the construction of the hasidic leader as male in relation to his metaphorically female (but effectively male) flock serves above all to stress the need to maintain the crucial union between them. The charismatic leader must reach out to the masses, and they in turn must 'cleave' to him, in order for the flow of spiritual and material divine 'bounty' to engulf them both. Their mutual dependence and accountability are likened to the ties that bind together a male–female couple in sexual union:

Men of matter and men of form are partners inasmuch as each looks out for the other: the former provide for the material needs of the latter and sustain them, while the latter oversee and guide the former along the upright path. This is alluded to by Rabah bar bar Hana, who referred to the place where earth and heaven touch each other.[52] Namely, the men of matter, who belong to the category of 'earth' [which in kabbalistic parlance refers to the female *sefirah* Malkhut], are united, by touching and kissing, with the men of form, who belong to the category of 'heaven' [kabbalistically alluding to Malkhut's male partner, the *sefirah* Tiferet].[53]

This vital connection between the tsadik and his flock is also often likened to the integrity of a single living organism in which both genders are combined: the tsadik as 'head', signifying the male 'form' or 'soul', is the spiritual component that animates the organism, while his followers are its female 'body', comprising the material organs and parts.[54] In advocating the organic union between them and expressing it in gendered terms, hasidism is drawing on the ancient tradition that likened God as male, and the Jewish people as female, to a flesh-and-blood couple in marital union.[55] The male tsadik is coupled with his 'female' flock as the male God is coupled with his 'bride' Israel. This is one of many intimations that the status of the tsadik in hasidism is closely analogous to that of God,[56] but in the present context it is important to note that femininity is being ascribed to the tsadik's male devotees, who are invested with the inherent materiality and corporeality that are traditionally attributed to women. Actual women never feature in the scheme and have clearly become redundant.

References to 'the female' become even further removed from any flesh-and-blood women when the categories of male and female are employed to distinguish between the two states of mind, or two alternative modes of operation, of the hasidic leader himself: 'When [the tsadik] engages in Torah or prayer, then he is on the level of the male, but when occasionally he discusses matters relating to God-fearing and ethics, this is called female';[57] 'The divine service of the tsadik may take two forms. One is to serve spiritually, and the other is to renew and purify himself even by way of corporeality. The mode of spiritual service is called Abraham, namely, [it comes] from the male side, while the mode of corporeal service is called Sarah . . . that is to say, the female side, which is called woman';[58] 'This may be what is alluded to by the verse "Live joyfully with the wife whom thou lovest" [Eccles. 9: 9]. For when [the tsadik] is on a high level, engaging in Torah and prayer, he is called man, which is not the case when he descends from this level to the level of the masses, at which point he is called woman. And when he accepts even this [lower level] joyfully and lovingly, uniting the two levels and raising them . . . this is alluded to by "Live joyfully with the wife whom thou lovest".'[59]

'Male' and 'female' are also used to create a typology of hasidic leadership:

Everything holy has a male and a female aspect. The tsadik who bestows [the divine bounty on others] is called male, but the tsadik who is not at that level of bestowing is called female.[60] There is the tsadik who, when he receives charity, does not intend it for his own pleasure and benefit but rather he intends that by means of it abundant good will be bestowed on the whole of Israel . . . This tsadik is called male, for even though he receives, his intention and desire are only to bestow . . . And there is the tsadik who receives charity, and intends it also for his own benefit, to provide him with food and sustenance. This tsadik is called female, because his intention is also to receive.[61]

In articulating this psycho-anthropological theory, the hasidic masters confine themselves to the allegorical or metaphorical use of gender categories while appearing to be unconcerned with the relationship between men and women as such. Ostensibly, their category of 'male' is just as distant from the concrete reality of any man as is the category of 'female' remote from the reality of any woman. The two categories feature as a pair, operating on the same level of abstraction, and each acquires its meaning by contrast with the other. But the relationship of the concept to the reality it signifies is not quite the same in each case. For inasmuch as the tsadik is always a man, his maleness is both notional and concrete. He may possess a female aspect or mode of operation, or else he may be ranked as a flawed, 'female' tsadik, but as an ideal type he is always a male in terms of both gender and sex. His followers, on the other hand, are men who have been collectively classified as notional females. Their gender is at odds with their sex, but it is capable of being transcended. For their notional female state points, above all, and in a language charged with erotic connotations, to the expectation that they will cleave or adhere to the male tsadik. By means of this they are integrated in him and restored, as it were, to maleness. This in turn enables them, through him, to cleave to a particular aspect of the godhead—one traditionally construed by the kabbalists as female. The situation of women is quite different. Their femaleness, which is as notional as it is concrete, appears to be irredeemable. Although in principle they, too, might be included in the call for ordinary people—all notional females—to cleave to the male tsadik, in reality the speculative literature of hasidism never addresses them in these terms (or indeed, in any other; as argued above, this literature does not address women at all, at least not until the turn brought about by the crisis of secularization and modernity in the twentieth century[62]). They are not present when the tsadik delivers his teaching to his assembled male hasidim, nor are they ever presumed to be reading it when it becomes available in print—always in Hebrew rather than Yiddish, the women's tongue. The female as an actual woman—or rather the notion of such a woman—concerns the hasidic masters only to the extent that her sexual allure is a threat to the spiritual integrity of men, who may or may not be able to rise to the challenge of sublimating it. In every other respect, she is effectively allegorized or metaphorized out of existence. Actual women do, of course, belong to the hasidic community by virtue of family tradition and ties if not by independent affiliation, but from the doctrinal point of view they are situated beyond its outer periphery. While they feature quite often in the hagiographical traditions, where they may be depicted in positive terms as pious, charitable, or steadfast in their faith in the tsadik,[63] the speculative teachings allow them to fall out of sight since, for all intents and purposes, they have been displaced as females by a feminized fraternity of exclusively male hasidim.

The absence of women from the hasidic framework for the cultivation and enhancement of spiritual life might be taken to be self-evident—the natural consequence of having emerged within a tradition that always excluded women from its formal frameworks of intellectual and spiritual pursuit. But the scandalous precedent of Sabbatianism, which became notorious, as we have seen, not least on account of the sexual depravity associated with its inclusive attitude to women, suggests the probability that in erecting their own impermeable gender barriers, the hasidic masters were not just conforming to a traditional gender norm, but rather they were recoiling with horror from the spectre of its breached boundaries. For while the Sabbatian movement incorporated women, addressed them, and gave them agency and voice, hasidic doctrine reduced them to the status of mute, irrelevant bystanders. This is particularly evident in the glaring contrast between the high profile and full legitimacy granted to the Sabbatian prophetesses, and the hasidic discomfort with the phenomenon of prophesying women.

Admittedly, prophetic revelation in general had been a problematic issue in rabbinic culture ever since the perceived cessation of ancient biblical prophecy. The rabbis of the early centuries of the Common Era reluctantly allowed it some limited outlets while always treating it with a certain measure of suspicion. They clearly valued the scholar or sage, who interpreted God's word as revealed in the Law, over and above the visionary, who claimed to be revealing it afresh.[64] Among the medieval and early modern kabbalists, prophetic revelations, often mediated by heavenly messengers or mentors, were not uncommon but rarely publicized or based on any claim to the full prophetic title, which was generally reserved for the biblical prophets alone.[65] The Sabbatian eruption of mass prophecy, fully acknowledged and labelled as such, was an unprecedented popular revival of the ancient apocalyptic tradition. It brought to the fore a large number and great variety of prophets and prophetesses, who broadcast the gospel of the redemption, enhanced its credibility with supernatural feats, and in a number of cases also articulated it in complex metaphysical terms. However, in the aftermath of Sabbatai Zevi's apostasy and his eventual demise, recognition that his messianic movement had failed, coupled with its persistence as a subversive sectarian heresy, revived, and even intensified, the traditional reservations about prophetic revelation, which had proved to be so liable to delude the faithful and lead them astray.[66]

The hasidic movement shared these reservations and was equivocal about prophecy from the start. It certainly credited its charismatic leaders with insight into future and past events, with the ability to fathom secret actions and thoughts, and to commune with otherworldly domains; above all it viewed their addresses to their followers as fresh revelations of nothing less than divinely inspired Torah. All these attributes clearly belonged to the stock-in-trade of the classical prophet, and it is not surprising that many tsadikim identified themselves with the biblical Moses—master of all prophets.[67] Nevertheless, they generally refrained from appropriating the prophetic title (which was more commonly attached to them by their detractors),[68] and apparently regarded prophetic insight as being rooted in some form of pathology, while at the same time fully acknowledging the veracity of its claims. A clear example of this ambivalence, linked explicitly to the memory of the Sabbatian heresy, occurs in the 'writer's preface' to *Shivḥei habesht* (In Praise of the Ba'al Shem Tov), written in the final decade of the eighteenth century by Dov Ber of Linits (Ilintsy), son-in-law of the Ba'al Shem Tov's personal scribe:

I myself have noticed as well that in the time between my youth and my old age, every day miracles have become fewer and marvels have begun to disappear. This happens because of our many sins. In earlier days when people revived after lying in a coma close to death, they used to tell about the awesome things they had seen in the upper world . . . Likewise my father-in-law . . . told about a man who had been lying in a coma in the holy community of Bershad. It was in the time when the sect of Sabbatai Zevi, may his name be blotted out, was stirring. That man was shown several places in the books, in which some rabbis had erred and were almost led astray by that sect. He was ordered to tell the rabbis the exact meaning of those portions. In his days there were also mad people who injured themselves with stones during the reading of the Torah, and who used to reveal people's sins to them and tell them which of their sins would cause their soul to wander restlessly. I remember that in my youth, in the village where I studied with a teacher, poor people once came to the *ḥeder* and were given a meal. Among them there was a woman possessed by an evil spirit, but they did not realize it. The teacher began to study the portion of the Torah with the children, but when he had recited two or three verses the evil spirit threw the woman down, and her husband came and asked the teacher to stop his instruction because the contaminated spirit within her could not stand anything holy. When he stopped she rose and sat at her place. Because of all these things, many repented and the faith in the heart of each Jew was strengthened.[69]

Genuine prophetic insight is being attributed here to the nearly dead 'after lying in a coma', or to self-harming 'madmen', whose pathology, alongside the pathology of spirit possession, is paradoxically prized for its power to instil faith, since the communications it conveys from the supernal worlds supply tangible proof of their existence. Given that the same type of prophetic insight is ascribed throughout the book to the Ba'al Shem Tov himself, as well as to some of his charismatic colleagues and associates,[70] it is clear that the prototype of the hasidic tsadik shares the faculty of prophecy with marginal figures caught up in the liminal states of near-death, possession, and madness.[71]

Another indication of hasidic ambiguity about the status of prophetic revelation occurs in Dov Ber of Linits's account of the prohibition on prophesying in the circle of Nahman of Kosów, the Ba'al Shem Tov's fellow charismatic and sometime rival:[72]

> I heard from the rabbi of our community that the famous rabbi, our teacher, Nahman of Kosów . . . used to send messages to the members of the holy group in the city, telling each of them what sins they had to correct in this world. Everything that he said was true, but they were very annoyed with his prophecies, because they had an agreement among them not to prophesy.[73]

The 'holy group' sends one of its members to challenge Nahman on his failure to observe their collective decision to desist from the practice of prophecy, but Nahman denies the allegation: 'I was no prophet, neither was I a prophet's son [Amos 7: 14]', and he embarks on a lengthy explanation, from which it emerges that he had gained his awareness of his colleagues' (as well as his own) secret sins, not by exercising his faculty of prophecy but rather through communications with a demonic figure—the impure soul of a deceased sinner, who had died while under the ban of excommunication.[74]

The explanation is bewildering. Why should the impure source of Nahman's prophetic insight render it more acceptable to the group than if it had originated in wholesome divine revelation? As Zvi Mark has observed: 'A paradoxical attitude emerges from the story, whereby prophecy inspired by the holy spirit is "forbidden", while prophecy deriving from the demonic realm is "permitted" and perhaps even desirable.'[75] Joseph Weiss has already suggested that the key to understanding the problematics of prophecy in Nahman's 'circle of pneumatics' was the likely Sabbatian context from which the circle emerged:

> Do these people fall into any already defined category of the religious history of eighteenth-century Judaism in Eastern Europe? The answer is that the members of the circle belong unmistakably to that pneumatic type of religious personality

> that was so abundantly represented in the history of the Sabbatian movement, i.e. to the type of the Sabbatian "prophet" . . . Beyond the striking similarity between the religious phenomena of the Sabbatian prophets and of the circle to which Nahman belongs, the fact that the pneumatic figures in both societies are called by the very same name, i.e. *navi*, suggests a historical link . . . One is tempted to suggest that he and his friends belonged to the last examples of a typically Sabbatian phenomenon in the religious history of later Judaism. G. Scholem ventured to trace back the historical origin of the Hasidic charismatic leader (*Ṣaddik*) to the Sabbatian prototype of the *navi*.[76] In this transformation of a Sabbatian type into a hasidic one, Nahman and his friends, belonging as they did, perhaps only peripherally, to both movements, have their place.[77]

Weiss goes on to conjecture that the circle's decision to stop prophesying was theologically motivated and 'marked the termination of their adherence to the Sabbatian belief', an interpretation, he argues, that 'would not be far-fetched in view of the historical transformation of Sabbatianism into hasidism'.[78] The suggestion that the circle might indeed have emerged from a covert Sabbatian background gains some support from the fact that Jacob Emden—that indefatigable campaigner against the messianic heresy—had implicated Nahman of Kosów in it (although Emden's suspicions were not always justified, especially not when they were based on distant rumours from Poland).[79] But even if neither Nahman nor his group had ever been involved with Sabbatianism,[80] the very fact that the practice of prophecy was itself so closely associated with it may have been the inhibiting factor that prompted the circle at some point—perhaps in response to such suspicions as were being raised by Emden—to abandon their own prophesying. Nahman and his colleagues would have been aware that their prophetic activities were too close for comfort to the discredited practices of the heretical Sabbatian prophets. Invocation of the holy spirit was dangerous; it conjured up memories of the extravagant claims that had been falsely made in its name. By contrast, Nahman's insistence that he had gained his prophetic insight only as a result of being approached by a lost soul, who had been excluded from Paradise and was seeking restoration to holiness, redefined his experience in pastoral terms[81] while disavowing its prophetic dimension, thereby taking the edge off its unsavoury Sabbatian associations. For these associations between prophecy and heresy persisted long after the events that had given rise to them. This is evident, for example, in the following denunciation of the false Sabbatian prophets by the

Galician hasidic master, Zevi Hirsch Eichenstein of Żydaczów (1763–1831), in the name of his teacher, Jacob Isaac, the Seer of Lublin (1745?–1815):

I have heard my master, of blessed memory, say of those disciples, in the notorious event[82] in the days of the Taz,[83] who formed themselves into a separate sect and profaned the divine name. He attributed it to the fact that they desired to have the mystical experience of [a revelation of] Elijah and the holy spirit and prophecy by means of unifications.[84] But they failed to preserve a proper balance and they did not humble their physical matter and remained impure. They failed to take proper care of themselves and walked in ways remote from their capacity. They performed unifications . . . without refining their physical matter. And so they depicted for themselves the higher forms from under the Chariot, with the result that lewd and adulterous forms got the better of them, Heaven save us, and what happened happened, Heaven spare us. This is what my master said in the name of the Baal Shem Tov, his soul is in Eden, that these fools studied this science without having any capacity for and knowledge of the awe and dread of Heaven, with the result that they took it all in a corporeal sense, and so they went astray.[85]

That hasidic anxieties surrounding prophecy were associated with its prominence in the Sabbatian milieu becomes even more plausible if we take into account the fact, first observed in this connection by Zvi Mark,[86] that Israel Yofeh, the Kopys printer who published the first edition of *Shivḥei habesht* at the very end of 1814, had also published, earlier in the same year—and apparently again in 1815—what may be termed the first Hebrew novel about Sabbatai Zevi and his movement. The book, *Me'ore'ot tsevi* (The Events [in the Life] of [Sabbatai] Zevi), also known as *Sipur ḥalomot vekets hapelaot* (Tale of Dreams, End of Wonders), was written anonymously by an author who had assimilated Haskalah values, and who set out to debunk the messianic movement as an entanglement with the demonic realm. It ascribed the success of Sabbatianism to the persuasive power of its prophets, who deluded the people, exploiting their credulity with displays of miraculous feats, but who had been empowered to perform them by the forces of 'the other side'—the metaphysical source of evil.

The prospect of publishing the first anthology of traditions 'in praise' of Israel Ba'al Shem Tov—by now celebrated as the venerable founder of the expanding hasidic movement—in such close proximity to the publication in the same year of a damning account of Sabbatai Zevi, and the potential popularity of both works,[87] must have troubled the printer-cum-publisher Israel Yofeh, who was himself a faithful follower of the Habad school of hasidism.[88] As Zvi Mark has observed, against the background of the publication of *Me'ore'ot tsevi*,

Israel Yofeh faced a serious problem with the image of the Besht as it emerged from the manuscript writings of Dov Ber of Linits . . . which he was eager to publish. From the very beginning of the work, the Besht was portrayed as a magician, endowed with supernatural powers, acknowledged by a possessed madwoman, and altogether uncomfortably reminiscent of the phenomenon of prophesying ignoramuses in the Sabbatian movement . . . What was to distinguish the Besht of *Shivḥei habesht* from the Sabbatian protagonists of *Me'ore'ot tsevi*?[89]

He goes on to propose the following solution:

The close proximity of the [two] books forced Israel Yofeh to re-edit *Shivḥei habesht* and to reorganize its opening section in a way that would allay such anxiety as would arise from any comparison between the Ba'al Shem Tov's 'praises' and the narrative of *Me'ore'ot tsevi*. For Israel Yofeh could assume with certainty that at least a substantial proportion of his customers who were going to read *Shivḥei habesht* would have earlier read *Me'ore'ot tsevi*, which he himself had published in the previous year, or else that they were bound to read the subsequent edition [of *Me'ore'ot tsevi*], which was due to be published in the same year in which he was also publishing *Shivḥei habesht*.[90]

Indeed, as he tells the reader in his preface to *Shivḥei habesht*, not only was Yofeh aware that the manuscript on which he was basing his edition 'had been copied over and over', so that 'errors would have increased in number until the meaning of the sentences would have been almost unrecognisable',[91] but he also makes the following declaration in the opening lines of the work itself:

The printer said: 'Since in the manuscripts from which I have copied these tales, the sequence of events and the revelation of the Besht—may his merit protect us, amen—are not in the right order, and because I heard everything in the name of *admor*,[92] whose soul rests in heaven, in the proper order and with the correct interpretation, I will print it first as it was heard from his holy lips, and after that point in the story, I will include what has been written in the manuscripts.'[93]

Scholars have long been aware that the published edition of *Shivḥei habesht* contained several layers of recension,[94] and that Yofeh's intervention in the text was much more than a thorough proofreading exercise or a mere reorganization of the material, designed to establish, as he claims, the correct sequence of events. His contribution, evidently based on the Habad tradition on the Ba'al Shem Tov's early life, reflects a certain ideological agenda, aiming to attenuate the practical-kabbalistic, magical dimension of his personality, and to highlight instead his stature as a distinguished spiritual leader. To achieve this, Yofeh prefaced Dov Ber of Linits's text with a cycle of some sixteen tales,[95] which he concluded with the following statement: 'Up to this point I heard the unfolding of these events in the name of *admor*, may his soul rest in heaven. The other events and miracles that occurred I shall print according to the manuscripts that I obtained.'[96]

These two editorial units—Yofeh's tale cycle, with which he introduces the volume, and Dov Ber of Linits's 'manuscript' text, representing an earlier and undoubtedly more authentic account transmitted by named individuals who were contemporaries and close associates of the Besht[97]—offer two ostensibly alternative versions of the Ba'al Shem Tov's prehistory and early life, during his years of anonymity, when he was disguised as an uncouth, uneducated brute, right up to the moment when he was ready to reveal his true nature in public. The relationship between the two units has been closely analysed by Moshe Rosman,[98] who, following Yehoshua Mondshine,[99] has also demonstrated that the division between them is not clear-cut. Yofeh's opening unit does, in fact, contain some sections which he had clearly detached from their original position in Dov Ber of Linits's manuscript and introduced as bracketed additions to his own cycle of tales.[100] His version of the Ba'al Shem Tov's life was not a comprehensive or systematic alternative to the 'manuscript' text. Rather, it was intended to amend and complement it in order to account for the transformation of the Besht, in the course of the two generations that elapsed between his death in 1760 and the publication of *Shivḥei habesht* in 1814, from a skilful manipulator of supernatural powers, which is how he was perceived by his contemporaries, and was still remembered by Dov Ber's informants when he produced his version in the mid-1790s, into the paragon of hasidic spiritual leadership that he became for Yofeh and his readership.[101]

A number of tales in Yofeh's account closely parallel and suggest the possibility that they may be adaptations or direct responses to the tales that feature in the 'manuscript' text.[102] Consequently, the differences that nevertheless distinguish them may be taken to be particularly instructive as to Yofeh's editorial intent. A striking example is the two parallel accounts of what is almost certainly a single occasion on which the Besht, while still disguised as an ignoramus, was revealed by a prophetically insightful person to be a holy man, endowed with supernatural powers.[103] Dov Ber of Linits's 'manuscript' account—the earlier version of the two—directly follows a brief description of the Besht's life in a small village where, during the entire week, he would 'retire into seclusion in a house-like crevice that was cut into the mountain', returning home to his wife only on the sabbath's eve. Throughout this period, while he was still concealing his preoccupation with study and prayer, his brother-in-law, Gershon of Kuty,[104] 'thought him to be an ignorant and boorish person, and he used to try to persuade his sister to obtain a divorce from him'.[105] At this point the account of his 'revelation' unfolds as follows:

Once the Besht came to a town where there was a madwoman who revealed to everyone his virtues and vices.[106] When the Besht, God bless his holy memory, came to the town, Rabbi Gershon asked the righteous rabbi, the head of the court of the holy community of Kuty, the righteous rabbi, the great light, our master and teacher, Moses, to take the Besht to this woman. Perhaps he would take to heart her reproaches and return to the proper path. And all of them went to her.[107]

The 'madwoman' of Kuty who can see through people's hearts and expose their secret actions or thoughts, who is moreover invested with the moral authority to reproach and return them 'to the proper path', is instantly recognizable as belonging to the type of the prophetically gifted woman we first encountered in Hayim Vital's accounts, and subsequently in numerous reports of the inspired Sabbatian prophetesses. The tale goes on:

When the rabbi of the holy community of Kuty entered, she said: 'Welcome to you who are holy and pure.' She greeted each one according to his merits. The Besht came in last and when she saw him she said: 'Welcome, Rabbi Israel', although he was still a young man. 'Do you suppose that I am afraid of you?' she said to him. 'Not in the least, since I know that you have been warned from heaven not to practise with holy names until you are thirty-six years old.'[108]

The madwoman, or rather—as we are led to understand—the spirit that has possessed her and speaks from her mouth, sees through the Besht's disguise, and instantly recognizes that he is, in fact, a practitioner of 'holy names'—a *ba'al shem* ('master of the name'), a practical kabbalist who knows how to tap the magical power of the divine names and to manipulate it to good effect, engaging in such practices as exorcism, healing, and the production of talismanic objects. This, indeed, is how the Besht was perceived during his own lifetime, and how he was still being portrayed in much of Dov Ber's 'manuscript' text.[109] At the same time, however, the woman is aware that 'heaven' has forbidden the Besht to exercise his supernatural skills, and therefore the spirit within her—clearly the source of her 'madness', which is tantamount to her faculty of prophecy—should not be susceptible to his power. The tale proceeds to describe how the Besht, who had been urged to exorcize the spirit, strikes a mutual agreement with it, whereby the spirit will exit the woman's body so long as the Besht does not divulge its name. Once the spirit departs, and the woman is 'cured' of both madness and prophecy, she abruptly disappears from the narrative, and the tale concludes with the Besht subduing some 'impure spirits' elsewhere.

The portrayal of the woman in the tale is extremely ambiguous: on the one hand, her prophetic insights are celebrated and widely held to be true; she is clearly respected and trusted by such eminent men as Gershon of Kuty and Moses, the town's rabbi—both well known as scholars and kabbalistic adepts.[110] On the other hand, she is labelled 'mad' and described as being possessed—the passive medium of revelations communicated by an impure spirit. Her prophetic skills, as Mark rightly observes,[111] are closely analogous to the Besht's (although neither is ever referred to by the problematic title 'prophet'), but it is clear that her powers have been classified as symptomatic of a certain pathology, while his are presented throughout the book as wholesome and divinely inspired. Dov Ber of Linits's 'manuscript' version depicts a late eighteenth-century environment in which the traditional type of prophetess (both Sabbatian and pre-Sabbatian) is evidently still present but is being relegated to the shady domain of spirit possession and madness. The privileged women who were at one time acknowledged as legitimate vehicles for revelations by the holy spirit are now perceived as tormented victims—mouthpieces of ghostly spirits seeking release from the grasp of the demonic realm. It is not by accident that the hagiographical literature of hasidism is so replete with exorcism narratives, in the vast majority of which the victims of possession are women or girls, who are being cured of their 'madness' by the tsadik acting as exorcist.[112]

Israel Yofeh's response to Dov Ber's 'revelation by madwoman' tale is to offer a comparable revelation tale of his own. With the exception of some variations in detail and one significant difference, it so closely resembles the basic structure and essential plot line of Dov Ber's tale that it is more than likely intended to function as its corrective.

Like Dov Ber's tale, Yofeh's version is preceded by a description—more elaborate but essentially the same—of the Besht's life of covert piety during his residence 'in a certain village, where he . . . built a house of seclusion in the forest. He prayed and studied there all day and all night every day of the week, and he returned home only on the Sabbath.'[113] His outward behaviour, however, as in Dov Ber's version of the tale, was such that his brother-in-law, Gershon of Kuty, 'thought that the Besht was a simpleton' and despaired of him as 'good for nothing'.[114]

On one occasion, when he visited his brother-in-law in town during the festival of Sukkot, the Besht appeared to be adopting a wholly inappropriate and presumptuous manner for a man in his humble station—praying by the eastern wall of the synagogue, which was traditionally reserved for the dignitaries of the community, and following, as if he was a learned kabbalist, the Zohar's admonition not to don phylacteries (*tefilin*) on the intermediate days of the festival. At this, Gershon of Kuty was provoked into action:

He went with [the Besht] to the rabbi of the community so that the rabbi would admonish him.[115] They considered the Besht to be a pious man, but 'an uncultured person is not sin-fearing [and neither is an ignorant person pious].'[116] The rabbi was a very righteous man. When they came to the rabbi's house, Rabbi Gershon kissed the mezuzah, but the Besht put his hand on the mezuzah without kissing it, and our master and rabbi, Rabbi Gershon, became angry with him over this as well. When they entered the rabbi's house, the Besht put aside his mask and the rabbi saw a great light. He rose up before the Besht. Then the Besht resumed the mask and the rabbi sat down. And this happened several times. The rabbi was very frightened, since he did not know who he was. Sometimes he seemed to be a holy person and at other times he seemed to be a common man. But when our master and rabbi, Rabbi Gershon, complained to him about the tefilin and the mezuzah, the rabbi took the Besht aside and privately said to him: 'I command you to reveal the truth to me.' And the Besht was forced to reveal himself to him. But the Besht commanded him in turn not to reveal anything that had transpired. When they came out the rabbi said to our master and rabbi, Rabbi Gershon: 'I taught him a lesson, but I think he would not knowingly commit a fault against our customs. He has acted in innocence.' Then the rabbi examined the mezuzah and they discovered that it had a defect.[117]

The essential contours of Yofeh's plot are the same as Dov Ber's: both depict the unmasking of the Besht by an individual who was expected to chastise him; both locate the episode in Kuty and share most of their protagonists in common. Some of the differences between them are but mirror-reflections of each other, while others are no more than variations of nuance and stress. For example, the madwoman in Dov Ber's 'manuscript' text brazenly announces that she, or rather the possessing spirit that has invaded her, is not in the least afraid of the Besht; she has fathomed his true nature but feels immune to his power, which she knows to be constrained 'from heaven'. By contrast, the rabbi of Kuty—her counterpart in Yofeh's tale—becomes very frightened on glimpsing the holiness of the Besht; he cannot reconcile it with the boorish behaviour of the man he has been charged to admonish. On the other hand, in Dov Ber's text the woman and her spirit are soon subdued by the Besht, reduced to pleading for mercy, and ultimately silenced, while in Yofeh's version the rabbi is allowed to maintain his authority and dignity throughout: he commands the Besht to reveal his true nature, and the Besht is forced to comply. Moreover, Yofeh's rabbi is 'a very righteous man', flawed by no more than his defective *mezuzah*, while Dov Ber's madwoman, revealed to be drawing her power from the impure spirit of a deceased sinner, is entirely embroiled in the evil associated with his crime; once she is freed from its influence, she simply disappears from the tale. At the same time, however, her prophetic insight as depicted by Dov Ber is clearer and sharper than that of Yofeh's rabbi: she can instantly see through the Besht's disguise, while the rabbi is puzzled by what he sees and cannot grasp it without the Besht's assistance. His prophetic faculty is inferior to the Besht's, while in Dov Ber's version the madwoman is endowed with an insight that matches the Besht's and is distinguished from it only by its impure origin. This renders the confrontation between them a struggle between the powers of the holy and the profane, a polarity that is totally absent from the Besht's encounter with the rabbi.

The most significant difference, however, between the two versions of the tale is the very substitution of a mad female with a righteous and highly respected male. In both accounts, Rabbi Gershon—exasperated with his brother-in-law's antics—resorts to a resident of Kuty, whom he believes to be capable of admonishing the Besht and putting him 'on the proper path'. But while according to Dov Ber, he turns for help to a prophetically inspired woman, in Yofeh's account the woman is nowhere to be found. She has been swept aside, her part in the plot ascribed instead to the town's rabbi—none other than the righteous Moses, who in the earlier version of the tale was instrumental in bringing the Besht to the woman whose role he now occupies himself. The capacity for genuine insight has been transferred from a deranged or possessed female to a traditional male figure of rabbinic authority. To Israel Yofeh and his readers, this must have seemed a more appropriate setting for the first exposure of the Besht as a holy man.

The elimination of the woman from this version of the tale appears to represent the final stage of a process of displacement that must have begun as a reaction to the infamous Sabbatian prophetesses. In the first stage, captured by Dov Ber, a woman who, in the Sabbatian context (as in Hayim Vital's sixteenth-century milieu), would have been highly valued and even venerated as the voice of divine revelation is reduced in stature by being labelled 'mad' and subsumed in the profanity of an impure spirit; her voice no longer communicates the holy but rather challenges and confronts it. Some twenty years later, when Yofeh was adapting Dov Ber's tale to the hasidic sensibilities of his own generation, the displacement of the prophesying woman had become complete: she has now disappeared from the landscape altogether, to be replaced by a rabbi who alone is privileged to perceive the holiness of the Besht. Not only does Yofeh's transposition of the scene dispose of the mad but insightful woman, it also has the effect of reconfiguring the Besht himself, most likely in the image of his own hasidic mentor, Shneur Zalman of Liady (Lyady).[118] His version of the tale implicitly aligns the Besht with the rabbinical world and its values (even though he outshines it with his unique brand of charisma) by depicting him in collusion with the rabbi, to keep secret his true identity and nature. This collusion in Yofeh's version echoes the collusion in Dov Ber's tale between the Besht and the woman, who agree to keep secret the identity and nature of her possessing spirit,[119] but the two collusions place the Besht in two diametrically opposed settings: rabbinic learning and authority on the one hand, spirit possession and madness on the other. Yofeh's version transplants the Besht from the madwoman's world to the rabbi's, a world in which there is no longer any room for even a trace, however debased, of the prophetic spirituality of women.

Admittedly, hasidic literature does occasionally refer to women who experience prophetic visions without being labelled mad or possessed by spirits. In *Shivḥei habesht* itself, the 'manuscript' text of Dov Ber of Linits relates in some detail the prophetic dreams of the wife of Abraham the Angel, son of the Magid of Mezhirech. In one of her dreams, a 'supreme council [the Sanhedrin] of venerable elders' informs her that her husband is soon to die. She pleads with the elders to spare him, and is granted 'as a gift' the prolongation of his life by twelve more years. Her husband—himself prophetically aware of her dream—'congratulated her and blessed her for the true plea which prolonged his time', and 'indeed, this was what happened to him'.[120] Subsequently her deceased father-in-law, the Magid of Mezhirech, regularly appears in her dreams, to warn her whenever imminent danger threatens. When she first communicates the Magid's warning to her husband he does not believe her. 'He said to her: "Why did he tell it to you and not to me?"' And yet his wife's dream comes true, and he suffers the consequences of ignoring her prophetic warning. On another occasion the Magid again warns her in a dream against embarking on a journey, despite being urged by two eminent tsadikim to travel and rejoin her husband. When it transpires soon afterwards that her husband has just died, 'the tsadikim were ashamed to face Rabbi Abraham's wife, because she had perceived the future better than they had'.[121] The narrative is remarkably unsparing in its acknowledgement of the woman's prophetic insight, which is shown time and again to be superior to the insight of everyone else around her.

Another hasidic source which is unstinting in its acknowledgement of a woman's prophetic gift is Nathan Sternharz's description of Feyge, mother of Nahman of Bratslav and granddaughter of the Besht:

> Towards the end of that year [1800], on the first day of Elul, his [Nahman's] daughter Edl was married. The wedding took place in Khmelnik, and the rebbe was present together with his entire family. His mother, the righteous Feyge, of blessed memory, also attended, and during the marriage ceremony she saw the [deceased] Ba'al Shem Tov, for, like a tsadik, she possessed the holy spirit, and all the tsadikim held her to be in possession of the holy spirit and of great spiritual insight. In particular, her brothers, the famous tsadikim, namely the saintly rabbi [Ephraim] of Sudyłków and the saintly rabbi, our master Rabbi Barukh [of Międzybóż], held her to be like one of the prophetesses.[122]

Notably, in likening Feyge to 'one of the prophetesses'—by which he must be referring to the small cluster of biblical women thus described and not to their more recent counterparts[123]—the author does not flinch from invoking the prophetic title, which the early hasidic sources were inclined to shun.[124] It may well be that by the time of writing, between 1824 and the author's death in 1845,[125] the designation 'prophet' had ceased to carry the Sabbatian associations it once conjured up, especially when used in reference to women. Now, not only could a woman be likened to a full-fledged biblical prophetess, she could simply herself be known by that title. An example is Yente the Prophetess, mother of Isaac of Drohobycz—a contemporary of the Besht and one of his fellow charismatics—and grandmother of Yehiel Mikhl of Złoczów—disciple of both the Besht and the Magid of Mezhirech, and a leading proponent of hasidism in Galicia. Although Yente is not mentioned in *Shivḥei habesht* or in any source close to her own, her son's, or even her grandson's lifetime, she features in a much later hagiographical source, tracing the family history of the grandson:

The wife of the saintly Rabbi Joseph Spravedliver,[126] mother of the saintly rabbi Isaac of Drohobycz, was called Yente the Prophetess. Once, while cleaning the house, she recited the Kedushah prayer [with its thrice 'Holy' response], and said that she had heard the angels say 'Holy' and therefore she said 'Holy' as well.[127]

Nevertheless, references to women endowed with prophetic insight remain extremely rare, and those that occur share one crucial feature in common: such women are invariably related to the most famous hasidic leaders of their day. As was suggested above,[128] their power is derived from their intimate association with illustrious male relatives, whose own charisma and reputation it serves to enhance. The singular tradition that ascribes this power to a woman who claimed it in her own right—the celibate Maid of Ludmir—demonstrates that she was viewed by her contemporary tsadikim as an aberration, or one possessed by an 'evil spirit', and at any rate a deviant who should be silenced, as indeed apparently she was, her career as a rebbe curtailed by marriage, and her memory effectively erased from the literary record of hasidism.[129]

Against the background of the bold Sabbatian redemptive vision which, as we have seen, had promised to deliver the equality and liberation of women—acknowledging their prophetic inspiration, investing them with power as autonomous agents, and fully engaging them en masse as an active constituency of the messianic movement—hasidism's disregard for women is particularly striking. It seems too regressive to be taken for granted as mere compliance with the gender norms that traditionally prevailed in the culture of rabbinic Judaism. The hasidic doctrine of hallowing the mundane, of rendering spiritual the corporeal and the material, simply begs to be interpreted as designed to facilitate the mobilization of women—defined in terms of 'body' or 'matter'—to usher in the transformation into 'spirit' or 'form'. Indeed, it could be argued that there never was a theological framework more conducive to the promotion of women to the privileged status of religious vanguard, for surely they embodied the greatest potential for realizing the collective goal. Their total exclusion from the enterprise therefore appears to be wilful if not downright perverse, and calls for an alternative explanation.

It is not as if hasidism might have been expected to accomplish the gender revolution that Sabbatianism strove to effect. The source of the potential it held for women was quite different from the one on which the Sabbatians drew. The egalitarian vision that prompted the Sabbatians to blur the halakhic distinctions between the sexes was based on the notion that the world they inhabited was governed by a new Law—that messianic Torah which transcended the halakhic framework and where all differentiation and distinction ceased. At the same time, their empowerment of women, exemplified most tangibly in the elevation of Eva Frank to the position of female messiah, was driven by the kabbalistic dynamics of the redemptive process—essentially a divine drama, which the heretics saw it as their mission to enact on earth. In that scenario the power of the female increases as the process approaches its climax, when she rises from the bottom to the top of the sefirotic tree, adorning it as 'a crown to her husband' (Prov. 12: 4). The hasidim, for their part, did not share the Sabbatians' sense of living in messianic times. With few exceptions, they viewed themselves as situated in a world of 'exile'—primarily a state of mind, which could be transcended and transformed into a state of 'redemption' by way of mystical experience mediated by the tsadik. If they were to allow women to join in and even lead this transformation, it would have been on the basis that they conceived of them as the very embodiment of earthly corporeality—base matter which concealed within it the capacity for soaring to the greatest spiritual heights. That hasidism shied away from engaging women in what was, after all, the logical conclusion of a principle that lay at its core might well be a measure of the bitter lesson it drew from the trauma of Sabbatianism. For the Sabbatian heretics had left behind a profound dread, above all, of the breached halakhic boundaries of sexual propriety. The sexual depravity imputed to their women was inextricably linked to their full engagement with the failed messianic project. It was an untimely eruption of female spirituality—a powerful force prematurely unleashed which was now to be stowed away, kept out of sight, and securely contained until the appointed time for its discharge, which was not to be until some unknown point in the distant messianic future.

Notes

1 Gershom Scholem's monumental *Sabbatai Ṣevi: The Mystical Messiah 1626–1676* (Princeton, NJ, 1973) remains the most exhaustive study of the messianic movement during Sabbatai Zevi's lifetime. Scholem's collected papers on the subsequent development of Sabbatianism appeared in two volumes, *Studies and Texts Concerning the History of Sabbatianism and Its Metamorphoses* [Meḥkarim umekorot letoledot hashabeta'ut vegilguleiha] (Jerusalem, 1974), and *Researches in Sabbatianism* [Meḥkerei shabeta'ut], ed. Y. Liebes (Tel Aviv, 1991). For the Ottoman and Turkish contexts see M. C. Baer, *The Dönme: Jewish Converts, Muslim Revolutionaries, and Secular Turks* (Stanford, Calif., 2009); C. Sisman, *The Burden of Silence: Sabbatai Sevi and the Evolution of the Ottoman Turkish Dönmes* (Oxford, 2015). See also M. Goldish, *The Sabbatian Prophets* (Cambridge, Mass., 2004); Y. Liebes, *On Sabbatianism and Its Kabbalah* [Sod ha'emunah hashabeta'it] (Jerusalem, 1995), and the two collections of Sabbatian documents translated into English by D. Halperin: *Sabbatai Zevi: Testimonies to a Fallen Messiah* (Oxford, 2007) and A. Cardozo, *Selected Writings*, trans. and introd. D. Halperin (New York, 2001). For the circle of Jacob Frank see P. Maciejko, *The Mixed Multitude: Jacob Frank and the Frankist Movement, 1755–1816* (Philadelphia, 2011).

2 For full documentation and analysis of women's involvement in the Sabbatian movement from its earliest beginnings, through the height of its success, to its last sectarian transmutations, see A. Rapoport-Albert, *Women and the Messianic Heresy of Sabbatai Zevi 1666–1816* (Oxford, 2011).

3 For the Greek origins of this conceptualization of the male–female dichotomy, of which, I believe, there are some early intimations in the classical rabbinic sources, but which was imported into medieval Jewish philosophy and became ubiquitous in the literature of Jewish thought, see ibid. 84–5 and n. 13 ad loc.

4 See ibid. 119–22.

5 On all this see ibid. 80–174.

6 The Hebrew for 'filthy', *mego'al*, plays on *go'el*, 'redeemer'.

7 This is a reference to the kabbalistic doctrine, associated with Isaac Luria, whereby the 'rectification' or restoration of the world to a state of perfection is the long-drawn-out process—culminating in the final redemption—of 'sifting', 'sorting', or extricating the world-sustaining vital particles of spiritual good ('nourishment') from the dead weight of material evil ('refuse') in which they are trapped.

8 M. Hagiz, *Shever poshe'im* (London, 1714; facsimile edn. Jerusalem, 1970), 71, quoted in G. Scholem, *Researches in Sabbatianism* (Heb.), 349. The final sentence is a citation from Mishnah *Avot* 3: 17, referring—sarcastically, here—to the feast that awaits the righteous in the eschatological World to Come. For Moses Hagiz as a vehement opponent of Sabbatianism see E. Carlebach, *The Pursuit of Heresy: Rabbi Moses Hagiz and the Sabbatian Controversies* (New York, 1990).

9 For sexuality as the defining characteristic of women see e.g. BT *Ber.* 24*a*, where a woman's little finger is likened to her genitals, and even an exposed 'hand's breadth' of her body, her leg, her voice, or her hair are considered her 'nakedness'. In the same vein *Derekh erets rabah*, 1: 13 urges men to refrain as much as possible from conversing with women, because 'a woman's conversation is nothing but lewd words [*divrei ni'ufim*]'. For the perception of female sexuality as an incontinent, menacing force which presents a constant threat to the integrity of men, see D. Boyarin, *Carnal Israel: Reading Sex in Talmudic Culture* (Berkeley, Calif., 1993), 77–106, where he is at pains to distinguish the predominantly positive attitude of classical rabbinic sources towards women and sex from Philo's condemnation of female sexuality as the source of all evil. At the same time, however, he concedes the presence of sexually 'misogynistic' texts within the midrashic corpus, and points to the growing anxiety about women's sexuality that became prevalent in later Judaism. It is clearly not by accident that an obscure reference to 'the affair of Beruriah', which is offered in the Babylonian Talmud as a possible explanation for the shameful flight of her husband, R. Meir, from Palestine to Babylonia (see BT *AZ* 18*b*), is developed in a medieval tradition recorded by Rashi into an account of her ignominious suicide following her seduction by one of her husband's disciples (see Rashi ad loc.). Beruriah's exceptional learning, which challenged the rabbinic dictum (BT *Shab.* 33*b*; BT *Kid.* 80*b*) that 'women are light-headed' (understood as lewd), and clashed implicitly with the view whereby teaching women Torah is tantamount to teaching them lewdness (see BT *Sot.* 20*a*), is thus associated with transgressive sexuality as a matter of course. A poignant statement of this sensibility, which persists in traditionalist circles to the present day, can be found in the recent memoirs of an Orthodox upbringing by Naomi Seidman, who writes: 'A boy might conceivably become an *apikores*, a heretic, but transgression in a girl could only mean something sexual' ('Reflections on a Belated Apostasy', *Contemplate: The International Journal of Cultural Jewish Thought*, 3 (2005/6), 55).

10 For prophesying women prior to Sabbatianism see Rapoport-Albert, *Women and the Messianic Heresy of Sabbatai Zevi*, 57–79.

11 For the phenomenon of mass prophecy in Sabbatianism, and the prominence of women in it, see ibid. 15–56.

12 The first to bring together all these phenomena and to define them as a continuous thread of female mystical spirituality, whose existence had been overlooked by Jewish historiography, was J. H. Chajes, in his 1999 doctoral dissertation, 'Spirit Possession', 202–7, and subsequently in several of his published works. See e.g. J. H. Chajes, *Between Worlds: Dybbuks, Exorcists, and Early Modern Judaism* (Philadelphia, 2003), 99–100.

13 See e.g. the condemnation of all contemporary messianic prophecy by Leyb ben Ozer, who concludes his 1718 account of the rise and fall of Sabbatai Zevi with the warning:

> We must not be impressed by those who perform awesome deeds, for they are all [driven] by the Other Side [Satan, the forces of evil], and we should keep as far away as possible from such people, since all they do is confound and disturb the worlds, causing nothing but adversity and leading to no good whatsoever. Rather, 'Thou shalt be perfect with the Lord thy God' [Deut. 18: 13], for we can do without prophets, and let none other but Elijah the Prophet herald good tidings, salvations, and consolations. (*The Story of Sabbatai Zevi* [Sipur ma'asei shabetai tsevi], trans. from original Yiddish manuscript (*Beshraybung fun shabsai tsvi*), with introd. and notes, Z. Shazar (Jerusalem, 1978), 209)

See also at n. 66 below.

14 See e.g. H. Kieval, *Languages of Community: The Jewish Experience in the Czech Lands* (Berkeley, Calif., 2000), 26–34, 37–64; W. McCagg, *A History of Habsburg Jews 1670–1918* (Bloomington, Ind., 1992), 22–6, 65–82; G. Scholem, *The Messianic Idea in Judaism and Other Essays on Jewish Spirituality* (New York, 1971), 170–1; A. G. Duker, 'Polish Frankism's Duration', *Jewish Social Studies*, 25 (1963), 297.

15 On the aversion to the Zohar and kabbalah during this period see I. Tishby, *The Wisdom of the Zohar: An Anthology of Texts*, trans. D. Goldstein (London, 1989), i. 43–50; B. Huss, 'Admiration and Disgust: The Ambivalent Re-canonisation of the *Zohar* in the Modern Period', in H. Kreisel (ed.), *Study and Knowledge in Jewish Thought* (Be'er Sheva, 2006), 203–7. See also M. A. Meyer (ed.), *German-Jewish History in Modern Times* (New York, 1996–8), i. 233–4, ii. 144. This is the sentiment to which Gershom Scholem referred as *Kabbala-Angst* ('Politik der Mystik: Zu Isaac Breuers "Neuem Kusari"', *Jüdische Rundschau*, 57 (17 July 1934), 2), and which, more recently, Mordecai Breuer described as 'Kabbalophobia' ('Fragments of Identity and Memory' (Heb.), in H. Pedaya and E. Meir (eds.), *Judaism: Topics, Fragments, Faces, Identities.*

Jubilee Volume in Honour of Rivka [Yahadut: sugyot, keta'im, panim, zehuyot. Sefer rivkah] (Be'er Sheva, 2007), 23). Notably, however, Rivka Horwitz has shown that some of the 18th- and early 19th-century *maskilim*, including Moses Mendelssohn himself, were not altogether ignorant of, or hostile to, kabbalah, treating it as a metaphysical doctrine which could be harmonized with rationalist Enlightenment values. She also highlights the survival of some strands of viable, if marginal, kabbalistic religiosity in 19th-century Germany, especially Bavaria, and the revival of interest in kabbalah by the turn of the 19th and 20th centuries. See R. Horwitz, *Multiple-Faceted Judaism* [Yahadut rabat panim] (Be'er Sheva, 2002), 11–235. For the debatable status of the kabbalah in late 18th-century Prague—a centre of clandestine Sabbatian-Frankist activity—during the chief rabbinate of Ezekiel Landau (1713–82), see S. Flatto, *The Kabbalistic Culture of Eighteenth-Century Prague: Ezekiel Landau (The 'Noda Biyehudah') and His Contemporaries* (Oxford, 2010). Flatto argues that 'Notwithstanding his protestations to the contrary . . . he [Landau] was immersed in kabbalah', and that mysticism played 'a pervasive role . . . in the community, in part thanks to Landau' (ibid. 227); and cf. Landau's sermon of September 1770, censored out of all the published editions of his sermons, in which he attacks in strong terms and warns against the three 'sects' he considered a threat to the religious integrity of his community—the kabbalists, the [Deist] philosophers, and the Sabbatian heretics. The sermon was published and analysed as a counter to Flatto's thesis in M. Kahana and M. K. Silber, 'Deists, Sabbatians, and Kabbalists in Prague: A Censored Sermon of R. Ezekiel Landau, 1770' (Heb.), *Kabbalah*, 21 (2010), 349–84. See also Flatto's rejoinder, 'Believing the Censor? A Response to 'Deists, Sabbatians, and Kabbalists in Prague: A Censored Sermon of R. Ezekiel Landau, 1770' (Eng.), *Kabbalah*, 24 (2011), 123–46.

16 Gershom Scholem and, following him, many other historians of kabbalah and hasidism believed the institution of the tsadik—the charismatic leader in hasidism—to have evolved out of the Sabbatian 'ideal type' of the charismatic prophet-messiah. See e.g. Scholem, *Major Trends in Jewish Mysticism* (New York, 1965), 333–4; id., *On the Mystical Shape of the Godhead: Basic Concepts in the Kabbalah* (New York, 1991), 124–6; id., 'The First Two Testimonies on the Relations between Hasidic Groups and the Ba'al Shem Tov' (Heb.), in id., *The Latest Phase: Essays on Hasidism by Gershom Scholem* [Hashalav ha'aḥaron: meḥkerei haḥasidut shel gershom shalom], ed. D. Assaf and E. Liebes (Jerusalem, 2008), 77–9; J. Weiss, 'Some Notes on the Social Background of Early Hasidism', in id., *Studies in Eastern European Jewish Mysticism* (Oxford, 1985), 10–12; and id., 'Beginnings of Hasidism' (Heb.), in A. Rubinstein (ed.), *Studies in Hasidism* [Perakim betorat haḥḥasidut uvetoledoteiha] (Jerusalem, 1977), 51–8. This view was challenged by Mendel Piekarz, who argued that much of the hasidic doctrine of the tsadik could have been drawn directly from the same kabbalistic sources that underlay the Sabbatian concept of the messiah, and thus that the emergence of charismatic leadership in hasidism could have altogether bypassed the discredited Sabbatian precedent. See M. Piekarz, *The Beginning of Hasidism: Intellectual Trends in Derush and Musar Literature* [Biyemei tsemiḥat haḥasidut: megamot ra'ayoniyot besifrei derush umusar] (Jerusalem, 1978), 299–302, and cf. A. Rubinstein, 'Between Hasidism and Sabbatianism' (Heb.), in id. (ed.), *Studies in Hasidism* (Heb.).

17 See M. Wilensky, *Hasidim and Mitnagedim* [Ḥasidim umitnagedim] (Jerusalem, 1970), i. 62, 66–7, 116 n. 3, 156, 240–1, 245, 256, 258–64, 268, 276, 304, 328–9, 346; ii. 16, 45–6, 75, 104, 141–2, 179–80, 209, 268, 292, 296, 321. See also S. Werses, *Haskalah and Sabbatianism: The Story of a Controversy* [Haskalah veshabeta'ut: toledotav shel ma'avak] (Jerusalem, 1988), 99–103.

18 See Werses, *Haskalah and Sabbatianism* (Heb.), 103–24.

19 See e.g. H. Graetz, *History of the Jews from the Earliest Times to the Present Day* (London, 1901), v. 396–9; D. Kahana, *A History of the Kabbalists, the Sabbatians, and the Hasidim* [Toledot hamekubalim, hashabeta'im vehaḥasidim], ii (Tel Aviv, 1926–7), *Even ofel*, 65; S. Dubnow, *The History of Hasidism* [Toledot haḥasidut] (Tel Aviv, 1960), 1–2.

20 This is implicit in the very presentation of Sabbatianism and hasidism as two consecutive chapters, representing two consecutive phases of the Jewish mystical tradition, in Gershom Scholem's influential *Major Trends in Jewish Mysticism*, where he also states this view explicitly (e.g. pp. 329–34), as he does elsewhere (e.g. 'The Neutralization of the Messianic Element in Early Hasidism', in id., *The Messianic Idea in Judaism*, and '*Devekut*', ibid. 221). See also M. Buber, *The Origin and Meaning of Hasidism* (New York, 1960), 29–40; I. Tishby and J. Dan, 'The Doctrine and Literature of Hasidism' (Heb.), in A. Rubinstein (ed.), *Studies in Hasidism* (Heb.), 251–3 and *passim*; Weiss, 'Some Notes on the Social Background of Early Hasidism', 11–13; id., 'Beginnings of Hasidism' (Heb.), 127–8, 133–4, 151, 169–70; and Rubinstein, 'Between Hasidism and Sabbatianism' (Heb.). But cf. Piekarz, *The Beginning of Hasidism* (Heb.), 278–9, 299–302, as well as M. Idel, *Hasidism: Between Ecstasy and Magic* (New York, 1995), 1–17, and id., 'Martin Buber and Gershom Scholem on Hasidism: A Critical Appraisal', in A. Rapoport-Albert (ed.), *Hasidism Reappraised* (London, 1996). Both Piekarz and Idel reject this view of the relationship between the two movements on philological and methodological grounds respectively.

21 For a critical evaluation of Horodetsky's interpretation of the Maid of Ludmir tradition and its subsequent ramifications in the literature, see Ch. 6 below. See also N. Deutsch, *The Maiden of Ludmir: A Jewish Holy Woman and Her World* (Berkely, Calif., 2003), 23–33. Deutsch's book is the latest attempt to construct the Maid's biography out of fragments of historical information, fleshed out by hagiographical and memoiristic accounts of doubtful historical value. For the cluster of publications and women-led events in the summer of 2004 which celebrated the Maid of Ludmir as an inspirational model, and included a pilgrimage to her supposed burial place in the Mount of Olives cemetery in Jerusalem on what purports to be the anniversary of her death, see e.g. Y. Levine Katz, 'In Memoriam Hannah Rachel, 1806–88' (Heb.), *Hatsofeh* (16 July 2004), 12; ead., 'The Events of the *Yahrzeit* of Hannah Rachel Verbermacher' (Heb.), *Mabua*, 43 (2004/5), 65–74; S. Friedlander Ben Arza, 'Hannah Rachel of Ludmir' (Heb.), *Kolekh: forum nashim datiyot*, 95 (1 Tamuz 2004), 3–4.

22 For the prophesying Sabbatian virgins, the practice of celibacy in the Frankist court (which was punctuated by ritual acts of transgressive sex), and its syncretistic cult of the redemptive 'Holy Maiden', see Rapoport-Albert, *Women and the Messianic Heresy of Sabbatai Zevi*, 23–56, 157–257.

23 An exception may be found in the eschatological theme of the elevation of women, and the intensification of female power, that occurs from time to time in the homiletical literature of hasidism. When it does it echoes the kabbalistic notion of the inversion of gender hierarchies in the messianic future, and is invariably featured in contexts that are devoid of any live messianic tension. Far from advocating the spiritual empowerment of women in the here and now, it serves primarily to highlight the contrast between the promise of this empowerment in the utopian future and its absence from the mundane reality of the present. It is decidedly in that reality that hasidism grounds itself, providing men with the means of transcending it only temporarily, as a subjective experience or mental exercise, and without ever challenging the existing world order or toppling its gender hierarchies. See on this Rapoport-Albert, *Women and the Messianic Heresy of Sabbatai Zevi*, 129–31 n. 65.

24 See e.g. R. Elior, '"The World is Filled with His Glory" and "All Men": Spiritual Renewal and Social Change in Early Hasidism' (Heb.), in M. Hallamish (ed.), *Alei shefer: Studies in the Literature of Jewish Thought Presented to Rabbi Dr Alexander Safran* [Alei shefer: meḥkarim besifrut hahagut hayehudit mugashim likhvod harav doktor aleksander safran] (Ramat Gan, 1990), 35; ead., *The Mystical Origins of Hasidism* (Oxford, 2006), 74–84; Tishby and Dan, 'The Doctrine and Literature of Hasidism' (Heb.), 258; T. Kauffman, *In All Your Ways Know Him: The Concept of God and Avodah Begashmiyut in the Early Stages of Hasidism* [Bekhol derakheikha de'ehu: tefisat ha'elohut veha'avodah begashmiyut bereshit haḥasidut] (Ramat Gan, 2009), 44–84. For the kabbalistic sources of this idea, on which hasidism undoubtedly drew, see Idel, *Hasidism: Between Ecstasy and Magic*, 17–18, 63–4, 215–18.

25 e.g. 'The ultimate purpose of man's creation is that he should convert matter to form' (Jacob Joseph of Połonne, *Toledot ya'akov yosef*, 109*b*, and see also ibid.

124*c*, 135*b–c*, 142*b*); 'Man must purify himself to such an extent that he would turn matter into form' (Elimelekh of Lizhensk, *No'am elimelekh*, ii. 401); 'Corporeality, namely eating and drinking and worldly affairs . . . must be introduced into holiness' (ibid. i. 279); 'Earthliness, that is, corporeality, must be raised . . . to holiness . . . that is to say, to the Upper World' (ibid. i. 14), and in many other places.

26 For the view that hasidism consecrated and thus affirmed the reality of earthly existence—the 'here and now' as it is—to the exclusion of any other, transcendent reality, see Buber, *The Origin and Meaning of Hasidism*, 114–49 and *passim*. For Scholem's rejection of this view, with the assertion that in consecrating the mundane, hasidism was effectively annihilating or denying its reality, see Scholem, 'Martin Buber's Interpretation of Hasidism', in id., *The Messianic Idea in Judaism*, 238–45.

27 Admittedly, some hasidic masters were concerned that the radical doctrine of 'worship through corporeality' might lend itself to vulgar interpretations by those who lacked the spiritual capacity for practising it authentically. Such people were liable to indulge in corporeal pleasures and worldly affairs while deluding themselves that they were thereby extracting the sacred from the profane. The solution to this problem lay in confining the practice of 'worship through corporeality' to the charismatic leaders of hasidism alone, while restricting the ordinary members of the community to normative devotional practices. See e.g. Meshulam Feibush Heller of Zbaraż, 'Yosher divrei emet', in *Likutim yekarim* (Jerusalem, 1974), 118–19 §§16–17; Elimelekh of Lizhensk, *No'am elimelekh*, ed. G. Nigal (Jerusalem, 1978), ii. 428.

28 Dov Ber of Mezhirech, *Or ha'emet* (Zhitomir, 1900), 31*b*. And see the parallel passages in id., *Or torah* (Jerusalem, 1968), 105, and in *Tsava'at harivash*, ed. J. I. Schochet (Brooklyn, 1975), 16*a* §90.

29 See *Yalkut shimoni*, i: *Devarim*, 'Va'etḥanan', §824.

30 See Gen. 39, and cf. BT *Sot.* 36*b*.

31 The consonants of the Hebrew word *tsiyun*, meaning an indication or a sign, are exactly the same as the consonants of the Hebrew name for Zion (*tsiyon*).

32 Dov Ber of Mezhirech, *Magid devarav leya'akov*, ed. R. Schatz-Uffenheimer (Jerusalem, 1976), 29–30 §15, and see also ibid. 331–3 §207. For the philosophical and kabbalistic sources of this theme, and its particular configuration in hasidic thought, see M. Idel, 'Female Beauty: A Chapter in the History of Jewish Mysticism' (Heb.), in I. Etkes et al. (eds.), *Within Hasidic Circles: Studies in Hasidism in Memory of Mordecai Wilensky* [Bema'agelei ḥasidim: kovets meḥkarim lezikhro shel profesor mordekhai vilenski] (Jerusalem, 2000), 317–34; id., *Kabbalah and Eros* (New Haven, 2005), 153–78. For clear reverberations of the Magid's homily in the teaching of Aaron of Apta (Opatów), see his *Or haganuz latsadikim* (Żółkiew, 1800), 10*b*, cited in Idel, *Kabbalah and Eros*, 171.

33 Women's experience of sexual arousal is hardly ever an issue in the classical rabbinic sources, which regularly focus on the sexual desire that women are assumed to arouse in men as a matter of course. For the construction of women as the embodiment of the sexual urge (*yetser*), to which all men are permanently susceptible, and the effective exclusion of women from the struggle to subdue it, in which the rabbis call on men alone to engage, see I. Rosen-Zvi, 'Do Women Have a *Yetzer*? Anthropology, Ethics, and Gender in Rabbinic Literature' (Heb.), in H. Kreisel, B. Huss, and U. Ehrlich (eds.), *Spiritual Authority: Struggles over Cultural Power in Jewish Thought* [Samkhut ruḥanit: ma'avakim al ko'aḥ tarbuti bahagut hayehudit] (Be'er Sheva, 2010), 21–34; id., 'Sexualising the Evil Inclination: Rabbinic "Yetzer" and Modern Scholarship', *Journal of Jewish Studies*, 60/2 (2009), 264–81; and id., 'Two Rabbinic Inclinations? Rethinking a Scholarly Dogma', *Journal for the Study of Judaism*, 39 (2008), 513–39.

34 As Moshe Idel points out ('Female Beauty' (Heb.), 317 and *Kabbalah and Eros*, 173), among the orthodox opponents of hasidism, the *mitnagedim*, the hasidic teaching on the sublimation of erotic thoughts was perceived as the deliberate pursuit of women in order to stimulate erotic thoughts and then to 'elevate' them. Thus David of Maków, an arch-opponent of hasidism, wrote: 'They walk idly, engaging in idle talk, saying that by walking in the marketplace and gazing at women they elevate their thought to God' (in Wilensky, *Hasidim and Mitnagedim* (Heb.), ii. 235). It is clear, however, that the Magid generally disapproved of any eye contact with women. The sublimation technique he outlines is intended for unavoidable chance encounters, and he introduces it with the following warning: 'One should avoid looking at coarse, corporeal things, and even more so at beautiful women, for this would be driven by sexual desire and amount to idolatry' (*Or ha'emet*, 31*a*). The Magid's disciple, Ze'ev Wolf of Zhitomir, reports in his name an incident dating back to his early life, apparently prior to his 'conversion' to the Ba'al Shem Tov's type of hasidism:

> I have heard from the Magid . . . that when he was a *melamed* [a teacher to young children] in a certain village, while he was sitting there in some corner, a nobleman arrived, accompanied by a beautiful whore, with her chest exposed right down to her breasts, as is their custom. He suddenly looked [at her] inadvertently, and became greatly distressed. He then began to reject [this] evil in the following way: [by focusing his mind on the thought] that she was created out of her parents' sexual fluids, out of the abominable foods from which she draws her beauty . . . that semen is as repulsive as snakes . . . and that her beauty and charm arise from such an utterly repulsive thing. [He concentrated on this thought so intensely] that he began to vomit in front of them. (Ze'ev Wolf of Zhitomir, *Or hame'ir*, 'Ḥayei sarah', 11*b*; and see the discussion of this passage in Idel, 'Female Beauty' (Heb.), 319–20)

As a method of extinguishing sexual desire, to focus on the 'repulsive' embryonic origins of the woman is comparable to focusing on her end as a decomposing corpse, but the next step, the transformation of the sexual desire she arouses into a vehicle for union with the Divine, is absent here and must represent a later stage in the development of the Magid's thinking.

35 The portrayal of biblical women in hasidic literature is the subject of a doctoral dissertation by my student, Yaffa Aronoff.

36 Very occasionally the female may also signify 'soul'. See e.g. Ephraim of Sudyłków, *Degel maḥaneh efrayim*, 'Tsav', 91: '"And if a man sell his daughter to be a maidservant" [Exod. 21: 7] . . . "his daughter"—this is the soul, which descends to this world', or Elimelekh of Lizhensk, *No'am elimelekh*, i. 96: '"And he . . . took his two wives" [Gen. 32: 23]; this may be interpreted to mean that a man has two wives, one is the wife whom the Creator . . . has commanded him to take in order to be fruitful and multiply, and the other is his holy soul.' For this ambivalence in the representation of women in hasidic homilies, see M. Rosman, 'Observations on Women and Hasidism' (Heb.), in D. Assaf and A. Rapoport-Albert (eds.), *Let the Old Make Way for the New* [Yashan mipenei ḥadash: meḥkarim betoledot yehudei mizraḥ eiropah uvetarbutam, shai le'imanu'el etkes] (Jerusalem, 2009), i. 155–8.

37 Dov Ber of Mezhirech, *Magid devarav leya'akov*, 180 §101, and see also ibid. 186 §111.

38 Menahem Mendel of Vitebsk, *Likutei amarim*, 37*a–b*, and see also ibid. 36*a*.

39 Jacob Joseph of Połonne, *Toledot ya'akov yosef*, 109*b*.

40 Ibid. 17*b*.

41 Id., *Tsafenat pa'ne'aḥ*, 209.

42 Elimelekh of Lizhensk, *No'am elimelekh*, i. 233.

43 Ibid. ii. 583.

44 J. I. Schneersohn, *Sefer hasiḥot* 5702 [1942] (Brooklyn, 1973), 141–3, from a teaching addressed by his father to the yeshiva students on Simhat Torah in 1900. Notably, Joseph Isaac Schneersohn, the sixth Lubavitcher Rebbe, who succeeded his father, Shalom Dovber, in 1920, proceeded, from the 1930s on, to mobilize women as an active Habad constituency, and pioneered their initiation in the speculative teachings of hasidism. This was a radical departure from the norm, which was to revolutionize the status of women in Habad, especially under the leadership of Joseph Isaac's successor, the last Lubavitcher Rebbe, Menachem Mendel Schneerson. The latter, without ever abandoning the traditional conceptualization of the female as material corporeality, was the first to incorporate and even privilege women in the enterprise of hallowing the mundane. In this he followed the paradoxical line of thinking, so characteristic of Habad, whereby it is precisely the darkest corporeal 'matter' that has the capacity for being refined into the purest and most luminous manifestation of spiritual 'form'. This potentiality was being actualized in his own time—the final decades of the 20th century—which he believed to signal the inauguration of the messianic age. See on all this below, Chs. 7 and 8.

45 Each of the two classes has a much wider range of designations, usually suggested by the particular vocabulary of each of the biblical verses or rabbinic dicta in which the hasidic masters often anchor the distinction between them. The dichotomous complementarity of the two classes is the central theme of many hasidic homilies and constitutes a fundamental principle of hasidism. For a review of the range of contrasting designations in the seminal writings of Jacob Joseph of Połonne, see G. Nigal, *Leader and Congregation: Opinions and Parables in the Beginning of Hasidism According to the Writings of R. Jacob Joseph of Połonne* [Manhig ve'edah: de'ot umeshalim bereshit haḥasidut al pi kitvei r. ya'akov yosef mipolna'ah] (Jerusalem, 1962), 58–60.

46 Jacob Joseph of Połonne, *Ketonet pasim*, 87.

47 Id., *Toledot ya'akov yosef*, 188*d*.

48 See e.g. BT *Ber.* 61*a*; *Gen. Rabbah* 8: 1.

49 Jacob Joseph of Połonne, *Ketonet pasim*, 95.

50 Id., *Toledot ya'akov yosef*, 121*b*, and see also id., *Tsafenat pa'ne'aḥ*, 394–5.

51 *Toledot ya'akov yosef*, 153*d*.

52 See BT *BB* 74*a*. The Aramaic for 'touch each other' here is *nashki*, which in Hebrew means primarily 'kiss'.

53 Ephraim of Sudyłków, *Degel maḥaneh efrayim*, 'Tsav', 91–2.

54 See Nigal, *Leader and Congregation* (Heb.), 58–65; id., *Rabbi Jacob Joseph of Połonne (Polna): Selected Writings* [Torot ba'al hatoledot: derashot rabi ya'akov yosef mipolna'ah lefi nose'ei yesod] (Jerusalem, 1974), 3–46; S. Dresner, *The Zaddik: The Doctrine of the Zaddik According to the Writings of Rabbi Yaakov Yosef of Polnoy* (London, 1960), 136–41; Weiss, 'Beginnings of Hasidism' (Heb.), 82–8.

55 See e.g. *Mekhilta derabi yishma'el*, 'Baḥodesh', 3: '"The Lord came from Sinai" [Deut. 33: 2] to receive Israel, as a bridegroom comes forth to meet the bride.' This is a common theme, most prominently underlying the rabbinic interpretation of the Song of Songs as an allegory of the love between God and Israel.

56 See above, Ch. 2, at nn. 75–96.

57 Elimelekh of Lizhensk, *No'am elimelekh*, ii. 315. When the tsadik prays or reveals his *torah* he is in direct contact with the Upper Worlds, from which he draws the divine 'bounty' to bestow it on the worlds below. This is his higher, 'male' mode of operation, as distinct from the lower, 'female' mode, which consists of mere guidance on upright religious and moral conduct (*musar*). For

a clear definition of *musar* as a lower level of instruction, in which *torah* may be 'clothed' in order to make it accessible to all, see N. Sternharz, *Ḥayei moharan*, i (Jerusalem, 1947), 'Nesiato le'erets yisra'el', 65 §19.

58 Elimelekh of Lizhensk, *No'am elimelekh*, i. 27–8.

59 Jacob Joseph of Połonne, *Toledot ya'akov yosef*, 36*b*.

60 Elimelekh of Lizhensk, *No'am elimelekh*, i. 168.

61 Ibid. 283.

62 On which see below, Chs. 6–8.

63 See e.g. G. Nigal, 'Women in the Book *Shivḥei habesht*' (Heb.), *Molad*, 31[241] (1974), 138–45, repr. in id., *Studies in Hasidism* [Meḥkarim baḥasidut] (Jerusalem, 1999), ii. 365–78; id., *Women in Hasidic Hagiography* [Nashim basiporet haḥasidit] (Jerusalem, 2005); Rosman, 'Observations on Women and Hasidism' (Heb.), 162–3.

64 See BT *BB* 12*a*, and the discussions in E. E. Urbach, *The World of the Sages: Collected Studies* [Me'olamam shel ḥakhamim: kovets meḥkarim] (Jerusalem, 1988), 9–49; A. J. Heschel, *Prophetic Inspiration After the Prophets: Maimonides and Other Medieval Authorities*, ed. M. M. Faierstein (Hoboken, NJ, 1996), 1–13. Cf. also Rapoport-Albert, *Women and the Messianic Heresy of Sabbatai Zevi*, 57–62.

65 There were exceptions, usually in the context of local messianic agitation, e.g. 'the Prophet of Avila' in Spain at the end of the 13th century, and other such popular figures known as prophets in pre-expulsion Spain, on whom only fragments of information have survived (see Y. F. Baer, *A History of the Jews in Christian Spain* (Philadelphia, 1966), i. 277–81; ii. 159–62, 356–8). Visionary-mystical activity is also attested in pre-kabbalistic circles in Germany and France during the 12th and 13th centuries, e.g. Rabbi Tröstlin, also known as Nehemiah ben Solomon, the Prophet of Erfurt, or Ezra, the Prophet of Montcontour (see Scholem, *Origins of the Kabbalah* (Princeton, NJ, 1987), 239–40; M. Idel, 'Some Forlorn Writings of a Forgotten Ashkenazi Prophet, R. Nehemiah Ben Shlomo Ha-Navi', *Jewish Quarterly Review*, 96 (2005), 188–96). For a review and discussion of the problematics of prophecy, see Heschel, *Prophetic Inspiration*, 13–67.

66 See n. 13 above. Mistrust of fresh prophetic revelation would seem to characterize the post-Sabbatian kabbalah generally. There is evidence for this in, for example, what has been termed the Lithuanian kabbalistic school, originating in Elijah, the Gaon of Vilna, and persisting among his disciples and followers from the 18th right through to the early 20th century. On this see Schuchat, 'Lithuanian Kabbalah as an Independent Trend of Kabbalistic Literature' (Heb.), *Kabbalah: Journal for the Study of Jewish Mystical Texts*, 10 (2004), 203–6.

67 See A. Green, 'Typologies of Leadership and the Hasidic Zaddiq', in id. (ed.),

Jewish Spirituality, ii: *From the Sixteenth-Century Revival to the Present* (New York, 1987), 146–9; M. Piekarz, *The Hasidic Leadership: Authority and Faith in Tsadikim as Reflected in the Hasidic Literature* [Hahanhagah haḥasidit: samkhut ve'emunat tsadikim be'aspaklaryat sifrutah shel haḥasidut] (Jerusalem, 1999), 16–22. For a typology of mystical prophecy, and the rightful claim that, despite their reluctance to acknowledge it by name, the hasidic masters displayed a range of prophetic powers rooted in a variety of earlier kabbalistic traditions, see Idel, 'On Prophecy and Early Hasidism', in M. Sharon (ed.), *Studies in Modern Religions, Religious Movements and the Babi-Baha'i Faiths* (Leiden, 2004), 41–75; id., 'The Besht as Prophet and Talismanic Magician' (Heb.), in A. Lipsker and R. Kushelevsky (eds.), *Studies in Jewish Narrative Presented to Yoav Elstein* [Ma'aseh sipur: meḥkarim basifrut hayehudit mugashim leyo'av elshtein] (Ramat Gan, 2006).

68 For the ironic use of the designation *nevi'im* (prophets) or the downright derogatory *nevi'ei sheker* (false prophets) in the anti-hasidic polemical literature of the late 18th century, see Weiss, *Studies in Eastern European Jewish Mysticism*, 39–40 n. 9, where he concludes: 'The conspicuous absence of any reference to this term in the Hasidic literature is no doubt due to the bad reputation of the word *navi* and has to be regarded as apologetical silence.' Weiss is not entirely accurate. Admittedly, the hasidic masters often endorse the classical rabbinic preference for the sage over the prophet, reiterating the notion that prophecy ceased with the last of the biblical prophets or the destruction of the Temple (see e.g. Epstein, *Ma'or vashemesh*, 'Vayigash', i. 113, 'Rimzei purim', i. 243; Simhah Bunem of Pshischa (Przysucha), *Kol mevaser*, 'Teshuvah', iii. 88 §16; Israel ben Sabbatai Hofstein of Kozienice, *Avodat yisra'el hashalem*, 'Likutim', 177; J. L. Alter, *Sefat emet al hatorah* (Jerusalem, 1997), iv: *Bemidbar*, 'Balak' 5649 [1889], 5650 [1890], and ibid. v: *Devarim*, 'Shofetim' 5652 [1892], 5661 [1901]). At times they even expressly disavow any claim to the prophetic title (see e.g. Menahem Mendel of Vitebsk's pastoral letters from the Land of Israel in J. Barnai, *Letters of Hasidim from the Land of Yisrael* [Igerot ḥasidim me'erets yisra'el] (Jerusalem, 1980), 146 no. 31, 167 no. 39, and 238 no. 63). And yet some are not averse to ascribing the status of prophecy to their own utterances (see e.g. Nahman of Bratslav in *Likutei moharan*, pt. II, *torah* 1, §8 and *torah* 8, §8, where—while acknowledging that there are no longer any prophets—he asserts that the 'spirit of prophecy' still rests upon every genuine 'leader', and he refers to the leader's prayer as prophecy, albeit without referring to himself as a prophet). They may also equate the tsadikim with prophets or with 'sons of prophets' (*benei hanevi'im*) by way of commentary on the biblical verses that mention these terms (e.g. Zevi Elimelekh of Dynów, *Agra dekhalah*, 'Shofetim', 198–9). Even Kalonymos Kalman Epstein (*Ma'or vashemesh*, 'Vayigash', i. 114) credits the 'great tsadikim', when they are attached to the supernal worlds, with the ability to prophesy and foretell the future, since 'the Shekhinah is speaking through their throats'. Nevertheless the claim to the title *navi* was rare and seems to have been viewed as problematic. Notably, the synonymous designation *ḥozeh* (seer), by which the founding father of Polish hasidism, Jacob Isaac Horowitz, the 'Seer of Lublin' (1745?–1815), became widely known, appears to be of late provenance and was not in use in the hasidic movement of his own lifetime (see D. Assaf, *Untold Tales of the Hasidim: Crisis & Discontent in the History of Hasidism* (Hanover, 2010), 266 n. 1, 274 n. 65). For a hasidic controversy in the mid-1860s about the cessation or otherwise of the holy spirit and the gift of prophecy 'in our own time', see id., 'The Clash over *Or Ha-Hayim*', *Modern Judaism*, 29/2 (May 2009), 194–225. See also the discussion in U. Gellman, 'Hasidism in Poland in the First Half of the Nineteenth Century: Typologies of Leadership and Devotees' [Ha-ḥasidut bepolin bamaḥatsit harishonah shel hame'ah hatesha esreh: tipologyah shel manhigut ve'edah], unpublished Ph.D. diss. (Hebrew University, 2011), 72–88.

69 *In Praise of the Baal Shem Tov*, ed. D. Ben-Amos and J. R. Mintz (Bloomington, Ind., 1970), 4 (with minor modifications to the translation), following the text of the first Hebrew edition (Kopys, 1814). The Berdiczów edition of the work (1815) has the following additional sentence here: 'And now, because of our many sins, these things have disappeared. There were also, in our generation, righteous men who revealed the secrets of the future, and by means of this, faith in God and the Torah was strengthened.'

70 See e.g. *In Praise of the Baal Shem Tov*, ed. Ben-Amos and Mintz, 234–5 §228; 63 §48, together with 67 §50, and time and again *passim*.

71 See Zvi Mark's analysis of madness as depicted in *Shivḥei habesht* (Mark, '*Dibbuk* and *Devekut* in *In Praise of the Baal Shem Tov*: Notes on the Phenomenology of Madness in Early Hasidism' (Heb.), in I. Etkes et al. (eds.), *Within Hasidic Circles* (Heb.), 247–86; id., *Mysticism and Madness in the Work of R. Nahman of Bratslav* [Mistikah veshiga'on biyetsirat r. naḥman mibratslav] (Tel Aviv, 2003), 18–46; this whole section has been omitted from the abridged English version of the book), which demonstrates that phenomenologically the madman and the tsadik are, indeed, closely analogous.

72 For the relationship between Nahman of Kosów and the Besht see above, Ch. 1, at nn. 12–17.

73 *In Praise of the Baal Shem Tov*, ed. Ben-Amos and Mintz, 208 §209.

74 Ibid. 208–10.

75 Mark, '*Dibbuk* and *Devekut*' (Heb.), 256; id., *Mysticism and Madness* (Heb.), 25.

76 See Scholem, *Major Trends in Jewish Mysticism*, 333–4; id., *Studies and Texts Concerning the History of Sabbatianism* (Heb.), 115; id., *The Latest Phase: Essays on Hasidism* (Heb.), 79–81, 238–40, and cf. above, at n. 20.

77 Weiss, *Studies in Eastern European Jewish Mysticism*, 29–30.

78 Ibid. 30.

79 See J. Emden, *Sefer hitabekut* (Lwów, 1877), 80*b*; id. [David Avaz], *Petaḥ einayim*, 14*b* (Altona, 1757).

80 Idel questions the Sabbatian background of the Kosów circle and its decision to desist from prophesying in the context of his overall rejection of Scholem's (and consequently also Weiss's) claim that hasidism had emerged from, and largely as a reaction to, Sabbatianism. See Idel, 'On Prophecy and Early Hasidism', 44–5; id., 'The Besht as Prophet' (Heb.), 122–4.

81 These terms are reminiscent of the Ba'al Shem Tov's mission to 'rectify' sinful souls and to secure their personal salvation as they seek admission to Paradise. Cf. e.g. the tale entitled 'The Besht and the Frog' in *In Praise of the Baal Shem Tov*, ed. Ben-Amos and Mintz, 24–6 §12, or the Ba'al Shem Tov's own report, in his letter to his brother-in-law, of his visionary encounter with innumerable souls pleading for his assistance in their endeavour to ascend to ever higher levels of the celestial worlds, in L. Jacobs, *Jewish Mystical Testimonies* (New York, 1977), 150.

82 An oblique reference to the appearance of Sabbatai Zevi and the mass messianic movement he inspired in the mid-1660s.

83 Taz is an acronymic reference to the celebrated talmudist and rabbi of Lwów, David ben Samuel Halevi (1586–1667), who became known by the title of his famous work *Turei zahav*, a commentary on a section of Joseph Caro's *Shulḥan arukh*. Swept up in the messianic frenzy which had erupted towards the end of his life, he appointed his two sons emissaries of his community, and in the spring of 1666 sent them to pay homage to Sabbatai Zevi, who was at that time imprisoned in Gallipoli. See Scholem, *Sabbatai Ṣevi*, 600–1, 620–7.

84 A kabbalistic technique whereby mental images of intertwining divine names, representing sefirotic integration, are contemplated, and they empower the practitioner to commune with the souls of the dead or with other supernal entities.

85 Z. H. Eichenstein, *Turn Aside from Evil and Do Good: An Introduction and a Way to the Tree of Life*, trans. with annotations and introd. by L. Jacobs (London, 1995), 83–4 (first published in Hebrew as *Sur mera va'aseh tov* (Lemberg, 1832)). The author goes on to guide the reader, basing himself on Hayim Vital's prophetic manual, *Sha'ar hakedushah*, on how to avoid being deluded by impure spirits and to attain the genuine holy spirit by means of Torah study, prayer, purification of the body's materiality, and the subduing of the evil inclination.

86 See Mark, '*Dibbuk* and *Devekut*' (Heb.), 268–74, 282–4; id., *Mysticism and Madness* (Heb.), 35–40.

87 The first edition of *Shivḥei habesht* (Kopys, 1814) was quickly followed in 1815 by two further editions, published in Berdiczów and Łaszczów respectively, as well as by a Yiddish edition, first published in Ostrog in the same year, and again in Korets (Korzec) in 1816. The publication history of *Me'ore'ot tsevi* is a little harder to establish. A Lemberg edition purporting to have been published in 1804 (under the title *Sipur ḥalomot vekets hapela'ot*) is taken by most bibliographers and scholars to have appeared only in 1824. Israel Yofeh first published the work (under the title *Me'ore'ot tsevi*) in Kopys, apparently in two editions, 1814 and 1815, of which only the latter is extant. The title page of this edition refers, without supplying any details, to an earlier edition which has 'sold out', necessitating republication. There are several subsequent editions. See also Mark, '*Dibbuk* and *Devekut*' (Heb.), 270 n. 62; Werses, *Haskalah and Sabbatianism* (Heb.), 220–6.

88 For Yofeh's affiliation with Habad see Heilman, *Beit rabi*, 149 (= 75*a*); M. Rosman, 'The History of a Historical Source: On the Editing of *Shivḥei habesht*' (Heb.), *Zion*, 58/2 (1993), 177–80.

89 Mark, '*Dibbuk* and *Devekut*' (Heb.), 272–3; id., *Mysticism and Madness* (Heb.), 38–9.

90 Mark, '*Dibbuk* and *Devekut*' (Heb.), 273–4; id., *Mysticism and Madness* (Heb.), 39.

91 *In Praise of the Baal Shem Tov*, ed. Ben-Amos and Mintz, 'The Printer's Preface', 2.

92 This is the honorific acronym of *adonenu, morenu verabenu* (our master, teacher, and rabbi), by which it is commonly assumed that Yofeh was referring to his late hasidic master, Habad's founder, Shneur Zalman of Liady, who had died two years previously. See *Shivḥei haba'al shem tov: A Facsimile of a Unique Manuscript, Variant Versions, and Appendices* [Sefer shivḥei habesht: faksimil miketav hayad hayeḥidi hanoda lanu veshinuyei nusaḥav le'umat nusaḥ hadefus], ed. Y. Mondshine (Jerusalem, 1982), 19 n. 37; Rosman, 'History of a Historical Source' (Heb.), 179–80; and cf. *In Praise of the Ba'al Shem Tov (Shivḥei Ha-Besht) with Introduction and Annotations* [Shivḥei habesht: mahadurah mu'eret umevo'eret], ed. A. Rubinstein (Jerusalem, 1991), 25 n. 23.

93 *In Praise of the Baal Shem Tov*, ed. Ben-Amos and Mintz, 6, with some modifications to the translation.

94 See e.g. E. Reiner, '*Shivḥei habesht*: Transmission, Editing, Printing' (Heb.), in *Proceedings of the Eleventh World Congress of Jewish Studies* (Jerusalem, 1994), division *c*, ii. 145–52; Rosman, 'History of a Historical Source' (Heb.); Rubinstein, 'The Revelation Stories in *Shivḥei habesht*' (Heb.), *Alei sefer*, 6–7 (1977), 157–86; *Shivḥei haba'al shem tov*, ed. Mondshine.

95 It is difficult to establish their precise number, since the Kopys edition does not number the tales, and it is not always possible to decide where one ends and the other begins. Subsequent editors have introduced various divisions of the narrative into numbered paragraphs. The English edition lists 'The Beginning of the Writer's Manuscript' as tale 17 (*In Praise of the Baal Shem Tov*, ed. Ben-Amos and Mintz, 32), counting sixteen discrete units in Yofeh's preceding cycle of tales.

96 Ibid. 31.

97 See Reiner, '*Shivḥei habesht*' (Heb.).

98 See Rosman, 'History of a Historical Source' (Heb.), 192–205.

99 See *Shivḥei haba'al shem tov*, ed. Mondshine, 20.

100 See Rosman, 'History of a Historical Source' (Heb.), 183–92.

101 See ibid. 202–5.

102 See ibid. 193, 202–5.

103 The relationship between the two tales was observed by Rubinstein ('Revelation Stories' (Heb.), 166), although following what is clearly an explanatory interpolation in the Korets (Korzec) Yiddish edition of *Shivḥei habesht*, he treated them as referring to two consecutive events. The tales were rightly juxtaposed as alternative accounts of the same event by Zvi Mark ('*Dibbuk* and *Devekut*' (Heb.), 252–7; id., *Mysticism and Madness* (Heb.), 22–6), whose analysis I follow here, even though his main concern is to establish the affinity between madness and prophecy, while mine is to highlight the gender boundaries of each.

104 See on him e.g. Heschel, *The Circle of the Baal Shem Tov: Studies in Hasidism*, ed. S. H. Dresner (Chicago, 1985), 44–112.

105 *In Praise of the Baal Shem Tov*, ed. Ben-Amos and Mintz, 34.

106 The town in question is clearly Kuty, as becomes apparent directly below.

107 *In Praise of the Baal Shem Tov*, ed. Ben-Amos and Mintz, 34.

108 Ibid.

109 For the Besht's primary role as a *ba'al shem*, and the status of *ba'alei shem* in his day, see G. Scholem, 'The Historical Figure of R. Israel Ba'al Shem Tov' (Heb.), in id., *The Latest Phase: Essays on Hasidism* (Heb.), 106–45; M. Rosman, *Founder of Hasidism: A Quest for the Historical Ba'al Shem Tov* (Berkeley, Calif., 1996), 11–26; I. Etkes, *The Besht: Magician, Mystic, and Leader*, trans. S. Sternberg (Waltham, Mass., 2005), 7–78.

110 See Weiss, *Studies in Eastern European Jewish Mysticism*, 34–8; Heschel, *The Circle of the Baal Shem Tov*, 45–7.

111 See above, at nn. 70–1.

112 See G. Nigal, *'Dybbuk' Tales in Jewish Literature* [Sipurei 'dibuk' besifrut yisra'el], 2nd edn. (Jerusalem, 1994), 229–63; id., *The Hasidic Tale*, trans.

E. Levin (Oxford, 2008), 208–11, 320–1; id., *Magic, Mysticism and Hasidism: The Supernatural in Jewish Thought* (Northvale, NJ, 1994), 67–133. For the ambivalent status of possession as 'religious madness'—a manifestation either of the holy spirit or of the demonic forces—see Chajes, *Between Worlds*, 119–38; Mark, *Mysticism and Madness* (Heb.), 18–46. By the 19th century, at least in the West, under the earlier impact of scepticism and the Enlightenment, this type of madness had been largely rationalized, psychologized, medicalized, and increasingly confined. On this see e.g. M. Foucault, *History of Madness*, ed. J. Khalfa, trans. J. Murphy and J. Khalfa (London, 2006); R. Porter, *Madness: A Brief History* (Oxford, 2002); A. Goldberg, *Sex, Religion, and the Making of Modern Madness: The Eberbach Asylum and German Society 1815–1849* (Oxford, 1999); T. S. Szasz, *The Manufacture of Madness* (London, 1971).

113 *In Praise of the Baal Shem Tov*, ed. Ben-Amos and Mintz, 27 §14.

114 Ibid. 26–7 §13.

115 The community in question is, again, Kuty, and the rabbi is the same Moses, head of the local rabbinical court. See *In Praise of the Ba'al Shem Tov*, ed. Rubinstein, 55 n. 4.

116 Mishnah *Avot* 2: 5.

117 *In Praise of the Baal Shem Tov*, ed. Ben-Amos and Mintz, 27–8 §14.

118 See Rosman, 'History of a Historical Source' (Heb.), 202–5.

119 See *In Praise of the Baal Shem Tov*, ed. Ben-Amos and Mintz, 35 §20.

120 Ibid. 96–7 §75.

121 Ibid. 97. For feminist readings of this tale see D. Biale, 'A Feminist Reading' (Heb.), 139–43; R. Dvir-Goldberg, 'Voice of a Subterranean Fountain: The Image of a Woman through the Hasidic Tale' (Heb.), *Jerusalem Studies in Jewish Folklore*, 21 (2001), 27–44.

122 Sternharz, *Ḥayei moharan*, i, 'Mekom yeshivato unesiotav', 54 §11.

123 See Rapoport-Albert, *Women and the Messianic Heresy of Sabbatai Zevi*, 57.

124 See above, at n. 68.

125 For the presumed time of writing see N. T. Koenig, *Neveh tsadikim* (Benei Berak, 1969), 76.

126 A nickname of Slavonic derivation meaning honest, just, righteous.

127 N. N. Donner, *Mayim rabim* (Warsaw, 1899), repr. in *Holy Books by the Disciples of the Ba'al Shem Tov* [Sefarim kedoshim mitalmidei ba'al shem tov], xviii (Brooklyn, 1984), 137. See also Heschel, *The Circle of the Baal Shem Tov*, 153; D. Assaf, 'A Messianic Vision among Volhynian Hasidim' (Heb.), *Gal-ed*, 20 (2006), 48 n. 36, and below, Ch. 6, n. 54. Donner's brief reference to Yente the Prophetess, which, to the best of my knowledge, is the earliest and only source for this tradition, gave rise to an elaborate Yiddish adaptation, which places

Yente within an unbroken tradition of illustrious hasidic prophetesses and claims that she adopted an ascetic lifestyle, abstained from conjugal relations, performed great miracles, and was proclaimed a prophetess by none other than the Besht himself. See M. Feinkind, *Female Rebbes and Famous Personalities in Poland* [Froyen rabonim un barimte perzenlekhkaytn in poylen] (Warsaw, 1937), 20–5. All this is entirely fictional, and clearly inspired by the oral traditions about the Maid of Ludmir and other female hasidic leaders, first noted by Horodetsky (on which see Ch. 6 below).

128 See above, pp. 276–7.

129 See ibid. Note, however, the possible allusion to her in a hasidic hagiographical source published in 1892 (Ch. 6, n. 43 below).

SIX

On Women in Hasidism: S. A. Horodetsky and the Maid of Ludmir Tradition

'THE JEWISH WOMAN was given complete equality in the emotional, mystical, religious life of Beshtian hasidism.' This statement was made in 1923 by S. A. Horodetsky in his book *Haḥasidut vehaḥasidim*, where he devoted a short chapter to 'The Jewish Woman in Hasidism'.[1] It was Horodetsky who first singled out the position of women in hasidism as an area of sufficient novelty and interest to merit particular discussion, and his view of the matter, now more than ninety years old, has been remarkably durable. In one form or another, acknowledged or unacknowledged, Horodetsky's findings as well as his analysis lie behind virtually every subsequent treatment of the subject in the popular, belletristic, and semi-scholarly literature about hasidism, as well as in the now growing library of works, of limited scholarly merit but considerable apologetic thrust, about

This essay arose from work carried out during 1984–5 at Harvard Divinity School, where I spent a most stimulating and enjoyable year as Visiting Lecturer and Research Associate to the Women in Religion programme. I am grateful to all my friends and colleagues there, and at the Center for the Study of World Religions, for wearing down my initial resistance to thinking in gender categories, and for pointing me in the direction of a new field of investigation, which has proved to be most rewarding.

Following the first publication of the essay, I was able to update it to some extent in preparation for the Hebrew version, first published in D. Assaf (ed.), *Zaddik and Devotees: Historical and Social Aspects of Hasidism* [Tsadik ve'edah: hebetim historiyim veḥevratiyim beḥeker haḥasidut] (Jerusalem, 2001), 496–527, and reprinted without any further revisions in my *Studies in Hasidism, Sabbatianism, and Gender* [Ḥasidim veshabeta'im, anashim venashim] (Jerusalem, 2015), 223–54. The present version contains the new material first added to that Hebrew version, as well as some additional references to sources of which I became aware only subsequently.

the position of women in Judaism generally.[2] Notably, the scholarly literature on the history of hasidism has generally ignored the subject, implicitly dismissing it as marginal or at any rate insufficiently documented to permit serious consideration.[3]

Horodetsky highlighted the equality he perceived between men and women in hasidism by contrasting it with the exclusion of women from active participation in the intellectual and devotional life of what he called 'official Judaism' or 'rabbinism'.[4] Deploying here the categories from which he was later to construct a framework for the interpretation of Jewish civilization as a whole, the categories of 'intellectual' versus 'emotional' Judaism,[5] he identified rabbinism as intellectual, while portraying the distinct mystical-messianic elements of the tradition, from which he believed hasidism to have evolved, as primarily emotional. Since he shared as a matter of course the common assumption that intellectuality was by nature a male attribute while the female temperament was innately emotional,[6] he was able to portray rabbinism as inherently, and so also effectively, the exclusive domain of men, while conceiving of mystical messianism, and ultimately hasidism, as inherently, and so historically, more accessible to women:

> Emotional religion, which transcends all rules and regulations; emotional Judaism, which knows no limitations or differentiation, accommodated the Jewish woman and allowed her much scope for direct involvement. [In] messianism . . . that popular movement which arose to liberate . . . pure faith and religious emotion from the yoke of innumerable laws and regulations . . . we see the Jewish woman taking part with the full ardour of her emotions. She played an especially important role in the messianic movement of Sabbatai Zevi, which produced women leaders of immense influence. With the rise of kabbalism, as it gradually descended from its esoteric heights to affect directly the spiritual lives of all the people, it also affected the life of the Jewish woman. The Lurianic kabbalah in particular had a great impact on the Jews of Poland in the sixteenth and seventeenth centuries, and the Polish Jewish woman was emotionally receptive to it in full.[7]

Horodetsky does not supply any evidence to support these far-reaching claims, and it is difficult to imagine what concrete instances he may have had in mind. In fact, the total absence of women from the Jewish mystical tradition as it has come down to us contrasts sharply with the relative prominence of women in the comparable traditions of both Christian and

Islamic mysticism.[8] Women did take part in such phenomena as mass prophecy inspired by Sabbatianism in its earlier phases, but they were not central to it and could hardly be conceived as 'leaders of immense influence'. Nor does this description fit any of Sabbatai Zevi's wives, who appear to have played no significant role in the development of the movement. Jacob Frank's daughter Eva does perhaps fit the bill a little better, but it would be absurd for Horodetsky to anchor his claims in this grotesque aberration of Jewish mystical messianism.[9] As for the receptivity of women to the Lurianic kabbalah in particular, or its special impact on their lives, there seems to be no evidence for it whatsoever.

It is only when he comes to his main subject of concern, the position of women in the hasidic movement, that Horodetsky is able to focus his argument more precisely. He identifies three areas in which the equality between men and women in hasidism is manifest:

1. Hasidism improved the position of women in the community and altogether strengthened Jewish family life by uniting husband and wife through their joint allegiance to the tsadik, an affiliation which acted as an equalizing force between the sexes.

2. Hasidism threw open the gates of scholarship to women by producing—in addition to works in Hebrew, which were accessible only to educated men—a large body of literature for women in the vernacular Yiddish. As a result, the largest obstacle on the way to women's spiritual and intellectual equality with men was removed.

3. Given the right circumstances, hasidism enabled some women to rise even to the ranks of the tsadikim, the predominantly male leaders of the movement. 'If the woman was worthy, nothing could stand in her way.'[10]

Every one of these claims may be qualified, countered, or quite plainly reversed. They appear to have been inspired by Horodetsky's Zionist feminism, combined with his evaluation of hasidism as anticipating, and so capable of providing an authentically Jewish model for, the rebirth of the Jewish nation on its land, cleansed of all the diaspora maladies of rabbinism.[11]

Considering his arguments in order, the following observations seem pertinent.

1. Far from improving the condition of women within hasidic family life, reinforced, as alleged, by the equality of husband and wife before the tsadik, hasidism can be seen as effecting precisely the opposite: *mitnagedim* and *maskilim* alike accused hasidism, with considerable justification, of undermining the institution of Jewish marriage and aggravating the condition of women by drawing young married men—the main recruits to the movement in its formative years[12]—away from their wives and children for periods ranging from several weeks to several months and more. They abandoned the women to fend for themselves materially[13] and, even more crucially, absented themselves at precisely those points in the Jewish calendar—the sabbath and festivals, the most popular times of assembly at the 'court' of the hasidic leader[14]—at which the presence of the husband and father was essential for proper ritual celebration at home.[15] In fact, as an emotionally charged and exclusively male fraternity grouped around the figure of the tsadik as father,[16] speaking of 'love' as the mutual relationship between the tsadik and his followers as well as among the members of the fraternity themselves,[17] celebrating the highest moments of communal activity at a 'table', during a 'meal', on the occasions traditionally set aside for domestic worship and festivity, hasidism provided an effective alternative to traditional family life. It did not, of course, renounce marriage formally or on a permanent basis, but it allowed its followers some room for periodic liberation from marital and family ties for the sake of the higher pursuit of spiritual invigoration.[18] In the early generations the hasidic movement offered young men the opportunity for an emotionally intense affiliation with a new, women-free spiritual family, an affiliation which entailed in some cases a partial or even complete break with the non-hasidic or anti-hasidic biological families of the recruits.[19] This separation diminished in time, as the initial affiliation with hasidism ceased to be a voluntary act by individual males and became more commonly inherited, encompassing whole families, which were now associated with one hasidic group or another by established family tradition.

Whether or not at this stage the position of hasidic women was significantly different from that of their non-hasidic counterparts is extremely difficult to assess. The general impression, however, is that women continued, on the whole, to be excluded from the life of the hasidic court. They did not usually accompany their husbands on their visits to the rebbe, although they could, at least in some courts, gain direct access to him in their own right, to be advised and blessed by him as were his male followers; but they did not attend the all-important sessions at his 'table', where he delivered his teachings to the exclusively male gathering of his followers.[20] It is difficult to estimate to what extent this degree of access, and its impact on the women's sense of active personal involvement with hasidism, differed from the access a non-hasidic woman would have had to a local rabbinic authority and her sense of involvement and identification with the values of what Horodetsky called rabbinism.

2. Hasidism did produce a considerable body of literature in Yiddish, but this was by no means created especially for women, nor did it represent an attempt to make universally accessible in Yiddish all that had been previously restricted to the Hebrew-reading male elite.

The translation of hasidic works from Hebrew into Yiddish[21] began relatively late, with the publication of the Yiddish version of *Shivḥei habesht* in 1815.[22] This appeared in several editions and versions a few months after the first Hebrew edition of the book was published at the end of 1814. Significantly, as well as being the first hasidic work to become available in Yiddish, *Shivḥei habesht* was also the first hasidic work which may be classified as belonging to the hagiographical genre—a genre that was never invested with the full legitimacy of the speculative-homiletical literature of hasidism, which began to appear in print more than three decades earlier.[23] Moreover, subsequent to this initial publication in both Hebrew and Yiddish, the development of hasidic hagiography was arrested—possibly because of its uncertain status—for at least another fifty years, to be renewed and to achieve popularity, if not full sanction, only in the second half of the nineteenth century.[24] The hagiographical collections which proliferated from this point on, whether they were written in Hebrew or in Yiddish or both, were not directed primarily at women, although women may well have formed a significant proportion of their readership.[25]

The point is that hasidism did not possess, at least not until relatively recently and for extraneous reasons, any ideology of women's education as such.[26] What it did possess was an internally controversial but nevertheless pervasive ideology of the dissemination of the teachings of hasidism as widely as possible, at such different levels of communication and varying degrees of exposure to its more radical esoteric aspects as were considered appropriate for different classes of recruits into the movement.[27] However much it was promoted from the start as a meritorious activity of the highest degree of holiness,[28] the telling, the hearing, and ultimately the reading of tales in praise of the saintly leaders of hasidism in Hebrew, and even more so in Yiddish, served as the lowest point of access into the hasidic orbit.[29] The tales captured the imagination even of ordinary, uneducated Jews, a class within which women had traditionally formed a sub-category.[30] It was only in this incidental capacity that women became a target audience for the hagiographical literature of hasidism. While it is doubtful (although it cannot be ruled out) that they constituted a significant element of the readership of the *Shivḥei habesht* when it was first published at the beginning of the nineteenth century, by the 1860s and 1870s, when the second wave of hasidic hagiography was beginning to flood the book market, it is much more likely that they did. By this time, as we have seen, the hasidic movement had become an affiliation into which one was born, within which one married, and which one passed on to one's offspring, both male and female. Whole families, including the women, became identified by their inherited association with particular hasidic groups. Although the women were no more directly involved in the devotional life of their community than they had been in the early days of the movement,[31] their hasidic identity was firmly established and would have fed on the hagiographical literature that was available to them.

However, alongside this popular literature in the vernacular, hasidism continued to produce, and ascribed the highest value to, a speculative-homiletical mystical and ethical literature of its own, which was published conservatively in Hebrew only, following the publication tradition of comparable works of this genre, a tradition which prevailed in the rabbinical world long before and beyond hasidism. These hasidic works largely consisted of Hebrew transcripts—effectively translations—and recensions of the sermons and discourses delivered orally in Yiddish (peppered with quotations from the Hebrew and Aramaic traditional sources), to an exclusively male audience, by the exclusively male tsadikim. Once in print—always in Hebrew—they remained virtually inaccessible to the women. Moreover, it was with this genre, and in Hebrew, rather than with the hagiographical genre and in Yiddish, that hasidism first launched itself in print in the 1780s and 1790s. In the three and a half decades between 1780 and 1815, from the publication of the first volume of hasidic homilies in Hebrew to that of the first volume of hagiographical tales in Yiddish, at least thirty hasidic books of the former type were published in Hebrew, and they formed an important element of the campaign for the wider dissemination of hasidism during the crucial stage of its expansion beyond the regions of its provenance.[32] It was during the same period that the internal hasidic controversy began about the degree to which it was appropriate to publicize the traditional esoteric, kabbalistic aspects of hasidism in print.[33] Significantly, though not surprisingly, throughout this debate no mention was ever made of women as a distinct class to be initiated into, or, conversely, to be excluded from, any particular level of instruction. Women might be implicitly classified together with 'the ignorant', but they were not explicitly addressed in the literature of hasidism.[34]

3. Horodetsky's final and most dramatic claim is that under the condition of equality between men and women in hasidism, certain women could attain even the position of tsadik, performing the same functions and exerting the same authority as their male colleagues. He begins his account of this by describing a number of mothers, sisters, and daughters (though, interestingly, not wives) of the most famous leaders of hasidism as 'endowed with divine inspiration', 'famous in the world of hasidism for . . . knowledge of rabbinic legends and tales of the lives of the tsadikim', 'influential', 'charitable', or 'sought after by many of the hasidim . . . for a blessing'.[35] Horodetsky does not supply any sources for these epithets. Some of them can be traced back to well-known and early hasidic works while others must be based on later oral traditions whose authenticity is difficult to establish.[36] Nevertheless, the fact that these women enjoyed considerable prestige and reputation in hasidic circles need not be questioned, however late or fragmentary the traditions which portray them in this light. After all, traditional Judaism, going as far back as the classical rabbinic sources, had always acknowledged the possibility that some of the glamour and authority generated by its most distinguished leaders in the realms of piety, humility, and even scholarly and halakhic acumen would reflect on the women most intimately associated with them, who were indeed well placed to acquire many such accomplishments through their proximity to these eminent men.[37] It is not surprising therefore that hasidism, a movement which, almost uniquely in the history of Judaism, had placed at the very centre of its theology and social organization the charismatic personality of the leader, should exploit this tradition to the full and allow the aura

of perfect scholarly, moral, and spiritual attributes, combined with supernatural powers surrounding the figure of the tsadik, to percolate to some of his female relations.

Horodetsky's account of these women is confined to reports of their personal virtues and informal influence in the hasidic world, which was facilitated by their proximity to the distinguished males to whom they were related. He interprets these reports, however, as suggesting that the women in question were considered to be fully fledged 'female tsadikim', and even cites one tradition whereby the brothers of Hannah Hayah of Chernobyl, all tsadikim in their own right and heirs to their famous father R. Mordecai of Chernobyl, had said 'that she was a tsadik just like them',[38] but he supplies no details to illustrate any formal, institutional aspects of her leadership or the leadership of any of the women he mentions in this connection. Such information is provided in abundance by subsequent authors in Yiddish, Hebrew, and more recently also in English and other languages. All are inspired by Horodetsky, but are more systematically, and perhaps more apologetically, concerned to produce a full record of the role of women in the history of Judaism, where hasidism invariably features as an exceptionally dignified chapter. Here we find descriptions of various daughters, mothers, and sisters (again, rarely wives) of the famous tsadikim, including all those originally mentioned by Horodetsky but also others,[39] operating as leaders of hasidic communities in their own right—regularly receiving *kvitlekh* and *pidyonot*, delivering hasidic and ethical teachings to a mixed male and female following (although the logistics of this are not always clear) at their formal, public 'tables', distributing *shirayim*, performing miracles, consulted as equals by their male colleagues, and often adopting rigorous standards of personal piety, displayed by the unusual practices for women of wearing *tsitsit*, as well as *talit* and *gartel* during prayer, and fasting on Mondays and Thursdays.[40] In some cases they are said to have engaged also in learned literary work and to have produced original hasidic writings.[41]

Most of this is reported without references to written documentation, and it appears in popular histories, belletristic works, personal memoirs, and newspaper articles published since the 1930s, but mostly after the Second World War and increasingly (although without any substantial additions to the information contained in the initial reports) in the past few decades, since the challenge of modern feminism has made women leaders in historical Judaism something more than a mere curiosity. Some of the female tsadikim described in this literature are located in the distant past of the beginnings of hasidism in the eighteenth century, but most are nineteenth-century figures and one or two appear to have lived to a very old age, well into the twentieth century, within the lifetimes and living memories of their popular biographers.[42] The lack of earlier, internal hasidic evidence for the institutional leadership of these women, coupled with the abrupt disruption, with the Second World War, of the eastern European hasidic world in which they are said to have operated, has made it virtually impossible to authenticate these late traditions. Nevertheless, as is generally the case with literary adaptations of oral traditions, allowing for a certain measure of exaggeration and romantic idealization, one must assume that they contain an element of truth. The important historical question, however, is not so much whether or not these prominent women existed, which is probable, but rather whether or not the phenomenon of independent female leaders was integrated into the ideology and organization of hasidism and considered to be fully legitimate.

The answer to this question is unequivocally negative. Hasidism did not evolve an ideology of female leadership, any more than it improved the position of women within the family or set out to educate them in Yiddish.

Significantly, it was not the internal literature of hasidism, not even the popular hagiographical works of the nineteenth and early twentieth centuries, that preserved the memory of these female tsadikim and celebrated them as authentic leaders. To the best of my knowledge, we do not possess a single volume of the 'praises' of any one of these women,[43] nor any collection of their teachings in hasidism, kabbalah, or ethics. If such writings exist, they have not been published and remain totally inaccessible. All the reports on the activities of female tsadikim in hasidism have emanated from the periphery of the hasidic world. They have been assembled by writers and scholars who, at best, like Horodetsky, were born into the heart of a hasidic environment before the two World Wars, and would have had good access to its living traditions, but who stepped out of this environment in later life and became exposed to a variety of modern ideologies through whose perspectives they now evaluated the experiences of their youth.[44] While the factual core of the traditions they report need not be questioned and may be essentially correct, the interpretation which they impose on it cannot be taken at face value.

No example can better illustrate this point than the case of Hannah Rachel, the Maid of Ludmir. Her story, in brief, is as follows. The only daughter of Monesh Verbermacher, a well-to-do and educated Jew, she was apparently born in or around 1806 (in some of the accounts the year of her birth is said to have been either 1815 or '*c.*1800', both of which are probably wrong; see in the appendix to the present chapter, pp. 335, 337) in the Volhynian town of Ludmir (Vladimir-Volynsky). From an early age she attracted attention by her beauty and unusual mental abilities: she studied the Bible in the original and learned to write in Hebrew, progressing to the study of talmudic *agadah*, Midrash, and halakhic works. She distinguished herself also by her extraordinary piety, praying with ecstasy three times a day, like a man. As soon as she came of age she was betrothed to a young man from her native city whom she had known and loved since childhood. However, once the engagement was announced, she was forced by custom to stop all contact with her groom until the wedding. This distressed the Maid and she gradually withdrew from society. During this period her mother died, and she began to isolate herself completely. She would spend whole days alone in her room, going out only to visit her mother's grave. On one of these visits in the cemetery she fell into unconsciousness followed by a prolonged and mysterious illness from which she eventually recovered, endowed, as she said, 'with a new and elevated soul'. She broke off her engagement and declared that she would not marry because she had 'transcended the world of the flesh'. From that time on she adopted the full rigour of male ritual observance, and absorbed herself in study and prayer. When her father died, she used her considerable inheritance to build a new *beit midrash* in Ludmir, where she lived in complete seclusion. She soon acquired a reputation for saintliness and miracle-work, and became known as 'the holy Maid of Ludmir'. Men and women from the neighbouring localities, among them scholars and rabbis, began to flock to what became her hasidic court. She would not allow anyone into her room but would address her teachings and blessings from behind the closed door to the many followers gathered in the adjacent room every sabbath, at the third meal. While her popular following grew, the response of the famous (and exclusively male) tsadikim of the region was negative. Some said that an evil or unclean spirit was speaking through her. Pressure was put on the Maid to abandon the practice of tsadikism and resume her rightful female role in marriage. R. Mordecai of Chernobyl, the most eminent tsadik brought into the case, is reported as saying: 'We do not know which famous tsadik's soul has transmigrated into this woman, but it is hard for the soul of a tsadik to find peace in the body of a woman.'[45] Through his intervention she finally agreed to marry,[46] but the marriage was never consummated and soon ended in divorce. She married again, but divorced once more, remaining a 'maid' to the end of her life. Her marriages, however unsuccessful, did nevertheless have the desired effect of putting an end to her career as a tsadik, and her following declined sharply. She spent her last years in the Holy Land, where she died in obscurity in old age.

This biographical sketch is based on what appears to be the earliest written report of the Maid of Ludmir—a short article in Russian published by S. A. Horodetsky in 1909.[47] All subsequent accounts, including Horodetsky's own adaptation of the material in his Hebrew book of 1923,[48] are derived from this original version.[49] Horodetsky informs his readers in a note[50] that his account is based on 'the reports of old women from Volhynia who remembered the Maid of Ludmir personally'. This suggests that no written accounts of the Maid were available to him. M. Klyachko, responding to Horodetsky's article in a note published in the same journal two years later,[51] adds a further detail to the story: apparently the Maid not only received supplicants in her own house but also travelled to the neighbouring towns and villages, where she preached in the synagogues. In addition, 'it is quite certain that she once travelled to Starokonstantinov [Konstantin Yashan, quite far from Ludmir], where the local women gathered and she delivered a religious sermon to them. Old women in Starokonstantinov still talk about this visit.' This report confirms the nature of the evidence: the author, like Horodetsky, is drawing on what he had heard from old women who claimed to have witnessed the events themselves. Interestingly, this report of the Maid conflicts with her reclusive image as it emerges from Horodetsky's tradition, as well as suggesting, in contrast to Horodetsky, that her leadership was primarily directed towards a female, not a male, following. Another detail is supplied by a later source in Horodetsky's name, although it is not present in his own accounts of the Maid's life: during her final years in the Holy Land, she was apparently involved, together with an old kabbalist, in a private and abortive attempt to bring about the advent of the messiah.[52]

Some of the subsequent versions of the story are richer in detail but clearly further removed from the oral sources, or else quite plainly construed as works of fiction—fanciful adaptations of the material contained in these first reports.[53] Common to all is the evaluation of the story as the most conclusive evidence for the 'equal opportunities' aspect of hasidism, which opened up to women full scope for publicly acknowledged intellectual and spiritual leadership. The fact, noted by Horodetsky and subsequently taken up by others, that the Maid of Ludmir was not related by family ties to any of the male tsadikim of her time is used to highlight the revolutionary novelty of the phenomenon, since the reports relating to her practice of tsadikism cannot be relegated to the more traditional category of associative authority, such that could always be derived by some women from their distinguished male relatives.[54]

While Horodetsky's account of the Maid in his 1923 Hebrew book contains no additional information to that which was available to him in 1909, his interpretation of the material had altered somewhat in the intervening years. The tone of the earlier version is restrained and cautious:

> In hasidism a modest, passive role is attached to a woman. From time to time she may approach a tsadik, pour out her soul before him and receive counsel and a blessing from him. Very rarely in the history of hasidism do we encounter active female characters who have influence on their surroundings. Among these holy women, who came close to the level of tsadik, is the enigmatic personality . . . immortalized in popular tradition under the name of the Maid of Ludmir.[55]

By 1923 Horodetsky had come to regard the same material as representing a radical change in the position of women, to which he referred as 'complete equality' with men in every aspect of the hasidic way of life.[56] Those few 'active female characters' who, in 1909, had been portrayed cautiously as 'coming close to the level of tsadik' were being celebrated by 1923 as 'veritable tsadikim', of whom the most remarkable and clear-cut example was the Maid of Ludmir—'one woman from amongst the masses [that is, rather than from the household of an established hasidic leader] who had merited, and risen to, the rank of a famous "female tsadik"'.[57] This shift in Horodetsky's perception may be accounted for in part by the fact that by the time when he was writing the later, Hebrew version of the story, he had been living in western Europe for some fifteen years, having left his native Ukraine in 1907 under the impact of the pogroms in the earlier years of the decade. By contrast, the first, Russian version in *Evreiskaya Starina* had been written while he was still freshly steeped in the atmosphere of the oral traditions he set out to record.[58] One must take into account also Horodetsky's exposure to Western society and culture during those years of university education and intellectual work in Zurich, Bern, and particularly Berlin, where German feminism, including Jewish feminism under the leadership of Bertha Pappenheim, was well in evidence.[59] All this, together with his growing involvement in the Zionist movement during the period when the Second and Third Aliyot were experimenting with the foundations of a revolutionary society in the Holy Land, where the women were to play, in theory if not always in practice, an equal part alongside the men,[60] may have combined to heighten Horodetsky's sensitivity to the issue of the equality of women. He now thought it to have been anticipated in an indigenously Jewish form by the emergence of female leaders in hasidism.[61]

There is little doubt, however, that the tradition that reached Horodetsky in itself, untainted by his later, extraneously inspired outlook, is authentic enough. His general credibility in this area is good: the Maid is said by some to have died in 1892 or 1895,[62] which suggests that she was thought to be still alive when Horodetsky was born in 1871. Moreover, the decisive intervention of R. Mordecai of Chernobyl in the course of events relating to the Maid (and he is the only tsadik whom Horodetsky mentions by name in this connection, although later accounts introduce others) puts the story within the orbit of the Chernobyl dynasty, from which Horodetsky was descended and with whose traditions he was intimately acquainted.[63] It is, rather, his interpretation of the tradition that needs to be examined critically.

Horodetsky presents the hasidic career of the Maid of Ludmir as a success story. It is his strongest evidence for the presence of egalitarian elements in hasidism, which he perceives as having liberated women from their traditional disabilities under rabbinism. In fact, the story reads much more convincingly as the record of a failure. To be sure, it echoes a certain aspiration or yearning, which may well have been profound and could have found expression in reality for a while, at a grassroots level, in a Christian environment which was not, after all, unfamiliar with holy maidens and female saints. Nevertheless, it constitutes the perfect exception which confirms the rule whereby no woman could legitimately claim the full powers of spiritual leadership in hasidism, any more than she could establish the legitimacy of such a claim at any previous stage in the development of Jewish mysticism (with the notable exception of the messianic heresy of Sabbatianism and its sectarian offshoots, on which see Chapter 5 above).

The story of the Maid is the story of a deviant, whose ultimate failure serves precisely to reinforce the boundaries which she attempts to cross, not to undermine them. It may suggest that deviance was 'in the air', and that a society which produces such a story senses that those boundaries are frail and in need of reinforcement; but it certainly does not reflect the programmatic eradication of boundaries which is implied in Horodetsky's interpretation and that of all those who follow him.

The first of these boundaries is confronted by the Maid while she is still acting out her role as a woman. She is engaged to a man she knows and loves, but she cannot accept the traditional constraint of total separation between the bride and groom before marriage.[64] The vulnerability of this particular boundary in the region and during the period in which the story arises is well attested. By the second half of the nineteenth century, eastern European *maskilim* were voicing their criticism of traditional marriage customs, while observing also the growing reluctance of young girls to comply with the parental discipline of totally unromantic, conventionally arranged marriages.[65] This criticism must have resounded within the traditional world under attack. The incidence of young girls who, rather than enter such a marriage, left home to gain a secular education and join radical political circles in the final decades of the tsarist regime in Russia was small, but not unheard of.[66] The story of the Maid may present an implicit warning against this danger, by making her rejection of pre-marital convention trigger off further and more serious deviation.

The Maid responds to the constraints of the traditional norm in male–female relations by altogether denying her female role. Her gender identity had been unstable from the start; her desire and aptitude for learning, as well as her ardour in prayer, were more fitting for a boy than for a girl. These childhood aberrations, however, could be tolerated and would more than likely have been curtailed by normal marital responsibilities. But the Maid does not outgrow them; instead she crosses the gender boundary in a spectacular way by embracing celibacy and claiming that, equipped with 'a new and elevated soul', she has 'transcended the world of the flesh'.[67]

Renunciation, and in particular the celibate life, was the path which led a large number of Christian and, to a certain extent, also some Muslim women to the publicly acknowledged and fully legitimate realization of their spiritual aspirations. Celibate asceticism, which strove to enhance spiritual existence by means of diminishing or transcending physicality, provided the means also of transcending physical, and especially sexual, differentiation. It thus secured a place for women, stripped of their worldly sexuality, alongside the men in the ranks of the saints and mystics of both Christianity and Islam. It is to be noted that virtually all the great female mystics of the Christian tradition were virgins. And even when, in the late Middle Ages, the ideal of virginity was spiritualized so that even married women and widows could be counted among the saints, this was only achieved through their ultimate renunciation of all worldly ties and the strict observance of celibacy, from which moment alone they saw themselves, and were recognized, as being free to join the mystical path.[68] Similarly, the Sufi tradition, despite the early and explicit denunciation of celibacy in orthodox Islam,[69] displayed ascetic tendencies from its earliest beginnings, and included among its most celebrated saints a number of women who had embraced the celibate life to transcend the limitations of their sex.[70] By contrast, rabbinic tradition unequivocally denied any access to this path to women. Its attitude to asceticism in general had always been ambivalent, but in certain circumstances, especially within spiritually or mystically orientated elitist circles, the practices of ritual and penitential asceticism, which could include prolonged periods of sexual abstinence, were accorded full legitimacy and even sanctity for men, albeit within the conflicting constraints of the world-affirming halakhah.[71] In women, on the other hand, such conduct was considered as inherently false, hypocritical, or self-deluding.[72]

The Maid's adoption of the ascetic, celibate life was a declaration of her spiritual-mystical and, probably, also her scholarly orientation, an orientation which had often been marked by the strict ascetic piety of the men who chose it.[73] This was particularly so following the emergence of the Safed kabbalah, whose strong ascetic inclination was popularized through a cluster of *musar* (conventionally, though somewhat misleadingly, rendered 'ethical') works promoting ascetic ideals.[74] These exerted a powerful, if problematic, influence on the hasidic ideals of mystical piety to which the Maid was trying to conform.[75] Had this tradition bestowed any legitimacy on the ascetic piety of women, the Maid might have found an outlet for it even within marriage, as did the men who managed to achieve it without altogether renouncing their halakhically prescribed obligations towards worldly existence. But in the lack of any legitimacy for this type of piety in women, and since no model was available in Judaism for an asexual spirituality that is oblivious of gender boundaries,[76] the Maid was forced to renounce her identity as a woman, only to embrace a false identity as a man, emulating the standard discipline of ritual observance, and so also the rigour of ascetic piety traditionally confined to males. As a 'false male' she could only be regarded as an aberration of nature and a social deviation. In traditional terms she was understood as having acquired the soul of a man, albeit a tsadik (but probably a 'fallen' tsadik, who had committed a serious transgression, most likely a sexual one, and who was being punished by transmigrating into her female body).[77] It is not surprising that the device to which R. Mordecai of Chernobyl is said to have resorted in attempting to rectify the situation was to force the Maid back into her female role by contracting a marriage. This was perfectly effective: from the moment that she resumed her natural role and social function, however reluctantly or inadequately, her claim to special spiritual powers was invalidated and her hasidic following abandoned her.[78] Her chastity, which survived two unconsummated marriages, was no longer 'holy' and became her private affair. Her final dispatch to the Holy Land, which is probably factual, amounted to her relegation to a safely remote corner of the nineteenth-century hasidic world—the method by which the movement is known to have disposed of some of its other embarrassments.[79]

This analysis of the story of the Maid exposes as false the claim, for which it has so often been cited as proof, that the hasidic movement pioneered the equality of men and women in Judaism.[80] Far from promoting such a novel ideal, hasidism embraced unquestioningly all the conceptions of women produced by classical rabbinic Judaism, as well as the kabbalistic association of women with the demonic realm,[81] and the concomitant representation by women of negative, material sexuality. This ought to be avoided by all men at all costs, or, at best, to be stripped of its corporeal exterior and 'raised' to the spiritual origin of all things by a small minority of spiritual giants from among the founding fathers of hasidism.[82]

◆

It is noteworthy that the relatively recent interest in the position of women in hasidism, pioneered by the Habad movement under the leadership of its sixth *admor*, Joseph Isaac Schneersohn (1880–1950), which was subsequently much enhanced by the seventh and last rebbe, Menachem Mendel Schneerson (1902–94), should have taken the form of a heightened concern primarily for the education of women in halakhic matters relating to their traditional female roles as wives and mothers, appealing to them as guardians of the Jewish identity of the younger generation.[83] The sixth *admor*'s direct appeal to women was prompted by the threat of modern secularism and assimilation, first in interwar Russia and Poland and eventually in the USA. With considerable insight, he identified in women a resource which had hardly been tapped before. He enlisted their energies in a campaign, not so much for the dissemination of hasidic doctrine specifically (although he did lay the foundations for the initiation of girls in the speculative teachings of the Habad school of thought) but for the very preservation of Orthodox practice and halakhic Judaism as such. This direction, which has opened up much scope for active participation by women, is authentic and legitimate by traditional yardsticks—however we value them—inasmuch as it is based on stressing, rather than obliterating, the difference between men and women in Judaism.[84]

APPENDIX

The Maid of Ludmir in Jerusalem

The oral tradition regarding the immigration of the Maid of Ludmir to the Holy Land and her residence in Jerusalem in the second half of the nineteenth century seems to be confirmed by archival documentation and is most likely based on historical fact. Patricia Madsen, a graduate student at Denver University, Colorado, whose MA dissertation concerned the literary reception of the Maid of Ludmir tradition, found a probable trace of the Maid in one of the five nineteenth-century censuses of the Jewish population in the Holy Land commissioned by the prominent financier, philanthropist, and spokesman for world Jewry, Moses Montefiore.[85] The census data were collected and noted approximately once a decade, in the years 1839, 1849, 1855, 1866, and 1875. They are preserved in bound manuscript volumes held in London by the Montefiore Endowment, on whose website they are now available in digitized form for online searches in both Hebrew and English.

MS Montefiore 537, entitled in Hebrew 'Statistical Accounts of the Holy Land Taken in the Year 5626 [= 1866] by order of Sir Moses Montefiore Bart. [= Baronet]' contains demographic data on all the local centres of Jewish population, divided into organizational units called *kolelim* (sing. *kolel*, lit. a 'collection' of people), corresponding to a range of distinct communities defined by common ethnicity, country of origin, and religious affiliation. All these units depended financially on their share of the *ḥalukah* (distribution) funds, which were regularly donated by the Jews of the diaspora to provide for their brethren living in the Holy Land.

The organizational unit that concerns us here is the *kolel* of the hasidim of Volhynia in Jerusalem. Founded in 1841, it was the first and most important hasidic *kolel* in the city, from which various other hasidic *kolelim* subsequently branched off.[86] The census data are arranged in several tables (*luḥot*), each with its own title defining it as referring to men (pp. 1–4), widows (pp. 5–7), male orphans (p. 8), female orphans (p. 9), synagogues (p. 10), study houses (p. 11), schools (p. 12), and communal associations (*ḥevrot*) (p. 13). The names of all the individuals and institutions listed in each of the tables appear in the first column, which is followed by several others stretching across the full breadth of the page. Each column has its own heading, and space is allocated for additional information relating to each of the names listed. Thus the 'Table of widows belonging to the holy community of the hasidic *kolel* of Volhynia who dwell in the holy city of Jerusalem, may it be built and established soon in our own days, ordered by our master . . . Moses Montefiore, may God protect him, in the year 5626 since the creation of the world [= 1866]', on page 7, under the heading 'These are their names', lists, among the other widows, 'the *rabanit* Rachel Hannah'. The title *rabanit* (a feminine form of rabbi) appears only rarely in this column, where most of the widows are listed by their first names only. It seems to refer, as it commonly does, to the wife (here widow) of a rabbi. But in the next column, headed 'Name of the deceased husband, heaven forbid', the space next to Rachel Hannah's name has been left blank, and it seems that information about her dead husband, whether or not he was a rabbi, was simply not available. The third column, headed 'Their birthplace', has 'from Ludmir' against her name, while the fourth column, 'Their age', offers '60'. This means that in 1866, the year of the census, this widow was 60 years old, suggesting that she was born in 1806. In the fifth column, under the heading 'Their time of arrival in the Holy Land', the figure 3 (represented by the Hebrew letter *gimel*) is entered, meaning that the widow Rachel Hannah had arrived in Jerusalem three years prior to the census, in 1863.[87] The next six columns, headed 'Nature of their income', 'Their occupation and work', 'Number of children', 'Names and ages of children', 'Names of sons over 13 / under 13', and 'Comments', were all left blank, not only against the name of Rachel Hannah but also against those of most of the other widows, and it seems that this information, too, was unavailable to the data collector. In the last column, headed 'Number of family members', the figure 1 was entered, indicating that Rachel Hannah lived on her own.

Admittedly, most of the traditions about the Maid of Ludmir, including Horodetsky's initial report and his subsequent elaborations on the story, refer to her as Hannah Rachel, not Rachel Hannah (with the exception of the rather muddled account in *Nifle'ot harabi*,[88] where she is called Hannah Sarah), but the census manuscripts are not altogether free of spelling mistakes and other scribal errors; the data they contain are not always accurate, and many basic items of information are absent. It is therefore not impossible that in this case the widow's first names were recorded in reverse order. Moreover, all the other details about her in the widows' table are perfectly compatible with the Maid of Ludmir tradition as it has come down to us. This makes it likely that Rachel Hannah, the 60-year-old widow from Ludmir, is, in fact, Hannah Rachel Verbermacher, the Maid of Ludmir.

This interpretation of the 1866 census reference to the widow Rachel Hannah becomes even more plausible if we compare it with another reference to a hasidic widow from the town of Ludmir, listed in the 1875 census (MS Montefiore 553), in the section devoted to the same Volhynian hasidic *kolel*. On pages 15–16 there is a table of all the *kolel*'s widows, arranged in similar (but not identically ordered) columns to those set out in the 1866 census. Here, in the first column, on page 16, which is again headed 'These are their names', we encounter 'the *rabanit*, the righteous [*tsadeket*] Hannah Rachel'. The two first names are listed in the correct order for the Maid of Ludmir, and the title *rabanit*, which, as observed above, is very rare in this document, has been coupled with the epithet 'righteous', which does not occur anywhere else in the lists of widows. It may well be more than a mere reference to Hannah Rachel's reputation for righteous deeds (which in itself would be out of place in an otherwise prosaic repository of demographic data) by alluding, somewhat awkwardly, to her status as a hasidic leader—tsadik, a term for which there is no equivalent standard feminine form.

In the second column her deceased husband's name is missing again, and in the third column her age is recorded as 69, which means that Hannah Rachel's age of 69 in 1875 is perfectly compatible with Rachel Hannah's age of 60 at the time of the 1866 census, nine years earlier. The year of her birth must therefore be 1806. These dates approximately match some of the late traditions about the Maid of Ludmir, according to which she was born in 1805.[89]

In the fourth column of the 1875 widows table, Hannah Rachel's birthplace is again noted as Ludmir, while in the fifth column the year of her arrival in the Holy Land is recorded as 1859—a discrepancy of some four years with 1863, which the 1866 census notes as Rachel Hannah's year of arrival. But this relatively minor discrepancy, in a document which, as noted above, is not free of mistakes and inaccuracies, does not diminish the likelihood that Rachel Hannah is one and the same as Hannah Rachel.

In the next column, 'Their occupation and work', Hannah Rachel is described in somewhat awkward Hebrew terms as an 'old woman [from] an elevated family' (*zekenah mishpaḥat ram*). This, too, is compatible with the tradition whereby the Maid of Ludmir was left a sizeable inheritance by her wealthy father (see above, p. 327). The phrase itself stands out as highly exceptional in the lists of widows' 'occupations and work', where the vast majority are described as 'seamstress', 'servant', 'bread seller', 'seller of various types of food', 'liquor seller', 'brewer', 'supported by her son', 'self-supporting', and above all the formula, repeated time and again: 'a life of poverty out of *ḥalukah* and *kedimah* [alternatively *kedumah*]'—two distinct elements of the *ḥalukah* funding system, which provided the majority of *kolel* members with their sole income. The next three columns—'Nature of their income', 'Number of children', and 'Age of sons—above 13 / below 13' were all left blank, while in the 'Number of family members' column the figure 1 appears again, and the last column, 'Comments', remains blank.

In light of all the above, it seems likely that the widow Hannah Rachel should be identified with the widow Rachel Hannah, and that both should be identified with the legendary Hannah Rachel, the Maid of Ludmir, who was known in her youth in Ludmir as a singular female tsadik, but who ended her life in old age as a solitary widow in Jerusalem.

Notes

1 S. A. Horodetsky, *Hasidism and Its Adherents* [Haḥasidut vehaḥasidim] (2nd edn., Tel Aviv, 1928–43), iv. 68; cf. the abridged one-volume edition in English, *Leaders of Hasidism* (London, 1928), 113, the chapter entitled 'The Maid of Ludmir'.

2 See e.g. D. L. Mekler, *From the Rebbe's Court (from Chernobyl to Talne)* [Fun rebins hoyf (fun chernobyl biz talne)] (New York, 1931), i. 209–45; J. S. Minkin, *The Romance of Hassidism* (3rd edn., Los Angeles, 1971), 345–7; M. Feinkind, *Female Rebbes and Famous Personalities in Poland* [Froyen rabonim un barimte perzenlekhkayten in poyln] (Warsaw, 1937), 21–69; M. Biber, 'The Maiden of Ludmir' (Heb.), *Reshumot: hame'asef ledivrei zikhronot le'etnografyah ulefolklor beyisra'el*, 2 (Tel Aviv, 1946), 69–76 (repr. in the *Ludmir Memorial Book* [Pinkas ludmir: sefer zikaron likehilat ludmir] (Tel Aviv, 1962), 295–302, where it is followed by an anonymous note in Yiddish, 'Di ludmirer moyd', 294–5, and a Yiddish poem by Kehat Kliger, 'Di ludmirer moyd davent', 301); Y. Twersky, *The Maiden of Ludmir* [Habetulah miludmir] (Jerusalem [1950]); S. Ashkenazi, *Woman in Jewish Perspective* [Ha'ishah be'aspaklaryat hayahadut] (Tel Aviv, 1953), i. 55–60; M. S. Geshuri, *Melody and Dance in Hasidism* [Hanigun veharikud baḥasidut] (Tel Aviv, 1959), iii. 366–70; E. Taubenhaus, *On the Path of the Individual* [Binetiv hayaḥid] (Haifa, 1959), 37–41 (I am grateful to Ezra Kahn, the former librarian of Jews' College London, for drawing my attention to this work); H. Rabinowicz, *A Guide to Hassidism* (New York, 1960), 102–13; N. Shemen, *Attitudes to Women* [Batsiung tsu der froy] (Buenos Aires, 1969), ii. 328–38; H. Rabinowicz, *The World of Hassidism* (London, 1970), 202–10; Y. Alfasi, *Hasidism* [Haḥasidut] (Tel Aviv, 1974), 242; S. Henry and E. Taitz, *Written Out of History* (Fresh Meadows, NY, 1983), 175–83; M. M. Brayer, *The Jewish Woman in Rabbinic Literature*, ii: *A Psychohistorical Perspective* (Hoboken, NJ, 1986), 37–48; G. Winkler, *They Called Her Rebbe: The Maiden of Ludmir* (New York, 1991) (thanks to David Assaf for directing me to this work); *The Dream Assembly of Rabbi Zalman Schachter-Shalomi*, collected and retold by H. Schwartz (New York, 1988), 161–8. The above list is more representative than exhaustive. N. Deutsch's *The Maiden of Ludmir: A Jewish Holy Woman and Her World* (Berkely, Calif., 2003) is the latest attempt to construct the Maid's biography out of fragments of historical information, fleshed out by hagiographical and memoiristic accounts of doubtful historical value. For the cluster of publications and women-led events in the summer of 2004 which celebrated the Maid of Ludmir as an inspirational model, and included a pilgrimage to her supposed burial place in the Mount of Olives cemetery in Jerusalem on what purports to be the anniversary of her death, see e.g. Y. Levine Katz, 'In Memoriam Hannah Rachel, 1806–88' (Heb.), *Hatsofeh* (16 July 2004), 12; ead., 'The Events of the *Yahrzeit* of Hannah Rachel Verbermacher' (Heb.), *Mabua*, 43 (2004/5), 65–74; S. Friedlander Ben-Arza, 'Han-

nah Rachel of Ludmir' (Heb.), *Kolekh: forum nashim datiyot*, 95 (1 Tamuz 2004), 3–4.

3 This was the position when the present chapter was first published in 1988. Since then, valuable contributions to the topic have been made by other scholars, often in relation or response to my claims. Some have modified or contested them, others arrived at somewhat different conclusions by redefining my questions or employing different methodologies, but all have undoubtedly enriched our knowledge and understanding of women's relationship to hasidism. Among the most significant contributions are N. Polen, 'Miriam's Dance: Radical Egalitarianism in Hasidic Thought', *Modern Judaism*, 12/1 (Feb. 1992), 1–21; id., 'Rebbetzins, Wonder-Children, and the Emergence of the Dynastic Principle in Hasidism', in S. T. Katz (ed.), *The Shtetl: New Examinations* (New York, 2009), 53–84; N. Loewenthal, 'Women and the Dialectic of Spirituality in Hasidism', in I. Etkes (ed.), *Within Hasidic Circles: Studies in Hasidism in Memory of Mordecai Wilensky* [Bema'agelei ḥasidim: kovets meḥkarim mukdash lezikhro shel mordekhai vilenski] (Heb. and Eng.) (Jerusalem, 1999), English section, 7*–65*; Deutsch, *The Maiden of Ludmir*; M. Rosman, 'Observations on Women and Hasidism' (Heb.), in D. Assaf and A. Rapoport-Albert (eds.), *Let the Old Make Way for the New: Studies in the Social and Cultural History of Eastern European Jewry Presented to Immanuel Etkes* [Yashan mipenei ḥadash: meḥkarim betoledot yehudei mizraḥ eiropah uvetarbutam shai le'imanuel etkes] (Jerusalem, 2009), i. 151–64; S. Stampfer, 'The Impact of Hasidism on the Jewish Family in Eastern Europe: Towards a Re-Evaluation' (Heb.), in Assaf and Rapoport-Albert (eds.), *Let the Old Make Way for the New* (Heb.), i. 165–84; H. Bar-Itzhak, 'The Legend of the Jewish Holy Virgin of Ludmir: A Folkloristic Perspective', *Journal of Folklore Research*, 46/3 (2009), 269–92; M. Wodziński, 'Women in Hasidism: A "Non-Sectarian" Perspective', *Jewish History*, 27/2–4 (Dec. 2013), 399–434; G. Sagiv, *Dynasty: The Chernobyl Hasidic Dynasty and Its Place in the History of Hasidism* [Hashoshelet: beit chernobyl umekomo betoledot haḥasidut] (Jerusalem, 2014), 129–35; D. Biale, 'A Feminist Reading of Hasidic Texts' (Heb.), in R. Levine Melammed (ed.), *'Lift up Your Voice': Women's Voices and Feminist Interpretation in Jewish Studies* [Harimi bako'aḥ kolekh: al kolot nashiyim ufarshanut feministit belimudei hayahadut] (Tel Aviv, 2001), 125–44; R. Goldberg, 'The Voice of a Subterranean Spring: The Image of a Woman as Reflected in the Hasidic Tale' (Heb.), *Jerusalem Studies in Jewish Folklore* 21 (2001), 27–44; ead., 'Rebbe Israel Ba'al Shem Tov and His Wife, and Other Women in Hasidic Tales' (Heb.), *Massekhet*, 3 (2005), 45–62; T. Kauffman, 'Two *Tsadikim*, Two Women in Labor, and One Salvation: Reading Gender in a Hasidic Story', *Jewish Quarterly Review*, 101/3 (2011), 420–38; T. El-Or, *Educated and Ignorant: Ultraorthodox Jewish Women and Their World* (Boulder, Colo., 1994).

4 Horodetsky, *Hasidism and Its Adherents* (Heb.), iv. 67–8.

5 See his *The Judaism of Intellect and the Judaism of Emotion* [Yahadut hasekhel veyahadut haregesh], 2 vols. (Tel Aviv, 1947).

6 For the presumed universality of this perception, and a feminist critique of it, see M. Zimbalist Rosaldo, 'Woman, Culture, and Society: A Theoretical Overview', in M. Zimbalist Rosaldo and L. Lamphere (eds.), *Woman, Culture, and Society* (Stanford, 1974), 29–30; N. Chodorow, 'Family Structure and Feminine Personality', ibid. 43–66; A. Oakley, *Sex, Gender and Society* (rev. edn., Aldershot, 1985), 49–78 and 79–98. See also M. Lowe and R. Hubbard (eds.), *Woman's Nature: Rationalizations of Inequality* (New York, 1983); J. N. Burstyn, *Victorian Education and the Ideal of Womanhood* (New Brunswick, NJ, 1984), 37, 70–83, 86–7.

7 Horodetsky, *Hasidism and Its Adherents* (Heb.), iv. 67–8.

8 See G. Scholem, *Major Trends in Jewish Mysticism* (New York, 1961), 37–8.

9 See G. Scholem, *Sabbatai Ṣevi* (Princeton, NJ, 1973), 124, 191–7, 254, 418–23, 799, 850–1, 855, 887–9; id., *Kabbalah* (Jerusalem, 1974), 302–8. For a totally different assessment of the position of women in the Sabbatian movement, closer to Horodetsky's impressionistic observations but fully anchored in evidence, see now my *Women and the Messianic Heresy of Sabbatai Zevi 1666–1816* (Oxford, 2011), where I entirely revise my earlier view, which was informed by Scholem's conclusions, arguing afresh that a gender-egalitarian women-liberationist agenda was inherent in Sabbatian eschatology from the outset, even though it did not always find fully articulated or consistent expression. This agenda was an integral element of Sabbatai Zevi's own redemptive vision, and it persisted in one form or another right up to and including the last sectarian transmutations of the messianic movement, both within and without the boundaries of Judaism. This had the effect of opening up to women the public arena of messianically charged hypernomian, anomian, and antinomian religious activism.

10 *Hasidism and Its Adherents* (Heb.), iv. 69.

11 See ibid., the chapter entitled 'Hasidism as It Is' ('Haḥasidut kemo shehi'), iv. 128–9:

> Let us admit the truth: official, legalistic Judaism is obsolete . . . This type of Judaism never agreed with the true spirit of the nation. Only through external factors—the Exile and all its ramifications—was it able to dominate the Jewish world . . . The question arises: how can this Judaism be reformed on the basis of the true foundations of Judaism? [This is an implicit rejection of the Reform movement, which Horodetsky considered to be based on extraneous foundations.] . . . This question is particularly pertinent now, when there is hope that, in time, many Jews will settle in the Land of Israel and lead a normal, independent life . . . What should be done there, in the Land of Israel, to this diaspora Judaism? . . . The time

> has come for the 'other' Judaism—the Judaism of emotion, of mysticism, of ecstasy . . . This type of Judaism does not need to be created; it does not need to be discovered in books and manuscripts. It is alive and well now, among thousands of Jews; it is hasidism . . . The immense spiritual force which is contained within hasidism will reveal itself in full once the movement has stripped off its diaspora guise . . . in the Land of Israel . . . Through hasidism . . . it should be possible to renew . . . the type of communal life which existed first among the Essenes and last among the hasidim. *Through hasidism it should be possible to put right the great wrong which legalistic Judaism had committed against the Jewish woman . . . whom hasidism has granted equal religious rights for the first time in Judaism.* [emphasis mine; A. R.-A.]

Horodetsky's notion that hasidism was capable of reforming Judaism from within, in preparation for the realization of the Zionist vision, is not dissimilar to the view held by others of his generation. Buber, for example, wrote:

> Moses Hess said that we cannot foresee the consequences of Hasidism if it will be taken up by the national movement. This is also my opinion. Because here, in Hasidism, we have something close to us in time, and its off-shoots reach into our very age. Hasidism is a great revelation of spirit and life in which the nation appears to be connected by an inner tie with the world, with the soul, and with God. Only through such a contact will it be possible to guard Zionism against following the way of the nationalism of our age, which, by demolishing the bridges which connect it with the world, is destroying its own value and its right to exist. (M. Buber, *The Origins and Meaning of Hasidism*, ed. and trans. M. E. Friedman (New York, 1966), 218, and cf. G. Scholem, 'Martin Buber's Interpretation of Hasidism', in id., *The Messianic Idea in Judaism* (London, 1971), 229; see also above, pp. 329–30)

Even Berdyczewski, whose attitude towards hasidism was extremely ambivalent, declared:

> Our ancestors, masters of arid 'knowledge', have traced the beginning of the new era in our recent history to Ben Menahem [Moses Mendelssohn] and his Haskalah, while we, the 'people of the heart', trace the beginning of our spiritual revival and liberation to that spiritual giant, R. Israel Ba'al Shem Tov, who, with his great spirit, became a luminary to the Jewish people . . . The hasidic movement seems to us to have revealed a great and sublime force which has acted on the depths of our national soul and revived our dry bones. (M. Y. Berdyczewski, 'About Hasidism' (Heb.), *Hamagid*, 6/33 (19 Aug. 1897), 264, cited in Z. Mark, 'Hasidism and Anarchy: The Intellectual and Autobiographical Foundations of the Story "Hahafsakah" by Micha Yosef Berdyczewski' (Heb.), *Tsafon*, 17 (n.d.), 231 n. 69)

12 See S. Dubnow, *The History of Hasidism* [Toledot haḥasidut] (Tel Aviv, 1960), 365, 369; J. Katz, *Tradition and Crisis*, trans. B. D. Cooperman (New York, 1993), 211–12 and 345 n. 21. For the interesting observation that young men in similar circumstances constituted the majority of recruits not only to hasidism but also to the Haskalah and Musar movements, and for similar reasons, see D. Biale, 'Eros and Enlightenment: Love Against Marriage in the East European Jewish Enlightenment', in A. Polonsky (ed.), *Poles and Jews: Renewing the Dialogue*, Polin: Studies in Polish Jewry 1 (1986), 49–67, especially 50–3, 57. Cf. below, n. 14.

13 This in itself was not necessarily as serious as it may sound, since, at least among the educated and wealthier classes, the women in any case often carried this burden alone or within their parental households, enabling their husbands to devote as much time as possible to their religious studies. The custom is amply documented, but see e.g. J. Katz, 'Marriage and Marital Relations at the End of the Middle Ages' (Heb.), *Zion*, 10 (1944), 33, 43; M. Rosman, 'To Be a Jewish Woman in Poland-Lithuania of the Early Modern Period' (Heb.), in I. Bartal and I. Gutman (eds.), *The Broken Chain: Polish Jewry through the Ages* [Kiyum veshever: yehudei polin ledoroteihem] (Jerusalem, 2001), ii. 428–34; S. Stampfer, *Families, Rabbis and Education: Traditional Jewish Society in Nineteenth-Century Eastern Europe* (Oxford, 2010), 128–9; T. Cohen, 'Women in Haskalah Fiction', in S. Feiner and D. Sorkin (eds.), *New Perspectives on the Haskalah* (London, 2001), 149–52. Eastern European *maskilim* were particularly critical of this aspect of traditional life, and they advocated the retreat of women from the marketplace to the home, after the model of the 19th-century ideal bourgeois marriage. See e.g. A. B. Gottlober, *Memoirs and Travels* [Zikhronot umasa'ot], selected and edited by R. Goldberg (Jerusalem, 1976), i. 86; cf. Biale, 'Eros and Enlightenment', 60.

14 See Dubnow, *The History of Hasidism* (Heb.), 353, 361–5. R. Nahman of Bratslav restricted the weekly sabbath visits to his court, allowing only a small number of close disciples to come each week. However, he made obligatory on all his followers the three annual pilgrimages to Bratslav on Rosh Hashanah, Shabat Hanukah, and Shavuot, of which the first was the most important. In addition he used to visit, on three sabbaths a year, the three communities in which the largest numbers of his followers were concentrated, and all would travel to see him there. See N. Sternharz, *Ḥayei moharan*, i (Jerusalem, 1947), 'Mekom yeshivato unesiotav', 59–60 §24. R. Shneur Zalman of Liady permitted all his followers to come to his court four times a year, for Simhat Torah, Shabat Hanukah, Purim, and Shabat Shuvah (Sabbath of Repentance—the sabbath preceding Yom Kippur). The sabbaths preceding each New Moon were also established as times of assembly, but R. Shneur Zalman continued to restrict attendance on these occasions to particular types of recruits in order to cope with the growing numbers of his followers, and he prohibited all visits on some of these sabbaths. See the Liozno Ordinances (Heb.), and the letters relating to them, in D. Z. Hillman, *Letters by the Author of the Tanya and His Contemporaries* [Igerot ba'al hatanya uvenei doro] (Jerusalem, 1953), 58–69, nos. 37–42. Cf. I. Etkes, *Rabbi Shneur Zalman of Liady: The Origins of Chabad Hasidism* (Waltham, Mass., 2014), 41–9.

15 For these complaints see the text of the ban against the hasidim, issued in Vilna in 1781, in M. Wilensky, *Hasidim and Mitnagedim* [Ḥasidim umitnagedim] (Jerusalem, 1970), i. 103 (based on Solomon Dubno's manuscript version); ii. 151 (the version embedded in David of Maków's *Shever poshe'im*). See also ii. 107, 159–60, 173; Israel Loebel, 'Sefer vikuaḥ', ibid. ii. 315; S. Maimon, *The Autobiography of Solomon Maimon* (London, 1954), 176 and his n. 1 ad loc.; J. Perl, *Uiber das Wesen der Secte Chassidim*, ed. A. Rubinstein (Jerusalem, 1977), 125. There is probable corroboration of this from within the hasidic literature. In a 'talk' (*siḥah*) of R. Nahman of Bratslav, recorded by R. Nathan Sternharz, his scribe, R. Nahman laments this situation and ascribes it to the machinations of Satan:

> I was told this by a certain man who was talking to him [to R. Nahman], of blessed memory, about the situation of [our] young men. It is very common for the relations between them and their wives to deteriorate. They separate for a while, and sometimes this results in the complete break-up of the marriage, Heaven forbid. He said that this was due to the activities of Satan, who is particularly concerned to spoil the domestic harmony of [our] young men, so that they would fall into his trap by means of this [namely, that through their separation from their wives and the concomitant cessation of their properly conducted conjugal relations, which results in sexual frustration and increased appetite, they would be driven to erotic fantasies and possibly illicit sex. A.R.-A.]. Satan lies in wait for them, to catch them in their youth by means of spoiling their domestic harmony, Heaven forbid, which he brings about by his cunning . . . And he spoke of this matter at length. (N. Sternharz, *Siḥot haran* [with *Shivḥei haran*] (Lemberg, 1901), 77*a* §261).

Interestingly, this is followed by an injunction 'to prize and honour one's wife . . . for the women suffer greatly' (ibid., §262). While reflecting a rare concern for the suffering of the women, this nevertheless confirms its perceived severity.

16 For the tsadik as 'father' see e.g. Ephraim of Sudyłków, *Degel maḥaneh efrayim* (Zhitomir, 1875), 'No'aḥ', 11; Menahem Mendel of Vitebsk, *Igerot hakodesh*, in *The Books of the Fathers of Hasidism in the Holy Land* [Sifrei avot haḥasidut be'erets hakodesh] (n.p., n.d.), ii. 25*a* no. 18; Elimelekh of Lizhensk, *No'am elimelekh*, ed. G. Nigal (Jerusalem, 1978), ii. 469; Jacob Isaac, the Seer of Lublin, *Zot zikaron*, in the series *The Holy Books of All the Disciples of the Holy Besht* [Sefarim hakedoshim mikol talmidei habesht hakadosh] (Brooklyn,

1981), ii. 66 (on the verse 'Even by the God of thy father', Gen. 49: 25); id., *Divrei emet* (ibid.), 25 (on the same verse); cf. the description of a hasidic gathering in E. Z. Hakohen Zweifel, *Shalom al yisra'el*, ed. A. Rubinstein (Jerusalem, 1972), ii. 31, 'Hashkafah letovah'. Zweifel claims in the same passage that 'the hasidim love and honour their wives, and they spend more money to adorn and beautify them than do the *mitnagedim*'. But this is in tune with the generally apologetic tone of the book, and is not reliable. A little further on (p. 32), however, Zweifel confirms that the prolonged stay at the court of the tsadik offers the hasid temporary relief from his domestic troubles by liberating him from his obligations to his wife and children. It should be noted that, alongside the analogy between the father and the tsadik as head of an alternative spiritual 'family', hasidic sources also compare the tsadik to a son in quite a different relation to God as father. See, for example, the index entry for father–son parables (*mishlei av*) in *Magid devarav leya'akov*, ed. R. Schatz-Uffenheimer (Jerusalem, 1976), 372.

17 See J. G. Weiss, 'Abraham Kalisker's Concept of Communion with God and Man', *Journal of Jewish Studies*, 6 (1955), 87–99 (repr. in id., *Studies in Eastern European Jewish Mysticism*, ed. D. Goldstein (Oxford, 1985), 155–69); Z. Gries, 'From Myth to Ethos—Towards a History of R. Abraham of Kalisk' (Heb.), in S. Ettinger (ed.), *A Nation and Its History* [Umah vetoledoteiha] (Jerusalem, 1984), ii. 117–43. Cf. Y. Liebes, 'The Messiah of the Zohar', in id., *Studies in the Zohar*, trans. A. Schwartz, S. Nakache, and P. Peli (Albany, NY, 1995), 37–43.

18 The pattern of periodic departures from home which could turn into prolonged stays, affording young married men little contact with their wives and families, was by no means unique to hasidism, although it was only hasidism that offered these young men an alternative focus for their social and emotional lives. This pattern was already prevalent among the students of the medieval Ashkenazi yeshivas, for whom the pursuit of scholarship away from their native towns was considered meritorious enough to legitimate the neglect of their halakhically prescribed sexual obligations to their wives. See e.g. M. Breuer, 'The Wanderings of Students and Scholars—A Prolegomenon to a Chapter in the History of the Yeshivas' (Heb.), in R. Bonfil, M. Ben-Sasson, and J. R. Hacker (eds.), *Culture and Society in Medieval Jewry: Studies Dedicated to the Memory of Haim Hillel Ben-Sasson* [Tarbut veḥevrah betoledot yisra'el biyemei habeinayim] (Jerusalem, 1989), 445–68; I. J. Yuval, 'An Ashkenazi Autobiography from the Fourteenth Century' (Heb.), *Tarbiz*, 55 (1986), 550–1, and his references in the notes ad loc. For the mid-19th century see e.g. E. Deinard, *Memories of My People* [Zikhronot bat ami] (St Louis, 1920), pt. I, 38–9, where he describes the *perushim* (abstinents) of the yeshiva at Eišiškės (Eishishok) in Lithuania:

> To a certain extent the yeshiva of Eišiškės enjoyed a higher status than the yeshiva of Volozhin. Eišiškės was not a place for young boys. Only fully grown men or married men were accepted there. They were called *perushim*, and most of them had obtained *semikhah* [rabbinic ordination] before arriving at Eišiškės. Anyone entering the *beit midrash* of the 'abstinents' would be awestruck. He would see before him some 100 young men, all standing . . . each at a small table called a *shtender*, with a volume of Gemara open in front of him . . . For twenty hours a day, and in some cases even longer, these men would stand on their feet without sitting down to rest for a moment . . . They are oblivious of the world . . . totally absorbed in another world, which is all spirit . . . Such . . . extraordinary enthusiasm is displayed by young men in their early years of marriage. They reject all the pleasures of life before they have had a chance to enjoy them. Their young, beloved wives stay at their parents' homes and take pride in their husbands, who exist on dry morsels of bread, sleeping on hard wooden benches at their place of study. They make no distinction between sabbath and festivals and ordinary weekdays [that is, they do not visit their wives even on the sabbath and festivals]. So they live at the yeshiva for seven years without a break, without breathing the fresh air of the world. Many of them do not even find time to remember their families by as much as a letter.

A different pattern of 'wanderings', or 'exile' for its own sake rather than to a particular, if distant, centre of scholarship, became prevalent in eastern European scholarly circles in the 19th century, and served as an ascetic discipline designed to concentrate the scholar's mental faculties on his studies and to eliminate all worldly distractions. See on this I. Etkes, 'Family and Study of Torah in Lithuanian Talmudist Circles in the Nineteenth Century' (Heb.), *Zion*, 51 (1986), 96–7; id., *Rabbi Israel Salanter and the Mussar Movement: Seeking the Torah of Truth* (Philadelphia, 1993), 17–21, 60. The most celebrated model for the sacrifice of domestic and marital comforts for the sake of Torah was, of course, the tannaitic sage R. Akiva (BT *Ned.* 50*a*), and the more ambiguously valued life-long celibate Ben Azai (BT *Yev.* 63*b*) was still venerated for his Torah scholarship. An extreme manifestation of the ideal of abstinence for the sake of scholarship can be found in the historically obscure but ethically unequivocal medieval document entitled *The Statutes of the Torah* [Ḥukei hatorah], on which see S. Assaf, *Sources for the History of Jewish Education* [Mekorot letoledot haḥinukh beyisra'el] (Tel Aviv, 1925), i. 6–16; E. Kanarfogel, 'A Monastic-Like Setting for the Study of Torah', in L. Fine (ed.), *Judaism in Practice from the Middle Ages through the Early Modern Period* (Princeton, 2001), 191–202. This document does not promote abstinence within marriage during periods of study, however long, but rather something approaching an ideal of male virginity until well into manhood for boys dedicated by their parents to intense study at 'the houses of the abstinents'. It is my impression that the tradition of renouncing all worldly pleasures, including conjugal relations, at least intermittently and within the halakhic constraints of the obligation to marry and procreate (which could be disposed of either early or late in life while leaving much scope for ascetic deprivation in between) was continuous, if not universal, in both scholarly and mystical circles, right up to and including hasidism. I have dealt with this in a lecture entitled 'Asceticism and Mysticism in the Jewish Tradition', which was delivered at the second Scholem Memorial Conference in Jerusalem in February 1986, and which I hope to publish elsewhere. For the position in early rabbinic literature see S. D. Fraade, 'Ascetical Aspects of Ancient Judaism', in A. Green (ed.), *Jewish Spirituality from the Bible through the Middle Ages* (London, 1986), 253–88, with which I am in full agreement. For further consideration of this issue see also Biale, *Eros and the Jews* (New York, 1992); D. Boyarin, *Carnal Israel* (Berkeley, 1993); E. R. Wolfson, *Language, Eros, Being: Kabbalistic Hermeneutics and Poetic Imagination* (New York, 2005), 296–332.

19 See Katz, *Tradition and Crisis* (New York, 1993), 212, 345 n. 23. See also N. Sternharz, *Yemei moharnat* (Benei Berak, 1956), pt. I, 11–13.

20 There are numerous reports by *mitnagedim* concerning the presence of women in the courts to seek a blessing from the rebbe. They often suggest all manner of licentious conduct between these women and the rebbe himself or the male hasidim present. See e.g. David of Maków in Wilensky, *Hasidim and Mitnagedim* (Heb.), ii. 66, 105, 137; Dubnow, *The History of Hasidism* (Heb.), 366. Dubnow is right in observing that these reports could well have been inspired by a distorted understanding of the early hasidic doctrine of the 'raising of wayward thoughts' (which the *mitnagedim* denounced vehemently), more than by any direct experience of hasidic practices of this sort. Notably, the reports which refer to the presence of women in the courts conflict, in the writings of the same authors, with the common complaint against the hasidim who flock to the courts while abandoning their wives at home. Cf. Wilensky's comment in *Hasidim and Mitnagedim* (Heb.), ii. 46. In addition, there are references to women visiting the tsadikim in their courts throughout the hasidic hagiographical literature of the 19th century. See e.g. M. Buber, *Tales of the Hasidim*, ii: *Later Masters* (New York, 1972), 111, 141, 204, 210, 293. By contrast, the Liozno Ordinances of R. Shneur Zalman of Liady (see n. 14 above), which divide the hasidim into distinct categories in order to regulate their visits to the court, make no mention of women at all. Nor does one hear of women among the hasidim who visited R. Nahman of Bratslav. There may well have been regional differences between the different courts in this respect, as well as differences in the personal styles of leadership adopted by various tsadikim. Both R. Nahman and R. Shneur Zalman disapproved of the more vulgar displays of miracle-working tsadikism, and may well have excluded women from their courts on the grounds that this was all that the women might have expected of them, barred as they were from hearing their hasidic *torah*. There are some testimonies—admittedly of late provenance—in both the Bratslav and the Habad tradition to the effect that R. Nahman and R. Shneur Zalman (and in the case of the latter all his pre-20th-century successors as well) never had any dealings with women (for more on this see below, Ch. 7). An interesting insight into the questionable desirability of women at the courts is supplied by Isaac ben Leyb Landau in his *Zikaron tov*, a collection of stories about the life of his venerated hasidic master, the *admor* Isaac (ben Mordecai) of Neshchiz—a miracle-working tsadik, whose modest collection of homilies, *Toledot yitsḥak*, was published by the same Isaac Landau shortly after the *admor*'s death in 1868. In *Zikaron tov* (Piotrków, 1892), now reprinted in vol. iii of the series *Sefarim hakedoshim mikol talmidei habesht hakadosh* (see n. 16 above), pt. II, 27*b* [54] §30 we read:

> Towards the end of his life he did not allow women to enter his house unless they were accompanied by their husbands. [If they came unaccompanied they could enter but] only for the purpose of paying him his *pidyon* money; otherwise he would speak to them through the window. He explained this by saying that he did not wish the women to frequent his court, since he could not bear the burden of dealing with the large crowds that were always coming to see him. However, it was his manner to offer simple explanations for actions which he had taken for sublime reasons known only to himself.

Although the phrasing is a little ambiguous, it seems that the 'large crowds' of visitors to which the author refers are not crowds of women specifically but rather the hasidic following of R. Isaac of Neshchiz as a whole. When these crowds became too large, the simplest method of pruning them was to discourage the women from coming. However, the author's speculation that R. Isaac's 'simple' explanation concealed a more sublime and esoteric reason reflects his sense that, at its face value, the *admor*'s explanation was not fully satisfactory. This suggests in the first instance that the policy of deliberately discouraging women from attending the court may have been unusual enough in this particular environment to require some further explanation, but it may allude also to the sexual, and therefore esoteric, direction of the *admor*'s sublime intention, a direction which would be pointed quite naturally by any address to women as a category.

In trying to assess the extent to which women were received in the courts, it is interesting to note the evidence of Sarah Schenirer, the founder of the Beit Ya'akov network of Orthodox schools for girls. She came from a Polish hasidic family—precisely the region from which many of the hasidic tales relating to women who visited the courts have emanated. She describes the situation in her youth, at the turn of the 19th and 20th centuries, as one in which, especially during the High Holidays, 'fathers and sons travel and those who can afford it make this journey several times a year. Thus they are drawn to Ger, to Bełz, to Alexander, to Bobo[v] . . . And we stay at home, the wives, the daughters with the little ones. We have an empty Yomtov' (Judith Grunfeld-Rosenbaum, an early collaborator of Sarah Schenirer, reminiscing about her friend's experience, in J. Grunfeld-Rosenbaum, 'Sara Schenierer—The Story of a Great Movement', in L. Jung (ed.), *Jewish Leaders* (New York, 1953), 410–11). The same situation is described in the following testimony of two sisters from the Galician town of Wieliczka, who belonged to a hasidic household affiliated with the court of Bełz: 'We were born to a strictly hasidic family . . . My father . . . was a Belzer hasid, and he often left his house and his family to travel to his rebbe' (cited from the *Wieliczka Memorial Book* in R. Manikin, 'The Development of the Idea of Religious Education for Girls in Galicia in the Modern Era' (Heb.), *Massekhet*, 2 (2004), 68 n. 9). It seems that, if women did visit the courts, their visits did not coincide with the times of regular assembly for the male hasidim, namely the sabbath and festivals. This impression is corroborated by the memoirs of E. Shmueli regarding the same region during the interwar period. He describes the men taking leave of their wives and small children, who stay at home while they, accompanied by their older sons, travel to the courts at the fixed times of assembly. See E. Shmueli, *In the Last Jewish Generation in Poland* [Bador hayehudi ha'aḥaron bepolin] (Tel Aviv, 1986), 15, and 9–110 *passim*. Cf. also S. Elberg, *Heavenly Warsaw* [Warsaw shel malah] (Benei Berak, 1969), 64. The book contains reminiscences about pre-war Warsaw. The author stresses the importance of leaving the home and the family behind when travelling to visit the rebbe, suggesting that the hasidim generally preferred to travel a long distance rather than visit a local rebbe precisely because this would take them away from their wives and children, who stayed behind. For additional information on the presence of women in the hasidic courts see below, pp. 372–81.

21 In fact, translations from Hebrew into Yiddish were generally retranslations from the vernacular Yiddish—in which the material was first narrated orally—with a view to publication, for which Hebrew was considered the more appropriate language. See C. Shmeruk, *Yiddish Literature: Aspects of Its History* [Sifrut yidish: perakim letoledoteiha] (Tel Aviv, 1978), 213, 218.

22 See ibid. 217.

23 See ibid. 205 ff.

24 See J. Dan, *The Hasidic Story—Its History and Development* [Hasipur haḥasidi] (Jerusalem, 1975), 189–95; Shmeruk, *Yiddish Literature: Aspects of Its History* (Heb.), 211; G. Nigal, *The Hasidic Tale* (Oxford, 2008), 64–74. For the persistence, well into the 20th century, of the hasidic ambivalence about the printing of such tales, see J. R. Mintz, *Legends of the Hasidim* (Chicago, 1968), 5–6.

25 Women could and may well have read this type of literature, which was, at least in some cases, expressly directed at them alongside the other two categories of readers who were not proficient in Hebrew—uneducated men and children. For example the introduction to the 1816 Korets (Korzec) Yiddish edition of *Shivḥei habesht* (fo. 1*b*) addresses the translation to 'all those people who do not know the Holy Tongue—men, women, and children'. Nevertheless the evidence that women actually read the Yiddish *Shivḥei habesht* is extremely sparse. See more on this below, Ch. 7, n. 5 and Appendix I.

26 See pp. 333–4 above and nn. 83–4 below. See also pp. 387–91, 439 ff. below.

27 This topic is discussed in N. Loewenthal's *Communicating the Infinite: The Emergence of the Habad School* (Chicago, 1990), 1–28. The book focuses on the Habad movement but surveys the position both before and outside it. See also id., 'The Apotheosis of Action in Early Habad', *Daat*, 18 (1987), vi–viii. Cf. Etkes, *Rabbi Shneur Zalman of Liady*, 209–11. For the distinction between the communication of hasidism by means of the *torah* and prayer of the tsadik, which are aimed at the superior class of learned hasidim, and his communication with simpler folk by means of common talk or tales and parables, see M. Piekarz, *Braslav Hasidism* [Ḥasidut braslav: perakim beḥayei meḥolelah, bikhtaveiha uvisefiḥeiha] (Jerusalem, 1972), 87–106. For a clear distinction between hasidic *torah* as a higher level of teaching, accessible to a select minority of disciples, and *musar* as a lower level, in which the same *torah* may be clothed in order to make it accessible to all, see Sternharz, *Ḥayei moharan*, i, 'Nesiato le'erets yisra'el', 65 §19.

28 See *In Praise of the Baal Shem Tov*, ed. D. Ben-Amos and J. Mintz (Bloomington, 1972), 'The Printer's Preface', 1. Cf. G. Scholem, 'The Neutralization of the Messianic Element in Early Hasidism', in *The Messianic Idea in Judaism*, 198–9, for the Sabbatian origin of this notion.

29 See Shmeruk, *Yiddish Literature: Aspects of Its History* (Heb.), 206–7.

30 See L. Jacobs, 'Woman', in *Encyclopaedia Judaica* (Jerusalem, 1972), xvi. 627.

31 See n. 20 above.

32 See Dubnow, *The History of Hasidism* (Heb.), 138 ff.

33 For this controversy, triggered by the publication of R. Shneur Zalman of Liady's *Tanya* in 1796, see Dubnow, *The History of Hasidism* (Heb.), 335–8; H. M. Heilman, *Beit rabi* (Berdiczów, 1903), 81–90 (= 41*a*–45*b*); A. J. Braver, 'On the Controversy between RSHZ and Abraham of Kalisk' (Heb.), *Kiryat sefer*, 1 (1924–5), 142–50, 226–38; E. Kupfer, 'New Documents on the Controversy between RSHZ of Liady, R. Abraham of Kalisk, and R. Barukh of Międzybóż' (Heb.), *Tarbiz*, 47 (1978), 230–7; R. Elior, 'The Minsk Debate' (Heb.), *Jerusalem Studies in Jewish Thought*, 1/4 (1982), 194–5; R. Haran, 'R. Abraham of Kalisk and R. Shneur Zalman of Liady—A Friendship Cut

Off' (Heb.), in R. Elior and J. Dan (eds.), *Rivka Schatz-Uffenheimer Memorial Volume* [Kolot rabim: sefer hazikaron lerivkah schatz-uffenheimer], Jerusalem Studies in Jewish Thought 13 (Jerusalem, 1996), ii. 399–428; Etkes, *Rabbi Shneur Zalman of Liady*, 208–59; Gries, 'From Myth to Ethos' (Heb.), 127–32.

34 One possible exception should be mentioned, although it seems marginal in this context. This is the booklet entitled *Poke'aḥ ivrim* by R. Shneur Zalman of Liady's son Dov Ber, the second leader of Habad (on this book see H. Lieberman, *Ohel raḥel* (New York, 1984), iii. 646–9; Shmeruk, *Yiddish Literature: Aspects of Its History* (Heb.), 199–200). Published in Yiddish in the second decade of the 19th century, the book offers advice on ethical matters and calls for repentance. The introduction addresses it to ordinary people who cannot read the many books on this subject which are available to the better-educated Hebrew readers (see *Poke'aḥ ivrim* (Brooklyn, 1955), 35). Although no mention of women as part of the anticipated readership is made in the introduction itself, women may well be addressed directly in ch. 17, p. 42: 'Similarly, the women who sit in between the shops should take great care not to indulge in conversation with the young men [who had been warned in the immediately preceding passage never to look at the women in the shops], because this is very harmful to the health of children, heaven forbid.' This suggests that a female readership could have been assumed by the author. However, the book clearly belongs to the ethical genre and, but for the identity of its hasidic author, displays no distinctly hasidic characteristics at all. *Musar* books in Yiddish had traditionally attracted a mixed male and female readership (see C. Shmeruk, *Yiddish Literature in Poland: Historical Studies and Perspectives* [Sifrut yidish bepolin: meḥkarim ve'iyunim historiyim] (Jerusalem, 1981), 43 ff.). I am grateful to Naftali Loewenthal for drawing my attention to this passage, although his interpretation of its significance is quite different from mine. See N. Loewenthal, 'Women and the Dialectic of Spirituality in Hasidism', in I. Etkes et al. (eds.), *Within Hasidic Circles: Studies in Hasidism in Memory of Mordecai Wilensky* [Bema'agelei ḥasidim: kovets meḥkarim mukdash lezikhro shel mordekhai vilenski] (Heb. and Eng.) (Jerusalem, 1999), English section, 22–4.

35 These are: Edl, the daughter of the Ba'al Shem Tov; her daughter Feyge, who was the sister of both R. Barukh of Międzybóż and R. Ephraim of Sudyłków, and the mother of R. Nahman of Bratslav; Rachel, the daughter of R. Joshua Heschel of Apta (Opatów); and Hannah Hayah, the daughter of R. Mordecai of Chernobyl. See Horodetsky, *Hasidism and Its Adherents* (Heb.), iv. 69.

36 For the status of Edl as a female tsadik, Horodetsky alludes to the tradition whereby the Ba'al Shem Tov had derived her soul, and so also her name, from the Torah, by constructing it out of the initial letters of the verse in Deut. 33: 2—'A fiery law unto them' (*esh dat lamo*). This tradition appears in *In Praise of the Baal Shem Tov*, ed. Ben-Amos and Mintz, 137. It concludes a story in which

Edl appears in a rather more negative light: the Ba'al Shem Tov was engaged in an ecstatic exposition of a certain point to one of his disciples. 'His face burned like a torch.' Suddenly Edl entered the room and summoned her father to dinner. The Ba'al Shem Tov's state of trance ended abruptly. He reproached Edl for interrupting him and explained that both the prophet Elijah and his own personal teacher from heaven, Ahiyah the prophet of Shiloh, had been present in the room but were driven away at the sound of Edl's voice, which had confused him. Far from displaying visionary capacities of her own, Edl by her very presence, which is robustly corporeal on two scores—her female nature and the food which she delivers—interferes with her father's spiritual endeavours and puts an end to his vision. In fact, this portrayal of Edl is sufficiently negative to raise suspicions with regard to the authenticity of the discrepant concluding 'praise'. It could well have been added to the original story by a later hand, more programmatically committed to the idealization not only of the Besht but also of all those associated with him (but cf. G. Nigal, 'Women in *Shivḥei habesht*' (Heb.), *Molad*, 31 (241) (1974), 143 for a totally different reading of this story). The Yiddish version of *Shivḥei habesht* sheds no light on the matter, since this story does not appear in it at all; see A. Yaari, 'Two Basic Editions of *Shivḥei habesht*' (Heb.), *Kiryat sefer*, 39 (1963–4), 557–8. For another tradition in the same book, in which Edl appears as a typical woman by conventional standards, devoid of any spiritual ambition or tsadik-like qualities but rather excluded from the ecstatic male fraternity of her father and his disciples, and seeking, like any ordinary woman, 'a blessing' from one of them in order to ensure that she would conceive a male child, see *In Praise of the Baal Shem Tov*, ed. Ben-Amos and Mintz, 223–4. Cf. also *Sefer sipurei kedoshim*, ed. G. Nigal (Jerusalem, 1976), 41. S. Ashkenazi adds to the account of Edl, which he derives from Horodetsky, the following information: 'The Besht considered her one of his disciples. With his permission she gave out magical remedies to the sick. In a letter she wrote to R. Shalom of Pogrebishche (dated Monday [of the week in which the Pentateuchal portion of] 'Genesis' [is read, in the year] 5547 [1787]), she reported on her father's conduct in study and worship' (*Woman in Jewish Perspective* (Heb.), 55). In a note on the same page Ashkenazi directs the reader to his source for this—the book *Butsina dinehora hashalem* 'by R. Barukh [of Międzybóż]', Edl's son. A book entitled *Butsina dinehora* does, indeed, contain traditions which are ascribed to R. Barukh of Międzybóż, and has been published many times since 1880. However, its relation to R. Barukh is problematic and probably false; see A. Schischa Halevi, 'About the Book *Butsina dinehora*' (Heb.), *Alei sefer*, 8 (1980), 155–7. The book *Butsina dinehora hashalem* is even more problematic in that it contains numerous additions from extraneous sources, put together by its modern editor-author Reuben Margaliot. It was first published by Margaliot through his bookselling business in Lemberg and printed in Biłgoraj in or around 1930.

The edition is undated but the date was suggested to me by Mr A. Schischa, on the basis of the fact that in 1931 Margaliot published and printed in Zamość the first part of *Butsina dinehora hashalem* as a separate pamphlet entitled *Mekor barukh* from the matrices of the first edition of the complete work. On *Mekor barukh* see Schischa in *Alei sefer*, 8 (1980), 157. I am grateful to Mr Schischa for his help in clarifying this point. The material portraying Edl as a disciple of the Besht, the author of letters and recipes for magical remedies, appears in *Butsina dinehora hashalem*, pt. I, *Mekor barukh*, 5–7. It contains three letters from the Besht to his daughter and one letter by her to R. Shalom of Pogrebishche, incorporated by Margaliot into his own sketch of R. Barukh's life. These letters are drawn from the notorious Kherson *genizah* of hasidic forgeries, and were copied by Margaliot from H. E. Bikhowsky, *Ginzei nistarot* (Jerusalem, 1924), pt. I, *Or yisra'el*, 9 no. 31, 10 no. 32, 16 no. 53; pt. II, *Or ne'erav*, 14–15 no. 33. On the Kherson *genizah* see Y. Rafael, 'The Kherson *Genizah*' (Heb.), in id., *On Hasidism and Its Adherents* [Al ḥasidut veḥasidim] (Jerusalem, 1991), 204–26, and Chs. 1 and 4 above. The most extensive collection of Kherson letters appeared in the Habad periodical *Hatamim*, published in Warsaw between 1935 and 1938. It was endorsed as authentic by the then leader of Habad, the *admor* Joseph Isaac Schneersohn, against the growing conviction of most scholars that the letters were all recent forgeries. For additional letters 'by' or 'to' Edl, see *Hatamim* (Kefar Habad, 1975), ii. 444 no. 111, 449–50 no. 143, 452 no. 154, 454 no. 163. Needless to say, all these letters are turn-of-the-last-century fabrications and can tell us nothing about Edl's role and status in the hasidic movement of her own time. Nevertheless, it is interesting to note that the forger, whose identity is not known but who clearly belonged to, or was intimately familiar with, the hasidic world of the end of the 19th century and the beginning of the 20th, did not attempt to 'promote' Edl to the rank of a fully fledged tsadik, but simply manufactured more information about her in line with the traditions contained in *Shivḥei habesht* and stressed her close relationship with her father. The Kherson letters lend themselves to a 'feminist' interpretation no more and no less than do the authentic traditions about women in hasidism. For an authentic model of female piety in *Shivḥei habesht*, which is unequivocal in its endorsement of traditional female virtues such as charity, humility, empathy, and compassion, while being totally innocent of any desire to 'liberate' women or to acknowledge their capacity for charismatic leadership, see the traditions on Rivaleh the Pious in *In Praise of Baal Shem Tov*, ed. Ben-Amos and Mintz, 120–2. Zeev Gries has suggested to me in a private communication that the Rivaleh tradition in *Shivḥei habesht* must be taken not at its face value but as an ironic condemnation of excessive piety, a quality which the classical rabbinic sources deplore, especially in women (cf. n. 72 below). This interpretation of the story seems to me possible but by no means certain, since various groups at various times in Jewish history did produce extreme norms of piety which would have been frowned upon, to say the least, by those among the sages who advocated a more sober balance between worldly pleasures and spiritual concerns, but which were nevertheless accepted as fully legitimate in their own context. Hasidism sprang from within an environment where such extreme norms of piety prevailed, and its reaction to them was by no means unequivocal (cf. n. 75 below). Rivaleh's extreme piety as it is portrayed in *Shivḥei habesht* could well have been valued positively, especially since, with the possible exception of her apparent idealization of poverty, it was free from the inclination towards ascetic mortification and sexual abstinence which characterized kabbalistic piety, and which would have been utterly unacceptable in a woman (cf. n. 18 above and nn. 72–4 below with the corresponding discussion in the main body of the text). Be that as it may, what is relevant at this point is the stress in *Shivḥei habesht* on Rivaleh's traditional female virtues, however extreme, and the total absence of any pneumatic or charismatic powers among her qualities.

Horodetsky's account of Edl's daughter Feyge is drawn from Sternharz, *Ḥayei moharan*, i, 'Mekom yeshivato unesiotav', 54 §11. This confirms that Feyge was, indeed, considered to be endowed with prophetic insight, and was able to 'see' the Besht at the wedding of her granddaughter, R. Nahman of Bratslav's daughter. But there is no indication whatsoever, in this passage or anywhere else in the Bratslav literature, that Feyge's visionary powers had made her a tsadik in her own right.

37 See the considerable amount of material on this, assembled uncritically but nevertheless a useful indication of the scope and continuity of this phenomenon, in Ashkenazi, *Woman in Jewish Perspective* (Heb.), i. 115–36.

38 Horodetsky, *Hasidism and Its Adherents* (Heb.), iv. 69.

39 See n. 2 above. The women are: Malkah of Trisk (Turiisk), daughter of R. Abraham of Trisk and granddaughter of R. Mordecai of Chernobyl; Perele, daughter of the Magid of Kozienice; Hayah, mother of R. Isaac Meir of Ger; Mirosh, daughter of R. Elimelekh of Lizhensk; Freyde, daughter of R. Shneur Zalman of Liady; Eydele, daughter of R. Shalom Roke'ah of Bełz; Hayah Moskowitz, daughter of R. Meir of Przemyślany; Sareleh, mother of Joshua Heschel of Olkusz and wife of Hayim Samuel of Chęciny (who was the grandson and heir of the 'Good Jew of Neustadt'); Hannah Berakhah, her daughter, who was the wife of R. Elimelekh of Grodzisk; Nehamah, daughter of R. Hayim of Sanz; and Sarah Shlomtse, daughter of R. Menahem Mendel of Żydachów. Sareleh of Chęciny and her daughter Hannah Berakhah appear to be among the very few wives rather than mothers, daughters, or sisters of the tsadikim who are said to have commanded a following in their own right. In the case of Sareleh, however, this appears to have begun only after her husband's death, when her son Joshua Heschel succeeded his father. See on her Feinkind, *Female Rebbes and Famous Personalities* (Yid.), 56–61; Ashkenazi,

Woman in Jewish Perspective (Heb.), i. 57–8; Shemen, *Attitudes to Women* (Yid.), ii. 328–9, and cf. n. 78 below.

40 See Feinkind, *Female Rebbes and Famous Personalities* (Yid.); Ashkenazi, *Woman in Jewish Perspective* (Heb.); Geshuri, *Melody and Dance in Hasidism* (Heb.); Shemen, *Attitudes to Women* (Yid.); Alfasi, *Hasidism* (Heb.), and Brayer, *The Jewish Woman in Rabbinic Literature*, ii.

41 On the literary and scholarly activities of Freyde, the daughter of R. Shneur Zalman of Liady, see Ashkenazi, *Woman in Jewish Perspective* (Heb.), i. 55–6; Shemen, *Attitudes to Women* (Yid.), ii. 328. This can be anchored in an authentic Habad tradition whereby R. Shneur Zalman of Liady used to teach hasidism to Freyde, and she would allow her brother, Dov Ber (who later succeeded R. Shneur Zalman), to hide in the room and listen, occasionally prompting his sister to ask their father for further clarifications. See Heilman, *Beit rabi*, 114 (= 57*b*). A letter addressed to R. Dov Ber, which explains in hasidic and kabbalistic terms the reasons why the time is not ripe for the disclosure of the date of the messianic advent, has been ascribed to Freyde and published several times. See e.g. M. Teitelbaum, *The Rabbi of Liady and the Habad Faction* [Harav miliadi umifleget ḥabad] (Jerusalem, 1970; 1st edn. Warsaw, 1914), i. 265; id., *Iyun tefilah* (Łódź, 1926), 38–9; Hillman, *Letters by the Author of the Tanya* (Heb.), 235–7 (in two distinct versions). Notably, however, Heilman expresses doubts about her authorship of this letter (*Beit rabi*, 114 (= 57*b*)), and Hillman is unsure of her authorship at least of the second version of the letter. The two versions were republished by Y. Mondshine in *Kerem ḥabad*, 1 (Kefar Habad, 1986), 100–1, and he ascribes both not to Freyde but to Dov Ber's friend and eventual rival, R. Aaron Halevi of Starosielce. Ashkenazi, in *Woman in Jewish Perspective* (Heb.), i. 56, states that 'after her death, manuscripts of her hasidic teachings were found, written to her brother, the *admor* David [*sic*], of blessed memory.' This must be a muddled reference to the same letter, and the addressee was R. Dov Ber. R. Shneur Zalman had no son by the name of David.

42 One such example is Sareleh of Chęciny as described by M. Feinkind in *Female Rebbes and Famous Personalities* (Yid.), 56–61. The chapter devoted to her ends with precise information concerning her death at the age of 99 in February 1937, 'Friday night, 15 Adar 5697, at 12 o'clock'. This must have been added by Feinkind's children, who published the book posthumously in 1937, their father having died in June 1935. See on him *Lexikon fun der nayer yidisher literatur* (New York, 1965–81), vii. 357–8. Another possible example is the dowager Rebbetsin Rivkah (1839–1914), widow of the fourth Habad leader, the *admor* Shemuel (1834–83), of whom it was reported by an eyewitness that she held her own 'table' like a rebbe. On her see below, Ch. 7, in and around n. 69.

43 The late Gedalyah Nigal, who examined most of the available hasidic hagiographical collections, confirmed to me in a personal communication that he

had not come across any references to female tsadikim in this literature. He did, however, point out one possible exception: a probable echo of the Maid of Ludmir tradition (on the tradition of her exceptional career as a full-fledged female tsadik see below) in *Zikaron tov* (see n. 20 above), where the author refers to 'a pious woman [*ishah kesherah*] in the town of Ludmir who was able to foretell the future' (pt. II, 15*a* §4). The reference appears in the middle of a rather obscure story featuring the main protagonist of *Zikaron tov*, R. Isaac of Neshchiz (son of R. Mordecai of Neshchiz, d.1868; see ibid. 20*a* §38), whose own prophetic insight is said to have corroborated the pious woman's prediction in regard to the imminent death of a certain man. An explicit reference to the Maid of Ludmir occurs, apparently for the first time, in a book published in Warsaw some twelve years earlier, in 1884. Significantly, however, this is not a hasidic work but rather a maskilic attack on rabbinic casuistry, where the notion of a female tsadik features incidentally only to be mocked (see on this work Ch. 7, n. 14 below). Such literary echoes of the Maid of Ludmir, however distant or hostile, suggest that the tradition about her career as a rebbe did circulate, at least orally, in late 19th-century eastern Europe, even though hasidic hagiography generally ignored or suppressed it. David Assaf has brought to my attention another explicit reference to the Maid of Ludmir, this time in a hasidic hagiographical source. This is *Nifle'ot harabi*—a collection of 'praises' dedicated to Jacob Isaac, the 'Seer of Lublin', by Pinhas Walden (son of Aaron Walden, author of *Shem hagedolim heḥadash*), which was published in Warsaw in 1911. The reference to the Maid reads as follows:

> When the girl Hannah Sarah [*sic*] of Ludmir, known [in Yiddish] as *dos ludmirer meydl*, acquired a reputation for her holy spirit and miracle work . . . the woman Racheli urged her brother to travel to Ludmir in the hope of learning [from the Maid] where their lost father might have ended up. She [presumably the Maid, though this is not clear] was advised to marry, but on the day of her wedding to the local scribe she was divorced because he [the groom] was frightened away before consummating the marriage. She then travelled to the holy city of Tiberias and died there. (*Nifle'ot harabi*, 88, §294).

Here the story of the Maid of Ludmir is confusingly interwoven with the story of 'the woman Racheli', and the Maid is referred to by the name Hannah Sarah rather than, as she is commonly known, Hannah Rachel (perhaps as a result of confusion, or in order to avoid confusion, with 'the woman Racheli'), but there is no doubt that the tradition of the Maid has been incorporated here in the hagiographical tradition of the Seer of Lublin and his disciples. This would seem to suggest that, contrary to my claim above, the tradition of the Maid *was* acknowledged, if only occasionally, in the literary tradition of hasidism. But this is not the case. Pinhas Walden directs his readers to his sole source of information about the Maid, and this turns out to be 'Samuel Abba Horodetsky of the community of Bern [in Switzerland]'. The reference is to Horodetsky's short article, the first ever to record the full story of the Maid of Ludmir, which appeared in the 1909 issue of the Russian scholarly periodical *Evreiskaya Starina* (see below, n. 47), two years prior to the publication of Walden's work in 1911. What emerges from this is an interesting process: 20th-century hasidic hagiography begins to absorb and internalize the findings of modern historical-ethnographic research. For more on this process see Ch. 4 above; I. Bartal, 'Simon the Heretic—a Chapter in Orthodox Historiography' (Heb.), in I. Bartal, E. Mendelsohn, and C. Turniansky (eds.), *Studies in Jewish Culture in Honour of Chone Shmeruk* [Keminhag ashkenaz upolin: sefer yovel leḥone shmeruk] (Jerusalem, 1993), 243–68.

44 For Horodetsky see below, at nn. 47–61, and above, in and around n. 11. In one form or another, all the authors listed in n. 2 can be said to have undergone a similar process of acculturation, although not necessarily in the same direction as did Horodetsky.

45 S. A. G. (the initials of Samuel Abba Horodetsky in Russian, where G and H are interchangeable), in his *Evreiskaya Starina* article (for full details see below, n. 47), 221.

46 *Leaders of Hasidism*, the abridged English version of Horodetsky's book (see n. 1 above), 116, is at odds with the Hebrew original in suggesting that the Maid 'became the wife of the celebrated Tzaddik, Rabbi Mordechai of Czernobyl, who prevailed upon her'. There is no trace of evidence for this, and it must be a mistake in translation by Horodetsky's wife Maria.

47 S. A. G. [S. A. Horodetsky], 'Ludmirskaya deva (Di ludmirer moyd)', *Evreiskaya Starina*, 1/2 (1909), 219–22. I am grateful to Simon Redlich, who helped me locate the article, and to Mark Pinson, who translated it for me into English.

48 See his *Hasidism and Its Adherents* [Haḥasidut vehaḥasidim] (2nd edn., Tel Aviv, 1943), iv. 65–71. Another adaptation of the same material appeared in one of his later works, *Immigrants to Zion* [Olei tsiyon] (Tel Aviv, 1947), 172–5. This contains a few minor additions, including the promotion of Rivaleh the Pious (see n. 36 above) to the rank of a female tsadik (p. 172).

49 For a list of these see n. 2 above.

50 'Ludmirskaya deva', 219.

51 M. Klyachko, 'Volynskie predaniya III: Eshche o Ludmirksoi deve', *Evreiskaya Starina*, 3/4 (1911), 391–2.

52 See Biber, 'The Maiden of Ludmir' (Heb.), 75 n. 7. Further details about the activities of the Maid during her old age in Jerusalem and Safed are supplied by Taubenhaus in a short chapter entitled 'At the Court of a Female Tsadik' (Heb.), in *On the Path of the Individual* (Heb.), 37–41, and in a note on p. 372.

The book is based on written material collected by the author, as well as on his personal reminiscences about his father, R. Meir Taubenhaus, who was one of the most outstanding figures in the 'old Yishuv' of Jerusalem and who later settled in Safed and pioneered the 'productivization' of Jewish life in that city. Drawing on his father's personal notes and diary, and on his own recollections, the author reports that as a young man R. Meir Taubenhaus (who was born in 1865) knew the Maid of Ludmir in Jerusalem, where she conducted herself 'as a Polish rebbe' and had a considerable following. R. Meir was so intrigued by her that he made a study of her career, and during one of his many journeys to eastern Europe (probably in the 1880s) he visited Ludmir and made extensive enquiries about her. However, Ephraim Taubenhaus' account of the Maid's early history in Poland adds practically nothing to Horodetsky's version and may well be dependent on it. He does not appear to be quoting it from his father's notes, as he does elsewhere in the book. For archival corroboration of the tradition that the Maid of Ludmir was resident in Jerusalem during this period (from 1859 or 1861), where she may well have died, see the Appendix to this chapter on pp. 334–52 above.

53 See especially Mekler, *From the Rebbe's Court* (Yid.); Twersky, *The Maiden of Ludmir* (Heb.); Schwartz (ed.), *The Dream Assembly of Rabbi Zalman Schachter-Shalomi*; Deutsch, *The Maiden of Ludmir*, Levine Katz, 'In Memoriam Hannah Rahel' and 'The Events of the *Yahrzeit*'; and Friedlander Ben-Arza, 'Hanna Rachel of Ludmir', all in n. 2 above.

54 The only other female tsadik portrayed as belonging to this category is Yente the Prophetess, who is said to have lived at the time of the Ba'al Shem Tov, in the middle decades of the 18th century. She is described as the daughter of a simple Galician Jew, and her husband, Joseph Spravedliver, was a follower of the Besht. (The name Spravedliver is a yiddishized form of the Polish *sprawiedliwy*, meaning just or righteous, an observation I owe to Gershon Hundert. This would seem to invest the husband with the proverbial righteousness of the biblical Joseph in kabbalistic tradition, while at the same time suggesting the legendary character of the tale.) Yente once accompanied him on a visit to the Besht, and on encountering him was so impressed by his ascetic piety that she decided to adopt it herself. On her return home she began to abstain from conjugal relations, take frequent ritual baths, fast, and pray intensely while wearing a prayer shawl like a man. When her husband complained to the Besht about his wife's irregular conduct, the Besht fully endorsed it, proclaiming Yente a prophetess. Once this became known, hasidim began to flock to her, seeking blessings and cures, which she apparently effected while refusing to accept *pidyon* money for her services, as was customary amongst the male tsadikim. For the earliest source of this tradition, dating from the turn of the 20th century, see above, p. 298. For later elaborations see Feinkind, *Female Rebbes and Famous Personalities* (Yid.), 20–5; Ashkenazi, *Woman in Jewish*

Perspective (Heb.) 55–6, and all the subsequent derivative accounts (n. 2 above). The story seems somewhat anachronistic and is almost certainly apocryphal. It is extremely vague in terms of time and place, and although the Ba'al Shem Tov did have a few early disciples from Galicia (see Dubnow, *The History of Hasidism* (Heb.), 101–4), Galicia did not become a part of the hasidic world until after the death of the Magid of Mezhirech in the 1770s. However, the story bears a few strikingly significant parallels to the Maid of Ludmir tradition. These include not only Yente's common background and lack of any connection to the household of a tsadik, but also her adoption of celibate asceticism. For the significance of this see above, pp. 332–3.

55 S. A. G. [S. A. Horodetsky], 'Ludmirskaya deva', 219. It seems, however, that Horodetsky's original wording in this opening paragraph of his article may have been far less reserved than the published version would suggest. This emerges from the postcard response of Simon Dubnow, the editor of *Evreiskaya Starina*, to Horodetsky's complaint that editorial interventions had altered and even reversed some of his arguments, a complaint which Dubnow dismisses by asserting his own view whereby 'women actually have no place whatsoever in active hasidism, and even in their daily lives they used to exclude women from the dining room table where the guests would be seated' (see more on this below, Ch. 7, n. 15). Without Dubnow's reservations and apparent editorial modifications, Horodetsky's original version might have already referred to the full equality of women in hasidism that he was eventually free to claim in his 1923 book.

56 See above, pp. 332–3.

57 Horodetsky, *Hasidism and Its Adherents* (Heb.), iv. 69.

58 See S. A. Horodetsky, *Pirkei zikhronot* (Tel Aviv, 1957), 72.

59 See M. Kaplan, *The Jewish Feminist Movement in Germany: The Campaigns of the Jüdischer Frauenbund, 1904–38* (Westport, Conn., 1979).

60 See N. Rein, *Daughters of Israel* (Harmondsworth, 1980), 25–43. D. Bernstein, *The Struggle for Equality: Women Workers in the Palestine 'Yishuv'* [Ishah be'erets yisra'el—hashe'ifah leshivyon bitekufat hayishuv] (Tel Aviv, 1987), 16–69.

61 See above, p. 320 and n. 11.

62 See Shemen, *Attitudes to Women* (Yid.), ii. 330, 338 (n. 5*a*).

63 For Horodetsky's hasidic pedigree see his *Pirkei zikhronot*, 11.

64 See above, p. 327.

65 See e.g. Gottlober, *Memoirs and Travels* (Heb.), 85–108, especially 98. This section of the autobiography appears, on the basis of internal evidence, to have been written in 1859 (see the editor's note on the same page). For Haskalah autobiography in general see S. Vilnai (Werses), 'Autobiography in the Haskalah Era' (Heb.), in id., *Trends and Forms in Haskalah Literature* [Megamot

vetsurot besifrut hahaskalah] (Jerusalem, 1990), 249–60; A. Mintz, 'Guenzburg, Lilienblum, and the Shape of Haskalah Autobiography', *Association of Jewish Studies Review*, 4 (1979), 71–110; M. Moseley, *Being For Myself Alone: Origins of Jewish Autobiography* (Stanford, Calif., 2005). For an analysis specifically of the maskilic critique of traditional marriage see Biale, 'Eros and Enlightenment', 49–67, especially 55, 61.

66 See S. Dubnow, *History of the Jews in Russia and Poland* (Philadelphia, 1918), ii. 243–4; L. Greenberg. *The Jews in Russia* (New Haven, 1944), 146–59, especially 151, 154; S. W. Baron, *The Russian Jew under Tsars and Soviets* (New York, 1964), 167; R. Stites, *The Women's Liberation Movement in Russia* (Princeton, 1978), 85, 133, 135–6, 150, 169, 270, 274–6; B. A. Engel, *Mothers and Daughters—Women of the Intelligentsia in Nineteenth-Century Russia* (Cambridge, 1983), 159.

67 See above, p. 327. For the ambiguous status of another reputedly powerful hasidic woman—Eydele, daughter of Shalom Roke'ah (1779–1869; founder of the Belz hasidic dynasty)—who seems to have combined the legitimate female model of wife and mother with the anomalous gender-bending behaviour that marked the career of the Maid of Ludmir, see below, Ch. 7, n. 138.

68 On the connection between mysticism and celibacy in a number of religious traditions see *Mistique et continence* in the series Études Carmélitaines (Bruges, 1952). For the virtual universality of celibacy among the Christian saints and mystics, especially the women, see P. Brown, 'The Notion of Virginity in the Early Church', in B. McGinn, J. Meyndorff, and J. Leclercq (eds.), *Christian Spirituality—Origins to the Twelfth Century* (London, 1986), 427–43; D. Weinstein and R. M. Bell, *Saints and Society* (Chicago, 1982), 73–99; S. Shahar, *The Fourth Order: Women in Medieval Society* [Hama'amad harevi'i: ha'ishah beḥevrat yemei habeinayim] (Tel Aviv, 1983), 57–65; E. Underhill, *Mysticism* (London, 1960), 198–231. For an indication of the sheer scope of the phenomenon of female mystics in the Christian tradition, see ibid., Appendix A, 'Historical Sketch of European Mysticism from the Beginning of the Christian Era to the Death of Blake', 453–73. For the late medieval spiritualization of virginity, but still within the confines of chastity, either by mutual consent within marriage or by the adoption of celibacy in later life, see C. Atkinson, '"Precious Balsam in a Fragile Glass": The Ideology of Virginity in the Later Middle Ages', *Journal of Family History* (Summer 1983), 131–43; D. Elliott, *Spiritual Marriage: Sexual Abstinence in Medieval Wedlock* (Princeton, NJ, 1993).

69 See Qur'an, *sura* 57, v. 27; *Encyclopaedia of Religion and Ethics* (New York, 1910), ii. 99–105.

70 See M. Smith, *Rabi'a the Mystic and her Fellow-Saints in Islam* (Cambridge, 1928), especially 165–75; A. Schimmel, *Mystical Dimensions of Islam* (Chapel

Hill, 1975), Appendix 2, 'The Feminine Element in Sufism', 426–35; S. Trimingham, *The Sufi Orders in Islam* (Oxford, 1971), 18, 114, 176, 232.

71 See n. 18 above.

72 See the explicit condemnation of the 'female ascetic' (*ishah perushah*) as a 'world destroyer' in the Mishnah and the Jerusalem Talmud (*Sot.* 3: 4), the Babylonian Talmud (*Sot.* 20*a* ff.), and the Tosafot ad loc. See also S. Lieberman, *Texts and Studies* (New York, 1974), 33, 35 ff., 39–40. Even though the Gemara raises the possibility that not all female ascetics are necessarily false, a long tradition of rabbinic interpretation, stretching from late antiquity through the medieval and early modern to the modern era, revolves round, or is anchored in, these classical sources and, almost without exception, persists in the unequivocal condemnation of ascetic piety in women. See, for example, the Maharal's comment on the same passage in *Sotah*, in Judah Loew ben Bezalel of Prague, *Perushei maharal miprag . . . le'agadot hashas* (Jerusalem, 1968), 52. For a few exceptions see A. Grossman, *He Shall Rule over You? Medieval Jewish Sages on Women* [Vehu yimshol bakh? Ha'ishah bemishnatam shel ḥakhmei yisra'el biyemei habeinayim] (Jerusalem, 2011), 142, 404–5, 521.

73 See n. 18 above.

74 See R. J. Z. Werblowsky, *Joseph Karo: Lawyer and Mystic* (Oxford, 1962), 38–83, 133–8, 149–51, 161–8; M. Pachter, 'The Concept of Devekut in the Homiletical Ethical Writings of 16th-Century Safed', in I. Twersky (ed.), *Studies in Medieval Jewish History and Literature* (Cambridge, Mass., 1984), ii. 171–230, especially 179, 186–7, 190–1, 195–7; J. Dan, *Jewish Mysticism and Jewish Ethics* (Seattle, 1986), 76–103, especially 82–7; L. Fine, *Physician of the Soul, Healer of the Cosmos: Isaac Luria and His Kabbalistic Fellowship* (Stanford, Calif., 2003), 65–74, 169, 179–80; P. B. Koch, *Human Self-Perfection: A Re-assessment of Kabbalistic Musar Literature of Sixteenth-Century Safed* (Los Angeles, 2015).

75 Although hasidism enjoys a popular image of robust this-worldliness, its orientation towards the material world and corporeal pleasures is complex, and by no means as unequivocally anti-ascetic as may be suggested by some of its most famous denunciations of self-mortification and its rejection of pessimism (*atsvut*) with regard to the moral frailty of human nature. For examples of hasidic anti-asceticism see *Tsava'at harivash*, ed. J. I. Schochet (Brooklyn, 1975), 14–16 §44–7; 18 §56. As against this posture, however, see in the same work pp. 2–3 §5–7; 12–13 §43*a*. The common assumption in hasidic scholarship is that hasidism reacted against, and differentiated itself consciously from, the powerful ascetic tendencies of the kabbalistic schools from which the movement had emerged in the middle of the 18th century. The ideal of *devekut* —mystical communion or union with God—which was promoted by hasidism to the top of its scale of values, is considered to be fundamentally non-ascetic, and is said to have ousted the ascetic ideal through direct progression from one posture to the other, a process which often manifested itself in the individual biographies of the early hasidic masters. (See e.g. *In Praise of the Baal Shem Tov*, ed. Ben-Amos and Mintz, 156 §133 with regard to R. Nahman of Horodenka's spiritual development; Dubnow, *The History of Hasidism* (Heb.), 78–80 with regard to the Magid of Mezhirech; A. J. Heschel, *The Circle of the Baal Shem Tov* (Chicago, 1985), 11–12 with regard to R. Pinhas of Korets.) In fact, asceticism and sexual abstinence were not uncommon practices in hasidism. As ideals of piety and saintliness, they coexisted with, rather than making way for, the more 'optimistic' approach to the problems of materiality and evil, an approach which has become so prominently associated with the Ba'al Shem Tov and his followers. For a discussion of this, primarily in the writings of R. Elimelekh of Lizhensk, see R. Schatz-Uffenheimer, 'On the Nature of the Tsadik in Hasidism' (Heb.), *Molad*, 144–50 (1960), 369–70, and G. Nigal's introduction to his edition of *No'am elimelekh* (Jerusalem, 1978), i. 69 ff. For the ascetic mortifications of R. Nahman of Bratslav see the discussion in A. Green, *Tormented Master* (Alabama, 1979), index, s.v. 'Asceticism'. For the presence of ascetic impulses in Chernobyl hasidism see G. Sagiv, 'The Rectification of the Covenant and the Element of Asceticism in Chernobyl Hasidism' (Heb.), in R. Elior (ed.), *'New Old Things': Myths, Mysticism and Controversies, Philosophy and Halakhah, Faith and Ritual in Jewish Thought through the Ages* ['Devarim ḥadashim atikim': mitos, mistikah ufulmus, filosofyah vehalakhah, emunah veritual bamaḥshavah hayehudit ledoroteiha], Jerusalem Studies in Jewish Thought 23 (Jerusalem, 2011), ii. 355–406. For the coexistence of the ascetic ideal and the ideal of joy in the kabbalistic *musar* literature before hasidism, see A. Shohet, 'On Joy in Hasidism' (Heb.), *Zion*, 16 (1951), 30–43. See also D. Biale, 'The Lust for Asceticism in the Hasidic Movement', in J. Magonet (ed.), *Jewish Explorations of Sexuality* (Providence, 1995), 51–64; id., *Eros and the Jews*, 121–48. For the post-war resurgence of sexual abstinence among a number of contemporary hasidic groups, see B. Brown, 'Kedushah: The Sexual Abstinence of Married Men in Gur, Slonim and Toledot Aharon', *Jewish History*, 27/2–4 (2013), 475–522. I intend to deal with this topic more extensively elsewhere.

76 See M. Idel, 'Métaphores et pratiques sexuelles dans la cabale', in C. Mopsik (ed.), *Lettre sur la sainteté* (Paris, 1986), 353–5, although I disagree with his view of the concomitant kabbalistic evaluation of sexuality and marriage in the human sphere as unequivocally positive. See n. 75 above.

77 See e.g. H. Vital, *Sha'ar hagilgulim* (Tel Aviv, 1963), 33, *hakdamah* 9. For the notion of transmigration of souls in the kabbalah generally, see G. Scholem, *On the Mystical Shape of the Godhead: Basic Concepts in the Kabbalah* (New York, 1991), 197–250; id., *Kabbalah* (Jerusalem, 1974), 344–50. The view that sinful men appear as women in their second incarnation can already be found in Plato, *Timaeus* (New York, 1929), 91.

78 The fact that most of the other women described as hasidic leaders in their own right were not the wives of reigning tsadikim but rather their widows, mothers, sisters, or daughters (see above, pp. 324–5 and n. 39) may belong in this context. If her relationship to the tsadik is marital, that is, sexual, the woman's powers, however great, are unequivocally confined within the boundary of her female role, and they are more likely to be perceived as being complementary rather than analogous to her husband's powers. Interestingly, marriage features as a solution to the problem of a spiritually ambitious young woman in a story reminiscent of the Maid of Ludmir tradition, which is associated with the arch-opponent of hasidism, the Gaon of Vilna: 'A certain maiden performed miracles, spoke of high and mighty things, and studied Zohar as well as other esoteric matters. The Gaon R. Elijah, of blessed memory, said: "When she marries, the spirit will depart from her", and this is just what happened' (A. Hakohen, *Keter rosh* [*Orkhot ḥayim*] (Jerusalem, n.d.), 29). The Gaon of Vilna, a supreme representative of what Horodetsky labels legalistic or intellectual Judaism (*The Judaism of Intellect and the Judaism of Emotion* (Heb.), ii. 346–86, especially 364–5), and R. Mordecai of Chernobyl, a prominent spokesman for that 'other' Judaism of Horodetsky's scheme, are portrayed as responding to the aberration of mystical spirituality in a woman in precisely the same way, despite the gulf between the hasidic and the mitnagdic perspectives in other respects. Altogether, this gulf was not as wide as might be suggested by the initial level of hostility between the two camps. Both shared a wide range of common sensibilities which were fundamental to traditional, halakhic Judaism. Cf. Z. Gries, 'The Hasidic Conduct (*Hanhagot*) Literature from the Mid-Eighteenth Century to the 1830s' (Heb.), *Zion*, 46 (1981), 228–36; id., *Conduct Literature: Its History and Place in the Life of Beshtian Hasidism* [Sifrut hahanhagot: toledoteiha umekomah beḥayei ḥasidei r. yisra'el ba'al shem tov] (Jerusalem, 1989), 142–4.

79 This is where the family of R. Shneur Zalman of Liady's son Moses were sent after his apparent conversion to Christianity. See Heilman, *Beit rabi*, 113–14 (= 57*a*–*b*). For his apostasy see S. Katz, 'Maskilic Letters Denigrating Hasidim' (Heb.), *Moznayim*, 10 (1940), 266–70, and all the bibliographical references cited there. Cf. R. Elior, 'The Controversy over the Legacy of Habad' (Heb.), *Tarbiz*, 49 (1979–80), 167–8. For a rather muddled but relatively early reference to the affair, brought to my attention by the late C. Abramsky, see L. Rosenthal's supplement, *Yode'a sefer*, to M. Roest, *L. Rosenthal'schen Bibliotek* (Amsterdam, 1875), ii. 164 no. 866 (the entry for *Likutei amarim* [*Tanya*]). For the most extensive account and critical discussion of the evidence on Moses' apostasy, drawing on previously unknown Russian archival documentation, see D. Assaf, *Untold Tales of the Hasidim: Crisis & Discontent in the History of Hasidism*, trans. D. Ordan (Hanover, 2010), 29–96 (although Assaf doubts that there was a connection between Moses' disgrace and his family's immigration to the Holy Land; see ibid. 40, and 251 n. 61).

80 For an attenuated version of this claim see Polen, 'Miriam's Dance', which draws on late hagiographical traditions about exceptional women who exercised public authority in hasidism, and treats one hasidic homily from *Ma'or vashemesh* by Kalonymos Kalman Epstein of Kraków (1754–1823) as an insight into the ideological foundations of this remarkable phenomenon. The homily concerns Miriam the Prophetess, Moses and Aaron's sister, who—following Moses' 'song unto the Lord' with which he celebrated the Israelites' miraculous crossing of the sea in flight from the Egyptians—led the Israelite women in their own recitation of a single verse of song (Exod. 20–1). Kalonymos Kalman depicts Miriam as having accessed at that moment of great salvation the eschatological domain from which she was briefly able to draw the highest spiritual and theurgic powers, thereby not only matching but even exceeding the powers of her brother Moses. This is interpreted in Polen's analysis as an indication of hasidism's 'radical [gender] egalitarianism'. However, his interpretation should be qualified by the observation that homiletical traditions about Israel's mythical past, in much the same way as eschatological traditions about Israel's utopian future, more often than not invert rather than reflect the reality of their authors. For more on this see below, pp. 432–5.

81 See I. Tishby, *The Wisdom of the Zohar: An Anthology of Texts*, trans. D. Goldstein (Oxford, 1989), i. 371–422; ii. 447–546; Scholem, *On the Mystical Shape of the Godhead*, 189–92; id., *Major Trends in Jewish Mysticism*, 37–8. Scholem offers the kabbalistic association between the feminine sphere and the demonic as the reason for the exclusion of women from the Jewish mystical tradition (ibid.). My own impression is that this association in the writings of the kabbalists was not novel but constituted a direct continuation of classical rabbinic and philosophical conceptions of women as more inclined to sorcery and witchcraft, more susceptible to ritual impurity, exhibiting a more intense and untamed sexuality, and altogether representing the material-physical element of creation rather than the nobler elements of form, intellect, or spirit. This was a perception of women which was common to Judaism, Christianity, and Islam, and yet it did not prevent their active participation in either of the other two mystical traditions as it did, according to Scholem, in the case of Jewish mysticism. The effective absence of women from all the records of the kabbalistic tradition (and all other varieties of Jewish mysticism and esotericism) cannot therefore be explained by what is, after all, a symptom rather than the cause of the condition.

82 Instances of this abound throughout the literature of hasidism. See e.g. *Tsava'at harivash*, 30–1 §90, and the parallels in the collections of teachings by the Magid of Mezhirech cited there in the notes; *Magid devarav leya'akov*, ed. A. I. Kahan (Jerusalem, 1971), 'Likutim ḥadashim', 1–142*b* (from *Or hame'ir* by R. Ze'ev Wolf of Zhitomir); Elimelekh of Lizhensk, *No'am elimelekh*, i. 280; N. Sternharz, *Likutei halakhot*, 'Yoreh de'ah', vol. i

(Jerusalem, 1950), 'Hilkhot gilu'aḥ', *halakhah* 4, §15–16, p. 476; 'Hilkhot nidah', *halakhah* 2, §7, p. 494; vol. ii (Jerusalem, 1953), 'Hilkhot reshit hagez', *halakhah* 5, §4, p. 538; 'Kelalim nora'im . . . dov ber mimezhirech', in Hayim Haykl of Amdur, *Ḥayim vaḥesed* (Jerusalem, 1970), 158. On worship 'through corporality' and the 'raising of wayward thoughts' as elitist ideals, see I. Tishby and J. Dan, 'Hasidic Doctrine and Literature' (Heb.), in *Encyclopaedia Hebraica* [Ha'entsiklopedyah ha'ivrit], xvii. 788–9 (repr. in A. Rubinstein (ed.), *Perakim betorat haḥasidut uvetoledoteiha* (Jerusalem, 1978), 274–5); Piekarz, *Braslav Hasidism* (Heb.), 95–7; T. Kauffman, *In All Your Ways Know Him: The Concept of God and Avodah Begashmiyut in the Early Stages of Hasidism* [Bekhol derakheikha da'ehu: tefisat ha'elohut veha'avodah begashmiyut bereshit haḥasidut] (Ramat-Gan, 2009), 260–5, 277–81, 301–5, 321, and *passim*; above, pp. 278–80.

83 Joseph Isaac's father, the *admor* Shalom Dovber, had already identified the crucially important part played by women in determining the degree of Jewish religious commitment of the younger generation. He wrote in 1902:

> Satan dances first among the women, to cast into them the filth of secularism. They then run their households in the spirit of secularism, take into their hands the guidance and education of their children, prevail upon their husband with their own frivolous notions, and send their sons to the [secular] teachers who corrupt them rather than to traditional, religious teachers. (*Igerot kodesh . . . shalom dovber* (Brooklyn, 1982), i. 274)

In terms which echo traditional rabbinic and kabbalistic notions of women's frivolity, and especially their sexual susceptibility to the influence of Satan (cf. n. 81 above), he blames them for starting the fashion for modern, secular education, as well as for lowering the standards of religious observance generally (ibid. i. 279). This evaluation of the responsibility of women for initiating the process of estrangement from tradition in many households is not without historical foundation. Lacking any formal traditional education themselves, but increasingly encouraged, unlike the boys, to acquire some secular accomplishments and skills in early life, women were more inclined and able to expose their children to secular European culture. This, after all, was the basis for the ideology of the Beit Ya'akov movement for the Orthodox Jewish education of women, which began some fifteen years after the *admor* Shalom Dovber had written the letter quoted above. (For the Beit Ya'akov movement see n. 20 above and Ch. 8, n. 42, below.) Shalom Dovber's endeavours to arrest the tide of secularism and assimilation were confined, however, to educational activities by and for men. It was his son and successor, R. Joseph Isaac Schneersohn, who drew the logical conclusion from his father's diagnosis of the malaise and prescribed a more directly effective remedy by harnessing women to positive action for the preservation of traditional Judaism. During his visit to the USA in 1929–30, where he was particularly struck by the estrangement of the younger generation of Russian Jews from all aspects of religious observance (see e.g. his letter from Baltimore, *Igerot kodesh . . . yosef yitsḥak* (Brooklyn, 1982), ii. 225–7), he set up what eventually became a whole network of 'Women's Associations for the Purity of the Family', spreading information in Hebrew, Yiddish, and English about the laws of ritual purity, encouraging women to teach others how to observe these laws meticulously, as well as providing the facilities for this (see ibid., editor's introduction, pp. 20–2, 224, 252). When he returned from America and settled for three years in Riga, he visited his followers in Lithuania and founded similar women's associations there, of which the first was in the town of Rokiškis (see ibid. 332). He repeatedly invited women to take the initiative in founding these associations (see e.g. ibid., vol. iv (Brooklyn, 1983), 12–13). In the same letter from Otwock, written in 1936 to the Habad community in the Holy Land, he wrote:

> It is the duty of the wives and daughters of the hasidim, may they live, to stand in the forefront of any enterprise for the strengthening of religion and Judaism in general, and in particular with regard to the purity of the family. This is an area which they must take entirely upon themselves in order to establish the foundations of the purity of the daughters of Israel. Naturally the men, the communities in general, and all their institutions must help them in whatever they require, but the entire area of family purity is the responsibility of the women. It is up to them to establish and sustain it in such a way that one woman alert another, the other yet another, and all the women should, in turn, alert their husbands, sons, and daughters. (ibid. 13)

The same letter makes it clear that, while he was not displeased with the initiation of women to a certain level of the teachings of hasidism as such so long as this was carefully supervised by their fathers or husbands (see more on this below, pp. 389-91), he was primarily interested in their contribution to the campaign for the reinforcement of Orthodox Jewish practice in general, and specifically in those areas where their influence as women could be most direct. Notably, this type of direct appeal to women to maintain 'the purity of the family' against the growing relaxation of strict Orthodox practice was not unique to Habad. During the same period similar initiatives directed at women were being taken by other Orthodox and Agudat Yisra'el circles more generally. In the winter of 1930, for example, R. Israel Meir Hakohen, the Hafets Hayim, delivered a sermon on this subject to an exclusively female audience in the Great Synagogue of Vilna, from which all the men had been barred for the occasion (although apparently some men gathered in the women's gallery). This was an unprecedented event, as the Hafets Hayim himself observed in his sermon (see on this M. M. Yoshor, *The Hafets Hayim: His Life and Work* [Haḥafets ḥayim, ḥayav ufo'olo] (Tel Aviv, 1959), ii. 506–12. See also below, Ch. 7, n. 98). After his installation in the USA in 1940, the *admor* Joseph Isaac

Schneersohn founded various other women's organizations, and his son-in-law and successor, R. Menachem Mendel Schneerson, continued in the same vein with extra vigour and purpose. He founded the Lubavitch Women's Organization and generated a vast literature for women as well as numerous frameworks for women's activism all over the world (for a sample of these see n. 84 below, and see more below, Ch. 8).

84 Habad publications for and by women invariably feature the traditional areas of Jewish female responsibility: the three commandments which apply specifically to women: modesty, maternal responsibilities, and the creation of a proper Jewish atmosphere in the home. Aggressively appealing to women outside the Orthodox sector of Judaism, who have inevitably become exposed to the modern feminist critique of 'patriarchy' in both its religious and secular manifestations, they are quite ingenious in appropriating feminist concerns and terminology, and exploiting precisely those areas of overlap between the female separatism of some of the more extreme feminists and the traditional separation of the sexes as practised in the strictest possible way within Habad. A discussion of the periodical abstinence from conjugal relations arising from the ritual impurity of women during and after menstruation—a feature of Orthodox Judaism which has been particularly offensive to modern Jewish feminists—can thus be entitled '"Space" For Myself' (see Yehudis Groner, in R. Schnall Friedfertig and F. Shapiro (eds.), *The Modern Jewish Woman—A Unique Perspective* (Brooklyn, 1981), 59–60); and the traditional women's festival of Rosh Hodesh (New Moon) is reinvigorated in much the same way as this has been done by some Jewish feminist groups attempting to create a new spirituality for women outside the conventional Orthodox framework (see M. M. Schneerson, *Letters by the Lubavitcher Rebbe to N'shei uBnos Chabad, 1956–1980* (Brooklyn, 1981), 31–2 of the English text, 28–9 of the Yiddish). In addition to these works see e.g. the Lubavitch Foundation of Great Britain, *A Woman of Valour—An Anthology for the Thinking Jewess* (London, 1976); Lubavitch Women's Organization, *Aura—A Reader on Jewish Womanhood* (New York, 1984); Lubavitch Women's Organization, *The Gift* (New York, 1985), on the sabbath, which has a particular relation to women; M. M. Schneerson, *Equal Rights* (a pamphlet which contains an adaptation and translation into English of 'an address given by the Lubavitcher Rebbe Shlita on the sixth of Tishrei 5745, the 20th Yartzeit of Rebbetzin Chana, the Rebbe's mother'), published and distributed in late 1984. There are numerous additional books, pamphlets, and journals for women in the same vein. The sense of being actively engaged and equally valued as men, resulting from the new opportunities which these initiatives have opened up to Habad women, is captured in the personal testimony of Shoshana Gelerenter-Liebowitz, 'Growing up Lubavitch', in S. Grossman and R. Haut (eds.), *Daughters of the King: Women and the Synagogue (A Survey of History, Halakhah, and Contemporary*

Realities) (Philadelphia, 1993), 238–42. On p. 239 she states:

> Lubavitch women don't ever feel secondary or deprived. Their lives are as busy as the men's. There is always so much activity. An equal responsibility for performing *mitzvot* rests with the males and females. All children are soldiers in *HaShem*'s army. The boys encourage non-observant men to wear *tefilin*; the girls ask women to light candles: equal roles.

85 I am grateful to Ms Madsen for drawing my attention to her discovery, and for granting me permission to report it in Appendix IV of the revised Hebrew version of the present essay, first published in 2001 in Assaf (ed.), *Zaddik and Devotees* (Heb.), 525–7, and more recently incorporated in my 2015 *Studies in Hasidism, Sabbatianism, and Gender* (Heb.), 252–4. Thanks are due also to Mr A. Prys, one of the librarians at what was once the Jews' College and later the London School of Jewish Studies library (where the census manuscript volumes were kept when I first inspected them), who pointed me to another probable reference to the Maid of Ludmir in an earlier census. The same two references were discovered independently, apparently at about the same time, by Nathaniel Deutsch, who reported the discovery in an article entitled 'New Archival Sources on the Maiden of Ludmir' (published in *Jewish Social Studies*, 9 (2002), 164–72) and subsequently integrated it in his 2003 monograph *The Maiden of Ludmir*, 193–4, 276 n. 10.

86 See A. M. Lunz, 'The *Ḥalukah*, Its Origin and History' (Heb.), *Yerushalayim*, 9 (1911), 208–9; B.-Z. Gat, *The Jewish Community in the Land of Israel in the Years 1840–1881* [Hayishuv hayehudi be'erets yisra'el bishenot [5]600–[5]641] (Jerusalem, 1963), 123.

87 When I first examined the original census manuscript, I read this figure as '5' (represented by the Hebrew letter *he*), but on subsequent inspection of the microfiche version, which was very clear, it appeared to be '3' (represented by the Hebrew letter *gimel*). This meant that the year of her arrival in the Holy Land was 1863, not 1861 as stated in the original Hebrew version of this appendix, a correction to which Deutsch (*The Maiden of Ludmir*, 276 n. 10) rightly drew attention.

88 See n. 43 above.

89 See Shemen, *Attitudes to Women* (Yid.), ii. 329. Shemen states that she died in 1895, at the advanced old age of 90 (ibid. 330), and he goes on the say (ibid. 338 n. 5*a*) that, according to some, the year of her death was 1892. His tradition contradicts Horodetsky's claim in his first, Russian-language, report ('Ludmirskaya deva', 219) that the Maid was born in or around 1815. Geshuri (*Melody and Dance in Hasidism* (Heb.), iii. 368) repeats the same claim without citing his source, which is, most likely, Horodetsky's report, and he adds that she died in Jerusalem in 1892.

SEVEN

The Emergence of a Female Constituency in Twentieth-Century Habad Hasidism

'On Women in Hasidism': Twenty Years On

In a paper first published twenty years ago, I set out to refute the notion that the hasidic movement brought about something of a feminist revolution in Judaism.[1] It was the early twentieth-century historian of hasidism, S. A. Horodetsky, who first claimed that the movement endowed women with 'complete equality in the religious life'[2]—a radical departure from the traditional norm, which he found manifested in a number of hasidic innovations. These ranged from women's direct, personal relationship with the charismatic leader (rebbe or tsadik), which established a new equality between the sexes within the family and the community; through the breakdown of the educational barrier of Hebrew—the language of traditional scholarly discourse in the male world of Torah learning—by virtue of an outpouring of hasidic books in Yiddish, the women's tongue; to 'the rise of the Jewish woman even to the level of tsadik; if she showed herself worthy of it, nothing could stand in her way'.[3]

Against these far-reaching claims I argued that, from its inception until the early twentieth century, hasidism was and remained predominantly the preserve of men. Far from granting women equal access to the rebbe, the

I thank Chava Turniansky and Naftali Loewenthal, who read the manuscript version of this essay and offered helpful comments and suggestions. Other friends and colleagues, especially fellow members of the 2007–8 hasidism group at the Hebrew University's Institute of Advanced Studies, have made many useful contributions, each of which is acknowledged with gratitude in the notes.

sabbath and festival assemblies at his court, and above all at his 'table'—the focal point of the hasidic gathering, where he delivered his personal *torah*—regularly excluded women. The male hasidim who travelled to the court would normally leave their women behind, thus periodically 'dropping out' of matrimony and its mundane obligations. The pilgrimages to the court offered them instead the spiritually invigorating experience of communal life within an emotionally charged, exclusively male fraternity, which functioned symbolically as an alternative to ordinary family life. Moreover, contrary to Horodetsky's claim, hasidism never embarked on a programme of Yiddish publications designed to create an educated female readership. The speculative literature of hasidism, with which, during the 1780s and 1790s, the movement first launched itself in print, was published exclusively in Hebrew and remained totally inaccessible to the Yiddish-reading female (and uneducated male) public. Only the later, popular but never fully sanctioned, hasidic hagiographical writings appeared in both Hebrew and Yiddish.[4] Women could and may well have read this type of literature, which was, at least in some cases, expressly directed at them (alongside other categories of readers who were not proficient in Hebrew—uneducated men and children),[5] but—somewhat surprisingly—the literary evidence that they actually read it is extremely sparse.[6] Nor did hasidism lend any support or legitimacy to the phenomenon of independent female tsadikim. The claim that it did was based on some late local rumours and oral traditions, which portrayed a small cluster of women as charismatic spiritual leaders, equal in status and power to the male tsadikim. As I argued in my essay, at grassroots level the hasidic movement did, in all probability, occasionally bring forth a type of woman whose spiritual powers were widely acknowledged in public, and who may have attracted a hasidic following of her own. In other words, it is not unlikely that word-of-mouth reports 'in praise' of such women, first committed to writing in modern ethnography[7] but subsequently fleshed out and greatly embellished in various genres of popular literature,[8] were based on recollections of actual historical events. However, the very tradition that attests to the existence of the most remarkable of all these women, the 'Maid of Ludmir', suggests that in 'official', exclusively male, hasidic leadership circles the possibility that a woman who conducted herself as a man might become a full-fledged tsadik in her own right was greeted with alarm. Viewed as an aberration of nature—subverting traditional norms and undermining the foundations of society—it was quickly, vigorously, and apparently thoroughly suppressed.[9]

In reality, up until the early decades of the twentieth century, when the entire Orthodox sector, hasidic and non-hasidic alike, woke up to the potential for enlisting the unexploited human resources of its womenfolk in the struggle against modernity and secularism,[10] the hasidic movement had no message of its own for women as one of its constituencies. Notably, at least one hasidic leader—Meir Rotenberg of Opatów (1760–1831), who, in 1824, was asked to defend the doctrines and practices of hasidism at his interrogation by the Polish Government Commission for Religious Confessions and Public Education—stated explicitly that 'women generally are not hasidim'.[11] Contrary to Horodetsky's claims, the hasidic movement possessed no ideology aspiring to equalize women's religious or social status to that of men, nor did it set out to educate them in Yiddish, or to elevate them to positions of authority as rebbes. This is evidenced not least by the thundering silence of all the eighteenth- and nineteenth-century hasidic literary sources, both speculative and hagiographical, on every single one of these supposed innovations.[12] Most notably, throughout this period the hasidic sources contain not a single reference to the Maid of Ludmir or to any other female tsadik of her type or, indeed, of any other.[13] The latter-day interest in such remarkable women would seem to have sprung entirely from Horodetsky's oral tradition, which he first recorded in 1909 as a mere curiosity, in sober terms,[14] but which, by the early 1920s, when preparing for publication in Hebrew his four-volume history of hasidism (the first ever to feature a short chapter entitled 'The Jewish Woman in Hasidism'), he had come to regard as evidence for women's unprecedented empowerment in hasidism—the eruption of fresh spiritual and social energies that could be harnessed to the project of Jewish national revival, with its own distinct, if never fully realized, female liberationist strand. Horodetsky now presented the women he had first described cautiously as 'very rarely in the history of hasidism, active female characters who have influence on their surroundings',[15] in terms that celebrated them as full-fledged tsadikim, harbingers, as it were, of the new, egalitarian society being created in Palestine by the Zionist movement, for which he believed hasidism to offer a viable traditionalist model.[16] This partisan re-evaluation of his early findings was subsequently picked up and elaborated by others. It was eventually revitalized within the ideological context of the latter part of the twentieth century, in apologetic response to the challenges of modern feminism, and has more recently been adopted by Orthodox feminist circles as an empowering model of female Jewish spirituality. But this had little to do with the socio-religious doctrines and gender norms of pre-twentieth-century hasidism.

Women in Pre-Twentieth-Century Habad

Against this background, throughout the period from the late 1700s to the turn of the twentieth century, there is nothing remarkable about the Habad Lubavitch record as regards the attitude to women. Admittedly, according to an internal Habad tradition of early twentieth-century provenance, Shneur Zalman of Liady (Lyady), the Habad school's founder, used to teach hasidism to his beloved daughter Freyde, and she would allow her brother, Dov Ber (who was eventually to succeed Shneur Zalman as leader), to hide in the room and listen to expositions of particular topics on which he had earlier asked her to probe their father.[17] But this apparently innovative model for the initiation of women in the speculative doctrines of hasidism must be recognized as belonging in the same tradition that acknowledged certain women's capacity to acquire scholarly or spiritual accomplishments by virtue of their intimate association with distinguished men—a tradition which found fresh expression in hasidism but predated it by many centuries.[18] More exceptionally, and possibly as a by-product of Freyde's reputation for being her father's student in hasidism, she has been credited with the authorship of a letter—written in a mixture of Hebrew and Yiddish, addressed to 'my beloved brother' (presumably Dov Ber), and published several times in more than one version under her name—which argued in kabbalistic and hasidic terms that the time was not ripe for the disclosure of the messianic end date. However, the attribution of the letter to Freyde is highly questionable. As argued convincingly by Y. Mondshine, it was almost certainly written by Aaron Halevi of Starosielce—Shneur Zalman's disciple and Dov Ber's close friend ('beloved brother'), who eventually became his rival in the contest for the succession to the leadership.[19]

Another factor, often taken to suggest that, from its earliest beginnings, the Habad school was marked by its concern for the Jewish education of women, is the publication in Shklov, in 1794, of Shneur Zalman's *Hilkhot talmud torah*,[20] in which he cited the traditional strictures against Torah study by women, but ruled that 'nonetheless, women too are duty-bound to study the *halakhot* which apply to them'. He proceeded to list some examples of these, and suggested that in classical rabbinic times women used to attend sabbath sermons in which 'the sage' would explain the *halakhot* that apply to everyone, which everyone should know, 'in a language that would be understood by women and uneducated men'.[21] It must be noted, however, that there was nothing innovative or unique about the substance of Shneur Zalman's ruling; it relied on a large body of earlier halakhic sources that advocated effectively the same, and—most significantly—did not give rise to any immediate effort to create a framework for women's education in Habad.[22] The frequent references to this halakhic ruling, scattered throughout the literature emanating from the teachings of the last Lubavitcher Rebbe[23]—for whom the education of women, their spiritual empowerment, and, indeed, their mobilization as an active hasidic constituency did become an important issue—are a characteristically anachronistic, modern Habad projection of twentieth-century concerns onto its eighteenth-century origins.[24] In the same vein, Naftali Loewenthal's presentation of two short Yiddish tracts, published by Dov Ber a few years after succeeding his father to the leadership (in 1817 and 1820 respectively),[25] as 'evidence of the desire to involve women in the hasidic path of Habad' remains unconvincing. Both works were clearly aimed at uneducated readers who had no access to Hebrew—a class within which women had always formed a subcategory—but they were not addressed specifically to women, contained no message pertaining primarily to them, and there is no evidence to suggest that they attracted a female readership.[26]

Women's Access to the Rebbe

While women, as a rule, were (and usually still are) excluded from the highlight of the hasidic gathering at the rebbe's 'table', the hagiographical sources of hasidism, as well as some anti-hasidic polemics of the final decades of the eighteenth century and the early decades of the nineteenth, suggest that women could obtain a private audience with the rebbe in order to submit their *kvitl* (the note on which their personal request would be inscribed), pay their *pidyen* (from the Hebrew *pidyon* meaning 'ransom'—the payment accompanying the *kvitl*), and receive his blessing in return.[27]

But this was by no means universal. The presence of women in the courts, and above all their admittance to an audience with the rebbe, were clearly perceived as problematic. Some hasidic leaders did not admit them at all, while others would do so only under certain constraints. In the 1920s the Munkács (Mukachevo) Rebbe, Hayim Eleazar Shapira (1872–1937), found it necessary to defend the tradition of his ancestors, the tsadikim 'of our own province' (but not necessarily, at least implicitly, those of other provinces), 'who allowed women to come before them with their requests', against the objection, raised by 'a certain sage', that, according to the Talmud, women were excluded from the Jew's duty to pay his respect to his teacher on the sabbath and festivals.[28] The Munkács Rebbe justified the practice of allowing women 'to pay their respect', that is, to be admitted to his presence—apparently not only on weekdays, the usual time for their visits to the court, but also on the sabbath and festivals, which were normally reserved for the gatherings of the male hasidim—on the grounds that this would provide the opportunity to 'reprove and instruct them in God's ways', so as to ensure that they would bring up their sons as Torah scholars, conduct themselves modestly, and run kosher households.[29] But this rationale for what was clearly viewed by some as the questionable practice of welcoming women to the courts would seem to point at the novel awareness in all Orthodox circles by this time that women should be mobilized in the cause of maintaining the allegiance to tradition of the younger generation, who were deserting it in droves in response to the appeal of a range of secularist ideologies (on which see more below).

By contrast, during the first half of the nineteenth century, Meir of Przemyślany (1783–1850) apparently decided to stop admitting women to his court. A number of letters by eminent contemporaries addressing him on this subject suggest that 'important women had pleaded with the highest rabbinic authorities of the day, seeking an introduction to the rebbe [of Przemyślany] that would allow them to visit and put their requests to him, but the rebbe responded in the negative'.[30] Isaac of Neshchiz (1789–1868) was similarly said, towards the end of his life,

> to have forbidden women from entering his house unless they were accompanied by their husbands, except for handing over their *pidyon* [probably not to the rebbe himself but to one of his attendants] . . . Otherwise he would only speak to a woman through the window. He explained that this was in order altogether to

discourage the women from coming, since he could no longer bear the burden of the masses flocking to his court.[31]

Women were denied personal access also to Israel of Ruzhin (1796–1850); they were allowed only to hand over their *kvitlekh* and *pidyon* money to his attendants, and this was apparently the practice at the court of Yerahmiel (d. 1839), son of the 'Holy Jew' of Pshischa (Przysucha) as well.[32] Of the Belzer Rebbe, Issachar Dov Roke'ah (1854–1926), Jiři Langer of Prague, who had stayed at his court for the entire duration of the First World War, reports that 'the saint never looks on the face of a woman. If he must speak to women—as, when he receives a *kvitl*—he looks out of the window while he speaks.'[33] And a late Habad hagiographical tradition, at pains to distinguish the Habad style of leadership (where, as is implicit in the tale, the rebbe never engages with women) from the practice of Ukrainian or—as most other hasidic schools are often referred to in the late Habad sources—'Polish' tsadikim, claims that 'it was customary for Mordecai of Chernobyl [1770–1837] to give blessings even to women, so long as they remained concealed behind a curtain'.[34] Another tale in the same collection attributes to Hillel of Porich (Parichi)—a Chernobyl hasid who was drawn to Habad and became a disciple of Dov Ber, the Mitteler Rebbe—the following statement, highlighting the superiority of Habad over Ukrainian hasidism in similar but more explicit terms: 'Let women and madmen travel to Vilednik [Veledniki, the seat of the Chernobyl tsadik Israel of Vilednik] while men and pietists [*ḥasidim*] travel to Lubavitch.'[35]

Shneur Zalman of Liady, like his younger contemporary Nahman of Bratslav, may indeed have been one of those hasidic leaders who refrained altogether from dealing with women. There is no direct evidence on this, but the probability is suggested by the absence of references to women from Shneur Zalman's Liozno Ordinances, which regulated the visits to his court of a range of well-differentiated, distinct classes of hasidim, apparently all male.[36] The same absence of references to women marks all of Nathan Sternharz's descriptions of the pilgrimages to Nahman of Bratslav's court,[37] about which at least one late Bratslav source states categorically: 'Women were not admitted to our rebbe's presence under any circumstances.'[38] Both Shneur Zalman and Nahman of Bratslav were critical of the 'vulgar' tsadikim of their day, who, rather than presenting their adherents with *torah* as an intellectual, spiritual, and moral challenge, offered them no more than their 'blessing', which was intended to resolve material problems of daily life, and entailed the expectation of miraculous feats—a style of 'tsadikism' from which both leaders strove to distance themselves.[39] Since women—excluded from all the occasions on which the rebbe would deliver *torah*—could only have come to the court in pursuit of such mundane 'blessings', both Shneur Zalman and Nahman of Bratslav apparently denied them access.

While the literary sources of Shneur Zalman's time permit us no more than to surmise his stance from the evidence of silence, the rich memoirist-hagiographical literature of twentieth-century Habad often claims that he, and most of his successors, refrained from dealing with women as a matter of policy. Admittedly these late Habad sources, as was suggested above, are all too often anachronistic, but in respect of the attitude to women their credibility is enhanced precisely by the fact that they run counter to what became the 'official' ideology and common practice of twentieth-century Habad (on which see below). Thus a modern anthology of Habad tales, published in three volumes during the 1970s, reads:

In a neighbouring town to Liozno there was a woman who had been deserted by her husband [an *agunah*] . . . The residents of the town advised her to go to the Old *Admor* [the standard Habad appellation of Shneur Zalman] in Liozno. Even though in those days he did not admit any women to his presence,[40] [they advised that] she should stand at his door and not leave until he gave her a clear answer, which is what she did. Every day she would stand at his door, loudly and tearfully pleading to be allowed in to see him. On one occasion, when the [male] hasidim arrived . . . they took pity and pleaded on her behalf. [As a result, when] she [next] stood behind the [closed] door, the *Admor* gave her a brief answer.[41]

Nor is there any contemporary evidence on the attitude to direct dealings with women of Shneur Zalman's son and successor, Dov Ber, the Mitteler Rebbe (1773–1827),[42] but a late hagiographical tale, recorded by one of his descendants, Azriel Zelig Slonim (d.1971), would seem to confirm that he, too, did not admit women to his presence:

In Velizh there lived R. Isaiah Eydels, who managed the business affairs of the wealthy and well-known R. Yeruham Dov Berlin. He said that once, on his way to Karlsbad, the Mitteler Rebbe visited Velizh and stayed at the house of that wealthy R. Yeruham Dov. R. Isaiah himself had been appointed by Yeruham Dov to attend on the rebbe throughout his visit. Naturally, a great crowd gathered from all over the region to hear [the Mitteler Rebbe's] *torah* and to obtain a private audience with him. The wife of the wealthy R. Yeruham Dov also wanted to enter, seeking the rebbe's blessing for viable offspring, but women were not admitted to the rebbe. It was decided that R. Isaiah the attendant . . . would plead for the woman and her entire family to be allowed in.[43]

Another hagiographical tale, however, suggests that at least once a year the Mitteler Rebbe would admit women and grant them his blessing, which had miraculous effect: 'As is well known, the Mitteler Rebbe was not in the habit of performing miracles, except on [the festival of] Lag Ba'omer.[44] Once, on Lag Ba'omer, a barren woman came to him and asked for a blessing. He advised her always to take a bite of food on waking up from her sleep. A year later she gave birth to twins.'[45] But the situation implied in this tale—which is of late provenance—whereby on Lag Ba'omer men and women seeking a blessing had equal access to Dov Ber, reflects the modern Habad practice of granting women private audiences with the rebbe. Since, as was suggested above, late traditions portraying the past in terms that are compatible with twentieth-century practice may be considered less credible than those that are at odds with it, the implicit claim in the present tale must be deemed less credible than the explicit statement to the effect that 'women were not admitted to the rebbe'.

Of the Mitteler Rebbe's son-in-law Menahem Mendel, 'the Tsemah Tsedek'—Habad's third leader (from 1828 until his death in 1866)—we are told by one of his followers in his memoirs that 'with the rebbe, R. Mendele, it was the custom that women were not allowed under any circumstances to enter his chamber with their requests'.[46] This is corroborated by some of Habad's more recent hagiographical tales:

Once a woman came to his holiness . . . the Tsemah Tsedek . . . She had been deserted by her husband for many years . . . and did not know what to do. Now, with the Tsemah Tsedek, women were not allowed to enter . . .[47]

A desperate woman, who kept miscarrying . . . came to his holiness . . . the Tsemah Tsedek. They did not allow her to enter, but she pushed her way in . . .[48]

At the time of his holiness, the Tsemah Tsedek . . . there was in Lubavitch a wealthy woman who was barren . . . Once she came wishing to enter the rebbe's chamber and ask him [for a blessing] about this, but the attendant (the *gabai* Hayim Dov Ber, who used to admit supplicants to their private audience with the rebbe) would not allow her in under any circumstances . . . She began to argue with him, but he persisted in his staunch refusal to allow her in.[49]

Another modern Habad tale suggests that, while his initial policy was not to admit any women, the Tsemah Tsedek, under the influence of his wife, eventually began to deal personally with desperate women, especially *agunot*—women who had been deserted by their husbands:

At first the . . . Tsemah Tsedek was not in the habit of granting women a private audience, until the occasion when his wife fell ill, and he came to visit her. He sat down and asked her: 'How are you?' and she replied: 'You should know, Mendel, that I am unwell on account of your transgressions, for many *agunot* have come to see you, and you refuse to let them in. You are totally indifferent to their misfortune, and this is why I am ill.' From then on the . . . Tsemah Tsedek began to grant private audiences to *agunot* and to other desperate women, whom he was able to help by miraculous means.[50]

Indeed, quite a number of tales in the same anthology refer to women in dire circumstances—mothers of critically ill children, women who miscarried repeatedly, childless widows in pursuit of release from marriage to a recalcitrant or untraceable levir, and especially deserted wives seeking remarriage—who were apparently received and helped by the Tsemah Tsedek despite the claim that he did not grant private audiences to women.[51] That he displayed sensitivity to the plight of such women, whether or not he ever received them personally, is evidenced by the Tsemah Tsedek's many responsa that deal with the halakhic dimension of their predicament, where his often lenient rulings were clearly designed to serve their interest.[52] The sixth Lubavitcher Rebbe, Joseph Isaac Schneersohn (1880–1950), basing himself on what he presents as the eyewitness account of his grandmother Rivkah (1834–1914)—wife of the fourth *admor*, Shemuel, and the Tsemah Tsedek's daughter-in-law[53]—refers in one of his historiographical letters to the case of an *agunah* who had come to the Tsemah Tsedek seeking permission to remarry. In the middle of the narrative, Joseph Isaac inserts a bracketed comment of his own, which is clearly designed to reconcile the conflicting traditions whereby, on the one hand, the Tsemah Tsedek did not admit any women to his presence, and on the other hand he concerned himself personally with the plight of many *agunot*. Joseph Isaac's comment suggests that at a certain point, presumably—as suggested by the tale quoted above—when the Tsemah Tsedek, under the influence of his wife, decided to attend to the requests for help he was receiving from desperate women, a compromise solution was found that allowed such women to plead their case without actually confronting him face to face:

My grandmother . . . told us that once a certain *agunah* came to . . . her father-in-law [the Tsemah Tsedek] . . . and brought with her an 11- or 12-year-old boy who was mute and hard of hearing. Several weeks passed, but owing to the large number of people coming [to the rebbe], her turn to be admitted to his presence had not arrived (as there was a time when *agunot* were permitted to stand in a room adjacent to his, with the door [between the two rooms] kept open; our rebbe would sit and listen to each woman's case and supplication, and then instruct his attendant . . . to tell her that she should travel to such and such a place, or enquire with such and such a rabbi, etc.).[54]

The *admor* Joseph Isaac goes on to relate that, while awaiting her turn to address the Tsemah Tsedek (which never arrived, although she did finally manage to smuggle her deaf-and-dumb son into his chamber, where the boy gave the rebbe her request note and was miraculously healed while also being told where his father, who was alive, could be found), the *agunah* sat with the Tsemah Tsedek's daughter-in-law, to whom she poured out her heart, 'bemoaning her ill fate, for her husband had been missing for seven years, and she had already been permitted [to remarry] by several rabbis, but would not do so without the *admor*'s consent'.[55] Although the tale is concerned primarily with the Tsemah Tsedek's reputation for supernatural powers, which the *admor* Joseph Isaac was eager to promote despite the traditional Habad disdain for miracle-working tsadikim,[56] it suggests that, while women's access to the Tsemah Tsedek was difficult to obtain and never fully direct, they could relate directly and intimately to a female member of his household. Another tale, transmitted by Azriel Zelig Slonim,[57] ascribes a similar function to Hayah Mushka, the Tsemah Tsedek's wife:

A certain *agunah* stayed in Lubavitch for many days, in the hope of learning from the rebbe where her husband might be found. When a very long time elapsed without her hearing anything from the rebbe, she burst into the rebbetsin's chamber, pleading with her to ask the rebbe for salvation on her behalf. The rebbetsin went in to the Tsemah Tsedek and complained about his failure to help this desperate woman find her husband, as he had revealed to dozens of other *agunot* where their husbands were to be found.[58]

According to another tale in the same collection, the Tsemah Tsedek's son—the fourth *admor*, Shemuel (1834–82)—refrained, like his father, from speaking to women but allowed them to hear his advice and blessing from behind the door, in an adjacent room:

A childless couple was about to divorce in compliance with the decree of the rabbinical court . . . Our people took pity on this couple, who had lived together amicably . . . and were now being forced to separate. They advised them to consult our rebbe . . . The couple agreed. The husband entered the rebbe's chamber and told him about his misfortune. The *admor* Shemuel was surprised and asked: 'Who has ruled that you should divorce?! No, no! I look to God to grant you long-living offspring.' The husband was astounded at this . . . for he had long abandoned all hope of children . . . Wishing that his wife should hear and be encouraged by the rebbe's words, he asked for her to be allowed to stand behind the door while the rebbe repeated his opinion and his blessing. On the next day, the husband entered again, and his wife, from behind the door, heard the rebbe forbid them to divorce and promise them long-living offspring.[59]

A generation later the fifth *admor*, Shalom Dovber (1861–1920), is still described in the memoirs of one of his followers as maintaining what appears to be his ancestral tradition of refusing, as a rule, to have direct dealings with women:

Women the rebbe [Shalom Dovber] would not admit at all, while—mutatis mutandis—gentiles were occasionally granted a private audience. Once a wealthy gentile woman came to Lubavitch and entered the rebbe's court, claiming that she had had some business dealings with a Jew who had deceived her. The Jew was denying the accusation, and she could not prove it. Her Jewish acquaintances advised her to turn to the Lubavitcher Rebbe, since he would be sure to influence that Jew . . . and this was why she had come. They informed her that the rebbe did not admit women but promised to put her case to him.[60]

Raphael Kahan, the narrator (born in 1897),[61] appends to this episode a personal childhood recollection, which throws more light on the procedure for dealing with women's requests in the Lubavitch court of Shalom Dovber's day (*c.*1905):

When I was 8 years old (we lived in Warsaw at that time) . . . my father conceived the idea of sending me to Lubavitch [to be admitted to Habad's Tomekhei Temimim yeshiva, which Shalom Dovber had founded in 1897] . . . My mother objected but my father . . . spoke to her at length, assuring her that she need not worry, since she could travel there with me and find me a good place to stay. Eventually she was persuaded and travelled with me to Lubavitch, where she rented a good place for me to stay and receive my meals . . . Mother then went to see the rebbe's wife . . . Shterna Sarah . . . and told her the reason for her visit. The rebbe's wife was surprised and asked: 'Should such a small child be sent away from home? Have you done this with your husband's consent?' My mother replied that she was acting under her husband's orders, and that she did not know whether or not he had consulted the rebbe in advance. The rebbe's wife advised her to consult the rebbe, but since he did not grant private audiences to women, my mother went to Samuel 'the inscriber' (who used to write down, for anyone who required his services, the notes on which personal requests were to be addressed to the rebbe),[62] and he wrote down what she had told him. The rebbe's attendant . . . then took me to the rebbe with my mother's request note. After the rebbe had read it (and I had no idea of what it said), he started examining me on my studies . . . Finally he asked me: 'Do you want to stay here?' I replied that I did. He asked further: 'Will you not miss your mother?' and I burst into tears. He then asked his attendant to instruct my mother to take me back home, and said that he himself would write to my father. I subsequently saw the letter which the rebbe had written to my mother [*sic*] . . . It said as follows: 'Your son is an infant who still needs his mother. In two years' time—so long as Messiah has not arrived, Heaven forbid—bring him back.'[63]

Notably, like Hayah Mushka, the Tsemah Tsedek's wife, or Rivkah his daughter-in-law[64]—wife of the fourth *admor*, Shemuel, and mother of the fifth, Shalom Dovber—Shterna Sarah (1860–1942), Shalom Dovber's wife, appears to be serving as a point of access to the rebbe's advice and help for a female supplicant, whom, by definition, the rebbe would not receive personally. Another late hagiographical tale traces the same procedure back to the lifetime of Habad's founder, Shneur Zalman of Liady. It suggests that while women were regularly denied direct access to the Old *Admor*, they could nevertheless address him through his wife Sterna, who acted as an intermediary, apparently pleading even on behalf of some non-Jewish women:

The wife of the Old *Admor* always pleaded on behalf of the women who came to him seeking his assistance or blessing . . . On one occasion she came to her husband and told him that one of their female relatives was in urgent need of fifty rubles. The old rebbe replied: 'Where might such a sum be obtained, if not from *kadokhes* [idiomatic Yiddish for 'nothing', 'thin air'; lit. 'fever']?' On the same day a wealthy gentile woman came to the rebbe's wife, pleading for the Old *Admor* to bless and heal her from the *kadokhes* [fever] that troubled her greatly. The rebbe's wife entered his room again and conveyed the gentile woman's request. The Old

Admor said: 'Did I not tell you this morning that only *kadokhes* would help our female relative? Tell this gentile woman to give the needy woman fifty rubles, and I shall pray for her full recovery.[65]

If indeed, as these tales suggest, the Lubavitcher Rebbe's wife (or other prominent female members of his household, such as his mother, daughter, or daughter-in-law, who were themselves either future or past rebbetsins) always functioned as a channel through which women could voice their personal concerns and obtain the rebbe's advice or blessing, then arguably, despite his refusal to deal with them directly, and their exclusion from his hasidic *torah*, the women who belonged to his community by virtue of their kinsmen's affiliation with him may be viewed as a distinct, albeit secondary, female Habad constituency—united by the connection to the rebbe through his wife, daughter, or daughter-in-law, and sharing a collective sense of Habad identity.[66] This, however, must be qualified by the observation that, unlike the men who, in addition to their private audiences with the rebbe, generally visited the court at regular times, heard the rebbe's *torah* together, and thus constituted a socially cohesive, spiritually empowered collective, the women, according to all the hagiographical sources, would turn to the rebbe's wife on an ad hoc basis and only as individuals, since there existed no frameworks within the court that would enable them to cohere and be empowered as a group.[67] To this extent, therefore, any notion of an active Habad (or, for that matter, any other hasidic) female constituency during the eighteenth and the whole of the nineteenth century must be viewed as being no more than tenuous.[68]

The Makeup of Female Hasidic Identities: Individual and Collective

Rebbetsin Rivkah: 'Of Hasidic Stock'

Even by the beginning of the twentieth century, there are as yet no indications that women were involved in the collective life of the Lubavitch court as a united, self-conscious Habad entity. One memoirist's testimony offers an interesting insight into the construction of an individual female hasidic identity during that period. Remarkably, it concerns not the wife of an ordinary hasid but the dowager Rebbetsin Rivkah—Shalom Dovber's mother, the matriarch of the household, who was apparently herself treated as a quasi-rebbe by the inner circle of the Lubavitch court.[69] According to this testimony, which the author, Hayim Mordecai Perlow (d. 1977), records as an event that he had witnessed himself, during the 1910 Simhat Torah celebration in Lubavitch Rebbetsin Rivkah urged her son to stop his address to the assembled hasidim. He had been speaking at length about his late father and the circumstances of his death, which was upsetting him to such an extent that he began to weep copiously. The crowded assembly hall was hot and stuffy, and soon everyone was aware that Shalom Dovber was unwell.

At this point his mother, the rebbetsin [who had come in from an adjacent room] . . . said to him: 'Surely, you must see that you cannot go on . . . Stop now . . . You will say what you want to say now on another occasion.' He replied with the following words (as they are imprinted on my memory, which may not be entirely accurate): 'Mother, I must give a "talk" [*siḥah* in Hebrew, here *a reyd* in Yiddish—a technical term for the less formal address by a Lubavitcher rebbe] and then deliver a "discourse" [*ma'amar* in Hebrew or *maymer* in Yiddish—his formal and usually very substantial lesson],' to which she replied: 'But if so, you can't.' He responded: 'Mother, surely, you are a hasidic Jewess [*a khsidishe yidene*]!' She replied: 'Whether or not I am a hasidic Jewess I do not know, but that I am of hasidic stock [*fun khsidim shtam*] is certain.'[70]

Appealing to her to share his own, and presumably also the hasidim's, sense that his duty as rebbe to deliver *torah* takes precedence over all other considerations, Shalom Dovber attempts to ascribe to his mother a hasidic consciousness of her own, which Rebbetsin Rivkah dismisses, insisting that as a woman, her connection to hasidism is a matter of genealogy alone.

Rebbetsin Shterna Sarah: Early Attempts at Mobilization of Habad Women

There are, nevertheless, at about this time, some intimations of a certain collective bond that existed between the younger rebbetsin, Shterna Sarah, and a group of female members of the Habad community, those who were permanently resident in the town of Lubavitch. This emerges from an account of the burglary that took place one night in Babinovichi, in the country house where Shalom Dovber and his family were spending the summer. 'The next day', when news of the burglary reached Lubavitch, 'almost all of the yeshiva teachers and supervisors came to see the rebbe . . . as well as many Lubavitch householders. And many townswomen, those who were particularly close [*hamekoravot*], came to see the rebbetsin.'[71] It is not clear precisely what the status of *mekoravot* amounted to, beyond the sheer geographical proximity that facilitated frequent visits to the court, but it undoubtedly implies the women's awareness of their affiliation with one another and with the Lubavitch court through their common personal connection to the rebbetsin.[72]

The first evidence, however, of women being harnessed to some collective action that went beyond their mutual personal bond with the rebbetsin was their mobilization in the cause of providing financial support for the Tomekhei Temimim yeshiva, a move that was apparently initiated and orchestrated by Shterna Sarah herself. This is described in the memoirs of Raphael Kahan, one of the early students of the yeshiva:

> There was a kitchen where the senior students of the yeshiva would eat (although some ate in the lodging houses at their own expense) . . . The rebbetsin, Shterna Sarah . . . set up a kitchen (not in the rebbe's court) also for the pupils of the lower classes,[73] where they were provided with lunch—a first course and a soup, with a little meat and bread, as much as they required, and this was known as 'the rebbetsin's soup'. She established a women's organization, and each one of the women made an annual contribution to the kitchen.[74]

Another memoirist who attended the yeshiva during approximately the same period provides a few more details about the younger pupils' kitchen:

> At that time,[75] Rebbetsin Shterna Sarah . . . launched her support project, which was called the rebbetsin's *krupnik* [barley soup].[76] Once a day she would provide a hot meal for the students in the lower classes: bread and occasionally some appetizer, and a hot dish with a little meat. She hired for this the services of Shimon Dovber Lifshits (on what terms I do not know), who kept an inn, which even in Lubavitch was not considered first rate, and it was arranged for us to have our meals there.[77]

Shterna Sarah's fundraising activities among the female members of the Habad community are highlighted in the literature emanating from her son, the sixth *admor*, Joseph Isaac: 'Rebbetsin Shterna Sarah . . . was particularly concerned with the maintenance of the Tomekhei Temimim yeshiva. She founded a world-wide women's organization, which sustained all the pupils in the preparatory classes.'[78] Admittedly, the reference here to the women's organization as 'world-wide' is something of an exaggeration, reflecting Joseph Isaac's own ambitious vision more than the reality of

Tomekhei Temimim in Lubavitch of his father's day.[79] This is evident from the published accounts of the rebbetsin's Damen Ferayn oyf Shtitse di Orme Kleyne Shiller in di Khadorim fun di Yeshive Tomkhey Tmimim[80] (the Ladies' Association for the Support of the Poor Junior Heder Pupils of the Tomekhei Temimim Yeshiva), as the organization was officially called. The rebbetsin first published the accounts in summary form in an autumn 1911 issue of the Habad children's weekly *Ha'aḥ*,[81] where she listed the overall expenditure and income figures for the three years from 1909 to 1911. A year later, in a booklet printed in St Petersburg towards the end of 1912, she published a breakdown of individual donors' names, places of residence, and amounts of donation, covering the period from the autumn of 1911 to the autumn of 1912.[82] Out of the 179 contributions listed, the vast majority had come from within the borders of the Russian empire, with only two from 'America', six from Königsberg, one from Munich, one from St Moritz (Switzerland), and one from Grosswardein (Austro-Hungary). Nevertheless, Shterna Sarah's recruitment of female donors from the wider Habad community—women who did not belong to the inner circle of her female Lubavitch 'intimates' but who were scattered in places as far from Lubavitch and from each other as Moscow, St Petersburg, Warsaw, Riga, Jakobstadt (Finland), or Kishinev[83]—was undoubtedly a novel initiative, creating for the first time a framework that would enable a female Habad constituency to emerge. It was clearly prompted by the urgent need to raise funds for the rapidly expanding yeshiva, and, most particularly, by Shalom Dovber's ambition for Tomekhei Temimim to provide communal accommodation and eating facilities for all its students (an ambition that was never fully realized). This he considered, on pedagogical grounds, to be preferable to the alternative traditional arrangement, whereby individual students would be accommodated in local lodging houses, while their meals would be provided by a rota of local householders who would each feed a student or two on a designated day of the week.[84]

Shterna Sarah's Ladies' Association, harnessing Habad's nascent female constituency to the charitable cause of supporting needy yeshiva students, was an east European Orthodox example of the type of Jewish women's voluntary organization that had been in existence in east central Europe and the West since the first half of the nineteenth century.[85] It was in evidence in the Russian empire as well, where, by the second half of the century, the wives of wealthy Jewish bankers and industrialists were becoming involved in philanthropy and had begun to set up a variety of Jewish women's charitable associations.[86] In 1882 the *maskil* Aleksander Zederbaum—from the pages of the *Yidishes folksblat*, which he edited—called on Jewish women to organize themselves into fundraising associations that would provide precisely the same support for young yeshiva students as Rebbetsin Shterna Sarah was to set up almost thirty years later:

> An earnest word to our Jewish daughters in Russia and in Poland! These days a new idea has come up: to set up a kitchen for many, which would cost very little and where the food would be good and clean. A midday meal [at such a kitchen] would surely be cheaper than what it costs for every yeshiva student to eat each day in another house. It is much better for every housewife [*baleboste*] to give a few kopeks a week to a general chest. Out of this a kitchen would be set up, with a table at which a healthy meal would be provided in a dignified fashion—free of charge to the poor and cheaply to the half-poor. If, for example, each decent housewife gave 10–15 kopeks a week, then for 10 kopeks one could have, in an economically run kitchen, a very good midday meal, with soup, meat, and bread . . . Therefore the ladies and the well-to-do women in the larger towns should undertake this task in earnest . . . first of all in their own town, where they should prompt the wealthy housewives to set themselves a weekly sum that would be paid into the Ladies' Chest—as much as their good hearts would allow and according to their circumstances. Then they should ask the women they know in the surrounding small towns to do the same.[87]

As a *maskil*, however, Zederbaum called on the women to provide support not only for the young *yeshive bokhers* but also for the equally poor Jewish 'pro-gymnasium' (pre-secondary school) students, and especially university students, whose conditions of deprivation and hardship he went on to describe at length in the same piece.

Shterna Sarah was thus introducing the Habad world of the early twentieth century to a mode of female voluntary action that was not unknown among the upper bourgeoisie of eastern European Jewry. Nor was she apparently being innovative in concerning herself with the provision of food not only for her husband's table but also for others visiting or staying at his court, which would seem to have been the traditional responsibility of a rebbetsin.[88] It is therefore difficult to determine whether her method of securing the provision of daily meals for the younger pupils of the yeshiva was primarily an extension of her traditional female role of charity and food provider, or whether, as a response to the novel situation created by the establishment of what was effectively the first modern yeshiva in the hasidic world, her initiative redefined her role by formally incorporating her, as fundraiser among the women, in Habad's 'senior management team', where, alongside her husband and son, she was engaged in the modernization of the court's mode of operation. The latter interpretation gains some support from fragments of information about Shterna Sarah's involvement in policy-making at the court, and her role as her husband's personal assistant. For example early in 1915, several months after the outbreak of the First World War, she was described as eagerly following the latest news from the front and 'constantly reading out to her husband newspaper articles about the course of the war'.[89] By the autumn of the same year she had apparently become sufficiently anxious to have initiated, and negotiated personally with three senior figures at the Lubavitch court, the possibility of abandoning the town of Lubavitch and moving the court away from the threat of the advancing German army:

After the High Holidays . . . everyone was pleased at the knowledge that this year [1915–16] the rebbe would not spend the winter abroad . . . since the First World War was going on and all the borders were closed. After Sukkot the rebbetsin . . . Shterna Sarah . . . summoned the *mashpi'a* [the yeshiva students' spiritual guide] S[amuel] G[runem] Esterman, the hasid Samuel Gurarye, and the hasid Samuel Mikhl Trainin to a meeting, putting it to them that since the German troops were approaching Minsk from one direction and Polotsk from the other, there was a risk that the Russian government would take important people hostage, and if the German army invaded, they, too, would take important people hostage. It might therefore be best for the *admor* to move to [one of] the towns of central Russia. The above-mentioned hasidim asked the rebbetsin: 'And what does the *admor* think about this?' She replied that in his opinion, they should move as soon as possible. It then became known that his holiness was soon to move to [one of] the towns of central Russia, but the matter had not been publicized as yet.[90]

In addition, Shterna Sarah's son, the *admor* Joseph Isaac, describes her as her husband's personal assistant not only in domestic but also in public affairs: 'Whenever . . . her husband the *admor* . . . Shalom Dovber went abroad, the rebbetsin would copy his papers and letters concerned with public affairs, and would assist him in his work.'[91] He also reports that she was in the habit, from the early years of her marriage, of copying out her husband's commentaries on the hasidic discourses of his predecessor, the *admor* Shemuel.[92]

And yet the court of Shalom Dovber's time did not turn to its emergent female constituency with anything other than the call to provide financial support for an educational establishment that was conceived in purely traditional terms as being exclusively male. This was the Tomekhei Temimim yeshiva, which was designed to nurture Habad's future elite core. It was envisaged as a vanguard of rigorously trained young men who would lead Shalom Dovber's campaign of resistance to the secular ideologies of Haskalah, Zionism, and socialism, while at the same time revitalizing Orthodox Judaism in the spirit of Habad and providing an alternative to the Lithuanian yeshivas, which had been attracting intellectually able young hasidim, and which Shalom Dovber believed to be a gateway to Haskalah.[93] Far from incorporating women in this vision as militant campaigners in their own right for the promotion of Orthodoxy and the spiritual values of Habad, he held them to be responsible for the falling standards of religious observance in the home, and thus for the growing estrangement from tradition of the younger generation. Having called attention to the 'dreadful conditions of the present time, [when] most of our youngsters are being swept away . . . by the rising tide of libertinism, which has taken root in their hearts as a result of numerous secular books written by heretics and deniers',[94] he went on to point the finger of blame at women for introducing their children to secular education and altogether undermining their commitment to religion. In terms that echo traditional rabbinic and kabbalistic notions of women's frivolity, and above all their susceptibility to sexual contamination by Satan,[95] Shalom Dovber wrote in 1902:

> Satan dances first among the women, to cast into them the filth of secularism. They then run their households in the spirit of secularism, take into their hands the guidance and education of their children, prevail upon their husbands with their own frivolous notions, and send their sons to the [secular] teachers who corrupt them, instead of sending them to traditional, religious teachers.[96]

The Court of Joseph Isaac: From 'Family Purity' to Hasidic Education for Women

While Shalom Dovber had identified women as a source of the malaise of secularism, his son and successor, the sixth *admor*, Joseph Isaac Schneersohn, drew the logical conclusion from his father's diagnosis. For the first time in the history of Habad, he personally addressed the 'wives and daughters of the hasidim' collectively and directly, calling on them to embrace and champion the cause of preserving Orthodox Judaism. During his visit to the United States in 1929–30, where he was hosted by local communities of Habad hasidim who had been settling in the New World since the start of the mass emigration from eastern Europe in the last decades of the nineteenth century, he was particularly shocked by the younger generation's total estrangement from religion. He felt that it was both essential and possible to draw them back into the fold:

I have met many young men who were born here and who, as a consequence of their education, are far removed from Torah knowledge. Out of ignorance of the strictures of both positive and negative commandments, they do not observe them . . . These dry bones . . . may yet be resurrected . . . I have come to the clear understanding that . . . these young men and women [may be reached] by the living word . . . written in a language they will understand, mild and clear, in *zhargon* [Yiddish] and in translation into the local [English] vernacular.[97]

One of the first steps he took was to embark on a campaign for Jewish 'family purity', calling specifically on women to organize themselves into ladies' associations that would initiate, facilitate, and ensure strict observance of the laws that required of them ritual immersion in a *mikveh* to mark the end of each monthly period of prescribed abstention from conjugal relations. He urged the more experienced women to engage in propaganda for the cause—to speak in public about the laws of ritual purity to female audiences, especially the young, and to spread written information in Hebrew, Yiddish, and English that would provide them with practical guidance on the subject.[98] On his return to eastern Europe, Joseph Isaac visited his followers in Lithuania, similarly calling on women to found 'family purity' associations, of which the first was soon established in Rokiškis.[99] In a letter sent in the autumn of 1936 from Otwock, near Warsaw, he wrote to one of his followers in the Holy Land:

It is the duty of the wives and daughters of the hasidim, may they live, to stand at the forefront of every enterprise that would strengthen religion and Judaism in general, and in particular family purity, which is an area that they must take entirely upon themselves so as to establish on a firm basis the purity of the daughters of Israel. Naturally all the men, the communities, and their institutions must help them in whatever they require. But family purity is entirely the responsibility of the women. It is up to them to establish and manage it in such a way that one woman would alert another, and the other [would alert] yet another, and so would all of them, with their husbands, their sons, and their daughters.[100]

It is not clear how effective the 'family purity' campaign as such, and other attempts to found ladies' associations in support, for example, of various branches of the Tomekhei Temimim yeshiva, might have been at the time,[101] but there is no doubt that the mobilization of women, and the positive encouragement of female activism, had become a pronounced policy of the sixth *admor*, and this was soon coupled by unprecedented endeavours to initiate women in the spiritual teachings of Habad hasidism.

When I first referred briefly to the latter in my essay on women in hasidism (Ch. 6 above), I presented Joseph Isaac as tolerating, rather than initiating, the instruction of women in Habad doctrines. It had been triggered by an individual request for guidance on behalf of a single young woman, for whom Joseph Isaac recommended exceptionally a limited level of hasidic instruction under careful male supervision. He was, after all, as I argued at the time, 'primarily interested in [women's] contribution to the campaign for the reinforcement of Orthodox Jewish practice in general, and specifically in those areas where their influence as women could be most direct'.[102] In that context the introduction of women to the speculative teachings of Habad must have been no more than a secondary concern of relatively little impact.[103] Since then, however, Naftali Loewenthal has demonstrated that what indeed began, in the winter of 1936, as a response to the unusual case of an individual young woman soon led to the creation of a pioneering framework for the instruction of women in Habad 'talks' and discourses, which consciously aimed to establish comparability and parity between, on the one hand, the lay association of Brothers of the Temimim (Ahei Hatemimim)—young men who were not themselves students of Tomekhei Temimim, but who would meet in the evenings on a regular basis to study Habad teachings as an expression of the ethos of the yeshiva[104]—and, on the other hand, the parallel association Sisters of the Temimim (Ahot Hatemimim), equally connected to the hasidic ethos of the yeshiva.[105] The latter began with a group of girls in Riga, who studied together Habad discourses in Yiddish under the supervision of three male 'shepherds' appointed by Joseph Isaac. The regular meetings of this Sister association lasted from 1937 until the Soviet invasion of Latvia at the end of 1940, which was followed by the Nazi liquidation of the community in

1941. Once the Riga group was established, Joseph Isaac called on women to follow its model by setting up Sister associations elsewhere, and at least one other Ahot Hatemimim group was active during the same period in New York, with Joseph Isaac closely monitoring and encouraging its activities.[106]

The sixth *admor* was thus instituting the regular instruction of women in hasidic doctrines—a radical departure from an educational tradition that generally exposed women to little more than a small repertoire of basic Jewish texts and the religious laws that applied to them, which at least some authorities (including Shneur Zalman of Liady[107]) had sanctioned. Joseph Isaac was clearly breaking new ground, although characteristically he anchored his innovation in what he implied was an established Habad tradition. In a letter sent from Otwock in the winter of 1937, he attributed to his father, the *admor* Shalom Dovber, the desire—supposedly expressed in detail and at great length in his 'talk' delivered at the 1899 Simhat Torah assembly of the hasidim in Lubavitch—for all fathers and teachers to focus for at least half an hour each day on the instruction in hasidic lore of boys and girls—'the sons and daughters of the hasidim'—equally and alike.[108] In another letter, written two years earlier, he had already projected this 'traditional' concern even further back, to the time of his grandfather the fourth *admor*, Shemuel, who allegedly reproached his followers (in Yiddish) for neglecting the hasidic education of their daughters:

> For true Habad stock [*in geza*] there is no difference between a son and a daughter. [But] the hasidim provide a hasidic education only to their sons, and they forget to initiate and educate their daughters in the paths of hasidism. The Or Hahayim[109] had daughters with whom he used to study the Pentateuch, and this became his *Or haḥayim* Torah commentary.[110]

There is no indication whatsoever, other than Joseph Isaac's claims above, that either the fifth *admor*, Shalom Dovber—who, as we have seen, was far from positive in his evaluation of women—or indeed his father the fourth *admor*, Shemuel, had ever concerned himself with the hasidic education of the wives and daughters of his followers.[111] Nor is there any evidence to suggest that attempts were ever made during either of their reigns to instruct women in the spiritual teachings of Habad. This, coupled with the fact that Joseph Isaac's references to their pronouncements on this issue coincided with the launch of his own programme of activating and integrating in Habad spirituality the female membership of his flock, suggests that he was fully aware that the novel practices he was advocating might be controversial, and that he needed to invoke the authority of the past if he was to establish their legitimacy.

After his escape from Europe in 1940 and the transfer of his court to New York, Joseph Isaac was fully engaged in the effort to recreate Habad's institutional frameworks and to establish its distinctive ethos on American soil. He did not lose sight of his 1930s experience of addressing the educational and spiritual needs of his activated female constituency. In 1942 he launched the Beit Rivkah network of Lubavitch schools, which followed the Beit Ya'akov model in providing a Jewish religious education for girls, but did not, apparently, feature the study of Habad's speculative teachings.[112] The next step in the process of integrating women in Habad in their own right, and the construction of a distinctly female hasidic consciousness in the Habad Lubavitch camp, was to be taken by his son-in-law and successor, the last Lubavitcher Rebbe. But Menachem Mendel Schneerson's vision of the role of women in the messianic age, which he expected to bring to full realization, lies beyond the scope of the present study.[113]

APPENDIX I

Did Women Read Hasidic Tales in Yiddish?

Iris Parush's pioneering study of the reading habits of eastern European Jewish women during the nineteenth century—the period in which hasidism was becoming a dominant force in much of the region—contains not a single reference to a woman reading a hasidic book, not even the popular *Shivḥei habesht* (In Praise of the Ba'al Shem Tov—the earliest hasidic hagiographical work, first published in Yiddish in 1815, only a few months after the publication of the first Hebrew edition at the end of 1814) or any of the subsequent collections of hasidic tales, which were being published in both Hebrew and Yiddish from the 1860s on.[114] The devotional Yiddish reading repertoire of all the women mentioned in the book, whether or not they were associated with the world of hasidism, appears to have consisted of collections of women's prayers (*tkhines*), traditional ethical (*musar*) tracts, Yiddish translations of the Pentateuch (*taytsh khumesh*),[115] and the anthology of homilies on the weekly Bible readings known as *Tsenerene*, to which may be added a small number of popular history books and medieval or early modern romances translated into Yiddish.[116]

More recently, however, in a personal communication subsequent to the publication of her book, Professor Parush supplied me with the only references she has encountered so far to a woman—a midwife and herbal healer—who was described as regularly reading on the sabbath, together with her two daughters, the *Shivḥei habesht* in addition to the *Tsenerene* and the usual range of devotional and ethical works available to them in Yiddish—a small 'library' in which all three women apparently became 'well versed, from cover to cover'.[117] The author of this description, Barukh Schwarz—a Hebrew teacher born in 1860 in the Ukrainian town of Balta—offers it as a recollection of his childhood in the agricultural colony of Helbinova, which would place the woman and her daughters in Podolia, in the sixties or early seventies of the nineteenth century. But even if this list of titles faithfully represents the contents of the women's 'library' rather than what a male author might have imagined to be the standard set of pious works read on the sabbath by women in 'their' language (notably, his list concludes with 'etc.', which may suggest that it was notional rather than actual), the inclusion of *Shivḥei habesht* does not in itself testify that the women who supposedly read it were thereby expressing a distinctive hasidic identity. In fact, there is no indication in Schwarz's account that the women and their family were in any way associated with hasidism. On the other hand, Shmarya Levin, when describing his own childhood in the small Belarusian town of Svisloch (Svislovitch) during the same period, reports that his mother, who came from a Habad family (but had married a *mitnaged*), used to tell her children 'hasidic stories and legends'.[118] It is not impossible that hasidic stories were circulating among women primarily as oral lore, without necessarily being read in the hasidic books that were becoming available in Yiddish.[119] This would seem to have been the case even of a prominent woman in the Habad court, Rebbetsin Rivkah (1837–1914), wife of the fourth *admor*, Shemuel. Her grandson—Joseph Isaac Schneersohn, the sixth Lubavitcher Rebbe—often credits her with oral traditions and tales about the early history of hasidism,[120] but when referring to her reading habits, he makes no mention of any hasidic books, listing only the *Tsenerene*, *Sheyres yisro'el* [She'erit yisra'el], and the Yiddish version of *Yosipon*,[121] from which apparently she read out every sabbath to a group of female relatives and associates.[122] By contrast, the Galician Haskalah activist and staunch opponent of hasidism, Joseph Perl, has a fictional female character not only reading but even studying the *Shivḥei habesht* in Yiddish.[123] This, however, must be read as one of his many satirical ploys, designed, in this case, to pour scorn on the recently published book and to present it as fanciful nonsense fit only for feeble-minded women; it can hardly be taken as evidence that real women were actually reading *Shivḥei habesht*, either in Hebrew or in Yiddish translation.[124] As late as 1889, a woman was described—probably in jest—as reciting by heart (presumably in Yiddish) hasidic tales from Aaron Walden's popular anthology *Kehal ḥasidim*[125] and from *Shivḥei habesht*, but her remarkable familiarity with these tales was credited entirely to her being possessed by the *dibuk* of a deceased man—uneducated and coarse (hence the likelihood that the Yiddish, not the Hebrew, version of the tales was being recited)—who had invaded her body and was speaking 'hasidism' from her throat. Once the *dibuk* was exorcised by a local tsadik, the woman instantly reverted to her natural state of being totally ignorant of the tales she had been reciting.[126]

All this, while depending largely on evidence deduced from the silence of the literary sources, which can never be conclusive, would seem to suggest that, even though much of the hagiographical (and, it should be noted, only the hagiographical) literature of hasidism was available in Yiddish and had been, at least in part, addressed to a female readership, women did not necessarily access it in print but may well have heard and transmitted it orally. This tentative conclusion must, however, be modified in light of the concrete evidence which has come to light only recently, through the newly discovered copy of the first Yiddish edition of *Shivḥei habesht*, published in Ostrog in 1815 and long considered lost. This copy—the only one now known to be extant—has been located by Jonatan Meir in the Russian National Library in St Petersburg. It contains, on the blank front page, the inscribed names of three successive female owners of the copy, with one of the inscriptions dated 1817 (although these inscriptions were not necessarily made by the hands of the female owners, who are described as 'the important' or 'the modest woman'—epithets which one would not normally use in reference to oneself). According to Meir, who has inspected numerous copies of various other Yiddish editions of the work, it is not at all uncommon to come across the signatures of female owners.[127] This indicates that women did apparently purchase and presumably read this first collection of hasidic hagiographical tales as soon as it became accessible to them in Yiddish. That they heard this type of material, transmitted it orally, and—as we now know—also read it in print may reflect, and could have reinforced, their affiliation with hasidism and its leaders, but there is no direct evidence to this effect, nor is it possible to reconstruct, on the basis of this assumption, the nature of their hasidic experience or sense of hasidic identity, especially not if they did not belong to the family circle of a ruling hasidic dynasty. What seems likely, at any rate, is that the mere publication of hasidic tales in Yiddish did not educate women or necessarily turn them into an active and equal constituency of the movement.

APPENDIX II

Powerful Women—In and Out of the Norm

S. A. Horodetsky—and following him, all subsequent versions of the story—points out that the Maid of Ludmir was unrelated by family ties to any of the male hasidic leaders of her day.[128] In this respect she is to be distinguished from other spiritually powerful women—all mothers, daughters, sisters, and especially widows of the well-known tsadikim (but not their wives, who, it seems, while functioning as sexual partners, could be ascribed complementary rather than equal or analogous powers to those attributed to their husbands).[129] According to Horodetsky's oral tradition, and some of the early hagiographical sources on which he draws,[130] the women who belonged to this latter category were endowed with extraordinary spiritual or prophetic insight and exercised a great deal of power and authority in the hasidic world. Nevertheless it is clear that they derived such power as they possessed from their affiliation to their illustrious male relatives, without ever functioning fully as their equals. An early twentieth-century Habad tradition ascribes an explicit statement to this effect to Shneur Zalman of Liady's widow, the dowager Rebbetsin Sterna, who is described as 'an eminent, modest, and influential woman, wise and extremely insightful'.[131] She not only acknowledges but is positively proud of the fact that her much-celebrated 'spirituality' and her power 'to make a *pidyon*', which she claims to be superior to those of her son—the reigning *admor*, Dov Ber, the Mitteler Rebbe—derive from nothing other than her intimate association during fifty years of marriage with her late husband, the founder of Habad.[132] A letter she wrote during this period (in 1817) to a certain Isaac Doktor of Dubrovno (Dubrowna),[133] in which she asked him to inform her of his mother's name, appears to confirm that she was, indeed, in the habit of 'making a *pidyon*' (for which, as for other magical procedures, the mother's name is required to establish the identity of the 'client').[134] This suggests that she was believed to possess supernatural powers, and that her blessings, which she granted like a rebbe, were credited with miraculous effect.

This phenomenon may be seen as the hasidic extension of an age-old tradition within rabbinic Judaism, which always acknowledged the capacity of receptive females to inherit or acquire by association something of the extraordinary intellectual or spiritual gifts that distinguished their eminent male relatives.[135] It is hardly surprising that hasidism, which placed the personality of the charismatic leader at the heart of both its doctrine and its social organization, should give more scope than ever before for the leader's charisma to reflect on his intimate associates, including his female relatives.[136]

The Maid of Ludmir was an exception not only in respect of her family background, which lacked the essential connection to a leading male figure in the hasidic camp, but also through her scholarly inclination and ascetic practices—traditionally viewed as inappropriate in women—and especially through her commitment to the celibate life, which gave rise to a popular perception of her 'holy virginity'. This was by far the most syncretistic, deviant aspect of her anomalous conduct, and it can account more than anything else for the apparent endeavours to suppress her activities on the part of the hasidic leadership of her day.[137] By contrast, the women who derived their spiritual authority from their intimate connection to the famous tsadikim had all conformed, through marriage and child-bearing, to their traditional gender role. Having thus fulfilled their primary female function, they were not perceived as breaching the norm and could exercise their extraordinary spiritual powers without attracting censure. This category of well-connected powerful women clearly provided a legitimate model of female authority in hasidism, which may be seen as a successful alternative to the failed model of the Maid of Ludmir.[138]

Nevertheless it should be noted that if such women ever held their own 'table' and delivered their own *torah*, as is being claimed in some twentieth-century hagiographies, then the hasidic movement did not choose to preserve any of their speculative teachings, and the pre-twentieth-century hagiographical literature, to the extent that it mentioned them at all, never depicted any of these women as tsadikim or quasi-tsadikim in their own right. There is little doubt that the incorporation of women in the charismatic leadership of the movement was far from being on the hasidic agenda during the eighteenth and nineteenth centuries. The earliest reference I have encountered so far to a woman being described in rebbe-like terms dates from 1902 and concerns Tsizye Hannah, the widow of Israel Abraham of Cherny Ostrov (1772–1814).[139] According to her great-grandson, 'she conducted herself as a rebbe after her husband's death, and the hasidim flocked to her as they had done to her husband in his lifetime. Once the holy man of God . . . Mordecai . . . of Chernobyl spent the sabbath in Cherny Ostrov and attended the third sabbath meal at her table.'[140] It is obvious that the author takes pride in his great-grandmother's reputation and high standing. He presents it as fully legitimate, and evidently considers the phenomenon of a woman being viewed by her hasidic environment as a rebbe important and exceptional enough to put it on record. But this sensibility was not commonly shared by contemporary authors and anthologists of hasidic hagiography. It was Horodetsky's Maid of Ludmir publication of 1909, and especially his 1923 presentation of the same material in female egalitarian terms, that provided a timely impetus for the romantic celebration of female rebbes in the subsequent literature, inspired by feminism, that sprang and proliferated above all on the periphery, and eventually well beyond the traditional world of east European hasidism.[141]

APPENDIX III

Women and Food at the Court

Although much has been written about the 'third sabbath meal' as a formative institution and hallmark of hasidism,[142] it is not clear who cooked or perhaps supervised the production of food for the rebbe's table, and precisely how or by whom the food was paid for.[143] The early hasidic sources, as well as the writings of those who set out to vilify or satirize the movement in its early stages, say practically nothing on the former, and not much that is unbiased by hostility to hasidism on the latter. Drawing on the scant and problematical material available, Haviva Pedaya has managed to trace the history and clarify the nature of the somewhat ambiguous relationship between the *pidyon* money, which the rebbe receives from his hasidim in return for his blessing, and the hospitality he offers them at his public table on the sabbath or at other festive occasions on which they visit him at his court, often lingering as his guests for extended periods. She suggested a certain evolution, from spontaneous communal meals at the rebbe's table in the intimate settings of the early period, when poverty was held to be a common religious ideal and when all the money received by the rebbe was spent on sustaining his assembled hasidim, to the more formal and complex financial arrangements that emerged later on, especially in the larger nineteenth-century courts, which maintained the rebbe and his household—at times in opulent and ostentatious style—by a regular flow of *pidyon* donations and various other streams of income.[144] But Pedaya did not raise the question of who was involved in the production of food for the communal meal, either in the early period of informal arrangements or later on at the fully institutionalized courts. In the absence of information from the early sources, and on the basis of no more than incidental remarks that appear here and there in the nineteenth- and twentieth-century memoirist and hagiographical sources (on which see below), one is forced to assume that this had always been the responsibility of female members of the rebbe's household, whether they prepared the food themselves or supervised the work of others.[145] What seems certain, at any rate, is that neither the women who belonged to the rebbe's family nor any other females engaged in the preparation of food for the court were admitted to the rebbe's table to partake of the communal meal, which always was and still remains an exclusively male affair. A late Habad tradition suggests that in the court of Shneur Zalman of Liady's time the exclusion of women applied even to the festive Seder table, which, more than any other Jewish ceremonial meal, is commonly celebrated in an all-inclusive family setting:

At the time of the great wedding in Zhlobin,[146] the rebbetsin [Sterna, wife of Shneur Zalman] met the wife of the holy Rabbi Levi Isaac of Berdiczów. In the course of conversation, the wife of Rabbi Levi Isaac mentioned an incident that had occurred once when she sat at the Seder table on the eve of Passover. Rebbetsin Sterna was surprised at this and asked: 'Does your husband permit you to be present at his Seder table?' The wife of Rabbi Levi Isaac replied: 'Yes!' In the following year the rebbetsin [Sterna] asked her husband [Shneur Zalman] to allow her to sit at the Seder table, just as the holy rabbi of Berdiczów allowed his wife the rebbetsin to do.[147] The rebbe agreed to this, and the rebbetsin sat at the table. When the rebbe reached the phrase [in the Haggadah text] '"and with a great manifestation" [Deut. 26: 8]—this refers to the revelation of the Shekhinah', he pointed with his holy finger at the *matsah* bowl, emphasizing the word 'this'. At that very instant the rebbetsin fainted. When she came round, the rebbe said to her: 'But you insisted on being present.'[148]

It seems clear that, according to this tradition, there was no room for the rebbetsin at the rebbe's Seder table since her place as a female was occupied by 'this', namely the *matsah* representing—for her husband and presumably also for all the male hasidim present—the divine female, the Shekhinah, who had come to rest among them. Whether this tradition preserves an authentic Habad memory of the early court practice, or whether it is based on familiarity with more recent Seders at the Lubavitch court,[149] it clearly reinforces the sense that the enhancement and prominence of the Shekhinah in the later kabbalah[150] did not enhance the status of women in hasidism but rather served to displace and thus to exclude them from the main hasidic arenas of divine service.[151] In more recent times, it appears that the women in the household of the last Lubavitcher Rebbe were indeed excluded from his Seder table, at least for as long as it was celebrated as a formal or semi-formal hasidic gathering: 'On the eve of Passover his mother the rebbetsin[152] would hold the Seder on the second floor of 770 [Eastern Parkway] (in the private apartment of the late [previous] rebbe, Joseph Isaac Schneersohn), where the [last] rebbe [Menachem Mendel Schneerson] held his Seders. She would sit together with the women in a separate room.'[153]

As regards the management and production of food for the rebbe's table and for the court as a whole, David Assaf has assembled a range of admittedly late hagiographical, memoirist, and belletristic sources which throw light on the workings of the nineteenth-century hasidic court economy, primarily within the orbit of the Ruzhin–Sadagora line. He considered the mechanisms by which the court strove to balance its income against the burden of providing not only spiritual but also material nourishment for the hasidim.[154] On the men and women involved in this enterprise, he writes:

Every court had a general manager, who was responsible for the logistics of the court and, in particular, for running the kitchen. This position demanded considerable practical and organizational ability, and was generally given to Hasidim who were not distinguished for their scholarly talents. Assisting the administrator were kashrut supervisors and accountants . . . The everyday life of the court—in particular the organization of the kitchen—was supervised by the rebbetsin, the Zaddik's wife, with the assistance of her daughters and daughters-in-law.[155]

It is not entirely clear from this what the actual responsibility of the rebbetsin and her daughters or daughters-in-law might have been, and how it complemented the operations of the 'general manager' and other male officials involved in running the court kitchen. It stands to reason, however, that in the early, more intimate and informal courts, and even in the largest and wealthiest, which were modelled in many other respects on the manorial establishments of the local nobility,[156] female members of the rebbe's household would oversee the supply and preparation of food, not only for the rebbe's family table but also for the many visitors to the court, whether or not they were directly involved in the day-to-day management or physical labour that this entailed.[157] Habad's twentieth-century memoirist-hagiographical literature certainly implies that the provision of food had been the responsibility of the women in the rebbe's household since the early beginnings of hasidism. For example the fifth rebbetsin, Shterna Sarah, who—as a family member recalled—had 'sent me sabbath dishes to the inn',[158] was said in this connection to have been responsible for the preparation of a festive Purim meal for 'approximately ten guests or more', like the Ba'al Shem Tov's daughter Edl in her day, who 'on the eve of every sabbath used to ask her father for how many guests she should prepare a sabbath meal'.[159] Of the first Habad rebbetsin, Sterna, Shneur Zalman of Liady's wife, it is said that 'when her daughter Freyde grew up, she passed on the responsibility for the kitchen to her, and she would do the cooking', although 'once, when a particularly important guest arrived, the holy Rebbe Shelomoh of Karlin, the rebbetsin [Sterna] naturally wanted to cook in his honour herself'.[160] The second rebbetsin, Sheyna, wife of the Mitteler Rebbe, is described as being 'very busy in the kitchen' on the day of her grandson Shemuel's wedding (in 1849). She was 'bothered and preoccupied, with many other women frantically running around her to carry out her instructions'.[161] The bride, Rivkah—the future fourth rebbetsin—was described by her grandson, the sixth *admor*, Joseph Isaac Schneersohn, as overseer of the 'court economy' (*kalkalat heḥatser*), a responsibility with which she was charged by her father-in-law, the Tsemah Tsedek, on the death of his wife, who had previously held the same position at the Lubavitch court.[162] Elsewhere Joseph Isaac relates that in her old age, as the dowager rebbetsin, Rivkah took it upon herself to feed the students admitted to her son's newly established yeshiva:

When father [Shalom Dovber], may he rest in Eden, founded the Tomekhei Temimim yeshiva in 1897, he did not wish to accept any money from people, so that they would not have any say in the management of the yeshiva. [As a result,] it was very difficult to organize the yeshiva. His mother, my grandmother, Rebbetsin Rivkah, may she rest in Eden, said to him: Why are you upset? What we eat—they [the students] will also eat! And this is just what happened. Those who were admitted to the yeshiva were fed by his mother, the righteous Rebbetsin Rivkah.[163]

Elsewhere, while again acknowledging his grandmother's commitment to feeding the students of the yeshiva, he adds: 'The rebbetsin would personally oversee the preparation of food for these students.'[164] A few years later, in 1901, the long-widowed Rivkah apparently instigated the conversion of her old marital quarters within the Lubavitch court into a kitchen and communal dining room for the senior students of the yeshiva.[165] And since the younger students were excluded from this facility, she provided, in her household within the precincts of the court, regular 'days' at her own table for some of the pupils in the preparatory classes and for many other visitors and guests: 'Almost every day several young pupils would eat at her table, some of them twice a week, some three times (in addition to family members who used to visit Lubavitch and stay with her for several months, especially those coming from the Holy Land . . . and other family members who regularly ate at her table).'[166]

Rebbetsin Rivkah is also said to have regularly distributed *lekakh* (honey cake) on the eve of the Day of Atonement to all the students of the yeshiva,[167] to various guests, to Lubavitch householders, and to her son, the reigning *admor*, Shalom Dovber,[168] while her daughter-in-law, Shterna Sarah—Shalom Dovber's wife—is said to have given *lekakh* to her son, the *admor* Joseph Isaac Schneersohn.[169] Notably, however, the distribution of *lekakh* at this time of year was a function subsequently performed for many years by the last Lubavitcher Rebbe himself and, according to him, also by his predecessor and father-in-law, Joseph Isaac Schneersohn.[170] Moreover, according to traditions assembled by Y. Mondshine, the distribution of *lekakh* was, and still is, performed by other male leaders of hasidism, and Joseph Isaac Schneersohn claims that it was originally performed by the Ba'al Shem Tov himself.[171] The attribution to Rivkah, or indeed to Shterna Sarah, of this particular function may therefore point to the possibility that the distribution of *lekakh* was not necessarily a symbolic enactment of the rebbetsin's traditional and specifically female role of food provider for the court, but rather that in performing this task, she was behaving as a quasi-rebbe and being treated as such by all those closely associated with the Lubavitch court.[172]

Alongside these fragments of information on the involvement of rebbetsins in the provision of food, the memoirist literature of twentieth-century Habad refers occasionally to men who were in charge of various aspects of food production and distribution as well as financial management, most specifically in connection with the Tomekhei Temimim yeshiva. For example Moses Nahman Garelik is described as the 'steward' (*sadran*) of the students' kitchen and dining room in Lubavitch;[173] at the branch of the yeshiva in Shchedrin the male bursar (*hamenahel hagashmi*) decided to economize by stopping the provision of dessert for the students' sabbath meal, a decision which was eventually overruled by the *admor* Shalom Dovber himself;[174] and tea for the students at Lubavitch was prepared by the gentile Pavlik.[175] It seems likely that by the early twentieth century the rebbetsin's role had begun to shift away from direct involvement with the kitchen or with oversight of the 'court economy'—a responsibility that was now increasingly being placed in the hands of male officials. The rebbetsin, modelling herself on what had become the social norm for the women of the upper bourgeoisie, was supporting her husband's projects in a more personal secretarial or even executive capacity,[176] as did Shterna Sarah when she first engaged her Damen Ferayn in a fundraising campaign, which was to pave the way for the emergence of Habad's female constituency.

Notes

1 See Ch. 6 above.

2 *Hasidism and Its Adherents* [Haḥasidut vehaḥasidim] (Tel Aviv, 1928–43), iv. 68.

3 Ibid. iv. 69.

4 For the questionable status of the hagiographical tales within hasidism see J. Dan, *The Hasidic Tale: Its History and Development* [Hasipur haḥasidi] (Jerusalem, 1975), 189–95; C. Shmeruk, *Yiddish Literature: Aspects of Its History* [Sifrut yidish: perakim letoledoteiha] (Tel Aviv, 1978), 210–11; G. Nigal, *The Hasidic Tale*, trans. E. Levin (Oxford, 2008), 66–74; *Shivhey Ha-Baal Shem Tov: A Facsimile of a Unique Manuscript, Variant Versions, and Appendices* [Sefer shivḥei habesht: faksimil miketav hayad hayeḥidi hanoda lanu veshinuyei nusaḥav le'umat nusaḥ hadefus], ed. Y. Mondshine (Jerusalem, 1982), 52–8.

5 See e.g. the introduction to the 1816 Korets (Korzec) Yiddish edition of *Shivḥei habesht*, 1*b*, which addresses the translation to 'all those people who do not know the Holy Tongue—men, women and children'. See also, on the same page, Naftali Hirsch Hakohen's approbation, in which he recommends the edition 'especially since most women, and members of their households, are eager to read this book, to peruse at leisure its saintly narratives and miracle tales on the holy sabbath'. Similarly the title pages of the Novy Dvor, 1816 and Żółkiew, 1817 Yiddish editions (reproduced in both Shmeruk, *Yiddish Literature: Aspects of Its History* (Heb.), 215–16, and *Shivhey Ha-Baal Shem Tov* (Heb.), ed. Mondshine, 29–30) address the translation to 'men and women' (Novy Dvor) or 'especially righteous women' (Żółkiew) who cannot read Hebrew. I am grateful to Chava Turniansky for reminding me that women were clearly included in the target audience of the Yiddish editions of the book.

6 See below, Appendix I.

7 See below, n. 14.

8 For a representative, but by no means exhaustive, list of such popular works see above, Ch. 6, n. 2. Nathaniel Deutsch's compelling study, *The Maiden of Ludmir: A Jewish Holy Woman and Her World* (Berkeley, 2003), constructs most of what purports to be the Maid's biography out of precisely such late, unverifiable, and at times conflicting, semi-fictional memoirist and other questionable sources, which by and large make up the 20th-century reception history of Horodetsky's Maid tradition more than they preserve independently any credible memory of her actual reality.

9 For an analysis of the Maid of Ludmir tradition, presenting her case as a failure rather than the success story suggested by Horodetsky's account, see above, Ch. 6. For a distinction between this failed model and a more successful alternative path to female power in hasidism, see below, Appendix II.

10 This was the background for the establishment of the Beit Ya'akov network of Orthodox schools for girls, which was initiated by Sarah Schenirer and which gained the approval of both the hasidic and the non-hasidic leadership of Agudat Yisra'el in interwar Poland. On this and other Orthodox appeals to women during the period see above, Ch. 6, n. 83, and below, Ch. 8, n. 44.

11 Meir of Opatów was answering the question: 'If a wife, unaccompanied by her

non-hasidic husband or a son of his who was still a juvenile, were to come to your congregation, would she be admitted?' His full answer was: 'They are free to come to the synagogue; however, women generally are not hasidim. Anyway, women and children come under the authority of the father, so that if it is not the father's will that they be hasidim, they cannot be accepted.' The full text of the interrogation was published in the original Polish in M. Wodziński, '"Sprawa chasydymów": Z materiałów do dziejów chasydyzmu w Królestwie Polskim', in K. Matwijowski (ed.), *Z historii ludności żydowskiej w Polsce i na Śląsku* (Wrocław, 1994), 235–9. A French translation appeared in id., 'L'Affaire des "Chasydymów": Matériaux pour l'histoire des Hassidim dans le Royaume de Pologne', *Tsafon: Revue d'études juives du Nord*, 29 (1997), 35–58, where Meir of Opatów's reference to women appears on p. 53; and an English version was incorporated in id., *Hasidism and Politics: The Kingdom of Poland, 1815–1864* (Oxford, 2013), 100–3, where the above exchange appears on p. 103. I am grateful to Marcin Wodziński for bringing it to my attention. Reference to the same interrogation, quoting Meir of Opatów's response to the question on women, appears also in G. Dynner, *Men of Silk: The Hasidic Conquest of Polish Jewish Society* (Oxford, 2006), 44, 182. However, Dynner takes Meir's exclusion of women from the category of hasidim to be 'patently false' (ibid. 44) or 'not accurate' (ibid. 182), presumably reading it as the tsadik's endeavour to refute the claim made by some of hasidism's opponents (both *mitnagedim* and *maskilim*) to the effect that women were 'the primary victims of the zaddikim', and that they often visited and brought them donations without their husbands' consent (ibid. 44). This charge may well underlie the interrogator's question concerning the wife and child of a non-hasid, as the *maskil* Abraham Stern, who reported negatively on hasidism to the Polish officials, had claimed that 'they would attempt to beguile and ensnare the younger and less sensible . . . particularly the female sex' (ibid. 158). At least one of the government reports which gave rise to the investigation in 1824 was probably inspired by Stern and accused the hasidim of enticing 'the gullible and those with less sense' to join their ranks (Wodziński, *Hasidism and Politics*, 85). Nevertheless, Meir's replies to the interrogator's questions generally ring defensive but true, and Dynner's conclusion from his anti-hasidic sources that 'women constituted a large proportion of hasidic adherents' (*Men of Silk*, 182) is misleading. While some women did visit some of the courts, with or without their husbands' permission, it is impossible to gauge their numbers or to guess what proportion they might have constituted of the total number of Polish hasidim—a figure which is in itself at best contested and at worst elusive. Moreover, quite a few of the anti-hasidic sources (produced by both *mitnagedim* and *maskilim*) suggest the opposite picture when they accuse the hasidim of abandoning their women at home when they travel to visit their rebbes; see e.g. M. Wilensky, *Hasidim and Mitnagedim* [Ḥasidim umitnagedim] (Jerusalem, 1970), i. 103; ii. 107, 151, 159–60, 173, 315; S. Maimon, *The Autobiography of Solomon Maimon* (London,

1954), 168; J. Perl, *Uiber das Wesen der Sekte Chassidim*, ed. A. Rubinstein (Jerusalem, 1977), 125; Wodziński, *Hasidism and Politics*, 82. Be that as it may, women's affiliation with the courts—the exceptional status of the wealthy hasidic patroness Temerel Bergson notwithstanding, as Dynner himself admits —was much more restricted than the men's, and was considered problematic or even undesirable by some of the hasidic leaders. On this, and on the limited extent to which women could count as a constituency of hasidism prior to the 20th century, see below.

12 I do not accept Nehemiah Polen's interpretation of a certain homily by the hasidic master Kalonymos Kalman Epstein (1751–1823) as representing an agenda of 'radical egalitarianism' that provides the theoretical underpinnings, as it were, for hasidism's alleged promotion in practice of women's spiritual powers (see N. Polen, 'Miriam's Dance: Radical Egalitarianism in Hasidic Thought', *Modern Judaism*, 12 (1992), 3–6, 8). It seems to me that the homily, which explores the mythical (biblical) past in terms of the utopian future, serves primarily, like other rabbinic, kabbalistic, and hasidic traditions of this kind, to highlight the contrast between a radically transformed but safely distant messianic World to Come and the prosaic reality of the present in the here and now, of which it is often portrayed as a provocatively fanciful inversion (see on this A. Rapoport-Albert, *Women and the Messianic Heresy of Sabbatai Zevi, 1666–1816* (Oxford, 2011), 119–29). In the absence of any evidence to suggest that Kalonymos Kalman Epstein was involved in any active messianic agitation, or indeed that he believed, like the Sabbatians in their day, that the messianic age had already dawned, and with it the inauguration of an 'upside-down' eschatological world order, his 'egalitarian' homily must be seen as belonging in this tantalizing but ultimately conservative tradition (see more on this ibid. 129–31 n. 65). The same can be said of two other hasidic homilies—both by Shneur Zalman of Liady—of which one is briefly discussed by Polen ('Miriam's Dance', 6) as a possible source for the same theme in Kalonymos Kalman's homily, and the other is elaborated by Yael Levine Katz ('The Voice of the Bride in the Future' (Heb.), in S. Raz (ed.), *The Religious Zionist Anthology in Memory of Zerach Warhaftig* [Kovets hatsiyonut hadatit lezekher zeraḥ varhaftig] (Jerusalem, 2001), 365–8). Here, too, in the absence of any indication that the author believed the messianic era to be imminent or to have already dawned in his own time, his homily must be seen as placing an emphasis at least as much on the persisting inferiority of the female in the present conditions of 'exile' as it is on the ultimate superiority she will achieve with the redemption at some distant point in the future, beyond foreseeable time.

13 A possible and, as far as I know, unique allusion to the Maid of Ludmir does, however, occur in one hasidic hagiographical work, published in the last decade of the 19th century. It mentions 'a pious woman' (*ishah kesherah*) in the town of Ludmir who was able to foretell the future. See I. Landau, *Zikaron tov*

(Piotrków, 1892), pt. II, 15*a* [29] §4. For the book and its author see above, Ch. 6, n. 20.

14 This was a short article in Russian, based—as he noted—on the '[verbal] accounts of old people in Volhynia'. See S. A. G. [Samuel Abba G/Horodetsky], 'Ludmirskaya deva (Di Ludmirer Moyd)', *Evreiskaya Starina*, 1/4 (1909), 219–22. I have encountered so far only one earlier reference to the Maid of Ludmir in a published source. It appeared in 1884, predating Horodetsky's initial report by two and a half decades. Significantly, however, this is not a hasidic source but rather a maskilic polemic, directed against a certain Barukh Esman of Kiev and his book of casuistry, *Sefer ḥad veḥalak*, published in Vilna some two years earlier, in 1882. Employing the language and literary conceits of Joseph Perl's satire *Megaleh temirin*, the polemicist ridicules Esman's daughter, portraying her as a famous rabbinic scholar and kabbalist,

> almost on a par with the Maid . . . of the town of Ludmir, who was subject in her day to the authority of the rebbe of Trisk. The only difference between them is that the Maid of Ludmir wore a *talit* and laid *tefilin* . . . paying no attention to the rabbis of her time, who had put her under *ḥerem* . . . because they feared that everyone would be misled into following her, taking her to be a tsadik, and all the hasidim would be drawn to her. About the present daughter, on the other hand . . . the rabbis will never say such a thing . . . Without a doubt, she, too, will soon don a fringed *talit* and lay *tefilin*, as befits her stature . . . and her uncle will no doubt soon find for her a lucrative rabbinic appointment . . . in Vilna. (See I. J. Weissberg, *Ga'on vashever* (pt. II of *Shever ga'on* by Mikhl ben Aaron David Gordon) (Warsaw, 1884), 44–5. I am grateful to Jonatan Meir for bringing this passage to my attention.)

While providing independent corroboration of Horodetsky's oral tradition, this account of the Maid of Ludmir confirms that her career as a rebbe attracted the unequivocal opposition of the hasidic leaders of her day, which accounts for the eradication of her memory from all the literary sources of hasidism prior to Horodetsky's 1909 publication. For an early (and fully acknowledged!) infiltration of Horodetsky's Maid tradition into hasidic hagiography, see M. M. Walden, *Nifle'ot harabi* (Warsaw, 1911), 88, which reads: 'The girl Hannah Sarah [should be Hannah Rachel; A.R-A.] of Ludmir, known as *dos ludmirer meydl*, became famous for her holy spirit and miracles (her entire story has been published in a periodical journal by Samuel Abba Horodetsky of Bern).' I am grateful to David Assaf for this reference.

15 S. A. G., 'Ludmirskaya deva', 219, and see the discussion above, Ch. 6. It seems, however, that Horodetsky's original wording in this opening paragraph of his article may have been far less reserved than the published version suggests. The original version may have already referred to the full equality of women in hasidism that Horodetsky was eventually to claim in his 1923 book.

This emerges from a postcard, dated 26 Jan.–8 Feb. 1910, which was sent to Horodetsky from the St Petersburg editorial office of *Evreiskaya Starina* by Simon Dubnow, the editor. Evidently responding to Horodetsky's complaint that editorial interventions had altered and even reversed some of his arguments, Dubnow wrote to him in Hebrew:

> As for the beginning of 'The Maid of Ludmir', about the role of women in hasidism—I do not remember how much of your wording I had altered, but I doubt that it would be possible to prove the 'opposite' of what was published, as women actually have no place whatsoever in active hasidism, and even in their daily lives the hasidim used to exclude women from the dining room table where the guests would be seated. (Gnazim Institute, Horodetsky archive, 35/848)

I am grateful to Gadi Sagiv for bringing this postcard to my attention.

16 For Horodetsky's background, his intellectual development, his exposure to both Zionism and feminism, and his evaluation of hasidism as a forerunner of both, see above, Ch. 6, in and around nn. 11 and 56–61; Deutsch, *The Maiden of Ludmir*, 23–33.

17 The tradition originates in H. M. Heilman's Habad history, *Beit rabi* (Berdiczów, 1902), 114 (= 57*b*) and 183 (= 92*a*) n. 2. See above, Ch. 6, n. 41, and cf. N. Loewenthal, 'Women and the Dialectic of Spirituality in Hasidism', in I. Etkes et al. (eds.), *Within Hasidic Circles: Studies in Hasidism in Memory of Mordecai Wilensky* [Bema'agelei ḥasidim: kovets meḥkarim lezikhro shel profesor mordekhai vilenski] (Jerusalem, 1999), English section, 22.

18 See below, at nn. 135–6. The same applies to Heilman's anecdote about Shneur Zalman's widow, Sterna, in which she herself attributes her spiritual powers to her long association with her late husband. See below, Appendix II.

19 See on all this above, Ch. 6, n. 41.

20 The work was subsequently incorporated in his halakhic compendium *Shulḥan arukh* and published posthumously in Kopys in 1814.

21 *Hilkhot talmud torah* (Brooklyn, 1968), fo. 11*a*–*b*, cited and discussed in Loewenthal, 'Women and the Dialectic of Spirituality in Hasidism', 20, and his 'Early Habad Publications in their Setting', in D. Rowland Smith and P. S. Salinger (eds.), *Hebrew Studies*, British Library Occasional Papers 13 (The British Library, 1991), 96–100. Loewenthal deals with this halakhic ruling in the sections of his essays entitled respectively 'Torah Study for Women: Early Stages' (p. 19) and 'Education for Women' (pp. 99–100), presenting it as the beginning of an unbroken tradition in Habad, which has always displayed exceptional concern for women's education, their spiritual empowerment, and their active engagement with hasidism. This view seems to project the truly innovative stance on the position of women in 20th-century Habad onto a

period long before this stance first emerged in response to the challenges of modernity. See more on this directly below.

22 Loewenthal himself admits this; see 'Women and the Dialectic of Spirituality in Hasidism', 25–6.

23 See e.g. M. M. Schneerson, *Likutei siḥot*, viii: *Bemidbar* (Brooklyn, 1991), the 1965 address on pericope 'Shelaḥ' (Yid.), 289; ibid., vol. xiv: *Devarim* (Brooklyn, 1999), the second 1974 address on pericope 'Ekev' (Heb.), 37–44, which is devoted in its entirety to women's obligation to study Torah (and to recite the blessing on Torah study), using Shneur Zalman's ruling as its starting point; ibid., vol. xxvii: *Vayikra* (Brooklyn, 1989), the 1984 last-day-of-Passover address (and several subsequent ones), explaining the universal directive, which includes women, to study Maimonides' *Mishneh torah*. The incorporation of women in the obligation to study Torah is anchored in Shneur Zalman's halakhic ruling in much of the Habad literature inspired by Menachem Mendel Schneerson's teachings. See e.g. U. Kaploun (ed.), *A Partner in the Dynamic of Creation: Womanhood in the Teachings of the Lubavitcher Rebbe, Rabbi Menachem M. Schneerson* (Brooklyn, 1994), 68–9; S. Handelman, 'Women and the Study of Torah in the Thought of the Lubavitcher Rebbe', in M. D. Halpern and C. Safrai, (eds.) *Jewish Legal Writings by Women* (Jerusalem, 1998), 143–78.

24 For this tendency of internal Habad historiography see above, Ch. 4; I. Bartal, '"Shimon ha-Kofer"—A Chapter in Orthodox Historiography' (Heb.), in I. Bartal, E. Mendelsohn, and C. Turniansky (eds.), *Studies in Jewish Culture in Honour of Chone Shmeruk* [Keminhag ashkenaz upolin: sefer yovel leḥone shmeruk] (Jerusalem, 1992), 243–68; N. Karlinsky, *Counter-History: The Hasidic Epistles from Erets Yisra'el: Text and Context* [Ḥasidut shekeneged: igerot haḥasidim me'erets yisra'el: hatekst vehakontekst] (Jerusalem, 1998).

25 These are *Poke'aḥ ivrim* and *Seder birkhot hanehenin*. See Loewenthal, 'Women and the Dialectic of Spirituality in Hasidism', 22–5; Shmeruk, *Yiddish Literature: Aspects of Its History* (Heb.), 199–200.

26 Loewenthal rightly observes ('Women and the Dialectic of Spirituality in Hasidism', 22–3) that *Poke'aḥ ivrim* (Brooklyn, 1955) (chs. 9 and 17, 38 and 42 in the original Yiddish, 64 and 70 in the Hebrew translation) contains two extremely unusual, albeit brief, references to women as the subjects rather than, as almost invariably in rabbinic literature, the objects of illicit erotic fantasies (in this case, 'bad dreams'), but even he admits that 'this may seem a rather dubious level of female emancipation'.

27 See above, Ch. 6, n. 20.

28 See BT *RH* 16*b*; *Suk.* 27*b*.

29 See Hayim Eleazar of Munkács, *Divrei torah*, cited in Y. Mondshine (ed.), *Kerem ḥabad*, 1 (1986), 53.

30 Y. Mondshine, 'The Friendly Relations between the Holy *Admor* Rabbi Meir of Przemyślany and the Holy Gaon Rabbi Shelomoh Kluger' (Heb.), *Naḥalat tsevi*, 4 (1991), 74, cited in H. Gertner, 'The Rabbinate and the Hasidic Movement in Nineteenth-Century Galicia: The Case of Rabbi Shelomoh Kluger' (Heb.), in Etkes et al. (eds.), *Within Hasidic Circles* (Heb. and Eng.), 73 n. 82.

31 I. Landau, *Zikaron tov* (Piotrków, 1892), reprinted in the series *The Holy Books of All the Disciples of the Holy Besht* [Sefarim hakedoshim mikol talmidei habesht hakadosh] (Brooklyn, 1981), pt. II, 27*b* §30.

32 See D. Assaf, *The Regal Way: The Life and Times of Rabbi Israel of Ruzhin* (Stanford, Calif., 2002), 282. See also the original Hebrew version of the same work, *Derekh hamalkhut* (Jerusalem, 1997), 385 n. 84.

33 J. Langer, *Nine Gates* (London, 1961), 11, quoted in Loewenthal, 'Women and the Dialectic of Spirituality in Hasidism', 28.

34 See R. N. Kahan, *Oral Traditions and Tales about Our Holy Rebbes* [Shemuot vesipurim meraboteinu hakedoshim] (Kefar Habad, 1977), iii. 315 §164. For the term 'Polish' hasidism in Habad parlance see A. Rapoport-Albert and G. Sagiv, 'Habad versus "Polish Hasidism": Towards the History of a Dichotomy' (Heb.), in J. Meir and G. Sagiv (eds.), *Habad Hasidism: History, Thought, Image* (Jerusalem, 2016).

35 Kahan, *Oral Traditions and Tales about Our Holy Rebbes* (Heb.) (Kefar Habad, 1974), ii. 50 §49. Israel of Vilednik [Novi Velednyky] (*c.*1788/9–1850) was a miracle-working tsadik and a disciple of Mordecai of Chernobyl.

36 See D. Z. Hillman, *Letters by the Author of the Tanya and His Contemporaries* [Igerot ba'al hatanya uvenei doro] (Jerusalem, 1953), 58–69, nos. 37–42; I. Etkes, *Rabbi Shneur Zalman of Liady: The Origins of Chabad Hasidism*, trans. J. M. Green (Waltham, Mass., 2015), 41–9. Nor is there any mention of women a generation later, in the comparable set of ordinances issued by Dov Ber, the Mitteler Rebbe, to regulate the flow of distinct classes of hasidim to his Lubavitch court in the early 1820s. *Igerot kodesh admor hazaken, admor haemtsa'i, admor hatsemaḥ tsedek*, i. (Brooklyn, 1980), 269–71 no. 20, and see the discussion, with full English translation of these, in N. Loewenthal, *Communicating the Infinite: The Emergence of the Habad School* (Chicago, 1990), 163–7.

37 On the regular pilgrimages to Nahman's court see e.g. N. Sternharz, *Ḥayei moharan*, i (Jerusalem, 1947), 'Mekom yeshivato unesiotav', 59–60 §24.

38 *Siaḥ sarfei kodesh* (Jerusalem, 1994), ii. 106 §313, published anonymously but based primarily on the Bratslav traditions of Levi Isaac Bender.

39 For Nahman's scornful remarks on the miracle-working, 'false' tsadikim of his day, see e.g. his *Likutei moharan* (New York, 1966), pt. II, 46–7 §15; Sternharz, *Hayei moharan*, ii, 'Ma'alat hamitkarvim elav', 22 §95; Abraham of Tulchin, *Sefer avaneiha barzel* [with *Sefer kokhevei or*] (Jerusalem, 1961), 8 §6. For

Shneur Zalman's disdain for this style of leadership see the discussion in Etkes, *Rabbi Shneur Zalman of Liady*, 28–9. See also the selection of Shneur Zalman's statements on this subject assembled in Y. Mondshine, *Migdal oz* (Kefar Habad, 1980), 320–6.

40 This would seem to imply that in other periods of his life Shneur Zalman did admit women, although the tales make no further mention of the matter. It may well be that the reference to 'in those days' is intended to distinguish Shneur Zalman's time from the author's own, by which stage women were regularly admitted to the presence of the seventh Lubavitcher Rebbe (on which see e.g. Loewenthal, 'Women and the Dialectic of Spirituality in Hasidism', 59; B. J. Morris, *Lubavitcher Women in America* (New York, 1998), 58).

41 Kahan, *Oral Traditions and Tales about Our Holy Rebbes* (Heb.), ii. 122 §134.

42 However, the absence of references to women from his own ordinances regulating the visits to Lubavitch of various classes of hasidim (on which see above, at n. 36) may suggest—albeit by way of evidence from silence, as far as it goes —that women were not part of what he viewed as his hasidic constituency.

43 Published in Mondshine, *Migdal oz*, 192 §92.

44 This is based on a claim by the sixth Lubavitcher Rebbe, Joseph Isaac Schneersohn (1880–1950), who has created much of modern Habad's often anachronistic historiographical tradition. See his *Hayom yom* (Brooklyn, 1976), 55, where the festival of Lag Ba'omer is said to have been the one time of year, eagerly anticipated by all the hasidim, at which the Mitteler Rebbe would 'perform miracles', especially miracles concerning children.

45 Kahan, *Oral Traditions and Tales about Our Holy Rebbes* (Heb.), iii. 259 §39.

46 P. B. Goldenstein, *Mayn lebens-geshikhte* (Petah Tikvah, 1928–9), cited in Hebrew translation in Y. Mondshine (ed.), *Kerem ḥabad*, 1 (1986), 61.

47 H. M. Perlow, *An Anthology of Tales* [Likutei sipurim] (Kefar Habad, 1966), 117 §36.

48 Ibid. 131 §64.

49 Ibid. 119 §38. Admittedly, in the latter two tales both women are said eventually to have managed to address the Tsemah Tsedek personally, one by forcing and the other by paying her way in, despite the general policy of denying women access to his presence.

50 Kahan, *Oral Traditions and Tales about Our Holy Rebbes* (Heb.), i. 54.

51 See ibid. i. 45–8; ii. 112 §124; iii. 266 §59, 268 §62, 309 §144, 319 §179. See also Mondshine, *Migdal oz*, 202 §108, 258 §28.

52 See his collection of responsa (by the title of which he himself became known) *Tsemaḥ tsedek, Even ha'ezer*, i (first published posthumously in Vilna in 1871; Brooklyn, 1994), 59*a*–147*b*, where nos. 48–89 (in fact, 88) are 'responsa on the laws of *agunot*', many of which are long, elaborate, and inclined to leniency. See

also the section 'Indices' (*maftehot*) at the end of the same volume, 79*a*–81*a*. In vol. ii of *Even ha'ezer* the sections on divorce and on levirate marriage similarly contain many responsa that reflect the endeavour to resolve cases in the interest of women who found it difficult to obtain halakhically valid release from marital ties to untraceable or recalcitrant men. It should be noted, however, that the Tsemah Tsedek was by no means unique in his concern for the predicament of women caught up in these halakhic conundrums. Halakhists had grappled with them for centuries (see e.g. M. Elon, *Jewish Law: History, Sources, Principles*, trans. B. Auerbach and M. J. Sykes, 4 vols. (Philadelphia, 1994), s.v. *agunah*), and in eastern Europe, in the course of the 19th century, when—as a result of increasing mobility and migration, the introduction of compulsory military service, and various other factors—instances of desertion, untraceability, and recalcitrance proliferated, a number of prominent halakhic authorities, such as Shelomoh Kluger (1785–1869), Isaac Elhanan Spektor (1817–96), and Moses Joshua Diskin (1817–98), became known for their endeavours to resolve them. See on this e.g. C. Y. Freeze, *Jewish Marriage and Divorce in Imperial Russia* (Hanover, 2002), 230–42; I. Levitats, *The Jewish Community in Russia, 1844–1917* (Jerusalem, 1981), 133–4; M. Baker, 'The Voice of the Deserted Jewish Woman, 1867–1870', *Jewish Social Studies*, 2/1 (1995), 98–123; H. Gertner, *The Rabbi and the City: The Rabbinate in Galicia and Its Encounter with Modernity, 1815–1867* [Harav veha'ir hagedolah: harabanut begalitsyah umifgashah im hamodernah, 1815–1867] (Jerusalem, 2013), 223–5, 270–2.

53 For Joseph Isaac's portrayal of his grandmother as a repository of orally transmitted family traditions, and one of his chief sources on hasidic history in general and Habad history in particular, see above, Ch. 4, at nn. 114 and 199; A. H. Glitzenstein, *Sefer hatoladot: rabi yosef yitshak schneersohn, admor morenu harav yosef yitshak* (Kefar Habad, 1976), i. 136–9; R. N. Kahan, *Lubavitch and Its Soldiers* [Lubavitch vehayaleiha] (Kefar Habad, 1983), 36–7; J. I. Schneersohn, *The History of Rebbetsin Rivkah* [Divrei yemei harabanit rivkah] (Brooklyn, 2003), 105–8 and *passim*. For a collection of additional references to Rivkah's reputation as a *ba'alat shemuah* (transmitter of oral lore), drawn largely from Joseph Isaac's writings, see *Crown of Royalty: The Rebbetzins of Chabad-Lubavitch of Seven Generations* [Ateret malkhut: shiv'ah dorot shel rabaniyot habad] (Brooklyn, 1998), 58–60 (where she is said to have written down the hasidic stories she had heard from all her female relatives, and to have received three manuscript collections of such stories written down by her father), 62–3, 69. A similar picture emerges from Malka Shapiro's memoirs, where her grandmother, the dowager Rebbetsin Sarah Devorah, is depicted as the source of oral traditions about the history of the Kozienice dynasty. See M. Shapiro, *The Rebbe's Daughter*, trans., ed., with introduction and commentary by N. Polen (Philadelphia, 2002), xxxii. 104–13.

54 *Igerot kodesh . . . yosef yitsḥak* (Brooklyn, 1982), ii. 93 no. 394 (sent from Riga in the summer of 1928). For another version of this tale see Mondshine, *Migdal oz*, 258 §29.

55 *Igerot kodesh . . . yosef yitsḥak*, ii. 94.

56 For the sixth *admor*'s own ambivalence about the celebration of miracles and the production of miracle tales, which he associated with the tradition of 'Polish' hasidism but advocated for Habad to adopt as an exigency of his own time, see above, Ch. 4, at nn. 186–202.

57 See above, at nn. 42–3.

58 Mondshine, *Migdal oz*, 208 §125. For more on the mediating function of female members of the rebbe's household, see directly below.

59 Ibid. 118–19 §154.

60 Kahan, *Lubavitch and Its Soldiers* (Heb.), 60–1.

61 I am grateful to Michoel Seligson for this information.

62 The same Samuel also used to transcribe and sell copies of Shalom Dovber's discourses. See Kahan, *Lubavitch and Its Soldiers* (Heb.), 25.

63 Ibid. 60–1 n. 1.

64 Rivkah appears to have functioned as a channel for women's concerns throughout the three stages of her life in the Lubavitch court: as a rebbe's daughter-in-law, as a rebbe's wife, and as a rebbe's mother. In 1909 she is still described as intervening successfully with her son, Shalom Dovber, on behalf of two candidates who had been refused admission to the yeshiva, or a widowed mother whose appeals to the rebbe to admit her two young sons to the yeshiva had been ignored for many weeks. See the selections from Israel Jacobsohn's memoirs, *Zikaron livnei yisra'el*, published by Y. Mondshine in *Kerem ḥabad*, 3 (1987), 242–3.

65 Kahan, *Oral Traditions and Tales about Our Holy Rebbes* (Heb.), ii. 111 §120. Another tale from a modern Habad anthology similarly suggests that Shneur Zalman's wife, Sterna, mediated a woman's request to her husband, although in this case the woman was subsequently able to consult the rebbe himself. See Perlow, *An Anthology of Tales* (Heb.), 60 §59. Cf. Kahan, *Oral Traditions and Tales about Our Holy Rebbes* (Heb.), ii. 49 §48: 'A woman once came to the Old *Admor* to ask that he pray for her daughter'. There is no reference here to Sterna's or anyone else's mediation; the tale seems to imply direct access to the Old *Admor* himself.

66 In the chapter in which he offers his generic characterization of 'hasidic life', Horodetsky, who was brought up in a Ukrainian hasidic milieu in the last quarter of the 19th century, presents the close relationship between the rebbetsin and what he terms 'the female hasid' (*haḥasidah*) as a common feature of all

hasidic courts:

> Even the 'female hasid', who sometime comes to the tsadik, either with or without her husband, is allowed to sit among the hasidim and listen to their discussions and tales about the holy tsadikim. She spends most of her visit at the court with the rebbetsin, the tsadik's wife, with whom she eats 'holy bread' on the sabbath and festivals, so that she, too, can taste the left-over food [*shirayim*] of the tsadik's table. (*Hasidism and Its Adherents* (Heb.), iv. 82)

67 This is in sharp contrast to the Sabbatio-Frankist movement and its sectarian fellowships, which addressed to women collectively a liberationist message of their own, and to which women belonged in their own right—whether with or without their husbands—and where they fully participated, either alongside or apart from the men, in every aspect of the ritual and devotional life of the messianic community. They thus formed a fully mobilized constituency of the movement. On all this see Rapoport-Albert, *Women and the Messianic Heresy of Sabbatai Zevi*.

68 For a consideration of women's hasidic identity both before and after affiliation to a particular court began, in the early 19th century, to be transmitted from one generation to the next and to encompass whole families, communities, and even whole regions, as well as the extent to which this identity may have differed from that of non-hasidic women, see above, pp. 321–2.

69 See e.g. Kahan, *Lubavitch and Its Soldiers* (Heb.), 36–7, 41, where she is described as 'holding a table' attended by her son, the rebbe, and the students of the Tomekhei Temimim yeshiva, or ibid. 29 n. 10, where she is said to have distributed *lekakh* [honey cake] on the eve of the Day of Atonement, granting a blessing to the narrator's younger brother. For the power and influence wielded by dowager rebbetsins generally see N. Polen, 'Rebbetzins, Wonder Children, and the Emergence of the Dynastic Principle in Hasidism', in S. T. Katz (ed.), *The Shtetl: New Evaluations* (New York, 2007), 53–84, concerning primarily the power to determine succession to the office of rebbe within the ruling family.

70 Perlow, *An Anthology of Tales* (Heb.), 228 §99. There exists another eyewitness account of what is evidently the same event, in the memoirs of Israel Jacobsohn (see above, n. 64). Jacobsohn's version, however, contains no reference to the exchange between the rebbe and his mother. See *Kerem ḥabad*, 3 (1987), 246.

71 Perlow, *An Anthology of Tales* (Heb.), 239 §114.

72 Assaf defines the comparable category of male *mekoravim* as 'intimates':

> a small group of Hasidim, consisting of those who accompanied the zaddik everywhere to assure him of always having a *minyan* for prayer. Among them were beadles and various functionaries who lived permanently in the zaddik's home, or very close by, and who were always at his service. The

hard core of this group were the *gabba'im*, who were the zaddik's most intimate advisers. The other intimates—valets, tutors, cantors, and ritual slaughterers—served the zaddik, his family, and his guests. These people were naturally expected to behave with the utmost discretion and loyalty, since they were in close contact with the zaddik and his family from morning to night. (*The Regal Way*, 278)

The female 'intimates' would hardly have served in any professional ritual capacities comparable to those of the males, but they might have attended on the rebbetsin and her children, and carried out various domestic duties, either for the rebbe's household or for the court as a whole.

73 For the formal hierarchy of grades in the Tomekhei Temimim yeshiva see N. Brawer, 'Resistance and Response to Change: The Leadership of Rabbi Shalom Dov Ber Schneersohn (1860–1920)', unpublished Ph.D. diss. (University College London, 2004), 243–6.

74 Kahan, *Lubavitch and Its Soldiers* (Heb.), 88.

75 From the context it is clear that the time in question was the spring of 1908.

76 In another version of the same memoir this soup is referred to as the rebbetsin's *krepkhen*. See the selections from Jacobsohn's memoirs published in *Kerem ḥabad*, 3 (1987), 245.

77 I. Jacobsohn (1890–1974), *Zikaron livnei yisra'el* (Brooklyn, 1996), Chabad Library CD-ROM, version 3, ch. 3 (for the year 1908). For yet another account of 'the rebbetsin's soup' by a former student of the yeshiva, see the memoirs of Hayim Eliezer Karasik (d.1960), published by Mondshine in *Kerem ḥabad*, 3 (1987), 264–5.

78 J. I. Schneersohn, *Sefer hasiḥot 5680–5687* [1920–7] (Brooklyn, 1994), 13, editorial note 12. The note originates in the obituary description of Shterna Sarah, which appeared first in *Hakeri'ah vehakedushah*, 3/29 (Feb. 1943), 4, marking the first anniversary of her death in New York, on 31 January 1942.

79 For the expansion of the yeshiva in its early decades, and Joseph Isaac's pivotal role as its young and energetic executive director on behalf of Shalom Dovber, see Brawer, 'Resistance and Response to Change', 271–82.

80 I have transliterated the Yiddish so as to reflect the original spelling as accurately as possible and in conformity with YIVO practice, although it contains a number of Germanized forms, which I have not restored to German.

81 The paper was edited by Moshe Rosenblum and was published in St Petersburg during 1911–12.

82 See the facsimile edition of both sets of accounts published by Mondshine in *Kerem ḥabad*, 3 (1987), 198–205. Most of the contributions were listed under the names of the female donors, but some included their husbands' names, and a few appeared under men's names alone. Some donations were listed as earmarked for particular purposes, and from this, together with the itemized list of expenditures for 1911–12 (ibid. 203), it is obvious that the money was used not only for the provision of regular meals but also for other basic needs, such as laundry, linen, and clothing. The total amounts raised per year, which rose from 809.80 rubles in 1909–10 to 2,062.89 rubles in 1911–12, were fairly substantial, equivalent at their height to the annual salary of a communal rabbi, or to half the annual salary of a Member of Parliament, the ruble at that time being valued at just over 50 American cents. I am grateful to Vladimir Levin for this assessment.

83 This wide dispersion is a reflection of the accelerated migration and urbanization processes which the Habad community, with the rest of the Jewish population of Imperial Russia, had been undergoing since the final decades of the 19th century. See on this e.g. J. Lestschinsky, *The Jewish People in Numbers: Jews throughout the World* (Yid.) (Berlin, 1922), 71–9; A. Kahan, 'The Impact of Industrialization in Tsarist Russia on the Socioeconomic Conditions of the Jewish Population', in id., *Essays in Jewish Social and Economic History*, ed. R. Weiss, with an introduction by J. Frankel (Chicago, 1986), 1–69, esp. 27–34; S. Stampfer, 'Patterns of Internal Jewish Migration in the Russian Empire', in Y. Ro'i (ed.), *Jews and Jewish Life in Russia and the Soviet Union* (Portland, Oreg., 1995), 28–47; *The YIVO Encyclopedia of Jews in Eastern Europe*, ii (New Haven, 2008), s.v. 'Population and Migration', 1427; 'Russia', 1612.

84 This had been the customary arrangement in the east European study houses, where the provision of food for the students was funded locally out of communal charity, as well as at Volozhin, the model for all the 19th-century Lithuanian yeshivas, where costs were covered by central institutional funds. See Brawer, 'Resistance and Response to Change', 261–7; id., 'The Founding of "Tomekhei Temimim" and Its Impact on the Habad Lubavitch Movement' (Heb.), in I. Etkes (ed.), *Yeshivot and Batei Midrash* [Yeshivot uvatei midrashot] (Jerusalem, 2006), 366; S. Stampfer, *The Lithuanian Yeshivas of the Nineteenth Century: Creating a Tradition of Learning* (Oxford, 2012), 9, 35, 121, 128, 155, 255, 273 n. 61, 307, 309, 310.

85 See e.g. M. A. Kaplan, *The Making of the Jewish Middle Class: Women, Family, and Identity in Imperial Germany* (New York, 1991), 192–227; P. E. Hyman and D. Ofer (eds.), *Jewish Women—A Comprehensive Historical Encyclopedia*, CD-ROM, Shalvi Publishing Ltd. (Jerusalem, 2006), s.v. 'Gratz, Rebecca (1781–1869)', 'Morgenstern, Lina (1830–1909)', 'Female Voluntarism', 'Philanthropy in the United States', 'Sisterhoods of Personal Service in the United States', 'Union of Jewish Women', 'National Council of Jewish Women'. In Budapest, Johanna Bischitz (née Fischer, 1827–98) founded in 1866 the Pest Israelite Women's Association, which provided relief for the poor, including a kosher soup kitchen. See *The YIVO Encyclopedia of Jews in Eastern Europe*, i. 191–2 (I am grateful to Gershon Hundert for this last reference, and to Moshe

Rosman for pointing out that this was the context of the rebbetsin's fundraising initiative).

86 Not much has been written about this. For brief general remarks see I. Levitats, *The Jewish Community in Russia, 1844–1917* (Jerusalem, 1981), 164, 167. V. Levin, 'Ocherk istorii evreiskogo shkolnogo obrazovanya v dorevolyutsionnom Peterburge', *Evreiskaya Shkola* (Jan.–Mar. 1993), 75) suggests that 'women's philanthropic circles for providing Jewish schoolchildren with clothing and dinners appeared only at the end of the 1860s', and he provides the example of the Ladies' Committee (p. 78) which operated under the aegis of the St Petersburg Community Board from 1873 until the collapse of the old regime. This, and a few other ladies' associations active in St Petersburg between 1873 and 1897, including the Ladies' Circle of the Society for the Promotion of Haskalah, are mentioned in V. Gessen's *K istorii Sankt-Peterburgskoi evreiskoi religioznoi obshchiny: Ot pervykh evreev do XX veka* (St Petersburg, 2000), 165, 176–7, 180–1, 190, 192. M. Beizer (*The Jews of St Petersburg: Excursions through a Noble Past* (Philadelphia, 1989), 293–4) refers to a 'Ladies' Circle to Provide the Fees for Pupils at Secondary Schools', which operated in the city between 1900 and 1915, and to a society chaired by Baroness Matilda Gintsburg, which provided cheap kosher food for students. In *Hamelits*, 21 (5 Sivan 5639 (1879)), col. 403, Elke Rosenberg, wife of the banker Hayim Joshua Heschel Rosenberg and sister of Baron Joseph Gintsburg, was praised for her philanthropic activities. In 1878 she set up in Kiev a Jewish women's association, which supported and cared for soldiers wounded in the Balkan war. There are also some references to her charitable projects in *Wanderer—The Memoirs of Yechezkel Kotik* [Na vanad: zikhronotav shel yeḥezkel kotik], ed., trans., and with an introduction by D. Assaf (Tel Aviv, 2005), ii. 177–8, 227. For details and a full discussion of Jewish women's charitable organizations in Kiev during the final decades of the czarist regime, see N. M. Meir, *Kiev, Jewish Metropolis: A History, 1861–1914* (Bloomington, Ind., 2010), 18, 212, 237–45. S. Ury refers to the 'Don't Overdress' women's organization, founded in Warsaw in 1904 by a group of 'respected women' who set out to fight the new fashion for 'excessive decoration and makeup' (*Barricades and Banners: The Revolution of 1905 and the Transformation of Warsaw Jewry* (Stanford, Calif., 2012), 64–5). In V. E. Kelner and D. A. Elyashevich (eds.), *Literatura o evereyakh na russkom yazyke, 1890–1947* (St Petersburg, 1995), 394–5, there is a list of reports by seventeen local women's institutions for social welfare, which existed within the Russian empire in towns of varying sizes, including St Petersburg, Warsaw, Vilna, Minsk, Pinsk, Uman, and Balta, between 1898 and 1916. Shaul Stampfer, who directed me to this source, suggests that the list is almost certainly far from comprehensive, and that Jewish women's organizations of this sort must have operated in many other localities throughout the empire during this period. At the same time, women's philanthropic organiza-

tions were being set up also in the Old Yishuv in Palestine (see the numerous references throughout P. B. Grayevsky's series of booklets *Daughters of Zion and Jerusalem* [Benot tsiyon viyerushalayim], nos. 1–10 (Jerusalem, 2000). I am grateful to David Assaf, Gershon Hundert, Vladimir Levin, and Shaul Stampfer for their help in assembling these references.

87 *Yidishes folksblat*, 2/41 (21 Oct. [2 Nov.] 1882), col. 622. I am grateful to Nurit Orchan for bringing Zederbaum's article to my attention, and to Chava Turniansky for her help in translating it from Yiddish.

88 See below, Appendix III.

89 B. S. Schneersohn, *Reshimot harabash* (Brooklyn, 2001), 115. Rabbi Barukh Shneur Schneersohn (1853–1926/8) was the great-grandson of the Tsemah Tsedek.

90 The memoirs of Y. Chitrik, *Reshimot devarim*, 4 vols. (New York, 1981–5), selection from i. 311 ff., published by Mondshine in *Kerem ḥabad*, 3 (1987), 270.

91 *Hakeri'ah vehakedushah*, 5.

92 J. I. Schneersohn, *Sefer hasiḥot 5703–5* [1943–5] (Brooklyn, 1996), 65, the section covering 1944 (reproduced in Hebrew in *Crown of Royalty* (Heb.), 109). This shift in the definition of the rebbetsin's role, which began with Shterna Sarah—away from direct involvement with food and towards a more personal-secretarial and even executive function—was carried through to the next rebbetsin, Nehamah Dinah—Joseph Isaac's own wife. She was apparently recruited, soon after her marriage in 1897, to help in the management of the newly founded Tomekhei Temimim yeshiva: 'Since there was no money for a secretary, the [future] rebbetsin would write the receipts etc. She did this in her house, which was no more than a room—the same room that served as a dining room, a study, a bedroom, and as the yeshiva office.' Later, after she became rebbetsin in 1920, she said that

> her husband, the rebbe, used to entrust to her various matters of public concern, such as the distribution of charity etc., especially when he was away from home. He highly valued her opinion on these matters. In 1944 he established a charity chest for the reinforcement of Judaism, which was directed by his wife the rebbetsin, jointly with an executive council. (*Crown of Royalty*, 135, 137)

93 For Shalom Dovber's motivation, and his aim in founding Tomekhei Temimim, see Brawer, 'The Founding of "Tomekhei Temimim"' (Heb.), 357–63; id., 'Resistance and Response to Change', 190–286. See also I. Lurie, 'Education and Ideology: The Beginnings of the Habad Yeshiva' (Heb.) in D. Assaf and A. Rapoport-Albert (eds.), *Let the Old Make Way for the New: Studies in the Social and Cultural History of Eastern European Jewry Presented to Immanuel Etkes* [Yashan mipenei ḥadash: meḥkarim betoledot yehudei mizraḥ eiropah uvetarbutam, shai le'imanu'el etkes] (Jerusalem 2009), i. 185–221.

94 *Igerot kodesh . . . shalom dovber* (Brooklyn, 1982), i. 273 no. 117.

95 See e.g. BT *Shab.* 33*b*, 146*a*; Zohar i. 126*a*; I. Tishby, *The Wisdom of the Zohar: An Anthology of Texts*, trans. D. Goldstein (London, 1989), i. 373–87.

96 *Igerot kodesh . . . shalom dovber*, i. 274 no. 117. See also ibid. i. 279 no. 117** (both letters were written in the summer of 1902). There was, of course, some truth in this accusation, inasmuch as women, who had traditionally been excluded at an early age from formal Jewish education, were often more involved than the men—at least among the better-off and educated classes—in the practical business of earning a living, which usually entailed direct dealings in the local vernacular with the non-Jewish environment. During the 19th and into the 20th century, they were increasingly being encouraged to acquire secular skills and accomplishments, such as arithmetic and foreign languages, with the help of private tutors, and eventually by attending public schools, gymnasia, and even institutions of higher education. They were thus much more exposed to secular European culture and its values than their husbands, whose experience was more often confined to traditional Jewish educational frameworks. See I. Parush, *Reading Jewish Women: Marginality and Modernization in Nineteenth-Century Eastern European Jewish Society*, trans. S. Sternberg (Waltham, Mass., 2004), 38–96.

97 *Igerot kodesh . . . yosef yitsḥak* (Brooklyn, 1982), ii. 225–7 no. 466. The letter was sent from Baltimore in January 1930.

98 See ibid., Shalom Dovber Levin's editorial introduction, 21. See also Loewenthal, 'Women and the Dialectic of Spirituality in Hasidism', 42–3; id., 'From "Ladies' Auxiliary" to "Shluhot Network"—Women's Activism in Twentieth-Century HABAD', in I. Bartal et al. (eds.), *A Touch of Grace: Studies in Ashkenazi Culture, Women's History, and the Languages of the Jews, Presented to Chava Turniansky* (Heb., Eng., and Ger.) [Ḥut shel ḥesed lekoved ḥavah turnianski] (Jerusalem, 2013), 73*–4*. Notably, the *admor* Joseph Isaac was not the only Orthodox leader during this period who was addressing women directly with an urgent call to observe the laws of 'family purity'. In the winter of 1930 Israel Meir Kagan, the Hafets Hayim, delivered a sermon on this subject to an audience of several thousand women in the main hall of the Great Synagogue of Vilna (from which the men had been barred for the occasion, but apparently filled the women's gallery). See M. M. Yoshor, *Haḥafets ḥayim, ḥayav ufo'olo* (Tel Aviv, 1959), ii. 506–12. The Yiddish text of the sermon (together with a Hebrew translation) was published in *Kol kitvei haḥafets ḥayim hashalem* (Jerusalem, 1990), 'Igerot uma'amarim', iii. 171–4 no. 77. I am grateful to Benny Brown for directing me to it. The volume contains several other pieces on the same subject: the treatise 'Sefer taharat yisra'el', 1–23 of the first pagination sequence; a 1928 Hebrew letter, jointly signed with Hayim Ozer

Grodzinsky, 36–7 no. 15 of the 'Igerot uma'amarim' section; and the Yiddish 'Ma'amar taharat hamishpaḥah', ibid. 230–46 no. 118.

99 See *Igerot kodesh . . . yosef yitsḥak*, ii. 332 no. 526.

100 Ibid. iv. 13 no. 873.

101 A letter written by Joseph Isaac from Philadelphia in the winter of 1929 (ibid. iv. 224 no. 465) celebrates the establishment of a women's association for 'family purity' in that city, and another, sent from New York in the early summer of 1930 (ibid. iv. 252–4 no. 482), refers to the existence of such an association in St Louis. But in the same letter he laments the general state of neglect in this field. In yet another letter, written in the summer of 1933, Joseph Isaac complains: 'Women's associations should have been set up in every place possible, but of course this takes labor and toil. And from time to time, rousing reading materials should be published for them, but, to my regret, all these plans of action and initiatives remain on paper, by way of good intentions alone' (ibid. iii. 8 no. 653). See also Loewenthal, 'From "Ladies' Auxiliary" to "Shluhot Network"', 74*, 76*.

102 See above, Ch. 6, n. 83.

103 This is how he seems to set his priorities in a letter from Otwock, written in the autumn of 1936, where he expresses his pleasure at hearing that in a number of Habad households, and among the students of Tomekhei Temimim, 'the wives and daughters read the narratives [embedded] in the "talks", and their husbands and fathers explain to them every single point of substance. I congratulate them on this . . . and may each girl prompt her [female] friends and acquaintances to read the "talk" and the narratives.' This, however, is directly followed by the much firmer 'but alongside this, it is the duty of the wives and daughters of the hasidim to stand at the forefront of every enterprise that would strengthen religion and Judaism in general, and in particular family purity' (cited above, at n. 100). He encourages the women to study the 'talks' but he commands them to campaign for strict religious observance.

104 For the establishment of Ahei Hatemimim in New York see *Igerot kodesh . . . yosef yitsḥak*, iv. 351 no. 1030; Loewenthal, 'Women and the Dialectic of Spirituality in Hasidism', 46.

105 It is not clear why the feminine singular *aḥot* rather than the plural *aḥyot* (comparable to the masculine plural of *aḥei*) was adopted, which would have better highlighted the analogous status of the two groups—clearly Joseph Isaac's intention. Quite possibly the slight discrepancy between the two matching designations arose simply from a failure to distinguish between the singular and plural forms of this feminine Hebrew word.

106 See the editorial introduction to *Igerot kodesh . . . yosef yitsḥak*, iv. 10–13, which provides references to all of Joseph Isaac's letters concerning the 'Brothers'

and the 'Sisters' of the Temimim, and see Loewenthal's detailed coverage of this topic in 'Women and the Dialectic of Spirituality in Hasidism', 44–51; id., 'From "Ladies' Auxiliary" to "Shluhot Network"', 77*–79*.

107 See above, pp. 371–2.

108 *Igerot kodesh . . . yosef yitsḥak*, iv. 186–7 no. 961.

109 Hayim ben Attar (1696–1743), the Moroccan scholar and author of the *Or haḥayim* commentary on the Pentateuch, by the title of which he himself came to be known.

110 *Igerot kodesh . . . yosef yitsḥak*, iii. 469 no. 818; it was first published in Warsaw in the winter of 1935 in the Habad periodical *Hatamim* (see the facsimile edn. (Kefar Habad, 1975), i. 172), and is quoted in part in Loewenthal, 'Women and the Dialectic of Spirituality in Hasidism', 44. I have not been able to trace any source for this account of Hayim ben Attar and his daughters. Ben Attar's biographies, as well as the numerous hagiographical traditions about him, make no mention of it at all but suggest, rather, that he was childless, and that despite the near-universality of monogamy in the Jewish world since medieval times, he had two living wives (and possibly even six!) precisely because he kept trying but repeatedly failed to produce offspring. See e.g. J. Nacht, *Mekor ḥayim* (Drohobycz, 1898), 10; R. Margaliot, *The Biography of Our Master Hayim ben Attar, Author of* Or Haḥayim [Toledot rabenu ḥayim ben atar ba'al or haḥayim] (Lwów, 1925), 45–6; B. Klar, *Rabbi Hayim ben Attar: His Immigration to the Land of Israel* [Rabi ḥayim ibn atar: aliyato le'erets yisra'el] (Jerusalem, 1951), 20 n. 16. See also D. Manor, 'Rabbi Hayim Ben Attar in Hasidic Writings' (Heb.), *Pe'amim*, 20 (1984), 88–110; G. Nigal, 'In Praise of R. Hayim ben Attar' (Heb.), in id., *West and East Studies* [Meḥkerei ma'arav umizraḥ] (Jerusalem, 2001), 99–120. Nevertheless, the reference to Ben Attar's practice of studying with his daughters features, in the context of women's education, in the subsequent Habad literature that derives from the writings of the sixth *admor* (see e.g. M. M. Schneerson, *Torat menaḥem–hitva'aduyot*, xx (5717 [1957]), pt. III, 177), who may well be its original source. His creative imagination could have conjured Ben Attar's daughters out of his knowledge that the Moroccan sage did not have any sons, and perhaps also his acquaintance with the tradition whereby Or Hahayim's sermons were so popular that even women flocked 'to his wives' chamber' in order to hear them (cited in E. Touitou, *Rabbi Hayim ben Attar and His Commentary* Or haḥayim *on the Torah* [Rabi ḥayim ben atar uferusho or haḥayim al hatorah] (Jerusalem, 1981), 14). In E. H. Carlebach (ed.), *A Memorial to the Holy Or Haḥayim and His Biography* [Yad or haḥayim hakadosh vetoledotav] (Hillside, NJ, 1981)—an anthology of works by or relating to Hayim ben Attar—the *admor* Joseph Isaac's statement on Ben Attar's studies with his daughters is cited as a source for this tradition (p. 355 §31). However, the same work, which reproduces, among other previously published texts, Reuben Margaliot's biography of the sage, contains two new editorial notes, which refer to Margaliot's comment on Ben Attar's childlessness (p. 53, nn. 103, 105). They suggest that the absence of sons should be taken to mean the presence of daughters, and this is cited as a generally held view in the name of the Belzer Rebbe, Aaron of Bełz (1880–1957), who may or may not have depended on Joseph Isaac Schneersohn as his source.

111 The very short fragment that survives from Shalom Dovber's Simhat Torah 'talk' of 1899 (5660) contains no reference to the instruction of boys and girls in hasidic lore. See his *Torat shalom—sefer hasiḥot* (Brooklyn, 2003), 3. The topic does feature as part of the same 'talk' in the more recent collection of supplements to *Torat shalom* (*Torat shalom—sefer hasiḥot (milu'im)*, i. 269), but this supplement is, in fact, a Hebrew translation of Joseph Isaac's Yiddish 'quotation' from his father's *siḥah* as it appears in his 1937 letter from Otwock (see above, at n. 108).

112 See Loewenthal, 'Women and the Dialectic of Spirituality in Hasidism', 52.

113 On this, see ibid. 58–62; id., 'From "Ladies' Auxiliary" to "Shluhot Network"'; id., '"Daughter/Wife of a Hasid" or "Hasidic Woman"?', *Mada'ei hayahadut*, 40 (2000), 25–8. And see pp. 447 ff. below.

114 See Parush, *Reading Jewish Women*. Two other scholars—Nathan Cohen, who has researched extensively the biographical and autobiographical Yiddish literature of the 19th century, and Nurit Orchan, who has studied the contribution of women to the Yiddish press of the same period—inform me that they have not come across any references to women reading *Shivḥei habesht* or any other hasidic book published in Yiddish.

115 The title *taytsh khumesh* could refer to any one of a number of Yiddish translations-cum-adaptations of the Pentateuch (though it is not clear when such translations began to be called by this name), on which see C. Turniansky, 'Towards the History of the "*Taytsh Khumesh*"—"*Khumesh mit Khiber*"' (Heb.), in *Considerations of Literature: Lectures in Honour of Dov Sadan on the Occasion of His Eightieth Birthday* [Iyunim besifrut: devarim shene'emru be'erev likhvod dov sadan bimelot lo shemonim shanah] (Jerusalem, 1988), 21–58.

116 See ibid. 59, 66–7, 137–8. On the emergence and function of this type of Yiddish literature see C. Turniansky, 'Yiddish and the Transmission of Knowledge in Early Modern Europe', *Jewish Studies Quarterly*, 15/1 (2008), 5–18.

117 See B. Schwarz, *My Life: My History and Memoirs* [Ḥayai: toledotai vezikhronotai] (Jerusalem, 1930), 162.

118 See S. Levin, *Childhood in Exile*, trans. M. Samuel (London, 1929), 6.

119 On women as transmitters of hagiographical traditions see M. Oron, 'The Woman as Narrator in Hasidic Tales: A Fictional Device or Preservation of

Tradition?' (Heb.), in D. Assaf et al. (eds.), *Studies in Eastern European Jewish History and Culture in Honor of Professor Shmuel Werses* [Mivilna liyerushalayim: meḥkarim betoledoteihem uvetarbutam shel yehudei mizraḥ eiropah mugashim liprofesor shemuel verses] (Jerusalem, 2002), 513–29.

120 See above, n. 53. For references to other female members of the ruling Habad family across the generations, all of whom are described as oral transmitters of early hasidic history and tales, see *Crown of Royalty* (Heb.), 76, 136, 198, 253–4, 267.

121 The Yiddish translation of the *Yosipon*, first published in Zürich in 1546, appeared in several subsequent editions, and was eventually published by Menahem Mann Amelander in Amsterdam, 1743, under the additional title of *Keter malkhut*, together with his own Yiddish sequel, *Keter kehunah*, under the additional title of *Sheyres yisro'el*, which took up the historical narrative of the *Yosipon* from the Second Temple period to the 18th century.

122 See Schneersohn, *The History of Rebbetsin Rivkah* (Heb.), 105–8. See also Joseph Isaac's essay 'The History of the Famous Hasidim' (Heb.), which appeared in Warsaw, in the Habad journal *Hatamim*, ii. 524, where he describes how, on Saturday nights, his grandmother Rivkah would tell him stories that she had read in her large volume of the *Tsenerene*. This is reproduced in *Crown of Royalty* (Heb.), 73, where there follows (p. 77) a Hebrew translation from one of Joseph Isaac's Yiddish discourses (*kuntres* 84, published in *Sefer ha-ma'amarim* 5711 (1951), 64). In it he claims that Rivkah herself, in the name of her mother-in-law, Hayah Mushka—the Tsemah Tsedek's wife—reported that 'the Old *Admor* [Shneur Zalman of Liady] had ordered that every Saturday night, following the sabbath meal, the women should *read* the weekly Torah portion from a *taytsh khumesh*, and in the afternoon—in winter, once the sabbath was over—they should *tell* hasidic stories' (emphases mine; A.R.-A).

123 See J. Perl, *Revealer of Secrets* (first published in Hebrew in 1819), trans. with an introduction and notes by D. Taylor (Boulder, Colo., 1997), 191 §112.

124 For a different assessment, however, taking the maskilic portrayal of women as avid readers of the Yiddish *Shivkhey habesht* to be reliable and wholly realistic, see S. Werses, 'Women in the Hasidic Courts as Reflected in Mitnagdic Polemics and Maskilic Satires' (Heb.), *Gal-ed*, 21 (2007), 33, 37–8, 46–7.

125 First published in Lemberg—in Hebrew in 1860 and in Yiddish in 1870.

126 See the report by a correspondent from Pułtusk in *Hamelits* of 16 Jan. 1889, 2–3. I am grateful to David Assaf for drawing my attention to it.

127 See J. Meir, 'The Lost Yiddish Editions of *Shivḥei habesht* (1815–1817)' (Heb.), *Kabbalah: Journal for the Study of Jewish Mystical Texts*, 39 (2017).

128 See Horodetsky, *Hasidism and Its Adherents* (Heb.), iv. 69.

129 On this see above, Ch. 6, at nn. 35–44 and 73–6, and see there nn. 39, 78.

For the special, liminal status of widows, who—no longer defined as women by their sexual nature and function—have been historically more free to pursue the path of ascetic piety in order to gain some spiritual or intellectual empowerment, see A. Rapoport-Albert, 'Glikl Hamel as a Widow' (Heb.), in ead., *Studies in Hasidism, Sabbatianism, and Gender* [Ḥasidim veshabeta'im, anashim venashim] (Jerusalem, 2015), 492–504.

130 For these see above, Ch. 6, n. 36.

131 See Heilman, *Beit rabi*, 109 (= 54*b*–55*a*), cited in Loewenthal, 'Women and the Dialectic of Spirituality in Hasidism', 21–2.

132 See Heilman, *Beit rabi*, 109 (= 55*a*). Another tradition, transmitted by Azriel Zelig Slonim (see above, at n. 43), similarly attributes to Rebbetsin Sheyna, wife of the Mitteler Rebbe, the belief that she acquired her spiritual powers from her husband. On the wedding day of her grandson, the future *admor*, Shemuel, 'she placed both her hands on his head, and in the presence of two witnesses she blessed him with the following words: "May all the powers that I have inherited from my husband pass on to you"' (Mondshine, *Migdal oz*, 213).

133 On him see Heilman, *Beit rabi*, 154 (= 74*b*).

134 See Zohar i. 84*a*. The letter, which appears to be genuine, was published by Y. Mondshine in *Bite'on ḥabad*, 15–16 (34–5) (1971), 10.

135 For this tradition see above, Ch. 6, at nn. 36–7, and n. 37; A. Grossman, *Pious and Rebellious: Jewish Women in Medieval Europe*, trans. J. Chipman (Waltham, Mass., 2004), 162–5, 194.

136 For a list of prominent hasidic women who fall into this category see above, Ch. 6, at nn. 38–42. See also the account of Sarah Horowitz Sternfeld of Chęciny—the 'Chentshiner Rebbetsin', who clearly conforms to the same type, in Polen, 'Miriam's Dance', 10–13. For Malka Shapiro's 'spiritual autobiography', depicting her early 20th-century upbringing as the daughter of a hasidic rebbe, while also commemorating the lives of her distinguished female relatives, including Perele, daughter of the Magid of Kozienice, who was reputed to be in possession of remarkable spiritual powers, see Shapiro, *The Rebbe's Daughter*.

137 For the repudiation of 'the ascetic woman' (*ishah perushah*) in rabbinic culture, see above, pp. 331–3.

138 For discussions highlighting this alternative model see Polen, 'Miriam's Dance', 11–15; Loewenthal, 'Women and the Dialectic of Spirituality in Hasidism', 12–15. On the unusual status of Eydele—daughter of Shalom Roke'aḥ (1779–1869), founder of the Belz dynasty—who seems to have combined elements of both the legitimate model of the powerful rebbe's daughter —married and a mother to several children—with the anomalous gender-bending career of the Maid of Ludmir, see Y. Bilu, 'The Woman Who Wanted To Be Her Father: A Case Analysis of Dibbuk Possession in a Hasidic Community', *Journal of Psychoanalytical Anthropology*, 8/1 (1985), 11–27; J. J. Lewis, '"Eydele, the Rebbe": Shifting Perspectives on a Jewish Gender Transgressor', *Journal of Modern Jewish Studies*, 6/1 (2007), 21–40, with references to earlier studies and sources on this case.

139 I am grateful to Rivka Dvir-Goldberg for bringing this to my attention.

140 From the approbation (*haskamah*) of Israel Abraham's great-grandson to the collection of his ancestor's teachings by Nathan Nata Donner of Kołbiel (Kolobel), *Menorat zahav* [first published in Warsaw in 1902] (Benei Berak, 2001), 7, reproduced in id., *Butsina kadisha* [hagiographical tales about Meshulam Zusya of Annopol, Israel Abraham's father, first published in Warsaw in 1912] (Benei Berak, 2001), 54.

141 See above, p. 326.

142 See e.g. A. Wertheim, *Laws and Customs in Hasidism* (Hoboken, NJ, 1992), 226–8, 252–4; J. G. Weiss, *Studies in East European Jewish Mysticism and Hasidism* (London, 1997), 31–4.

143 Cf. David Assaf's observations in *The Regal Way*, 268–9, on the dearth of evidence as regards the day-to-day practicalities of managing the hasidic court.

144 See H. Pedaya, 'On the Development of the Socio-Religious-Economic Model in Hasidism: *Pidyon*, *Ḥavurah*, and Pilgrimage' (Heb.), in M. Ben-Sasson (ed.), *Religion and Economy: Connections and Interactions* [Dat vekalkalah; yaḥasei gomelin] (Jerusalem, 1995), 311–73. For the various streams of income flowing to the 19th-century hasidic court see Assaf, *The Regal Way*, 285–309.

145 There are a few references in *Shivḥei habesht* to the involvement of the Besht's wife and daughter in the provision of food and wine for his table. See *In Praise of the Baal Shem Tov*, ed. D. Ben-Amos and J. R. Mintz (Bloomington, 1970), 80–1 §61; 137 §114. For evidence from 20th-century sources see below, n. 155.

146 This was the 1807 wedding of Beyle—daughter of the Mitteler Rebbe—and Yekutiel Zalman, grandson of Levi Isaac of Berdiczów. See *Crown of Royalty* (Heb.), 239.

147 To the extent that this late hagiographical tradition is susceptible of historical scrutiny, it is perhaps possible to explain this alleged difference between the two households by viewing Shneur Zalman's conduct as being governed by his role of rebbe, whose Seder is a public 'table' event at his hasidic court, while assuming that Levi Isaac, who served as a communal rabbi throughout his life, maintained a different relationship with his congregants and did not share his Seder table with them but rather celebrated in a conventional domestic setting, which included his wife. Alternatively, the difference might be explained in terms of the variation in hasidic practice on this point, which persists to the present day (see below, n. 153).

148 *Crown of Royalty* (Heb.), 26–7, drawn from *Kefar ḥabad*, 490 (28 Aug. 1991), 21, where the story is published for the first time, together with a whole cycle of Habad traditions drawn from the archive of the late Hayim Elijah Mishulovin, who was known as a transmitter of oral Habad lore (*ba'al shemuah*), and whose chain of informants is traceable back to Shneur Zalman of Liady's lifetime (see ibid. *Kefar ḥabad*, 19).

149 On this see directly below.

150 See M. Idel, 'Jewish Mysticism among the Jews of Arab/Moslem Lands', *Journal for the Study of Sephardic and Mizrahi Jewry*, 1/1 (Feb. 2007), 31–4; M. Cordovero, *Ma'ayan Ein Ya'akov: The Fourth Fountain of the Book Elimah* [Ma'ayan ein ya'akov lerabi mosheh kordovero], ed. with notes by B. Sack, introd. by S. Asulin et al. (Be'er Sheva, 2009). See also G. Scholem, *On the Mystical Shape of the Godhead: Basic Concepts in the Kabbalah* (New York, 1991), 187–9, 192–4; Y. Jacobson, 'The Aspect of the "Feminine" in the Lurianic Kabbalah', in P. Schäfer and J. Dan (eds.), *Gershom Scholem's Major Trends in Jewish Mysticism 50 Years After* (Tübingen, 1993), 239–55; B. Roi, *Love of Shekhinah: Mysticism and Poetics in the Tikunei Zohar* [Ahavat hashekhinah: mistikah ufoetikah betikunei hazohar] (Ramat Gan, 1917).

151 See on this above, Ch. 5.

152 Hannah Schneerson, Menachem Mendel Schneerson's mother (d.1964), was not a rebbetsin in the sense of a hasidic rebbe's wife but is referred to by the ambiguous title of *harabanit*. This can mean the wife of a rabbi, which she was, having married Levi Isaac Schneerson (1878–1944), great-grandson of the Tsemah Tsedek, who served as rabbi of Ekaterinoslav (Dnepropetrovsk) between 1909 and 1939.

153 A. S. Bukiet (ed.), *Em hamalkhut* (Kefar Habad, 2001), 60. This was confirmed, in a private communication, by Rabbi Shmuel Lew of London, who writes:

> The Seder at the rebbe's was more likely a Farbrengen type of activity (at least during many periods during the history of Chabad rebbes), which was attended by many Chasidim (in addition to the guests at the table), in which case I would imagine that it would not be appropriate for it to be a mixed event . . . Our rebbe's Seder from 5711 (1951) through 5730 (1970) was 'upstairs', the second floor of 770, the apartment of the previous rebbe, R. Yosef Yitzchak. I would imagine that what took place was a continuation of the custom with his [the last rebbe's] father-in-law [Joseph Isaac], namely, that there was over a Minyan present, and many Chasidim would come along at different stages of the evening. The previous rebbe would talk as well; it was his style of 'farbrengen', to speak at Yomtov

meals. Our rebbe would generally not speak at the table (certainly not formally) . . . In those years the women sat in a room (a kitchen) not far away, off a small corridor in the apartment. The rebbe's wife, Rebbetsin Chaya Mushka, would stand outside that room, in the corridor, for the Rebbe's Kidush. After the wife of the previous rebbe (Rebbetsin Nechama Dina) passed away on 10 Tevet 5731 [7 Jan. 1971], these meals discontinued upstairs, and the rebbe then held the Seder in his home on President Street, and in later years in the library apartment next door to 770, together with the rebbetsin (and the live-in help, Rabbi S. B. Gansbourg), until her passing in 5748 (1988).

I am grateful to Rabbi Lew for this information. For a collection of Habad Seder night customs, suggesting some variation of practice across the generations, especially as regards the number of guests sharing the rebbe's Seder table, and the question whether or how many hasidim and yeshiva students would be allowed to join it at certain stages of the proceedings, see Mondshine, *Otsar minhegei ḥabad—nisan–sivan* (Jerusalem, 1996), 115–18. On p. 118 Mondshine provides some comparative information on the degree to which the rebbe's Seder table was considered a public hasidic event at some of the other hasidic courts. From this, too, it emerges that practice varied. As for the presence of women—apparently at the courts of both the fourth and the fifth Lubavitcher rebbes, the household women held their Seder in the same room as the men but at a separate table. At other hasidic courts practice varied, from the relegation of household women to a separate room, through their incorporation in the same room but at a separate table, to their full inclusion (e.g. in Bełz) with the men at the rebbe's table (see ibid. 118–19).

154 See Assaf, *The Regal Way*, 285–309.

155 Ibid. 283. The observation regading women's involvement is based on a reference to Feyge (ibid. 396 n. 76, and cf. the fuller information supplied in the original Hebrew version of the book, *Derekh hamalkhut*, 386 n. 97), the wife of David Moses of Czortków (1827–1903), who 'complained that she did not have enough money to cover the cost of sustaining the holy court', which appeared in a hagiographical source first published in 1930; on the description of Miriam, wife of Abraham Jacob of Sadagora (1819–83), who, according to a short story by S. Y. Agnon, managed the kitchen and organized the supply of food to her husband's court; and on the account of Sarah Tsiporah, wife of Abraham Matityahu of Ştefăneşti (1848–1933), who features in a family memoir published for the first time in 1981. For the problematic nature of such sources and the methodology of drawing on them, see Assaf's introduction to *The Regal Way*, 21–8.

156 See on this ibid. 274; A. Teller, 'Hasidism and the Challenge of Geography: The Polish Background to the Spread of the Hasidic Movement', *AJS Review*, 30/1 (2006), 18–24.

157 For the function of female members of the Polish nobility as mistresses of their households who oversaw the work of servants engaged in the production of food, see M. Bogucka, *Women in Early Modern Polish Society, Against the European Background* (Aldershot, 2004), 33.

158 *Reshimot harabash*, 107–8.

159 Ibid. 133.

160 Kahan, *Oral Traditions and Tales about Our Holy Rebbes* (Heb.), ii. 37.

161 Azriel Zelig Slonim's tradition, in Mondshine, *Migdal oz*, 213.

162 See *Hakeri'ah vehakedushah*, 1/5 (Feb. 1941), 6.

163 J. I. Schneersohn, *Likutei diburim*, (Yid.) ii (Brooklyn, 1984), pt. III, 512 (reproduced in translation from Yiddish into Hebrew in *Crown of Royalty* (Heb.), 74–5).

164 *Igerot kodesh . . . yosef yitsḥak*, ii. 428 no. 584.

165 See M. Rosenblum, 'Divrei yemei hatemimim', *Kerem ḥabad*, 3 (1987), 49–50.

166 Jacobsohn, *Zikaron livnei yisra'el*, 15 n. 26, and with slight variations in Mondshine's version, published in *Kerem ḥabad*, 3 (1987), 241.

167 This practice may have sprung from the eve-of-fast custom of handing out sweetmeats at the synagogue or cemetery gates. See Y. T. Lewinsky, *Encyclopedia of Folklore, Customs, and Tradition in Judaism* [Entsiklopedyah shel havai umasoret bayahadut] (Tel Aviv, 1975), 246; A. I. Sperling, *Sefer ta'amei haminhagim umekorei hadinim* (Jerusalem, 1972), 327 §733.

168 See Kahan, *Lubavitch and Its Soldiers* (Heb.), 29.

169 See Y. Mondshine, *Otsar minhegei ḥabad—elul–tishrei* (Jerusalem, 1995), 181 §34.

170 See M. M. Schneerson, *Sefer hasiḥot 5750* (1990), 23.

171 See Mondshine, *Otsar minhegei ḥabad—elul–tishrei*, 181–3.

172 Cf. above, n. 69.

173 See Jacobsohn, *Zikaron livnei yisra'el*, selections published in *Kerem ḥabad*, 3 (1987), 250.

174 See Karasik's memoirs (above, n. 77), 264.

175 See selections from Iser Gutin's memoirs, *Kur oni*, published by Mondshine in *Kerem ḥabad*, 3 (1987), 272.

176 See above, pp. 385–6.

EIGHT

From Woman as Hasid to Woman as 'Tsadik' in the Teachings of the Last Two Lubavitcher Rebbes

The Pre-Twentieth-Century Background

The exceptionally inclusive attitude to women that has become a hallmark of contemporary Habad Lubavitch has been traced back to the very beginnings of this early school of hasidism. However, the historical record of Habad, from its inception in the late 1700s to the early decades of the twentieth century, does not distinguish its attitude to women from the male exclusivity that marks the hasidic movement as a whole.[1] The factors cited to suggest that the contemporary stance has evolved from early ideological foundations, rooted in the special gender sensibilities of Habad's first leaders, include (1) the internal Habad tradition of early twentieth-century provenance whereby Shneur Zalman of Liady (Lyady), Habad's founder (1745–1813), used to teach hasidism to his daughter Freyde, who has even been credited with the authorship of a letter containing speculative teachings of her own; (2) the publication in Shklov, in 1794, of Shneur Zalman's *Hilkhot talmud torah*, in which he cited the traditional strictures against women's Torah study but ruled that 'nonetheless, women, too, are duty bound to study the *halakhot* that apply to them'; and (3) the two Yiddish tracts, *Poke'aḥ ivrim* and *Seder birkhot hanehenin*, published in 1817 and 1820 respectively by Shneur Zalman's son and successor, Dov Ber, the Mitteler Rebbe (1773–1827), which have been presented as 'evidence of the desire to involve women in the hasidic path of Habad' on the grounds that they were written in a language that was accessible to women, and that the former tract referred unusually, if briefly, to women's own sexual urges while the latter was halakhically applicable to men and women alike.[2] Each of these supposed factors can be shown to depend on an unconvincing interpretation of the facts or on sheer error.

First, while Freyde may well have been taught hasidism by her father, this neither sprang from nor led to any innovative early Habad model for the initiation of women in the speculative doctrines of hasidism; it must be recognized as belonging in the long-established rabbinic tradition that credited certain women with scholarly or spiritual accomplishments by virtue of their intimate association with illustrious male relatives—a tradition which found fresh expression in hasidism but predated it by many centuries.[3] That Freyde belonged to this exceptional category of well-connected women, empowered not so much in their own right as through close proximity to distinguished men, is corroborated by another Habad tradition, recorded in the same twentieth-century source, which ascribes to Freyde's widowed mother, the dowager Rebbetsin Sterna, the proud declaration that her own spirituality, and her ability 'to make a *pidyon*' (to receive petitions for, and to grant, efficacious blessings like a rebbe)[4]—powers that she claimed to be superior to those of her son, the reigning *admor*, Dov Ber—derived from nothing other than her association with her late husband, Shneur Zalman, during fifty years of marriage.[5] As for the attribution to Freyde of the letter containing kabbalistic speculations on the date of the messianic advent, it has been proved to be erroneous; the actual author was in all probability Aaron Halevi of Starosielce (1766–1828), Shneur Zalman's disciple and his son's rival in the contest for the Habad leadership.

Second, Shneur Zalman did indeed sanction women's study of the ritual laws that apply specifically to them, but there was nothing innovative or unique about this ruling; it relied on a large body of earlier halakhic sources that advocated effectively the same, and, most importantly, did not generate any Habad framework for women's education. Such a framework only emerged a century and a half later, in response to changing historical circumstances. The frequent references to this halakhic ruling, scattered throughout the literature emanating from the teachings of Menachem Mendel Schneerson, the last Lubavitcher Rebbe[6]—for whom, as will be discussed below, the education of women, their spiritual empowerment, and their mobilization as an active hasidic constituency *did* become an important issue—are a characteristically anachronistic, modern Habad projection of contemporary concerns onto its eighteenth-century origins.[7]

Third, the two Yiddish tracts published by Dov Ber were clearly aimed at uneducated readers who had no knowledge of Hebrew—a class within which women had always formed a sub-category; but they were not addressed specifically to women, contained no message pertaining primarily to them, and there is no evidence to suggest that they attracted a female readership.[8]

Women as a rule were (and usually still are) excluded from the highlight of the hasidic gathering at the rebbe's table, where he delivers his personal teaching. However, the hagiographical sources of hasidism, as well as some anti-hasidic polemics of the final decades of the eighteenth century, suggest that women could obtain a private audience with the rebbe in order to submit their *kvitl* (the note on which their personal petition would be inscribed), pay their *pidyon* (Hebrew for 'ransom'—the payment accompanying the submission of a *kvitl*[9]), and receive his blessing in return.[10] But this was by no means universal. The presence of women in the hasidic courts and, above all, their admittance to a personal audience with the rebbe were clearly perceived as problematic. Some hasidic leaders did not admit them at all, while others would do so only under certain constraints.[11] A late Habad hagiographical tale, at pains to distinguish the Habad style of leadership—where, as is implicit in the tale, the rebbe never engages with women—from the practice of Ukrainian (or, as most other hasidic schools are often referred to in the late Habad sources, Polish[12]) tsadikim, claims that 'it was customary for Mordecai of Chernobyl [1770–1837] to give blessings even to women, so long as they remained concealed behind a curtain'.[13] Another tale in the same collection attributes to Hillel of Porich (Parichi)—a Chernobyl hasid who was drawn to Habad and became a disciple of Dov Ber, the Mitteler Rebbe—the following statement, highlighting more bluntly this particular aspect of the superiority of Habad over Ukrainian hasidism: 'Let women and madmen travel to Vilednik [Novi Velidnyky, the seat of the tsadik Israel of Vilednik[14]] while [real] men and pietists [*ḥasidim*] travel to Lubavitch.'[15]

Shneur Zalman of Liady may indeed have been one of those hasidic leaders who refrained altogether from dealing with women. There is no direct evidence of this in any of the contemporary sources, but the absence of references to women from his Liozno Ordinances, which regulated the visits to his court of a range of well-differentiated, distinct classes of hasidim, apparently all male, suggests the probability. Moreover, Shneur

Zalman is known to have distanced himself from the style of hasidic leadership that consisted primarily of the distribution of 'blessings'. These blessings were credited with the power to resolve material problems of daily life, and entailed the expectation of miraculous feats, which Shneur Zalman firmly disavowed, insisting that what he could offer his hasidim was intellectual, spiritual, and moral guidance by means of his *torah* (teaching). Since women were excluded from the occasions on which he would deliver his *torah*, they could only have come to the court in pursuit of blessings. It therefore stands to reason that he did not grant them private audiences and generally did not encourage their visits to his court. This impression is strengthened by a cluster of anecdotes, drawn from the rich hagiographical and memoirist literature of twentieth-century Habad, which explicitly state that Shneur Zalman of Liady, and following him most of his successors, refrained from dealing with women as a matter of policy. Admittedly these late Habad sources are all too often anachronistic, but as regards the attribution to virtually every one of the pre-twentieth-century Habad leaders of the policy of having 'no dealings with women', their credibility is enhanced precisely because they run counter to what became, in the course of the twentieth century, the 'official' Habad line of engaging with women, incorporating and even promoting them as activists—a policy that continues to distinguish Habad Lubavitch hasidism to the present day.[16]

All this suggests that the hasidic identity and personal hasidic experience of pre-twentieth-century women born or married into the Habad fold—either to the families of rank-and-file hasidim or even, as we have seen, to the ruling dynasty—must have been at least as circumscribed and as contingent on the Habad affiliation of their menfolk as those of women born or married into any other branch of hasidism.[17]

Nor is there any evidence of a particular interest in women in pre-twentieth-century Habad doctrine. The hasidic discourses of the leaders, like those of other hasidic masters, never address a female audience, and to the extent that women feature in them at all—either collectively, as the gender category 'female', or individually, in reference most commonly to female protagonists of the Hebrew Bible—they are routinely allegorized. As such, they serve to allude to one or another of the female divine *sefirot*, to the restrictive, harsh, judgmental forces that emanate from the feminine domain of the 'left-hand-side', or else they signify one of the attributes traditionally marked by the philosophers and the kabbalists as feminine

—passivity, receptivity, and, above all, material corporeality, whereby as 'matter' or 'body' they are schematically juxtaposed with their standard male counterparts, 'form' or 'soul'.[18] Moreover, in some of the classical hasidic sources, the ontological categories of male and female are applied to a corresponding pair of anthropological or sociological categories, distinguishing as quintessentially 'male' the spiritual elite—the hasidic masters themselves—from the mass of common people constituting their (all-male) hasidic following, who are classified as corporeal or material and are labelled 'female'. In other contexts, the male–female dichotomy is employed to create a typology of hasidic leaders (again, all male) where the ideal tsadik is classified as male while the one who falls short of the ideal is classified as female. At yet other times, the gender dichotomy is used to discern the fluctuating balance of male and female qualities, states of mind, or modes of operation that may be displayed involuntarily, or else deliberately employed, at different times and in different circumstances, by one and the same tsadik.[19]

In the Habad homilies, as in the kabbalistic sources on which they draw, the dichotomous presentation of male and female is less concerned to draw anthropological, sociological, or psychological distinctions between particular types or classes of men, and tends to assume a more universal or cosmic character, but there, too, the category 'female' is liable to feature as a trait or a mode of operation that is ascribed to men.[20] In fact, throughout the speculative literature in which hasidism articulated its formative doctrines, references to 'woman', 'femininity', or 'the female' have very little to do with actual women. More often than not they are allegorized out of existence or else displaced by a 'feminized' fraternity of male hasidim. The idea of a flesh-and-blood woman does feature from time to time as an object of male desire, and thus a threat to the spiritual integrity of men who strive to focus their minds on the endeavour to attain communion with God. To cope with the distraction of erotic thoughts triggered by the encounter with an attractive woman, they are advised to sublimate or 'raise' these thoughts by contemplating the transience of the woman's corporeal beauty, which will degenerate in time to the point where she would be utterly repulsive. This in turn enables the men to recognize, and shift their attention to, the permanent, pure, spiritual source of all beauty, which is God, who then becomes the true object of their desire. While the chance encounter with the attractive woman thus triggers for the men an encounter with God, the woman herself is oblivious of the experience and totally excluded from it: she plays no part in the contemplative exercise, is not herself spiritually transformed, and her irredeemably corporeal allure is erased from the men's minds once the lust she has aroused in them has been converted into spiritual yearnings. At this point the woman becomes redundant and simply falls out of sight.[21]

There is, however, one theme—part of the kabbalistic legacy of hasidism—that celebrates a much-empowered female, matching and ultimately supplanting the male as the dominant gender category. It occurs in discussions that focus on the dynamics of the redemptive process, whereby the cosmic female gradually ascends from the lowest to the highest levels of the sefirotic hierarchy, culminating in her installation at its very head. Discussions of this process are usually anchored in the biblical verses 'a woman shall encircle a man' (Jer. 31: 22) and 'an excellent woman is a crown to her husband' (Prov. 12: 4). The former is taken to allude to the reversal of gender roles, when the female shall appropriate the traditional active, 'giving', 'bestowing', or 'emanating' attributes of the male, and the latter is understood as pointing to the inverted gender hierarchy whereby 'woman' shall rise above 'her husband'. Variations on this eschatological theme feature from time to time in Shneur Zalman of Liady's homilies. For example:

On the face of it, it seems easier for a person to adhere to God by way of Love [the attribute associated with the male] rather than Awe [the attribute associated with the female], which [latter] may be achieved [only] with great difficulty. But the deeper understanding of this is that even though down below Love is greater than Awe, up above Awe is greater than Love. This may be explained by the following illustration. Ostensibly it is surprising to find that Abraham was told: 'In all that Sarah says to you, hearken to her voice' [Gen. 21: 11], for surely, Abraham belongs to the [male, active] category of 'bestower' [*mashpi'a*] and Sarah to the [female, passive] category of 'receiver' [*mekabel*]. How, then, could Abraham receive from Sarah? . . . In truth, however, down below the Patriarchs were bestowers and the Matriarchs receivers, but up above the Matriarchs were higher than the Patriarchs, as [will be the case] in the messianic future, which is alluded to by the verses 'an excellent woman is a crown to her husband' and 'a woman shall encircle a man'. For the [female] category of receiver shall rise above the category of the male, and the Patriarchs will receive from the Matriarchs. As regards Abraham, Isaac, and Jacob, the Sages said that God had given them a foretaste of the World to Come[22] . . . For this reason, even in their own time, there was something about the level of the Matriarchs that was higher than that of the Patriarchs, and this is why Scripture said, 'In all that Sarah says to you, hearken to her voice.'[23]

The biblical Matriarchs and Patriarchs are understood primarily in symbolic, sefirotic terms, and the future ascent of the 'female category' refers first and foremost to the ascent of the divine female. However, the distinction between 'up above' and 'down below' runs through the whole passage, and the biblical Matriarchs, who were exceptional enough as living human beings to be allowed to sample in their earthly lifetime something of the eschatological inversion of the gender hierarchy, are presumed to be historical. Combined, these two factors suggest that this inversion of male and female will manifest itself not only on the cosmic-divine plane but also on the plane of living humanity, albeit a humanity that has been purified and perfected by the time of, or rather by means of, the messianic redemption.

The same applies to another context in which Shneur Zalman observes the eschatological supremacy of the female. This is the difference between the wording of the sixth and the seventh marriage benedictions.[24] The former concludes with 'blessed are thou, God, who gladdens the groom and the bride', while the latter concludes with the slight variation 'who gladdens the groom *with* the bride'. In Shneur Zalman's understanding of the blessings, the difference between them alludes to the distinction between the exilic reality of his own time and the messianic future. For him, the sixth benediction, where reference to the bride's joy follows, and thus is secondary to, and dependent on, the groom's—a state of affairs which, for the time being, reflects the inferior status of the female—alludes to the contemporary exilic state. On the other hand, the seventh benediction alludes to the messianic future, for the situation is reversed: the joy of the bride is primary, while the groom's joy, appended to it by the preposition 'with', is derived from, and dependent on, the bride's. Here, too, the inverted positions of the bride and groom symbolically represent the inversion that will occur 'up above', in the sefirotic hierarchy, but at the same time they are intended to allude to the future inversion of the gender hierarchy in the lives of flesh-and-blood women and men, as is suggested by the fact that Shneur Zalman incorporates the theme and elaborates on it in his wedding homilies and blessings for betrothals and marriages.[25]

However, Shneur Zalman's expositions of this topic (like the homily on the same eschatological theme by the contemporary hasidic master, Kalonymos Kalman Epstein of Kraków (1751–1823),[26] draw their rhetorical force and full effect precisely from the contrast they highlight between the familiar reality of the present and the fanciful upside-down world of the messianic future. In this respect the theme belongs in a long tradition of eschatological speculation depicting the Future to Come as being utterly new and different from, or even a complete inversion of, the present. The tradition has its origins in the utopian strand of biblical prophecy, but it was developed in startlingly provocative terms in some classical rabbinic and medieval kabbalistic sources, where the inauguration of a new messianic Law was envisaged as entailing the abrogation of the commandments. This messianic Law derives from the divine unity that lies above and beyond the multiplicity that marks the creative processes of differentiation and restriction. In the new Law even the distinction between right and wrong, which gave rise to the halakhic prohibitions of the old Law, no longer obtains, so that the forbidden becomes permitted, including—perhaps specifically—the strictest prohibitions, for example of ritually unclean meat or of illicit sexual relations.[27]

By contrasting the reality of the present with a tantalizing fantasy of the future, this tradition serves above all to affirm, rather than challenge or subvert, the authority of the old Law, which, for the time being, will continue to govern the familiar world order. The tradition becomes subversive only in the context of acute messianic tension, when the Future to Come is believed to have arrived and to be unfolding in the here and now, as some Sabbatian and Frankist heretics apparently believed. But in the absence of any sense of messianic urgency in Shneur Zalman's teachings, which present a particularly spiritualized brand of personal eschatology, and without a shred of historical evidence that he was involved in active messianic agitation, there is no reason to suppose that he expected the conventional gender hierarchy to be transcended or reversed in the persisting 'exilic' reality of his time. His expositions of the theme effectively placed as much emphasis on the inferiority of the female in the present as they did on the ultimate superiority she would achieve in the messianic future, which, as far as he was concerned, lay beyond the earthly dimensions of time and place.[28]

The same can be said of all the subsequent nineteenth-century Habad leaders, in whose teachings this eschatological theme features from time to time, often as elaborations on Shneur Zalman's homilies, in reference to the same biblical verses, and similarly without the slightest indication that the inverted or transcended gender hierarchy of the messianic future is felt to be imminent or manifest in the mundane reality of the present.[29] Habad did not display a more urgent sense of messianic mission until the early twentieth century, when turbulent contemporary events began to be interpreted in apocalyptic terms. Notably, it was during the same period that the movement was beginning to re-evaluate the position of women within its ranks.

In what follows I propose to review these two concurrent developments, and to examine the relationship between them in order to determine whether, or to what extent, the gradual transformation of Habad women in the course of the twentieth century—from individual 'wives and daughters of the hasidim' situated on the outer periphery of hasidic life to a mobilized constituency of female hasidim imbued with a sense of mission and operating at its centre—was conceived as a move towards the realization of a messianic future in which the female—both earthly and divine—was to occupy her rightful place alongside, or even above, her male partner.

Twentieth-Century Developments

As I have demonstrated elsewhere, already during the leadership of Shalom Dovber, the fifth Lubavitcher Rebbe (1860–1920), Habad women were for the first time addressed directly, as a group, in an attempt to harness them to an important cause—a pioneering initiative that may have laid the foundations for what would eventually emerge as the fully engaged female hasidic constituency of Habad. But this initiative, while emanating from the headquarters of the movement at the Lubavitch court, was not taken by the rebbe himself and was not expressed in his teachings, which continued to concern, and be addressed exclusively to, his male hasidim. Rather, it was his wife, Rebbetsin Shterna Sarah (1860–1942), who, towards the end of the first decade of the new century, launched a fundraising campaign targeting women in the Habad fold throughout the Russian empire and beyond. She urged the women to contribute to the maintenance of the junior students at the expanding Tomekhei Temimim yeshiva, established by her husband in Lubavitch in 1897. To this end she founded a Habad 'ladies' association' (*damen ferayn*)—unprecedented in the hasidic world but modelled on what had become a fairly standard mode of philanthropic activity among women who belonged to the upper echelons of the Jewish bourgeoisie. Contributions from women throughout the widely dispersed Habad community were evidently forthcoming: the rebbetsin published the association's income and expenditure figures for 1909–11, and a year later provided a breakdown of 179 individual donors' names, places of residence, and amounts of donation for the period from 1911 to 1912.[30]

This initiative, which mobilized women to charitable action (a traditional female virtue) in the name of a vital Habad cause, betrayed something of the modernization processes that the Lubavitch court was undergoing at the time, despite its entrenched ideological opposition to various manifestations of modernity. However, the cause itself, the Tomekhei Temimim yeshiva, was conceived in purely traditional terms as being exclusively male. It was designed to nurture Habad's future elite core, which Shalom Dovber envisaged as a vanguard of rigorously trained, dedicated young men who would lead his campaign of resistance to the secular ideologies of Haskalah, Zionism, and socialism, while at the same time revitalizing Orthodox Judaism in the spirit of Habad, and providing an alternative to the Lithuanian yeshivas, which he believed to be a gateway to secularism.[31] His wife's appeal to the female members of hasidic households throughout the Habad world was a modern means of realizing Shalom Dovber's anti-modernist vision, couched in urgent messianic terms as the antithesis of what he perceived to be the false, secularist messianic promise of Zionism.[32] But his anti-Zionist messianic rhetoric contained no intimations of the inverted gender hierarchy that was a hallmark of kabbalistic eschatology. The theme of the female's future installation above the male as 'a crown to her husband', or her 'encircling' of the male as she assumes his active and bestowing functions, does feature from time to time in Shalom Dovber's discourses, but only in abstruse theosophical contexts that are quite distinct and apparently free from the apocalyptic tension that marks his anti-Zionist pronouncements.[33] Moreover, far from incorporating women in his endeavours to bolster Orthodox practice and to promote the spiritual values of Habad, which he regarded as the only means of expediting the messianic advent, he held women responsible for the falling standards of religious observance in the home, and thus for the growing estrangement from tradition of the younger generation. In terms that echo old rabbinic and kabbalistic notions of women's 'frivolity' and their inherent susceptibility to sexual pollution by Satan,[34] he wrote in the summer of 1902:

Satan dances first among the women, to cast into them the filth of libertinism. They then run their households in the spirit of libertinism, taking charge of the guidance and education of their children. With their frivolous notions they prevail upon their husbands to dismiss the traditional religious teachers and to send their sons instead to the [secular] teachers who corrupt them.[35]

In another letter, written a month later, he blamed women for their immodest appearance, for neglecting the laws of ritual purity, and for exerting an altogether negative influence on their 'God-fearing' husbands, who tolerate their improprieties and allow them to lead their children astray:

We should pay attention to the collapse [of standards] in the homes of our God-fearing brethren. In most cases their households are run in a manner which is entirely at odds with their own God-fearing conduct. The wantonness of the women's uncovered hair has become so commonplace that hardly a single household is free from it. It has come to be viewed as a permissible thing, and the husbands feel no obligation to resist it and to put things right. Even if at first a husband would find it difficult [to tolerate such conduct], eventually he resigns himself to it without displaying any signs of displeasure [with his wife], and similarly with his daughter. Nor is he in the least worried or distressed by their blatant disregard for the cardinal laws of ritual purity, whereby they implicate their husbands in grave sin and transgression, Heaven forbid.[36]

While Shalom Dovber, who had identified women as a source of the malaise of secularism, excluded them from direct participation in his anti-secularist projects, his son and successor, Joseph Isaac Schneersohn, the sixth Lubavitcher Rebbe (1880–1950), drew the logical conclusion from his father's diagnosis and tackled the malaise at its apparent source. For the first time in the history of Habad he, as reigning *admor*, personally turned to 'the wives and daughters of the hasidim', calling on them to champion the cause of preserving Orthodox Judaism. This was in 1929–30, during his visit to the United States, where he was hosted by local Habad hasidim who had been settling in the New World since the start of the mass emigration from eastern Europe in the last two decades of the nineteenth century. Shocked by the lack of Jewish education and religious observance he encountered among the young, he was fired by the belief that it was essential and possible to draw this lost generation back into the fold. One of his first moves was to launch a campaign for the promotion of Jewish 'family purity', calling specifically on women to take the matter into their hands by setting up ladies' associations, whose members would be committed, and strive to commit others, to strict observance of the laws that required of women ritual immersion in the *mikveh* at the end of each period of prescribed abstention from conjugal relations. In a letter sent from New York to Chicago in the summer of 1930, he wrote:

Family purity is in a derelict state. To re-establish . . . it on a proper basis it is necessary to found a ladies' association dedicated to family purity (as they have done in St Louis). The purpose of the association would be (*a*) to bring together and unite the women who observe family purity, and (*b*) to engage in propaganda in order to persuade young women to enrol in the Association for Family Purity . . . The most important thing is to make every effort to ensure that the activists in this matter would be the women themselves. They will be the ones who inspire and organize. One should find young women who, with God's help, have a great capacity for influencing others. We have seen tangible evidence that when they take upon themselves this kind of activity, they are successful, with God's help.[37]

In the spring of 1931, a few months after his return to Riga—his place of residence (always referred to as temporary) since his flight from the Soviet Union in 1927, Joseph Isaac visited his followers in Lithuania, where he similarly called on the women to found family purity associations, of which the first was soon established in Rokiškis (Rakiszki).[38] And in the autumn of 1936, by which time he had settled in Poland, he wrote from Otwock, near Warsaw, to one of his followers in the Holy Land:

It is the duty of the wives and daughters of the hasidim . . . to stand at the forefront of every enterprise that would strengthen religion and Judaism in general, and in particular family purity, which is an area that they must take entirely upon themselves so as to establish on a firm basis the purity of the daughters of Israel.[39]

Rather than blaming them for the decline of religious observance, as his father had done, Joseph Isaac positioned women at the forefront of his campaign for the revival of strict Orthodox practice and challenged them to become religious activists in their own right.[40] Admittedly this challenge, which focused on the standard halakhic norms of Orthodox Judaism rather than promoting Habad's own hasidic ideals and lore, is hardly likely to have turned these female activists from 'wives and daughters of the hasidim' into full-fledged hasidic members of the Habad community, but appealing to them as an important human resource would seem to have been a step in this direction, and there are other indications that, from the mid-1930s on, Joseph Isaac was willing to entertain precisely this kind of transformation. During this period he created new frameworks that were expressly designed to impart to women something of the distinctive ethos and even —under careful male guidance—the speculative teachings of Habad hasidism.[41] In the 1936 letter cited above, where he called on women to 'strengthen religion and Judaism in general', he also commented, favourably enough, on the pioneering Beit Ya'akov network of Orthodox schools for girls, which inculcated in its pupils a strong commitment to Judaism but—despite the hasidic background of its founder, Sarah Schenirer—did not include in the curriculum any instruction in hasidic lore as such.[42] For this reason Joseph Isaac qualified his approval of Beit Ya'akov with the following remarks (in which every mention of the terms hasidism, hasidim, and hasidic is to be understood as referring to the hasidic path of Habad):

I have already said regarding this that the wives of the Temimim [students of the Tomekhei Temimim yeshiva] should set up societies and associations for the daughters of the hasidim, to enhance [their grasp of] every aspect of hasidism by means of guidance and education, [imparting] a hasidism-filled spirit, such as once dwelt in the hasidic households of old . . . It is an important aim of my talks[43] to grant the wives and daughters of the hasidim the opportunity to engage with the hasidic path . . . It gives me great pleasure to learn that, in a number of Habad households and among the Temimim, wives and daughters are reading the stories [that feature] in the talks, while their husbands and fathers explain to them each subject matter thoroughly. I congratulate you on this . . . and it is a *mitsvah* and an obligation for each woman to encourage her [female] friend and acquaintance to read the talk and the stories [within it].[44]

Naftali Loewenthal has charted the development of Joseph Isaac's innovative programme, which enabled young Lubavitch women to engage with Habad's special ethos and spiritual teachings. The initial trigger was provided, towards the end of 1935, by the request for guidance from one of Joseph Isaac's hasidim in Riga, in respect of a girl whose future father-in-law had asked him to instruct her in the doctrines of hasidism. Joseph Isaac responded positively to this unusual request. He even claimed that his grandfather, the fourth *admor*, Shemuel, had already acknowledged that hasidism should be taught to daughters just as much as to sons.[45] He encouraged the girl's prospective teacher to introduce her gradually to a carefully selected repertoire of Habad texts, and offered him pedagogical advice. By 1937, with Joseph Isaac's encouragement and blessing, a group of girls eager to study hasidism was formally established in Riga as an association named Sisters of the Temimim,[46] no doubt signalling its members' identification with the educational goals of the Tomekhei Temimim yeshiva. A year later another Sisters association, modelled on the Riga group, was founded in New York.

Joseph Isaac made it clear that the Sisters of the Temimim were on a par with their male counterpart, the association of Brothers of the Temimim, which was established at about the same time and consisted of young men who were not themselves students of the Tomekhei Temimim yeshiva but who met in the evenings to study Habad teachings as an expression of the yeshiva's ethos. The Sisters of the Temimim similarly met on a regular basis to study together under expert male guidance, tackling selections from Shneur Zalman's *Tanya*, the rebbe's own talks, as well as some of his spiritually demanding discourses, which Joseph Isaac urged them to translate into Yiddish in order to make them more widely accessible. He even wrote personally to one member of the Riga group, providing her with guidance on meditation and the methodology of contemplative study.[47] During a brief stay in Riga in early 1940, on the eve of his escape from Poland to the United States, he agreed to receive the local Sisters group and addressed them with a talk in much the same way as he would address a gathering of his male hasidim. The girls' group functioned until the Soviet invasion of Latvia at the end of 1940, which was closely followed by the Nazi liquidation of the Jewish community in 1941. By 1942, having established his court in Brooklyn, Joseph Isaac launched the Lubavitch network of schools for girls known as Beit Rivkah or Beit Sarah, in which the New York association of Sisters of the Temimim was initially involved and eventually subsumed.[48]

Notably, during precisely the same period, Joseph Isaac was developing his own apocalyptic interpretation of the turbulent events he had experienced during the interwar years, from the upheavals of the Russian revolution and civil war, through persecution under Stalin, to the mounting wave of antisemitism and the rise of the Nazis to power, culminating in the outbreak of the Second World War and the unfolding horrors of the Holocaust. Like his father, he believed that this unprecedented sequence of catastrophic events, coupled with the persisting decline of religious faith and observance, was fulfilling the conditions of utmost depravity and despair that were traditionally believed to augur the messianic advent. He often expressed himself on this subject in his letters and talks. In the summer of 1933, for example, he wrote from Marienbad to his followers in Russia:

Anyone who pays attention to what is going on in the world is bound to see that the present time is the Holy Sabbath's Eve, just prior to the lighting of the candles. With God's help, Friday evening is here. All the trials and tribulations that have already been and those that are currently experienced are but the immersion in boiling water that disposes of all filth, to welcome the 'good guest'[49] whom all our Jewish brethren throughout the world (including the Holy Land) are expecting to come soon, in our own days, Amen.[50]

From 1940, soon after his departure from Poland, and throughout the war years, in an outpouring of letters from his newly established Brooklyn court, Joseph Isaac consistently advocated that the violence raging in the world must be recognized as the apocalyptic war that will obliterate all evil and cleanse the earth in preparation for the final redemption, and also that the sufferings of the Jews of Europe were nothing other than 'the birth pangs of the messiah'. He repeatedly proclaimed the imminence of the redemption while warning that if world Jewry, and especially the religiously indifferent American Jews who had been lulled into a false sense of security, would not immediately repent by reverting to strict halakhic observance and putting their trust in God rather than relying on the Allied Forces to save them from the bitter fate of their European brethren, the messianic mission would be aborted and the world would sink further into chaos.[51] In the same vein, he published urgent public appeals in the Jewish press and made regular (anonymous) contributions to the journal he launched in 1940 under the title *Hakeri'ah vehakedushah*,[52] in which he broadcast his urgent messianic message, pressing for a 'fiery awakening' of universal repentance, on which alone the redemption depended. This message was captured by the slogan that featured prominently in all the issues of the journal, and in all of Joseph Isaac's letters and public proclamations during this period: *Le'altar liteshuvah, le'altar lige'ulah* ('forthwith repentance, forthwith redemption').[53]

Hakeri'ah vehakedushah ceased publication in 1945, as soon as the war was over, when Joseph Isaac's predictions about the course of the events and their final outcome failed to come true. At the same time references to the messiah and the slogan 'forthwith repentance, forthwith redemption' all but disappeared from his writings. It seemed as though the messianic fervour that marked his leadership up until then had suddenly subsided, although, as Naftali Loewenthal has argued, this does not mean that it died out. Rather, his focus on the redemption had shifted from the apocalyptic-national to the mystical-personal dimension, which was more in line with the pre-twentieth-century Habad approach to eschatology. Loewenthal has demonstrated that the two dimensions, which are inherent in the messianic orientation of hasidism in general, coexisted all along in Joseph Isaac's conceptualization of the redemption, each dimension finding expression in a distinct mode of communication: the former, highly apocalyptic, dimension was expressed in his letters, publications in the press, and (generally unsuccessful) attempts to capture the arena of Jewish public opinion, while the latter, predominantly concerned with the mystical concept of messianic redemption as 'a revelation of the inner essence of the divine', featured in the talks and discourses he addressed to the intimate circle of his followers, from which—even during the war years, when messianic tension reached unprecedented heights—the apocalyptic notion of the redemption was virtually absent.[54]

As we have seen, Joseph Isaac was concerned during the same period to mobilize women, first as promoters of halakhic observance and subsequently also as students of Habad spirituality. Moreover, during the war, driven by the urgent need to spread his messianic message, he set up, in October 1940, the international organization of Mahaneh Yisra'el (Camp of Israel), which aimed to prevent the catastrophe from running its full destructive course by the purely religious means of disseminating awareness of its messianic import and calling for mass Jewish repentance through strict halakhic observance. The organization actively sought to incorporate women in this project, as 'in all the important events of Jewish history the women proved to be more faithful and more practical than the men'.[55] It created a special 'women's division', to which it ascribed the important task of reaching out to households that had become alienated from halakhic Judaism, urging them to re-embrace it, especially in the spheres of family purity, sabbath observance, and the education of children.[56] Could all these efforts to mobilize women, calling on their exemplary historical record, which revealed their superior capacity and aptitude for coping with crisis, spring from Joseph Isaac's sense that the messianic future was now dawning, and that therefore female power was on the ascent, in line with the kabbalistic dynamic of the redemption?

The women involved in Joseph Isaac's projects, especially those who were engaged not only in the promotion of standard Orthodox practice but also in the study of Habad discourses and talks, must have been empowered by the experience. They may have effectively become his female hasidim, even though Joseph Isaac continued to call them the wives, daughters, and sisters of his male followers—perhaps simply because he found it awkward to address them by the feminine form of the term 'hasid', which in Hebrew (*ḥasidah*) is more readily understood as the homonym 'stork' than the female pietist.[57] Be that as it may, the Sisters of the Temimim surely did cohere as a female hasidic circle, accessing and studying the rebbe's teachings like many of his male hasidim. But even if Joseph Isaac did consider them full-fledged members of his hasidic flock, or if they had themselves developed a sense of belonging to it in their own right, their numbers (of which there is no record) seem to have been very small—perhaps no more than two dozen or so in each of the two Sisters groups, in Riga and New York.[58] Even his 1930s attempts to create, in both America and Europe, a vast network of women's 'family purity' associations was a disappointing failure, as Joseph Isaac himself acknowledged in his letters,[59] while the network of Beit Rivkah schools for girls he established in America in 1942 struggled to survive during the 1940s and did not provide instruction in any specifically hasidic or Habad texts.[60] Most 'wives and daughters of the hasidim' would have continued to depend on their family ties for their sense of belonging to the Lubavitch fold. Moreover, there is no indication that Joseph Isaac conceived of the mobilization of women for his cause in terms of anticipating the messianic future, in which the conventional gender hierarchy would be inverted or effaced. Notably, in the talk he addressed to the Riga Sisters of the Temimim on the eve of his departure for the United States he invoked the verse in Proverbs 'an excellent woman is a crown to her husband' without making any mention of the inverted gender hierarchy to which, as he was certainly aware, it commonly referred in traditional kabbalistic and Habad parlance:

King Solomon [as the presumed author of the book of Proverbs] gave the good, pious [*frume*] Jewish woman the title of 'excellent woman' [*eshet ḥayil*, alternatively rendered 'woman of valour'], which means a woman who has power. A woman's power is evident in the way she conducts her household, and also in the conduct of her husband and children. This is why [the verse] 'an excellent woman is a crown to her husband' means not only the crown of the children she has raised but the crown of her husband in his own right.[61]

Rather than exploiting the verse to inspire his all-girl audience with the promise of the female's rise to supremacy in the redemptive scheme of things, or to urge them to engage in religious activism by adopting the 'active', 'bestowing' mode of operation in line with the eschatological inversion of gender attributes, Joseph Isaac takes the crown to symbolize the authority that a woman exercises over her family in her home by virtue of being the one who determines how the household is run—which in turn determines the conduct of both her children and her husband even when they are not at home. This is an acknowledgement of women's power within women's traditional domestic sphere, not in any eschatological scenario of inverted gender status and roles.

In another of his talks, delivered in Otwock in 1938, Joseph Isaac tells a story that celebrates the self-sacrifice and ingenuity of a virtuous wife, who, in her afterlife, is granted a place in the paradisal 'palace of righteous women'.[62] The reference to this palace clearly echoes the description in the Zohar (iii. 167*b*) of six (or seven) heavenly palaces populated by myriads of righteous women, who appear to be free from all their earthly female duties and obligations, occupying themselves instead with nothing other than the ritual, spiritual, and intellectual pursuits that are traditionally the preserve of men: prayer, songs of praise, the performance of all the commandments from which, as women, they had been precluded while living on earth, and even speculation on the mystical rationales for the commandments.[63] Despite a few minor concessions to the conventional gender hierarchy, such as the observation that the righteous women's 'garments of light' shine less brightly than the comparable men's garments, or the attribution of the women's afterlife glory to some crucial service each had rendered in life to an important male figure, this unique description was evidently sensed to be extremely empowering of women; it was plucked out of its arcane kabbalistic context and subsequently found its way, through popular Yiddish translations and adaptations of the zoharic text, to the early modern Ashkenazi devotional literature for women, where the empowering features of the zoharic source were subtly enhanced, while the few more demeaning elements were excluded.[64] If Joseph Isaac wished to frame his mobilization of women in eschatological terms, this zoharic depiction of the afterlife as an 'upside-down world' where women have transcended all their earthly gender limitations would have served him as an obvious vehicle. As it was, while alluding to the zoharic account, he chose to ignore its most revolutionary features, focusing instead on the one element that reinforced rather than overturned the conventional gender norms—an element which the female author of the Yiddish adaptation of the text for women had seen fit to exclude. This is the traditional female virtue of the self-sacrificing, enabling wife, who renders her husband a crucial service which allows him to pursue the male goal of becoming a Torah scholar, and to rise to the elevated status of a 'hidden tsadik'.

Joseph Isaac did not conceive of the activation of women in kabbalistic terms as an expression of the dynamic of the messianic process, even though he clearly believed this process to be approaching its climax. This is corroborated by the themes he chose to highlight in his address 'to the Jewish women' during his visit to Riga in 1934:

Twice in our holy Torah, in two contexts that relate to the whole of the Jewish people—the Giving of the Torah [at Sinai] and the [Israelites'] contributions to the building of the Tabernacle—you, women, were mentioned before the men[65] . . . The Giving of the Torah was not a one-time event of the past; it is an ongoing process. In the life of the Jewish family, the Giving of the Torah means giving one's children a Torah education, sending the sons to a *ḥeder* run by God-fearing teachers with strict supervision and guidance, and educating the daughters under the guidance and supervision of women who are pious and kind-hearted . . . But before providing the children with a Torah education . . . it is necessary to speak to their mothers. Jewish women, the fate of our children is in your hands. Their whole future—good or, Heaven forbid, bad—depends on their education, and the heavy burden of their education rests entirely on you . . . The second occasion on which the women were mentioned before the men was at the collection of contributions for the construction of the Tabernacle—the Sanctuary—and all its vessels. The Sanctuary is not a temporal, one-time building. Rather, every Jewish home builds a Sanctuary, as Scripture says, 'And let them make me a Sanctuary that I may dwell among them' [Exod. 25: 8]. When God wished to grant us Jews the great gift of making a Sanctuary for His holy name . . . he asked for our contributions . . . and the first to offer their contributions were the women . . . who brought four kinds of jewellery . . . According to Ibn Ezra's interpretation,[66] these were earrings, nose rings, finger rings, and arm bracelets. The construction of a Sanctuary in family life requires collaboration between husbands and wives, but the first contributions . . . are the woman's, who donates her 'jewellery' for the sake of her children's education . . . Her first contribution is the earring, which signifies listening carefully to the words of the holy Torah and its sages on how to educate the children and run the Jewish home, as well as listening carefully to what one's sons and daughters say among themselves and each with his or her friends . . . The second kind of jewellery is the nose ring, which signifies the sense of smell. One should be very sensitive to the kind of company one's children are keeping, and make enquiries to find out if such friendships are appropriate. The third kind of jewellery is the finger ring, which signifies . . . that one should point the children to the proper way of conducting themselves, and thoroughly explain to them the positive consequences of following the proper path, as well as the negative consequences of straying from it, Heaven forbid . . . The fourth kind of jewellery is the arm bracelet, [indicating that] children should be brought up with a firm hand, not only when they are disobedient but even when they are obedient . . . as this injects liveliness into their studies, to ensure that they study diligently and with perseverance . . . Rashi interprets *kumaz* [the fourth kind of jewellery] as alluding to the women's commandment of family purity.[67] I am sure that it is not necessary to speak of this with all those present here, but I wish to say that the women who observe it meticulously . . . should not be satisfied with their own good conduct but must make every effort to explain to their [female] friends, with delicacy and tact, the importance of observing the laws of purity.[68]

This was the essential agenda, which Joseph Isaac advocated most consistently, and which undergirded all his projects for women even once he began to address their spiritual needs. His appeal to women did not spring from his apocalyptic interpretation of contemporary events but rather from the pragmatic realization that as a large and hitherto untapped human resource, women within Orthodoxy could play a valuable part in the struggle to resist 'the epidemic-germs' of secularism, which threatened 'to annihilate, God forbid . . . the people of Abraham's God'.[69] The pioneering framework of Sisters of the Temimim, which initiated women in the mystical doctrines of Habad, never catered for more than a small minority of spiritually ambitious girls, whose interest in study and contemplation was never allowed to take precedence over their engagement with the spheres of action outlined in the address to women quoted above. The female students and practitioners of Habad spirituality were expected to demonstrate their credentials above all as practical religious activists within their traditional gender roles rather than as mystics who have been transported to a transcendent eschatological domain where gender roles are inverted and the female gains supremacy over the male. As Loewenthal observes in this connection, 'The goal is empowerment and activism—but maintaining the conventional structure of society.'[70]

On the Brink of the Final Redemption

Joseph Isaac had activated women by appealing to them personally as a collective entity, enlisting them in the struggle against the encroachment of secularism into the Orthodox world, and enabling them to gain access to the teachings of Habad, but it was under the leadership of his son-in-law and successor, Menachem Mendel Schneerson (1902–94), that Habad's constituency of female hasidim was to emerge fully for the first time. This was the culmination of a process of mobilization that had begun in the 1930s, but it marked a fundamental change in the nature of women's relationship to Habad.

The transformation of Menachem Mendel's female flock into an active constituency of female hasidim has been described in some detail by Loewenthal, who focused especially on the empowerment of women within the Habad institution of *sheliḥut* (mission), where husband-and-wife teams are sent out as emissaries (*sheluḥim*) to centres of Jewish population—whether large and thriving or remote and totally alien to Orthodox Judaism—the world over, with the outreach mission of spreading Jewish knowledge, religious observance, and Habad lore.[71] To illustrate the matter-of-course hasidic identity of a late twentieth-century Habad woman, he cited the following anecdote from a letter by a prominent female emissary (*sheluḥah*), the American-born Nechoma Greisman, one of the movement's most charismatic and influential activists, who died prematurely in 1992. In her letter she described how a Jewish doctor, who treated her when she broke her arm in a swimming accident, 'saw [in her], for the first time in his life, a living chassid. What really surprised him was that the chassid was not an elderly Yiddish speaking man with a long white beard, but rather a young American girl who speaks English and goes swimming.'[72] As a measure of the change effected by the last two Lubavitcher rebbes in this respect, it is instructive to compare Nechoma Greisman's robust identity as a female Habad hasid with the totally different early twentieth-century sense of affiliation with the movement, which was reportedly articulated by the most eminent woman at the Lubavitch court of the time, the dowager Rebbetsin Rivkah—mother of the then reigning *admor*, Shalom Dovber. In response to her son's teasing admonition: 'Mother, surely you are a hasidic Jewess [*a khsidishe yidene*]' she replied: 'Whether I am a hasidic Jewess I do not know, but that I am of hasidic stock [*fun khsidim shtam*] is certain.' The rebbetsin could not seriously entertain the notion that she was herself a hasid. As a woman, her connection to hasidism was entirely a matter of genealogy.[73]

Genealogy ceased to be the chief factor defining women's hasidic identity almost as soon as Menachem Mendel succeeded to the leadership of Habad. In 1952, less than a year after taking office, he founded the international Lubavitch Women's Organization, first in the Holy Land and Australia, and a year later in the United States and several other countries.[74] Notably, the Hebrew name he proposed for the organization was Agudat Neshei Uvenot Habad, which clearly echoed Joseph Isaac's standard mode of address to the women in his camp as *neshei uvenot haḥasidim*—'the wives and daughters of the hasidim', but the substitution of 'the hasidim' with 'Habad' was highly significant: it made it clear that, from now on, the women's connection to Habad was direct rather than being contingent on their husbands' and fathers' affiliation. The Hebrew name could have been translated into English as the Association of the Wives and Daughters of Habad—somewhat awkward but still retaining the echo of Joseph Isaac's style of address to women, which was preserved in the Hebrew version of the name. But the ambiguity of the Hebrew *nashim* and *banot*, which could mean either 'wives and daughters' or 'women and girls', allowed for the adoption of the latter option, which better reflected the new Habad standing of women and girls, who were now called on to see themselves as connected to the movement in their own right.[75]

There is some indication that the notion of such a novel organization, which was meant to give women a public presence in Habad, was not immediately greeted with enthusiasm by the men around the Lubavitch court. In the original stencilled publication of the Yiddish transcript of Menachem Mendel's 1952 Simhat Torah talk (unedited by the author), where he called for the immediate establishment of the women's organization and set out its aims,[76] the substantial section devoted to this topic was omitted, with only the brief note, 'Section 9: the talk about the establishment of Neshei Habad', leaving a trace of its existence.[77] The full text became available with the 1997 publication of the Hebrew translation, where the topic of women covers sections 10 to 13.

His predecessor had mobilized women primarily as a strategy for coping with what he perceived to be the apocalyptic crisis of his day, but his vision of the redemption that was directly to follow was devoid of those gender-revolutionary elements that were inherent in kabbalistic eschatology, whereas Menachem Mendel Schneerson, from the very beginning of his term of office, and increasingly from the 1980s on, as the messianic tension he generated became more explicit and continued to rise,[78] framed his own empowerment of women in eschatological terms that invoked all the earlier Habad references to the inverted gender hierarchy of the messianic future.[79] He charged them with a new sense of urgency, signalling that the time was rapidly approaching when 'an excellent woman is a crown to her husband' and 'a woman shall encircle a man'. In the summer of 1952, for example, in a Yiddish letter dated 21 Tamuz 5712 and addressed to a male follower who appears to have been complaining about his wife, he wrote:

When one thinks about one's wife, one must always remember that the whole Congregation of Israel [*keneset yisra'el*], and every Jew individually, is called a woman in relation to the King of Kings, the Holy One, blessed be He. And when one prays to God that He, blessed be He, would conduct Himself with the Congregation of Israel, whom He calls 'my wife', [in such a way as] to fill their heart with yearnings for the good [namely, for perfect union], it is well known that the stirring from above comes through the stirring from below. One should [therefore] similarly conduct oneself with one's own wife, as the Gemara says [BT *Yev.* 62*b*], one should honour her more than one honours oneself, especially when one considers that we are standing at the end of the Exile, and the perfect Redemption is nigh . . . when 'a woman shall encircle a man', and this alone brings on a sense of respect and care for one's wife, making one see her as a daughter of Abraham, Isaac, and Jacob even if she has a fault, which in most cases is entirely a fault in the husband's conduct.[80]

And again he writes, towards the end of 1956, endorsing his father-in-law's innovation—and extending its scope—of teaching women not only the canonical texts of Judaism but also the spiritual doctrines of Habad hasidism:

Even though the hasidic discourses contain profound matters, surely, with regard to everything that was handed down at the Giving of the Torah, that is, the whole of the Torah, it was written, 'Thus you shall say to the house of Jacob' [Exod. 19: 3], 'These are the women.'[81] This means that the Torah was given to the women, too, and the only difference [distinguishing it from giving the Torah to the men] was in the manner of giving, for in reference to women, Scripture says 'you shall say', namely, [speak] gently.[82] The same applies to the doctrines of hasidism, where the only difference is in the manner of saying and explaining things, but as for the actual studying, women are certainly able to and should study just like the men, so long as things are explained to them in a style . . . that is appropriate to them. From this it becomes clear that those topics [in my discourses] that were discussed here during the month of Tishrei, and were then transmitted and repeated [to all the male hasidim], should be transmitted and repeated also to the women of Israel, which is, moreover, a matter of cardinal importance, since the women have a great advantage in respect of the conduct of Jewish homes . . . And when they transmit and repeat these teachings to all types of Jews, using the distinct modes of explanation that are appropriate for each type, the distinction (including the distinction between men and women) would bring about the true unity of the children of Israel . . . to the point when the promise of the messianic future, that 'a woman shall encircle a man', would be fulfilled.[83]

The insistence that true unity would be achieved precisely by its opposite, 'distinction' (the literal Hebrew is 'division'—*hitḥalekut*), is characteristic of the paradoxical turns of phrase with which Menachem Mendel's teachings are strewn, springing from a fundamental principle of Habad theology, which he turned into the central theme of his messianic teaching. This is the conceptualization of the redemption as the revelation of God's most concealed essence (or the 'inner dimension' of Torah) throughout the lower levels of existence, which are unable to perceive it at present, but which would become so totally imbued with godliness once it is fully revealed that there would be no difference at all between 'above' and 'below'.[84] Moreover, this most sublime and inaccessible divine essence—the essence that remained concealed throughout the processes of divine self-revelation which brought forth the whole of creation and its history—will manifest itself most powerfully precisely within the lowest of all levels, the base material world that we inhabit, which would become God's 'dwelling-place in the lower worlds' (*dirah bataḥtonim*).[85]

The paradoxical insight that opposites converge, whereby the lowest has the potentiality of being the highest, the darkest the brightest, and the coarsest the most subtle and refined, finds frequent expression in Menachem Mendel's references to the inversion of the hierarchical relations that mark the corresponding female–male, woman–man, receiver–

giver, body–soul, or corporeality–spirituality binaries—a dialectical vision of the messianic future which has already begun to inform the present. Thus he encourages one of his followers to enjoy a summer vacation in the countryside in order to strengthen his body, because the body, which pietists had traditionally scorned and mortified, should have its base appetites 'clothed in holiness in anticipation of the fulfilment of its assigned goal, [which is] not only to stop distracting the spirit and to offer it help, but rather "a woman [the body] shall encircle [give, nourish, bestow godliness on] a man [the soul]"'.[86] Elsewhere he takes the Hebrew word for 'body'—*guf*, which has the additional reflexive sense of 'self'—to point at the body's special affinity with the very essence of the divine self (*etsem umahut dilema'alah*), which 'takes pleasure, as it were, in the body below, since in the messianic future the superiority of the body is destined to be revealed, so that even the soul would receive its vitality from the body, as in "a woman shall encircle a man". This is the good that will be visible and revealed just as it is, [and] which the body, too, will be able to grasp and sense.'[87] In the same vein, Menachem Mendel highlights women's 'special affinity with the redemption' not only in the messianic future but even in the messianic present—a theme he develops out of his father-in-law's famous talk, in which he observed that women took precedence over men at all the important moments in Israel's history:[88]

Moreover—and this is the main point—women have a special relationship to the redemption. Our sages said: 'By virtue of the righteous women of that generation, Israel were redeemed when they came out of Egypt.'[89] By the same token, it was said about the future redemption . . . that it would come by virtue of the righteous women of that generation . . . especially since it is explained in the writings of the Ari [Isaac Luria][90] . . . that the generation of the future redemption is a reincarnation of the generation that came out of Egypt. Accordingly, the righteous women of our generation, by whose virtue we are being redeemed, are the very same righteous women by whose virtue they came out of Egypt. And since our own generation is the last generation of exile and the first of the redemption . . . my father-in-law . . . strove to have an effect especially on the women, so as to speed up the redemption by virtue of the righteous women of our generation. In addition, the supremacy of Jewish women is emphasized not only on the grounds that they bring on the redemption but also and above all in respect of the redemption itself. As is well known and explained in kabbalistic and hasidic books, in the messianic future the supremacy of the [female] *sefirah* Malkhut [the lowest of the ten gradations of the divine emanation] will be revealed, because its root lies above all the other *sefirot* [the male ones, which emanate and bestow], as Scripture says: 'a woman shall encircle a man', and 'an excellent woman is a crown to her husband'.[91]

Women's divine service, unlike the service of the men, anticipates by its nature the full revelation of the Divine in the messianic future, as is evident from the fact that they focus their service on their home, which they turn into 'a dwelling-place' fit for God when he comes to inhabit 'the lower worlds':

To serve God does not mean to withdraw from the world; it rather means to serve God within the world and together with the world, beginning with one's own home, which is to be run in such a way that the Shekhinah would dwell within it, as Scripture says, 'They shall make me a sanctuary that I may dwell among them' [Exod. 25: 8].[92]

Indeed, women are spiritually empowered precisely through action *within* the world rather than by quietistic withdrawal to the divine infinitude, which, Menachem Mendel implies, tends to be the prerogative of men. In other words, women adopt the Lower Unity mode of revealing the godliness that is concealed within every aspect of mundane reality, while men, or at least some men, are more inclined to adopt the Upper Unity mode of self-absorption within the transcendent realm of the Divine. Menachem Mendel makes quite clear the Habad preference for the Lower Unity mode in terms of the eschatological goal of drawing down God's very essence, which would reveal itself when it comes to dwell among its worldly creatures:[93]

The Patriarchs and the Matriarchs are the fathers and mothers of every Jew. This means that the Patriarchs and the Matriarchs have bequeathed their legacies to every Jew, and every Jew possesses these two legacies. From the Patriarchs he has the aspect of Hokhmah [Wisdom, the second highest and sometimes the first of the *sefirot* or divine gradations, associated with the male], the capacity for self-abnegation and the Upper Unity, while from the Matriarchs he has the aspect of Binah [Insight, the third of the gradations, associated with the female]—the capacity for the annihilation of material existence and the Lower Unity. Now, since the ultimate aim is [to create] 'a dwelling-place [for God] in the lower worlds', and not, on the contrary, to withdraw from the world but rather to make the world itself a vessel for godliness, therefore, even though Binah [as the female divine gradation] receives from [the male] Hokhmah, there is here an advantage of the Matriarchs over the Patriarchs, which is why Scripture says, 'In all that

Sarah says to you, hearken to her voice' [Gen. 21: 12].[94]

Finally, women's power is surprisingly, but not unwittingly, portrayed in terms that the founding fathers of hasidism had reserved exclusively for the charismatic male leader, the tsadik. In a talk addressed to the 1984 annual convention of the Habad Women's Organization, held on 6 Tishrei, his mother's twentieth *yahrzeit*, Menachem Mendel again highlighted the advantage of the woman over the man, regardless of the conventional marital hierarchy that places her in an inferior position to her husband:

Our Sages said: 'If a man brings wheat, does he chew the wheat?[95] Rather, this is done by the woman, who is his "helpmate" [Gen. 2: 18], for she makes bread out of the wheat for human consumption.' Admittedly, the man is the one who bestows, as 'a man brings wheat', but at the same time it is the woman who has the advantage, because it is through her that the wheat becomes fit for human consumption.

Menachem Mendel goes on to quote a passage from Shneur Zalman's *Likutei torah*,[96] where the notion that the wife prepares food for her husband is presented as being at odds with the promise that the husband makes in her *ketubah* to cherish and feed her. The contradiction is resolved by the idea that, while the main flow of supernal grace does indeed derive from the male, who is the bestowing aspect of the Divine, such grace is liable to be purely spiritual, and it would not materialize on earth in the form of provisions that are required for sustenance. That such material provisions do in fact flow to earth is due entirely to the wife—'for the sake of his wife [*bishvil ishto*]'.[97]

Menachem Mendel now resumes his own analysis of the theme:

It is necessary to explain more precisely the expression *bishvil ishto*. According to the teaching of the Besht,[98] who was explaining our Sages' statement that 'the whole world is sustained for the sake of [*bishvil*] my son Hanina',[99] the word *bishvil* is to be understood as deriving from *shevil*, meaning pathway. A pathway is a channel, for he opened up a channel and a pathway for the abundance to flow down, in other words, the channel for the descent and the drawing down of the abundance of the utmost good out of the essence of the Divine itself, in order that it would become an apparent and revealed good—this is effected by the [female] *sefirah* Malkhut above, and in the same fashion below by every Jewish woman.[100]

Ostensibly this is yet another common observation on the analogous modes of operation of the divine female above and her human counterpart, who represents her in the world below. And yet, as Menachem Mendel was fully aware, the metaphor of the channel had long been associated with the figure of the quintessentially male tsadik, who alone was viewed within hasidism as capable of drawing down and bestowing the flow of divine abundance, both spiritual and material. Clearly, there is no suggestion here that any Habad woman could function as a tsadik, as the quality of the channel is not attributed to any extraordinary individual but rather is fragmented and distributed widely to 'every Jewish woman'. Nevertheless the use of the metaphor in this connection is striking.

A little further on in the same 1984 talk, Menachem Mendel applies to women yet another early hasidic formula that was traditionally associated only with the tsadikim and alluded to their supernatural powers. This is the formula 'children, [long] life, and sustenance' (*banei, ḥayei, umezonei*), which captures the three areas of greatest material need, and for which the tsadik is expected to provide by drawing down the material bounty that flows through the 'channel' linking heaven and earth, a channel which—according to Jacob Joseph of Połonne's comment on the statement he attributes to the Besht[101]—the tsadik himself constitutes. The formula originates in a talmudic statement attributed to Rabah: '[Long] life, children, and sustenance depend not on merit but on destiny.'[102] In the hasidic world it is most commonly associated with Elimelekh of Lizhensk (Leżajsk; 1717–87), in whose homilies it occurs many times.[103] Menachem Mendel uses a variant of the formula, which originates in the *Yekum purkan* prayer, recited after the reading from the Torah on sabbaths and festivals. In it the three elements of the talmudic formula appear alongside a longer list of pleas for divine assistance, but Menachem Mendel employs, with one minor modification, only the three that are associated with the tsadik in hasidism, where they have come to signify specifically his power to ensure the material wellbeing of his followers. Here this power is invested in the women's lighting of the candles! Moreover, Menachem Mendel extends the traditional scope of the formula from the drawing down of material good to include also, or rather above all, the power to draw down the 'true' and 'inner' good, by which he refers to nothing less than the messianic advent. After urging the women to spread the practice of lighting sabbath and festival candles, he promises:

Surely they [the women] will do all this joyfully, and with the utmost speed, because by means of this they would enhance (as it were) the speed at which God's blessings are drawn down to deliver the apparent and revealed good of 'children, [long] life, and abundant sustenance' during these last days of exile, and how much more so as regards the drawing down of the true good, the general good, and the inner good—the true and perfect redemption by means of our righteous messiah.[104]

Conclusion

Twentieth-century Habad hasidism effected a transformation in the relationship of women to the rebbe, to the Habad ethos, and to Habad's particular brand of mystical spirituality. It thereby created a unique constituency of full-fledged female Habad hasidim. Joseph Isaac Schneersohn, the sixth Lubavitcher Rebbe, was the first to recognize the potential for this transformation. Prompted to activate women by a sense of apocalyptic crisis, which—since it was to be followed by the redemption—could be overcome only through the urgent mobilization of every human resource at his disposal, he took the unprecedented step of addressing the women in his flock, personally appealing to them for the first time as a collective body. He thus established a direct connection with all the 'wives and daughters' of his hasidim, who up until then would have had few unmediated dealings with him, and even those would have been on an ad hoc and purely individual basis, in contrast to the contact he maintained regularly with the assemblies of his male hasidim. Although we have no direct testimonies to this effect from the women who responded to his call in the 1930s and early 1940s, it seems likely that those who were harnessed to his cause by forming 'family purity' associations—especially the girls who cohered as small groups engaged in regular study of Habad teachings, particularly his own—regarded Joseph Isaac as 'their' rebbe in much the same way as did his male hasidim. He even conducted what must be the first women's *farbrengen* (a Habad hasidic gathering at which the rebbe delivers his teaching) with the Sisters of the Temimim association in Riga in 1940.

By the beginning of the 1950s this small-scale pioneering experiment, abruptly curtailed by the Holocaust in Europe and initially failing to strike roots in the United States, was quickly institutionalized by Joseph Isaac's successor, Menachem Mendel Schneerson. Schneerson, whose own messianic project entailed the reconstruction of Habad as an international movement, founded the Lubavitch Women's Organization, which formalized the status of women in Habad as full-fledged members of the hasidic community. He regularly addressed his female hasidim at the special *farbrengens* for women held during the annual conventions of the Women's Organization in Crown Heights, and he granted them numerous private audiences. He also generated various institutional frameworks that empowered women, gave them agency and voice, and challenged them to act as his personal emissaries, playing a prominent role in the execution of his outreach agenda.[105] In parallel, and as an explicit response, to the rise of the post-war feminist movement, especially its non-Orthodox Jewish religious manifestations, he offered women a militant brand of counter-feminism that denounced the goals of women's liberation and equal rights, which he saw as a denigrating subversion of women's inherently powerful nature and crucially important God-given tasks.

His counter-feminism ascribed supreme value to all the traditional female virtues and roles.[106] But these were now to be exercised within a vastly expanded domestic sphere—women's natural habitat, which was being stretched to include not only the home but also 'the surrounding environment, the classroom, and the school'. There women were encouraged to be visible and active despite the traditional notion that 'the king's daughter is all glorious within' (Ps. 45: 13), that is, within the confines of the home.[107] This expanded domestic sphere, where women were put in charge, came to symbolize God's eschatological home. It was the material world He will occupy just as soon as He comes to dwell in the Lower Worlds.

All this was played out in the context of mounting messianic expectations, framing the empowerment of women in terms of the female's rise from her inferior position as 'receiver' to the superior position of one who 'bestows'. In this eschatological connection Menachem Mendel—himself unquestionably the one and only tsadik to all his hasidim, and to many of them the messiah—was able to invest 'every Jewish woman' with the unique quality of the hasidic tsadik without this potentially revolutionary notion ever downgrading his own unparalleled status or threatening to overturn the traditional order of society.

Notes

1 For the position of women in the hasidic movement see above, Ch. 6; M. Rosman, 'Observations on Women and Hasidism' (Heb.), in D. Assaf and A. Rapoport-Albert (eds.), *Let the Old Make Way for the New* [Yashan mipenei

ḥadash: meḥkarim betoledot yehudei mizraḥ eiropah uvetarbutam, shai le'imanu'el etkes] (Jerusalem, 2009), i. 151–64; M. Wodziński, 'Women and Hasidism: A Non-Sectarian Perspective', *Jewish History*, 27/2–4 (Dec. 2013), 399–434.

2 See N. Loewenthal, 'Women and the Dialectic of Spirituality in Hasidism', in I. Etkes et al. (eds.), *Within Hasidic Circles: Studies in Hasidism in Memory of Mordecai Wilensky* [Bema'agelei ḥasidim: kovets meḥkerei ḥasidut lezekher mordekhai vilenski] (Heb. and Eng.) (Jerusalem, 1999), English section, *19–*26.

3 For this tradition see above, Ch. 6, at n. 37, and Ch. 7, Appendix II; A. Grossman, *Pious and Rebellious: Jewish Women in Medieval Europe*, trans. J. Chipman (Waltham, Mass., 2004), 162–5, 195. For a list of prominent hasidic women who fall into this category, see above, Ch. 6, pp. 324–6, and n. 39. See also the account of Sarah Horowitz Sternfeld of Chęciny, the Chentshiner Rebbetsin, who clearly belongs in this type, in N. Polen, 'Miriam's Dance: Radical Egalitarianism in Hasidic Thought', *Modern Judaism*, 12 (1992), 10–13. For Malka Shapiro's spiritual autobiography depicting her early 20th-century upbringing as the privileged daughter of a hasidic rebbe, while also commemorating the lives of her distinguished female relatives, including Perele, daughter of the Magid of Kozienice, who was reputed to be in possession of remarkable spiritual powers, see M. Shapiro, *The Rebbe's Daughter*, trans. N. Polen (Philadelphia, 2002), xxxii, 104–13. For the power and influence exerted by these women in their husbands' or their sons' courts see id., 'Rebbetzins, Wonder-Children, and the Emergence of the Dynastic Principle in Hasidism', in S. T. Katz (ed.), *The Shtetl: New Evaluations* (New York, 2007), 53–84; for this category of powerful women in the Chernobyl dynasties see G. Sagiv, *Dynasty: The Chernobyl Hasidic Dynasty and Its Place in the History of Hasidism* [Hashoshelet: beit chernobyl umekomo betoledot haḥasidut] (Jerusalem, 2014), 129–35; id., '"*Yenuka*": On Child Leaders in Hasidism' (Heb.), *Zion*, 76/2 (2011), 169–72.

4 For the institution of *pidyon*, see below, n. 9.

5 See H. M. Heilman, *Beit rabi* (Warsaw, 1904), 109 (= 55*a*), cited in Loewenthal, 'Women and the Dialectic of Spirituality in Hasidism', *21–*2. A letter by Sterna, written during this period (1917) to Isaac Doktor of Dubrowna (see on him Heilman, *Beit rabi*, 154 (= 77*b*)), seeking to know his mother's name—an essential component of the petition for a blessing, by which the petitioner is identified—appears to confirm that she was, indeed, in the habit of 'making *pidyon*'. The letter was published by Yehoshua Mondshine in *Bite'on ḥabad*, 15–16 (34–5) (1971), 10.

6 See above, Ch. 7, n. 23.

7 For this tendency of internal Habad historiography see above, pp. 219 ff., and Ch. 7, n. 24.

8 On the surprising paucity of literary evidence for a female readership of hasidic works published in Yiddish, even when women were expressly included in the target audience, see above, Ch. 7, Appendix I. For a fully annotated discussion and critical evaluation of all the factors referred to above, see pp. 371–2.

9 For the origins and evolution of this hasidic institution see A. Wertheim, *Law and Custom in Hasidism*, trans. S. Himelstein (Hoboken, 1992), 241–8; H. Pedaya, 'On the Development of the Socio-Religious-Economic Model in Hasidism: *Pidyon*, *Ḥavurah*, and Pilgrimage' (Heb.), in M. Ben-Sasson (ed.), *Religion and Economy: Connections and Interactions* [Dat vekalkalah; yaḥasei gomelin] (Jerusalem, 1995), 311–73. For an analysis of the structure and gendered characteristics of the *kvitl* see Wodziński, 'Women and Hasidism', 414–15.

10 See above, Ch. 6, n. 20.

11 For a range of strategies adopted for dealing with the problem of women in the courts, and the degree to which women could gain direct access to the rebbes, see above, pp. 372–4. See also Wodziński, 'Women and Hasidism', 413–20.

12 For 'Polish' hasidism in Habad parlance see A. Rapoport-Albert and G. Sagiv, 'Habad versus "Polish Hasidism": Towards the History of a Dichotomy' (Heb.), in J. Meir and G. Sagiv (eds.), *Habad Hasidism: History, Thought, Image* [Ḥasidut ḥabad: historyah, hagut, dimuy] (Jerusalem, 2016).

13 R. N. Kahan, *Oral Traditions and Tales about Our Holy Rebbes* [Shemuot vesipurim meraboteinu hakedoshim] (Kefar Habad, 1977), iii. 315 §164.

14 On Israel of Vilednik (*c.*1789–1850), a miracle-working tsadik, see Yehoshua Mondshine's biographical introduction 'Ve'eleh toledot' in Israel of Vilednik, *She'erit yisra'el* (Monsey, 1998), 13–44; G. Sagiv, 'The Chernobyl Hasidic Dynasty: Its History and Thought from Its Beginning to the Eve of the First World War' [Ḥasidut chernobil: toledoteiha vetoroteiha mereshitah ve'ad erev milḥemet ha'olam harishonah], Ph.D. diss. (Tel Aviv University, 2009), 84, 215, and *passim*.

15 Kahan, *Oral Traditions and Tales about Our Holy Rebbes* (Heb.), ii. 50 §49.

16 For all this see above, pp. 374–81. The anecdotes do, however, suggest that, while women were denied direct access to the Habad rebbes, they could try to obtain their advice or blessing indirectly, through the intermediacy of the eminent female members of the rebbes' households—their mothers, wives, daughters, or daughters-in-law. See on this pp. 380–1 above.

17 During his 1824 interrogation by the Polish authorities, the tsadik Meir Rotenberg of Apta (Opatów) said explicitly that women in their own right were simply 'not hasidim'. The full Polish transcript of this interrogation was published in English translation by Marcin Wodziński in his *Hasidism and Politics: The Kingdom of Poland, 1815–1864* (Oxford, 2013), 100–3, where the

question regarding women appears on p. 103. See also the discussion above, Ch. 7, n. 11. A late Bratslav tradition transmitted by Levi Isaac Bender implicitly confirms the same hasidic perspective on the status of women: 'Our rebbe once said: Why don't you initiate [*mekarvim*] your wives and turn them into female hasidim [*ḥasidot*]? [Here the question is repeated in Yiddish, the language in which it would presumably have been posed—a device often employed in these hasidic traditions to highlight the authenticity and accuracy of an attribution.] Surely, this would make it easier for a man to conduct himself in a proper hasidic and God-fearing manner' (*Siaḥ sarfei kodesh*, ii. 7 §14). The same tradition, with some variations, appears also in the Bratslav periodical *Mabu'ei hanaḥal*, 5/58 (1982), 32:

> 'Women seek life' [after BT *Kid.* 34*a*]. Our rebbe, of blessed memory, used to say to his men: Why don't you make your wives female hasidim [the question is again repeated in Yiddish] by discussing with them [topics relating to] God-fearing and hasidism, so that they, too, like their husbands, would grasp the hasidic path and attain all levels of holiness?

(I am grateful to Jonatan Meir for bringing this version to my attention.) Notably, while both versions implicitly confirm that Nahman of Bratslav did not perceive women as members of his hasidic community, each ascribes to him quite a different rationale for turning them into hasidim in their own right. According to the first version, he had in mind primarily the interest of his male followers, whose wives' initiation into hasidism would facilitate their own pursuit of the hasidic path, while the second version suggests that he valued the notion of the female hasid as such. It is doubtful that Nahman ever entertained the prospect of turning his followers' wives into female hasidim—an ambition which reflects the 20th-century sensibilities of the modern transmitter of the tradition rather than Nahman's own concerns nearly 200 years earlier. Nevertheless Nahman did, on one occasion, apparently lament the frequent breakdown of marital harmony among the young hasidim who abandoned their wives for extended periods, insisting that 'one should honour and prize one's wife . . . for the women suffer greatly' (N. Sternharz, *Siḥot haran* [with *Shivḥei haran*] (Lemberg, 1901), 77*a* §§261–2). This early testimony may have given rise to the 20th-century 'feminist' slant of the tradition. That women today are still not viewed as hasidim in their own right emerges from Tamar El-Or's anthropological study of the Gerer community in Israel. She quotes a statement by a female teacher, who says to her class of girls: 'You know, after all, that there are no women Hasidim, right? [Laughter in the room.] There are only daughters of Hasidim and wives of Hasidim' (*Educated and Ignorant: Ultraorthodox Jewish Women and Their World* (Boulder, Colo., 1994)), 103, cited in Loewenthal, 'Women and the Dialectic of Spirituality in Hasidism', *53, where he offers some modifications of this view.

18 This is a characteristic feature of the homiletical literature of hasidism. See

Rosman, 'Observations on Women and Hasidism' (Heb.), 155–7, and pp. 280–1 above. The allegorized female may, however—in Habad homilies as in others—at times also signify 'soul', albeit 'soul' in its feminine, receptive mode, as it stands in relation to the masculine divine 'giver', rather than in its more common masculine mode, when it is juxtaposed with the feminine category of 'body' or its equivalent 'corporeality'. For an example of this see Shneur Zalman of Liady, *Ma'amerei admor hazaken haketsarim* (Brooklyn, 1981), 137. For this ambivalence in the representation of women in hasidic homilies in general, see Rosman, 'Observations on Women and Hasidism' (Heb.), 156–8. For the conventional use of the categories of male and female in Shneur Zalman of Liady's discourses, see e.g. *Likutei torah* (Brooklyn, 1976), 'Emor', 32*a*; 'Matot', 84*b–c*; 'Va'ethanan', 7*d*; 'Ekev', 17*c*; *Torah or* (Brooklyn, 1976), 'Vayeḥi', 54*c*; 'Beshalaḥ', 64*c*; 'Megilat ester', 94*a*; *Ma'amerei admor hazaken 5566* [1806] (Brooklyn, 2004), i. 403; *Ma'amerei admor hazaken 5569* [1809] (Brooklyn, 2005), 64, and much more. Even at the turn of the 20th century, the fifth Lubavitcher Rebbe, Shalom Dovber, was still allegorizing women as corporeality when he called on the students of the Tomekhei Temimim yeshiva, which he had founded in 1897 as a means of combating Haskalah, Zionism, and other secular ideologies, to behave like soldiers on the eve of battle, of whom the rabbis had said that, in order not to leave their wives 'anchored' (*agunot*) in the event that they did not survive to return home, '"everyone who went out in the wars of the house of David wrote a bill of divorcement for his wife" [BT *Shab.* 56*a*] . . . because to be a soldier in the war of the house of David one must first divorce [oneself from] all corporeal things in which worldly men engage' (Joseph Isaac Schneersohn (Shalom Dovber's son and the sixth Lubavitcher Rebbe), *Sefer hasiḥot 5702* [1942] (Brooklyn, 1973), 141–3, from an address by his father to the yeshiva students on Simhat Torah in 1900).

19 See on this pp. 281–4 above.

20 For instances of this see e.g. *Likutei torah*, 'Matot', 84*b–c*; 'Shir hashirim', 41*d*; *Ma'amerei admor hazaken 5566* [1806], i. 403.

21 See on this pp. 277–80 above.

22 See BT *BB* 16*b*–17*a*.

23 Shneur Zalman of Liady, *Ma'amerei admor hazaken 5569* [1809], 64. See also the numerous parallel discussions, e.g. ibid. 82, 84; *Ma'amerei admor hazaken 5572* [1812] (Brooklyn, 2006), 129; *Likutei torah*, 'Shir hashirim', 15*c*.

24 Shneur Zalman's treatment of this theme is explored and illustrated in Y. Levine-Katz, 'The Voice of the Bride in the Future' (Heb.), in S. Raz (ed.), *The Religious Zionist Anthology in Memory of Zerah Warhaftig* [Kovets hatsiyonut hadatit lezekher zeraḥ varhaftig] (Jerusalem, 2001), 365–8, and cf. the updated version in *Kolech: forum nashim datiyot*, <http:www.kolech.com/show.asp?id=

29984> (accessed 17 July 2011). See also the discussion in E. R. Wolfson, *Open Secret: Postmessianic Messianism and the Mystical Revision of Menaḥem Mendel Schneerson* (New York, 2009), 206–9; W. Tworek, 'Time in the Teaching of Rabbi Shneur Zalman of Liadi', Ph.D. diss. (University College London, 2014), 207–53; id., 'Time and Gender in the Teachings of R. Shneur Zalman of Liady' (Heb.), in Meir and Sagiv (eds.), *Habad Hasidism*, 57–74.

25 See Shneur Zalman of Liady, *Seder tefilot mikol hashanah al pi nusaḥ ha'ari z"l* (Kopys, 1816), 'Derushim leḥatunah', i. 36*c*–*d*, 40*d*; 'Birkat erusin venisu'in', i. 43*a*–*d*.

26 For an analysis and partial translation of this theme in Kalonymos Kalman's *Ma'or vashemesh* see Polen, 'Miriam's Dance', 1–21. Polen points out (p. 6) the presence of the theme in one of Shneur Zalman's homilies, suggesting that it may have served as one of Kalonymos Kalman's sources. Another source for the same eschatological motif may well have been the collection of sermons by Ephraim of Luntshits (Łęczyca), *Keli yakar* (Lublin, 1602), 57*a*, 58*a*, cited in Y. Chovav, *Maidens Love Thee: The Religious and Spiritual Life of Jewish Ashkenazi Women in the Early Modern Period* [Alamot ahevukha: ḥayei hadat veharuaḥ shel nashim baḥevrah ha'ashkenazit bereshit ha'et haḥadashah] (Jerusalem, 2009), 84–6.

27 See on all this A. Rapoport-Albert, *Women and the Messianic Heresy of Sabbatai Zevi 1666–1816* (Oxford, 2011), 119–31.

28 For Shneur Zalman's harmonistic response to the provocative talmudic notion of the abrogation of the commandments in the messianic future, and its zoharic version whereby the old Law of differentiation emanating from the Tree of Knowledge, which distinguishes good from evil, will be superseded by the new, messianic Law emanating from the Tree of Life, in which this distinction has been transcended, see his *Likutei amarim—tanya* (Brooklyn, 1973), 'Igeret hakodesh', ch. 26, 142*a*–5*b*; *Torah or*, 'Bereshit', 3*c*–*d*. There is, however, no apocalyptic tension in this messianic doctrine, despite the fact that Shneur Zalman did apparently predict that 1843 would be the year of the Redemption (see *Ma'amerei admor hazaken al parshiyot hatorah vehamo'adim* (Brooklyn, 1982), i. 419–23). For scholarly presentations of Shneur Zalman's eschatology as a 'neutralized' doctrine, primarily concerned with the inner experience of personal redemption, see R. F. Foxbrunner, *Habad: The Hasidism of Shneur Zalman of Lyady* (Northvale, 1993), 85–8, 91–2; D. Schwartz, *Habad's Thought* (Heb.), 271–82. See also I. Tishby, 'The Messianic Idea and Messianic Trends in the Formative Period of Hasidism' (Heb.), in id., *Studies* in *Kabbalah and Its Branches* [Ḥikerei kabalah usheluḥoteiha] (Jerusalem, 1993), ii. 510–15, where he challenges Gershom Scholem's claim that, with few exceptions, early hasidism had 'neutralized' the messianic idea (for the full articulation of this thesis—itself a response to Tishby's challenge—see G. Scholem, 'The

Neutralization of the Messianic Element in Early Hasidism', in id., *The Messianic Idea in Judaism* (London, 1971), 176–202). But even Tishby admits that messianism features relatively marginally in Shneur Zalman of Liady's doctrine, despite the fact that he refers to his generation in Lurianic terms as originating in the 'heels' of Primordial Man, that is, in the 'lowest'—the most corrupt and degraded—phase in the history of the world, the phase directly preceding the messianic advent. See ibid. 511–12.

29 For reverberations of this eschatological theme, as captured by the same two biblical verses, in the teachings of the second Habad leader, Dov Ber, the Mitteler Rebbe, see e.g. his *Sha'arei teshuvah* (Brooklyn, 1983), 'Sha'ar hatefilah', 49*a*; *Ner mitsvah vetorah or* (Brooklyn, 1974), 'Sha'ar ha'emunah', 54*b*; *Ma'amerei admor ha'emtsa'i, derushei ḥatunah* (Brooklyn, 1991), ii. 401, 504, 539, 578, 635, 637. For the same theme in the teaching of his successor, the third rebbe, Menahem Mendel, the Tsemah Tsedek, see his commentary on Psalms, *Yahel or* (Brooklyn, 1953), 355, 703. For the fourth rebbe, Shemuel of Lubavitch, see e.g. *Likutei torah, torat shemuel 5627* [1867] (Brooklyn, 1981), 8; *Likutei torah, torat shemuel 5632* [1872], vol. i (Brooklyn, 1999), 112–13, 220; ibid. vol. ii (Brooklyn, 2000), 360, 550; *Likutei torah, torat shemuel 5673* [1873], vol. i (Brooklyn, 1994), 260; *Likutei torah, torat shemuel 5640* [1880] (Brooklyn, 2004), 180–1, 183, 373, 375; *Likutei torah, torat shemuel 5641* [1881] (Brooklyn, 2006), 265, 573. For his son and heir, the fifth rebbe, Shalom Dovber, see below, n. 35. For an analysis of this theme in the teachings of both Dov Ber, the Mitteler Rebbe, and Shalom Dovber, see Wolfson, *Open Secret: Postmessianic Messianism*, 209–13.

30 A facsimile edition was published by Yehoshua Mondshine in *Kerem ḥabad*, 3 (1987), 198–205. For a full discussion of this see pp. 382–7 above.

31 For Shalom Dovber's motivation and his aims in founding Tomekhei Temimim, see N. Brawer, 'The Founding of "Tomekhei Temimim" and Its Impact on the Habad Lubavitch Movement' (Heb.), in I. Etkes (ed.) *Yeshivot and Batei Midrash* [Yeshivot uvatei midrashot] (Jerusalem, 2006), 357–68; I. Lurie, 'Education and Ideology: The Beginnings of the HaBaD Yeshiva' (Heb.), in D. Assaf and A. Rapoport-Albert (eds.), *Let the Old Make Way for the New*, i. 185–221.

32 For Shalom Dovber's anti-Zionist messianism see A. Ravitzky, *Messianism, Zionism, and Jewish Religious Radicalism* [Hakets hameguleh umedinat hayehudim] (Tel Aviv, 1993), 29–35, 250, 264; M. Friedman, 'Habad as Messianic Fundamentalism: From Local Particularism to Universal Jewish Mission', in M. E. Marty and R. Scott Appelby (eds.), *Accounting for Fundamentalism: The Dynamic Character of Movements* (Chicago, 1994), 332–8; id., 'Messiah and Messianism in Habad Lubavitch Hasidism' (Heb.), in D. Ariel-Joel et al. (eds.), *The War of Gog and Magog: Messianism and the Apocalypse in Judaism—Past and*

Present [Milḥemet gog umagog: meshiḥiyut ve'apokalipsah bayahadut—be'avar uveyameinu] (Tel Aviv, 2001), 176–97; S. Ratsabi, 'Anti-Zionism and Messianic Tension in the Speculative Thought of Rabbi Shalom Dovber' (Heb.), *Hatsiyonut*, 20 (1996), 77–101; D. Schwartz, *Habad Thought From Beginning to End* [Maḥshevet ḥabad mereshit ve'ad aḥarit] (Ramat Gan, 2010), 286–8.

33 See e.g. S. D. Schneersohn, *Hemshekh 5672* [1912], Written but not Said, iii (Brooklyn, 1977), 1029; *Kuntres uma'yan mibeit adonai* (Brooklyn, 1969), 75, 6: 1. See also the analysis of id., *Sefer hama'amarim 5659* [1899] (Brooklyn, 1991), 97–8 in Wolfson, *Open Secret: Postmessianic Messianism*, 211–13.

34 See e.g. BT *Shab.* 33*b*, 146*a*; Zohar i. 126*a*; I. Tishby, *The Wisdom of the Zohar: An Anthology of Texts*, trans. D. Goldstein (London, 1989), i. 373–87.

35 *Igerot kodesh . . . shalom dovber* (Brooklyn, 1982), i. 274 no. 117.

36 Ibid. i. 279 no. 117**; see also ibid. iii. 364 no. 798*.

37 *Igerot kodesh . . . yosef yitsḥak* (Brooklyn, 1982), ii. 252–3 no. 482, partly quoted in Loewenthal, 'Women and the Dialectic of Spirituality in Hasidism', *42–*3. See also *Igerot kodesh . . . yosef yitsḥak*, ii. 224 no. 465.

38 See *Igerot kodesh . . . yosef yitsḥak*, ii. 332 no. 526.

39 *Igerot kodesh . . . yosef yitsḥak*, iv (Brooklyn, 1983), 13 no. 873.

40 Orthodox attempts to mobilize women by harnessing them to the cause of family purity were not unique to Habad. For the wider 1930s context see above, Ch. 7, n. 98. For the apparently limited success, if not downright failure, of Joseph Isaac's family purity campaign see Ch. 7, at and in n. 101; N. Loewenthal, 'From "Ladies' Auxiliary" to "Shluhot Network"—Women's Activism in Twentieth-Century HABAD', in I. Bartal et al. (eds.), *A Touch of Grace: Studies in Ashkenazi Culture, Women's History, and the Languages of the Jews Presented to Chava Turniansky* (Yid., Eng., and Ger.) [Ḥut shel ḥesed lekoved ḥavah turniansky] (Jerusalem, 2013), 74*, 76*.

41 Joseph Isaac often claimed that his father, Shalom Dovber, and even his grandfather, the fourth *admor*, Shemuel (1834–82), had reproached their followers for neglecting the hasidic education of their daughters, urging them to provide the same instruction in hasidic lore 'to the sons and daughters of the hasidim, equally and alike', but this is most likely one of Joseph Isaac's characteristic projections of the present onto the past, anchoring his own innovation in what he construes as an old Habad tradition. See above, p. 390.

42 On Beit Ya'akov see D. Weissman, 'Bais Yaakov: A Historical Model for Jewish Feminists', in E. Koltun (ed.), *The Jewish Woman* (New York, 1976), 139–48; ead., 'Bais Yaakov: A Women's Educational Movement in the Polish Jewish Community: A Case Study in Tradition and Modernity', MA thesis (New York University, n.d.); Loewenthal, 'Women and the Dialectic of Spirituality in Hasidism', *26–*41; id., 'Spiritual Experience for Hasidic Youths and Girls

in Pre-Holocaust Europe—A Confluence of Tradition and Modernity', in A. Mintz and L. Schiffman (eds.), *Jewish Spirituality and Divine Law* (Jersey City, 2005), 432–40; A. Kaniel, 'Beys Yankev', in *The YIVO Encyclopedia of Jews in Eastern Europe* (New Haven, 2008), i. 175–6; A. Oleszak, '"The Borderland": The Beys Yaakov School in Kraków as a Symbolic Encounter between East and West', in M. Galas and A. Polonsky (eds.), *Jews in Kraków*, Polin: Studies in Polish Jewry 23 (2011), 277–90.

43 In Hebrew *siḥot*—the less formal, Yiddish addresses by the Habad rebbe to his followers, which may contain tales, historical narratives, and discussions about aspects of Habad thought, as distinct from the formal, speculative teachings, which are referred to as discourses—*ma'amarim*. For the historical development and characterization of all the distinct elements that make up the Habad literary corpus see A. Roth, 'The Habad Literary Corpus, Its Components and Distribution as the Basis for Reading Habad Text' [Hakorpus hasifruti haḥabadi: rekhivav vehafatsato kevasis likri'at tekst ḥabadi], Ph.D. diss. (Bar-Ilan University, 2012), 62–135.

44 *Igerot kodesh . . . yosef yitsḥak*, iv. 13 no. 873, cited in part in Loewenthal, 'Women and the Dialectic of Spirituality in Hasidism', *43.

45 But see above, n. 41.

46 In Hebrew the name appears as the singular *aḥot hatemimim* (Sister of the Temimim; although *aḥot* can also be read as the construct form *aḥvat*, meaning 'Sisterhood of'), but it is rendered both Sisters and Sisterhood of the Temimim in a letter by Joseph Isaac that was originally published in English (see *Igerot kodesh . . . yosef yitsḥak*, iv. 362 no. 1037). It is not impossible that the Hebrew singular *aḥot* was mistaken for the construct-state plural *aḥyot*, as the final syllable of the singular coincides with a standard plural marker for Hebrew feminine nouns. In view of the comparability Joseph Isaac was eager to establish between this group and its male counterpart, the Brothers of the Temimim, the reading Sisters seems most likely.

47 There is a much earlier letter in which Joseph Isaac offers personal guidance on hasidic study to a woman. It was written in Hebrew, with sprinklings of Yiddish, sometime between 1910 and 1915—five to ten years prior to his succession as rebbe—to Sonia Rosenblum (1896–1974), member of the prominent Gurarie family of Habad hasidim, whose brother, Shemaryah Gurarie, would later marry Joseph Isaac's eldest daughter. The letter appears to be a response to a communication from Sonia in which she expressed her frustration with what she perceived to be her limited ability to grasp and apply the hasidic teachings she was studying on her own. Joseph Isaac was not in the least surprised or perturbed to learn that she was seriously engaged in the study of complex Habad texts, and he willingly offered her, at some length, encouragement in the form of a detailed analysis distinguishing between the emotional

and the intellectual modes of apprehension. Interesting though the letter is as evidence that some women were studying Habad teachings long before any formal framework for women's hasidic education was established by Joseph Isaac, it nevertheless places Sonia Rosenblum within that small category of women who had always been able to achieve such accomplishments by virtue of their connection to highly distinguished men (see above, at nn. 3–5). The letter to Sonia was published in *Igerot kodesh . . . yosef yitsḥak*, i. 96–9 no. 57. For a full description and analysis see E. Rubin, 'Emotive Intelligence: A Letter to Sonia Rozenblum by Rabbi Yosef Yitzchak Schneersohn', <http://www.chabad.org/blogs/blog_cdo/aid/1744944/jewish/Emotive-Intelligence-A-Letter-to-Sonia-Rozenblum-by-Rabbi-Yosef-Yitzchak-Schneersohn.htm> (accessed 24 Jan. 2012). I am grateful to Eli Rubin for drawing this letter and his article to my attention. See also the references to a few other women from prominent Habad families who were apparently studying Habad teachings on their own in Loewenthal, 'Women and the Dialectic of Spirituality in Hasidism', *25–*6 n. 59, *54–*5.

48 On all this see Loewenthal, 'Women and the Dialectic of Spirituality in Hasidism', *42–*57; id., '"Daughter/Wife of Hasid" or: "Hasidic Woman"?' *Mada'ei hayahadut*, 40 (2000), Eng. section, 21*–8*; id., 'Spiritual Experience for Hasidic Youths', 440–8; id., 'From "Ladies' Auxiliary" to "Shluhot Network"'. See also the editorial introduction to *Igerot kodesh . . . yosef yitsḥak*, iv. 10–13, and above, pp. 387–91.

49 After BT *Ber.* 58*a*, clearly in reference to the messiah.

50 *Igerot kodesh . . . yosef yitsḥak*, ii. 531 no. 633.

51 See e.g. ibid. v. 37 no. 1162, 359–60 no. 1444, 361–7 no. 1447, 427 no. 1489, 435 no. 192; ibid. vi. 63 no. 1601, 193 no. 1705, 204 no. 1714, 209 no. 1718, 306–7 no. 1782, 310 no. 1784, 311 no. 1785, 337 no. 1794, 338–9 no. 1795, 340 no. 1796, 354 no. 1806, 372 no. 1824, 392 no. 1838, 394–5 no. 1840, 419 no. 1897, 430–42 no. 1867; ibid. vii. 97 no. 1930, 105 no. 1932, 125 no. 1946, 159 no. 1962, 173 no. 1976, 191 no. 1988, 371 no. 2126.

52 A phrase taken from the liturgical hymn 'Ha'aderet veha'emunah', originating in the mystical *heikhalot* literature, where it refers to the angelic declaration (*keri'ah*) of God's sanctity (*kedushah*). Joseph Isaac employed the phrase in the sense of a call, a summons, or an invitation (*keri'ah*) to holiness, namely, to strict observance of the Law as preparation for the messianic advent. See his own explanation in *Igerot kodesh . . . yosef yitsḥak*, v. 359 no. 1444. In the journal itself the phrase is translated into English literally and rather enigmatically as 'Reading and Holiness' (see e.g. *Hakeri'ah vehakedushah*, 1/5 (Feb. 1941), 8; 1/8 (May 1941), 5, 15).

53 There is considerable scholarly literature about all this. See e.g. G. Greenberg, 'Mahaneh Israel-Lubavitch 1940–45: Actively Responding to Khurban', in

A. A. Berger (ed.), *Bearing Witness to the Holocaust, 1939–89* (New York, 1991), 141–63; id., 'Redemption After Holocaust According to Mahane Israel-Lubavitch 1940–45', *Modern Judaism*, 12 (1992), 61–84; id., 'The Sect of Catastrophe: Mahane Israel-Lubavitch 1940–45', in M. Mor (ed.), *Jewish Sects, Religious Movements, and Political Parties* (Omaha, 1992), 165–84; R. Elior, 'The Lubavitch Messianic Resurgence: The Historical and Mystical Background 1939–96', in P. Schäfer and M. Cohen (eds.), *Toward the Millennium: Messianic Expectations from the Bible to Waco* (Leiden, 1998), 383–93; Friedman, 'Messiah and Messianism in Habad-Lubavitch Hasidism' (Heb.), 207–15.

54 See N. Loewenthal, 'The Neutralisation of Messianism and the Apocalypse', in R. Elior and J. Dan (eds.), *Rivka Schatz-Uffenheimer Memorial Volume* [Kolot rabim: sefer hazikaron lerivkah shatz-uffenheimer] (Heb. and Eng.) (Jerusalem, 1996), English section, ii. 59*–69*.

55 'Kol kore fun der "maḥne yisroel" tsu di yidishe froyen', *Hakeri'ah vehakedushah*, 1/11 (Aug. 1941), 12.

56 See Mahaneh Yisra'el's public appeal to women in S. D. Levin, *History of Habad in the USA—1900–1950* [Toledot ḥabad be'artsot haberit bashanim tav-resh-samekh–tav-shin-yud] (Brooklyn, 1988), 310. See also Greenberg, 'The Sect of Catastrophe', 167; id., 'Mahane Israel-Lubavitch', 149–50.

57 The feminine term *ḥasidah* (pl. *ḥasidot*) in the sense of 'female pietist' occurs very rarely in the pre-modern Hebrew sources, perhaps on account of its ascetic connotations, as ascetic attributes are generally considered inappropriate in women. In the medieval Ashkenazi *Sefer ḥasidim* (Book of the Pietists), for example, where the masculine form appears on almost every page, the feminine occurs no more than three times—twice in both the Bologna and Parma editions, and once in the Bologna edition alone, although the first of the instances in both editions does not refer to a pious woman but rather to the homonymic term 'stork' mentioned in Deut. 14: 18. For the Bologna edition see *Sefer ḥasidim*, ed. R. Margaliot (Jerusalem, 1957), 61 §10, 146 §135, 532 §1015. For the Parma edition see *Sefer ḥasidim*, ed. J. Wistinetzki, with an introduction by J. Freimann (Frankfurt am Main, 1924), 240 §875, 437 §1826. It seems that only in a martyrological context could a woman, having suffered a violent death for her faith, be more readily described as *ḥasidah*. See e.g. *Sefer gezerot ashkenaz vetsarfat*, ed. A. M. Habermann (Jerusalem, 1971), 25, 32, 34, 73, 165. See also Wodziński, 'Women and Hasidism', 405 n. 15.

58 The memorial volume for Latvian Jewry, B. Eliav, M. Bobe, and A. Kremer (eds.), *The Jews of Latvia: Memorial Book* [Yahadut latviyah: sefer zikaron] (Tel Aviv, 1953), pl. 67, contains a group photograph of the Riga Sisters of the Temimim featuring twenty-six girls. See the discussion and the facsimile photograph in H. Hasidov, '"The Sister of the Temimim Group" in Riga' (Yid.), *Di yidishe heym*, 22/3 (1981), 12–22. The article includes an anonymous

Yiddish transcript of Joseph Isaac's talk, which he personally addressed to the girls when the group visited him during his brief stay in Riga in 1940, shortly before his departure to the United States. A somewhat different picture emerges from the testimony of Israel Jacobsohn—one of the three male 'shepherds' appointed by Joseph Isaac to oversee the activities of the New York Sisters group—who claims that by the late 1930s in Riga, fifty-eight girls were enrolled in three such Lubavitch female study groups. See his contribution to *Di yidishe heym*, 8/3 (1967), 11, cited in B. J. Morris, *Lubavitcher Women in America: Identity and Activism in the Postwar Era* (Albany, NY, 1998), 37. According to the oral testimony of a member of the New York Sisters group, 'an average of ten girls would attend each meeting' (cited in Loewenthal, 'Women and the Dialectic of Spirituality in Hasidism', *50 n. 146).

59 See above, Ch. 7, n. 101.

60 See Loewenthal, 'Women and the Dialectic of Spirituality in Hasidism', *51–*2; Morris, *Lubavitcher Women*, 38–42; Levin, *History of Habad in the USA* (Heb.), 284–93.

61 Hasidov, '"The Sister of the Temimim Group" in Riga' (Yid.), 18.

62 See J. I. Schneersohn, *Likutei diburim* (Yid.) (Brooklyn, 1984), ii. 1400, the talk delivered on the last day of Passover.

63 For a discussion of this passage as an example of the eschatological inversion of mundane reality, see Rapoport-Albert, *Women and the Messianic Heresy of Sabbatai Zevi*, 123–31.

64 See C. Weissler, *Voices of the Matriarchs* (Boston, 1998), 76–85.

65 See e.g. *Shemot rabah*, 28: 2; Rashi on Exod. 19: 3, and Nahmanides on Exod. 35: 22.

66 See Ibn Ezra on Exod. 35: 22.

67 See Rashi on Exod. 35: 22, where he interprets *kumaz* as a jewel inserted into the vagina. Joseph Isaac takes this reference to female genitalia to be an allusion to the laws of family purity, one of the issues that preoccupied him at the time.

68 J. I. Schneersohn, *Likutei diburim* (Yid.), ii. 1141–8.

69 Transcript of Joseph Isaac's 1940 talk to the Riga Sisters of the Temimim, in Hasidov, '"The Sister of the Temimim Group" in Riga' (Yid.), 18.

70 Loewenthal, '"Daughter/Wife of Hasid" or: "Hasidic Woman"?', 24*. Elsewhere Loewenthal suggests that Joseph Isaac's emphasis was on women's empowerment through action *within* the world rather than through mystical absorption in the divine infinitude, and that this reflected the general Habad preference for the Lower Unity mode of interacting with the Divine. See Loewenthal, 'Women and the Dialectic of Spirituality in Hasidism', *47. For the wider Habad context of the Upper–Lower Unity polarity see id.,

'"The Lower Unity": Joining Mystical Quest and Reality in the First Century of Habad', *BDD—Bekhol derakheikha da'ehu*, 16 (Aug. 2005), 57–73; id., '"Reason" and "Beyond Reason" in Habad Hasidism', in M. Hallamish (ed.), *Alei shefer: Studies in Jewish Thought in Honor of Alexander Shafran* [Alei shefer: meḥkarim besifrut hehagut hayehudit mugashim likhvod harav dr aleksander shafran] (Ramat Gan, 1990), English section: 109*–26*.

71 See Loewenthal, '"Daughter/Wife of Hasid" or: "Hasidic Woman"?', 25*–8*; id., 'Women and the Dialectic of Spirituality in Hasidism', *58–*62; id., 'From "Ladies' Auxiliary" to "Shluhot Network"'.

72 M. Miller (ed.), *The Nechoma Greisman Anthology—Wisdom from the Heart* (Jerusalem, 1993), 180, cited in Loewenthal, '"Daughter/Wife of Hasid" or: "Hasidic Woman"?', 27*, and in Hebrew in E. Weil, 'The Beginning of the Women's Era: Women and Femininity in the Teaching of the Lubavitcher Rebbe' (Heb.), *Akdamot*, 22 (2009), 79.

73 For a full discussion of this episode in the context of the construction of female hasidic identities see pp. 381–2 above.

74 These are the dates as listed in *Hayom yom*, a calendar for the Hebrew year 5703 (1942–3), which was compiled by Menachem Mendel Schneerson and first published in 1943. It has since been reprinted many times, with the addition, in the later editions, of a year-by-year account of key events in Menachem Mendel's leadership. See the Brooklyn, 1993 edn., 'Shalshelet hayaḥas', 22. See also Menachem Mendel's 1952 talk, delivered on Simhat Torah (of 5713), in which, after referring to his late father-in-law's concern for the hasidic education of women, he launched the idea of the Habad women's organization:

> In order to reinforce this, it is necessary to establish an 'association of Habad women [or wives] and girls [or daughters] [*agudat neshei uvenot ḥabad*]', so that together they would learn the *halakhot* that apply to them, discuss educational matters, and study hasidic talks, stories about the tsadikim, etc., which would inject greater vitality into both their study of the *halakhot* and their educational deliberations. (M. M. Schneerson, *Torat menaḥem—hitva'aduyot* (Brooklyn, 1997), vii. 116)

On the same occasion he announced that this organization had just been founded in the Holy Land, and urged all those present to establish it in New York by the following sabbath (ibid. 117). Some studies of Menachem Mendel, or of the position of women in Habad during his leadership, offer conflicting dates for the establishment of the women's organization. See e.g. Morris, *Lubavitcher Women*, 55, who states that it was founded in 1955; Y. Kraus, *The Seventh: Messianism in the Last Generation of Habad* [Hashevi'i: meshiḥiyut bador hashevi'i shel ḥabad] (Tel Aviv, 2007), 56, who offers 1952; and Weil, 'The Beginning of the Women's Era' (Heb.), 61, who dates it to 1953. The confusion may be due to the probability that the organization was formally established at different times in different places during the early 1950s.

75 The association became known variously as the Lubavitch Women's Organization, Women's Organization of Lubavitch, The Women's and Girls' Division [of the Lubavitch Foundation of Great Britain], Agudat Hasidei Habad: Women's and Girls' Association, Agudat Neshei Habad, Agudat Hasidei Habad—Irgun Benot Habad, and so on. 'Wives and Daughters' do not feature among the names of the organization's numerous branches.

76 See above, n. 74.

77 See *Siḥot kodesh mikevod kedushato admor shelita milubavitch 5713* [1952–3], *bilti mugah* (Brooklyn, 1994), 'Yom simḥat torah 5713', 55. I am grateful to Naftali Loewenthal for drawing this omission to my attention.

78 For a division of Menachem Mendel's career into decades, each marked by the intensification of certain trends, with the 1980s singled out as the point at which messianic expectations became the most public agenda of Habad, see Kraus, *The Seventh* (Heb.), 56–91, especially 77 ff.

79 See above, pp. 432–5.

80 M. M. Schneerson, *Likutei siḥot 38, al parshiyot hashavua, ḥagim umo'adim*, book 9, vol. iv (Brooklyn, 2006), 188 (published also in his *Igerot kodesh . . . menaḥem mendel 5711* [1951] (Brooklyn, 2007), vi. 201–2 no. 1718).

81 See e.g. *Midrash shemot rabah* 28: 2.

82 See Rashi's comment on Exod. 19: 3.

83 M. M. Schneerson, *Torat menaḥem—hitva'aduyot 5717* [1956–7], vol. xviii, pt. I, 191. For the halakhic basis Menachem Mendel supplied for instructing women in the doctrines of Habad hasidism see Loewenthal, 'Women and the Dialectic of Spirituality in Hasidism', *52; id., 'From "Ladies' Auxiliary" to "Shluhot Network"', 82*; Weil, 'The Beginning of the Women's Era' (Heb.), 66–9; S. Handelman, 'Women and the Study of Torah in the Thought of the Lubavitcher Rebbe: A Halakhic Analysis', in M. Halperin and C. Safrai (eds.), *Jewish Legal Writings by Women* (Jerusalem, 1998), 142–77.

84 This refers back to Shneur Zalman of Liady's formulation of the idea as 'above and below are the same', which occurs dozens of times in his writings. See e.g. *Torah or*, 'Lekh lekha', 11*d*, 'Vayetse', 22*b*, 'Beshalaḥ', 66*c*; *Likutei torah*, 'Vayikra', 4*d*.

85 This is a rather simplistic presentation of the dialectics of Habad's messianism. For full analyses see R. Elior, *The Paradoxical Ascent to God: The Kabbalistic Theosophy of Habad Hasidism* (Albany, 1993); D. Schwartz, *Habad's Thought from Beginning to End* [Maḥshevet ḥabad mereshit ve'ad aḥarit] (Ramat Gan, 2010), esp. 271–318. For an analysis of Menachem Mendel's messianic doctrine see A. Dahan, '"Dira Batahtonim": The Messianic Doctrine of Rabbi Menachem Mendel Schneerson (the Lubavitcher Rebbe)' [Dirah bataḥtonim: mishnato hameshiḥit shel r. menaḥem mendel shneerson (harabi milubavitch)',

Ph.D. diss. (Hebrew University, 2006); Wolfson, *Open Secret: Postmessianic Messianism*.

86 M. M. Schneerson, *Igerot kodesh, Summer 5715* [1955] (Brooklyn, 1999), xi. 129 no. 3514.

87 Id., *Igerot kodesh 5717* [1957] (Brooklyn, 1989), xiv. 279 no. 5041.

88 For this talk by Joseph Isaac see above, pp. 445–6.

89 BT *Sot.* 11*b*.

90 See H. Vital, *Sha'ar hagilgulim* (Jerusalem, 1963), 54, *hakdamah* 20.

91 M. M. Schneerson, *Torat menaḥem—hitva'aduyot 5752* [1992] (Brooklyn, 1994), ii. 183–4.

92 Id., *Letters by the Lubavitcher Rebbe to N'shei uBnos Chabad 1956–80* (Brooklyn, 1981), Yiddish section, 13.

93 For the Upper–Lower Unity polarity in Habad, and for the general preference for the latter, see above, n. 70.

94 M. M. Schneerson, *Likutei siḥot* (Brooklyn, 2006), iv. 1068–9 (from a talk dated 13 Tamuz 5722 (1962)).

95 BT *Yev.* 63*a*. The context is a discussion about the ways in which a wife may be a helpmate to her husband.

96 'Zot haberakhah', 100*a*.

97 BT *BM* 59*a*.

98 See Jacob Joseph of Połonne, *Ben porat yosef* (Korzec, 1781), 'Vayeḥi', 63*b*, citing the Besht.

99 BT *Ber.* 17*b*.

100 M. M. Schneerson, *Torat menaḥem—hitva'aduyot 5745* [1985], 106–7.

101 See above, n. 98.

102 BT *MK* 28*a*.

103 See e.g. Elimelekh of Lizhensk, *No'am elimelekh*, ed. G. Nigal (Jerusalem, 1978), i. 43.

104 M. M. Schneerson, *Torat menaḥem—hitva'aduyot 5745*, 109.

105 For a detailed account of the development of these frameworks see Morris, *Lubavitcher Women*; Loewenthal, 'From "Ladies' Auxiliary" to "Shluhot Network"', 86*–89*.

106 For Menachem Mendel's counter-feminism, see e.g. his *Torat menaḥem—hitva'aduyot 5745*, 128—37. See also the discussion in Morris, *Lubavitcher Women*, 127–35.

107 From the private audience granted on Tuesday, 29 Tishrei 5742 (1981) to a visiting group of Beit Rivkah and Beit Sarah pupils from the Holy Land.

Bibliography

AARON OF OPATÓW, *Keter shem tov* [Zholkva (Żółkiew), 1794–5], 2 vols. (Brooklyn, NY, 1972).

—— *Or haganuz latsadikim* (Żółkiew, 1800).

AESCOLY (WEINTRAUB), A. Z., *Hasidism in Poland* [Haḥasidut bepolin], introd. D. Assaf, Mivḥar: Studies and Sources in the History and Culture of Eastern European Jewry (Jerusalem, 1999).

—— *Introduction à l'étude des hérésies religieuses parmi les juifs: La Kabbale—Le Hasidisme* (Paris, 1928).

AHAD HA'AM, *Selected Essays*, trans. L. Simon (Philadelphia, 1912).

ALFASI, Y., *Encyclopedia of Hasidism: Personalities* [Entsiklopedyah laḥasidut: ishim], ed. Y. Rafael, 3 vols. (Jerusalem, 1986).

—— *Hasidism* [Haḥasidut] (Tel Aviv, 1974).

ALTER, J. L., *Sefat emet al hatorah* (Jerusalem, 1997).

ALTSHULER, M., *Between Nationalism and Communism: The Evsektsia in the Soviet Union, 1918–1930* [Hayevsektsyah biverit hamo'atsot, bein le'umiyut lekomunizm] (Tel Aviv, 1980).

ASHKENAZI, S., *Woman in Jewish Perspective* [Ha'ishah be'aspaklaryat hayahadut] (Tel Aviv, 1953).

ASSAF, D., *Beguiled by Knowledge: An Anatomy of a Hasidic Controversy* [Hetsits venifga: anatomyah shel maḥloket ḥasidit] (Haifa, 2012).

—— 'The Clash over *Or Ha-Hayim*', *Modern Judaism*, 29/2 (May 2009).

—— 'A Messianic Vision among Volhynian Hasidim' (Heb.), *Gal-ed*, 20 (2006).

—— *The Regal Way: The Life and Times of R. Israel of Ruzhin* [Derekh hamalkhut: r. yisra'el meruzhin umekomo betoledot haḥasidut] (Jerusalem, 1997); Eng. edn.: *The Regal Way: The Life and Times of Rabbi Israel of Ruzhin* (Stanford, 2002).

—— *Untold Tales of the Hasidim: Crisis & Discontent in the History of Hasidism* (Hanover, 2010).

—— (ed.), *Zaddik and Devotees: Historical and Social Aspects of Hasidism* [Tsadik ve'edah: hebetim historiyim veḥevratiyim beḥeker haḥasidut] (Jerusalem, 2001).

—— JOSEPH DAN, and IMMANUEL ETKES (eds.), *Studies in Hasidism* [Meḥkerei ḥasidut] (Jerusalem, 1999).

ASSAF, S., 'On the History of the Rabbinate' (Heb.), in id., *Be'oholei ya'akov* (Jerusalem, 1943).

—— *Sources for the History of Jewish Education* [Mekorot letoledot haḥinukh beyisra'el], 2 vols. (Tel Aviv, 1925).

ATKINSON, C., '"Precious Balsam in a Fragile Glass": The Ideology of Virginity in the Later Middle Ages', *Journal of Family History* (Summer 1983).

AZULAI, A., *Ḥesed le'avraham* (Amsterdam, 1685).

BACON, G. C., 'East European Jewry from the First Partition to the Present', in G. D. Hundert and G. C. Bacon, *The Jews in Poland and Russia: Bibliographical Essays* (Bloomington, 1984).

BAER, Y. F., *A History of the Jews in Christian Spain*, 2 vols. (Philadelphia, 1966).

—— 'The Religious Social Tendency of *Sefer ḥasidim*' (Heb.), *Zion*, 3 (1938).

BAKER, M., 'The Voice of the Deserted Jewish Woman, 1867–1870', *Jewish Social Studies*, 2/1 (1995).

BAŁABAN, M., *History of the Frankist Movement* [Letoledot hatenuah hafrankit] (Tel Aviv, 1935).

BAR-ITZHAK, H., 'The Legend of the Jewish Holy Virgin of Ludmir: A Folkloristic Perspective', *Journal of Folklore Research*, 46/3 (2009).

BARNAI, J., *Letters of Hasidim from the Land of Israel* [Igerot ḥasidim me'erets yisra'el] (Jerusalem, 1980).

—— 'Some Clarifications on the Land of Israel's Stories of "In Praise of the Baal Shem Tov"', *Revue des études juives*, 146 (1987).

BARON, S. W., *The Jewish Community*, 3 vols. (Philadelphia, 1942).

—— *The Russian Jew under Tsars and Soviets* (New York, 1964).

BARTAL, I., 'The Immigration of R. Eleazar of Amsterdam to the Land of Israel in 1740' (Heb.), in J. Michman (ed.), *Studies on the History of Dutch Jewry* [Meḥkarim al toledot yahadut holand], vol. iv (Jerusalem, 1984); repr. in I. Bartal, *Exile in the Homeland* [Galut ba'arets: yishuv erets yisra'el beterem tsiyonut] (Jerusalem, 1994).

—— 'Simon the Heretic—a Chapter in Orthodox Historiography' (Heb.), in I. Bartal, E. Mendelsohn, and C. Turniansky (eds.), *Studies in Jewish Culture in Honour of Chone Shmeruk* [Keminhag ashkenaz upolin: sefer yovel leḥone shmeruk] (Jerusalem, 1993).

Be'ibei hanaḥal [supplement to *Likutei moharan*] (New York, 1966).

BEIZER, M., *The Jews of St Petersburg: Excursions through a Noble Past* (Philadelphia, 1989).

BEN-SASSON, H. H., *Ideology and Leadership: Views of Society among Polish Jews at the End of the Middle Ages* [Hagut vehanhagah: hashkafoteihem haḥevratiyot shel yehudei polin beshalhei yemei habeinayim] (Jerusalem, 1959).

—— 'The Personality and Historical Impact of the Gra' (Heb.), *Zion*, 31 (1966).

BERDYCZEWSKI, M. Y., 'About Hasidism' (Heb.), *Hamagid*, 6/33 (19 Aug. 1897).

BERGER, D., *The Jewish–Christian Debate in the High Middle Ages: A Critical Edition of the Nizzahon Vetus* (Philadelphia, 1979).

BERNSTEIN, D., *The Struggle for Equality: Women Workers in the Palestine 'Yishuv'* [Ishah be'erets yisra'el—hashe'ifah leshivyon bitekufat hayishuv] (Tel Aviv, 1987).

BIALE, D., 'Eros and Enlightenment: Love Against Marriage in the East European Jewish Enlightenment', in A. Polonsky (ed.), *Poles and Jews: Renewing the Dialogue*, Polin: Studies in Polish Jewry 1 (1986).

—— *Eros and the Jews* (New York, 1992).

—— 'A Feminist Reading of Hasidic Texts' (Heb.), in R. Levine Melammed (ed.), *'Lift up Your Voice': Women's Voices and Feminist Interpretation in Jewish Studies* [Harimi bako'aḥ kolekh: al kolot nashiyim ufarshanut feministit belimudei hayahadut] (Tel Aviv, 2001).

—— 'The Lust for Asceticism in the Hasidic Movement', in J. Magonet (ed.), *Jewish Explorations of Sexuality* (Providence, 1995).

BIBER, M., 'The Maiden of Ludmir' (Heb.), *Reshumot: hame'asef ledivrei zikhronot le'etnografyah ulefolklor beyisra'el*, 2 (Tel Aviv, 1946); repr. in *Ludmir Memorial Book* [Pinkas ludmir: sefer zikaron likehilat ludmir] (Tel Aviv, 1962).

BIKHOVSKY, H. E., *Ginzei nistarot* (Jerusalem, 1924).

BILU, Y., 'The Woman Who Wanted To Be Her Father: A Case Analysis of Dibbuk Possession in a Hasidic Community', *Journal of Psychoanalytical Anthropology*, 8/1 (1985).

BLAU, T., 'Writings of the *Admor* Joseph Isaac' (Heb.), in *Al hasifrut haḥabadit* (n.p., Kehot Publication Society, 1969).

BODEK, M. M., *Seder hadorot mitalmidei habesht z"l (Seder hadorot heḥadash)* [Lemberg, 1865] (Lublin, 1927).

BOYARIN, D., *Carnal Israel: Reading Sex in Talmudic Culture* (Berkeley, Calif., 1993).

BRAWER, A. Y., 'On the Dispute between R. Shneur Zalman of Liady and R. Abraham Hakohen of Kalisk' (Heb.), *Kiryat sefer*, 1 (1924–5).

—— *Studies in Galician Jewry* [Galitsyah viyehudeiha] (Jerusalem, 1956).

BRAWER, N., 'The Founding of "Tomekhei Temimim" and Its Impact on the Habad Lubavitch Movement' (Heb.), in I. Etkes (ed.), *Yeshivot and Batei Midrash* [Yeshivot uvatei midrashot] (Jerusalem, 2006).

—— 'Resistance and Response to Change: The Leadership of Rabbi Shalom Dov Ber Schneersohn (1860–1920)', Ph.D. diss. (University College London, 2004).

BRAYER, M. M., *The Jewish Woman in Rabbinic Literature*, ii: *A Psychohistorical Perspective* (Hoboken, NJ, 1986).

BREUER, M., 'Fragments of Identity and Memory' (Heb.), in H. Pedaya and E. Meir (eds.), *Judaism: Topics, Fragments, Faces, Identities. Jubilee Volume in Honour of Rivka* [Yahadut: sugyot, keta'im, panim, zehuyot. Sefer rivkah] (Be'er Sheva, 2007).

BREUER, M., 'The Wanderings of Students and Scholars—A Prolegomenon to a Chapter in the History of the Yeshivas' (Heb.), in R. Bonfil, M. Ben-Sasson, and J. R. Hacker (eds.), *Culture and Society in Medieval Jewry: Studies Dedicated to the Memory of Haim Hillel Ben-Sasson* [Tarbut veḥevrah betoledot yisra'el biyemei habeinayim] (Jerusalem, 1989).

BROKMAN, M., *Migdal david* (Piotrków, 1930), repr. in *Sefarim kedoshim migedolei talmidei ba'al shem tov hakadosh*, vol. iii (Brooklyn, NY, 1981).

BROWN, B., 'Kedushah: The Sexual Abstinence of Married Men in Gur, Slonim and Toledot Aharon', *Jewish History*, 27/2–4 (2013).

BROWN, P., 'The Notion of Virginity in the Early Church', in B. McGinn, J. Meyndorff, and J. Leclercq (eds.), *Christian Spirituality—Origins to the Twelfth Century* (London, 1986).

BUBER, M., *Or haganuz* (Tel Aviv, 1977).

—— *The Origin and Meaning of Hasidism*, ed. and trans. M. E. Friedman (New York, 1960).

—— *Tales of the Hasidim*, 2 vols. (New York, 1972).

BÜCHLER, A., *Studies in Sin and Atonement* (Oxford, 1928).

BUKIET, A. S. (ed.), *Em hamalkhut* (Kefar Habad, 2001).

BURSTYN, J. N., *Victorian Education and the Ideal of Womanhood* (New Brunswick, NJ, 1984).

Butsina dinehora (Lemberg, 1884).

CARDOZO, A., *Selected Writings*, trans. and introd. D. Halperin (New York, 2001).

CARLEBACH, E., *The Pursuit of Heresy: Rabbi Moses Hagiz and the Sabbatian Controversies* (New York, 1990).

CARLEBACH, E. H. (ed.), *A Memorial to the Holy Or Haḥayim and His Biography* [Yad or haḥayim hakadosh vetoledotav] (Hillside, NJ, 1981).

CARLYLE, T., *On Heroes, Hero-Worship and the Heroic in History* (London, 1840).

CHAJES, J. H., *Between Worlds: Dybbuks, Exorcists, and Early Modern Judaism* (Philadelphia, 2003).

CHAZAN, R., *Fashioning Jewish Identity in Medieval Western Christendom* (Cambridge, 2004).

CHITRIK, Y., *Reshimot devarim*, 4 vols. (New York, 1981–5).

CHODOROW, N., 'Family Structure and Feminine Personality', in M. Zimbalist Rosaldo and L. Lamphere (eds.), *Woman, Culture, and Society* (Stanford, Calif., 1974).

CHOVAV, Y., *Maidens Love Thee: The Religious and Spiritual Life of Jewish Ashkenazi Women in the Early Modern Period* [Alamot ahevukha: ḥayei hadat veharuaḥ shel nashim baḥevrah ha'ashkenazit bereshit ha'et haḥadashah] (Jerusalem, 2009).

COHEN, G., *The Book of Tradition by Abraham Ibn Daud* (London, 1967).

COHEN, T., 'Women in Haskalah Fiction', in S. Feiner and D. Sorkin (eds.), *New Perspectives on the Haskalah* (London, 2001).

CORDOVERO, M., *Ma'ayan Ein Ya'akov: The Fourth Fountain of the Book Elimah* [Ma'ayan ein ya'akov lerabi mosheh kordovero], ed. with notes by B. Sack, introd. S. Asulin et al. (Be'er Sheva, 2009).
—— *Pardes rimonim* (Jerusalem, 1962).
Crown of Royalty: The Rebbetzins of Chabad-Lubavitch of Seven Generations [Ateret malkhut: shiv'ah dorot shel rabaniyot ḥabad], ed. A. Cohen (Brooklyn, 1998).
DAHAN, A., '"Dira Batahtonim": The Messianic Doctrine of Rabbi Menachem Mendel Schneerson (the Lubavitcher Rebbe)' [Dirah bataḥtonim: mishnato hameshiḥit shel r. menaḥem mendel shneerson (harabi milubavitch)'], Ph.D. diss. (Hebrew University, 2006).
DAN, J., *The Esoteric Theology of Ashkenazi Hasidism* [Torat hasod shel ḥasidut ashkenaz] (Jerusalem, 1968).
—— *The Hasidic Tale: Its History and Development* [Hasipur haḥasidi] (Jerusalem, 1975).
—— *The Hebrew Story in the Middle Ages* [Hasipur ha'ivri biyemei habeinayim: iyunim betoledotav] (Jerusalem, 1974).
—— *Jewish Mysticism and Jewish Ethics* (Seattle, 1986).
—— 'On the History of the "Praises" Literature' (Heb.), *Jerusalem Studies in Jewish Folklore*, 1 (1982).
DAVIES, N., *God's Playground: A History of Poland*, 2 vols. (Oxford, 1981).
DEINARD, E., *Memories of My People* [Zikhronot bat ami] (St Louis, 1920).
DEUTSCH, N., *The Maiden of Ludmir: A Jewish Holy Woman and Her World* (Berkely, Calif., 2003).
—— 'New Archival Sources on the Maiden of Ludmir', *Jewish Social Studies*, 9 (2002).
DINUR, B.-Z., *With the Turn of the Generations* [Bemifneh hadorot] (Jerusalem, 1955).
DONNER, N. N., *Mayim rabim* (Warsaw, 1899), repr. in *Holy Books by the Disciples of the Ba'al Shem Tov* [Sefarim kedoshim mitalmidei ba'al shem tov], xviii (Brooklyn, 1984).
—— *Menorat zahav* (Warsaw, 1902); reproduced in N. N. Donner, *Butsina kadisha* (Warsaw, 1912; repr. Benei Berak, 2001).
DOV BER OF MEZHIRECH, *Magid devarav leya'akov*, ed. R. Schatz-Uffenheimer (Jerusalem, 1976); ed. A. I. Kahan (Jerusalem, 1971).
—— *Or ha'emet* (Zhitomir, 1900).
—— *Or torah* (Jerusalem, 1968).
DOV BER BEN SHEMUEL OF LINITS, *Shivḥei habesht* (Berdiczów, 1815).
DOV BER SHNEURI OF LUBAVITCH (the Mitteler Rebbe), *Ma'amerei admor ha'emtsa'i, derushei ḥatunah*, ii (Brooklyn, 1991).
—— *Ner mitsvah vetorah or* (Brooklyn, 1974).
—— *Poke'aḥ ivrim* (Brooklyn, 1955).
—— *Sha'arei teshuvah* (Brooklyn, 1983).
See also *Igerot kodesh . . . admor ha'emtsa'i . . .* below

DRESCHER MAYSE, E., 'Beyond the Letters: The Question of Language in the Teachings of Rabbi Dov Baer of Mezritch', Ph.D. diss. (Harvard University, 2015).

DRESNER, S. H., *The Zaddik: The Doctrine of the Zaddik According to the Writings of Rabbi Yaakov Yosef of Polnoy* (London, 1960).

DREZNITS, S., *Shivḥei ha'ari* (Warsaw, 1863).

DUBNOW, S., *The History of Hasidism* [Toledot haḥasidut] [1930–1] (Tel Aviv, 1960).

—— *History of the Jews in Russia and Poland*, 3 vols. (Philadelphia, 1916–20).

DUKER, A. G., 'Polish Frankism's Duration', *Jewish Social Studies*, 25 (1963).

DVIR-GOLDBERG, R., 'Rebbe Israel Ba'al Shem Tov and His Wife, and Other Women in Hasidic Tales' (Heb.), *Massekhet*, 3 (2005).

—— 'Voice of a Subterranean Fountain: The Image of a Woman through the Hasidic Tale' (Heb.), *Jerusalem Studies in Jewish Folklore*, 21 (2001).

DYNNER, G., *Men of Silk: The Hasidic Conquest of Polish Jewish Society* (Oxford, 2006).

EICHENSTEIN, Z. H., *Sur mera va'aseh tov* (Lemberg, 1832); Eng. edn. *Turn Aside from Evil and Do Good: An Introduction and a Way to the Tree of Life*, trans. with annotations and introd. Louis Jacobs (London, 1995).

EISENSTADT, MEIR, *Panim me'irot* (Sulzbach, 1733).

ELBERG, S., *Heavenly Warsaw* [Varsha shel ma'lah] (Benei Berak, 1969).

ELIAV, B., M. BOBE, and A. KREMER (eds.), *The Jews of Latvia: Memorial Book* [Yahadut latvyah: sefer zikaron] (Tel Aviv, 1953).

ELIMELEKH OF LIZHENSK, *No'am elimelekh* [Lemberg, 1788]; ed. G. Nigal, 2 vols. (Jerusalem, 1978).

ELIOR, R., 'Between *Yesh* and *Ayin*: The Doctrine of the Zaddik in the Works of Jacob Isaac, the Seer of Lublin', in A. Rapoport-Albert and S. J. Zipperstein (eds.), *Jewish History: Essays in Honour of Chimen Abramsky* (London, 1988).

—— 'The Controversy over the Legacy of Habad' (Heb.), *Tarbiz*, 49 (1980).

—— *Israel Ba'al Shem Tov and His Contemporaries: Kabbalists, Sabbatians, Hasidim, and Mitnagedim* [Yisra'el ba'al shem tov uvenei doro: mekubalim, shabeta'im, ḥasidim umitnagedim], 2 vols. (Jerusalem, 2014).

—— 'The Lubavitch Messianic Resurgence: The Historical and Mystical Background 1939–96', in P. Schäfer and M. Cohen (eds.), *Toward the Millennium: Messianic Expectations from the Bible to Waco* (Leiden, 1998).

—— 'The Minsk Debate' (Heb.), *Jerusalem Studies in Jewish Thought*, 1/4 (1981–2).

—— *The Mystical Origins of Hasidism* (Oxford, 2006).

—— *The Paradoxical Ascent to God: The Kabbalistic Theosophy of Habad Hasidism* (Albany, NY, 1993).

—— *The Theory of Divinity of Hasidut Habad: Second Generation* [Torat ha'elohut bador hasheni shel ḥasidut ḥabad] (Jerusalem, 1982).

—— '"The World is Filled with His Glory" and "All Men": Spiritual Renewal and Social Change in Early Hasidism' (Heb.), in M. Hallamish (ed.), *Alei shefer: Studies in Jewish Thought in Honour of Alexander Shafran* [Alei shefer: meḥkarim besifrut hehagut hayehudit, mugashim likhvod harav dr aleksander shafran] (Ramat Gan, 1990).

ELLIOTT, D., *Spiritual Marriage: Sexual Abstinence in Medieval Wedlock* (Princeton, NJ, 1993).

ELON, M., *Jewish Law: History, Sources, Principles*, trans. B. Auerbach and M. J. Sykes, 4 vols. (Philadelphia, 1994).

EL-OR, T., *Educated and Ignorant: Ultraorthodox Jewish Women and Their World* (Boulder, Colo., 1994).

EMDEN, J., *Sefer hitabekut* (Lwów, 1877).

—— [David Avaz], *Petaḥ einayim* (Altona, 1757).

Encyclopaedia of Religion and Ethics, ed. J. Hastings, 12 vols. (New York, 1908–27).

ENGEL, B. A., *Mothers and Daughters—Women of the Intelligentsia in Nineteenth-Century Russia* (Cambridge, 1983).

EPHRAIM OF LUNTSHITS, *Keli yakar* (Lublin, 1602).

EPHRAIM OF SUDYŁKÓW, *Degel maḥaneh efrayim* (Zhitomir, 1875).

EPSTEIN, K. K., *Ma'or vashemesh* [Breslau, 1842], 2 vols. (Jerusalem, 1986).

ESMAN, B., *Sefer ḥad veḥalak* (Vilna, 1882).

ETKES, I., *Ba'al hatanya: Rabbi Shneur Zalman of Liady and the Origins of Habad Hasidism* [Ba'al hatanya; rabi shneur zalman milady vereshitah shel ḥasidut ḥabad] (Jerusalem, 2011).

—— *The Besht: Magician, Mystic and Leader* (Waltham, Mass., 2005).

—— 'Family and Study of Torah in Lithuanian Talmudist Circles in the Nineteenth Century' (Heb.), *Zion*, 51 (1986).

—— *The Gaon of Vilna: The Man and His Image* (Berkeley, Calif., 2002).

—— 'Hasidism as a Movement: The First Stage', in B. Safran (ed.), *Hasidism: Continuity or Innovation?* (Cambridge, Mass., 1988).

—— *Rabbi Israel Salanter and the Mussar Movement: Seeking the Torah of Truth* (Philadelphia, 1993).

—— 'R. Meshullam Feibush Heller and His Conversion to Hasidism', *Studia Judaica*, 3 (1994).

—— *Rabbi Shneur Zalman of Liady: The Origins of Chabad Hasidism*, trans. J. M. Green (Waltham, Mass., 2015).

—— et al. (eds.), *Within Hasidic Circles: Studies in Hasidism in Memory of Mordecai Wilensky* [Bema'agelei ḥasidim: kovets meḥkarim mukdash lezikhro shel mordekhai vilenski] (Heb. and Eng.) (Jerusalem, 1999).

ETTINGER, S., 'The Hasidic Movement: Reality and Ideals', *Cahiers d'histoire mondiale: Journal of World History*, 11/1–2 (1968); repr. in H. H. Ben-Sasson and S. Ettinger (eds.), *Jewish Society through the Ages* (New York, 1971), and in G. D. Hundert (ed.), *Essential Papers on Hasidism* (New York, 1991).

ETTINGER, S. (ed.), *A Nation and Its History* [Umah vetoledoteiha], vol. ii (Jerusalem, 1984).

FEINKIND, M., *Female Rebbes and Famous Personalities in Poland* [Froyen rabonim un barimte perzenlekhkaytn in poylen] (Warsaw, 1937).

FINE, L., *Physician of the Soul, Healer of the Cosmos* (Stanford, Calif., 2001).

FISHMAN, D., 'Preserving Tradition in the Land of Revolution: The Religious Leadership of Soviet Jewry, 1917–1930', in J. Wertheimer (ed.), *The Uses of Tradition: Jewish Continuity in the Modern Era* (New York, 1992).

FLATTO, S., *The Kabbalistic Culture of Eighteenth-Century Prague: Ezekiel Landau (the 'Noda Biyehudah') and His Contemporaries* (Oxford, 2010).

FOIGEL, M. M., 'The Holy Rabbi Zevi Hirsh of Nadvorna and His Disciples' (Heb.), *Kovets siftei tsadikim*, 7 (Kislev 5755 [1994]).

FOUCAULT, M., *History of Madness*, ed. J. Khalfa, trans. J. Murphy and J. Khalfa (London, 2006).

FOXBRUNNER, R. A., *Ḥabad: The Hasidism of R. Shneur Zalman of Liady* (Northvale, NJ, 1993).

FRAADE, S. D., 'Ascetical Aspects of Ancient Judaism', in A. Green (ed.), *Jewish Spirituality from the Bible through the Middle Ages* (London, 1986).

FREEZE, C. Y., *Jewish Marriage and Divorce in Imperial Russia* (Hanover, 2002).

FRIEDLANDER BEN ARZA, S., 'Hannah Rachel of Ludmir' (Heb.), *Kolekh: forum nashim datiyot*, 95 (1 Tamuz 2004).

FRIEDMAN, M., 'Habad as Messianic Fundamentalism: From Local Particularism to Universal Jewish Mission', in M. E. Marty and R. Scott Appelby (eds.), *Accounting for Fundamentalism: The Dynamic Character of Movements* (Chicago, 1994).

—— 'Messiah and Messianism in Habad Lubavitch Hasidism' (Heb.), in D. Ariel-Joel et al. (eds.), *The War of Gog and Magog: Messianism and the Apocalypse in Judaism—Past and Present* [Milḥemet gog umagog: meshiḥiyut ve'apokalipsah bayahadut—be'avar uveyameinu] (Tel Aviv, 2001).

GAT, B.-Z., *The Jewish Community in the Land of Israel in the Years 1840–1881* [Hayishuv hayehudi be'erets yisra'el bishenot [5]600–[5]641] (Jerusalem, 1963).

GELERENTER-LIEBOWITZ, S., 'Growing up Lubavitch', in S. Grossman and R. Haut (eds.), *Daughters of the King: Women and the Synagogue (A Survey of History, Halakhah, and Contemporary Realities)* (Philadelphia, 1993).

GELLMAN, U., 'The Great Wedding at Ustila: The History of a Hasidic Myth' (Heb.), *Tarbiz*, 80/4 (2013).

—— 'Hasidism in Poland in the First Half of the Nineteenth Century: Typologies of Leadership and Devotees' (Heb.) [Haḥasidut bepolin bamaḥatsit harishonah shel hame'ah hatesha-esreh: tipologyah shel manhigut ve'edah], Ph.D. diss. (Hebrew University, 2011).

GERSHUNI, A. A., *Judaism in Soviet Russia: Towards a History of Religious Persecution* [Yahadut berusyah hasovyetit: lekorot redifot hadat] (Jerusalem, 1961).

GERTNER, H., *The Rabbi and the City: The Rabbinate in Galicia and Its Encounter with Modernity, 1815–1867* [Harav veha'ir hagedolah: harabanut begalitsyah umifgashah im hamodernah, 1815–1867] (Jerusalem, 2013).

—— 'The Rabbinate and the Hasidic Movement in Nineteenth-Century Galicia: The Case of Rabbi Solomon Kluger' (Heb.), in I. Etkes et al. (eds.), *Within Hasidic Circles: Studies in Hasidism in Memory of Mordecai Wilensky* [Bema'agelei ḥasidim: kovets meḥkarim mukdash lezikhro shel mordekhai vilenski] (Heb. and Eng.) (Jerusalem, 1999).

GESHURI, M. S., *Melody and Dance in Hasidism* [Hanigun veharikud baḥasidut], 3 vols. (Tel Aviv, 1959).

GESSEN, V., *K istorii Sankt-Peterburgskoi evreiskoi religioznoi obshchiny: Ot pervykh evreev do XX veka* (St Petersburg, 2000).

GLITZENSTEIN, A. H., *Rabbi Israel Ba'al Shem Tov* [Yisra'el ba'al shem tov] (Kefar Habad, 1975).

—— *Sefer hatoladot: rabi yosef yitsḥak schneersohn, admor morenu harav yosef yitsḥak*, 4 vols. in 3 (Kefar Habad, 1971–4).

GOLDBERG, A., *Sex, Religion, and the Making of Modern Madness: The Eberbach Asylum and German Society 1815–1849* (Oxford, 1999).

GOLDENSTEIN, P. B., *Mayn lebens-geshikhte* (Petah Tikvah, 1928–9).

GOLDISH, M., *The Sabbatian Prophets* (Cambridge, Mass., 2004).

GOTTLOBER, A. B., *Memoirs and Travels* [Zikhronot umasa'ot], 2 vols., ed. R. Goldberg (Jerusalem, 1976).

GRAETZ, H., *History of the Jews from the Earliest Times to the Present Day*, 5 vols. (London, 1901).

GRAYEVSKY, P. B., *Daughters of Zion and Jerusalem* [Benot tsiyon viyerushalayim], nos. 1–10 (Jerusalem, 2000).

GREEN, A., 'Around the Maggid's Table: *Tsadik*, Leadership, and Popularization in the Circle of Dov Baer of Miedzyrzecz' (Heb.), *Zion*, 78/1 (2013).

—— *Tormented Master: A Life of Rabbi Nahman of Bratslav* (Tuscaloosa, Ala., 1979).

—— 'Typologies of Leadership and the Hasidic Zaddik', in id. (ed.), *Jewish Spirituality*, ii: *From the Sixteenth Century Revival to the Present* (New York, 1987).

—— with E. LEADER, A. E. MAYSE, and O. N. ROSE (eds.), *Speaking Torah: Spiritual Teachings from around the Maggid's Table*, 2 vols. (Woodstock, Vt., 2013).

GREENBERG, G., 'Mahaneh Israel-Lubavitch 1940–45: Actively Responding to Khurban', in A. A. Berger (ed.), *Bearing Witness to the Holocaust, 1939–89* (New York, 1991).

—— 'Redemption after Holocaust According to Mahane Israel-Lubavitch 1940–45', *Modern Judaism*, 12 (1992).

—— 'The Sect of Catastrophe: Mahane Israel-Lubavitch 1940–45', in M. Mor (ed.), *Jewish Sects, Religious Movements, and Political Parties* (Omaha, 1992).

GREENBERG, L., *The Jews in Russia* (New Haven, 1944).
GRIES, Z., *Conduct Literature* [Sifrut hahanhagot: toledoteiha umekomah beḥayei ḥasidei r. yisra'el ba'al shem tov] (Jerusalem, 1989).
—— 'From Myth to Ethos: Towards a Portrait of R. Abraham of Kalisk' (Heb.), in S. Ettinger (ed.), *A Nation and Its History*, ii: *The Modern Era* [Umah vetoledoteiha, ii: Ha'et haḥadashah] (Jerusalem, 1984).
—— 'The Hasidic Conduct (*Hanhagot*) Literature from the Mid-Eighteenth Century to the 1830s' (Heb.), *Zion*, 46 (1981).
—— 'Hasidism: The Present State of Research and Some Desirable Priorities', *Numen*, 34/1 (1987).
GROSSMAN, A., 'Family Pedigree and its Role in Early Ashkenazi Jewish Society' (Heb.), in I. Etkes and Y. Salmon (eds.), *Studies in the History of Jewish Society in the Middle Ages and in the Modern Period* [Perakim betoledot haḥevrah hayehudit biyemei habeinayim uva'et haḥadashah, mukdashim leya'akov kats] (Jerusalem, 1980).
—— *He Shall Rule Over You? Medieval Jewish Sages on Women* [Vehu yimshol bakh? Ha'ishah bemishnatam shel ḥakhmei yisra'el biyemei habeinayim] (Jerusalem, 2011).
—— *Pious and Rebellious: Jewish Women in Medieval Europe*, trans. J. Chipman (Waltham, Mass., 2004).
GRUNFELD-ROSENBAUM, J., 'Sara Schenierer—The Story of a Great Movement', in L. Jung (ed.), *Jewish Leaders* (New York, 1953).
HAGIZ, M., *Shever poshe'im* (London, 1714; facsimile edn. Jerusalem, 1970).
HAKOHEN, A., *Keter rosh* [*Orkhot ḥayim*] (Jerusalem, n.d.).
HALECKI, O., *A History of Poland* (London, 1978).
HALPERIN, D. J., *Sabbatai Zevi: Testimonies to a Fallen Messiah* (Oxford, 2007).
HALPERN, I., *Eastern European Jewry: Historical Studies* [Yehudim veyahadut bemizraḥ eiropah] (Jerusalem, 1968).
—— (ed.), *The Jewish People in Poland* [Beit yisra'el bepolin] (Jerusalem, 1953).
—— 'R. Levi Isaac of Berdiczów and the Decrees of the State in His Time' (Heb.), in id., *Eastern European Jewry: Historical Studies*.
—— 'Torah and Mitsvah Societies and the Expanding Hasidic Movement' (Heb.), in id., *Eastern European Jewry: Historical Studies*.
HANDELMAN, S., 'Women and the Study of Torah in the Thought of the Lubavitcher Rebbe', in M. D. Halpern and C. Safrai (eds.), *Jewish Legal Writings by Women* (Jerusalem, 1998).
HARAN, R., 'R. Abraham of Kalisk and R. Shneur Zalman of Liady—a Friendship Cut Off' (Heb.), in R. Elior and J. Dan (eds.), *Rivka Schatz-Uffenheimer Memorial Volume* [Kolot rabim: sefer hazikaron lerivkah schatz-ufenheimer] vol. ii, Jerusalem Studies in Jewish Thought 13 (Jerusalem, 1996).
HASIDOV, H., '"The Sister of the Temimim Group" in Riga' (Yid.), *Di yidishe heym*, 22/3 (1981).

Hatamim, 2 vols. (Kefar Habad, 1975).

HAVLIN, S. Z., 'Letter to the Editor' (Heb.), *Yeshurun: me'asef torani*, 4 (1998).

HAYIM HAYKL OF AMDUR, *Ḥayim vaḥesed* (Jerusalem, 1970).

HAYMAN, A. P., *Sefer Yeṣira*, Texts and Studies in Ancient Judaism 104 (Tübingen, 2004).

HAZAN, A., *Avaneiha barzel*, in id., *Sefer kokhevei or* (Jerusalem, 1961).

HEILMAN, H. M., *Beit rabi* (Berdiczów, 1902).

HENRY, S., and E. TAITZ, *Written Out of History* (Fresh Meadows, NY, 1983).

HESCHEL, A. J., *The Circle of the Baal Shem Tov: Studies in Hasidism*, ed. S. H. Dresner (Chicago, 1985).

—— *Prophetic Inspiration After the Prophets: Maimonides and Other Medieval Authorities*, ed. M. M. Faierstein (Hoboken, NJ, 1996).

—— 'R. Gershon Kutover: His Life and Emigration to the Land of Israel' (Heb.), *Hebrew Union College Annual*, 23, pt. II (1951).

HILLMAN, D. Z., *Letters by the Author of the Tanya and His Contemporaries* [Igerot ba'al hatanya uvenei doro] (Jerusalem, 1953).

HOFSTEIN, I., *Avodat yisra'el hashalem* (Munkács, 1929).

HOFSTEIN, M. E. B, *Vayeḥal mosheh* (Lemberg, 1863).

HORODETSKY, S. A., *Hasidism and Its Adherents* [Haḥasidut vehaḥasidim], 4 vols. (2nd edn., Tel Aviv, 1928–43).

—— *Immigrants to Zion* [Olei tsiyon] (Tel Aviv, 1947).

—— *The Judaism of Intellect and the Judaism of Emotion* [Yahadut hasekhel veyahadut haregesh], 2 vols. (Tel Aviv, 1947).

—— *Leaders* of *Hasidism* (London, 1928).

—— [S. A. G.], 'Ludmirskaya deva (Di ludmirer moyd)', *Evreiskaya Starina*, 1/2 (1909).

—— *Pirkei zikhronot* (Tel Aviv, 1957).

HORWITZ, R., *Multiple-Faceted Judaism* [Yahadut rabat panim] (Be'er Sheva, 2002).

HUNDERT, G. D., 'The Conditions in Jewish Society in the Polish-Lithuanian Commonwealth in the Middle Decades of the Eighteenth Century', in A. Rapoport-Albert (ed.), *Hasidism Reappraised* (London, 1996).

—— (ed.), *Essential Papers on Hasidism* (New York, 1991).

—— 'Some Basic Characteristics of the Jewish Experience in Poland', in A. Polonsky (ed.), *Poles and Jews: Renewing the Dialogue*, Polin: Studies in Polish Jewry 1 (1986).

HUSS, B., 'Admiration and Disgust: The Ambivalent Re-canonisation of the *Zohar* in the Modern Period', in H. Kreisel (ed.), *Study and Knowledge in Jewish Thought* (Be'er Sheva, 2006).

HYMAN, P. E., and D. OFER (eds.), *Jewish Women—A Comprehensive Historical Encyclopedia*, CD-ROM (Jerusalem, 2006).

IDEL, M., 'The Besht as Prophet and Talismanic Magician' (Heb.), in A. Lipsker and R. Kushelevsky (eds.), *Studies in Jewish Narrative Presented to Yoav Elstein* [Ma'aseh sipur: meḥkarim basifrut hayehudit mugashim leyo'av elshtein] (Ramat Gan, 2006).

—— 'Female Beauty: A Chapter in the History of Jewish Mysticism' (Heb.), in I. Etkes et al. (eds.), *Within Hasidic Circles: Studies in Hasidism in Memory of Mordecai Wilensky* [Bema'agelei ḥasidim: kovets meḥkarim lezikhro shel profesor mordekhai vilenski] (Jerusalem, 2000).

—— *Hasidism: Between Ecstasy and Magic* (Albany, NY, 1995).

—— 'Jewish Mysticism among the Jews of Arab/Moslem Lands', *Journal for the Study of Sephardic and Mizrahi Jewry*, 1/1 (Feb. 2007).

—— *Kabbalah and Eros* (New Haven, 2005).

—— 'Martin Buber and Gershom Scholem on Hasidism: A Critical Appraisal', in A. Rapoport-Albert (ed.), *Hasidism Reappraised* (London, 1996).

—— 'Métaphores et pratiques sexuelles dans la cabale', in C. Mopsik (ed.), *Lettre sur la sainteté* (Paris, 1986).

—— 'Modes of Cleaving to the Letters in the Teachings of Israel Baal Shem Tov: A Sample Analysis', *Jewish History*, 27/2–4 (2013).

—— 'On Prophecy and Early Hasidism', in M. Sharon (ed.), *Studies in Modern Religions, Religious Movements and the Babi-Baha'i Faiths* (Leiden, 2004).

—— 'Some Forlorn Writings of a Forgotten Ashkenazi Prophet, R. Nehemiah Ben Shlomo Ha-Navi', *Jewish Quarterly Review*, 96 (2005).

Igerot kodesh admor hazaken, admor ha'emtsa'i, admor hatsemaḥ tsedek, 2 vols. (Brooklyn, 1980, 1993).

In Praise of the Baal Shem Tov, ed. D. Ben-Amos and J. R. Mintz (Bloomington, Ind., 1970).

In Praise of the Ba'al Shem Tov (Shivhei Ha-Besht), with Introduction and Annotations by Avraham Rubinstein [Shivḥei habesht: mahadurah mu'eret umevo'eret. Avraham Rubinstein] (Jerusalem, 1991).

ISRAEL OF VILEDNIK, *She'erit yisra'el* (Monsey, 1998).

JACOB ISAAC, THE SEER OF LUBLIN, *Divrei emet*, in *The Holy Books of All the Disciples of the Holy Besht* [Sefarim hakedoshim mikol talmidei habesht hakadosh], vol. ii (Brooklyn, 1981).

—— *Zot zikaron*, in *The Holy Books of All the Disciples of the Holy Besht* [Sefarim hakedoshim mikol talmidei habesht hakadosh], vol. ii (Brooklyn, 1981).

JACOB JOSEPH OF POŁONNE, *Ben porat yosef* [Korzec, 1781] (New York, 1954).

—— *Ketonet pasim* (New York, 1950).

—— *Toledot ya'akov yosef* (Korzec, 1780; repr. Jerusalem, 1966).

—— *Tsafenat pa'ne'aḥ* [Korzec, 1782] (New York, 1954).

JACOBS, L., *Hasidic Prayer* (London, 1972).

—— 'Hasidism and the Dogma of the Decline of the Generations', in A. Rapoport-Albert (ed.), *Hasidism Reappraised* (London, 1996).

—— *Jewish Mystical Testimonies* (New York, 1977).

—— *Seeker of Unity: The Life and Works of Aaron of Starosselje* (London, 1966).

—— 'Woman', *Encyclopaedia Judaica*, vol. xvi (Jerusalem, 1972).

JACOBSOHN, I., *Zikaron livnei yisra'el* (Brooklyn, 1996).

JACOBSON, Y., 'The Aspect of the "Feminine" in the Lurianic Kabbalah', in P. Schäfer and J. Dan (eds.), *Gershom Scholem's Major Trends in Jewish Mysticism 50 Years After* (Tübingen, 1993).

Jewish Mystical Autobiographies: Book of Visions and Book of Secrets, trans. and introd. M. M. Faierstein (New York, 1999).

JUDAH LOEW BEN BEZALEL OF PRAGUE, *Perushei maharal miprag . . . le'agadot hashas* (Jerusalem, 1968).

KAGAN, I. M., *Kol kitvei haḥafets ḥayim hashalem*, 4 vols. (Jerusalem, 1990).

KAHAN, A., 'The Impact of Industrialization in Tsarist Russia on the Socioeconomic Conditions of the Jewish Population', in id., *Essays in Jewish Social and Economic History*, ed. R. Weiss, with an introduction by J. Frankel (Chicago, 1986).

KAHAN, R. N., *Lubavitch and Its Soldiers* [Lubavitch veḥayaleiha] (Kefar Habad, 1983).

—— *Shemuot vesipurim meraboteinu hakedoshim*, 3 vols. (Kefar Habad, 1974–7).

KAHANA, A., *Sefer haḥasidut* (Warsaw, 1922).

KAHANA, D., *A History of the Kabbalists, the Sabbatians, and the Hasidim* [Toledot hamekubalim, hashabeta'im vehaḥasidim], 2 vols. (Tel Aviv, 1926–7).

KAHANA, M., and M. K. SILBER, 'Deists, Sabbatians, and Kabbalists in Prague: A Censored Sermon of R. Ezekiel Landau, 1770' (Heb.), *Kabbalah*, 21 (2010).

KAIDANER, J., *Sipurim nora'im* (Lemberg, 1875).

KALLUS, M., 'The Relation of the Baal Shem Tov to the Practice of Lurianic Kavvanot in Light of his Comments on the Siddur Rashkov', *Kabbalah: Journal for the Study of Jewish Mystical Texts*, 2 (1997).

KANARFOGEL, E., 'A Monastic-Like Setting for the Study of Torah', in L. Fine (ed.), *Judaism in Practice from the Middle Ages through the Early Modern Period* (Princeton, 2001).

KANIEL, A., 'Beys Yankev', in *The YIVO Encyclopedia of Jews in Eastern Europe*, vol. i (New Haven, 2008).

KAPLAN, M. A., *The Jewish Feminist Movement in Germany: The Campaigns of the Jüdischer Frauenbund, 1904–38* (Westport, Conn., 1979).

—— *The Making of the Jewish Middle Class: Women, Family, and Identity in Imperial Germany* (New York, 1991).

KAPLOUN, U. (ed.), *A Partner in the Dynamic of Creation: Womanhood in the Teachings of the Lubavitcher Rebbe, Rabbi Menachem M. Schneerson* (Brooklyn, 1994).

KARLINSKY, N., *Counter-History: The Hasidic Epistles from Erets Yisra'el: Text and Context* [Ḥasidut shekeneged: igerot haḥasidim me'erets yisra'el: hatekst vehakontekst] (Jerusalem, 1998).

KARLINSKY, N., 'The Dawn of Hasidic-Haredi Historiography', *Modern Judaism*, 27/1 (2007).

KATZ, J., 'Marriage and Marital Relations at the End of the Middle Ages' (Heb.), *Zion*, 10 (1944).

—— *Tradition and Crisis*, trans. B. D. Cooperman (New York, 1993); originally published in Hebrew as *Masoret umashber* (Jerusalem, 1958).

KATZ, S., 'Maskilic Letters Denigrating Hasidim' (Heb.), *Moznayim*, 10 (1940).

KAUFFMAN, T., *In All Your Ways Know Him: The Concept of God and Avodah Begashmiyut in the Early Stages of Hasidism* [Bekhol derakheikha da'ehu: tefisat ha'elohut veha'avodah begashmiyut bereshit haḥasidut] (Ramat Gan, 2009).

—— 'Two *Tsadikim*, Two Women in Labor, and One Salvation: Reading Gender in a Hasidic Story', *Jewish Quarterly Review*, 101/3 (2011).

KELNER, V. E., and D. A. ELYASHEVICH (eds.), *Literatura o evereyakh na russkom yazyke, 1890–1947* (St Petersburg, 1995).

Keneset hagedolah vedivrei ḥakhamim (Lemberg, 1869).

KIENIEWICZ, S., et al. (eds.), *History of Poland* (Warsaw, 1968).

KIEVAL, H., *Languages of Community: The Jewish Experience in the Czech Lands* (Berkeley, Calif., 2000).

KLAR, B., *Rabbi Hayim ben Attar: His Immigration to the Land of Israel* [Rabi ḥayim ibn atar: aliyato le'erets yisra'el] (Jerusalem, 1951).

KLIER, J. D., *Russia Gathers Her Jews: The Origin of the 'Jewish Question' in Russia, 1772–1825* (Dekalb, Ill., 1986).

KLYACHKO, M., 'Volynskie predaniya III: Eshche o Ludmirksoi deve', *Evreiskaya Starina*, 3/4 (1911).

KOCH, P. B., *Human Self-Perfection: A Re-assessment of Kabbalistic Musar-Literature of Sixteenth-Century Safed* (Los Angeles, 2015).

KOENIG, N. T., *Neveh tsadikim* (Benei Berak, 1969).

KOKHAV LEV [STERNHARZ], A., *Tovot zikhronot* [appended to Nahman of Cherin's *Yeraḥ ha'eitanim*] (Jerusalem, 1951).

KOTIK, Y., *Wanderer—The Memoirs of Yechezkel Kotik* [Na vanad: zikhronotav shel yeḥezkel kotik], ed., trans., and introd. D. Assaf (Tel Aviv, 2005).

KRASSEN, M., *Uniter of Heaven and Earth: Rabbi Meshullam Feibush Heller of Zbarazh and the Rise of Hasidism in Eastern Galicia* (Albany, NY, 1998).

KRAUS, Y., *The Seventh: Messianism in the Last Generation of Habad* [Hashevi'i: meshiḥiyut bador hashevi'i shel ḥabad] (Tel Aviv, 2007).

KUPFER, E., 'New Documents on the Controversy between RSHZ of Liady, R. Abraham of Kalisk, and R. Barukh of Międzybóż' (Heb.), *Tarbiz*, 47 (1978).

LANDAU, I., *Zikaron tov* (Piotrków, 1892), in *The Holy Books of All the Disciples of the Holy Besht* [Sefarim hakedoshim mikol talmidei habesht hakadosh], vol. iii (Brooklyn, 1981).

LANGER, J., *Nine Gates* (London, 1961).

LESTSCHINSKY, J., *The Jewish People in Numbers: Jews throughout the World* [Dos yidishe folk in tsifern: di yidn in der gorer velt] (Berlin, 1922).
—— *The Jews in Soviet Russia: From the October Revolution to the Second World War* [Hayehudim berusyah hasovyetit: mimahapekhat oktober ad milḥemet ha'olam hasheniyah] (Tel Aviv, 1953).
LEVIN, S., *Childhood in Exile*, trans. M. Samuel (London, 1929).
LEVIN, S. D., *The History of Habad in the Soviet Union, 1917–1950* [Toledot ḥabad berusyah hasovyetit [5]678–[5]710] (Brooklyn, 1989).
—— *The History of Habad in the USA—1900–1950* [Toledot ḥabad be'artsot haberit bashanim tav-resh-samekh–tav-shin-yud] (Brooklyn, 1988).
LEVIN, V., 'Ocherk istorii evreiskogo shkolnogo obrazovanya v dorevolyutsionnom Peterburge', *Evreiskaya Shkola* (Jan.–Mar. 1993).
—— and D. STALIŪNAS, '*Lite* in the Jewish Mental Maps', in D. Staliūnas (ed.), *Spatial Concepts of Lithuania in the Long Nineteenth Century* (Boston, 2016).
LEVINE KATZ, Y., 'The Events of the *Yahrzeit* of Hannah Rachel Verbermacher' (Heb.), *Mabua*, 43 (2004/5).
—— 'In Memoriam Hannah Rachel, 1806–88' (Heb.), *Hatsofeh* (16 July 2004).
—— 'The Voice of the Bride in the Future' (Heb.), in S. Raz (ed.), *The Religious Zionist Anthology in Memory of Zerach Warhaftig* [Kovets hatsiyonut hadatit lezekher zeraḥ varhaftig] (Jerusalem, 2001).
LEVINSON, I. B., *Emek refa'im*, in id., *Yalkut rival* (Warsaw, 1878).
LEVITATS, I., *The Jewish Community in Russia, 1772–1844* (New York, 1943).
—— *The Jewish Community in Russia, 1844–1917* (Jerusalem, 1981).
LEWINSKY, Y. T., *Encyclopedia of Folklore, Customs, and Tradition in Judaism* [Entsiklopedyah shel havai umasoret bayahadut] (Tel Aviv, 1975).
LEWIS, J. J., '"Eydele, the Rebbe": Shifting Perspectives on a Jewish Gender Transgressor', *Journal of Modern Jewish Studies*, 6/1 (2007).
Lexikon fun der nayer yidisher literatur, 8 vols. (New York, 1965–81).
LEYB BEN OZER, *The Story of Sabbatai Zevi* [Sipur ma'asei shabetai tsevi], trans. from the original Yiddish manuscript (*Beshraybung fun shabsai tsvi*), with introd. and notes, Z. Shazar (Jerusalem, 1978).
LIEBERMAN, H., 'How Hasidism is "Studied" in Israel' (Heb.), in id., *Ohel raḥel*, vol. i (New York, 1980).
—— *Ohel raḥel*, 3 vols. (New York, 1980-4).
LIEBERMAN, S., *Texts and Studies* (New York, 1974).
LIEBES, Y., 'The Messiah of the Zohar', in id., *Studies in the Zohar*, trans. A. Schwartz, S. Nakache, and P. Peli (Albany, NY, 1995).
—— *On Sabbatianism and Its Kabbalah* [Sod ha'emunah hashabeta'it] (Jerusalem, 1995).
—— 'R. Nahman's General *Tikun* and His Attitude to Sabbatianism' (Heb.), *Zion*, 45/3 (1980).

Likutim yekarim [Lemberg, 1792] (Jerusalem, 1975).

LOEBEL, I., 'Sefer vikuaḥ', in M. Wilensky, *Hasidim and Mitnagedim* [Ḥasidim umitnagedim], vol. ii (Jerusalem, 1970).

LOEWENTHAL, N., 'The Apotheosis of Action in Early Habad', *Daat*, 18 (1987).

—— *Communicating the Infinite: The Emergence of the Habad School* (Chicago, 1990).

—— '"Daughter/Wife of a Hasid" or "Hasidic Woman"?', *Mada'ei hayahadut*, 40 (2000).

—— 'Early Habad Publications in their Setting', in D. Rowland Smith and P. S. Salinger (eds.), British Library Occasional Papers 13 (London: British Library, 1991).

—— 'From "Ladies' Auxiliary" to "Shluhot Network"—Women's Activism in Twentieth-Century HABAD', in I. Bartal et al. (eds.), *A Touch of Grace: Studies in Ashkenazi Culture, Women's History, and the Languages of the Jews, Presented to Chava Turniansky* [Ḥut shel ḥesed lekoved ḥavah turnianski] (Heb., Eng., and Ger.) (Jerusalem, 2013).

—— '"The Lower Unity": Joining Mystical Quest and Reality in the First Century of Habad', *BDD—Bekhol derakheikha da'ehu*, 16 (Aug. 2005).

—— 'The Neutralisation of Messianism and the Apocalypse', in R. Elior and J. Dan (eds.), *Rivka Schatz-Uffenheimer Memorial Volume* [Kolot rabim: sefer hazikaron lerivkah shatz-ufenheimer] (Heb. and Eng.) (Jerusalem, 1996), vol. ii, English section.

—— '"Reason" and "Beyond Reason" in Habad Hasidism', in M. Hallamish (ed.), *Alei shefer: Studies in Jewish Thought in Honor of Alexander Shafran* [Alei shefer: meḥkarim besifrut hehagut hayehudit mugashim likhvod harav dr aleksander shafran] (Ramat Gan, 1990), English section.

—— 'Spiritual Experience for Hasidic Youths and Girls in Pre-Holocaust Europe—A Confluence of Tradition and Modernity', in A. Mintz and L. Schiffman (eds.), *Jewish Spirituality and Divine Law* (Jersey City, 2005).

—— 'Women and the Dialectic of Spirituality in Hasidism', in I. Etkes (ed.), *Within Hasidic Circles: Studies in Hasidism in Memory of Mordecai Wilensky* [Bema'agelei ḥasidim: kovets meḥkarim mukdash lezikhro shel mordekhai vilenski] (Heb. and Eng.) (Jerusalem, 1999), English section.

LORBERBAUM, M., '"Attain the Attribute of *Ayin*": The Mystical Religiosity of *Magid devarav leya'akov*' (Heb.), *Kabbalah: Journal for the Study of Jewish Mystical Texts*, 31 (2014).

LOWE, M., and R. HUBBARD (eds.), *Woman's Nature: Rationalizations of Inequality* (New York, 1983).

Lubavitch Foundation of Great Britain, *A Woman of Valour—An Anthology for the Thinking Jewess* (London, 1976).

Lubavitch Women's Organization, *Aura—A Reader on Jewish Womanhood* (New York, 1984).

—— *The Gift* (New York, 1985).

LUNZ, A. M., 'The *Ḥalukah*, Its Origin and History' (Heb.), *Yerushalayim*, 9 (1911).

LURIE, I., 'Education and Ideology: The Beginnings of the Habad Yeshiva' (Heb.), in D. Assaf and A. Rapoport-Albert (eds.), *Let the Old Make Way for the New: Studies in the Social and Cultural History of Eastern European Jewry Presented to Immanuel Etkes* [Yashan mipenei ḥadash: meḥkarim betoledot yehudei mizraḥ eiropah uvetarbutam, shai le'imanu'el etkes], vol. i (Jerusalem 2009).

MCCAGG, W., *A History of Habsburg Jews 1670–1918* (Bloomington, Ind., 1992).

MACIEJKO, P., *The Mixed Multitude: Jacob Frank and the Frankist Movement, 1755–1816* (Philadelphia, 2011).

MAGID, S., *Hasidism Incarnate: Hasidism, Christianity, and the Construction of Modern Judaism* (Stanford, Calif., 2014).

MAHLER, R., *Hasidism and Haskalah* [Haḥasidut vehahaskalah begalitsyah uvepolin hakongresa'it bamaḥatsit harishonah shel hame'ah hatesha-esreh] (Merhavyah, 1961).

—— *Hasidism and the Jewish Enlightenment: Their Confrontation in Galicia and Poland in the First Half of the Nineteenth Century*, trans. E. Orenstein, A. Klein, and J. Machlowitz Klein (Philadelphia, 1985).

MAIMON, S., *Salomon Maimons Lebensgeschichte*, ed. J. Fromer (Munich, 1911); Eng. trans.: *The Autobiography of Solomon Maimon*, trans. J. Clark Murray (London, 1954); Heb. trans.: *Ḥayei shelomoh maimon* (Tel Aviv, 1942).

MANIKIN, R., 'The Development of the Idea of Religious Education for Girls in Galicia in the Modern Era' (Heb.), *Massekhet*, 2 (2004).

MANOR, D., 'Rabbi Hayim ben Attar in Hasidic Writings' (Heb.), *Pe'amim*, 20 (1984).

MARGALIOT, E., *Ma'aseh nora'ah venifla'ah . . . merabi zalmina . . .* (Czernowitz, 1863).

MARGALIOT, R., *The Biography of Our Master Hayim ben Attar, Author of Or Haḥayim* [Toledot rabenu ḥayim ben atar ba'al or haḥayim] (Lwów, 1925).

MARK, Z., '*Dibbuk* and *Devekut* in *In Praise of the Baal Shem Tov*: Notes on the Phenomenology of Madness in Early Hasidism' (Heb.), in I. Etkes et al. (eds.), *Within Hasidic Circles: Studies in Hasidism in Memory of Mordecai Wilensky* [Bema'agelei ḥasidim: kovets meḥkarim mukdash lezikhro shel mordekhai vilenski] (Heb. and Eng.) (Jerusalem, 1999).

—— 'Hasidism and Anarchy: The Intellectual and Autobiographical Foundations of the Story "Hahafsakah" by Micha Yosef Berdyczewski' (Heb.), *Tsafon*, 17 (n.d.).

—— *Mysticism and Madness in the Work of R. Nahman of Bratslav* [Mistikah veshiga'on biyetsirat r. naḥman mibratslav] (Tel Aviv, 2003).

—— *The Scroll of Secrets: The Hidden Messianic Vision of R. Nachman of Breslav* (Brighton, Mass., 2010).

Matsref ha'avodah [Königsberg, 1858] (Zhitomir, 1865).

MEIR, J., *Imagined Hasidism: The Anti-Hasidic Writings of Joseph Perl* [Ḥasidut medumah: iyunim bikhtavav hasatiriyim shel yosef perl] (Jerusalem, 2013).

—— 'The Lost Yiddish Editions of *Shivḥei habesht* (1815–1817)' (Heb.), *Kabbalah: Journal for the Study of Jewish Mystical Texts*, 39 (2017).

—— *Michael Levi Rodkinson and Hasidism* [Shivḥei rodkinson: mikha'el levi frumkin-rodkinson vehaḥasidut] (Tel Aviv, 2012).

—— 'The Politics of Printing *Sefer likutei tefilot*' (Heb.), *Zion*, 80/1 (2015).

—— and G. SAGIV (eds.), *Habad Hasidism: History, Theology and Image* [Ḥabad: historyah, hagut vedimuy] (Jerusalem, 2016).

MEIR, N. M., *Kiev, Jewish Metropolis: A History, 1861–1914* (Bloomington, Ind., 2010).

MEIR BEN SIMEON OF NARBONNE, *Milḥemet mitsvah*, MS Parma 2749.

MEKLER, D. L., *From the Rebbe's Court (from Chernobyl to Talne)* [Fun rebins hoyf (fun chernobyl biz talne)], 2 vols. (New York, 1931).

MENAHEM MENDEL OF PRZEMYŚLANY, *Darkhei yesharim* (Zhitomir, 1805).

MENAHEM MENDEL OF VITEBSK, *Igerot hakodesh*, in *The Books of the Fathers of Hasidism in the Holy Land* [Sifrei avot haḥasidut be'erets hakodesh], vol. ii (n.p., n.d.).

—— *Likutei amarim* [Lemberg, 1911] (Brooklyn, 1961).

Me'ore'ot tsevi (Kopys, 1815).

MESHULAM FEIBUSH HELLER OF ZBARAŻ, *Derekh emet* (n.p., n.d.).

—— 'Yosher divrei emet', in *Likutim yekarim* (Jerusalem, 1974).

MEYER, M. A. (ed.), *German-Jewish History in Modern Times*, 4 vols. (New York, 1996–8).

MICHAELIS, O., 'The Path of Love and Awe in the Doctrine of the Magid R. Ber of Mezhirech' [Ahavah veyir'ah betorat hamagid mimezrich], MA thesis (Tel Aviv University, 2013).

MICHELSOHN, A., *Ohel elimelekh* (Przemyśl, 1910).

MILLER, M. (ed.), *The Nechoma Greisman Anthology—Wisdom from the Heart* (Jerusalem, 1993).

MINKIN, J. S., *The Romance of Hassidism*, 3rd edn. (Los Angeles, 1971).

MINTZ, A., 'Guenzburg, Lilienblum, and the Shape of Haskalah Autobiography', *Association of Jewish Studies Review*, 4 (1979).

MINTZ, J. R., *Legends of the Hasidim* (Chicago, 1968).

MONDSHINE, Y., 'The Books of *Matsref ha'avodah* and *Vikuḥa rabah*' (Heb.), *Alei sefer*, 5 (1978).

—— 'The Friendly Relations between the Holy *Admor* Rabbi Meir of Przemyślany and the Holy Gaon Rabbi Solomon Kluger' (Heb.), *Naḥalat tsevi*, 4 (1991).

—— 'Is It Really a Praise from *Shivḥei habesht*?' (Heb.), *Tarbiz*, 51 (1982).

—— *Migdal oz* (Kefar Habad, 1980).

—— *Otsar minhegei ḥabad—elul–tishrei* (Jerusalem, 1995).

—— *Otsar minhegei ḥabad—nisan–sivan* (Jerusalem, 1996).

—— 'The Story of R. Zalmina: Fictional Tales about the Old *Admor*' (Heb.), *Kerem ḥabad*, 4/2 (1992).

MORRIS, B. J., *Lubavitcher Women in America: Identity and Activism in the Postwar Era* (Albany, NY, 1998).

MORTIMER, R. C., *The Origins of Private Penance in the Western Church* (Oxford, 1939).

MOSELEY, M., *Being for Myself Alone: Origins of Jewish Autobiography* (Stanford, Calif., 2005).

Mystique et continence: Travaux scientifiques du VIIe Congrès international d'Avon, Études Carmélitaines (Bruges, 1952).

NACHT, J., *Mekor ḥayim* (Drohobycz, 1898).

NAHMAN OF BRATSLAV, *Likutei moharan* (New York, 1966).

—— *Sefer hamidot* [Mohilev, 1811] (New York, 1965).

NIGAL, G., 'A Chapter in the History of the Hasidic Tale' (Heb.), in *Sefer sipurei kedoshim*, ed. G. Nigal (Jerusalem, 1977).

—— *'Dybbuk' Tales in Jewish Literature* [Sipurei 'dibuk' besifrut yisra'el], 2nd edn. (Jerusalem, 1994).

—— 'Hasidic Doctrine in the Writings of R. Elimelekh of Lizhensk and His Contemporaries' [Mishnat haḥasidut bekhitvei rabi elimelekh milizhensk uvenei doro], Ph.D. diss. (Hebrew University, Jerusalem, 1972).

—— *The Hasidic Tale*, trans. E. Levin (Oxford, 2008).

—— 'In Praise of R. Hayim ben Attar' (Heb.), in G. Nigal, *West and East Studies* [Meḥkerei ma'arav umizraḥ] (Jerusalem, 2001).

—— (ed.), *Jacob Kaidaner,* Sipurim nora'im*: The Tales of a Habad Hasid* [Ya'akov kaidaner, sipurim nora'im: sipurav shel ish ḥabad] (Jerusalem, 1992).

—— *Leader and Congregation: Opinions and Parables in the Beginning of Hasidism According to the Writings of R. Jacob Joseph of Połonne* [Manhig ve'edah: de'ot umeshalim bereshit haḥasidut al pi kitvei r. ya'akov yosef mipolna'ah] (Jerusalem, 1962).

—— *Magic, Mysticism and Hasidism: The Supernatural in Jewish Thought* (Northvale, NJ, 1994).

—— *Rabbi Jacob Joseph of Połonne (Polna): Selected Writings* [Torot ba'al hatoledot: derashot rabi ya'akov yosef mipolna'ah lefi nose'ei yesod] (Jerusalem, 1974).

—— 'A Study in the History of the Hasidic Tale' (Heb.), in G. Nigal (ed.), *Sefer sipurei kedoshim* (Jerusalem, 1977).

—— 'Women in the Book *Shivḥei habesht*' (Heb.), *Molad*, 31[241] (1974), repr. in id., *Studies in Hasidism*, vol. ii [Meḥkarim baḥasidut] (Jerusalem, 1999).

NIGAL, G., *Women in Hasidic Hagiography* [Nashim basiporet haḥasidit] (Jerusalem, 2005).

OAKLEY, A., *Sex, Gender and Society*, rev. edn. (Aldershot, 1985).

OLESZAK, A., '"The Borderland": The Beys Yaakov School in Kraków as a Symbolic Encounter between East and West', in M. Galas and A. Polonsky (eds.), *Jews in Kraków*, Polin: Studies in Polish Jewry 23 (2011).

ORON, M., 'The Woman as Narrator in Hasidic Tales: A Fictional Device or Preservation of Tradition?' (Heb.), in D. Assaf et al. (eds.), *Studies in Eastern European Jewish History and Culture in Honor of Professor Shmuel Werses* [Mivilna liyerushalayim: meḥkarim betoledoteihem uvetarbutam shel yehudei mizraḥ eiropah mugashim liprofesor shemuel verses] (Jerusalem, 2002).

PACHTER, M., 'The Concept of *Devekut* in the Homiletical Ethical Writings of 16th-Century Safed', in i. Twersky (ed.), *Studies in Medieval Jewish History and Literature*, vol. ii (Cambridge, Mass., 1984).

PALMER, P. F. (ed.), *Sacraments and Forgiveness: History and Doctrinal Development of Penance, Extreme Unction and Indulgences*, Sources of Christian Theology 2 (Westminster, Md., 1960).

PARUSH, I., *Reading Jewish Women: Marginality and Modernization in Nineteenth-Century Eastern European Jewish Society*, trans. S. Sternberg (Waltham, Mass., 2004).

PEDAYA, H., 'On the Development of the Socio-Religious-Economic Model in Hasidism: *Pidyon*, *Ḥavurah*, and Pilgrimage' (Heb.), in M. Ben-Sasson (ed.), *Religion and Economy: Connections and Interactions* [Dat vekalkalah; yaḥasei gomelin] (Jerusalem, 1995).

Peri ha'arets (Zhitomir, 1867; facsimile edn. Jerusalem, 1970).

PERL, J., *Megaleh temirin* (Vienna, 1819); Eng. edn. *Revealer of Secrets*, trans. with an introduction and notes by D. Taylor (Boulder, Colo., 1997).

—— *Uiber das Wesen der Sekte Chassidim aus ihren eigenen Schriften gezogen im Jahre 1816*, ed. with introduction and annotations by A. Rubinstein (Jerusalem, 1977).

PERLOW, H. M., *An Anthology of Tales* [Likutei sipurim] (Kefar Habad, 1966).

Pe'ulat hatsadik (Jerusalem, 1981).

PIEKARZ, M., *The Beginning of Hasidism: Intellectual Trends in Derush and Musar Literature* [Biyemei tsemiḥat haḥasidut: megamot ra'ayoniyot besifrei derush umusar] (Jerusalem, 1978).

—— *Braslav Hasidism* [Ḥasidut braslav] (Jerusalem, 1972).

—— *The Hasidic Leadership: Authority and Faith in Tsadikim as Reflected in the Hasidic Literature* [Hahanhagah haḥasidit: samkhut ve'emunat tsadikim be'aspaklaryat sifrutah shel haḥasidut] (Jerusalem, 1999).

PLATO, *Timaeus* (New York, 1929).

POLEN, N., 'Miriam's Dance: Radical Egalitarianism in Hasidic Thought', *Modern Judaism*, 12/1 (Feb. 1992).

—— 'Rebbetzins, Wonder-Children, and the Emergence of the Dynastic Principle in Hasidism', in S. T. Katz (ed.), *The Shtetl: New Examinations* (New York, 2009).

PORTER, R., *Madness: A Brief History* (Oxford, 2002).

PORUSH, S. H., *Encyclopedia of Hasidism: Works* [Entsiklopedyah laḥasidut: sefarim], ed. Y. Rafael (Jerusalem, 1980).

RABINOWICZ, H., *A Guide to Hassidism* (New York, 1960).

—— *The World of Hassidism* (London, 1970).

RABINOWITSCH, W. Z., *Lithuanian Hasidism* (London, 1970).

RAFAEL, Y., 'The Kherson *Genizah*' (Heb.), in Y. Rafael, *On Hasidism and Its Adherents* [Al ḥasidut veḥasidim] (Jerusalem, 1991).

—— 'Shivḥei habesht', in Y. Rafael, *On Hasidism and Its Adherents* [Al ḥasidut veḥasidim] (Jerusalem, 1991).

RAPOPORT-ALBERT, A., 'Glikl Hamel as a Widow' (Heb.), in ead., *Studies in Hasidism, Sabbatianism, and Gender*.

—— '*Katnut*, *Peshitut*, and *Eini Yode'a* in Nahman of Bratslav' (Heb.), in ead., *Studies in Hasidism, Sabbatianism and Gender*.

—— *Studies in Hasidism, Sabbatianism, and Gender* [Ḥasidim veshabeta'im, anashim venashim] (Jerusalem, 2015).

—— *Women and the Messianic Heresy of Sabbatai Zevi 1666–1816* (Oxford, 2011).

—— and G. SAGIV, 'Habad versus "Polish Hasidism": Towards the History of a Dichotomy' (Heb.), in J. Meir and G. Sagiv (eds.), *Habad Hasidism: History, Theology and Image* [Ḥabad: historyah, hagut vedimuy] (Jerusalem, 2016).

RATSABI, S., 'Anti-Zionism and Messianic Tension in the Speculative Thought of Rabbi Shalom Dovber' (Heb.), *Hatsiyonut*, 20 (1996).

RAVITZKY, A., *Messianism, Zionism, and Jewish Religious Radicalism* [Hakets hameguleh umedinat hayehudim] (Tel Aviv, 1993).

REDDAWAY, W., et al. (eds.), *The Cambridge History of Poland*, 2 vols. (New York, 1978).

REIN, N., *Daughters of Israel* (Harmondsworth, 1980).

REINER, E., '*Shivḥei habesht*: Transmission, Editing, Printing' (Heb.), in *Proceedings of the Eleventh World Congress of Jewish Studies*, vol. ii (Jerusalem, 1994), division *c*.

RODKINSON (FRUMKIN), M. L., *Shivḥei harav* (Lemberg, 1864).

—— *Toledot amudei ḥabad* (Königsberg, 1876).

—— *Toledot ba'alei shem tov* (Königsberg, 1876).

ROEST, M., *Catalog der Hebraica und Judaica aus der L. Rosenthal'schen Bibliothek*, 2 vols. (Amsterdam, 1875).

ROI, B., *Love of Shekhinah: Mysticism and Poetics in Tikunei hazohar* [Ahavat ha-shekhinah: mistikah ufo'etikah betikunei hazohar] (Ramat Gan, 2017).

ROSENTHAL, J., *Sefer yosef hamekane* (Jerusalem, 1970).

ROSEN-ZVI, I., 'Do Women Have a *Yetzer*? Anthropology, Ethics, and Gender in Rabbinic Literature' (Heb.), in H. Kreisel, B. Huss, and U. Ehrlich (eds.), *Spiritual Authority: Struggles over Cultural Power in Jewish Thought* [Samkhut ruḥanit: ma'avakim al ko'aḥ tarbuti bahagut hayehudit] (Be'er Sheva, 2010).

—— 'Sexualising the Evil Inclination: Rabbinic "Yetzer" and Modern Scholarship', *Journal of Jewish Studies*, 60/2 (2009).

—— 'Two Rabbinic Inclinations? Rethinking a Scholarly Dogma', *Journal for the Study of Judaism*, 39 (2008).

ROSMAN, M., 'The Besht's Letters: Towards a New Assessment' (Heb.), in D. Assaf, J. Dan, and I. Etkes (eds.), *Studies in Hasidism* [Meḥkerei ḥasidut] (Jerusalem, 1999).

—— *Founder of Hasidism: A Quest for the Historical Ba'al Shem Tov* (Berkeley, Calif., 1996; 2nd edn. Oxford, 2013).

—— 'The History of a Historical Source: On the Editing of *Shivḥei habesht*' (Heb.), *Zion*, 58/2 (1993).

—— 'The Image of Poland as a Centre of Torah Learning after the 1648 Persecutions' (Heb.), *Zion*, 51 (1986).

—— 'In Praise of the Ba'al Shem Tov: A User's Guide to the Editions of *Shivhei haBesht*', in G. D. Hundert (ed.), *Jews in Early Modern Poland*, Polin: Studies in Polish Jewry 10 (1997).

—— 'Jewish Perceptions of Insecurity and Powerlessness in Sixteenth- to Eighteenth-Century Poland', in A. Polonsky (ed.), *Poles and Jews: Renewing the Dialogue*, Polin: Studies in Polish Jewry 1 (1986).

—— 'Miedzyboz and Rabbi Israel Baal Shem Tov', in G. D. Hundert (ed.), *Essential Papers on Hasidism: Origins to Present* (New York, 1991).

—— 'Observations on Women and Hasidism' (Heb.), in D. Assaf and A. Rapoport-Albert (eds.), *Let the Old Make Way for the New* [Yashan mipenei ḥadash: meḥkarim betoledot yehudei mizraḥ eiropah uvetarbutam, shai le'imanu'el etkes], vol. i (Jerusalem, 2009).

—— 'To Be a Jewish Woman in Poland-Lithuania of the Early Modern Period' (Heb.), in I. Bartal and I. Gutman (eds.), *The Broken Chain: Polish Jewry through the Ages* [Kiyum veshever: yehudei polin ledoroteihem], vol. ii (Jerusalem, 2001).

ROTH, A., 'The Habad Literary Corpus, Its Components and Distribution as the Basis for Reading Habad Text' [Hakorpus hasifruti haḥabadi: rekhivav vehafatsato kevasis likri'at tekst ḥabadi], Ph.D. diss. (Bar-Ilan University, 2012).

ROTHENBERG, J., *The Jewish Religion in the Soviet Union* (New York, 1971).

RUBIN, E., 'Emotive Intelligence: A Letter to Sonia Rozenblum by Rabbi

Yosef Yitzchak Schneersohn', <http://www.chabad.org/blogs/blog_cdo/aid/1744944/jewish/Emotive-Intelligence-A-Letter-to-Sonia-Rozenblum-by-Rabbi-Yosef-Yitzchak-Schneersohn.htm>, accessed 24 Jan. 2012.

RUBINSTEIN, A., 'Between Hasidism and Sabbatianism' (Heb.), in id. (ed.), *Studies in Hasidism* (Heb.).

—— 'A Praise from *Shivḥei habesht*' (Heb.), *Tarbiz*, 35 (1966).

—— 'The Revelation Stories in *Shivḥei habesht*' (Heb.), *Alei sefer*, 6–7 (1977).

—— 'Studies in the History of Hasidism' (Heb.), in id. (ed.), *Studies in Hasidism* (Heb.).

—— (ed.), *Studies in Hasidism* [Perakim betorat haḥasidut uvetoledoteiha] (Jerusalem, 1977).

RUDERMAN, P., 'An Overall Perspective on the Tsadikim and on the Hasidim' (Heb.), *Hashaḥar*, 6 (1875).

SA'ADYAH GAON, *Emunot vede'ot*, ed. Slucki (Leipzig, 1864).

SACK, B., 'Man as Mirror and the Theory of Mutual Responsibility' (Heb.), *Da'at*, 12 (1984).

—— 'Three Times of Redemption in R. Moses Cordovero's *Or yakar*' (Heb.), in Z. Baras (ed.), *Messianism and Eschatology* [Meshiḥiyut ve'eskhatologyah] (Jerusalem, 1984).

SAFRIN, I. J., *Megilat setarim*, ed. N. Ben-Menahem (Jerusalem, 1944).

SAGIV, G., 'The Chernobyl Hasidic Dynasty: Its History and Thought from Its Beginning to the Eve of the First World War' [Ḥasidut chernobil: toledoteiha vetoroteiha mereshitah ve'ad erev milḥemet ha'olam harishonah], Ph.D. diss. (Tel Aviv University, 2009).

—— *Dynasty: The Chernobyl Hasidic Dynasty and Its Place in the History of Hasidism* [Hashoshelet: beit chernobil umekomo betoledot haḥasidut] (Jerusalem, 2014).

—— 'The Rectification of the Covenant and the Element of Asceticism in Chernobyl Hasidism' (Heb.), in R. Elior (ed.), *'New Old Things': Myths, Mysticism and Controversies, Philosophy and Halakhah, Faith and Ritual in Jewish Thought through the Ages* ['Devarim ḥadashim atikim': mitos, mistikah ufulmus, filosofyah vehalakhah, emunah veritual bamaḥshavah hayehudit ledoroteiha], Jerusalem Studies in Jewish Thought 23, vol. ii (Jerusalem, 2011).

—— '"*Yenuka*": On Child Leaders in Hasidism' (Heb.), *Zion*, 76/2 (2011).

SCHATZ-UFFENHEIMER, R., *Hasidism as Mysticism: Quietistic Elements in Eighteenth-Century Hasidic Thought* (Princeton, NJ, 1993).

—— 'On the Nature of the Tsadik in Hasidism' (Heb.), *Molad*, 18/144–5 (1960).

SCHIMMEL, A., *Mystical Dimensions of Islam* (Chapel Hill, 1975).

SCHISCHA HALEVI, A., 'On the Book *Butsina dinehora*' (Heb.), *Alei sefer*, 8 (1980).

SCHNALL FRIEDFERTIG, R., and F. SHAPIRO (eds.), *The Modern Jewish Woman—A Unique Perspective* (Brooklyn, 1981).

SCHNEERSOHN, B. S., *Reshimot harabash* (Brooklyn, 2001).

SCHNEERSOHN, J. I., 'Avot haḥasidut', *Hatamim*, 2 vols. (Kefar Habad, 1975).

—— *Hayom Yom: From Day to Day*, ed. M. M. Schneerson (Brooklyn, 1988).

—— *The History of Rebbetsin Rivkah* [Divrei yemei harabanit rivkah] (Brooklyn, 2003).

—— *Igerot kodesh . . . yosef yitsḥak*, 17 vols. (Brooklyn, 1982–2011).

—— *Likutei diburim* (Yid.), 2 vols. (Brooklyn, 1984).

—— *Sefer hasiḥot 5680–5687* [1920–7] (Brooklyn, 1994).

—— *Sefer hasiḥot 5702* [1942] (Brooklyn, 1973).

—— *Sefer hasiḥot 5703–5* [1943–5] (Brooklyn, 1996).

—— *Sefer hazikhronot* (Heb.), 2 vols. (Kefar Habad, 1985).

—— *The 'Tzemach Tzedek' and the Haskala Movement* (Brooklyn, 1969).

SCHNEERSOHN, M. M. (the Tsemah Tsedek), *Tsemaḥ tsedek, Even ha'ezer*, 2 vols. [Vilna, 1871] (Brooklyn, 1994).

—— *Yahel or* (Brooklyn, 1953).

See also *Igerot kodesh . . . hatsemaḥ tsedek* above

SCHNEERSOHN, S. D., *Hemshekh 5672* [1912], Written but not Said, vol. iii (Brooklyn, 1977).

—— *Igerot kodesh . . . shalom dovber*, 5 vols. (Brooklyn, 1982–6).

—— *Kuntres uma'yan mibeit adonai* (Brooklyn, 1969).

—— *Sefer hama'amarim 5659* [1899] (Brooklyn, 1991).

—— *Torat shalom* (Brooklyn, 1957; 2nd edn. Brooklyn, 2003).

SCHNEERSOHN, SHEMUEL, *Likutei torah, torat shemuel 5627* [1867] (Brooklyn, 1981).

—— *Likutei torah, torat shemuel 5632* [1872], 2 vols. (Brooklyn, 1999).

—— *Likutei torah, torat shemuel 5633* [1873], 2 vols. (Brooklyn, 1994).

—— *Likutei torah, torat shemuel 5640* [1880], 2 vols. (Brooklyn, 2004).

—— *Likutei torah, torat shemuel 5641* [1881] (Brooklyn, 2006).

SCHNEERSON, M. M., *Igerot kodesh . . . menaḥem mendel*, 32 vols. (Brooklyn, 1987–).

—— *Letters by the Lubavitcher Rebbe to N'shei uBnos Chabad, 1956–1980* (Brooklyn, 1981).

—— *Likutei siḥot*, 39 vols. (Brooklyn, 1962–2001).

—— *Sefer hasiḥot 5750* (1990).

—— *Siḥot kodesh mikevod kedushato admor shelita milubavitch 5713* [1952–3], *bilti mugah* (Brooklyn, 1994).

—— *Torat menaḥem–hitva'aduyot 5710–23*, 36 vols. (Brooklyn, 1992–2007).

—— *Torat menaḥem–hitva'aduyot 5742–52*, 43 vols. (Brooklyn, 1990–4).

SCHOLEM, G., 'Devekut, or Communion with God', in id., *The Messianic Idea in Judaism*.

—— 'The First Two Testimonies on Hasidic Groups and the Besht' (Heb.), in id., *The Latest Phase: Essays on Hasidism* [Hashalav ha'aḥaron: meḥkerei haḥasidut shel gershom shalom], ed. D. Assaf and E. Liebes (Jerusalem, 2008).
—— 'The Historical Figure of R. Israel Ba'al Shem Tov' (Heb.), in id., *The Latest Phase: Essays on Hasidism by Gershom Scholem* [Hashalav ha'aḥaron: meḥkerei haḥasidut shel gershom shalom], ed. D. Assaf and E. Liebes (Jerusalem, 2008).
—— *Kabbalah* (Jerusalem, 1974).
—— *Major Trends in Jewish Mysticism* (New York, 1961).
—— 'Martin Buber's Interpretation of Hasidism', in id., *The Messianic Idea in Judaism*.
—— *The Messianic Idea in Judaism and Other Essays on Jewish Spirituality* (New York, 1971).
—— 'The Neutralization of the Messianic Element in Early Hasidism', in id., *The Messianic Idea in Judaism*.
—— 'On Israel Löbel and His Anti-Hasidic Polemics' (Heb.), in Gershom Scholem, *The Latest Phase: Essays on Hasidism by Gershom Scholem* [Hashalav ha'aḥaron: meḥkerei haḥasidut shel gershom shalom], ed. D. Assaf and E. Liebes (Jerusalem, 2008).
—— *On the Mystical Shape of the Godhead: Basic Concepts in the Kabbalah* (New York, 1991).
—— *Origins of the Kabbalah* (Princeton, NJ, 1987).
—— 'The Polemic against Hasidism and Its Leaders in the Book *Nezed ha-Dema*' (Heb.), in id., *The Latest Phase: Essays on Hasidism* [Hashalav ha'aḥaron: meḥkerei haḥasidut shel gershom shalom], ed. D. Assaf and E. Liebes (Jerusalem, 2008).
—— 'Politik der Mystik: Zu Isaac Breuers "Neuem Kusari"', *Jüdische Rundschau*, 57 (17 July 1934).
—— 'Reflections on *Wissenschaft des Judentums*' (Heb.), in id., *Explications and Implications: Writings on Jewish Heritage and Renaissance* [Devarim bego: pirkei morashah uteḥiyah] (Tel Aviv, 1975).
—— *Researches in Sabbatianism* [Meḥkerei shabeta'ut], ed. Y. Liebes (Tel Aviv, 1991).
—— *Sabbatai Ṣevi: The Mystical Messiah 1626–1676* (Princeton, NJ, 1973).
—— 'The Science of Judaism: Then and Now', in id., *The Messianic Idea in Judaism*.
—— *Studies and Texts Concerning the History of Sabbatianism and Its Metamorphoses* [Meḥkarim umekorot letoledot hashabeta'ut vegilguleiha] (Jerusalem, 1974).
SCHUCHAT, R., 'Lithuanian Kabbalah as an Independent Trend of Kabbalistic Literature' (Heb.), *Kabbalah: Journal for the Study of Jewish Mystical Texts*, 10 (2004).

SCHWARTZ, D., *Habad's Thought from Beginning to End* [Maḥshevet ḥabad mereshit ve'ad aḥarit] (Ramat Gan, 2010).

SCHWARZ, B., *My Life: My History and Memoirs* [Ḥayai: toledotai vezikhronotai] (Jerusalem, 1930).

SCHWARZ, M., *The Jews in the Soviet Union* (Syracuse, NY, 1952).

Sefer gezerot ashkenaz vetsarfat, ed. A. M. Habermann (Jerusalem, 1971).

Sefer ḥasidim (Bologna edn.), ed. R. Margaliot (Jerusalem, 1957).

Sefer ḥasidim (Parma edn.), ed. J. Wistinetzki, introd. J. Freimann (Frankfurt am Main, 1924).

Sefer sipurei kedoshim, ed. G. Nigal (Jerusalem, 1976).

SEGAL, Y. H., *Beit halevi* (Lemberg, 1910).

SEIDMAN, N., 'Reflections on a Belated Apostasy', *Contemplate: The International Journal of Cultural Jewish Thought*, 3 (2005/6).

SELTZER, R. M., 'The Secular Appropriation of Hasidism by an East European Jewish Intellectual: Dubnow, Renan, and Besht', in A. Polonsky (ed.), *Poles and Jews: Renewing the Dialogue*, Polin: Studies in Polish Jewry 1 (1986).

SHAHAR, S., *The Fourth Order: Women in Medieval Society* [Hama'amad harevi'i: ha'ishah beḥevrat yemei habeinayim] (Tel Aviv, 1983).

SHAPIRO, M., *The Rebbe's Daughter*, trans. and ed., with introduction and commentary, N. Polen (Philadelphia, 2002).

SHAROT, S., *Messianism, Mysticism, and Magic: A Sociological Analysis of Jewish and Religious Movements* (Chapel Hill, NC, 1982).

SHEMEN, N., *Attitudes to Women* [Batsiung tsu der froy], 2 vols. (Buenos Aires, 1969).

Shivḥei haba'al shem tov: A Facsimile of a Unique Manuscript, Variant Versions, and Appendices [Sefer shivḥei habesht: faksimil miketav-hayad hayeḥidi hanoda lanu veshinuyei nusaḥav le'umat nusaḥ hadefus], ed. Y. Mondshine (Jerusalem, 1982).

Shivḥei habesht (Berdiczów, 1815).

Shivḥei habesht (Łaszczów, 1815).

Shivḥei habesht, ed. S. A. Horodetsky [Berlin, 1922] (Tel Aviv, 1947).

Shivḥei habesht, ed. B. Mintz (Tel Aviv, 1961).

Shivḥei habesht, ed. I. Yofeh (Kopys, 1814).

Shivḥei habesht (Yid.) [Korzec, 1816] (Jerusalem, 1965).

SHMERUK, C., 'The Jewish Community and Jewish Agricultural Settlement in Soviet Belorussia (1918–1932)' [Hakibuts hayehudi vehahityashevut hayehudit bebelorusyah hasovyetit], Ph.D. diss., Heb. with Eng. summary (Hebrew University, 1961).

—— 'The Social Implications of Hasidic Ritual Slaughtering' (Heb.), *Zion*, 20 (1955); repr. in *A Call for a Prophet*, ed. I Bartal (Jerusalem, 1999).

——*Yiddish Literature: Aspects of Its History* [Sifrut yidish: perakim letoledoteiha] (Tel Aviv, 1978).

——*Yiddish Literature in Poland: Historical Studies and Perspectives* [Sifrut yidish bepolin: meḥkarim ve'iyunim historiyim] (Jerusalem, 1981).

SHMUELI, E., *In the Last Jewish Generation in Poland* [Bador hayehudi ha'aḥaron bepolin] (Tel Aviv, 1986).

SHNEUR ZALMAN OF LIADY, *Hilkhot talmud torah* (Brooklyn, 1968).

——*Likutei amarim—tanya* (Brooklyn, 1973).

——*Likutei torah* (Brooklyn, 1976).

——*Ma'amerei admor hazaken 5566* [1806], 2 vols. (Brooklyn, 2004).

——*Ma'amerei admor hazaken 5569* [1809] (Brooklyn, 2005).

——*Ma'amerei admor hazaken 5572* [1812] (Brooklyn, 2006).

——*Ma'amerei admor hazaken haketsarim* (Brooklyn, 1981).

——*Ma'amerei admor hazaken al parshiyot hatorah vehamo'adim*, 2 vols. (Brooklyn, 1982).

——*Seder tefilot mikol hashanah al pi nusaḥ ha'ari z"l* (Kopys, 1816).

——*Torah or* (Brooklyn, 1976).

See also *Igerot kodesh admor hazaken* . . . above

SHOHET, A., 'On Joy in Hasidism' (Heb.), *Zion*, 16 (1951).

SHULVASS, A., 'Torah Study in Poland and Lithuania' (Heb.), in I. Halpern (ed.), *The Jewish People in Poland* [Beit yisra'el bepolin], vol. ii (Jerusalem, 1953).

Siaḥ sarfei kodesh, 8 vols. (Jerusalem, 1994–2009).

SIMHAH BUNEM OF PSHISCHA, *Kol mevaser* (Ra'ananah, 1991).

SIMON, E., and J. E. HELLER, *Ahad Ha'am: The Man and His Works* [Aḥad ha'am: ha'ish ufo'olo] (Jerusalem, 1955).

SISMAN, C., *The Burden of Silence: Sabbatai Sevi and the Evolution of the Ottoman Turkish Dönmes* (Oxford, 2015).

SMITH, M., *Rabi'a the Mystic and her Fellow-Saints in Islam* (Cambridge, 1928).

SPERLING, A. I., *Sefer ta'amei haminhagim umekorei hadinim* (Jerusalem, 1972).

STAMPFER, S., *Families, Rabbis, and Education: Traditional Jewish Society in Nineteenth-Century Eastern Europe* (Oxford, 2010).

——'The Impact of Hasidism on the Jewish Family in Eastern Europe: Towards a Re-Evaluation' (Heb.), in D. Assaf and A. Rapoport-Albert (eds.), *Let the Old Make Way for the New: Studies in the Social and Cultural History of Eastern European Jewry Presented to Immanuel Etkes* [Yashan mipenei ḥadash: meḥkarim betoledot yehudei mizraḥ eiropah uvetarbutam shai le'imanuel etkes], vol. i (Jerusalem, 2009).

——*Lithuanian Yeshivas of the Nineteenth Century: Creating a Tradition of Learning*, trans. Lindsey Taylor-Guthartz (Oxford, 2012).

——'Patterns of Internal Jewish Migration in the Russian Empire', in Y. Ro'i (ed.), *Jews and Jewish Life in Russia and the Soviet Union* (Portland, Oreg., 1995).

STANISLAWSKI, M., *Tsar Nicholas I and the Jews: The Transformation of Jewish Society in Russia, 1825–1855* (Philadelphia, 1983).

STERN, E. Z., *Siḥot yekarim* (Satu-Mare, n.d.).

STERNHARZ, N., *Ḥayei moharan*, 2 vols. (Jerusalem, 1947).

—— *Likutei halakhot*, 8 vols. (Jerusalem, 1940–63).

—— *Likutei tefilot* (Jerusalem, 1957).

—— *Shivḥei haran* (Lemberg, 1901).

—— *Siḥot haran* [with *Shivḥei haran*] (Lemberg, 1901).

—— *Yemei moharnat* (Benei Berak, 1956).

STITES, R., *The Women's Liberation Movement in Russia* (Princeton, 1978).

SZASZ, T. S., *The Manufacture of Madness* (London, 1971).

TAUBENHAUS, E., *On the Path of the Individual* [Binetiv hayaḥid] (Haifa, 1959).

TAYLOR, D., *Joseph Perl's Revealer of Secrets: The First Hebrew Novel* (Boulder, Colo., 1996).

TEITELBAUM, M., *Iyun tefilah* (Łódź, 1926).

—— *The Rabbi of Liady and the Habad Faction* [Harav miliadi umifleget ḥabad], 2 vols. (Warsaw, 1914).

TELLER, A., 'Hasidism and the Challenge of Geography: The Polish Background to the Spread of the Hasidic Movement', *AJS Review*, 30/1 (2006).

—— 'The Słuck Tradition Concerning the Early Days of the Besht' (Heb.), in D. Assaf, J. Dan, and I. Etkes (eds.), *Studies in Hasidism* [Meḥkerei ḥasidut] (Jerusalem, 1999).

TISHBY, I., 'The Messianic Idea and Messianic Trends in the Formative Period of Hasidism' (Heb.), in id., *Studies* in *Kabbalah and Its Branches* [Ḥikerei kabalah usheluḥoteiha], vol. ii (Jerusalem, 1993).

—— *Mishnat hazohar* (Jerusalem, 1971); Eng. trans. *The Wisdom of the Zohar: An Anthology of Texts*, trans. D. Goldstein, 3 vols. (Oxford, 1989).

—— and J. DAN, 'The Doctrine and Literature of Hasidism' (Heb.), in *Encyclopaedia Hebraica* [Ha'entsiklopedyah ha'ivrit], xvii. 788–9; repr. in A. Rubinstein (ed.), *Studies in Hasidism* [Perakim betorat haḥasidut uvetoledoteiha] (Jerusalem, 1977).

Toledot ha'ari, ed. M. Benayahu (Jerusalem, 1967).

TOUITOU, E., *Rabbi Hayim ben Attar and His Commentary* Or haḥayim *on the Torah* [Rabi ḥayim ben atar uferusho or haḥayim al hatorah] (Jerusalem, 1981).

TRIMINGHAM, S., *The Sufi Orders in Islam* (Oxford, 1971).

Tsava'at harivash, ed. J. I. Schochet (Brooklyn, 1975).

TURNIANSKY, C., 'Towards the History of the "*Taytsh Khumesh*"—"*Khumesh mit Khiber*"' (Heb.), in *Considerations of Literature: Lectures in Honour of Dov Sadan on the Occasion of His Eightieth Birthday* [Iyunim besifrut: devarim shene'emru be'erev likhvod dov sadan bimelot lo shemonim shanah] (Jerusalem, 1988).

—— 'Yiddish and the Transmission of Knowledge in Early Modern Europe', *Jewish Studies Quarterly*, 15/1 (2008).

TWERSKY, Y., *The Maiden of Ludmir* [Habetulah miludmir] (Jerusalem [1950]).

TWOREK, W., 'Time and Gender in the Teachings of R. Shneur Zalman of Liady' (Heb.), in J. Meir and G. Sagiv (eds.), *Habad Hasidism: History, Theology and Image* [Ḥabad: historyah, hagut vedimuy] (Jerusalem, 2016).

—— 'Time in the Teaching of Rabbi Shneur Zalman of Liadi', Ph.D. diss. (University College London, 2014).

UNDERHILL, E., *Mysticism* (London, 1960).

URBACH, E. E., 'Études sur la littérature polémique au moyen-age', *Revue des études juives*, 197–8 (1935).

—— *The Sages: Their Concepts and Beliefs* (Cambridge, Mass., 1987).

—— *The World of the Sages: Collected Studies* [Me'olamam shel ḥakhamim: kovets meḥkarim] (Jerusalem, 1988).

URY, S., *Barricades and Banners: The Revolution of 1905 and the Transformation of Warsaw Jewry* (Stanford, Calif., 2012).

Vikuḥa rabah (Munkács, 1894).

VILNAI (WERSES), S., 'Autobiography in the Haskalah Era' (Heb.), in id., *Trends and Forms in Haskalah Literature* [Megamot vetsurot besifrut hahaskalah] (Jerusalem, 1990).

VITAL, H., *Sha'ar hagilgulim* (Tel Aviv, 1963).

—— *Sha'ar hamitsvot* (Tel Aviv, 1962).

WALDEN, A., *Shem hagedolim heḥadash* (Warsaw, 1870).

WALDEN, P., *Nifle'ot harabi* (Warsaw, 1911).

WATKINS, O. D., *A History of Penance*, 2 vols. (London, 1920).

WEIL, E., 'The Beginning of the Women's Era: Women and Femininity in the Teaching of the Lubavitcher Rebbe' (Heb.), *Akdamot*, 22 (2009).

WEINRYB, B. D., *The Jews of Poland* (Philadelphia, 1973).

WEINSTEIN, D., and R. M. BELL, *Saints and Society* (Chicago, 1982).

WEISS, J. G., 'The Beginnings of Hasidism' (Heb.), *Zion*, 16 (1951); repr. in A. Rubinstein (ed.), *Studies in Hasidism* [Perakim betorat haḥasidut uvetoledoteiha] (Jerusalem, 1977).

—— 'The Besht's Method of Torah Study' (Heb.), in H. J. Zimmels, J. Rabbinowitz, and I. Feinstein (eds.), *Essays Presented to Chief Rabbi Israel Brody on the Occasion of His Seventieth Birthday* (London, 1968).

—— 'A Circle of Pneumatics in Pre-Hasidism', *Journal of Jewish Studies*, 8 (1957); repr. in id., *Studies in Eastern European Jewish Mysticism*.

—— 'The Kavvanoth of Prayer in Early Hasidism', *Journal of Jewish Studies*, 9 (1958); repr. in id., *Studies in Eastern European Jewish Mysticism*.

—— 'Megilat setarim' (Heb.), *Kiryat sefer*, 44 (1969).

WEISS, J. G., 'R. Abraham Kalisker's Concept of Communion with God and Man', *Journal of Jewish Studies*, 6 (1955); repr. in id., *Studies in Eastern European Jewish Mysticism*.

—— 'Some Notes on the Social Background of Early Hasidism', in id., *Studies in Eastern European Jewish Mysticism*.

—— *Studies in Braslav Hasidism* [Meḥkarim beḥasidut bratslav] (Jerusalem, 1974).

—— *Studies in Eastern European Jewish Mysticism*, ed. D. Goldstein (Oxford, 1985; 2nd edn. Oxford, 1997).

WEISSBERG, I. J., *Ga'on vashever* (Warsaw, 1884).

WEISSLER, C., *Voices of the Matriarchs* (Boston, 1998).

WEISSMAN, D., 'Bais Yaakov: A Historical Model for Jewish Feminists', in E. Koltun (ed.), *The Jewish Woman* (New York, 1976).

—— 'Bais Yaakov: A Women's Educational Movement in the Polish Jewish Community: A Case Study in Tradition and Modernity', MA thesis (New York University, n.d.).

WERBLOWSKY, R. J. Z., *Joseph Karo: Lawyer and Mystic* (Oxford, 1962).

WERSES, S., *Haskalah and Sabbatianism: The Story of a Controversy* [Haskalah veshabeta'ut: toledotav shel ma'avak] (Jerusalem, 1988).

—— *Joseph Perl and His Literary Legacy* [Ginzei yosef perl], ed. J. Meir (Tel Aviv, 2013).

—— 'Women in the Hasidic Courts as Reflected in Mitnagdic Polemics and Maskilic Satires' (Heb.), *Gal-ed*, 21 (2007).

WERTHEIM, A., *Law and Custom in Hasidism*, trans. S. Himelstein (Hoboken, NJ, 1992).

WIENER, M., *Judaism in the Era of Emancipation* [Hadat hayehudit bitekufat ha'emantsipatsyah], trans. L. Zagagi (Jerusalem, 1974).

WILENSKY, M., *Hasidim and Mitnagedim* [Ḥasidim umitnagedim], 2 vols. (Jerusalem, 1970).

WILSON, B. R., 'A Typology of Sects', in R. Robertson (ed.), *Sociology of Religion* (London, 1969).

WINKLER, G., *They Called Her Rebbe: The Maiden of Ludmir* (New York, 1991).

WODZIŃSKI, M., 'L'Affaire des "Chasydymów": Matériaux pour l'histoire des Hassidim dans le Royaume de Pologne', *Tsafon: Revue d'études juives du Nord*, 29 (1997).

—— *Hasidism and Politics: The Kingdom of Poland, 1815–1864* (Oxford, 2013).

—— *Haskalah and Hasidism in the Kingdom of Poland: A History of Conflict* (Oxford, 2005).

—— '"Sprawa chasydymów": Z materiałów do dziejów chasydyzmu w Królestwie Polskim', in K. Matwijowski (ed.), *Z historii ludności żydowskiej w Polsce i na Śląsku* (Wrocław, 1994).

—— 'Women in Hasidism: A "Non-Sectarian" Perspective', *Jewish History*, 27/2–4 (Dec. 2013).

WOLFSON, E. R., *Open Secret: Postmessianic Messianism and the Mystical Revision of Menaḥem Mendel Schneerson* (New York, 2009).

YA'ARI, A., 'Two Basic Editions of *Shivḥei habesht*' (Heb.), *Kiryat sefer*, 39 (1964).

YERUSHALMI, Y. H., *Zakhor: Jewish History and Jewish Memory* (Seattle, 1982).

The YIVO Encyclopedia of Jews in Eastern Europe, ed. G. D. Hundert, 2 vols. (New Haven, 2008).

YOSHOR, M. M., *The Hafets Hayim: His Life and Work* [Haḥafets ḥayim, ḥayav ufo'olo], 2 vols. (Tel Aviv, 1959).

YUVAL, I. J., 'An Ashkenazi Autobiography from the Fourteenth Century' (Heb.), *Tarbiz*, 55 (1986).

ZEVI ELIMELEKH OF DYNÓW, *Agra dekhalah* (New York, 1964).

ZIMBALIST ROSALDO, M., 'Woman, Culture, and Society: A Theoretical Overview', in M. Zimbalist Rosaldo and L. Lamphere (eds.), *Woman, Culture, and Society* (Stanford, 1974).

The Zohar: Pritzker Edition, trans. D. C. Matt, vol. v (Stanford, Calif., 2009).

ZWEIFEL, E. Z. HAKOHEN, *Shalom al yisra'el*, 3 vols. (Zhitomir, 1868–9; Vilna, 1873); partial reprint, ed. A. Rubinstein (Jerusalem, 1972).

Index

A

Aaron (disciple of Nahman of Bratslav) 166, 167, 168–9, 174
Aaron of Apta 306 n.32
Aaron of Belz 420 n.120
Aaron of Karlin 40, 119 n.201, 154 n.46
Aaron Halevi of Starosielce 101 n.73, 354 n.41, 371, 428
Abraham (father of Phinehas of Korets) 74, 120–1 n.210
Abraham (patriarch) 280, 283, 432
Abraham the Angel (son of the Magid):
  leadership issues 24, 45, 84–5 n.2, 100 n.76, 102–3 n.76, 114 n.176, 217–19, 223–4, 256 n.121, 257 n.124
  wife, 297
Abraham of Kalisk:
  Belarus hasidim 49, 100 n.68, 116 n.187, 252 n.102, 260 n.146
  disciple of the Magid 3, 39–40, 42–3
  dispute with Shneur Zalman of Liady 39, 62, 78, 116 n.187
  emigration to Erets Yisra'el 66, 260 n.146, 116 n.187, 252 n.102, 260 n.146
  foundation of court 3, 39–40, 42–3, 98 n.57
  friendship with Nahman of Bratslav 59–60
  relationship with the Magid 42–3, 64, 98 n.57, 100 n.72, 116 n.187
  role after death of the Magid 66
  style of hasidism 42–3, 78
Abraham of Szarogród 207, 208–10, 214, 247 n.41
Abraham of Trisk 353 n.39
Abraham Hazan of Tulchin 173, 189 n.19, 192 nn.38, 39
Abraham Jacob of Sadagora 425 n.155
Abraham Matityahu of Ştefăneşti 425 n.155
Adam Ba'al Shem 214–16, 250–1 n.88
Aescoly, Aaron Zeev 201, 206, 208
Ahad Ha'am 199–200
Akiva (tannaitic sage) 109 n.131, 345 n.18
Alexander I, Tsar 63, 230
Aryeh Judah Leyb (Mokhiah of Połonne) 28–9, 32, 72, 137
Aryeh Leyb (Zeyde of Shpola) 60, 64, 86 n.5, 148–9, 180
Asher of Karlin 85 n.5, 119 n.201
Assaf, David 355 n.43, 398–9
Avigdor, deposed rabbi of Pinsk 85 n.5, 164
Azulai, Abraham 159 n.76

B

Ba'al Shem Tov (the Besht, Israel ben Eliezer):
  circle of 26–9, 31–3, 45, 72–4, 77, 90 n.17, 94–5 n.36, 137, 140
  company of 'secret tsadikim' 216–17, 219, 222–3, 227–31, 233, 236, 260 n.152
  confession to 167, 190 n.26, 191 n.35
  conventional account of 23–4, 42, 78
  daughter Edl 350–2 nn.35, 36, 399
  death of 11, 18, 34, 36–8, 45, 97 n.53, 208
  descendants 54–9, 61, 108–9 nn.123, 124, 225
  devekut 5, 125–30, 134–6, 143
  disciples as associates 3, 26–30, 32–6
  distribution of *lekakh* 401
  Dov Ber of Linits's account of 290–3, 296–7
  Dubnow's account of 2–3, 6, 201
  forged correspondence 13, 97 n.37, 210, 213–14, 216–17, 250–1 n.88
  'founder' of hasidic movement 2, 4, 6, 10–11, 23, 289
  God of 138–9
  granddaughter Feyge 16, 297, 353 n.36
  grandson Barukh of Międzybóż 54–6, 58–9, 152 n.19, 225

Ba'al Shem Tov (*cont.*):
grandson Ephraim of Sudyłków 156 n.54
great-grandson Nahman of Bratslav 54, 56–9, 61
Habad 'biography' of 250–1 n.88
historical figure of 200–10
image of 6, 246 n.48, 290–1
Israel Yofeh's account of 291–4
Joseph Isaac Schneersohn's account of 227–33, 241–2, 263 n.165
Kherson documents 210, 213–19, 222–3, 250–1 n.88
knowledge of the Law 247 n.46
leadership 10, 23, 26–9, 54–5, 78, 87 n.10, 93 n.33, 218, 227
letters by 244 n.17
manufactured evidence for 207, 208, 210, 214–16, 218–19, 222–3
method of study 136, 153 n.38, 156 n.52
miracles 88 n.10, 139, 241
mission to 'rectify' sinful souls 313 n.81
name 2, 212
period of concealment 203, 216–17, 222, 227, 236, 260 n.152, 291–6
powers of 27–8, 88 n.10, 136, 139, 141, 292–3
prayer 141–2
prophetic insight of 287
region of residence 208, 250 n.81
relationship with 'disciples' 26–9
relationship with God 138–40
relationship with the Magid 96–7 n.47
relationship with Nahman of Kosów 26–8, 29, 78, 89–90 n.16, 137, 287
role as a *ba'al shem* 4, 315 n.109
role in formation of hasidism 10, 72
Scholem's account of 5–6, 151–2 n.9, 246 n.36
scribe 286
Shivḥei habesht, see *Shivḥei habesht*
son Zevi 34, 36, 84–5 n.2, 102 n.76, 217–18, 228, 259 n.146
sources for history of 12–14, 202–6
status of 2–3, 10–12, 26–9, 33–4, 38, 54–5, 115–16 n.184, 246 n.38, 341 n.11
'streams of wisdom' 96 n.47, 251–2 n.93, 259 n.143
successor 34–9, 218–19, 226
teachings 126–31, 144, 156 n.54
Bałaban, Majer 214
Barukh (father of Shneur Zalman of Liady) 233
Barukh of Międzybóż:
Butsina dinehora attribution 56, 351 n.36
character 54
court 80, 85 n.5
friction with contemporaries 55
grandson of the Besht 54, 56, 58, 108 n.123, 109 n.124, 225, 258 n.134
leadership claim 54–5, 58
relationship with Nahman of Bratslav 58–9, 60, 78, 112 n.152
relationship with Shneur Zalman of Liady 55–6, 60, 86 n.5, 106 n.115, 108 n.123, 109 n.124, 225, 258 n.134
relationship with the Zeyde of Shpola 64
on rise to leadership 106 n.109
on role of tsadik 152 n.19
sister Feyge 297, 350 n.35
Beit Rivkah schools 391, 440, 443, 470 n.107
Beit Sarah schools 443, 470 n.107
Beit Ya'akov schools 347 n.20, 364 n.83, 391, 402 n.10, 439
Belarus:
Abraham of Kalisk's congregation 40, 49, 66, 67, 100 n.68, 116 n.187, 252 n.102, 260 n.146
annexed to Russia 23, 49, 51
Habad hasidism in 117 n.188, 224, 236, 252–3 n.102
Lubavitch town 113 n.161, 236
Menahem Mendel of Vitebsk's hasidim 49, 66, 67, 100 n.68, 224, 252 n.102, 260 n.146
Shneur Zalman of Liady's position 66, 67, 86 n.5, 224, 252 n.102, 260 n.146
Ben Attar Hayim (Or Hahayim) 390, 419–20 nn.109, 110
Ben Azai 109 n.131, 345 n.18
Bender, Levi Isaac 103 n.81, 191 n.30, 192 n.38, 459 n.17
Berdiczów, conferences 63, 64, 114 n.173

Bergson, Temerel 404 n.11
Beruriah 301 n.9
Besht, the, *see* Ba'al Shem Tov
Beyle, daughter of the Mitteler Rebbe 423 n.146
body–soul binary 30, 33, 128–9, 133, 195 n.58, 260 n.152, 271, 280, 281, 283, 299, 301 n.9, 431, 451
bone-aches 167, 190 n.26, 195 n.58
Brokman, Mordecai 70
Buber, Martin 5, 6, 158 n.72, 341 n.11

C

Carlyle, Thomas 199
celibacy and sexual abstinence, *see* sex
Chajes, J. H. 302 n.12
Chernobyl hasidism:
  asceticism 361 n.75
  dynasty 103 n.77, 119 n.201, 330, 457
Coenen, Thomas 272
Cohen, Nathan 420 n.114
confession:
  absolution 9, 174–5, 186
  addressed directly to God 182, 186
  adherence to the tsadik 164, 177–8
  before the Ari 163–4, 186
  before Nahman of Bratslav 165–98, 192 n.38
  Christian 161–2, 186, 187
  ended at Nahman of Bratslav's court 180–1, 185
  hitkarvut (initiation) 166–9, 171–2, 174, 178–81, 189 n.21
  initiation ceremony 165–74, 180–1
  Jewish attitudes to 162–3, 187
  origin of institution in Bratslav 186–7
  viduynikes (confessors) 168, 172, 180, 181, 193 n.42, 194 n.44
Conversos 273–4
Cossack uprising (1648) 2, 231, 261 n.156
Council of Four Lands 47, 52–3, 86–7 n.6, 105 n.101, 247 n.46
Czartoryski family 205

D

David of Lelów 69–70, 119 n.201
David of Maków 95 n.40, 97 n.48, 164–5, 307 n.34
David Moses of Czortków 425 n.155
Deutsch, Nathaniel 367 n.85, 402 n.8
devekut (communion with God):
  attaining 8, 125, 127, 135–6, 140, 143
  Besht's teachings 5, 125–31, 134–6, 141, 143
  constant 125–7, 143
  for members of spiritual elite 8, 9, 31, 140
  gap between ordinary people and 'spiritual men' 129–30, 133–6, 144
  kabbalistic idea of 124–6, 141–2, 143
  Magid's position on 144–5
  Menahem Mendel of Przemyślany's position 155–6 n.52
  Meshulam Feibush Heller's position 143
  Nahman of Kosów's position 125–6
  Scholem's account of in hasidism 5–6, 8, 124, 132–3, 155 n.47
  tsadik's role in 70, 145–6
Dinur, Ben-Zion 4–5, 6, 27, 90 n.17, 136–7, 139
Dov Ber (the Mitteler Rebbe):
  agricultural policy 230
  attitude to women 375–6
  daughter 423 n.146
  disciples 374, 429
  dispute with Aaron Halevi 101 nn.73, 74, 428
  false accusations against 232
  miracles 376, 409 n.44
  mother 394–5, 428
  ordinances 408 n.36
  sister's education 371
  teachings 462 n.29
  wife 422 n.132
  Yiddish works 350 n.34, 427, 429
Dov Ber of Linits 12, 286, 287, 290–3, 296–7
Dov Ber of Mezhirech, *see* Magid of Mezhirech
Dresner, Samuel 36, 144, 158 n.72
Dubnow, Simon:
  on Berdiczów conferences 63, 64
  construction of hasidic history 2–4, 8, 9
  criticisms of hagiographical sources 212

Dubnow, Simon (*cont.*):
history of hasidism 1–4, 247 n.38, 250 n.67
on image of the Besht 201–2
on reports of women at hasidic courts 346 n.20
on rise of hasidism 261–2 n.156
on women's position in hasidism 358 n.55, 406 n.15

E

Edl, daughter of the Ba'al Shem Tov 350–2 nn.35, 36, 399
Edl, daughter of Nahman of Bratslav 297
Eichenstein, Zevi Hirsch 289, 313 n.85
Ein Sof (infinity) 177–8
Eisenstadt, Meir 163
Eleazar of Amsterdam 205, 246 n.34
Elijah, the Ba'al Shem of Worms 233
Elijah ben Solomon Zalman, *see* Vilna Gaon
Elijah of Sokołówka 142
Elimelekh of Grodzisk 353 n.39
Elimelekh of Lizhensk:
on affinity of souls 68–9, 123 n.243
brother Zusya 99 n.66, 115 n.184, 172
daughter 353 n.39
death 119 n.201
disciple of the Magid 3, 115–16 n.184
disciples 69, 101 n.74, 118 n.194
on female soul 308 n.36
on role of tsadik 147, 309 n.57
successor to the Magid 115–16 n.184, 257 n.129
successors 119 n.201
use of formula 'children, long life and sustenance' 454
Elior, Rachel 256 n.120, 262 n.156
Emden, Jacob 207, 209–10, 214, 247 n.41, 288
Enlightenment, Jewish (Haskalah):
autobiographical genre 245 n.19
Habad campaign against 232, 280–1, 387, 436
relationship with hasidism 211–13, 238, 260 n.152
see also *maskilim*
Ephraim of Luntshits 461 n.26
Ephraim of Sudyłków 107 n.120, 156 n.54, 297, 308 n.36, 350 n.35
Epstein, Kalonymos Kalman, of Kraków 119 n.200, 311–12 n.68, 363 n.80, 404 n.12, 434
eschatology:
elevation of the female 305 n.23, 432–3, 436, 449
Habad approach 434–5, 442, 449, 452, 456
inversion of gender hierarchy 305 n.23, 432–3, 436, 444, 446, 449
kabbalistic 305 n.23, 436, 449
Sabbatian 273, 340 n.9
'upside-down' world order 404 n.12, 434, 445
women in Paradise 271, 444
Esman, Barukh 405 n.14
Ettinger, Shmuel 24, 25, 93–4 n.33
exorcism 293
Eydele, daughter of Shalom Roke'ah of Bełz 353 n.39, 359 n.67, 422–3 n.138
Ezra, the Prophet of Montcontour 310 n.65

F

Feyge, granddaughter of the Besht, mother of Nahman of Bratslav 16, 59, 297, 350 n.35, 353 n.36
Flatto, Sharon 303 n.15
food at hasidic court 396–401
Foxbrunner, R. F. 256 n.120
Frank, Eva 299, 320
Frank, Jacob 207, 270, 272, 320
Frankists:
court 271, 305 n.22
disputation in Lwów 207, 209, 214, 232, 256 n.121
messianism 207, 270, 434
rabbinic campaign against 105 n.101
relationship with hasidism 231–2
sex and celibacy 305 n.22
women's position 412 n.67
Freyde, daughter of Shneur Zalman of Liady 353 n.39, 354 n.41, 371, 399, 427–8

G

Galicia:
  agricultural settlement of Jews 230
  annexed to Austria 23
  anti-hasidic agitation 259 n.146, 276
  arrival of hasidism 215, 358 n.54
  ḥerem against hasidim 42
  Israel Loebel in 105 n.96
  Israel of Ruzhin in 50
  maskilim and hasidim 276
  mitnagedim and hasidim 23, 42
Garelik, Moses Nahman 401
Gedaliah of Linits 80
gender:
  'female' in hasidism 280–4, 430–1, 436–7
  female and male *sefirot* 280, 430–1
  female relatives of tsadikim 395
  hierarchy in hasidism 15, 16, 19, 443–4, 446
  inverted gender hierarchy 305 n.23, 432–5, 436, 443–5, 446, 449–51
  Jewish law 272
  norms in hasidism 371, 427
  norms in rabbinic Judaism 299
  Sabbatianism 299
  tsadik and followers 283–4
  violation of gender boundary 15, 331, 333, 359 n.67
Gershon of Kuty 29, 32, 90 n.17, 213–14, 216, 292–5
Glitzenstein, Abraham H. 114 n.180, 115 n.184
Gottlober, Abraham Ber 49–50, 63–4
Graetz, Heinrich 212
Greisman, Nechoma 447
Gries, Zeev 116 n.187, 156 n.52, 253 n.102, 352 n.36
Gurarie, Shemaryah 464 n.47

H

Habad:
  area of influence (nineteenth century) 49–50
  attitude to miracle-working 241–2, 260–1 n.152, 378
  Belarusian 117 n.188, 224
  'biography' of the Besht 250–1 n.88
  centralized court 66
  definition of Habad path 239
  education of women 371, 389–91, 406 n.21, 464–5, n.47, 468 n.74
  'family purity' associations 388–9
  founder 56, 219, 238, 314 n.92, 380
  hagiography 225–6, 236–7, 238–9, 242–3, 266 n.192, 374–6, 429, 430
  Hatamim (periodical) 100 n.67, 220, 352 n.36
  historians 221–2, 238, 255–6 n.118
  historiography 13–14, 62–3, 65–8, 102 n.76, 107–8 n.123, 221–5, 252–3 n.102, 256 n.120
  history (*Beit rabi*) 82
  Joseph Isaac Schneersohn's work 13–14, 225–7, 230–4, 236–7, 239–43, 257 n.130, 258 n.136
  Kherson *genizah* 13, 219–20, 253 n.109
  Ladies' Association 383–5, 401, 435–6
  leadership 109 n.124, 114–16 nn.180, 184, 119 n.201, 230–3, 240, 257 n.126, 260 n.147, 374, 429
  Lubavitch headquarters 236
  Lubavitch Women's Organization 366 n.83, 448, 455–6, 469 n.75
  messianism 148, 469 nn.78, 85
  'Polish' hasidism 49, 117 n.188, 239–42, 266 n.193, 374, 411 n.56
  productivization policy 230, 260 n.152
  publications for and by women 366 n.84
  Seder night customs 397–8, 425 n.153
  sheliḥut (mission) 447
  Sisters of the Temimim 389–90, 440, 443, 446, 455
  speculative teachings 243, 265 n.188, 308 n.44, 334, 389, 391, 427–8, 439, 464 n.43
  Tomekhei Temimim yeshiva 387; *see also* Schneersohn, Shalom Dovber; Tomekhei Temimim yeshiva
  transmission of oral lore 410 n.53, 424 n.148
  twentieth-century 16–17, 19, 62, 375, 385, 430, 447, 455
  Upper/Lower Unity 452, 467–8 n.70

Habad (*cont.*):
women in pre-twentieth-century Habad 371–2, 394–401, 427–35
women in twentieth-century Habad 17, 375, 385, 435–47, 447–55
women's position 16–18, 242–3, 308 n.44, 333–4, 364–7 nn.83–4, 368–470
Hakeri'ah vehakedushah (journal) 441, 465 n.52
Halpern, Israel 63, 64
Hannah Berakhah, daughter of Sareleh of Chęciny 353 n.39
Hannah Hayah of Chernobyl 325, 350 n.35
hasidism:
ascetic piety in 114 n.176, 344–6 n.18, 357–8 n.54, 360–1 n.75
ascetic-mystical background 10, 11, 18
Belarusian 113 n.161, 116 n.187, 224, 252 n.102, 260 n.146
centralist tendencies in leadership after 1772? 53–62
centralized? 3, 6, 10, 23, 25–6, 33–4, 43–4, 47, 66
conferences (meetings) of tsadikim 62–8, 77–8, 114 n.173
courts 3, 11, 25, 39–40, 44, 49, 71, 77, 79–83, 218, 239–40, 397
decentralized? 3, 6, 11, 23–5, 37, 38–9, 45–6, 48, 53, 65
'democratization' of mystical ideals 6, 7, 8, 9, 18, 30, 138
elitist movement 8, 9, 138–43
female hasidim 411–12 n.66, 435, 443, 447, 455–6
'feminized' fraternity of male hasidim 284, 431
first generation 3, 27, 84 n.2, 125, 133
food at hasidic courts 396–401
fraternities 25, 73, 78, 276–7, 321, 369
gender hierarchy 15, 16, 19, 443–4, 446
hagiographical tradition 12, 13, 32, 202–3, 206–10, 212–17, 225, 228, 229, 233, 236–8, 255 n.118, 265 n.186, 293, 332–3, 356 n.43, 391, 393–4, 396
historiography 12, 14, 36, 206, 207, 210, 218, 249 n.64, 261 n.156
ideological framework in relation to organizational change 68–83
independence of courts 24, 25, 39, 44, 47, 65
leadership in the time of the Ba'al Shem Tov 26–38
leadership in the time of the Magid 38–45
'men of matter' and 'men of form' 8, 16, 30, 32, 129, 133, 135, 281, 282
opposition to 4, 6, 10, 11–12, 18, 52–3, 181, 231–2, 253 n.102, 259 n.146, 262–3 n.165
origins 2, 4, 6, 8, 10, 11
popular movement 3, 7, 8, 10
presence of women in courts, *see* women
rival groups 263 n.166
Sabbatianism and 90 n.17, 110 n.135, 215, 263 n.166, 275–6, 287–300, 303–4 n.16, 304 n.20, 313 n.80
'secret' 259 n.146
Seder table at hasidic courts 397–8, 424–5 n.153
speculative literature 217, 241, 284, 322–3, 369–70, 431
speculative teachings 33, 39, 79, 221, 237–8, 243, 284, 308 n.44, 334, 371, 396, 428
structural continuity and change 23–6
structure of leadership after 1772 45–53
three-generation chronology 2–3, 4, 6, 9–12
women's place 7, 15–16, 17–19, 318–25, 333–4
'worship through corporeality' 8, 31, 125, 130, 306 n.27
Haskalah, *see* Enlightenment
Hayah, mother of Isaac Meir of Ger 353 n.39
Hayah Moskowitz, daughter of Meir of Przemyślany 353 n.39
Hayah Mushka, wife of the Tsemah Tsedek 377, 378, 380, 400, 421 n.122, 425 n.123
Hayim Haykl of Amdur 164–5
Hebrew 126, 135–6, 176, 322–4, 368–9, 464 n.46

Heilman, Hayim Meir 82–3, 255–6 n.118, 354 n.41
Heschel, A. J. 26, 34–6, 137, 139
Heschel, Abraham Joshua of Apta 118 n.194, 350 n.35
Heschel, Joshua of Olkusz 353 n.39
Hess, Moses 341 n.11
Hillel of Porich 429
hitkarvut (drawing near, initiation) 44, 120 n.210, 166–9, 171–2, 174, 178–81, 189 n.21
Horodetsky, Samuel Abba:
  background 330, 411 n.66
  on Barukh of Międzybóż 55
  on Maid of Ludmir 7, 15, 304 n.21, 328–31, 336, 356 n.43, 367 n.89, 394, 396
  on messianism 319–20
  on women's place in hasidism 7, 14–15, 277, 318–20, 368, 396, 405–6 n.15
  use of oral tradition 405 n.14
Horwitz, Rivka 303 n.15

I
Ibn Ezra 124, 445
Idel, Moshe 304 n.20, 307 n.34, 313 n.80
Isaac, son-in-law of the Magid of Tirhavitsa 171–3
Isaac of Drohobycz 26, 72, 298
Isaac ben Mordecai of Neshchiz 347 n.20, 355 n.43, 373–4
Isaac Doktor of Dubrovno 395
Isaac Judah Yehiel Safrin of Komarno 116 n.184
Isaac Meir of Ger 353 n.39
Israel, Magid of Kozienice 85 n.5, 119 n.201
Israel ben Eliezer, *see* Ba'al Shem Tov (the Besht)
Israel of Ruzhin 50, 100 n.68, 104 n.90, 374
Israel of Vilednik 374, 429
Israel Abraham of Cherny Ostrov 396
Israel Löbel 37, 97–8 n.53
Israel Meir Kagan (Hakohen), the 'Hafets Hayim' 417 n.98
Issachar Dov Roke'ah (the Belzer Rebbe) 374
Itskovitch, Samuel and Gedaliah 204

J
Jacob Isaac (the Jew of Pshiskhah) 100–1 n.73, 101 n.74, 148
Jacob Isaac Horowitz (the Seer of Lublin):
  denunciation of Sabbatian prophets 289
  dispute with the Jew of Pshiskhah 100–1, n.73, 101 n.74
  hagiographical tradition 355 n.43
  status on death of the Magid 116 n.184, 257 n.129
  title 312 n.68
Jacob Joseph of Połonne:
  distinction between 'men of matter' and 'men of form' 30–1, 33, 131, 133–5, 144, 155 n.52, 158 n.72, 305 n.25
  expulsion as rabbi of Shargorod 121 n.210
  hagiographical account of 32
  leadership question 35–7, 78
  parable recorded by 128, 151 n.8
  relationship with the Besht 28, 31, 95 n.36, 137, 156 n.54, 200–1
  relationship with the Magid 35, 37, 78, 200
  relationship with non-hasidic community 72
  role in formation of hasidism 10, 72
  on role of tsadik 145, 454
  on worship through corporeality 130
  writings 3, 4, 8, 90 n.17, 92–3 n.33, 145, 151 n.9, 281, 309 n.45
Jacob Kadaner 108 n.123, 265 n.186
Jacob of Satanów 120 n.203
Jacob of Smiła 87 n.10
Jacobs, Louis 147
Jacobsohn, Israel 411 n.64, 412 n.70, 467 n.58
Joel of Nemirov 200
Joseph Spravedliver 298, 357 n.54
Judah Eliezer 180–1
Judah Hasid 94 n.36, 271
Judah Leyb Hakohen of Annopol 257 n.124
Judah Leyb Pistiner 135

Judah Loew ben Bezalel of Prague 360 n.72

K

kabbalah:
  asceticism 84 n.2, 90 n.17, 125, 332, 353 n.36, 360 n.75
  association of women with demonic realm 333, 363 n.81
  concept of *devekut* 5, 124–5, 126, 141–2, 143
  confession as theurgy 186
  doctrine of affinity of souls 68, 70–1, 73, 80–3
  elite circles of adepts 138–40
  Enlightenment attitudes to 275, 303 n.15
  female and male *sefirot* 280, 430–1
  inversion of gender hierarchies 305 n.23, 436, 443–4
  kelipot 175
  Lurianic 5, 126, 163–4, 186, 319–20
  Lurianic *kavanot* 141
  Luria's powers as confessor 163–4
  messianism 5, 275, 305 n.23
  perceptions of women 363 n.81, 364 n.83, 387, 436–7
  'pre-hasidic' circles of kabbalists 90 n.17
  relationship with rabbinic establishment 262–3 nn.165, 166
  retreat from the world 278
  righteous women in afterlife 444
  Sabbatianism 269–70, 275, 299
  sefirah Malkhut 134, 174–5, 194–5 n.57, 279, 282, 451–2
  Shekhinah 398
  speculations about messianic end date 354 n.41, 371, 428
  unifications (*yiḥudim*) 126, 313 n.84
Kahan, Raphael 379, 383
Karlin 154 n.46, 119 n.201
Katz, Jacob 122 n.221
kelipot ('evil husks') 175–6
Kherson *genizah*:
  collection presented to Shalom Dovber 219, 248 n.59, 253 n.109
  connection with Habad historiography 219, 256 n.120
  contents 210, 213–18, 253 n.109
  correspondence between the Magid and his disciples 99–100 n.67
  date of production 212, 220
  discovery 210, 220, 221–2
  exposed as forgeries 214, 220
  forgeries 13, 56, 97 n.47, 210–11
  Habad view of 13–14, 219–20, 224–5, 251 n.88
  identity of forgers 248 n.56
  Joseph Isaac's defence of 13–14, 103 n.76, 220–1, 222, 242, 248 n.56, 352 n.36
  Joseph Isaac's use as source 222–5, 227, 232, 242, 257 n.124
  letters supposedly written by the Besht 250–1 n.88
  Margaliot's use as source 56, 352 n.36
  Menachem Mendel Schneersohn's view of documents 220, 253 nn.103, 109
  motivations of forgers 211, 212–13
  publication 352 n.36
  Shalom Dovber's collection of documents 219, 248 n.59
  Shalom Dovber's view of 219–20, 248 n.59, 253 n.109
  unpublished material 253 n.109
Khmelnytsky, Bohdan 2
Kluger, Shelomoh 408 n.30, 410 n.52
Klyachko, M. 328
kolelim 335–7
Kosów 27, 313 n.80
Kozienice, hasidic dynasty 119 n.201, 410 n.53
Kuty 90 n.17, 212–13, 295, 315 n.106, 316 n.115

L

Landau, Ezekiel 303 n.15
Landau, Isaac ben Leyb 347 n.120
Langer, Jiři 374
Lelów, hasidic leadership 119 n.201
Levi Isaac of Berdyczów:
  disciple of the Magid 3
  disputes 39, 85 n.5
  grandson 423 n.146
  instructions to Abraham Joshua Heschel 118 n.194

meeting of communal leaders 63–4
relationship with the Magid 95 n.40
Seder table 397, 423–4 n.147
virtues praised by Nahman of Bratslav 59, 80, 112 n.152
visited by Nathan Sternharz 80
Levin, Shmarya 392
Levinson, Isaac Ber 165
Leyb ben Ozer 302 n.13
Lieberman, Haim 246 n.36, 248 n.56
Lifshits, Shimon Dovber 383
Likutei moharan 57, 149–50, 174–5, 178, 181, 183–4
Lithuania:
anti-hasidic agitation 259 n.146
Habad in 49–50, 365 n.83, 388, 438
hasidic centre in Karlin 40
ḥerem against hasidim 42, 51, 52
kabbalah study 262 n.165, 310 n.66
mitnagedim 23, 38, 53, 99 n.63, 208, 232, 259 n.145, 262–3 n.165
Radziwiłł estates 204
Shneur Zalman's position 67
yeshivas 387, 414 n.84, 436
Lizhensk, hasidic leadership 119 n.201
Loewenthal, Naftali 350 n.34, 372, 389, 439, 442
Lubavitch Women's Organization 366 n.83, 448, 455–6, 469 n.75
Luria, Isaac (the Ari):
doctrine of 'rectification' of the world 301 n.7
gift of physiognomy 163–4
God of 138–9
hagiographical tales 203–4
kavanot 141–3
on redemption by virtue of righteous women 451
tsimtsum 148–9, 160 n.91
Lwów 207–9, 214, 232, 256 n.121, 323 n.83

M

madness:
female spirituality 275
'religious' 316 n.112
story of the Besht and the madwoman 292–3, 295–6
Madsen, Patricia 334
Magid of Mezhirech, the (Dov Ber):
accession to hasidic leadership 34–7, 39, 84 n.2, 95 n.40, 96–7 n.47, 109 n.124, 228, 232
attitude to women 278–80, 307–8 n.34
charismatic authority 38, 252 n.93
court 3, 79, 200
daughter-in-law 297
death 3, 9, 12, 23, 24–5, 38, 45, 48, 108 n.123, 258 n.136
'democratization' of mystical ideals 138
on *devekut* 143, 144
disciples 3, 4, 6, 11, 24–5, 39–45, 54, 62–3, 65, 77, 100 n.68, 136–7
Dubnow's view of 3
forged correspondence 219, 256 n.120
hagiographical account 32
influence 38–9
leadership role 3, 6, 10, 24, 43, 54, 62, 65, 99 n.61, 218
on Lurianic *kavanot* 142, 143
powers 29
relationship with Abraham of Kalisk 42–3, 64, 98 n.57, 100 n.72, 116 n.187
relationship with the Besht 74, 96–7 n.47
role in formation of hasidism 10, 72
son, *see* Abraham the Angel
on status of tsadik 144–5
'streams of wisdom' 96 n.47, 251–2 n.93, 259 n.143
successor 24–5, 38, 48, 53, 65–7, 84 n.2, 102–3 n.76, 114 n.176, 115 n.184, 217–19, 223–4, 226, 257 nn.124, 126, 129
teachings 3, 39, 79, 142–7, 278–80, 363 n.82
Mahaneh Yisra'el (Camp of Israel) 442
Maid of Ludmir, the (Hannah Rachel Verbermacher):
allusions to 355–6 n.43, 367 n.85, 404 n.13, 405 n.14
biographical sketch 327–8
celibacy 277, 298, 331–3, 395
comparisons with 358 n.54, 359 n.67, 362 n.78

Maid of Ludmir (*cont.*):
construction of biography 304–5 n.21, 328–9, 338 n.2, 356–7 n.52, 402 n.8
critical analysis of tradition on 331–3
failed model of female authority 395, 402 n.9
family background 327, 337, 394, 395
Horodetsky's work 7, 14–15, 317 n.127, 328–30, 355–6 n.43, 367 n.89, 394, 396, 406 n.15
in Jerusalem 305 n.21, 334–7, 356–7 n.52
reputation 305 n.21, 327–8
story of a deviant 15, 298, 331–3, 369–70
Maimon, Solomon 40, 74, 75–7, 99 n.63, 121 n.217
Maimonides 161, 407 n.23
Malkah of Trisk 353 n.39
Malkhut (*sefirah*) 134, 175–7, 179, 186, 194–5 n.57, 279, 282, 451–3
Margaliot, Reuben 56, 107 nn.118, 120, 121, 351–2 n.36, 420 n.110
Mark, Zvi 287, 289–90, 293, 315 n.103
marriage:
agunot 281, 375, 377–8
barrier to women's spiritual authority 328, 362 n.78
benedictions 433
effects of hasidic male fraternities 321, 343 n.15
Maid of Ludmir 298, 327–8, 331, 333, 395
traditional customs 331
of tsadikim 65
views of *maskilim* 321, 331, 342 n.13
of yeshiva students 344–5 n.18
maskilim:
anti-hasidic campaign 51, 232, 263 n.166, 276
anti-hasidic writings 50, 254–5 n.117, 261 n.156
views on hasidic confession 164, 165, 188 n.16, 191 n.37
views on hasidic tales 237, 238
views on hasidic women 321, 405 n.14
views on kabbalah 303 n.15
views on traditional marriage 331
women's fundraising organizations 385
Meir (tannaitic sage) 301 n.9
Meir, Jonatan 393
Meir of Przemyślany 353 n.39, 373
Meir Rotenberg of Opatów 370, 402–3 n.11, 458 n.17
Menahem Mendel, Magid of Bar 128
Menahem Mendel of Przemyślany 35, 45, 95 n.40, 97 n.49, 155–6 n.52
Menahem Mendel of Vitebsk:
on the Ba'al Shem Tov 87 n.10
death of 66, 260 n.146
departure for Erets Yisra'el 66, 67, 116 n.187, 252 n.102
disciple of the Magid 3, 224
disciples 100 n.68
leadership 3, 40, 49–50
Lithuanian 256 n.123
pastoral letters 311 n.68
relationship with Abraham of Kalisk 42, 98 n.57
relationship with *mitnagedim* 232
status in Minsk 98 n.58
succession issue 223–4, 257 n.126
views on miracle-working tsadikim 87–8 n.10
Menahem Mendel of Żydachów 353 n.39
Mendel of Kotsk 148
Mendelssohn, Moses 212, 303–4 n.15, 341 n.11
Meshulam Feibush Heller of Zbaraż 143, 159 n.76
Meshulam Zusya of Annopol 257 n.124, 423 n.140
messianism:
end date 354 n.41, 371, 428
Frankist 207, 270
Habad 148, 469 nn.78, 85
inversion of gender hierarchies 305 n.23, 432–5, 436, 443–4, 446, 449–51
kabbalistic 5, 275, 305 n.23
Menachem Mendel Schneerson's project 17, 391, 449–52, 454, 455–6
Nahman of Bratslav's 57–8, 61–2, 103 n.77, 118–19 n.200, 149–50, 198 n.91
prophetesses 15, 273–5, 276

role of women 17–18, 391, 449–50
Sabbatian 269, 271–3, 285, 288, 299–300, 404 n.12
miracles and wonders:
female relatives of tsadikim 325
Habad attitude 241–2, 260–1 n.152, 378
Isaac of Neshchiz 347
Israel of Vilednik 408 n.35, 458 n.14
Joseph Isaac Schneersohn's views 241–2, 411 n.56
Maid of Ludmir 327, 355 n.43, 405 n.14
miracle-working tsadikim 60–1, 87–8 n.10, 237, 238
Mitteler Rebbe 376, 409 n.44
Nahman of Bratslav's view 60–1, 346–7 n.20, 408 n.39
publication of 286, 291
Shneur Zalman of Liady's view 238–9, 260–1 n.152, 346–7 n.20, 430
Yente the Prophetess 316–17 n.127
Miriam, wife of Abraham Jacob of Sadagora 425 n.155
Miriam the Prophetess 363 n.80
Mirosh, daughter of Elimelekh of Lizhensk 353 n.39
Mishulovin, Hayim Elijah 424 n.148
mitnagedim (hasidic opponents of the Bratslav group) 193 n.42
mitnagedim (rabbinic opponents of hasidism):
anti-hasidic writings 164–5
Belarusian 40
campaign against hasidism 51–3, 71, 77–8, 85 n.5, 109 n.124, 119 n.203, 208, 232, 258 n.134
hasidic resistance to 10, 42, 229, 252–3 n.102, 344 n.16
ḥerem (excommunication) of Vilna against hasidim 51–2
hostilities between hasidim and *mitnagedim* 23, 43, 48, 62–3, 65, 68, 73–6, 100 n.72, 232
Lithuanian 38, 53, 99 n.63, 208, 232, 259 n.145, 262–3 n.165
Nathan Sternharz's conversion to hasidism 79, 81
opposition to hasidism 4, 116 n.187, 231–2, 263 n.166, 307 n.34
'*perushim*' 193 n.42
rise of 122 n.221
view of hasidic confession 181
view of hasidic prayer 184
view of hasidic women 321, 346 n.20, 403 n.11
Mitteler Rebbe, *see* Dov Ber
Mokhiah of Połonne, the, *see* Aryeh Judah Leyb
Mondshine, Yehoshua:
on attitudes to hagiographical tales 249 n.60
on authorship of Freyde's letter 354 n.41, 371
on distribution of *lekakh* 401
on editorial units of *Shivḥei habesht* 291
publication of *Shivḥei habesht* 89 n.14, 251 n.88
on rebbe's Seder table 425 n.153
on tales of early hasidic leaders 265 n.188
use of sources 257 n.130
Montefiore, Moses 334–5
Mordecai of Chernobyl:
attitudes to women 362 n.78, 374, 396, 429
case of Maid of Ludmir 327–8, 330, 333
daughter 325, 350 n.35
granddaughter 353 n.39
leadership 119 n.201
Mordecai of Krzemieniec 80
Mordecai of Neshchiz 60, 355 n.43
Moses 131, 177–8, 199–200, 280, 286, 363 n.80
Moses of Kuty 90 n.17, 292, 293, 296, 316 n.115
Moses of Lelów 119 n.201
Moses Elyakim Briah of Kozhnitz 159 n.76
Moses Hagiz 273, 301 n.8
Moses Leyb of Sasów 118 n.194
Moses Zevi of Savran 184
Munkács Rebbe (Hayim Eleazar Shapira) 373

N

Naftali Hirsch Hakohen 402 n.5

Naftali of Ropczyce 215
Naftali Zevi Shapira of Odessa 248 n.56
Nahman of Bratslav (Moharan):
absolution of followers after confession 174–5
asceticism 180, 361 n.75
attitude to the Besht 58–9, 110 nn.133, 135
attitude to women 347 n.20, 374–5, 459 n.17
biography 64, 148
Bratslav circle 103 n.81, 148
claim to supreme leadership 56–7
'concealed' leadership 57–8, 61–2, 110 n.135, 112 n.152, 149
confession institution 9, 165–74, 176–80, 186–7, 190–1 nn.30, 37, 192 n.38
confession institution ended 180–2, 185, 187
daughter's marriage 297, 353 n.36
death 148, 149, 150, 160 n.92, 181, 197 n.78, 198 n.91
dispute with Barukh of Międzybóż 58–9, 60, 78, 112 n.152
dispute with Shpola Zeyde 78, 86 n.5, 148–9, 184
identifying with the Ari 204
identifying with Moses 195 n.61
initiation ceremony for followers 165–6, 189 n.19
leadership 54, 56–8, 61–2
Likutei moharan 57, 118 n.200, 149–50, 174–5, 178, 181, 183–4, 194 n.46
on marital relations 343 n.15, 459 n.17
messianic role 57–8, 61–2, 103 n.77, 118–19 n.200, 149–50, 198 n.91
mother 16, 297, 350 n.35
Nathan Sternharz's relationship with 57, 64, 75, 79–80, 81, 103–4 n.81, 149, 178, 181, 193 n.42, 197 n.78, 245 n.19
pilgrimages to court 342 n.14, 374, 408 n.37
recruiting followers 165–6
relationship with the Besht 58–9, 61, 89 n.16, 110 n.135, 139–40, 190 n.26
relationship with other tsadikim 59–60, 111–12 n.152, 183
relationship with Shneur Zalman of Liady 111 nn.144, 150
Sipurei ma'asiyot 237
teachings 8, 92 n.32, 111 n.152, 118 n.200, 131–2, 149–50, 172, 174–8, 183–4, 194–5 nn.46, 57
title 189 nn.18, 19
travels 58, 60, 187, 190 nn.22, 24, 192 n.38, 342 n.14
True Tsadik 140, 148, 150, 178, 182–4, 186
'tsadik of the generation' 56–7, 112 n.152, 118–19 n.200
tsadik's role 9, 54, 56–7, 131–2, 139–40, 148, 183–4, 198 nn.91, 92
views on miracle-working tsadikim 60–1, 346–7 n.20, 408 n.39
views on prophecy 311 n.68
Nahman of Cherin 192 n.39
Nahman of Horodenka 45, 94 n.36, 110 n.135, 133
Nahman of Kosów:
advocate of constant *devekut* 125–6
analysis of traditions relating to 88 n.12
disciples 28, 89 n.15
occupation 126
powers 27, 29
relationship with the Besht 26–8, 29, 78, 90 n.16, 137, 287
role in formation of hasidism 72, 90 n.17
views on prophecy 287, 288
Nahman of Tulchin 104 n.81, 184, 192 n.39
Nahmanides 124, 126
Nathan, *see* Sternharz
Nehamah, daughter of Hayim of Sanz 353 n.39
Nehamah Dinah, wife of Joseph Isaac Schneersohn 416 n.92, 425 n.153
New York:
Joseph Isaac Schneersohn in 235–6, 391, 438
Sisters of the Temimim 390, 418 n.104, 440, 443, 467 n.58
Nicholas I, Tsar 230

O

Orchan, Nurit 420 n.114
Ozer of Uman 193 n.42

P

Parush, Iris 391–2
Pavlitch (Pawołocz), ritual blood accusation 204
Perele, daughter of the Magid of Kozienice 353 n.39, 422 n.136, 457 n.3
Perl, Joseph 51, 95 n.40, 237, 393, 405 n.14
Perlow, Hayim Mordecai 382
Philo 301 n.9
physical desire as vehicle to spiritual yearnings 127–9, 151–2 nn.8–9, 279–80, 307 n.34, 431
pidyon (payment accompanying the submission of a *kvitl*) 165, 167, 170, 283, 325, 347, 372, 373, 374, 397, 429
  criticisms of custom 165
  origins 423 n.144, 458 n.9
  Rebbetsin Sterna's powers 394–5, 428
  relationship between payment and hospitality 397
  women paying 347 n.20, 372–4, 429
  Yente the prophetess's refusal to accept 357 n.54
Piekarz, Mendel 303–4 n.16
Pinhas of Korets:
  Bratslav tradition on 80
  disciples 28
  father 74, 120–1 n.210
  hagiographical account of 32
  leadership 35, 45
  relationship with the Besht 26–7, 28, 94 n.36, 121 n.210, 137
  relationship with Jacob Joseph of Połonne 35
  relationship with the Magid 35, 78, 121 n.210
  role in formation of hasidism 10, 72
Pinhas of Ostrog 55
Podolia:
  the Besht's region of residence 208, 229–30, 250 n.81
  foundation of hasidism 117 n.188
Poke'aḥ ivrim 350 n.34, 407 nn.25, 26, 427
Poland (Polish–Lithuanian Commonwealth):
  boundaries of estates 25
  Cossack uprising 231
  disintegration of 23, 47, 51, 66, 86 n.6
  effects of partitions on Jewish community 23, 49, 51
  expansion of hasidism 47
  foundation of hasidic courts 3
  hasidic leaders 241
  ḥerem 52
  Joseph Isaac Schneersohn's career in 221, 227, 240, 438, 440–1
  Lurianic kabbalah in 319
  partitions 23, 48, 49, 51, 53
  'Polish' hasidism, *see* Habad
  Republic 240
  separation of hasidic community after partition 23, 49
  travel documents 104 n.81
  women's fundraising associations 385
Polen, Nehemiah 363 n.80, 404 n.12
prophecy:
  biblical 285, 311 n.68, 434
  condemnation of messianic 302 n.13
  Feyge's reputation 297–8
  hasidic view of 285–9, 311 n.68
  madwoman's faculty of 293
  messianic prophecy 275
  messianic prophetesses 15–16, 273–4, 293
  Sabbatian 15, 273–5, 288–9, 320
  Sabbatian prophetesses 273, 274–5, 276, 285, 292, 293, 296
  Yente the Prophetess 298, 317 n.127, 357 n.54
Pshiskhah, the 'Jew of', *see* Jacob Isaac

R

Rabah bar bar Hana 282, 454
Rachel, daughter of Joshua Heschel of Apta 350 n.35
Radziwiłł, Prince 204
Rapoport, Hayim Hakohen 209
Rashi 109 n.131, 301 n.9, 446
Riga:
  Joseph Isaac Schneersohn in 240, 241, 365 n.83, 438, 440, 443–4, 445–6

Riga (*cont.*):
Joseph Isaac Schneersohn's address to Sisters of the Temimim (1940) 388–90, 440, 443–4, 455, 467 n.58
Rivaleh the Pious 352–3 n.36, 356 n.48
Rivkah, Rebbetsin, wife of the fourth *admor* Shemuel 392
channel for women's concerns 380, 411 n.64
hasidic identity of 381–2, 447–8
reading 392–3, 421 n.122
role in community 354 n.42, 399–401
transmitter of oral lore 242, 377, 392, 410 n.53
wedding 399
Rodkinson, Michael Levi 56, 151–2 n.9, 225, 265 n.186, 266 n.192
Romania 50
root-affinity of souls 68–73, 80, 82–3, 94 n.33, 118 n.194, 119 n.200
Rosenberg, Elke 415 n.86
Rosenblum, Sonia 464–5 n.47
Rosman, Moshe 205–6, 291
Równe, meeting of Magid's disciples (1772) 42–3, 62–4, 68, 77, 98 nn.57, 58, 100 n.72
Rubinstein, Avraham 35, 95 n.40, 204
Ruderman, Pesah 238

S
Sa'adyah Gaon 127–8, 151–2 n.9
Sabbatai Zevi:
apostasy 269, 285
coronation ceremonies 271
as human incarnation of the Divine 270
life and death 269, 285, 302 n.13, 313 n.83
messianic movement 313 n.82, 319
publication of novel about 289–90
redemptive vision 340 n.9
sexual transgression 272
wives 271, 272, 274, 320
Sabbatianism:
apostasy 105 n.101
the Besht's view of 209
gender egalitarianism 271–2, 298–9
hasidism's relationship with 275–6, 284–9, 299
legacy 299–300
libertinism 271–3
mass prophecy 285, 320
messianic movement 269, 319
messianism 434
opposition to 207, 273
in Poland 105 n.101
prophetesses 15, 273, 274–5, 276, 285, 292, 293, 296
redemptive vision 270, 298, 340 n.9
survival 269–70
waning 275
women's role 270–2, 319–20, 340 n.9, 412 n.67
women's sexuality 16
Samson of Shepetovka 59
Samuel Isaac 166–9, 174
Sarah, matriarch 432–3
Sarah, wife of Sabbatai Zevi 271, 274
Sarah Devorah, Rebbetsin 420 n.53
Sarah (Sareleh) Horowitz Sternfeld of Chęciny (the Chentshiner Rebbetsin) 353 n.39, 354 n.42, 422 n.136, 457 n.3
Sarah Shlomtse, daughter of Menahem Mendel of Żydachów 353 n.39
Sarah Tsiporah, wife of Abraham Matityahu of Ştefăneşti 425 n.155
Schatz-Uffenheimer, Rivka 143
Schenirer, Sarah 347–8 n.20, 402 n.10, 439
Schiper, Ignacy 200, 206, 208
Schneersohn, Barukh Shneur 416 n.89
Schneersohn, Joseph Isaac (sixth *admor*):
addresses to Riga women 440, 443–4, 445–6, 455, 467 n.58
apocalyptic vision of world events 440–2, 455
on Ben Attar (Or Hahayim)'s daughters 390, 419–20 n.110
on the Besht 14, 222–3, 227–8, 255 n.117, 260 n.152
on the Besht's successor 102 n.76
biography 259 n.138
'Brothers' and 'Sisters' of the Temimim 389, 440, 443, 446, 455, 466–7 n.58, 467 n.69
career 226–7, 232–3, 413 n.79

court in New York 227, 391, 424–5 n.143, 441
daughters 102 n.76, 464 n.47
defence of Kherson *genizah* 13–14, 103 n.76, 220–1, 222, 242, 248 n.56, 352 n.36
definition of Habad path 239
on distribution of *lekakh* 400–1
family purity campaign 365 n.83, 388–9, 417 n.98, 418 n.103, 438, 442–3, 446, 455, 463 n.40, 467 n.67
on father's use of Kherson material 219–20, 248 n.59, 253 n.109
grandmother 392, 399–400, 410 n.53, 421 n.122
on Habad tradition 98 n.57
on hagiographical production in Habad 242
on hasidic historiography 254–5 n.117
on hasidic leadership 230–3, 260 n.152
historiographical writings of 13–14, 65–8, 84–5 n.2, 108 n.123, 113 n.161, 221–2, 234–6, 242–3, 258 n.136, 409 n.44
on the Magid's successor 102–3 n.76, 223–4, 226
Memoirs 236–7
messianism 441–3, 445
mother 383–4, 386, 400
organization of women's groups 17, 365 n.83, 388–91, 418 n.101, 438–40, 443, 467 n.58
policies towards women 308 n.44, 333, 364–5 n.83, 387–91, 417 n.98, 437–9, 443–7, 448, 455, 463 nn.40, 41, 464–5 n.47, 467 n.70
on 'Polish' hasidism 117 n.188, 239–42
portrayal of hasidism 261–2 n.156, 263 n.165
publication of talks 254 n.111
Riga address to Jewish women 445–6
secret activities 14, 114–15 n.180, 226–7
silence on Abraham of Kalisk 116 n.187
on the Tsemah Tsedek 377–8
use of hagiographical sources 225–6, 258 n.136
use of Kherson material as source 222–5, 227, 232, 242
view of miracles 241–2, 411 n.56
wife 416 n.92, 425 n.153
Schneersohn, Menahem Mendel (the Tsemah Tsedek, third *admor*):
agricultural policy 230
area of influence 50
campaign against Enlighteners 232, 254 n.113
death 50, 104 n.88
exclusion of women 376–7
grandson of Shneur Zalman of Liady 108 n.123
name 260 n.152
teachings 462 n.29
wife 377, 378, 380, 400, 421 n.122
women's appeals to 378–9, 409 n.49, 409–10 n.52
Schneersohn, Shalom Dovber (fifth *admor*):
anti-Zionist messianism 436, 462 n.32
burglary of house 382
discourses 240, 259 n.143, 411 n.62, 436
exclusion of women 379, 437
on hasidic education 390, 463 n.41
Kherson documents 219, 248 n.59
mother 380, 381–2, 400, 411 n.64, 447–8
on 'Polish' hasidim 266 n.193
talk on father's death 382
Tomekhei Temimim yeshiva 17, 280–1, 384, 387, 400, 401, 435–6, 460 n.18, 462 n.31
view of women 17, 280–1, 364 n.83, 387, 390, 435–7, 460 n.18
wife 17, 379–80, 382–3, 386, 400, 435–6
Schneersohn, Shemaryahu 255 n.118
Schneersohn, Shemuel (fourth *admor*) 399, 422 n.132, 439
Schneerson, Hannah 424 n.152
Schneerson, Levi Isaac 424 n.152
Schneerson, Menachem Mendel (last Lubavitcher Rebbe):
career 469 n.78
counter-feminism 18, 456, 470 n.106
death 61
foundation of Lubavitch Women's Organization 448, 455–6

Schneerson, Menachem Mendel (*cont.*):
Hayom yom 468 n.74
messianic doctrine 17, 391, 449–52, 454, 455–6, 469 nn.78, 85
mother 398, 424 n.152
policies towards women 17–18, 308–9 n.44, 334, 366 n.83, 391, 407 n.23, 428, 447–56
Simhat Torah talk (1952) 448, 468 n.74
view of Kherson documents 220, 253 nn.103, 109
on women 449–55
Scholem, Gershom:
on concept of *devekut* 5–6, 8, 124, 132–3, 155 n.47
on consecration of the mundane 306 n.26
on 'democratic' approach of hasidism 6, 132–3
on early opposition to hasidism 6, 207–8, 246 n.36
on exclusion of women from mystical tradition 363 n.81
on extra-hasidic references to the Besht 246 n.36
on messianic idea in early hasidism 5, 461 n.28
on origins of hasidism 304 n.20, 313 n.80
on origins of the hasidic tsadik 288, 303 n.16
speculation on Adam Ba'al Shem 215
on women in Sabbatianism 340 n.9
Schwarz, Barukh 392
Seder birkhot hanehenin 407 n.25, 427
Seder table, rebbe's 397–8, 424–5 n.153
Seer of Lublin, *see* Jacob Isaac Horowitz
Sefer hahasidut 107 n.121
Sefer ḥasidim 162, 466 n.57
Sefer kokhevei or 110 n.135. 166, 168, 171–3, 197 n.78
Sefer likutei tefilot 181
Sefer yetsirah 194 n.56
sefirot 134, 174–6, 186, 280, 299, 430, 432–3, 451–3
Seidman, Naomi 301 n.9
sex:
abstinence 332, 345–6 n.18, 353 n.36, 361 n.75, 366 n.84
celibacy 305 n.22, 331–3, 345 n.18, 359 n.68, 395
conception without sexual desire 203
confessions 168, 191 n.37
dangers of conjugal separation 343 n.15
eschatological speculation 434
female sexuality 301 n.9, 307 n.33, 333, 427
at Frankist court 305 n.22
kabbalistic views 353 n.36, 361 n.76, 363 n.81
nocturnal emission 180, 191 n.37
prohibited unions 271
in Sabbatianism 270, 272–3, 284–5, 299–300
segregation 270–1
sublimation of female sexuality 278–9, 307–8 n.34
tsadik and his followers 282–4
wives of tsadikim 324, 325, 362 n.78, 394
women's nature 16, 18–19, 271, 273, 277–8, 364 n.83, 387, 437
Shalom Dovber, *see* Schneersohn
Shalom of Pogrebishche 80, 351–2 n.36
Shalom Roke'ah of Bełz 353 n.39, 359 n.67, 422 n.138
Shapiro, Malka 410 n.53, 422 n.136, 457 n.3
Shargorod (Szarogród) 28, 75, 121 n.210
Shekhinah 131, 134, 147, 398, 452
Shelomoh of Karlin 49, 85–6 n.5, 100 n.68, 119 n.201, 266 n.193, 399
Sheyna, Rebbetsin, wife of Mitteler Rebbe 399, 422 n.132
Shivḥei habesht (In Praise of the Ba'al Shem Tov):
on the Besht's circle 26–9, 32–3, 137, 140
on the Besht's knowledge of ritual law 247 n.46
on the Besht's prayer 141
on the Besht's wife and daughter 423 n.145
on 'common people' 32–3
editions 87 n.10, 89 nn.14–16, 204, 209, 213, 214–18, 228, 234, 237–8, 289–91, 314 n.87, 322

on expulsion of Jacob Joseph of Połonne 121 n.210
first publication 202, 209, 322, 391
Habad influence 113 n.161, 251 n.88
on heavenly 'streams of wisdom' 259 n.143
on individuals joining the Besht and his circle 74
intention of 12–13
on the Magid's status 96 n.47, 251–2 n.93
on relations between the Besht and Nahman of Kosów 27–8
as source 202–7, 209
status as sacred literature 248–9 n.60
typological models for 203, 206
on woman's prophetic dream 297
women reading 323, 349 n.25, 391–4, 402 n.5, 420 n.114, 421 n.124
on women's piety 351–3 n.36
'writer's preface' 206, 286
Yiddish versions 89 n.14–16, 204, 209, 322, 391
Shmeruk, Chone 25
Shmueli, E. 348 n.20
Shneur Zalman of Liady:
attendance at his court 342–3 n.14
daughter Freyde 353 n.39, 354 n.41, 371, 399, 427–8
death 119 n.201
disciple of the Magid 3, 56, 108 n.123, 113 n.162, 219, 223, 224, 258 n.136
disciples 428
dispute with Abraham of Kalisk 39, 62, 78
eschatology 432–4, 461–2 n.28
exclusion of women 347 n.20, 374–5, 380–1, 390, 397–8, 409 n.40, 423–4 n.147, 429–30
family circle 101 nn.73, 74, 108 n.123, 113 n.161, 252 n.102, 255 n.118, 380–1
father 233
founder of Habad 232, 238, 252–3 n.102
on gender roles 432–5, 453
hasidic leadership 14, 49, 65, 66–8, 85–6 n.5, 109 n.124, 115–16 n.184, 224, 227, 229, 233, 257 n.126, 259–60 n.146
imprisonment 111 n.144, 232, 258 n.134
letter from Abraham of Kalisk 98 n.57
letter to Abraham of Kalisk 42, 62–3, 68, 98 nn.57, 58, 100 n.72
Liozno Ordinances 343 n.14, 346 n.20, 374, 429
on messianism 401–2 n.28
not mentioned in *Shivḥei habesht* 113 n.161, 252 n.102
petition against 164
powers 219
relationship with Barukh of Międzybóż 55–6, 60, 86 n.5, 106 n.115, 108 n.123, 109 n.124, 225, 258 n.134
relationship with the Besht 56, 108 n.123, 109 n.124, 225–6, 257–8 n.131, 260 n.152, 296
relationship with Nahman of Bratslav 59–60
ruling on women's studies 371–2, 407 n.23, 427, 428
son Dov Ber (the Mitteler Rebbe) 101 nn.73, 74, 230, 232, 350 n.34, 371, 375, 394–5, 427, 428
son Moses 255 n.118, 362 n.79
view of miracle-working 238–9, 260–1 n.152, 346–7 n.20, 430
wife Sterna 380–1, 394–5, 397–8, 399, 406 n.18, 411 n.65, 428
works 111 n.150, 371–2, 404 n.12, 427, 432–3, 440, 453, 460 n.18, 461 n.26
Shterna Sarah, Rebbetsin (wife of the fifth *admor* Shalom Dovber):
bond with female members of Habad community 382–3
cooking 399
distribution of honey cake 400–1
obituary description 413 n.78
pleading women's cases with husband 17, 380
role as husband's assistant 386, 416 n.92
women's philanthropic group 17, 383–6, 401, 435–6
Sisters of the Temimim 389–90, 418 n.105, 418–19 n.106, 440, 443, 446, 455
Slonim, Azriel Zelig 375, 378

Stern, Abraham 403 n.11
Sterna, Rebbetsin, wife of Shneur Zalman of Liady:
cooking 399
place at rebbe's Seder table 397–8
pleading women's cases with husband 380–1, 411 n.65
powers 394–5, 406 n.18, 428, 457 n.5
Sternharz, Abraham 166, 173, 181, 192 n.39. 194 n.46
Sternharz, Nathan:
autobiography 245 n.19
on conference of hasidic leaders 64
on confessions 181–4
conversion from *mitnaged* to hasid 75–7, 79–81, 181, 193 n.42
death 121 n.217
on death of Nahman 197 n.78
description of Feyge 297
descriptions of pilgrimages to Nahman's court 374
on initiation of Yudl 189 n.19
journey to Erets Yisra'el 121 n.217, 180
Likutei halakhot 174, 178
Likutei tefilot 149, 184–5
list of dates 190 n.30, 194 n.46
list of tsadikim 112 n.152
on Nahman's visit to Shneur Zalman 111 n.144
records of Nahman of Bratslav's teachings 8, 57, 343 n.15
as source 192 n.39
travels 103–4 n.81

T
Taubenhaus, Ephraim 357 n.52
Taubenhaus, Meir 357 n.52
Taz (David ben Samuel Halevi) 289, 313 n.83
Teitelbaum, Mordecai 255–6 n.18, 354 n.41
tikunim 141, 171, 174, 179–80, 181
Tomekhei Temimim yeshiva:
admission to 379–80
aims 387, 436, 440
foundation 280, 400
instructions to students 280–1
women's support 383–4, 389, 400–1, 416 n.92, 435–6, 439
Tovot zikhronot 166, 168, 171, 173
Tree of Knowledge 271, 461 n.28
Tree of Life 271–2, 461 n.28
Tröstlin (Nehemiah ben Solomon), the Prophet of Erfurt 310 n.65
tsadik, tsadikim:
analogous to God 146, 148, 282
conferences 62–8
as 'father' 321, 343–4 n.16
female relatives 276, 324, 325, 353 n.39, 362 n.78, 394
female tsadikim 15, 325–6, 329, 337, 355 n.43, 356 n.48, 357 n.54, 369–70
figure of tsadik 4, 5, 7, 9, 132, 146, 321, 325, 344 n.16, 454
hereditary family link 46–7, 80, 82, 83
intimates (*mekoravim*) 412–13 n.72
marriages of 65, 114 n.174
miracle-working 60–1, 87–8 n.10, 237, 238
root-affinity of souls 68–73, 80, 82–3, 94 n.33, 118 n.194, 119 n.200
'secret' 216–17, 219, 222–3, 227–31, 233, 236, 260 n.152, 264 n.176
sphere of influence 25
wives 324, 325, 353 n.39, 362 n.78, 394
tsadikism 4, 30, 60, 61, 138, 147, 375
Tsemah Tsedek, *see* Schneersohn, Menahem Mendel
Tsizye Hannah, widow of Israel Abraham of Cherny Ostrov 396

U
Ukraine 2, 231, 329

V
Verbermacher, Hannah Rachel, *see* Maid of Ludmir
Verbermacher, Monesh 327, 337
viduy devarim (confession) 170, 173–5, 179, 182, 186
viduynikes (confessors) 168, 172, 180–1, 193 n.42, 194 n.44
Vilna Gaon, the (Elijah ben Solomon Zalman):
campaign against hasidism 4, 10, 11–12, 51, 99 n.63, 105 n.99

death 4
ḥerem proclamation against hasidism 51–2
kabbalist 263 n.165, 310 n.66
on miracle-working maiden 362 n.78
status and reputation 99 n.61
Vital, Hayim 117 n.192, 274–5, 292, 296, 313 n.85
Volhynia:
centre of hasidic movement 40, 116 n.188
'conventions' of the Magid's disciples in 67
foundation of hasidism 117 n.188
Habad in 49–50
hasidic schools in, compared with Habad 239, 240–1
kolel of the hasidim of Volhynia in Jerusalem 335–6
Maid of Ludmir 327–8, 335–6, 405 n.14

W
Walden, Aaron 38, 393
Walden, Pinhas 355–6 n.43
Weiss, Joseph:
on the Besht's circle 27, 72, 137, 139
on doctrine of descent of tsadik 145
on language of orally transmitted texts 92 n.33
on Lurianic *kavanot* 141
on Nahman of Kosów's 'holy fraternity' 90 n.17
on practice of confession 164
on prophecy in Nahman of Kosów's circle 287–8
on prophets 311 n.68
on traditions transmitted in name of the Besht 156 n.54
on tsadik as intermediary 187
Wilensky, Mordecai 97–8 n.53
women:
access to rebbe 372–81, 429, 458 n.16
agunot 281, 375, 377–8
ascetic piety of 317 n.127, 331–3, 360 n.72, 395, 422 n.129, 466 n.57
celibacy 332, 360 n.68
charitable associations 383–5, 415–16 n.86, 435–6
education of girls in tsarist Russia 331
education in Habad 17, 334, 364–6 n.83, 371–2, 389–91, 406–7 n.21, 439–40, 463 n.41, 464–5 n.47, 468 n.74
education in hasidism 322, 370, 390, 419 n.110
education in secular culture 417 n.96
educational barrier of Hebrew 368–9
educational networks of schools for girls 347 n.20, 364 n.83, 391, 402 n.10, 439, 440, 443, 470 n.107
excluded from spiritual life of hasidic community 321–2, 369, 373–5, 429
'family purity' 365 n.83, 388–9, 417 n.98, 418 n.103, 438, 442–3, 446, 455, 463 n.40, 467 n.67
female hasidic identities in Habad 381–7, 430, 447–8
food at hasidic court 396–401
from 'female purity' to hasidic education 387–91
Habad Ladies' Association (Damen Ferayn) 383–5, 401, 435–6
Habad publications 366 n.84
hasidic identity 321–2, 370, 381–2, 394, 402–4 n.11, 412 n.68, 447–8, 459–60 n.17
hasidic literature for or about 7, 15–16, 284, 296–7, 320, 322–6, 369, 393–6
in hasidism 368–71, 458–9 n.17
Mahaneh Yisra'el (Camp of Israel) 'women's division' 442
marriage, *see* marriage
messianic catalysts 17–18
powerful women—in and out of the norm 394–6
presence in the courts 276–7, 321–2, 346–8 n.20, 373, 403–4 n.11, 425 n.153, 429
in pre-twentieth-century Habad 371–2
prophetesses 15, 273–5, 276
reading habits 391–4, 429, 458 n.8
receptive to Lurianic kabbalah? 319–20
'Satan dancing among' 17, 364 n.83, 387, 437

women (*cont.*):
sexuality 16, 18–19, 271, 273, 278–9, 301 n.9, 333, 363 n.81
'stork' homonym for female pietist 443, 466 n.57
transmitters of early hasidic history and hagiographical tales 420–1 n.119, 421 n.120
transmitters of oral lore 410 n.53
widows 422 n.129
Woszczyło revolt (1740s) 204–5

Y

Yehiel Mikhl of Złoczów 42, 80, 96 n.47, 154–5 n.46, 165, 251–2 n.93, 298
Yekutiel Zalman, grandson of Levi Isaac of Berdiczów 423 n.146
Yente the Prophetess 298, 316–17 n.127, 357–8 n.54
Yerahmiel, son of the 'Holy Jew' of Pshischa 374
Yeruham Dov Berlin 375–6
yeshivas 344–5 n.18
see also Tomekhei Temimim yeshiva
Yiddish:
account of Yente the Prophetess 317 n.127
biographical and autobiographical literature 420 n.114
editions of *Shivḥei habesht* 89 nn.15, 16, 204, 209, 214, 216–17, 238, 314 n.87, 315 n.103, 322, 349 n.25, 391, 393, 402 n.5
female readership 349 n.25, 350 n.34, 369, 391–4, 421 n.124, 458 n.8
hagiographical works 215, 265 n.186, 313, 323, 369
hasidic literature for women 7, 320, 322–3, 402 n.5
Joseph Isaac Schneersohn's policies 388, 440
press 236, 238, 420 n.114
publication of hasidic tales 265 nn.185, 186, 323, 391, 394
sermons and discourses 323, 417 n.98, 421 n.122, 448
tracts for uneducated readers 372, 427, 429
translation of hasidic works into 322–3
translations from Hebrew into 348 n.21, 392, 444–5
Tsenerene 392
Women's Associations 365 n.83
women's education 326, 370, 389
women's tongue 284, 368
works on female leadership 325
Yosipon, Yiddish version 392–3
Yofeh, Israel 87 n.10, 113 n.161, 289–91, 293–6
Yudl 166–9, 174, 190 n.24

Z

Zederbaum, Alexander 385
Ze'ev Wolf of Zhitomir 307 n.34
Zevi, son of the Besht:
leadership question 34, 36, 84–5 n.2, 102 n.76, 217–18, 228, 259 n.146
residence 205
Zevi Aryeh of Ołyka 60
Zevi Elimelekh of Dynów 311 n.68
Zevi Hirsch Eichenstein of Żydaczów 289, 313 n.85
Zionism:
combating 280, 387, 436, 460 n.18
gender egalitarianism 277, 320, 330, 370
intellectuals 7, 200
nationalist issues 341 n.11
Zohar:
mixed-sex study groups 272
parable of the prince 151 n.8
on phylacteries 294
quoted in order of service 106 n.112
on the righteous 146, 160 n.89
on righteous women in paradise 271, 444
women's study of 271, 362 n.78
Zoref, Heschel 215
Zusya of Annopol 40–1, 80, 99 n.66, 115 n.184, 171–2
Zweifel, Eliezer Zvi Hakohen 152 n.9, 191 n.37, 344 n.16